Lecture Notes in Computer Science   9180

Commenced Publication in 1973
Founding and Former Series Editors:
Gerhard Goos, Juris Hartmanis, and Jan van Leeuwen

More information about this series at http://www.springer.com/series/7409

P.L. Patrick Rau (Ed.)

Cross-Cultural Design

Methods, Practice and Impact

7th International Conference, CCD 2015
Held as Part of HCI International 2015
Los Angeles, CA, USA, August 2–7, 2015
Proceedings, Part I

Springer

Editor
P.L. Patrick Rau
Department of Industrial Engineering
Tsinghua University
Beijing
P.R. China

ISSN 0302-9743   ISSN 1611-3349   (electronic)
Lecture Notes in Computer Science
ISBN 978-3-319-20906-7   ISBN 978-3-319-20907-4   (eBook)
DOI 10.1007/978-3-319-20907-4

Library of Congress Control Number: 2015942813

LNCS Sublibrary: SL3 – Information Systems and Applications, incl. Internet/Web, and HCI

Printed on acid-free paper

Springer International Publishing AG Switzerland is part of Springer Science+Business Media (www.springer.com)

Foreword

The 17th International Conference on Human-Computer Interaction, HCI International 2015, was held in Los Angeles, CA, USA, during 2–7 August 2015. The event incorporated the 15 conferences/thematic areas listed on the following page.

A total of 4843 individuals from academia, research institutes, industry, and governmental agencies from 73 countries submitted contributions, and 1462 papers and 246 posters have been included in the proceedings. These papers address the latest research and development efforts and highlight the human aspects of design and use of computing systems. The papers thoroughly cover the entire field of Human-Computer Interaction, addressing major advances in knowledge and effective use of computers in a variety of application areas. The volumes constituting the full 28-volume set of the conference proceedings are listed on pages VII and VIII.

I would like to thank the Program Board Chairs and the members of the Program Boards of all thematic areas and affiliated conferences for their contribution to the highest scientific quality and the overall success of the HCI International 2015 conference.

This conference could not have been possible without the continuous and unwavering support and advice of the founder, Conference General Chair Emeritus and Conference Scientific Advisor, Prof. Gavriel Salvendy. For their outstanding efforts, I would like to express my appreciation to the Communications Chair and Editor of HCI International News, Dr. Abbas Moallem, and the Student Volunteer Chair, Prof. Kim-Phuong L. Vu. Finally, for their dedicated contribution towards the smooth organization of HCI International 2015, I would like to express my gratitude to Maria Pitsoulaki and George Paparoulis, General Chair Assistants.

May 2015
Constantine Stephanidis
General Chair, HCI International 2015

HCI International 2015 Thematic Areas and Affiliated Conferences

Thematic areas:

- Human-Computer Interaction (HCI 2015)
- Human Interface and the Management of Information (HIMI 2015)

Affiliated conferences:

- 12th International Conference on Engineering Psychology and Cognitive Ergonomics (EPCE 2015)
- 9th International Conference on Universal Access in Human-Computer Interaction (UAHCI 2015)
- 7th International Conference on Virtual, Augmented and Mixed Reality (VAMR 2015)
- 7th International Conference on Cross-Cultural Design (CCD 2015)
- 7th International Conference on Social Computing and Social Media (SCSM 2015)
- 9th International Conference on Augmented Cognition (AC 2015)
- 6th International Conference on Digital Human Modeling and Applications in Health, Safety, Ergonomics and Risk Management (DHM 2015)
- 4th International Conference on Design, User Experience and Usability (DUXU 2015)
- 3rd International Conference on Distributed, Ambient and Pervasive Interactions (DAPI 2015)
- 3rd International Conference on Human Aspects of Information Security, Privacy and Trust (HAS 2015)
- 2nd International Conference on HCI in Business (HCIB 2015)
- 2nd International Conference on Learning and Collaboration Technologies (LCT 2015)
- 1st International Conference on Human Aspects of IT for the Aged Population (ITAP 2015)

Conference Proceedings Volumes Full List

1. LNCS 9169, Human-Computer Interaction: Design and Evaluation (Part I), edited by Masaaki Kurosu
2. LNCS 9170, Human-Computer Interaction: Interaction Technologies (Part II), edited by Masaaki Kurosu
3. LNCS 9171, Human-Computer Interaction: Users and Contexts (Part III), edited by Masaaki Kurosu
4. LNCS 9172, Human Interface and the Management of Information: Information and Knowledge Design (Part I), edited by Sakae Yamamoto
5. LNCS 9173, Human Interface and the Management of Information: Information and Knowledge in Context (Part II), edited by Sakae Yamamoto
6. LNAI 9174, Engineering Psychology and Cognitive Ergonomics, edited by Don Harris
7. LNCS 9175, Universal Access in Human-Computer Interaction: Access to Today's Technologies (Part I), edited by Margherita Antona and Constantine Stephanidis
8. LNCS 9176, Universal Access in Human-Computer Interaction: Access to Interaction (Part II), edited by Margherita Antona and Constantine Stephanidis
9. LNCS 9177, Universal Access in Human-Computer Interaction: Access to Learning, Health and Well-Being (Part III), edited by Margherita Antona and Constantine Stephanidis
10. LNCS 9178, Universal Access in Human-Computer Interaction: Access to the Human Environment and Culture (Part IV), edited by Margherita Antona and Constantine Stephanidis
11. LNCS 9179, Virtual, Augmented and Mixed Reality, edited by Randall Shumaker and Stephanie Lackey
12. LNCS 9180, Cross-Cultural Design: Methods, Practice and Impact (Part I), edited by P.L. Patrick Rau
13. LNCS 9181, Cross-Cultural Design: Applications in Mobile Interaction, Education, Health, Transport and Cultural Heritage (Part II), edited by P.L. Patrick Rau
14. LNCS 9182, Social Computing and Social Media, edited by Gabriele Meiselwitz
15. LNAI 9183, Foundations of Augmented Cognition, edited by Dylan D. Schmorrow and Cali M. Fidopiastis
16. LNCS 9184, Digital Human Modeling and Applications in Health, Safety, Ergonomics and Risk Management: Human Modeling (Part I), edited by Vincent G. Duffy
17. LNCS 9185, Digital Human Modeling and Applications in Health, Safety, Ergonomics and Risk Management: Ergonomics and Health (Part II), edited by Vincent G. Duffy
18. LNCS 9186, Design, User Experience, and Usability: Design Discourse (Part I), edited by Aaron Marcus
19. LNCS 9187, Design, User Experience, and Usability: Users and Interactions (Part II), edited by Aaron Marcus
20. LNCS 9188, Design, User Experience, and Usability: Interactive Experience Design (Part III), edited by Aaron Marcus

21. LNCS 9189, Distributed, Ambient and Pervasive Interactions, edited by Norbert Streitz and Panos Markopoulos
22. LNCS 9190, Human Aspects of Information Security, Privacy and Trust, edited by Theo Tryfonas and Ioannis Askoxylakis
23. LNCS 9191, HCI in Business, edited by Fiona Fui-Hoon Nah and Chuan-Hoo Tan
24. LNCS 9192, Learning and Collaboration Technologies, edited by Panayiotis Zaphiris and Andri Ioannou
25. LNCS 9193, Human Aspects of IT for the Aged Population: Design for Aging (Part I), edited by Jia Zhou and Gavriel Salvendy
26. LNCS 9194, Human Aspects of IT for the Aged Population: Design for Everyday Life (Part II), edited by Jia Zhou and Gavriel Salvendy
27. CCIS 528, HCI International 2015 Posters' Extended Abstracts (Part I), edited by Constantine Stephanidis
28. CCIS 529, HCI International 2015 Posters' Extended Abstracts (Part II), edited by Constantine Stephanidis

Cross-Cultural Design

Program Board Chair: P.L. Patrick Rau, P.R. China

- Zhe Chen, P.R. China
- Yu-Liang Chi, Taiwan
- Paul L. Fu, USA
- Zhiyong Fu, P.R. China
- Sung H. Han, Korea
- Toshikazu Kato, Japan
- Pin-Chao Liao, P.R. China
- Dyi-Yih Michael Lin, Taiwan
- Rungtai Lin, Taiwan

- Jun Liu, P.R. China
- Yongqi Lou, P.R. China
- Ta-Ping Lu, Taiwan
- Liang Ma, P.R. China
- Alexander Mädche, Germany
- Sheau-Farn Max Liang, Taiwan
- Katsuhiko Ogawa, Japan
- Huatong Sun, USA
- Hsiu-Ping Yueh, Taiwan

The full list with the Program Board Chairs and the members of the Program Boards of all thematic areas and affiliated conferences is available online at:

http://www.hci.international/2015/

HCI International 2016

The 18th International Conference on Human-Computer Interaction, HCI International 2016, will be held jointly with the affiliated conferences in Toronto, Canada, at the Westin Harbour Castle Hotel, 17–22 July 2016. It will cover a broad spectrum of themes related to Human-Computer Interaction, including theoretical issues, methods, tools, processes, and case studies in HCI design, as well as novel interaction techniques, interfaces, and applications. The proceedings will be published by Springer. More information will be available on the conference website: http://2016.hci.international/.

General Chair
Prof. Constantine Stephanidis
University of Crete and ICS-FORTH
Heraklion, Crete, Greece
Email: general_chair@hcii2016.org

http://2016.hci.international/

Contents – Part I

Cross-Cultural Product Design

A Brand Construction Strategy of Digital Cultural and Creative
Empowerment in Local Cultural Industries. 3
    Tsen-Yao Chang and Kuo-Li Huang

The Effects of Form Ratio in Product Design. 15
    Chiu-Wei Chien, Chih-Long Lin, and Rungtai Lin

Pilot Study on the Application of Light-Absorbing Fabric in Sport Fashion. . . . 24
    Chiui Hsu and Po-Hsien Lin

A Design Strategy of Cultural and Creative Products on the Global Market. . . 36
    Chi-Hsien Hsu and Wang-Chin Tsai

Chinese Cultural Values in User Experience Design of Kids' Home
Products. 49
    Xiaojun Huang and Linong Dai

Cross-Cultural User Experience Design Helping Product Designers
to Consider Cultural Differences. 58
    Florian Lachner, Constantin von Saucken, Florian 'Floyd' Mueller,
    and Udo Lindemann

A Product Service System Design for Fitness Activities Based on Active
Ageing a Proposal of Fitness for Xishan Style Council 71
    Yin Liang and Davide Fassi

A Study of the Accessible Approach to Replace the Reservoir Silt Glaze
with New Formula 83
    Chi-Chang Lu and Po-Hsien Lin

Humanism Presented in Taiwan Cochin Ceramic Design 96
    Huei-Mei Shih

Designing Wearable Device-Based Product and Service Ecosystem 108
    Xiaohua Sun, Yongqi Lou, Tong Li, and Qi Wang

From OEM to OBM - A Case Study of Branding Taiwan 116
    Hui-Yun Yen, Yu-Ju Lin, Yige Jin, and Rungtai Lin

Research on Service-Driven Feature of Industrial Designers Under
the Background of Industry Convergence.   128
    Qing Zhang, Chen Cheng, Junnan Ye, and Wei Ding

Cross-Cultural Design Methods and Case Studies

Comparison of User Responses to English and Arabic Emotion Elicitation
Video Clips   141
    Nawal Al-Mutairi, Sharifa Alghowinem, and Areej Al-Wabil

Understanding Gratifications of Watching Danmaku Videos – Videos
with Overlaid Comments   153
    Yue Chen, Qin Gao, and Pei-Luen Patrick Rau

User's Individual Needs Oriented Parametric Design Method of Chinese
Fonts.   164
    Qijun Duan and Xiaoli Zhang

Dramatic Sketches: A New Interaction Design Resource
for Communicating Contextual Factors   176
    Fuad Ali EL-Qirem and Gilbert Cockton

A Formal Method for Evaluating the Performance Level of Human-Human
Collaborative Procedures   186
    Dan Pan and Matthew L. Bolton

The Effect of Tactile Feedback on Mental Workload During the Interaction
with a Smartphone   198
    Peter Rasche, Alexander Mertens, Christopher Schlick,
    and Pilsung Choe

Brazilian Cultural Differences and Their Effects on the Web Interfaces
User Experience   209
    Tales Rebequi Costa Borges de Souza, Marcelo Morandini,
    and João Luiz Bernardes Jr.

A Pilot Study of Exploring the Relationship Between Dechnology Product
and Product Personality   221
    Wen-Zhong Su, Hsi-Yen Lin, Chi-Ying Hung, and Pei-Hua Hung

An Innovation Design for Hazardous Chemical/Gases Disaster Detection
and Analysis Equipment by Using Cross-Cultural User Scenarios
and Service Design   232
    Sheng-Ming Wang, Cheih Ju Huang, Lun-Chang Chou,
    and Pei-Lin Chen

Based on Action-Personality Data Mining, Research of Gamification
Emission Reduction Mechanism and Intelligent Personalized Action
Recommendation Model   241
   Yangbo Xu and Yi Tang

Design of a Clothing Shopping Guide Website for Visually Impaired
People   253
   Huiqiao Yang, Qijia Peng, Qin Gao, and Pei-Luen Patrick Rau

Co-design: An Investigation Through Interviewing Expert in Europe   262
   Shu Yuan, Hua Dong, and Zi Chen

Investigation into Designing of Elderly Products Intending for the User's
Behavior Experiencing.   274
   Ning Zhang, Yajun Li, Ming Zhou, and Zhizheng Zhang

Research on Product Affective Image by the Way of Empathic Design   283
   Meiyu Zhou, Xiaowen Yang, Peilong Liang, and Pei Xu

Design, Innovation, Social Development and Sustainability

A Study on the Balance and Optimization Measures in Industry-University
Collaborative Innovation of Interaction Design   293
   Jianxin Cheng, Miao Liu, and Junnan Ye

The Research and Practice Framework for Designing the Digital Social
Innovation   303
   Zhiyong Fu and Zirui Huang

Defining the Middle Ground: A Comprehensive Approach to the Planning,
Design and Implementation of Smart City Operating Systems.   316
   Christopher Grant Kirwan

Review on Interaction Design for Social Context in Public Spaces   328
   Xu Lin, Jun Hu, and Matthias Rauterberg

Diagnosis on Corporate Culture and Construction: A Case Study of Limin
Chemical Co., Ltd.   339
   Lin Ma, Xueli Wang, and Xiaopeng He

When Human-Centered Design Meets Social Innovation: The Idea
of Meaning Making Revisited.   349
   Jin Ma

Design Process as Communication Agency for Value Co-Creation in Open
Social Innovation Project: A Case Study of QuYang Community
in Shanghai   361
   Dongjin Song, Susu Nousala, and Yongqi Lou

Design for Sustainable Behaviour   372
  Xu Sun, Qingfeng Wang, Nan Wang, Charlie Sugianto So,
  and Yan Wang

Preliminary Study: Influence of Cultural Differences on the Innovation
Process Between Chinese and Germans   381
  Liuxing Tsao, Philip Alexander Behr-Heyder, and Liang Ma

From Invisible to Visible: The Evolution of Space Formation
of the Nineteenth Century Christian Missionary Work in Taiwan   392
  Yin-Chun Tseng, Kun-Chen Chang, Fu-Kuo Mii, and Chiu-Wei Chien

Exploring Socioeconomic and Sociocultural Implications of ICT Use:
An Ethnographic Study of Indigenous People in Malaysia   403
  Norazlinawati Walid, Emma Nuraihan Mior Ibrahim, Chee Siang Ang,
  and Norlaila Md. Noor

Stakeholder Engagement: Applying Dechnology in a Technology-Oriented
Organization.   414
  Chih-Shiang (Mike) Wu, William Huang, Pei-Lin Chen,
  and Tung-Jung Sung

Author Index   427

Contents – Part II

Cultural Aspects of Social Media and Mobile Services

Culturally Appropriate Design of Mobile Learning Applications
in the Malaysian Context 3
   Shamsul Arrieya Ariffin and Laurel Evelyn Dyson

How Online Social Network and Wearable Devices Enhance Exercise
Well-Being of Chinese Females? 15
   Hao Chen, Ting-Yu Tony Lin, Qiaochu Mu, and Pei-Luen Patrick Rau

Social Media Design Requirements for the Collectivist
International Students 22
   Kanrawi Kitkhachonkunlaphat and Mihaela Vorvoreanu

"Faith to Go or Devil's Work" – Social Media Acceptance
in Taboo-Related Usage Contexts 34
   Judith Leckebusch, Sylvia Kowalewski, Chantal Lidynia,
   and Martina Ziefle

The Impact of Natural Utilization of Traditional Chinese Cultural Elements
on the User Experience in Mobile Interaction Design 46
   Tian Lei, Xu Liu, Lei Wu, Tianjian Chen, Yuhui Wang, Luyao Xiong,
   and Shuaili Wei

Service Design Towards Sustainable Lifestyle in the Context
of Mobile Internet 57
   Xueliang Li, Miaosen Gong, and Dongjuan Xiao

From Technology to Design: A Case Study of Netizen's Perception Toward
Dechnology Products 68
   Hsi-Yen Lin, Wen-Zhong Su, Pei-Hua Hung, and Chi-Ying Hung

From Customer Satisfaction to Customer Experience: Online Customer
Satisfaction Practice in International E-commerce 80
   Yanyang Liuqu, Xinheng Fan, and Paul L. Fu

E-Commerce Purchase Intention in Emerging Markets: The Influence
of Gender and Culture 90
   Dimitrios Rigas and Nazish Riaz

Cultural Capital at Work in Facebook Users' Selection of Different
Languages 101
   Jieyu Wang and Satarupa Joardar

Culture for Transport and Travel

Applying Soundscape to Creating an Interactive and Cultural
Centered Experience 113
   Hsiu Ching Laura Hsieh and Chiao Yu Hwang

Design of Vehicle-to-Vehicle Communication System for Chinese
and German Drivers 121
   Xiang Ji, Lukas Haferkamp, Chieh Cheng,
   Muanphet Charunratanavisan, Andreas Neuhaus, Na Sun,
   and Pei-Luen Patrick Rau

Investigation of a Driver-to-Driver Communication Method
Through Rear Window Display for Chinese 129
   Na Liu, Ruifeng Yu, Deyu Wang, and Yunhong Zhang

On the Qualitative Research Approach and Application
of the "VTIO" Model Based on Cultural Differences:
A Case Study of Changan Ford Mazda Automobile Co., Ltd 140
   Lei Liu and Lin Ma

Driving Safety Considered User Interface of a Smartphone:
An Experimental Comparison 150
   Sanaz Motamedi, Mahdi Hasheminejad, and Pilsung Choe

Exploring Smart-Car Space in Urban India 161
   Sarita Seshagiri and Aditya Ponnada

Ask Local: Explore a New Place Like Locals 174
   Cagri Hakan Zaman, Federico Casalegno, Meng Sun,
   and Kulpreet Chilana

Culture for Design and Design for Culture

Analysis of Emotional Design and Cultural Product Narrative
Communication Model. 187
   Miao-Hsien Chuang and Jui-Ping Ma

From Design to Humanity - A Case Study of Costumer Value
Toward Dechnology Products 197
   Chi-Ying Hung, Pei-Hua Hung, Wen-Zhong Su, and Hsi-Yen Lin

From Design to Technology: A Case Study of Children's Perception
Toward the Dechnology Products 209
   Pei-Hua Hung, Chi-Ying Hung, Hsi-Yen Lin, and Wen-Zhong Su

Monster Design and Classifier Cognition 222
   Larry Hong-lin Li

Design of Literature Management Tool   230
   Xiaojing Liao

Emotion and Perception: A Case Study of Aesthetic Response
to Frith's Narrative Painting "The Railway Station".   241
   Po-Hsien Lin, Mo-Li Yeh, and Jao-Hsun Tseng

Traditional Western Art Elements in Disney Animations, Elite Influence
in Mass Culture Through the Prism of the Frankfurt School   252
   Nai-Hsuan Lin and Shwu-Huoy Tzou

From Dechnology to Humart – A Case Study of Taiwan Design
Development   263
   Rungtai Lin, John Kreifeldt, Pei-Hua Hung, and Jun-Liang Chen

Human Factors Perspective of Dancing Props Design: A Case Study
of "Feiyan's Dancing on Palms".   274
   Jao-Hsun Tseng and Po-Hsien Lin

The Application of Chinese Poem "*Yu Mei Ren*" in Design   285
   Mo-Li Yeh, Hsi-Yen Lin, Ming-shean Wang, and Rungtai Lin

Cultural Identification and Innovation–A Study on the Design of Exhibition
and Dissemination System for a City's Cultural Heritage
Under the New Media Context   294
   Lie Zhang and Wen Zhang

Culture for Health, Learning and Games

Paper Catalog and Digital Catalog - Reading Behaviors of College Students
in Taiwan.   307
   Yu-Ju Lin, Hui-Yun Yen, Chiui Hsu, Yige Jin, and Po-Hsien Lin

"Break the Language Great Wall" (RedClay): The Language Learning
Application   318
   Ting-Yu Tony Lin, Benoit Serot, Maxime Verlhac, Marie Maniglier,
   Na Sun, and Pei-Luen Patrick Rau

Interact Through Your Data: Collective Immersive Experience Design
for Indoor Exercises   328
   Xu Lin, Linkai Tao, Bin Yu, Yongyan Guo, and Jun Hu

Leap-Motion Based Online Interactive System for Hand Rehabilitation   338
   Zhe Liu, Yingzhi Zhang, Pei-Luen Patrick Rau, Pilsung Choe,
   and Tauseef Gulrez

From Dechnology to Humart: A Case Study of Applying Nature
User Interface to the Interactive Rehabilitation Design   348
    Jui Ping Ma, Na Ling Huang, Miao Hsien Chuang, and Rungtai Lin

Physician Communication Behaviors that Predict Patient Trust
in Outpatient Departments   361
    Manrong She, Zhizhong Li, and Pei-Luen Patrick Rau

Cultural Difference on Team Performance Between Chinese and Americans
in Multiplayer Online Battle Arena Games   374
    Huiwen Wang, Bang Xia, and Zhe Chen

Defining Design Opportunities of Healthcare in the Perspective
of Digital Social Innovation   384
    Dongjuan Xiao, Miaosen Gong, and Xueliang Li

The Service System Study on Children's Hospital-Bed Nursing
Based on Multi-level Experience   394
    Linghao Zhang, Chang Zhang, Sheng Huang, and Sichun Xiao

Field Study on College Students' Uses and Gratifications of Multitasking
Interaction with Multiple Smart Devices.   407
    Yubo Zhang and Pei-Luen Patrick Rau

Author Index   417

Cross-Cultural Product Design

Cross-Cultural Product Design

A Brand Construction Strategy of Digital Cultural and Creative Empowerment in Local Cultural Industries

Tsen-Yao Chang[1(✉)] and Kuo-Li Huang[2]

[1] Department of Creative Design, National Yunlin University of Science
and Technology, Douliu, Yunlin County, Taiwan
changty8908@gmail.com
[2] Department of Visual Communication Design, Southern Taiwan University,
Tainan, Taiwan
z3z@mail.stust.edu.tw

Abstract. The study introduces digital technology into local industry development, thus building a brand model and creating cultural experimental value to build cross-border brand equity and reduce time expense for design and marketing. The concept of brand model intends to promote in the form of value-added benefits and international business opportunities into industries. Subsequently, the upgrading and transformation of the traditional industry is promoted, driving industry value, the cultural tourism industry, and local brand development. The study is expected to assist local industries in determining their advantages, integrating local stories into brand marketing, and seeking potential opportunities to create brand value through digital marketing. This way, the local industry can be integrated into a sustainable industry chain or settlement. A typical local economy should also be encouraged to grow sustainably so that the local brand can be introduced to the international market and the local industry scale can be expanded.

Keywords: Cultural and creative industries · Local brand development · Digital marketing · Brand value

1 Introduction

The local industries of Taiwan are taken as examples. Taiwan, with an area of 35,980 km^2, features different geographical landscapes, distinct crops and strong local favors, all of which benefit the development of the country's cultural creative industry. The well-developed international tourism industry provides a perfect opportunity with which to develop local industries. As local tourism is promoted, creative tourism should be advanced along with local software and hardware, including compound management and experience marketing. Governments at all levels have promoted industrial transformation from the local industries to a tourism factory or mini-industry, allowing preservation and popularization of local culture and activation of local assets. Therefore, instead of creating a pick-and-mix design to destroy the whole picture, cultural resources can be combined with the concept of integrated brand-to-market

© Springer International Publishing Switzerland 2015
P.L.P. Rau (Ed.): CCD 2015, Part I, LNCS 9180, pp. 3–14, 2015.
DOI: 10.1007/978-3-319-20907-4_1

service design to create enjoyable experience. In addition, it can also lead to the application of digital technology to create new values and experiences that, in turn, can help maintain awareness among the local people. The study introduces digital technology into local industry development, thus building a brand model and creating cultural experimental value to build cross-border brand equity and reduce time expense for design and marketing. The company will benefit in the form of value-added benefits and international business opportunities. Subsequently, the upgrading and transformation of the traditional industry is promoted, driving industry value, the cultural tourism industry, and local brand development.

2 Literature Review

In the development of local tourism, and the arousal of sense of natives caused by globalization, the people, culture, geography, property and scenery with local feature will be a key factor of developing local economy, while culture and creativity could create business opportunity through the added value and service of digital technology, providing real estate with different strategic thinking. Thus, based on culture and economy, this study tries to explore the local property development and strategic approach of brand management.

2.1 Local Characteristic Culture and Creative Economy

Culture plays an irreplaceable role in brand and local industry, the elements such as emotional resonance and story possessed by culture have created infinite possibility of economic value, providing the best counter to highlight national feature. Localized life culture has gradually become a development direction of Taiwan's cultural creation; local feature is also the thinking point of local cultural creation in the development of community. In the 1980s and 1990s, in the face of cultural infiltration in consumer market by foreign mass culture, Taiwanese was evoked to think about native consciousness, reflection on self-identity and cultural criticism, started positive self cultural updating and reconstruction to create plentiful and real local life culture, and then the global culture in Taiwan coexisted harmoniously (Hsiao 2002; Liao 1996). For the managers of local industry and designers, they can understand the opinion of ethnic group effectively and the demand of market by culture, on the other hand, they can bring culture into industry and endow industry with depth through culture, promoting consumer behavior to a kind of experience of life attitude and culture. In addition, from the opinion of consumer, when industry and designer are creating consumption value by using cultural code, the commodity contacted by consumers is not only consumer goods, but also contain the cultural implication, which create deep emotional and sensitive connection.

Because of the relationship with economy, culture is made and produced to appear as various kinds of physical commodity and sightseeing; while economic activities have made economic behavior produce emotional recognition, heterogeneity and distinguishing degree due to elements such as story with cultural connotation and emotion.

Thus, there is a mutual benefit relationship between culture and economy (Lash and Urry 1994). The traits of culture such as diversification, uniqueness and distinguishing degree, making it one of the selling points of marketing, for local residents, culture is the element which is closely related to life, while it is exactly the trait of marketing, by digging local culture, culture has become the important core value in current marketing, design and community construction.

2.2 Service Experience Creating New Value of Brand

In the era of emphasizing experience economy, the products and service sold by enterprise have to produce unique value through experience design, and the introduction of service design is made by integrated service design system plan to consider using what kind of ways to create a service experience more perfectly and provide consumers with an innovative experience. Pine and Gilmore (1998) thought the difference between "Experience Economy" and traditional economy (agricultural economy, industrial economy) is that Experience Economy pursues the shaping of sensibility and experience to build and provide activities for consumers to recollect, besides, also pay attention to the interaction between consumers and commodity. However, service design refers to the people who has contacted and accepted service, brand, product, environment and connection between each other (Evenson 2006). Schmitt (1999) classifies experience into 5 kinds, namely sense, emotion, thinking, action and relation, these can be seen as a strategic experience module, by cooperating with its purpose and appeal, to choose one of them to apply independently or integrate them into a whole experience.

Generally speaking, both service design and experience economy pays attention to a kind of consumer experience context and interaction. Service design pays attention to explain the function and shape from consumer's point of view, helping industry to provide innovative service or improve existing service, making customer side product and service establish more useful, available and desired traits, as well as taking the feasibility, service efficiency of the application of service provider and enterprise side (Yang and Huang 2011; Moritz 2005). Compared to general traditional design, service design is a kind of more macro design activity plan and procedure. If service provides customers with a kind of experience, service design should pay more attention to provide customers with a series of desired unique experience design (Ho and Sung 2014). The main idea of service design is to make the boundary between service providers (designers) and service receivers (consumers) fuzzy and become the participants in the process of co-creating experience, producing the concept of Co-creation (Yang and Huang 2011; Brown 2009). The thinking of observation and user-centered can be applied in different issues and field to create different opinion and thinking direction. However, when performing service design, the integrity of content, all-dimensional consideration planning, including communication, environment and behavior, etc. must be taken into consideration, no matter in what kind of ways to express, consistency, easy-to-use and strategic combination must be presented (Hollins and Hollins 1991), so as to provide suitable service solution based on field domain, connecting local, tourism, service and experience to create innovative content of creative tourism.

2.3   Opportunities of Adding Value by Digitalization for Local Industry Branding

In the past, Taiwan enterprises widely believed that talking about "brand" is vague and unpractical, as the transformation of industry and the changing of consumer's interests, due to the gradual formation of "brand value" concept, making enterprises confront "brand" and pay attention (Lo and Lin 2007). The things brand differs from other competitive products or service are the following three functions: first, explicit function of distinguishing, such as brand name, mark, symbol, special color or font, etc., making brand produce uniqueness and easy to distinguish; second, implicit function of cohesion. Such as social responsibility, spirit pursuit and value orientation, which is regarded as the bridge between internal personnel and external consumer; third, function of market orientation. Brand is growing in market, which is the result of consumer's recognition; there will be no brand without consumer (Tsai 2009). The items involved in the three functions of brand contain Interdisciplinary professional knowledge connotation, from the distinguishing strategy of brand, spiritual value to market value, the construction of brand requires strategic operation with integrity and creating the opportunity of brand digital marketing through new media.

The so called "new media" connect people who use media in different places and time to form a community by using digital, website and interactive technology, so as to conduct group interaction, from which share information or experience, and then achieve the marketing mode of transmitting information (Ryan and Jones 2009). New social media mostly appear on website; the content is chosen or created by users, which is mostly published by people with the same interest. From the one-way information delivery in Web1.0 to the Web2.0 bilateral interaction social times, website platform is gradually transformed from customer service to citizen-oriented concept (Chen 2010). Digital technology has provided the new marketing opportunity, the business environment on social media is no longer the same as traditional media mode, always advertising or promoting products, it has to pay more time and energy to interact with members in social groups to achieve marketing performance (Ku and Lee 2014). In the ear of Web2.0, users have become information sharer, providing interaction mode between users as well as between users and website. The continuous development of digital technology brings great convenience to human life, making the relation between digital and life much closer.

2.4   Summary

The uniqueness in culture and life, in addition to endow town with character and life, when introducing design into local field to observe, plan and design, the diversification and feature of local culture will be the key point of local brand development and integrating design strategy. This study can help promote the brand development of the local economy, integrate local cultural features with the tourism brand, and facilitate the localization of industries in Taiwan by introducing digital technology. The cultural identity of a local industry is explored based on the settlements of villages and towns (or space, field, and strongpoint). Characteristic enterprises are regarded as a brand to build a test base. Local industries have a small business scope and may be unfamiliar with the concept of "brand management". Thus, products with good quality are often sold with poor marketing strategies. The study is expected to assist local industries in determining their advantages, integrating local stories into brand marketing, and seeking potential opportunities to create brand value through digital marketing. The study introduces service design and brand strategy into the local cultural industry as well as promotes industry transformation and brand marketing.

3 Research Method

The study has three stages. In the first stage, literature review and current case study were conducted to explore and determine the current conditions and resources of local brands in Taiwan. Lectures on brand image and planning were held. Experienced experts and scholars were invited to share their experiences. In addition, workshops on creative service design and creative brand strategies were provided to motivate the participants. They were also guided to visit villages and towns to obtain first-hand experience. A design project on local branding was proposed as a primary test, thus providing the relevant experience of brand operation and foundation for the formulation of a theory.

In the second stage, the results and theoretical foundation in the first stage were adopted to investigate the application of digital technology in brand management and operation. A project on the application of digital content service in the local industry was designed and proposed. The formulated theory was applied through practical operations.

In the third stage, research data were collected to build a local brand strategy pattern in accordance with local conditions. Through the evaluation of digital tools and research results from case analysis, a creative marketing pattern is built by integrating the digital technology into the distinct branding of the local industry.

4 Results and Discussions

The study analysis is divided into three major parts to propose the perception based on different study methods and steps for the current phase. At first, the expert speeches are analyzed to learn the opinions of the experts with practical experience towards the brand operation strategy. Then it hosts the workshop that introduces the service design tools through practical operation and diagnoses the existing local brands in Taiwan through the strategy of service design, so as to understand the current situation of local brand operation and outline the feasible strategy patterns in the future. Finally, the academic and industrial experts are invited to discuss about the opportunities for brand development in the future, and to propose the related suggestions and illustrations. To sum up the views in each phase, it integrates and proposes the operation strategy patterns of introducing the digital service into local brand operation.

4.1 Expert's Brand Speech: Value, Strategy and Profits

The study invites 10 experts with the practical experience related to brand operation, to share their experience in the speeches on the topics of local operation, brand strategy and design planning. It expects the experts could share the strategy experience and opinions of brand operation within the short speech by summary and brief elaboration. The study further conducts interview for the experts and analyzes their opinions towards brand establishment through the transcript codes, which are taken as the foundation and direction of the propositions in the follow-up studies. For the practical experience shared by the 10 experts, it analyzes and summarizes three major directions of brand operation, namely, 1. Value- sustainable operation of local specialties, 2. Strategy- brand positioning and marketing channels, and 3. Profits-Business features and patterns, as detailed below:

1. Value- sustainable operation of local specialties
   Developing brand and design from the perspective of caring locality, the experts consider the local spirits and features as the core of brand development, so as to strengthen the correlation of brand and locality that can become the irreplaceable brand distinction and create the brand identity. For the brand design plan from the perspective of local specialties, the core value must return to the local place, so as to build favorable operation interaction with the locals. Finally, it repays the locals and creates the opportunities for sustainable operation.

2. Strategy- brand positioning and marketing channels
   The brand planning strategy requires strict investigation and study. It conducts design service and visual planning suitable to the development of brand essence, so as to create the overall consistency of brand development. The product value is planned and the target consumer groups are defined through the brand positioning. Various problems related to the consumers and market orientation can determine the brand and product design strategies and conditions. Through the design diagnosis, problem digging and design positioning before the brand is promoted to the market, it can create brand and product and release them to the market in the test phase. In this way, it can create the profitable opportunities and save costs. Different positioning can determine the design operation direction and idea. Therefore, before a new brand and new design is released to the market, it requires strict analysis and strategy formulation. By doing so, it can discover the special stories and values of the products, grasp and magnify the characteristics, as well as strengthen the brand characteristics and finally produce identity and memory in the minds of the consumers. During this process, it must have quite good interaction and mutual trust relationship with the brand.

3. Profits- business features and patterns
   The current industrial pattern focuses on the consumption mechanism at the consumer end to gain profits, while the design itself is a business idea. Thus, the design originality can't ignore the thinking mode in the business field. During the operation, it first requires a full research and investigation on the cases of different brands, and then designs the optimal solution based on different positions and properties of the cases. With a clear thought and objective cutting point, it formulates the

strategies and resolves problems by following the five steps of observation, imitation, cultivation, understanding, and creation. Moreover, it discovers the special stories and values of the products, grasps and magnifies the characteristics, as well as strengthens the brand characteristics and finally produces identity and memory in the minds of the consumers. During this process, it must have quite good interaction and mutual trust relationship with the brand. It values the teamwork and interaction, and insists on the direction of brand positioning. The brand operation must closely combine the design with the channels, so as to match different channels to different customer groups and work out different design proposals. At the meantime, it must conduct market analysis and channel planning.

4.2 Brand Strategy Workshop: See Brand Innovation Opportunity from Service Design

After the experts share the experience, the study hosts the brand strategy workshop. It intends to introduce the service design to review the 7 local brand cases in Taiwan, find out the problems and clarify the current situation of the brands. The detailed instruction content includes building the fundamental concept of service design, introducing the service design tools, as well as the service design practice and brand strategy planning. The participants generate insights from service design through the analysis on the local industrial brands, draw the sustainable operation blueprint with the brand strategy planning, discover and increase the possibilities for the local industrial to develop international brands.

During the workshop operation, the study introduces a total of 10 service design tools for different phases of design process, as shown in Fig. 1.

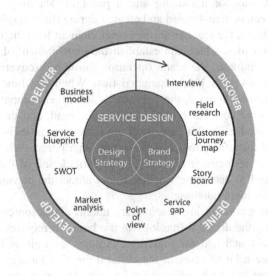

Fig. 1. Service design tools introduced for each phase

In the middle and ending phases of the workshop, the participants are required to think about the use of each service tool and provide feedbacks. To sum up the opinions of the participants, 4 of the 10 service design tools provide the greatest assistance for them during the process of brand strategy positioning, namely, "Customer Journey Map", "Storyboard", "Service Blueprint" and "Business Model Canvas", which can match the process of using the service tools. "Customer Journey Map" analyzes the customer positioning, and can help the participants sort and analyze the current situation of brand and service in a systematical way. "Storyboard" sorts the service order, and finds out whether there are some missing items or whether the logical is improper. The content of "Service Blueprint" clearly allocates the resources and manpower, and outlines the overall content and rules. "Business Model Canvas" presents the overall outlook of the brand and service. After clarifying various content items of the brand, it utilizes "Business Model Canvas" to review whether there are some missing parts from the core value to the profitability pattern, so as to think about the final positioning of the brand value. From the feedbacks of the participants, it is learned when introducing the service design tools into the brand; it can start from the process of problem diagnosis, strategy planning, resource allocation and business model, so as to facilitate the brand to build complete and comprehensive view.

4.3   In-depth Expert Interviews: Strategic Ideas from Concept to Profits

1. Story— Create brand value with story emotion
   The local development must find out the core value. This view is proposed repeatedly in different stages of the study process, which is taken as the core and key to the local brand development. The core value is from the local culture, including the local people, landscapes, industries, and etc. For these local values, it must find out a way for marketing and a point for standing. In this way, the economic value can be transformed and created during the cultural preservation and inheritance. Wherein, the story is an important element to strengthen and magnify the local characteristics, which can establish the development of local brands and the characteristic value of the brand operation through discovering the emotional value of the stories with local characteristics. When the functionalities of the product show minor difference, the consumer can further compare the sentimental elements such as the core value conveyed by the brand, and the cultural emotion contained in the product. In this case, what the consumer values is the spiritual story of the brand, and manufacturing persistence and finer points. When the consumer's concern transfers the focus, it depends on the formulation of the spiritual connotation of the brand to determine whether it can attract the consumer continuously and further makes them purchase.
2. Integration— Integration of interdisciplinary talents and resources
   When introducing the digital technology in the brand, it requires a communication role between the brand and the digital technology, as well as the resource integration. There are a lot of cases in the cultural creative industry which apply the digital technology to obtain value-added benefits. However, for the local brands,

they haven't obtained a deep understanding on and contact with the digital techniques and technologies, so they can't capture the market trend and technological application precisely. Therefore, it requires the communication media role which can understand the language between these two. In this way, the industries can benefit and cooperate with each other, as well as create the value-added opportunities.

- Positioning roles of interdisciplinary talents
  The terms and ideas adopted by the designers are different from that of the general managers or the technological developers, who are inclined to use the sentimental ones, but know how to apply the rational investigation tools. Therefore, the role positioning of the designers should be more open in the process of the brand operation, so they can participate in the overall process, and design the work that is closer to the brand requirements and customer demands. However, the technology and culture show a significant difference in the rational and sentimental orientation. Thus, the industrial experts with practical experience emphasize that the professional talents that play the bridge role are required to shorten the time and cost spent on the communication. Such interdisciplinary talents can be positioned as the role of managers or consultants, who create the innovative market opportunities through the understanding of the technology and the combination with the requirements of brand originality.
- Integration and application of technical resources
  Beside the integration of talents, the resource integration is also crucial. The management talents acquiring the knowledge from the both parties know how to communication with people from different industries. Furthermore, it needs to make good use of the resources and integrate them to maximize the strengths and benefits between the industries. Moreover, it must know how to use the resources at hand to seek assistance. For example, when seeking support from the government, it must clearly know which resources are in need. That can help get to the point directly and obtain the most support and assistance. The resource integration can create the synergistic effect that can link points into planes.

3. Digitalization— Communication, interaction and cost-saving
The digital technology should be considered as a tool used to create ideas and concept implementation. Moreover, it provides the operators and the consumers with a communication bridge, and helps the industries save cost, and so on. With the nature of service, the digital technology can help create value-added opportunities and reduce the operation costs for different industries if it is applied properly.

- Building communication bridge with the consumers
  With the era changes, the modern consumer groups show an increasingly high acceptance and dependency level. The digital message communication has become an indispensable part for promotion of modern brands, which can help shorten the communication cost and increase the brand visibility. Besides, the digital way also allows the brand operators to have the most direct contact and

interaction. The royal consumers supporting the brand can be cultivated in the communities. With these supporters, the brand operation can be maintained steadily. The word-of-mouth marketing effect of the network media makes the operators which show high requirements and persistence on the self-quality can create outstanding performance even without the advertisement exposure. All these are the benefits for the brand communication brought by the digital technology.

- Providing diverse assistance for the industries to save entrepreneurship cost
The application of digital technology in the entrepreneurship of cultural creative industry can be divided into different phases to provide different benefits and effects. In the founding phase, it can take advantage of the network features, such as low cost and high communication efficiency to make the brand contact with the consumers earlier. In this way, it tests the acceptance level of the market with lower cost. In the development phase, when the customers and consumer groups are gradually fixed, the network interaction can maintain the communication with the consumers. Moreover, it can provide service to stabilize the consumer groups. In addition, when the operation tends to be stable, it can introduce the product innovation and development, create different product items and perform the brand value innovation through the value-added benefit of the digital technology. Moreover, it communicates with the consumers constantly, and takes it as the way to keep in line with the preference of the consumers in the new era.

4. Commercialization — Diversified business models
In the process of developing local brands, how can we find a balancing point between the profits and the cultural value, and will the industrial development based on the commercial value fail to consider the cultural reality and make the application mere formality. In terms of the strategy of business model, the creative cultural operators can think about diversified business models in addition to the cost reduced by using the digital technology as stated above. The operation system can be divided into the profit department and development department. The former selects to operate with high market acceptance degree, stable case sources and low risk, so as to create stable revenue sources for the enterprise and the brand. At the meantime, the latter invests into the development of the creative and innovative ideas for the core perception of the brand, which is not restricted by whether the product will have immediate benefits and returns. The diversified operation strategy allows the local culture to strengthen the investment into the culture when developing the brand. The key for enterprise profits is not at the core value development end. Since the development end needs cultivation and test, so it may not obtain the market response immediately. However, with the time passing by, it can develop the consumer groups show recognition towards the brand perception, so as to create the long-tail effect in the enterprise. To achieve sustainable operation, the enterprise must think the return flow about from multiple perspectives. The operators cannot only think about gaining profits from the consumers, but also work out various profitable means. The profits can be gained by not only selling products, but also

selling advertisements and even providing services. Moreover, the operation subjects can be B-to-C or B-to-B, and even C-to-C. Also it can create stable operation and development with various profitable means.

5 Conclusion and Recommendations

After the constant operation is achieved, the enterprise should not stagnate. Under stable development, it must keep in line with the market preference and maintain the communication with the consumers. Furthermore, it can conduct development and innovation based on the customer preference, so as to achieve the goal of sustainable operation. To achieve sustainable operation, the practical consideration is to gain profits immediately. With the economic benefits, it can expand the business into industry, attract more talents and create more employment opportunities and new opportunities in the market.

In the enterprise operation cycle from founding phase, development phase, stablization phase to recession phase, the operation strategies in different phases must be centered with core value, so as to maintain the consistency of brand operation. Moreover, the strategic planning shall be performed based on the profitable means, manpower utilization and technological investment. Due to different brand stability, the operation strategies in each phase have different requirements of various talents and technologies. In the initial foundation phase, it could first plan the future development strategies for the overall operation, and then make adjustments according to the actual operation situation and the changes of market environment. By doing so, when entering the recession phase, the enterprise can develop new businesses based on the previous experience accumulation, or make transformation with various assets, so as to create the sustainable cycle. In terms of the brand operation, how to make innovation based on the times change and the technological advancement? It must keep good interaction with the consumers in addition to practicing the core value mainly based on the local culture. This can maintain the stable return flow and create opportunity of sustainable operation. The key echoes with the proposition of the study, namely, the assistance of

Fig. 2. Model of local brand operation strategies

Communication with the Consumers brought by the digitalization. Moreover, the promotion of digitalization depends on the talent cultivation and integration. These parts that are correlated with each other closely can create a new innovation point of brand operation strategy in the core value, strategy, integration, digital and commercial profits (Fig. 2).

Acknowledgment. The author gratefully acknowledges the financial support for this research provided by the Ministry of Science and Technology of Taiwan under Grant No. MOST 103-2420-H-224-003.

References

Chen, Y.-C.: Citizen-centric e-government services: understanding integrated citizen services, understanding integrated citizen services information systems. Soc. Sci. Comput. Rev. **28**(4), 427–442 (2010)

Brown, T.: Change by design: how design thinking transforms organisations and inspires innovation. HarperCollins, New York (2009)

Evenson, S.: Theory and Method for Experience Centered Design. Carnegie Mellon University, Pittsburg (2006)

Ho, S.S., Sung, T.J.: The development of academic research in service design: a meta-analysis. J. Des. **19**(2), 45–66 (2014)

Hollins, B., Hollins, G.: Over the Horizon: Planning Products Today for Success Tomorrow. Wiley, Chichester (1991)

Hsiao, H.H.M.: Coexistence and synthesis: cultural globalization and localization in contemporary Taiwan. In: Berger, R., Huntington, S.P. (eds.) Many Globalizations: Cultural Diversity in the Contemporary World, pp. 48–67. Oxford University Press, New York (2002)

Ku, C.K., Lee, Y.Y.: Social media marketing: an example in National Taiwan Museum. Taiwan Nat. Sci. **33**(2), 94–103 (2014)

Lash, S., Urry, J.: Economies of Signs and Space. Sage, London (1994)

Liao, P.: The case of the emergent cultural criticism columns in Taiwan's newspaper literary supplements: Global/Local dialectics in contemporary Taiwanese public culture. In: Wilson, R., Dissanayake, W. (eds.) Global/Local: Cultural Production and the Transnational Imaginary, pp. 337–347. Duke University Press, Durham (1996)

Lo, K., Lin, P.C.: An investigation on the cognitive model of high-brand-value identity design. J. Des. **12**(4), 1–20 (2007)

Moritz, S.: Service design: practical access to an evolving field. Unpublished master's thesis, Koln International School of Design, Cologne (2005)

PineII, B.J., Gilmore, J.H.: Welcome to experience economy. Harvard Bus. Rev. **76**, 97–105 (1998)

Ryan, D., Jones, C.: Understanding Digital Marketing: Marketing Strategies for Engaging the Digital Generation. Kogan Page, Philadelphia (2009)

Schmitt, B.H.: Experiential Marketing: How to Get Customers to Sense, Feel, Think, Act, and Relate to Your Company and Brands. Free Press, New York (1999)

Tsai, C.T.: Exploring school brand building and marketing management. J. Res. Elementary Secondary Educ. **23**, 139–160 (2009)

Yang, Z.F., Huang, Z.J.: Service Design Tools and Methods. Taiwan Design Center, Taipei (2011)

The Effects of Form Ratio in Product Design

Chiu-Wei Chien(✉), Chih-Long Lin, and Rungtai Lin

Graduate School of Creative Industry Design, National Taiwan University of
Arts, Ban Ciao City, Taipei 22058, Taiwan
chiewei@gmail.com, cl.lin@ntua.edu.tw,
rtlin@mail.ntua.edu.tw

Abstract. Product personalities are often designated for market segmentation
during product marketing, and product appearance is usually an important aspect
for determining product personality. Rational and emotional are the two opposite adjectives with the most resonance during interpretation of the properties of
product forms. Among the researches on form ratio, the golden ratio is the most
historic. In this study the questionnaire survey of two group variables of
"rational and emotional properties" and "preference" among 5 kinds of ratio
states of 4 kinds of basic forms has been carried out for the purposes of
(1) figuring out the correlation among the backgrounds of respondents, the form
preference, and the rational and emotional perception, and (2) the difference in
rational and emotional perceptions of different forms. This study is also aimed at
the impacts of ratio variations of different forms on the rational and emotional
properties. Both the online questionnaire and questionnaire in paper copy have
been implemented simultaneously in this experiment for two weeks. In the end
230 online questionnaires and 220 paper copies of questionnaires have been
collected, and there are 417 valid questionnaires out of the total of 450 questionnaires. The results of these questionnaires have led to two conclusions: 1.
The one with the highest significance of impact on rational and emotional
properties and preference level is the college attended, followed by the gender.
2. The smaller aspect ratio of rectangular, the more rational it will be. The
smaller aspect ratio of the organic form, the more emotional is will be.

Keywords: Rational and emotional · Form · Aspect ratio

1 Introduction

The two opposite adjectives of rational and emotional for interpretation and description
of human personalities can also be used for interpretation and description of specific
human behaviors for achieving certain objectives, such as the behavior of product
design. Since the collection of human personality characteristics can be used for
describing certain product [1], another question is can the product properties be used to
explain how to infer the product functionality personality from the designed appearance
[2]. Among the researches on form ratio, the golden ratio is the most historic. In late
19th century the German psychologist Gustav Fechner (1801–1887) began the research
on human special reaction to golden section rectangle, and he noticed that the buildings
of different cultures actually shared the same aesthetic preference with respect to the

© Springer International Publishing Switzerland 2015
P.L.P. Rau (Ed.): CCD 2015, Part I, LNCS 9180, pp. 15–23, 2015.
DOI: 10.1007/978-3-319-20907-4_2

golden section rectangle [3]. The purpose of this study is to (1) figuring out the correlation among the backgrounds of respondents, the form preference, and the rational and emotional perception, and (2) the difference in rational and emotional perceptions of different forms.

2   Literature Review

2.1   Investigation of Form Ratio

The experiment of Gustav Fechner was repeated by Charles Lalo (1877–1953) in 1908 with a more scientific approach [4]. Based on the results of experiments in two different eras, the variation of preference levels corresponding to different rectangle aspect ratio from 1:1 to 2:5 is as shown in Fig. 1 [5]. The experiments by Fechner and Lalo are based on the main target of preference on 5:8 golden ratio. However, the result of this study indicates that the preferences on 1:1 square, 1:2 rectangle (twice the size of square) and 2:5 rectangle (the one with the greatest ratio in the experiment) have shown changes. From the perspective of ratio similarity, 1:2 is closer to golden ratio than 2:5, yet the preference level of 1:2 is obviously lower than 2:5. As indicated by the variation curve in Fig. 1, the peak of preference level is at the golden ratio 5:8, and the lowest point of the decreasing ratio to the left is at 5:6, and the lowest point of the decreasing ratio to the right is at 1:2. And the difference values of 5:6 with respect to 1:2 and 5:8 are both close to 0.4. The preference level going past the lowest point will be rising again, such that the preference levels of 1:1 and 2:5 are both showing upward trend.

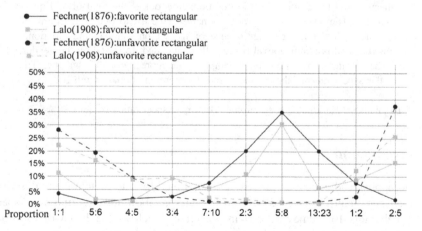

Fig. 1. Comparing figure of rectangle preference (on the basis of Elam (2001), this study rearrange).

Lin [6] suggested in the research on the ratio of automobile exterior dimensions that the aspect ratios of automobiles are mostly distributed at 1:2.618, which equals the golden rectangle plus another square. The rectangle based on the golden ratio of 1:1.618 is the one with the best static beauty, and the rectangle based on the ratio of

1:2.618 is the one with the best dynamic beauty. Yang [7] suggested that the ratio of cute form created by human varies in accordance with the ratio of infant, and the features created by the ratios of large head, small body, and fat and short limbs are exactly the cute factors perceived by the respondents. It indicates that the changes of ratios are influential to the properties of organic form.

2.2 The Rational and Emotional Properties

Kant (Immanuel Kant, 1724–1804) introduced the philosophical discourse of rationality and emotion in the book of The Critique of Pure Reason [8]. In recent years the pair of contrary adjectives "rational and emotional" has been used in researches of multiple orientations. The definitions of rational and emotional product properties can be dating back to 1980s, when Aaker and Shansby once defined product properties as: [The combination of various explicit and intrinsic features and properties of products which can be sensed by the consumers [9]. due to the market position requirement of product marketing. Japanese scholars have classified products based on whether or not the consumer is rational, thus leading to rational products and emotional products. The rational product properties are mostly product function, product quality, product price, and vendor reputation. The emotional product properties include consumer happiness, atmosphere, and fashion [10]. Hung and Chen [11] investigated the impacts of novelty of product appearance and aesthetic preferences, which included three basic dimensions of semantics — trend, complexity, and emotion. Among them, the contrary adjectives used for the emotion is "rational-emotional". This is for the definition and classification of properties for products entering the marketing stage. In this study the investigation is focused on the positioning of rational and emotional product personality at the design stage by product designer, or the future product properties which have been determined at the product planning by product planner before development design.

3 Research Method

In this study the questionnaire survey method has been used for the survey of the two group variables, [rational and emotional properties] and [preference], of 5 kinds of ratio states of 4 kinds of basic forms. The experiments of Fechner and Lalo are focused on the ratio of rectangle, while the experiments of Rong-Tai Lin are focused on the ratio of curve-shaped car. This study is focused on the design elements of three basic shapes — square, equilateral triangle and circle [12]. Even though the equilateral triangle is the basic element, its sharp angle feature can be visually irritant such that it is rarely used for actual products. Therefore, after eliminating the equilateral triangle and adding the curve shape and rounded square (which is frequently seen among modern industrial products such as iPhone), there are the basic states of the four forms. So there will be varying aspect ratios from 1:1, to 1:2 and 1:5, and the multiplied area of these three ratios will be the same. With the additional vertical and horizontal angles, there are a total of 5 ratios, which means there are 20 ($4 \times 5 = 20$) different figures serve as the sample for the first stage of experiment as shown in Fig. 2, where the numbers are shown below the figures. These 20 figures in this study are produced by the software of Corel DRAW12 in 1.5 mm black lines with white background.

Both the online questionnaire and questionnaire in paper copy have been implemented simultaneously in this experiment for two weeks. In the end 230 online questionnaires and 220 paper copies of questionnaires have been collected, and there are 417 valid questionnaires out of the total of 450 questionnaires. The basic information of the respondents are as shown below: female 221, male 196; age of 16–25: 269, age of 26–35: 58, age of 36–45: 62, age of 56–65: 4, age of 66–75: 1; education level: elementary school 2, senior high/vocational high school 22, bachelor degree 328, Master degree 53, Ph.D. 12; college attended: design and arts 230, science and engineering/electrical engineering/computer science 128, others 59; occupation: student 247, design and artwork 52, others 51, engineers 30, teachers 22, management positions 15. The questionnaire data is subject to SPSS data analysis. The first step is the reliability analysis on the two groups of combined variables of "rational and emotional properties" and "preference level" (hereinafter referred to as the two groups of combined variables), which leads to the Cronbach $\alpha = 0.746$ and 0.853 respectively. With both number greater than 7, they indicate high reliabilities.

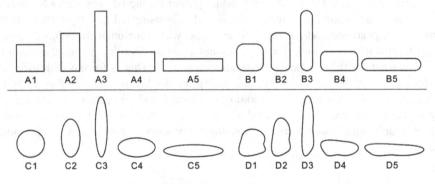

Fig. 2. Forms with no

4 Results and Discussions

4.1 The Cross Analysis Between the Backgrounds of Respondents and the Two Groups of Combined Variables

In this study the two-way multivariate analysis of variance (Two-Way MANOVA) has been used for the effect analysis of the interaction between the five basic information of respondent– gender, age, educational level, college attended, and occupation, and the "perception of rational and emotional properties" and "preference level". The one with the most significant impact on the "perception of rational and emotional properties" and "preference level" is the "college attended", followed by "gender" and "age". The occupation and educational level are not showing significant results. The next step is to figure out the difference between the reactions generated by different groups of combined variables by Independent Sample T Test. The [college attended] is the first to be analyzed, where the original eight categories of the college attended on the questionnaire are simplified to three major categories: College of Science and Engineering (Science/Engineering/Electrical Engineering/Computer Science), College of Design and Arts (Design and Arts) and others (literature/society, commerce/management, medical/biology and others). And the Science and Engineering (N = 128) and Design and Art (N = 230) accounted for 85 % of the respondents are taken as the grouping variables. With the two groups of combined variables of [perception of rational and emotional properties] and [preference level] as the test variables, those with significance of Sig.(2-taied) < 0.05 are listed along with the mean values as shown in Table 2. The result of age is not showing any significance due to that most respondents are with the age of 16–25 (N = 269).

Table 1 indicates that in the group of [rational and emotional properties] there are C3, C4 and C5 (all in oval series) with significance in terms of the difference in perception of Science and Engineering and Design and Arts backgrounds. The respondents with science and engineering background have higher perception of rational and emotional properties of oval shape than the average value of those with

Table 1. Independent sample t test in different majors

		F	Sig.	Sig.(2-taied)	Mean
C3-rational and emotional	SE	1.111	.293	.005	4.32
	DA			.004	3.92
C4-rational and emotional	SE	.387	.534	.004	4.37
	DA			.003	3.93
C5-rational and emotional	SE	.029	.865	.004	4.27
	DA			.004	3.85
B1-preference	SE	.000	.992	.000	4.91
	DA			.000	4.24
D1-preference	SE	.573	.450	.000	2.88
	DA			.000	3.87
B2-preference	SE	.860	.354	.000	4.57
	DA			.000	3.91
D2-preference	SE	2.329	.128	.000	2.96
	DA			.000	3.66
D3-preference	SE	1.267	.261	.002	3.09
	DA			.002	3.77
B4-preference	SE	.104	.748	.000	4.63
	DA			.000	3.95
D4-preference	SE	.478	.490	.005	3.18
	DA			.005	3.73
D5-preference	SE	2.982	.085	.000	3.03
	DA			.000	3.83

Only list Sig.(2-taied)< 0.05

SE = Science and engineering, DA = Design and Art

design and art background. In the group of [preference level] there are: B1, D1, B2, D2, D3, B4, D4 and D5, which fall into the round shapes of B series and the organic shapes of D series. Those with higher preference levels among respondents with science and engineering backgrounds than respondents with design and art backgrounds are: B1, B2 and B4, which are round shape, and horizontal and vertical 1:2 oval shapes; Those with higher preference levels among respondents with design and art backgrounds than respondents with science and engineering backgrounds are: D1, D2, D3, D4 and D5, which include all organic shapes of various aspect ratios.

4.2   Correlation Between Two Group Variables

The correlation between the two groups of combined variables of [rational and emotional properties] and [preference level] is as shown by the correlation matrix generated by Bivariate Correlation Analysis in Table 2. Among the 20×20 variables with γ value of * or **, 16 variables are with significance and 4 variables are without any significance. The 4 variables inside the borders of Table 2 without any significance are: A1 rational and emotional properties $\times$ A1 preference level, A2 rational and emotional properties $\times$ A2 preference level, A4 rational and emotional properties $\times$ A4 preference level, and D4 rational and emotional properties $\times$ D4 preference level.

Table 2. Correlation between two group variables

Preference rational & emotional	A	B	C	D
1 γ	−.036	.186**	.196**	.140**
Sig.(2-tailed)	.460	.000	.000	.004
2 γ	.007	.301**	.302**	.180**
Sig.(2-tailed)	.879	.000	.000	.000
3 γ	.146**	.305**	.296**	.251**
Sig.(2-tailed)	.003	.000	.000	.000
4 γ	.073	.272**	.327**	.072
Sig.(2-tailed)	.139	.000	.000	.144
5 γ	.115*	.263**	.272**	.242**
Sig.(2-tailed)	.019	.000	.000	.000

**Sig. = 0.01(2-taied),*Sig. = 0.05(2-taied)

From these 4 matrices with no significance, it appears that the standard deviations of [rational and emotional properties] of A1and A2 are rather small (0.814 and 0.877), and the standard deviations of A4 and D4 are rather large (2.642 and 2.452). The rest of standard deviations are all between 1.241–1.934, indicating that the respondents have more concentrated rational and emotional properties with respect to A1 and A2, and for A4 and D4 they are more scattered. The mean values of [preference level] of all four groups are all around 3.5 with standard deviations between 1.6–1.7. The analysis on the 4 groups (with solid line border) with no significance is as shown below:

(1) A1 square rectangle is the one with the lowest mean value among all 20 figures at 1.31, and the lowest standard deviation at 0.814. This indicates that the perception of respondents is consistent to regard A1 as the one with the most rational properties among all 20 figures; with $\gamma = -.036$, it indicates that respondents consider this figure to be rather rational, which is negatively correlated with the preference level, and the correlation between rational level and preference level is not significant. (2) The $\gamma = 0.007$ of A2 is the lowest among all 20 figures, indicating the least correlation between the [rational and emotional properties] and [preference level]. The $\gamma = 0.073$ of A4 also falls into the category of low significance. The figures of A2 and A4 are mostly identical, with the only difference in the horizontal and vertical aspect ratios. Yet it has led to different results. In terms of the mean value, the vertical A2 is 1.51. (3) The horizontal A4 is 1.80. On average, the respondents believe that the vertical rectangle with the aspect ratio of 1:2 is more rational than the vertical one, yet the high standard deviation of A4 indicates greater difference in rational perception of the horizontal one, and the vertical one is focused on the rational perception. (4) D4 is 1:2 vertical organic shape, and $\gamma = 0.073$ indicates insignificance just like A4. The mean value of 5.46 is leaning towards emotional, and the standard deviation of 2.452 indicates a big difference in the perceptions among respondents.

4.3 Discussions

1. As compared to those with design and arts backgrounds, the one with science and engineering backgrounds prefer round shape, and 1:2 vertical and horizontal oval shape, and they think 1:2 vertical oval shape and 1:5 vertical and horizontal oval shape are more emotional. It appears that the emotional acceptance of those with science and engineering backgrounds is only limited to the oval shape among all four forms (rectangle, radius angle rectangle, round/oval, organic shape). The acceptance with respect to the organic shapes with more complicated curvatures. In contrary, those with design and art backgrounds prefer organic shapes, yet they don't have any significance with respect to the emotional properties of organic shapes, which means those who received trainings of higher shaping capability should be more sensitive to the forms. This has increased the requirement of assessment value of form properties, which has also led to relatively higher acceptance of high order composite curves.
2. Among the four series of figures of A, B, C, and D, A series is for rational properties, D series is for emotional properties, and C and D series are neither rational nor emotional, which are categorized as mean value based on the [rational and emotional properties] of respondents with respect to the C series. Therefore, the radius angle rectangle of the B series is equipped with both the linear and curve shaping element. In terms of the curvature of figure, round shape and oval shape are curves with regular curvatures excluding the straight line with zero curvature, and it is unlike the organic shape which is composed of curves of multiple curvatures. This is why it is in between rectangle, radius angle rectangle, and organic shapes, and determined by respondents as the mean value among all four figures. The radius

angle rectangle is not determined by respondents as the mean value because it contains straight lines, whose rational level will affect the respondents.

3. In terms of the preference level of ratio, the preference level of 1:2 is higher than 1:5 because it is more stable and thus more comfortable and safety when it comes to the human visual stimulation. And the preference level of 1:1 ratio of B1 and C1 of the B and C series are higher than other ratios, while the preference levels of B1 and C1 are the highest among all figures. It indicates that, compared to the rectangle and organic shape which are located on the two ends of rational and emotional, figures located in between rational and emotional yet leaning towards rational, such as basic figures of non-extreme radius angle rectangle and round shape with 1:1 ratio, usually have the highest acceptance as compared to the deformation and forms based on other ratios.

As for the products with either rational or emotional forms, the eventual purpose is to pursue high consumer preference level. In this study, the forms with high preference levels are those of B and C series. These forms of mean value are between the most rational and emotional forms— radius angle rectangle and round/oval shapes; so it appears that most people prefer forms with higher stability, better balance, and high visual comfort.

Mugge [2] has suggested that the product design with right angle shape generally comes with a kind of business type and serious personality. Contrarily, the product design based on radius angle shape is considered to be the more cheerful, naughty, and childish personality, which has proved the positive correlation between the curvature and business type personality. The result of experiment I of this study has revealed that the right angle rectangle is considered rational, the radius angle rectangle is with increased emotional level, and round shape and organic shape with more curves and curvature variations are with less rational level and more emotional level. The business type and serious personality shares the same personality property formed by logical reasoning and principles as the rational properties, thus indicating the rational property of form is explicit, which is best represented by the right angle rectangle. As Kant said, emotion is a kind of intuitive perception, which is also known as intuition. Intuition varies from person to person. As a result, the result of experiment I reveals that the respondent background of college attended has significantly affected the difference between the emotional property of form and the preference level of respondents. Therefore, those with design and arts backgrounds prefer organic shapes, yet they don't have higher recognition with respect to the emotional properties and organic shapes. In other words, those who are more sensitive to the forms have relatively increased the assessment requirements of form properties, and higher acceptance with respect to the high order composite curves.

5 Conclusions

In this study the questionnaire survey of two group variables of "rational and emotional properties" and "preference" among 5 kinds of ratio states of 4 kinds of basic forms has been carried out. The conclusions including the impacts of backgrounds of respondents and the form ratios are as shown below:

1. Among all background conditions of respondents, those with the highest signifi-cance affecting the perception of rational and emotional properties and preference levels is the college attended followed by gender, while the age and educational level have no impact at all.
2. The rectangles with smaller aspect ratios are more rational, and the organic shapes with smaller aspect ratios are more emotional.

Acknowledgements. The authors gratefully acknowledge the support for this research provided by the Ministry of Science and Technology under Grant No. MOSY-103-2410-H-144-003 and MOST-103-2221-E-144-001.

References

1. Govers, P.C.M., Schoormans, J.P.L.: Product personality and its influence on consumer preference. J. Consum. Market. **22**(4), 189–197 (2005)
2. Mugge, R.: The effect of a business-like personality on the perceived performance quality of products. Int. J. Des. **5**(3), 67–76 (2011)
3. Fechner G.T.:Vorschule der Aesthetik. Breitkopf & H¨artel, Leipzig (1876)
4. Lalo, C.: L'esth'etique Exp'erimentale Contemporaine. Alcan, Paris (1908)
5. Elam, K.: Geometry of Design: Studies in Proportion and Composition. Princeton Architectural Press, New York (2001)
6. Lin, R.T.: The study of dimension proportion of car. J. Ming Chi **18**, 69–96 (1986)
7. Yang, H.C.: Study in ratio of lovable form. Master thesis of Graduate School of Design, National Taiwan University of Technology (2001)
8. Kant, I., Guyer, P., Wood, A.W. (eds.): Critique of Pure Reason. Cambridge University Press, Cambridge (1998)
9. Aaker, D.A., Shansby, G.J.: Positioning your product. Bus. Horiz. **25**, 56–62 (1982)
10. Atsushi, I., Masahiro, M., Masahito, T., Kazuo, S.: Emotional Consumption, Rational Consumption – What Type of Consumer Are You? Ye Chiang, Taipei (1989) (Trans. Cheng MH)
11. Hung, W.K., Chen, L.L.: Effects of novelty and its dimensions on aesthetic preference in product design. Int. J. Des. **6**(2), 81–90 (2012)
12. Hu, H.S.: Basic Design-Intellectual, Rational and Emotional. Wu-Nan, Taipei (2009)

Pilot Study on the Application
of Light-Absorbing Fabric in Sport Fashion

Chiui Hsu[1(✉)] and Po-Hsien Lin[2]

[1] Department of Material and Fiber, Oriental Institute of Technology,
Taipei, Taiwan
hsu.chiui@msa.hinet.net
[2] Graduate School of Creative Industry Design, National Taiwan University
of Arts, New Taipei, Taiwan
t0131@ntua.edu.tw

Abstract. In the 21st century, social change has quickened and intensified, resulting in humanity now facing many new challenges. With China, the United States, the European Union, and Japan shifting their focus towards low-carbon, environmentally friendly policies as the basis of future economic development. According to fashion industry observers, the use of natural and energy-saving forward-looking fabrics is already part of this global trend, and will continue to influence the clothing industry in the future. In terms of research and development of clothing materials, recent results from Taiwan far outstrip those of other countries. In the past six years, research into light-absorbing fibers has not only echoed the international trend towards energy-saving and environmental protection, but has also produced a new and unique technology, unmatched elsewhere. However, whether in terms of cost or actual technical application, new textile materials are invariably subjected to certain restrictions during the early stage of development, and currently, light-absorbing fabrics are at such basic stage of development. In this study, a survey was conducted to determine the potential demand for using advanced materials in sportswear. Respondent exercise habits were categorized, and sportswear needs for various sports activities were analyzed. The attributes of sportswear for the top three sports were analyzed and input into a matrix to stimulate diverse design ideas. It is hoped that "needs", "choice" and "thinking" can be incorporated into future product design strategies to clearly demonstrate the core value of applying advanced light-absorbing fabric to sports fashion.

Keywords: Fibers · Forward-looking technology · Performance fabric · Health and energy-saving · Sport fashion

1 Introduction

Historically, material development and human development are closely related, and each era has its representative material, which is the driving force behind social development and technological progress. Therefore, new material development and breakthrough are milestones of human civilization. After the 1960s, with the development of modern fiber technology, high-tech fiber technology has made great strides

© Springer International Publishing Switzerland 2015
P.L.P. Rau (Ed.): CCD 2015, Part I, LNCS 9180, pp. 24–35, 2015.
DOI: 10.1007/978-3-319-20907-4_3

worldwide, and has driven the boom in global sportswear market. Since the 1980s, Taiwan has been the world's core technology center for manufacturing functional material (Nikkan Kogyo Shimbun 1999).

The Taiwan Textile Research Institute (TTRI) is a major textile R&D institute in Taiwan, and owns unique high-end technology. Since the functional light-absorbing fabric is gradually demonstrating its unique attraction and advantages, investment into researching its development and application has already begun with support from the Innovative and Cutting-Edge Technology Program by the Ministry of Economic Affair Department of Industrial Technology. However, it seems that the development of applications for this advanced material is currently limited to interior décor. Hence effective promotion of its application in sportswear would quickly make it a favorite with designers and the sports fashion market.

The purposes of this study are:

1. Invite industry experts and designers to experiment with light-absorbing fabric. Then based on user perception of its attributes, outline possible end designs for sportswear.
2. Analyze survey to determine the needs of sportswear users to delineate the core value of design application for light-absorbing fabric.
3. Use the morphological method to identify the elements and construction of different types of urban sportswear. Illustrate these elements in a matrix to enhance application ideas for the light-absorbing fabric, and formulate a leading multi-strategy design module.

2 Literature Review

In recent years, fashion trends have revolved around Sports Fashion. The implementation of a two-day weekend in Taiwan has changed social trends, aroused health consciousness, and gradually set in motion a Lifestyle of Health and Sustainability (LOHAS) (Ray 1998). According to Turnbull and Wolfson (2002), exercise enhances positive emotions. Szabo (2003) also proposed that exercise reduces negative emotions such as anxiety and sadness, and domestic research have also shown that exercise is effective in reducing anxiety. These are the reasons for the health awareness, the pursuit of physical health and emotional health, and the motivation to exercise.

According to Schmitt, "Eliciting a response to an event usually begins with involvement". When urban dwellers can personally experience exercise at any given time, exercising becomes an urban trend and epidemic, and people begin to perceive exercise as trendy activities. For example, the Taipei Fu Bang Marathon, Taipei Highway Marathon, the PUMA Night Run, Mizuno Marathon Relay or 308 Marathon are suitable jogging activities for the family. Pine and Gilmore (1999) also pointed out that "experience is that conscious awareness of good feelings that arises when a person's emotion, physical strength, intellect and even spirit reach a certain level". More people are paying attention to and participating in less strenuous activities such as jogging, cycling, brisk walking and dancing, and correspondingly, they begin to experience a sense of well-being.

Currently, to satisfy the health lifestyle and safety concern of night time exercising by the public, many fashion brands such as TOPSHOP × ADIDAS, ADIDAS × FARM, PUMA × ASOS are promoting the use of special function material and collaborating with other industries. Urban exercise has gradually led the trend in jogger and biker apparel, with styles that are practical but fashionable (The Femin 2014). Particularly at night, poor visibility and recognition render running risky, and therefore it is safer to wear clothing with safety designs such as reflective strips or logos to make it easier to discern the runner. Using light-absorbing fabric in sportswear design is like having reflective strips so that urban dwellers can also safely exercise at night.

In this study, the sample selected for the experiment was white knitted fabric developed by Taiwan Textile Research Institute (TTRI). The light-absorbing fiber is not only consistent with international energy saving trend (Money 2009), but also leads the world with a unique core/shell construction that coats the luminescent material with polyester so that after several hours of absorbing indoor or outdoor light, it can emit light during the night. The non-toxic, washable, non-radiation "light-absorbing" fabric complies with world trend to "exercise, save energy, and protect the environment" (Chang and Chang 2009), and compared to other materials, its warmth, comfort and glow are unrivalled. In 2014, TTRI created its own LUMI LONG Light-Absorbing Finer brand. Initially there was little collaboration with fashion product design, and current applications are mainly limited to home products. Environmentally friendly fabric has become the global focus of green design, and as a green conscious material, the application of light-absorbing fiber to sports fashion could have significant advanced implication for healthy and safe living.

3   Methodologies

This research is a two-stage study. Stage 1 comprised literature review, collection of light-absorbing samples, analysis of urban exercise trend, and subject selection. Experts were invited to participate in the experiment and interviews, and the feedback analyzed in conjunction with various designs.

Stage 2 of the research comprised experiential testing by the experts. After testing the new fabric, the experts proposed ideas for product development based on user perception, thereby offering a more professional perspective and insight (Wang et al. 2005). In Chap 4, the top 3 sports and apparel design constructions are designated on the x-axis, and using a morphological approach, the attributes of sportswear were examined. For each sports type, elements from the 8 corresponding apparel styles designated along the y-axis were selected. The use of this matrix stimulates ideas for design strategies, and facilitates creative application for light-absorbing fabric.

The light-absorbing fabric produced by the TTRI was selected as the experimental object sample instead of other household light-absorbing fabrics produced by other manufacturers because the denier count of the TTRI fabric is finer, more stable and consistent with world technology and quality, and appropriate as end-fabric for apparels (Shiu 2010). The object sample, variables, subjects, sampling unit and time frame of this experiential study are as follow:

1. Object sample: 1 piece of light-absorbing knit fabric manufactured by the TTRI: 45″ × 15″.
2. Research variables: light source and intensity, exposure time, light storage time.
3. Research subjects: Textile developers and designers, urban dwellers with exercise habit, college students in design. Table 1 shows the subjects and subject characteristics.
4. Experiment and Interview: After experientially testing the light-absorbing fabric, the users proposed ideas for product needs and sportswear application from a user perspective. Table 2 shows the questionnaire items and answers.
5. Time frame: For natural or artificial light absorption, and due to the schedule and time limitation of the subjects, the researchers collected the questionnaires about two weeks after implementing the experiment.

Since this is a pilot study focusing on the future design application of advanced materials, subjects with textile industry or design background and exercise habits were selected. The subjects in the experiment and survey were divided into four groups. Group 1 comprised 3 professional textile developers; Group 2, 5 professional fashion designers; Group 3, 10 individuals with regular exercise habit; and Group 4, 15 college students in design. There were a total of 33 subjects, with 15 males and 18 females, ranging in age from 20 to 60. The subjects had a strong sense of health awareness. Subject information are as shown below.

Table 1. The 4 groups of professionals.

Subjects	Background Information	Profession
G.1	Fiber developer, fabric planner or fabric designer	Industrial developer/fabric product designer
G.2	Women's brand apparel designer, sportswear business, fashion planner	Industrial planner/apparel designer
G.3	Those who exercise 3 or more times per week over past years	Those with exercise habits/athletes
G. 4	Household products, visual and multi-media design field	Design students in public or private universities

This success of this pilot study on the application direction of light-absorbing fabric is contingent on whether the subjects can identify with the new material, therefore the most important part of the process is experiencing the fabric, followed by their perspective on application. The research variables are type and intensity of light source, exposure time, and light storage time. Prior to the experiment, the subjects were asked to view and describe the light-absorbing fabric. After the experiment, the process was recorded, followed by a 2–4 item narrative questionnaire. The questionnaire items are:

1. Describe your first impression of the fabric.
2. After experiencing the fabric, what ideas do you have for its application?
3. Within the last year, what are your 2 most frequent types of indoor/outdoor sports? How many times per week?
4. From the perspective of a sportswear user, how do you hope to see light-absorbing fabric used?

4 Results and Discussion

Thirty-three subjects completed the experiential test, and 32 questionnaire responses were collected, of which 28 were valid for comprehensive content analysis. Responses from the following subjects were given priority:

1. Those who recorded at least 3 or more of the experimental variables.
2. Those who provided comprehensive user perspective application ideas for the light-absorbing attributes. Since the light-absorbing experiment is the most critical part of the experience, only subjects who have experienced the day time light-absorbing and night time light-storing attribute of the fabric had a basis from which to propose application ideas for the new fabric. Therefore, based on the degree and completeness of experience, 28 questionnaires were selected while the remaining 4 questionnaires were excluded due to their incomplete descriptions.
3. Responses from the 28 questionnaires on light-absorbing material were summarized, and the content analysis illustrated as follow:

Based on the general condition of their eyesight, the 28 subjects were divided into 2 groups:

Group 1: Aged 20–43 years old, normal vision, with about 250–300° myopia.
Group 2: Aged 48–60 years old, 200–300° presbyopia.

Given the non-radiation luminosity, the Group 2 subjects felt that with or without myopic glasses or reading glasses, there was no significant difference in their perception of brightness. The results of the experiment are summarized in Table 2.

Light-absorbing materials are characterized by their ability to absorb and release light energy. After exposure to the sun or light, they are luminous in the dark. Absorption of outdoor natural sunlight is quick and effective, and brightness retention is much longer than for indoor artificial light. When used in fiber or textile products, they are soft and comfortable to the touch, can be cut, dyed, and withstand repeated washing. They are also safe, reliable and green. Their affinity for natural light, unlimited cycles of light absorption, retention and emission, and permanent use make them an energy saving green product.

After experiencing the light-absorbing fabric, the subjects not only felt a sense of novelty, but also believed that such a technological material should not be limited to being perceived as cool, but that other functional applications should be carefully considered. Night safety was a key selling point of this fiber, particularly for places or activities that require high visibility, such as sports and hunting gear, rigging cable, and interior carpeting of theater and aircraft. The light retention attribute of the fabric rendered it highly suitable for use as safety illumination or warnings in outdoor sports, functional products, sports fashion, shoes and bags. Other uses for outdoor rescue, medical or disability care were also proposed, such as emergency packages, senior health care, infant supplies, optical sensor clothing, shoes or schoolbag for elementary school children. Using light-absorbing materials for the shoulders life jackets, or stitching the material into the upper body of lifejackets, can to enhance sea search and rescue in sunless condition. The material was also deemed suitable for entertainment purposes such as 3C accessory or wearable products, nightclubs, pub or cool fashion.

Table 2. Summary of the light-absorbing fabric experiment.

Light Absorbing Test Type of Light Source	Light Absorbing Test Exposure Time	Retention Test Retention time and continuity of illumination in the dark
Artificial light source —white light Artificial ligh source (a) —yellow light	1. 1 hour of exposure to artificial light source	Showed no significant brightness. Lasted about 5 -10 minutes
	2. 1-2 hours of exposure to artificial light source	Emitted faint brightness. Lasted about 20 -25 minutes
	3. 3 or more hours of exposure to artificial light source	Emitted stronger brightness. Lasted about 35-40 minutes.
Artificial light source (b) —General fluorescent tubes	1. 1 hour of exposure to artificial light source	Showed no significant brightness. Lasted about 5 -10 minutes.
	2. 1-2 hours of exposure to artificial light source	Emitted faint brightness. Lasted about 15-20 minutes.
	3. 3 or more hours of exposure to artificial light source	Emitted stronger brightness. Lasted about 30-40 minutes.
Natural light source © —sunlight * Weather – clear/cloudy	1. 1 hour of exposure	2½ hours of significant brightness.
	2. 2 hours direct sunlight exposure on a clear day.	3½ hours of significant brightness.
Natural light source —sunlight * Weather – clear	3. 1 hour 15 minutes direct sunlight exposure at noon on a clear day.	Almost 8 hours of significant brightness.
Natural light source * Weather–sometimes clear, sometimes cloudy	4. 11 hours of exposure	Almost 9 hours of significant brightness.

(a)   (b)   (c)

* Regardless of white, yellow or fluorescent light, absorption of artificial indoor light was not high. An average of a 2-hour exposure produced about 30 minutes of light retention.
* Absorption of natural outdoor sunlight was rapid. An average of an 1-hour exposure produced about 2 hours of light retention
* The degree of direct natural sunlight and cloudiness affected light-absorbing brightness and retention time. Retention time was proportional to the brightness of the sunlight and exposure time.

In terms of the types of sports, the most frequently engaged activities were biking, swimming, jogging, mountain climbing, qigong, ball games, strolling and dancing. Of these, nighttime jogging, brisk walking and strolling were most frequent, followed by biking and mountain climbing. There were also 4 times more outdoor activities than indoor activities. The top 3 sports favored by the subjects were jogging and biking after work, and weekend mountain climbing, which accounted for 52.1 % of the sports selection, and with 70 % occurring after work. Survey of subjects' experience with sportswear found common demands, namely comfort, health, and safety. Evidently, light-absorbing fabric and future industry for urban exercise will be closely linked (Table 3).

Table 3. Application ideas for light-absorbing fabric from the perspectives of sportswear users.

User Needs / Sports Trend	Modern style / functional material / safety features /user-friendly design
Jogging 1	Reflective strip design / Elastic knee, ankle and wrist bands / loose Raglan sleeves / moisture control/ stretchable/ sweat absorbent/breathable / non-restrictive sleeves / functional material
Biking 2	High-contrast, double-sided reflective elastic strips/ back zipper design / comfortable / breathable / moisture control fabric / highly breathable armpits / forward curving patterns / fit / convenient pocket /fitting arms / 3D tailoring
MountainClimbing 3	Reflective strip design / comfortable and loose / moisture control /stretchable / sweat absorbent / breathable / non-restrictive sleeves or pants/ stretchable / functional material

The light-absorbing fabric tested by the subjects had absorbed light during the day, and emitted light in the dark. Table shows that among the subjects, having reflective strips or light-absorbing fabric in sportswear was a common need. Two of the subjects enjoyed early morning and nighttime walking or jogging, and hoped to see light-absorbing fabric used in jogging apparel. Therefore, integrating light-absorbing fabric into daytime wear design can allow nighttime joggers to feel relaxed and unafraid, and satisfy the safety needs of those who exercise after work.

4.1 Developing Leading Design Strategies

Pioneered in 1947 by Zwicky (Jones 1980), morphological analysis is currently used by many scholars as a design strategy to develop ideas in different fields such as domestic and foreign products, furniture and fashion design (Chen and Lai 2009). Based on the premise of improving urban sportswear and safety design, this study used systemic survey and content analysis to analyze the types of sportswear. Independent attributes were first de-constructed. The deconstructions were then inserted into a matrix to enhance inspiration for design application strategies for light-absorbing fabric.

Clothes design is complex, requiring not only creativity and fashion sense, but also comfort. Factors affecting the appearance of clothing include line, shape, texture and color, and the resulting contour and surface effect directly impacts visual aesthetics. However, in terms of sportswear, discussion of function is unavoidable, and the construction, form, material, and especially the strong performance demand must satisfy the functional needs of sportswear users. In particular, precise tailoring, pattern, sewing technique and the experience of sports experts are factors critical to the success of the sportswear design.

The types of sportswear depend on the sports function and safety considerations, and therefore the fabric, secondary materials, tailoring and shape vary accordingly. In terms of design, the human frame and appearance, which can mainly be divided into the head, limbs and torso (Jeng 1982), govern the design and inspire the construction of the apparel. In terms of clothing construction, 8 body structures significantly affect the pattern and performance of the apparel, and as shown in Fig. 1, the corresponding patterns deemed appropriate for the light-absorbing fabric are: head—hat style, neck–collar style, shoulder—should style, hand—sleeve style, chest—chest style, waist and hip—waist and hip lines, thigh—pants style, foot-shoe. As shown in Table 4, these could be individually marked on the matrix. The attributes of the type of sportswear (or selection) for each type of sports were then inserted into the vertical axis (y-axis) of the matrix. As shown in the matrix in Fig. 8, the design style are designated by the items A1, A2, B1, B2, C1, C2 … H1, H2. The more the design attributes or types of sports, the larger the strategy configuration.

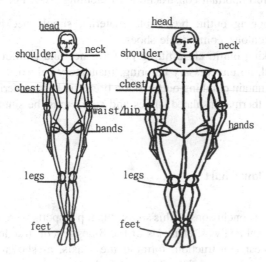

Fig. 1. 8 body structures affecting pattern and function (compiled by this study)

Table 4. Basic matrix for the sportswear form.

Design structure sports choice	A head hat style	B neck style	C shoulder shoulder style	D hand sleeve style	E chest chest style	F waist & hip	G thigh pants style	H foot shoe style
1 Jogging apparel attributes	Style A1	Style B1	Style C1	Style D1	Style E1	Style F1	Style G1	Style H1
2 Biking apparel attributes	Style A2	Style B2	Style C2	Style D2	Style E2	Style F2	Style G2	Style H2
3 Mountain climbing apparel attributes	Style A3	Style B3	Style C2	Style D3	Style E3	Style F3	Style G3	Style H3

The functional needs of clothing vary according to the type of sports. A complete sports outfit is called a set, such as a set of jogging outfit or a set of biking outfit. A set of jogging outfit would comprise items such as a vest T-shirts, long pants or shorts, jacket, hand and jogging shoes. In addition to tops, a set of biking outfit may comprise items such as leg warmers, over sleeves, biking pants and shoes. However, the attribute deconstruction of an outfit is based on a single item of clothing. For example, a jogging top comprises the collar style, sleeve style, chest style and waist contour. Changing the parts of an outfit is integral to outfit construction. The combination of deconstructed details forms the different attributes of an outfit, and contributes to the overall style construction of the outfit. Based on the original prototype, the attributes of shape and shoulder measurement of tops, the chest and waist-hip ratio, or armhole measurement and activity level are important constructions of clothing style. For example,

1. Attributes of jogging outfit: breathable material, simple neckline, close fitting shoulder, light contour, comfortable shoes.
2. Attributes of biking outfit: close fitting performance and comfortable, well-fitting and well tailored, no unnecessary tailoring, mandatory helmet.
3. Attributes of mountain climbing outfit: Wide brims on hats, material must be warm, water-proof and thermal insulated, shoes and socks must be suitable for mountain climbing.

4.2 Three-Step Flow Chart

Step 1. Based on the conclusions of this study, the top 3 sports were delineated. Using morphological analysis, elements of the 8 design constructions were used for the sportswear construction, forming the x-axis, as shown in Table 8. The attribute descriptions of each part of the sportswear formed the y-axis, resulting in 8 patterns and 24 types of sportswear for each type of sports

Step 2. The attributes and design elements of the different types of sportswear were listed. Based on the relationship between the attributes and functional construction of the sportswear, the elements were combined into creative ideas, forming the rows and columns of patterns in the matrix, such as A1, A2, B1, B2, C1, C2, as shown in Table 5.

Step 3. Based on preference, functional attributes and design constructions were selected. With clear corresponding functional attributes and clear intersecting relationship among the corresponding design constructions, selected designs in the matrix are marked and coded so the information then developed and transformed into designs. Hence the greatest advantage of such a matrix is its capacity for a diversity of ideas, thereby enhancing the quality of design strategies for sports fashion.

A systematic selection strategy for attribute construction inspires application ideas for light-absorbing fabric and functional materials. Based on construction needs and attributes, a design can be integrated, reinforced and converted into the new design and style. Figure 2 shows the design transformation.

Table 5. Matrix design strategy code: (A1B2C3D3E3F1G3H3), that is (1, 2, 3, 3, 3, 1, 3, 3)

Design Construction / Sports Type	A Hat Style	B Collar Style	C Shoulder Style	D Sleeve Style	E Chest Style	F Waist -Hips	G Pants Style	H Shoes Style
1.Jogging Apparel Attributes								
2.Biking Apparel Attributes								
3 Mountain climbing Apparel Attributes						2 8,(		

※ Ideas for apparel construction and design: cap, small collar, flat should, composite
fiber Raglan sleeves, wide hip hem, layered elastic culottes, tight elastic
stockings, heavy duty low ankle shoes. Easy, carefree and stylish.

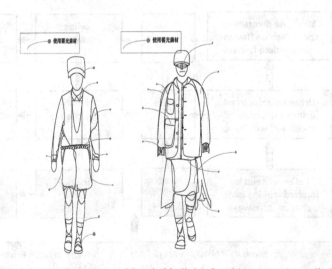

Fig. 2. Design transformation draft: designs with suitable light-absorbing areas (compiled from this study)

5 Conclusions and Suggestion Recommendations

Besides working hard for their living, the average office workers also seek adequate leisure and exercise to maintain a sense of health and security. Maslow's (Abraham H. Maslow) theory of hierarchy of needs divides needs into 5 levels, namely physical needs, safety needs, social needs, esteem needs and self-actualization needs. He believes that everyone has the need to grow, but that lower level needs must be met before pursuing higher aesthetic needs. In other words, regardless of general physical activities or specific exercise, both are health-promoting behaviors (Ni 2004). However, well-designed and functional light-absorbing sportswear can enhance a sense of safety and agility during exercise, and increase health awareness.

Using "experience" to explore future product design, this study clearly demonstrated the core value of applying light-absorbing fabric to sports fashion. The study also constructed a pilot model of design application for light-absorbing material, as shown in Fig. 3. On one hand, information about the technological material was obtained through experience, and on the other hand, perception of user need was based on experience and learning. Such complete "emotional empathy" is integral to the "need" to "choice" to "thinking" decision-making process of developers. Experiencing the fabric, and understanding and empathizing with sports safety needs enhanced the "More ATTEN-TION, More PATIENCE and Willing to learn & use" process of needs assessment, thereby making usefulness and physical safety the core of sports fashion design. In addition, the attitude of "health-safety", "friendly-function" and "fashion-feeling" are expressed in sports fashion design. In conclusion, this experiential pilot design module can be further applied to other high-end advanced materials to further the understanding of new technological materials, increase the added value of creative design application, and enhance design education. It is hoped that the 「HS + 4F」 concept can be further studied, verified and developed for style design in sports fashion.

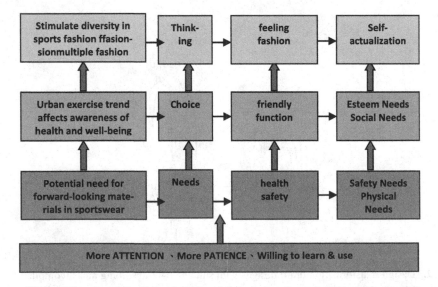

Fig. 3 Pilot model for light-absorbing fabric design (compiled from this study)

References

From ettoday: Nikkan Kogyo Shimbun: Development trend in functional fiber. High-Tech Fiber. http://www.ettoday.net/news (1999). Accessed 25 Jan 2015

Ray, P.: The Cultural Creatives: How 50 million People are Changing the World. Harmony Books, New York (1998)

Turnbull, M., Wolfson, S.: Effects of exercise and outcome feedback on mood: evidence for misattribution. J. Sport Behav. **25**(4), 394–406 (2002)

Szabo, A.: The acute effects of humor and exercise on mood and anxiety. J. Leisure Res. **35**(2), 152–162 (2003)

From wiki: Maslow Needs Hierarchy Theory. http://wiki.mbalib.com/zh-tw/

Hung, C.S.: Fitness, emotions and mental health. Univ. Phys. Educ. Sports **72**, 156–161 (2003)

Schmitt, B.H.: Experiential Marketing: How to Get Customers to Sense, Feel, Think, Act, and Relate to Your Company and Brands. Free Press, New York (1999)

Pine, B.J., Gilmore, J.H.: The Experience Economy: Work is Theatre and Every Business a Stage. Harvard Business School Press, Boston (1999)

From The Femin. http://thefemin.com/2014/04/sports-x-fashion/ (1999)

From Money: Green Philosophy—A Great Business and Investment Opportunity. http://www.richage.net. Accessed 26 Nov 2009

Chang, S.W., Chang, S.S.: Transportation textile products/product technology. Taiwan Text. Res. J. **19**(1), 1–5 (2009)

Wang, J.C., Lin, M.C., Chen, T.C.: Use of quality functions in the development of outdoor recreational clothing design. J. Des. **10**(2), 29–41 (2005)

Shiu, J.Y.: Fashion express. Taiwan Text. Fed. **29** (2010)

Jones, J.C.: Design Methods-Seeds of Human Future. Wiley, New York (1980)

Chen, H.J., Lai, C.F.: Morphological analysis of western clothing - renaissance clothing as case example. J. Des. **14**(1), 19–42 (2009)

Jeng, J.M.: Pattern recognition in humans. Sci. Mon. **13**(10), 14–22 (1982)

Ni, F.S.: Composition Art-plane Formation. Henan University Press, Henan (2004)

A Design Strategy of Cultural and Creative Products on the Global Market

Chi-Hsien Hsu[1][✉] and Wang-Chin Tsai[2]

[1] Department of Culture-Based Creative Design,
National Taitung Junior College, Taitung 95045, Taiwan
assah16@gmail.com
[2] Department of Product and Media Design, Fo Guang University,
Jiaoxi 26247, Yilan County, Taiwan
wachtsai@mail.fgu.edu.tw

Abstract. As the promotion of cultural and creative industries has become a trend in the current economic development strategies of various countries, the global market has gradually moved its focus towards local styles, and creative design applications have become a global competitive advantage of an industry. Therefore, the main purpose of this study is to investigate the effectiveness evaluation index and design strategy on cultural and creative products of consumer cognition and preference. First, we undertook a preliminary survey by means of literature review and opinions from a group of experts, and selected representative product samples and evaluation indices. Afterward, we analyzed the results of the questionnaire survey and found that cultural and creative products have distinct identity for participants. Furthermore, the participants considered that the main attributes affecting the overall presentation of a product, in order of degree of influence were "material, product function, aesthetic image, design quality, appearance style".

Keywords: Design strategy · Cultural and creative product

1 Introduction

With changing customers' demands and perceptions, the consumer market advances in an era of experience and aesthetic economics. In market economies characterized by profusion, corporations engage in activities and products filling their offerings with design, experience, ambiance, aesthetics, symbols and meaning [1, 2]. The distinctness of local culture and the structure of innovation-knowledge become the national core competency.

Europe and the United States specialize in taking traditional craft heritage items and combining them into brand marketing, developing them into fine boutique products such as Georg Jensen silver carving utensils and jewelry, Hermes handbags and scarves, Royal Copenhagen porcelain and so forth, attracting droves of consumers around the world. In recent years, Taiwan has also tried marketing cultural stories through creative design, commercializing local features and developing products of

© Springer International Publishing Switzerland 2015
P.L.P. Rau (Ed.): CCD 2015, Part I, LNCS 9180, pp. 36–48, 2015.
DOI: 10.1007/978-3-319-20907-4_4

distinct character, in the hope of injecting vibrancy into cultural industries and local industrial economies.

And as traditional culture is being used increasingly in design creativity, all kinds of conflict and controversy continue to arise on account of the different perspectives of the adherence of cultural workers to their traditional cultural values, the unrestrained vigor and ingenuity of creative design professionals, and the global marketing considerations of industry and commercial entities. This highlights the fact that cultural products are a kind of cross-industrial product, as well as the difficulties that will be encountered during processing. How to make cultural and creative design genuinely able to take into account both cultural heritage and global consumer demand is a question that as yet remains unanswered.

The purpose of this study is, specifically, to explore the views of consumer groups towards cultural and creative design and the differences in their evaluation of design. The research results can be used as a reference for design development in the relevant cultural and creative industries, as well as a reference to be used when preparing product development strategies.

2 Design Trend and Cultural Creativity

Each country has its own unique traditional customs, lifestyle and cultural style. With changing consumer needs, in addition to functionality and practicability, products today must be oriented toward consumer awareness and product demand [3]. Design has now become an innovative driving force for creating market opportunities. More advanced countries tend to treat design as an asset of economic advantage, and use it to promote their own image in the international community [4].

At present, the development of cultural and creative industries has become an important economic strategy, which is not only able to promote local and regional economic development, but also able to raise the quality of cultural life [5]. And traditional craft industries all over are focusing on both creativity and modernity, making every effort to ensure their craftwork can adapt to the needs of contemporary society. Handicraft design is both the cultural achievement of the handicraft business and also an inheritance of tradition [6]. For example, the Niigata in Japan, by its rich history of craftsmanship with creation of centennial values, has been pleased to present "Hyakunen-Monogatari" program to the world since 2005. This collection of crafts was designed to support as well as create a better style [7].

Because the influence of art and culture extends to the industry value chain, industry must create aesthetic innovations on the basis of consumer culture [8]. Therefore, product development that emphasizes cultural value, local characteristics and aesthetics has become critical to the design process. For example, Alessi has developed a unique evaluation equation theory, which is divided into the four items of communication, emotion, price and functionality. These are used as a basis for evaluation in selecting products for development [9].

3 Consumers' Expectations Towards Design

Good products must possess the ability to inspire the cultural codes of consumers. Only through leaving the consumer with a product imprint, and the interpretation of cultural codes can a deep emotional link be established between products and the consumer [10, 11]. Designers use sense of texture, shape, design and ornamentation properties, and through their design creativity give meaning to products, so that apart from a product providing features at the functional level, it may also be able to provide people with a further experience at the emotional level [12, 13].

When a product design has qualities of emotional awareness, then it can help user lines of thought turn from the rational to the emotional. Simply put, the design can take one from satisfaction with functionality to an emotionally moving experience. As to the memory and impression consumers have of products, consumption will not be limited to tangible objects, commodities have now evolved into being emotional, value, and cultural carriers. The value that consumers really want to buy is a stream of consciousness, or cultural codes [14]. Just as Europeans and Americans like the TALES of mythical rock ornaments, the reason for buying them may not be merely because they are China's Han Dynasty "Portrait Bricks," but rather that they are an emotional expression of Eastern culture.

The significance of a product can be divided into two dimensions: the designer's conceptual model, and the user's mental model; the ideal situation would be that the two must coalesce into one, for there to be a successful design [15]. In practice however, the designer's interpretation of the product and the user's interpretation are not necessarily the same. Many products possess ingenuity and innovation in their design, but are not commercially successful. Hence, the discrepancy between the perception and understanding of designers and users has consistently been a conundrum of the design and development process, which scholars and experts seek to overcome [16, 17].

4 Research Method

Product styles in response to consumer demand or market positioning vary with trends in the cultural and creative industries. There are products which have the appeal of geographical and cultural features, products which carry out design innovative, products which stress their abilities to move people emotionally, products aimed at meeting global marketing strategies, and so on. This study carries out a comprehensive investigation and analytical discussion.

This study used questionnaire survey methods, as well as MDS and SPSS statistical analysis to explore products with cultural and creative appeal, when entering international market competition, and the factors of cognitive design and evaluation which influence consumer groups. It thereby provides a reference for cultural and creative design-related fields of study or for industry. The questionnaires' execution was divided into two phases: the pre-survey and the formal questionnaire survey. The main purpose of the pre-survey was to collect product samples and design evaluation

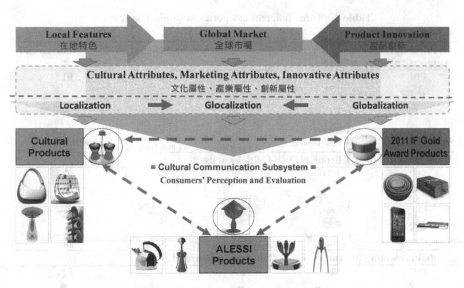

Fig. 1. The research framework

attributes, in accordance with the follow-up phase of the formal questionnaire. The study framework is shown in Fig. 1.

4.1 Selection of Stimulus Products and Evaluation Attribute

The study first conducted a pre-survey, extracting product sampling and design evaluation attributes in the three orientations of local features, product innovation, and global market [18–20]. After the initial screening, the results then went through the questionnaires and opinion surveys of nine experts in the three fields of cross-culture, innovation and industry. In accordance with the three orientations of local features, product innovation, and global market five product samples (a total of 15 samples) were selected (Table 1), and from these trans-orientation products were picked out as typical representative category products; P08 "Mr. & Mrs. Chin" salt and pepper set, P11 "Steamer Set" steamer pot, and P14 "Mandarin" Squeezer with goblet. All three possess elements of local features, product innovation and global market, though to differing degrees. In addition, 15 generally representative design evaluation attributes were selected.

4.2 Participants and Procedure

In this study, there were 373 of participants of the questionnaire survey which were deemed valid, of which 107 were males and 266 females. These participants were mainly college, undergraduate and graduate students, and all had taken more than one year of professional education in their respective fields of training. Participants can be divided into three main areas according to their educational background, namely, 119

Table 1. Three different categories of product samples

Local feature products – From Taiwan e-Learning and Digital Archives Commercial Application Competitions				
P01	P06	P08	P10	P15
"Ripple" martini cup	"Pinban Boat" handbag	"Mr. & Mrs. Chin" salt and pepper set	"Pearls Dropping on the Jade Plate" piggy bank	"Tile" magazine rack
Innovative products – From 2011 IF Gold Awards				
P02	P04	P09	P11	P13
"iPhone 4" smartphone	"Family Bowls" tableware	"Clever Little Bag" shoe packaging system	"Steamer Set" steamer pot	"USB-Clip" USB flash drive
Global marketing products – From Italian fashion brand Alessi				
P03	P05	P07	P12	P14
"Anna G." corkscrew	"Fruit Mama" fruit bowl	"9091" kettle	"Juicy Salif" citrus squeezer	"Mandarin" Squeezer with goblet

people from arts and humanities-related faculties, 106 from design-related faculties, and 148 from communication and business management-related faculties.

Before the participants actually filled in the questionnaire, we prepared a 10-min explanation to let the participants understand our research goal and the procedure of the survey. For this reason we explained to the participants the 15 experiment samples with pictures and written text. In the first part of the questionnaire participants fill in their personal information. The second part consists of the participant's design evaluation and the analysis of their perception of the experiment samples; we asked the participants to indicate their responses on a 9-point Likert scale according to their real feelings and experiences. Finally we asked the participants to select the product samples they like as well as important design qualities from 15 product samples and representative qualities, and rate them according to their preference.

5   Results and Analysis

The questionnaire survey results were first analyzed with Multi-dimension Scaling Analysis (MDS) to construct the participants' cognitive preferences space, and then using SPSS statistical software was used to carry out analysis and exploration. When using MDS, five tools are usually used to analyze data: KYST, INDSCAL, MDPREF, PREFMAP and PROFIT. And through the cognitive space constructed by MDPREF, we can at the same time explore the results of participants' attribute cognition and stimulus preferences [21, 22].

5.1 Analysis of Preference Data in Attribute Vectors

After the completion of survey data archiving, the MDPREF software program was used, to identify potential assessment factors according to the participant's evaluation attributes, to construct the cognitive space of participants. Table 2 shows that the cognitive space of this study can reach an explanatory power of 85.55 % in Factor II, and reach an explanatory power of 96.09 % in Factor III. After Factor III, the decline rate in the explanatory power eases.

After analysis of the aforementioned cognitive space factor figures, further verification was made of the design evaluation attributes covered by each factor. In MDPREF data analysis, the components comprising the evaluation attribute of each factor could be found (Table 2). In Factor I, there was an obvious grouping phenomenon for attributes: A03, A01, A02, and A04. In the Factor II, there was another obvious grouping phenomenon for attributes: A11, A14, A13, A06, A05, A12, A07, A10, A09, and A15; however the weighting for A10, A09, and A15 was lower, and could be divided into subgroups for exploration. Attribute A08 was representative evaluation attribute for the Factor III.

In the preferential cognitive space framed by MDPREF, product samples (stimulus) are expressed as point coordinates, while evaluation attribute are expressed as vector quantities. And the correlation coefficient (between −1 and +1) is the data

Table 2. Proportion of variance of fifteen attributes

Attributes	Population Matrix (Vectors)		
	Factor I	Factor II	Factor III
A01 cultural characteristic	**-0.9890**	0.1001	-0.1090
A02 evocation of feelings	**-0.9836**	-0.1338	-0.1212
A03 background story	**-0.9964**	-0.0376	-0.0760
A04 special meaning	**-0.9589**	-0.2238	0.1743
A05 aesthetic image	-0.2583	**-0.9265**	0.2737
A06 innovative level	0.3559	**-0.9343**	0.0232
A07 design quality	0.2899	**-0.9188**	-0.2679
A08 product function	0.2821	-0.2328	**-0.9307**
A09 overall presentation	0.0289	**-0.8593**	-0.5107
A10 material	0.1631	**-0.8665**	-0.4717
A11 show self	-0.0060	**-0.9997**	0.0224
A12 pleasure	-0.0366	**-0.9209**	-0.3881
A13 unique idea	0.1326	**-0.9510**	0.2794
A14 appearance style	-0.1514	**-0.9656**	0.2116
A15 imagination	-0.2790	**-0.7970**	0.5357
Variance (%)	**50.93%**	**34.62%**	**10.54%**
Cumulative (%)	**50.93%**	**85.55%**	**96.09%**

Table 3. Correlation matrix of fifteen attributes

Correlation Matrix of Subjects														
A01	A01													
A02	23.59	A02												
A03	12.12	15.36	A03											
A04	29.65	21.42	21.25	A04										
A05	83.68	69.48	75.85	60.75	A05									
A06	113.77	103.68	108.10	97.87	45.14	A06								
A07	110.28	96.81	103.38	96.10	46.69	24.76	A07							
A08	101.57	97.08	101.64	112.05	96.57	73.72	58.43	A08						
A09	93.50	81.67	**87.56**	85.68	50.88	40.55	23.38	48.37	A09					
A10	101.27	**88.98**	95.27	**90.42**	51.79	44.24	24.54	52.61	19.73	A10				
A11	94.43	84.57	**86.97**	77.71	38.07	31.68	32.18	78.23	38.38	44.62	A11			
A12	**90.66**	78.76	84.15	81.51	49.07	37.10	30.40	56.65	22.03	37.60	34.80	A12		
A13	103.63	**93.01**	96.46	82.65	33.15	24.08	37.34	**89.74**	49.83	51.30	27.03	42.52	A13	
A14	**87.94**	77.10	80.06	68.38	27.92	38.02	42.26	**90.36**	47.13	52.57	17.86	40.64	24.69	A14
A15	82.87	71.30	74.88	59.20	27.04	52.29	61.35	111.90	66.67	69.70	42.17	58.09	33.19	28.79	A15

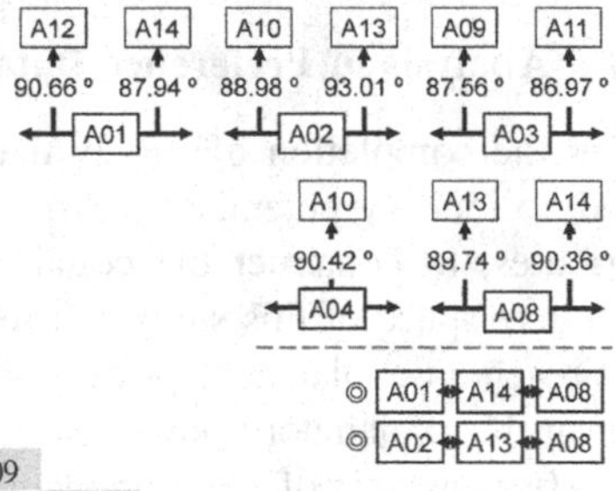

Diagram (right side):

A12   A14   A10   A13   A09   A11
90.66°   87.94°   88.98°   93.01°   87.56°   86.97°
↓ A01 ↓   ↓ A02 ↓   ↓ A03 ↓

A10   A13   A14
90.42°   89.74°   90.36°
→ A04 →   ↓ A08 ↓

◎ A01 — A14 — A08
◎ A02 — A13 — A08

corroboration of the test of degree of correlation between the vector quantity. Converted into an intersection angle, for example, the correlation coefficient is 0 (ACOS = 0), expressing no relevance whatsoever between the two vector quantities, when its vector quantity intersection angle is equal to 90°, this expresses the participant's independent preference cognitive system, can be interpreted as a representative axial direction of preferential cognitive space [21, 22].

After ordering the evaluation attributes of the correlation coefficients, they were converted into intersection angles, as shown in Table 3. Observing the vector intersection angles of the evaluation attributes, a more obvious presentation of completely unrelated evaluation attributes can be found, and these evaluation attributes are: A01 and A12, A01 and A14; A02 and A10, A02 and A13; A03 and A09, A03 and A11; A04 and A10; A08 and A13, A08 and A14.

The above relevant angles shown are all within the scope of that which can be studied, indicating that they are mutually independent factors. A two-dimensional cognitive space can be framed, taking into consideration the amount of variation in the explanatory power of the cognitive space factors, A08 is the representative evaluation attribute of Factor III, thus a mixed selection can be made taking "A01-A14-A08" and "A02-A13-A08" as the main independent factors of the two groups, commonly representing interpretation as three dimensional factors constituting preference cognitive space (Table 4).

Table 4. Stimulus coordinates of the MDPREF solution

Stimulus Product		Normalized Stimulus Matrix (Points)		
		Factor I	Factor II	Factor III
P01		0.1927	-0.1825	0.4492
P02		0.2742	-0.4449	-0.6489
P03		0.0144	-0.1931	0.0112
P04		-0.3801	0.0011	-0.1946
P05		0.1283	0.0463	0.2252
P06		-0.3645	0.1671	0.0244
P07		0.1546	0.1471	-0.0297
P08		-0.3255	0.1691	0.0095
P09		0.2658	0.0011	-0.1581
P10		-0.1414	-0.2997	0.0740
P11		-0.2271	0.1017	-0.2328
P12		0.1686	-0.2541	0.4252
P13		0.4802	0.6633	-0.1024
P14		-0.2499	0.1862	0.0746
P15		0.0098	-0.1087	0.0733

5.2   Analysis of Preference Data in Stimulus Products

According to data MDPREF analysis, each products projection value of each evaluation attribute vector quantity, constituting the coordinate values of preference cognitive space, showing the preferences for each product sample in evaluation attribute vector quantities. Matching evaluation attribute component values, a preference cognitive space can be drawn, as shown in Fig. 2. From the collective vector quantities of the two groups, "A01-A14-A08" and "A02-A13-A08", we can explore the product's representative significance and relationships in the three factor's space.

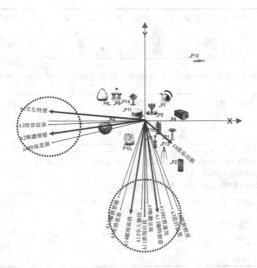

Fig. 2. Preference space from a three-dimensional MDPREF analysis

From the cognitive space framed by MDPREF, an approximation of distribution circumstances for each product sample can be seen; proceeding then by sorting product samples projection in axial projection values, we can interpret possible hidden significance in the cognitive space (Table 5). The MDPREF program's SECOND SCORE MATRIX data output, provides from cognitive space, a matching evaluation attribute vector quantity orthographic projection for each product sample. The size of the projection values indicates the sorting order of participant's assessment stimulus product for each product attribute. When the value of the projection is higher, this indicates greater relevance of the stimulus attribute to the participant, and vice versa.

Based on the MDPREF solution, a three-dimensional configuration is confirmed to construct a preference space. In Table 5, the main factors affecting participants' preference evaluation could be identified as: (1) "Cultural sensibility" dimension, which consists of cultural attributes including: cultural characteristic (A01), evocation of feelings (A02), background story (A03) and special meaning (A04). (2) "Qualia experience" dimension, which consists of innovative attributes including: aesthetic image (A05), innovative level (A06), design quality (A07), show self (A11), pleasure (A12), unique idea (A13), appearance style (A14), overall presentation (A09), material (A10), imagination (A15). (3) "Market orientation" dimension, which consists of product function (A08) in marketing attributes.

When the cognitive space of product samples features a grouping phenomenon, this demonstrates that product samples have similar evaluation attribute characteristics, and when the position of product samples is separated, this demonstrates that products possess different characteristics.

In cognitive space of the X-Y axes, it can be found that product samples P4, P6, P8, P11, P14 feature a grouping phenomenon, but P4 is slightly different in that it also has

Table 5. Dimension interpretation of MDPREF analysis

| P04 | P06 | P08 | P14 | P11 | P10 | P15 | P03 | P05 | P07 | P12 | P01 | P09 | P02 | P13 |

X– ... X+

Cultural sensibility ←————————————→ Rational functionality
● cultural characteristic (A01), evocation of feelings (A02), background story (A03) and special meanin (A04)

| P02 | P10 | P12 | P03 | P01 | P15 | P04 | P09 | P05 | P11 | P07 | P06 | P08 | P14 | P13 |

Y– ... Y+

Qualia experience ←————————————→ Nothing new
● aesthetic image (A05), innovative level (A06), design quality (A07), show self (A11), pleasure (A12), unique idea (A13), appearance style (A14)
● overall presentation (A09), material (A10), imagination (A15)

| P02 | P11 | P04 | P09 | P13 | P07 | P08 | P03 | P06 | P15 | P10 | P14 | P05 | P12 | P01 |

Z– ... Z+

Market orientation ←————————————→ Conceptual functionality
● product function (A08)

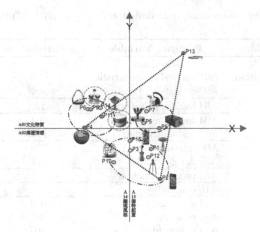

Fig. 3. Group stimulus space from X-Y Dimension for MDPREF analysis

a "cultural sensibility" dimension (X-axis), and is the most representative product sample of this; product samples P5, P7, P9 feature a grouping phenomenon; product samples P1, P2, P3, P10, P12, P15 also feature a grouping phenomenon, but P2 is slightly different in that it also has a "qualia experience" dimension (Y-axis), and is the most representative product sample of this; and P13 product samples exist entirely independently, and moreover are the product samples with the least "cultural sensibility" and "qualia experience" (Fig. 3).

5.3 Multiple Regression Analysis of Evaluation Indices to Predict "Product Preference"

To gain a deeper understanding of the key factors influencing the participants' overall perception of a product, this study used linear regression analysis, with multiple independent variables to predict the dependent corresponding variable values, and according to the size of the independent variables' explanatory power, from a number of independent variables, examined the effects and dependant variables [23]. Comprehensively predicting the overall presentation impression of products' through the participants' perception of design attributes, and consequently one by one exploring the attributes which will affect the design attributes of the overall presentation, the results are shown in Table 6. R-squared (determinant coefficient) was 0.866, indicating that independent variables possess an 86.6 % dependant variable explanatory power. The Durbin-Watson test was 1.820; a test result of between 1.5 and 2.5 indicates that no self-correlation exists between independent variables [24].

Overall, participants considered the major positive significant relevant attributes influencing the overall presentation of products, were A05, A07, A08, A10, and A14, of which the beta values of A10 and A08 were larger, demonstrating that they have greater predictive power towards their overall product presentation; while A02 and A03 constituted a significant negative correlation with the overall presentation of the

Table 6. Multiple regression analysis of design attributes to predict "overall presentation"

Dependent Variable	Predictor Variable	β-distribution	t	Sig.
	(Constant)		2.548	.011
A09 overall presentation	A01 cultural characteristic	.066	1.571	.117
(N=373)	A02 evocation of feelings	-.098	-2.029	.043*
	A03 background story	-.128	-2.406	.017*
	A04 special meaning	.064	1.327	.185
	A05 aesthetic image	.197	4.196	.000***
	A06 innovative level	.070	1.237	.217
	A07 design quality	.171	2.873	.004**
R² = 0.866	A08 product function	.255	7.101	.000***
	A10 material	.313	7.453	.000***
	A11 show self	-.031	-.803	.422
Durbin-Watson Test	A12 pleasure	.085	1.943	.053
= 1.820	A13 unique idea	-.107	-1.647	.101
	A14 appearance style	.151	2.692	.007**
	A15 imagination	-.028	-.691	.490

product, demonstrating that participants believe that the more clear the use of attributes of a background story and evocation of feelings are, the lower the overall presentation of the product.

6 Conclusions and Suggestions

Culture creativity is a new factor for economic development; a country's development is not only dependent on its scientific and technological capability any more, but on the ability to create local culture, lifestyle and taste and to add value with a combination of art and business. Furthermore, in the era of aesthetic economy, a product must possess charm, beauty and an emotional and pleasant element in order to stand out from the other competitors on the market.

This study used analysis of the results of MDS and SPSS questionnaire surveys to explore the product design evaluation and views of consumer groups towards the local characteristics, product innovation, and global marketing of products. Products "Family Bowls" tableware (P4), "Pinban Boat" handbag (P6), "Mr. & Mrs. Chin" salt and pepper set (P8), "Mandarin" Squeezer with goblet (P14), "Steamer Set" steamer pot (P11), "Pearls Dropping on the Jade Plate" piggy bank (P10), each come from different design concepts, different design objectives, and the product designs of different company operational strategies. In the cognitive space of participants' preferred attributes, they displayed a significant grouping phenomenon, demonstrating that design attributes of cultural sensibility dimensions possess a clear identifying ability; in another word, cultural and creative products have a significant qualities of recognition for participants.

The participants considered that the main attributes affecting the overall presentation of a product, in order of degree of influence were material (A10), product function

(A08), aesthetic image (A05), design quality (A07), appearance style (A14); and that the more clear the use of attributes of background story (A03), evocation of feelings (A02) are, the lower the overall presentation of the product. Through survey and analysis of participants' design evaluations, this study provides strategic direction to the design and marketing fields in their development of new global products. Taiwan's Future design styles and the development of her cultural and creative industries can derive greater application and value from this.

References

1. Pine II, B.J., Gilmore, J.H.: The Experience Economy: Work Is Theater & every Business a Stage. Harvard Business School Press, Boston (1999)
2. Dobers, P., Strannegård, L.: Design, lifestyles and sustainability. Aesthetic consumption in a world of abundance. Bus. Strategy Environ. **14**(5), 324–336 (2005)
3. Norman, D.A.: Emotional Design: Why We Love (or Hate) Everyday Things. Basic, New York (2004)
4. Raulik, G., Cawood, G., Larsen, P.: National design strategies and country competitive economic advantage. Des. J. **11**(2), 119–135 (2008)
5. Chia, H.L.: The spring up of cultural and creative industries. In: Summary of Cultural and Creative Industries, 2nd edn, pp. 4–53. Wu-Nan Culture enterprise, Taipei (2008) (in Chinese, semantic translation)
6. United Nations Educational, Scientific and Cultural Organization: The Diversity of Cultural Expressions (2006). http://www.unesco.org/bpi/pdf/memobpi36_culturaldiversity_zh.pdf
7. Niigata Industrial Creation Organization: Hyakunen - Monogatari from Niigata Japan (2005). http://www.nico.or.jp/hyaku/english/concept/
8. Shih, P.C.: Cipher of Aesthetic Economic. Business Weekly, Taipei (2009). (in Chinese, semantic translation)
9. Lin, M.H.: Alessi: DreamWorks of Italian Design Boutique. Sungood, Taipei (2005). (in Chinese, semantic translation)
10. Rapaille, C.: The Culture Code: An Ingenious way to Understand Why People around the World Live and Buy as They Do. Crown Business, New York (2007)
11. Liu, W.K.: Introduction to emotion password. In: The Culture Code: An Ingenious way to Understand Why People around the World Live and Buy as They Do, pp. 14–16. Bookzone, Taipei (2007) (in Chinese, semantic translation)
12. Verganti, R.: Design, meanings, and radical innovation: a metamodel and a research agenda. J. Prod. Innov. Manage. **25**, 436–456 (2008)
13. Tun, F.W.: Legends as sources of inspiration: product design inspired by the legend of "the Dragon's nine sons". J. Des. **16**(4), 75–90 (2011). (in Chinese, semantic translation)
14. Cheng, C.C.: Marketing and planning for culture code (2009). http://media.career.com.tw/college/college_main.asp?CA_NO=349p349&INO=133
15. Norman, D.A.: The Design of Everyday Things. Basic Books, New York (1988)
16. Chu, P.Y., Chen, L.C., Yu, W.S.: Extracting the emotional index and developing the evaluation method for the perceived value of products. J. Des. **15**(1), 25–49 (2010). (in Chinese, semantic translation)
17. Chu, P.Y.: Exploring the emotional dimensions on product design with a decision analysis model. Unpublished doctoral dissertation, Tatung University, Taipei (2011) (in Chinese, semantic translation)

18. Alessi. http://www.alessi-funclub.com.tw/
19. iF Design Award (2011). http://www.ifdesign.de/index_e
20. National Science Council: Taiwan e-learning and digital archives program. http://teldap.tw/
21. Ke, K.J.: Understanding mascots–a case study of mascot in athletic game. Unpublished master's thesis, National Taiwan University of Science and Technology, Taipei (1996) (in Chinese, semantic translation)
22. Lin, R., Lin, P.C., Ko, K.J.: A study of cognitive human factors in mascot design. Int. Ind. Ergon. **23**, 107–112 (1999)
23. Chen, K.Y., Wang, C.H.: Advanced Statistical Analysis Using SPSS and AMOS, 2nd edn. Wu-Nan, Taipei (2011). (in Chinese, semantic translation)
24. Rong, T.S.: SPSS and Research Methodology. Wu-Nan, Taipei (2009)

Chinese Cultural Values in User Experience Design of Kids' Home Products

Xiaojun Huang and Linong Dai(✉)

Shanghai Jiaotong University, No.800 Dongchuan Rd., Shanghai,
People's Republic of China
Miduo1@sjtu.edu.cn, Lndai@126.com

Abstract. Home has great influence on kids' formation of personalities because it is the first environment where they grow up. It represents parents' living and educational values. In this study, the authors use the methodology of Ethnography and POEMS, discuss the subject about how to apply the essence of traditional Chinese cultural values to the experience design of kids' home products, and put it into practice.

Keywords: Kids' home products · Chinese cultural values · User experience design

1 Introduction

According to Freud's psychoanalytic theory of personality, personality is composed of 5 stages. The period from 0 to 6 year old was deemed as the most important stage about personality development, which laid the foundation for the personality patterns in adulthood. In China, kids are raised at home from 0 to 3 year old, and then they go to kindergarten from 4 to 6 year old, at the same time they still take 5 h even more time in their family lives. Huang Baiqing and other researchers believe that in environment factors, the family is the main place for (kids') personality development, because the key period of the formation of (kids') personalities and social behaviors happens in home [1].

The kids' home environment, including the building of space and products, holds family activities, and it represents the parents' living and educational values. As kids live in home for a long period, the environment will shape their habits, influence their perception of the world subtly, and ultimately impact their values and personality formation.

In recent years, the youth in China had good chance to get in touch with the Western culture and their advanced technology. Then there are a great deal of useful ideas about home education introduced, such as respect for humanity, guidance by law, and creativity stimulation. At the same time, the youth also showed backtracking of traditional culture. There come a lot of Chinese culture classes with the courses of calligraphy, Guqin, Chinese zither and Chinese painting. Some areas, especially in educational institutions restored ancient ritual in classes to provide kids with the experience of traditional Chinese culture.

© Springer International Publishing Switzerland 2015
P.L.P. Rau (Ed.): CCD 2015, Part I, LNCS 9180, pp. 49–57, 2015.
DOI: 10.1007/978-3-319-20907-4_5

Family education plays a great important role in China. As the old saying goes, regulating the family, country and the world. 'Home' is very important as the source and foundation of self-cultivation. Chinese famous education experts Xiong Bingqi noted that the profound traditional culture had already contained rich and valuable resources of moral education [2]. In the home environment, Chinese parents try to cultivate a young generation who has the characteristic of Chinese features and broad perspective of the world through the subtle influence of traditional Chinese culture and the guidance of Western education concepts. It brings higher needs to the design for family environment and home products.

Home environment consist of the space and the products, which must comply with the users' concept and carry their behavior. However, the kids' home products in the market are largely identical with only minor differences. The research shows that kids' furniture products in China pay much attention to the adaption for kids' physiological changes, which correspond to the human dimensions and security in traditional ergonomic [3]. For the matter, it does not come to the subdivision design with sociological significance of different life style and educational value [4]. In consequence, this study will discuss how to apply the Chinese cultural values into kids' home products design emphatically, which will facilitate the healthy growth of kids' personality.

2 Methodology

The authors collected the data to analyze the living environment, educational concepts and kids' home products of different families by the methodology of ethnographic. Then we organized the data with the framework of POMES (people, object, environment, message, service), structured the user needs, and chose out the ones relevant with Chinese cultural values. Then the authors explored the possible development of kid's home products with Chinese cultural values, and applied them in practice.

2.1 Ethnography Research

Ethnography is a field in Anthropology. It is the meaning of "human portrait" and a kind of the same ethnic people "direction or life" portrait [5]. In other words, ethnographic study is to allow designers to understand the lives, behavior, needs, values, and beliefs of real users [6].

This research had conducted a survey of twelve families in Shanghai and recorded data of their living environments, educational concepts and kids' home products with the methodology of Ethnography by field observation, in-depth interview and focus group (Fig. 1). The authors not only research the kids' use space, but also recorded the overall layout, furniture style, usage, and style preference of testing families.

2.2 POEMS Analysis

Through the accumulation of a long research, we accessed to a rich array of data, and entered all the data into an Excel spreadsheet in accordance with the construction of

Fig. 1. Photos in real families [7]

	Behavior	Time	Behavior Description	Actor Gender	Actor Identity	Actor Age	Object	Environ-ment	Information	Service	Behavior Motivation	unsati-sfied	Advice	Observer/Use View	Motion Evaluation	Recognition Evaluation
2	刚刚入睡	晚上	姑婆来探望	男	孩子	6个月	无	客厅	月子里的孩子单人行为		月子里的无	无	只要是	4	4	4
3	在太姥姥	下午	去探望太姥	女	太姥姥	老年人	无		在父亲的两个大人之单多人行为		太姥姥要无	无	无	4	4	4
4	在婴儿床	下午	在婴儿里	男	孩子	6个月	婴儿床	卧室	三个月之内单人行为（睡觉		无	无	无	4	4	3
5	婴儿床	上午	现在的婴儿床 (10月)	与之前的婴儿	婴儿床、枕头	卧室		现在会翻身了单人行为（睡觉		现在小空间大整体来			4	4	3
6	在婴儿床	中午	在婴儿里	男	孩子	6个月	婴儿床、软帐	卧室	这个时期的多单人行为（睡觉，防		买回来得蚊帐用户按		5	4	3
7	刚睡醒	下午	在婴儿床里	男	孩子	7个月	婴儿床、玩具	卧室	玩具逗宝宝、单人行为（哄宝宝、		无	无	无	4	5	3
8	阿姨在逗	下午	在婴儿床里	女	保姆	中年	婴儿床、玩具	卧室	玩具逗宝宝、单人行为（哄宝宝、		无	无	无	4	5	3
9	婴儿床	上午	婴儿床	无	无	无	无	无	婴儿床与大床单人行为（一个大人在孩子）							[
10	逗孩子玩	下午	逗孩子玩	女	保姆	中年	婴儿床、玩具	卧室	孩子刚睡醒 单人行为			婴儿床婴儿床看目录	3	4	5
11	睡觉	下午	在床上睡觉	女	姥姥	30+	原儿床、孟祖	卧室	刚想90%哄和单人行为		拎了屋缝手	子	安静的	4	4	5

Fig. 2. Data with POEMS framework in excel

POEMS (Fig. 2). POEMS is a design analysis framework created by Illinois Institute of Technology School of Design, which considered people, object, environment, message, service and other factors synthetically. It is suitable for analysis of large amounts of qualitative data.

We cluster large amounts of original data, and analyze all the needs of users (Fig. 3). The study found that there are two types of users for the kids' home environment and products. One are the kids, whose needs of physical and mental development vary with their different personalities. And the other are the parents, who are the buyers of the kids' home products, as well as the one using products with kids. Parents' educational values play a main role in the process of decision-making, which contain a large number of traditional cultural values.

We catalogue all the needs of users about kids' home products and environment in Fig. 3. Through re combing and clustering, we divide them into basic physiological needs and psychological needs. Then we divide the psychological needs into individual and group ones. As we can see, group psychological needs are closely related to the sociality, culture, and values of families. Since many family education praise Western values in excess before, the kids will meet problems in integrating into the social groups when they grow up. However, Chinese culture contains a large number of educational perspectives on how to get along well with others, which will lead kids to a positive group psychology. The reason for this is that Chinese culture bases on the

kids needs	common needs of kids and parents	parents needs	
role play, self presentation, communication, privacy, expression of emotion, imitation, please their parents (correspond with the authority)	cultivate temperament, cultivate sentiment, respect	children centered, develop independent personality, family show, family external contact, authority, cultivate habit	group psychological needs
develop independent personality, recognition, exploration, emotion, entertainment, fitness	convenience, comfort, beauty and nattiness	privacy, finance, witness growth	indivisual psychological needs
basic physiological needs, well care, mistake tolerance, durability	information, storage, regulation, temperature, ventilation, illumination	guardianship, in the custody of others (correspond with guardianship), hygiene, security, health, movement, products with single feature	basic physiological needs

Fig. 3. Users needs of kids' home products and environment

group and focuses on individual duties and obligations, while Western culture bases on the individual and focuses on individual freedoms and rights [8].

For example, some parents have the need of "authority" while kids have the need of "please their parents". This pair of needs reflect the relationship between parents and their kids, which is closely related to the "filial piety" in Chinese traditional education. Besides, "filial piety" is the core of "benevolence" in Confucianism [9]. In the field observation, it shows as parents guide their children's values, teach them how to get along with others, train their behavior norms, and their children need to comply with the guidance. They are very typical Chinese cultural values.

3 Chinese Cultural Values in User Experience Design of Kids' Home Products

Chinese traditional culture was dominated by Confucianism, which permeates every aspect of traditional social life, and shaped the thoughts, personalities, ways of thinking and feelings of the Chinese nation. It also constructed the unique social structure of China. Confucianism attaches great importance to family education. In Confucian's view, parents need to train and edify their children, help them to form good views and develop good habits of conduct and ethics in long term from an early age, which will benefit their growth.

Confucianism believes that in family education you should take "benevolence" as the core, "integrity" as the basic premise to conduct yourself, "propriety" as the basic criterion to manage interpersonal relationship, and "rectitude" as the important content to develop your morality [9]. In the above four aspects, "integrity" and "rectitude" are close to contemporary Western educational view.

The traditional educational value of "integrity" refers to keeping promise and conforming deeds with words. For children, "integrity" requires the development of their self-discipline and honesty. To help children form the moral integrity, the design of products always comply with the philosophy that form follows function. These types of products often show the nature texture of the materials. It is also a good way to be used by children themselves to cultivate their good habits of independence. A good example is the home products with Scandinavian style, which is functional and also popular in the market. Therefore, we will not discuss this educational value in this paper.

The traditional educational value of "rectitude" emphasizes that we should comply with the moral principle when we obtain something and cannot be greedy. For children, they should establish the awareness of environmentally friendly. To help children form the virtue of "rectitude", the design of kids' home products should reflect the sustainability. There are several examples of green design in the market. Therefore, we will not discuss this value as well.

This paper makes a comparison between the traditional Chinese cultural and educational views and the kids' home products in the market, and finds that the products are lack of reflection with the views of "benevolence" and "propriety". In consequence, this study will focus on these two aspects.

The rhesis in <Shangshu> said that "to show integrity to the people by the virtue of forgiveness and kindness". It is the source of "benevolence". It's the root of "benevolence" to honor parents and respect brothers for Confucius. As for kids' family education, there are two meanings of "benevolence", one is the filial duty for the elder, the other is the love to all things on earth, which can be interpreted as the harmony among the heaven, the earth and human. This cultural value can be expressed by meet the needs of kids, which include "comply with parents", "express emotion", and "imitate parents".

"Propriety" shows as rigid social hierarchy and ethical rules in ancient China. Confucius said: "To subdue one's self and return to propriety, is perfect virtue." (<The Analects of Confucius and Yan Yuan>) Family is the first step for kids from individual to group and society. They understand the structure and hierarchy of the group by experiencing the order of family, and learn about the relationship with others by experiencing the internal modest and external respect with parents' words and deeds. The corresponding needs of parents include "family show" and "family external contact", while that of kids include "contact", "privacy", and both needs of parents and kids include "respect".

3.1 Space Design and Atmosphere Creation

Traditional Chinese atmosphere of the indoor environment often reflects ethical and moral concepts. These values were integrated into a unique aesthetic form, and reflected in a variety of design for layouts and spaces [10]. The overall sequence of propriety space separates from interior to exterior, which will show the level of progressive spatial relations. Quadrangle is a typical example of spatial consequence. In current kids' room design, the game, study and rest area often mixed together. However, the kids' life should be distinguished inside from outside, and dynamic from static states. For instance, children need to be acquainted with the rule that the living room

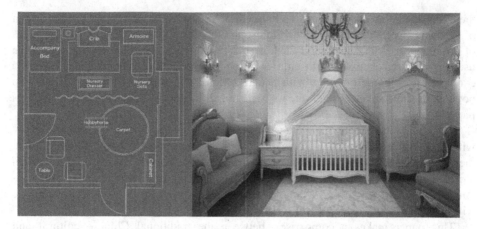

Fig. 4. Space and layout design of baby room for Princess Cisy [11]

and dining room are relative public spaces where the family members gather and interact, while the bedroom is a private space with dignity where other people cannot enter rashly, especially for parents' room. The authors apply this concept to the design for kids' room in two situations. When the space is limited, it will be better to perform the kids' social, play and other dynamic activities in the living room. Kids' rooms are functional areas mainly for static activities such as resting and learning. If the kids' rooms have larger space, then it can be divided into two main functional areas for actively playing and resting or studying alone, which will train the kids to establish good habits in their lives.

Although the style of Princess Cisy Series [11] is western and classical, it reflects the traditional Chinese family culture with connotation (Fig. 4). The baby room is divided into private and public spaces. The private space is a static and private area where the baby rest and diapered, while the public spaces is a dynamic and relative group gathering area where the baby play games and have social activities. The disposition of the furniture is centered and symmetrical, which will highlight its classic and grandeur. Growing in environment with layout and style like this, kids will make sense of the difference of interior and exterior, the propriety of dynamic and static movement, and the order of behavior.

3.2   Product Design and Behavior Cultivation

Repetitive behavior will form a habit, and the consistent habit will shape people's perceptions and attitudes. The function and the way to use a good product can bring positive influences on kids' behaviors. It can be a way to help kids form a traditional cultural concept of healthy personalities.

To balance the needs of kids as well as their parents in the kids' home products design can achieve a harmonious parent-child interaction, which will cultivate kids' love to their parents. It will avoid kids to be self-centered and stimulate the behavior of caring for parents. In the example of "Star Rescue - Luke" [11] (Fig. 5), which is a table

Fig. 5. "Star Rescue - Luke" parent-child table design [11]

especially designed for pupil and their parents to co-read. Kids will use the long side of the table to do homework or read, while parents can use the short side, where provide enough space for the tablet or reading books. There is a bunch of electric plugs on the table with many USB ports, and parents can easily recharge their phone or tablet. There are two cup trays with the sweet function of heating and cooling. In conclusion, adding features for adults in kids' furniture can cultivate kids' respect for parents, which is also a good expression of traditional philosophy of "benevolence".

3.3   Visual Design and Aesthetic Edification

Visual elements may convey rich cultural symbols. However, the kids' products design in the current market is lacking of Chinese elements. Chinese culture has its own unique aesthetic of imitating nature, which reflects the world view of "*Man and Nature Harmonization*". We will take the "blue-and-white porcelain" baby furniture collection (Fig. 6) for example. Blue-and-white is also called china flower, whose patterns are from the shapes of all things on earth. It is also the understanding of the world of Chinese. "Blue" symbolizes "Lucky" in traditional culture, and it is the love to all things on earth for ancient Chinese, which is also an expression of "benevolence". Using traditional patterns of blue and white on kids' furniture design provides them with a dignified and orderly environment, which will unconsciously influence kids to grow up as genteel, generous people with good propriety in the future.

Fig. 6. "Blue-and-white porcelain" baby furniture collection [11]

4 Conclusion

This study started from the lives of real users and found the relevance between their needs and family educational values, and then we emphasized the influence of lack of "benevolence" and "propriety" in kids' home products design. After that, we give advice about products design especially for these two educational values. The development of this study will help Chinese designers create more products fitting the Chinese cultural values, in consequence provide carrier for the healthy personalities of kids. However, the study had its limits in data support because of few research samples and the foundation of qualitative research. In addition, this study focuses on the influence of parents in kids' home products design, and does not discuss the problem which will caused by the difference of kids' personalities. So it is more suitable to the parent-led families.

Acknowledgements. This study was completed by the cooperation of Shanghai ForU Sleep Technology Co., Ltd. and Shanghai Jiaotong University. All the products presented above are original designs from ForU. Thanks a lot!

References

1. Huang, B., Hong, J., Xu, X.: The personalities and features of family environment of children with attention deficit hyperactivity disorder. Chin. J. Clin. Rehabil. (2003)
2. Xiong, B.: Activate the potential of traditional culture, make up the short board of moral education. Xinhua Daily Telegraph (2013)
3. The survey report of kids furniture. Kunming University of Science and Technology. (2012) http://wenku.baidu.com/view/782b3a84d4d8d15abe234e2b.html

4. On the spread of ethnographic research methods (2006). http://eng.hi138.com/journalism-and-communication-papers/200605/4631_on-the-spread-of-ethnographic-research-methods.asp#.VX4jHGSqqkp

5. Dai, L., Xu, B.: Human factors design research with Persona for kits set in Shanghai middle-class family. In: HCII2013

6. Dai, L.: Contemporary design philosophy, 《Contemporary design thinking当代设计研究理念》. Shanghai Jiaotong University Press (2009)

7. Participants provided by Shanghai ForU Sleep Technology Co., Ltd

8. Ma, S.: The main difference between Chinese and Western cultures in intercultural communication. People's Tribune (2012)

9. Cheng, C.: Confucian educational concept of family development and its contemporary value. Res. Educ. Hist. (2006)

10. Ji, Y., Tan, X., Wen, S.: Impact of confucian aesthetic upon modern indoor design concept. Shanxi Arch. (2014)

11. Products in Figure 4, 5, 6, 7 were originally designed by Shanghai ForU Sleep Technology Co., Ltd

Cross-Cultural User Experience Design Helping Product Designers to Consider Cultural Differences

Florian Lachner[1], Constantin von Saucken[2(✉)],
Florian 'Floyd' Mueller[1], and Udo Lindemann[2]

[1] Exertion Games Lab, RMIT University, Melbourne, Australia
lachner@gmx.de, floyd@floydmueller.com
[2] Institute of Product Development, Technische Universität München,
Munich, Germany
{saucken,lindemann}@pe.mw.tum.de

Abstract. User experience (UX) designers aim to create a product that causes a pleasant emotional reaction in order to generate an enjoyable memory. However, emotions are subjective and diverse because of cultural differences. As a consequence, cultural differences in UX design are often considered only as theoretical exercises. In this paper, we aim to bridge the gap between theoretical cultural studies and practical application. We analyze established cultural dimensions as well as notes from observational studies, business presentations and ethnographic interviews. Finally, we present "Cultural Personas", application-oriented tools that characterize derived cultural differences. That supports designers to consider a culturally sensitive UX and thereby to develop better, more enjoyable products.

Keywords: Country culture · Cross-cultural design · Cross-cultural evaluation · Personalities · Psychology · Personas · Storytelling

1 Introduction

Users' experiences are embedded in a specific social and cultural context, including associated emotions, expectations, and individual preferences [1]. For user experience (UX) designers these contexts are difficult to anticipate as they are biased by their own culture, whereas considering cultural differences is crucial to design better products in globalized markets [2]. Culture is a commonly used term with a variety of characterizations and descriptions. Definitions range from the collective knowledge and associated behavioral patterns within national, ethnic or regional groups to a population's field of action, containing objects, institutions, ideas, and values [3]. An established definition from Hofstede [4] describes culture as intellectual programming of peoples' minds. However, the field of UX design misses effective tools that support a systematic approach to consider cultural differences in design processes and faces the challenge to incorporate such tools in organization frameworks [5].

© Springer International Publishing Switzerland 2015
P.L.P. Rau (Ed.): CCD 2015, Part I, LNCS 9180, pp. 58–70, 2015.
DOI: 10.1007/978-3-319-20907-4_6

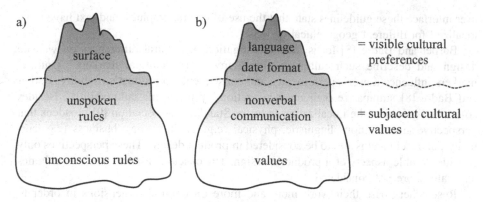

Fig. 1. Iceberg model (a) from Hoft (1995) and (b) associated UX characteristics

Hoft [6] suggests the use of descriptive models to provide a better understanding of cultural characteristics and presents the cultural Iceberg model. Analogous to an ice-berg (Fig. 1), where approximately only ten percent is visible above the water surface, this model states that only ten percent of cultural characteristics, such as date formats or language, are easily recognizable. Consequently, ninety percent of cultural characteristics, such as nonverbal communication or values, are difficult to identify and easy to ignore. The cultural Iceberg model provides the basis of understanding for analyzing existing research projects and for the traceability of our approach.

In this paper, we aim to bridge the gap between theoretical cultural studies and application to support a culturally sensitive UX design practice. Based on the cultural Ice-berg model we analyze established cultural dimensions as well as notes from field observations and interviews to address subjacent cultural aspects such as unspoken and unconscious rules. We present "cultural personas" – application-oriented tools that are inspired by traditional personas and support designers during the development process to localize their product in order to design for a better UX.

2 Related Work

Previous research works already investigate how cultural differences should be considered in UX design processes. Most of them base their approaches on cultural dimensions, mainly addressing visible cultural preferences on a culture's surface (Fig. 1). The following section defines cultural dimensions and provides an overview over existing cross-cultural design approaches identifying the research gap for this work.

2.1 Cross-Cultural Design Approaches

The influences of cultural differences on a product's user interface have already been taken into account in academia and industry. In interaction design, it goes all the way back to Apple's Macintosh Human Interface Guidelines [7]. With a focus on the visible user interface these guidelines state that the use of colors, graphics, and text have to be localized for different geographical regions.

Barber and Badre [8] focus their investigation of cultural differences on website design and describe such culture-specific elements as "cultural markers". Cultural markers influence a user's performance and consequently a product's usability. Barber and Badre [8] summarize their characterization by the term "culturability". Besides colors and graphics, the Localization Industry Standards Association [9] broadens that perspective and mentions linguistic, physical (e.g. modification), business (e.g. currency), and technical issues to be considered in product design. These perspectives only consider visible aspects of a product's design. Unconscious aspects, such as attitudes and values, are not considered.

Researchers base their work more and more on cultural dimensions in order to respect cultural differences in UX design (Fig. 2). Existing approaches either focus on a specific use case, a theoretical framework or analyze visible cultural preferences, neglecting subjacent cultural values.

Hsieh [10] evaluates visible cultural preferences on websites based on cultural dimensions for the specific use cases in Australian and Taiwanese contexts (Fig. 2a). Eune and Lee [11] analyze subjacent cultural values with respect to usage patterns and user perceptions of mobile phones (Fig. 2d). In contrast, Zakour [12] provides a conceptual model based on the technology acceptance model (TAM) while Eugene et al. [13] present a cultural relevance design framework. However, both approaches illustrate cultural differences merely theoretically (Fig. 2b/e). Liu and Keung [14] link cultural dimensions to a website's user interface elements and provide a tool to be used by website designers – considering usability aspects but without subjacent cultural values (Fig. 2c).

2.2   Research Gap and Research Question

We identified a number of research approaches that explore cultural differences in UX design by presenting use cases or by providing a rather abstract theoretical framework. Application-oriented tools to support designers only consider usability aspects, thus remaining at the visible surface of the cultural Iceberg Model. In conclusion, there is

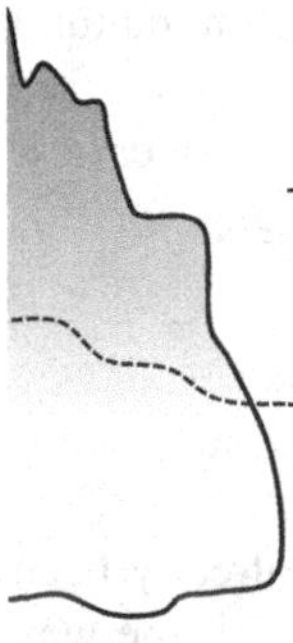

	Use Case	Theoretical Framework	Tool
visible cultural preferences	a) Hsieh (2014)	b) Zakour (2009)	c) Liu & Keung (2013)
subjacent cultural values	d) Eune & Lee (2009)	e) Eugene et al. (2009)	f) Research Gap

Fig. 2. Cross-cultural design studies (a–e) and research gap (f)

a research gap in self-explanatory tools considering subjacent cultural values being easy to use – such tools are highly appreciated by industrial designers [15]. In this paper, we address this gap by presenting an application-oriented tool that enables designer to effectively consider subjacent cultural values in UX design (Fig. 2f). We address the research question how we can help designers to consider UX-related cultural values in UX design processes.

3 Research Methodology

The goal of this research is to help designers to consider UX specific cultural differences, thus bridging the gap between theory and practical application. Therefore, we follow a two-step approach to gather relevant data. Firstly, we took notes during business related industry presentations, and conducted field observations and interviews (Sect. 3.2). Secondly, we supplement this qualitative data with culture-oriented literature review (Sect. 3.3). To ensure a structured approach we base our data collection and analysis process on the customer experience interaction model (Sect. 3.1).

3.1 Customer Experience Interaction Model

We take the customer experience interaction model (CEIM) as the background for our understanding of UX (Fig. 3). It provides a holistic view on the interaction of users

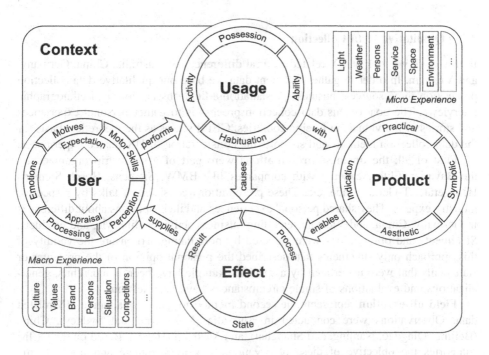

Fig. 3. Customer experience interaction model CEIM [16]

with products. CEIM incorporates different relevant models and views from the disciplines of engineering, human factors, industrial design and psychology [16].

CEIM is based on the block diagram of human machine system [17] – a classic ergonomics perspective with the goal to improve the working task fulfillment by adapting the machine, its interface and the environment impact to the user's capacity. It focuses the human machine interaction with relevant ports (sensory organs, muscular system and user interface). Since UX requires a stronger consideration of the human perception and processing, CEIM details the user element by emotions and motives [16].

CEIM enlarges the classic functional understanding of products by indication, aesthetic and symbolic aspects. UX is more than just fulfilling tasks in a most efficient manner. The emotional value and experience by using an expensive sports car can be the result not only of great driving properties (practical function) but also of the pleasant exterior and interior design considering shape and materials (aesthetic function) as well as the prestige through product and brand (symbolic function) [16].

The UX caused by the user-product interaction is highly dependent on the surrounding context: The micro experience context represents the physical environment that rather disturbs the interaction: light, weather or space conditions. By contrast, the macro experience context stands for the social surrounding impacting the reflective UX. It represents the culture, society and corresponding values the user in embedded in.

In this work, CEIM serves as a basis for systematically classifying the following research findings, observations and interview data in an UX framework.

3.2 Qualitative Data Collection

In this work we look at UX related cultural differences of Australia, China, Germany, and Vietnam. In order to gather sufficient data we base our qualitative data collection process on three sources: business presentations, field observation, and ethnographic interviews. The goal of this data collection process is to gather personal experiences and stories of individuals in foreign countries. CEIM serves as the theoretical basis for the data collection methods and supports the consideration of UX related experiences.

First of all, the **business presentations** were part of a study trip organized by the Bavarian Elite Academy with companies like BMW, Siemens, Bosch Siemens Hausgeräte, T-Good, Linde, etc. These presentations consisted of talks by respective industry experts. They shared personal experiences and their opinions about differences in Germany, China, and Vietnam regarding business activities, lifestyle, and products. Statements and observations were gathered by note taking. To ensure the validity of this approach only statements that described the personal opinion of the presenter or statements that were underlined by a specific example have been noted. Thus, generalizations and evaluations of single circumstances have been left out.

Field observation represents the second method to gather qualitative UX-related data. Observations were conducted in Australia (Melbourne and Sydney), China (Beijing, Qingdao, Nanjing, and Shanghai), and Vietnam (Hanoi). Based on the CEIM categories the objective of these observations was to recognize and note specific incidents regarding human behaviors, human-product interaction, product appearances, and environmental aspects, that seemed to be unusual or unexpected from the author's perspective. Having identified such an incident the situation was initially and retro-spectively recorded in detail using Excel.

In order to avoid subjectivity and ensure validity of the qualitative data the industry presentations and field observations have been complemented by **ethnographic interviews**. Therefore we conducted 10 interviews, via Skype or in person, each about 45 min, with participants (9 Ph.D. students and 1 professor) from in total 5 different countries. The interviews were semi-structured with a certain amount of key questions based on the CEIM sub-categories. Focus of the interviews was to identify and discuss situations that contained unusual situations or interactions in foreign countries. Therefore, the participants were asked not only to explain but to compare recognizable situations with their home country or other countries. Thus it was possible to avoid a judgmental bias of specific cultures. In total the 10 participants were able to describe situations in about 10 different countries with a clear focus on Australia and Germany. All interviews have been recorded, transcribed, and analyzed together with the notes from the presentations and observations following a structured analysis process (Sect. 3.4).

3.3 Cultural Dimensions

Cultural dimensions are independent characteristics that describe a culture's prefer-ences to answer basic problems that are common to all societies [4], such as the relation to authority or the relationship between the individual and the society [18]. The main application of cultural dimensions is to distinguish cultural differences at a national level [19].

Hofstede [4] describes five established cultural dimensions: **Power Distance** (the extent of inequalities and hierarchy that a society tolerates), **Uncertainty Avoidance** (the level of stress that is caused by unclear and ambiguous situations), **Individualism versus Collectivism** (how strong individuals are integrated in and feel responsible for a social group), **Masculinity versus Femininity** (the degree of differentiation of gender roles), and **Long-term versus Short-term Orientation** (the preferred focus of people's time orientation, on the future or the present). These dimensions are widely used and recognized in cross-cultural research projects due to Hofstede's extensive survey [12]. Therefore, they provide an ideal basis for the underlying research question.

In contrast, Edward T. Hall presents the following cultural dimensions to describe general cultural differences: **perception of space** (the physical distance that is per-ceived as comfortable) [20], the **context of communication** (whether communication is rather implicit or explicit, designated as high-context or low-context cultures) [21], and the **perception of time** (cultures that prefer to complete one task or more tasks simultaneously, designated as monochromic or polychronic cultures) [22]. Hall's dimensions represent the second set of dimensions that is commonly used in cross-cultural studies, as these dimensions are also more focused on human values than general beliefs [12]. Consequently, these dimensions, the context of communication and the perception of time in particular, represent a sensible supplement to Hofstede's dimensions for our research approach.

Kluckhohn and Strodtbeck [23], Trompenaars and Hampden-Turner [24], and Schwartz [25] have presented further cultural dimensions. These dimensions do not distinctly differ from Hofstede's and Hall's dimensions, besides their naming [12]. In general, these dimensions also represent a society's overall problems, describing the relationship between humans, between humans and the environment as well as the perception of time and space. Consequently, in cross-cultural design these dimensions are usually only used to describe certain dimensions more detailed.

3.4   Analyzing Cultural Differences

We base our analysis on the structuring content analysis according to Mayring [26] to derive UX-related cultural differences from the underlying variety of diverse statements. The structuring content analysis is used to find similarities within documented communication and to derive strategies or measures of actions related to this communication [26].

Our analysis process follows the steps of the structuring content analysis: Initially, a category system has to be elaborated to structure the gathered statements. In this project, we choose the existing CEIM categories as it holistically describes UX and has already been used as a framework to effectively structure and conduct the described field observation and qualitative interviews.

Secondly, all of the notes from the presentations and the field observations as well as relevant statements from the interview transcripts are assigned to one CEIM-category and an associated sub-category. Following this process, 599 allocations have been assigned based on the notes and transcripts using Excel. Within these 599 allocations some statements are listed more often as multiple assignments are necessary for statements that suit to several categories.

Thirdly, the categories and sub-categories provide the basis to paraphrase the assigned statements. By paraphrasing the statements they are broken down to the basic message and are easier to understand and analyze. Finally, we looked at each category and sub-category to identify cultural differences and similarities. Thus, we were able to derive culture specific UX design characteristics, which are presented in the following section.

4   Results

In order to bridge the gap between the theory and practical application, the results from the literature review, e.g. evaluation of cultural dimensions, and analysis process get translated into an effective tool. Firstly, the following section describes the identified UX-related differences between the countries Australia, China, Germany, and Vietnam. Secondly, we discuss the "Cultural Persona" as a practical tool for developers and designers. Thirdly, there is a short discussion about possible areas of application within the product creation process.

4.1 Cultural Differences in User Experience Design

In this work we focus on the countries Australia, China, Germany, and Vietnam. This is due to the facts that most qualitative data was gathered within the interviews targeting these countries as well as that general conditions allowed the conduct of field observations in these countries and enabled the participation in industry presentations in China and Vietnam. The cultural dimensions represent the theoretical basis for this research project. The cultural scientists Hofstede and Hall describe established and suitable dimensions for UX design processes.

Hofstede et al. [18] explicitly describe the characteristics of more than 75 countries, including our target countries. They identified Australia and Germany as rather individualistic (personal achievements are important) and as countries with a rather low power distance (equalized distribution of power) but higher uncertainty avoidance (unknown circumstances are avoided). China and Vietnam show opposite results in these dimensions. Besides Vietnam, a feminine country (more consensus-oriented), Australia, China, and Germany are labelled as rather masculine (preference for material rewards). With regard to time orientation, China and Germany focus more on the future (long-term orientation) whereas Australia and Vietnam are described as short-term oriented (values are related to the past).

Hall [21, 22] does not provide explicit country information in his work. With regard to his dimensions context of communication (Contextuality) and perception of time (Time Perception), western-oriented cultures can be described as low-context (communicators are expected to be straightforward, concise, and efficient) and monochronic (time is perceived in a linear fashion, one thing after another) cultures, Asian cultures as the opposites: high-context and polychronic.

In addition to the comparison of established cultural dimension the analysis of the notes from the industry presentations, field observations, and transcribed interviews provide valuable insights in UX-related cultural differences. The identified aspects in this step of our research focused on general UX-related differences as illustrated in CEIM (Sect. 3.1). For each country five noticeable aspects have been derived from our data. In the following each aspect is stated and briefly described by mentioning an associated note or quote from our qualitative data set:

- **Australia.** People in Australia pay attention to their identification and an affiliation to a social group ("Every Australian I have talked to said the Victoria Bitter is kind of the student beer, you drink it because you are a student"), they prefer a trendy design with themed or unique features ("Buildings often have a fancy facade in Melbourne") as well as regulations and simplicity ("It is obligatory to wear a helmet when you ride a bike"). Australians are laid-back ("I don't think I have experienced such hospitality like that in any other place"), their lifestyle is influenced by living in a rather removed area ("Everything in general is more expensive").
- **China.** Chinese people pay a lot of attention to avoid conflicts ("Emotions are rather withheld emotions to save their face") and personal relationships are very important to them ("Food and drinks are always shared within the group when you are in a restaurant"). In general people in China appreciate a flashy, expensive

looking design ("Our products in China a very colorful and bigger") and place value on a product's first impression ("Almost every present you received was very much as you say, nicely packed"). Environmental and social differences however make China a very diverse country ("China is like many countries in one").

- **Germany.** Germans appreciate functionality ("In Germany the aesthetics are strongly related to the technical features of a product") and prefer high quality products ("Germans rather spend a little extra and it might not look as fancy but it will work better for a longer period"). Germans put a lot of value on individualism ("In Germany it was not about the brands it was about the look") and appreciate efficient processes ("The size of the country and how everything is compacted into it is very obvious"). Although relationships are important for Germans they are in general initially reserved towards strangers ("You really have to make a real big effort to become a part of a community").

- **Vietnam.** Superstition ("A fortune-teller had to approve our office floor plan") and social conditions ("The differences between public and private hospitals are immense") have a great influence on the Vietnamese lifestyle. They have a strongly anchored Vietnamese culture ("Radio stations mostly play Vietnamese songs") that is more and more influenced by western values ("Young Vietnamese define status by having an iPhone and a Honda Airblade"). While the daily routine in Vietnam is rather hectic, Vietnamese are usually quite relaxed and friendly ("Nobody gets angry when you ignore their right of way").

4.2 Cultural Personas in Design Process

Personas are mainly used to support a designer's focus and by providing a common basis for communication [27]. They help to create a mutual language, to create empathy towards the user and thus to make better decisions [28]. Consequently, personas are usually created within a specific design project with specific requirements for a defined target group. However, our cultural personas have been created independently from any product or design project.

From our perspective they serve three different needs along the product development process: (1) Cultural personas can provide a basic understanding in target group definition and requirements engineering. At this stage of the development process a design team can identify suitable target markets by matching product characteristics with cultural UX-preferences. (2) Designers can adjust or add product features or characteristics to suit cultural regions, i.e. localizing a product. Localizing products and services is an important factor based on an ongoing trend towards globalization [29]. (3) Cultural personas provide a basic understanding in cultural differences and a basis for a shared communication regarding cultural aspects in UX design. Especially in time consuming design processes it is difficult to develop cultural knowledge from scratch but cultural personas can help to consider cultural differences to design better products.

4.3 Cultural Persona Form Sheet

The cultural persona is a two-page document containing a theoretical basis derived from suitable cultural dimensions and the findings from the qualitative data analysis (Fig. 4). The results are illustrated in three blocks – from general to detail.

Firstly, the cultural dimensions by Hofstede [4] and Hall [20–22] are presented to get a feeling for general preferences, values and characteristics of the culture. We illustrated the selected dimensions with slide controls to indicate that each manifestation is rather a tendency than an absolute value. Moreover, the dimensions were renamed to avoid scientific abstractions and enhance their comprehension, e.g. Hofstede's [4] dimensions "femininity vs. masculinity" is named "motivation" as it describes what people drives. A brief description and a graphic icon explain the dimensions' tendencies.

Secondly, the findings of the qualitative data analysis are shown below the cultural dimensions. Every country's specific characteristics are symbolized by an icon and illustrated by three associated quotes from the interviews or observational notes. Thirdly, two personas per country summarize relevant cultural characteristics to enhance a designer's comprehension. We based the creation of these personas on the approach of Adlin and Pruitt [28] and included a photo, a distinctive quote as well as information about the persona's personal life, the environment, and likes/dislikes. We filled this data set with the results from the analysis (Sect. 4.1) as well as with information from the analysis of the cultural dimensions. Furthermore, we included two

Fig. 4. Cultural persona form: front page (left) and reverse side (right)

quantitative aspects, such as the population or age distribution, from CIA's World Factbook [30] or Think with Google [31].

5 Conclusion and Limitations

We discussed the customer experience interaction model (CEIM) that provides a holistic perspective on user experience (UX) and allowed us to systematically gather and analyze observable experiences. We did that based on statements and stories from industry presentations, field observations, and interviews. Our intention was to identify subjective experiences representing UX-related cultural differences. Thereby, we gathered data for evaluations regarding the countries Australia, China, Germany, and Vietnam. In addition to this qualitative data collection, we reviewed and compared established cultural dimensions, particularly from Hofstede [4] and Hall [20–22].

Both, the insights from our literature review and qualitative data analysis, provided the basis for the creation of cultural personas. A cultural persona is a two-page tool that contains culture-specific and UX-related country information and is illustrated by two fictitious, representative individuals per country. This tool can be used to communicate and understand cultural differences in the entire product development process and to identify and implement culturally sensitive product aspects.

With CEIM and the analysis approach of Mayring [26] we created a structured framework for this research project. However, we were only able to gather enough data for four countries, whereas further investigations can provide supplementary insights in UX-related cultural differences regarding other countries. Furthermore, the whole research was conducted from a western perspective while additional insights from researchers with other cultural backgrounds can complement and adjust the developed cultural personas. Moreover, it must be tested in development projects to see if they serve their aspired objectives. It has to be particularly evaluated if the presentation of only two personas is sufficient to take cultural differences in UX design into account. A web-based version of the developed cultural personas can thereby support the distribution and modifiability of the tool.

All in all we, see cultural personas as a top-level tool that enhances the understanding and communication in UX design processes and allows designers to consider UX-related cultural differences to create culturally targeted, hence better products.

References

1. Roto, V., Law, E., Vermeeren, A., Hoonhout, J. (eds.): User experience white paper. http://www.allaboutux.org/files/UX-WhitePaper.pdf
2. Del Galdo, E.M., Nielsen, J.: International User Interfaces. Wiley, New York (1996)
3. Thomas, A.: Kultur und Kulturstandards. In: Thomas, A., Kinast, E.-U., Schroll-Machl, S. (eds.) Handbuch Interkulturelle Kommunikation und Kooperation. Vandenhoeck & Ruprecht, Göttingen (2005)
4. Hofstede, G.: Culture's Consequences. Comparing Values, Behaviors, Institutions, and Organizations Across Nations. Sage, Thousand Oaks (2001)

5. Marcus, A.: Cross-cultural user-experience design. In: Barker-Plummer, D., Cox, R., Swoboda, N. (eds.) Diagrams 2006. LNCS (LNAI), vol. 4045, pp. 16–24. Springer, Heidelberg (2006)
6. Hoft, N.: Developing a cultural model. In: Del Galdo, E.M., Nielsen, J. (eds.) International User Interfaces, pp. 41–73. Wiley, New York (1996)
7. Apple Computer, Inc.: Macintosh Human Interface Guidelines. Addison-Wesley, Reading (1995)
8. Barber, W., Badre, A.: Culturability: the merging of culture and usability. http://research.microsoft.com/en-us/um/people/marycz/hfweb98/barber/
9. Localization Industry Standards Association (LISA): The globalization industry primer. http://www.acclaro.com/assets/files/downloads/whitepapers/lisa_globalization_primer.pdf
10. Hsieh, H.C.L.: Evaluating the effects of cultural preferences on website use. In: Rau, P. (ed.) CCD 2014. LNCS, vol. 8528, pp. 162–173. Springer, Heidelberg (2014)
11. Eune, J., Lee, K.-P.: Cultural dimensions in user preferences and behaviors of mobile phones and interpretation of national cultural differences. In: Aykin, N. (ed.) IDGD 2009. LNCS, vol. 5623, pp. 29–38. Springer, Heidelberg (2009)
12. Zakour, A.B.: Information technology acceptance across cultures. In: Zaphiris, P., Ang, C.S. (eds.) Human Computer Interaction, pp. 132–153. IGI Global, Hershey (2009)
13. Eugene, W., Hatley, L., McMullen, K., Brown, Q., Rankin, Y., Lewis, S.: This is who I am and this is what I do: demystifying the process of designing culturally authentic technology. In: Aykin, N. (ed.) IDGD 2009. LNCS, vol. 5623, pp. 19–28. Springer, Heidelberg (2009)
14. Liu, P., Keung, C.: Defining cross-culture theoretical framework of user interface. In: Rau, P. (ed.) HCII 2013 and CCD 2013, Part I. LNCS, vol. 8023, pp. 235–242. Springer, Heidelberg (2013)
15. von Saucken, C., Lindemann, U.: User-centered design for research: following our own recommendations. In: Proceedings of the International Conference on Advanced Design Research and Education (ICADRE14), pp. 118–122. Singapore (2014)
16. von Saucken, C., Gomez, R.: Unified user experience model: enabling a more comprehensive understanding of emotional experience design. In: Salamanca, J., et al. (eds.) Proceedings of the Colors of Care. Ediciones Uniandes, Bogotá (2014)
17. Schmidtke, H.: Ergonomie. Hanser, München (1993)
18. Hofstede, G., Hofstede, G.J., Minkov, M.: Cultures and Organizations. Software of the Mind. McGrawHill, New York (2010)
19. Chakraborty, J., Norcio, A.F.: Cross cultural computer gaming. In: Aykin, N. (ed.) IDGD 2009. LNCS, vol. 5623, pp. 13–18. Springer, Heidelberg (2009)
20. Hall, E.T.: The Hidden Dimension. Doubleday, Garden City (1969)
21. Hall, E.T.: Beyond Culture. Doubleday, New York (1989)
22. Hall, E.T.: The Dance of Life: The Other Dimensions. Anchor Books, New York (1989)
23. Kluckhohn, F.R., Strodtbeck, F.L.: Variations in Value Orientation. Greenwood, Westport (1961)
24. Trompenaars, F., Hampden-Turner, C.: Riding the Waves of Culture. Understanding Cultural Diversity in Business. Nicholas Brealey, London (1998)
25. Schwartz, S.H.: A theory of cultural values and some implications for work. Appl. Psychol. 48, 23–47 (1999)
26. Mayring, P.: Qualitative Inhaltsanalyse. Beltz, Weinheim (2003)
27. Pruitt, J., Grudin, J.: Personas: practice and theory. In: Arnowitz, J., Chalmers, A., Swack, T. (eds.) Proceedings of the 2003 Conference on Designing for User Experiences, pp. 1–15. ACM, New York (2003)

28. Adlin, T., Pruitt, J.: Putting personas to work: using data-driven personas to focus product planning, design, and development. In: Sears, A., Jacko, J.A. (eds.) The Human-Computer Interaction Handbook. Taylor & Francis, New York (2008)

29. Sturm, C.: Studien zur transkulturellen Benutzbarkeit mobiler Endgeräte. http://www.freidok.uni-freiburg.de/volltexte/2343/pdf/Dissertation_Sturm.pdf

30. CIA: The world factbook. https://www.cia.gov/library/publications/the-world-factbook/

31. Think with Google: Our mobile planet. https://think.withgoogle.com/mobileplanet/en/

A Product Service System Design for Fitness Activities Based on Active Ageing a Proposal of Fitness for Xishan Style Council

Yin Liang[✉] and Davide Fassi

Department of Design, Politecnico Di Milano, Milano, Italy
yl401402@hotmail.com, davide.fassi@polimi.it

Abstract. This paper is about a design proposal for the "Style Council" (Xishan Style Council is local government department which take charge of organizing cultural and fitness activities. http://wt.jsxishan.gov.cn/zgxswtj/.) of Xishan, Wuxi, China to offer a service which help the residents, especially the elders, to do fitness in a healthy and social interactive way. It aims not only to improve physical health but also to build up a friendly relationship among the neighbors.

This service will be developed under the active ageing policy (WHO 2002) released by WHO (World Health Organization) followed by the Chinese government too. Because of this policy, many fitness spaces emerged and equipment was produced under the help of sponsors and "sports administration" (Sports Administration is a government department which take charge of Sports Events, training athletes, improving the physical fitness and exercise etc. http://www.sport.gov.cn/.). Nowadays local government has the mission to integrate fitness resources including sponsors, fitness groups, coaches and temporary spaces to build up a fitness system which elders can easily join. But this top-down fitness system is not working well in many places.

In this proposal, we analyze this integration work in Xishan with the aim to modify and improve it toward a lifestyle which bring both physical and psychological health to people.

According to the Social innovation journey (Fassi et al. 2013) after having investigated the user's needs, we design a service system which aims to offer multi- experienced fitness activities for elders and encourage sponsors to support this activity.

Keywords: Fitness life style · Active ageing · Social innovation · Service design

1 Introduction

As China is coming into super ageing society (Zhang 2011), fitness activities for elders have become a serious social challenge in urban contexts. Even if great effort has been paid by government and local enterprises, elders still find it hard to have an appropriate

© Springer International Publishing Switzerland 2015
P.L.P. Rau (Ed.): CCD 2015, Part I, LNCS 9180, pp. 71–82, 2015.
DOI: 10.1007/978-3-319-20907-4_7

fitness space. In east China, rapid urbanization and large amount of old migrants make the public space crowded both for normal use (walk paths, rest areas, shopping squares) and for fitness one (square dancing etc.). This resulted directly in the conflict between those people who are using these spaces in their free time (i.e. fitness people) and local resident who are suffering from the noisy or overusing of their living place.

To deal with this problem, Chinese government released "active ageing" and "health ageing" policy to invite companies and NGOs to take part in the fitness program. Beside this, "National Fitness Program" was launched in 2011. This plan has invested a large sum of money in fitness equipment, coach training and holding fitness events. During the past 4 years, community fitness programs are wildly developed. Unfortunately, this top-down public fitness system have given rise to a large burden on government, that's why many local governments started to invite non-government sectors to deal with the problems like capital shortage, engagement, social participation etc.

On the other hand, many companies are taking these national wild fitness activities as opportunities. Sponsors cooperate with residents in many ways to enhance their social influence but cooperation are limited due to reliance, information accessibility and weak organization.

This applied research is focusing on helping Xishan "Style Council" to effectively cooperate with sponsors, residents and other stakeholders to improve the local fitness system of activities.

2 Background

Square dancing is one of the most popular fitness activity in Chinese towns. It is basically done by a team of people usually meeting after dinner (6–8 pm) in public spaces (i.e. squares, parks, underground stations, large sidewalks etc.) to train themselves for contemporary dance performances guided by a team-leader. This activity has a long history rooted in the Chinese culture to cooperate and spending their free time together. The aging people who had experienced the cultural revolution in their teens, started to look for new activities to practice during in their spare time as ways to keep fit (Chen 2011). In the last years due to the renewal of many public spaces, new development urban system and the people ageing, the square dancing is being considered more as a problem than an opportunity by the local people. In Xishan District, Local Style Council believes it is a cost-effective activity for the elders. The positive aspects are obvious, elders socialize and interact through dancing, moreover, dancers bring vitality to the city. To support square dancing, Xishan Style Council has planned to involve more public spaces including more than 30 school playgrounds and to employ almost 900 coaches to tutor elder people, with the aim to reduce the negative impact of square dancing, make it work under the control of "neighborhood committee"[1]. Style Council hopes to build up a system according to two main aspects:

---

[1] Neighbourhood community is a self-management organization at the grassroots level in China. They are in charge of mediation of disputes among the people and activity organization.

1. Use public social resources like coaches, temporary spaces and school equipment so to not create new spaces;
2. Pay more attention to the local residents, their needs, habits and environmental wellness.

To help improving the actual system through a product service system design approach we started a research activity by analyzing the user needs in-the-field we firstly did field research and analyzed the needs of different stakeholders. This gave us some insights about fitness habits in urban contexts and feedback by the local residents. Both of them were useful to start to identify the design opportunities and then the outputs.

3 Design Methods

3.1 Design Process

"Solutions to many of the world's most difficult social problems don't need to be invented, they only need to be found, funded and scaled" (Rodin 2007).

To deal with the community fitness problem, we first found some effective existing solutions. Further we interviewed several stakeholders including government officers, sponsors and participators to find a new fitness life style which can be scaled in Xishan.

We used a user-centered design approach based on questionnaires, survey ethnography research to develop possible scenarios where elders could get more sense of belonging, respect and wellness (Fig. 1).

3.2 Analyze Existing Solutions and Problems

The currently running fitness policy brings positive impact to residents but it still in need of some improvements. To make it work better and extend its coverage to more people, we figured out some effective solutions based on the in-the-field research then analyze the positive and negative aspect of these cases.

Cooperation with Sponsors. Sponsors including shop owners, banks and local companies play an irreplaceable role in the existing fitness system in Xishan. They have a strong will to support the fitness activities especially square dancing, while dancers also hope to get uniforms, video equipment and financial support from

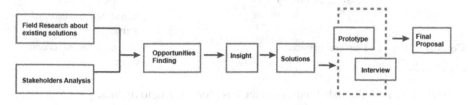

Fig. 1. The overall methodology of this project

sponsors. In the cooperation between sponsors and Style Council, there is benefit on both sides. According to the active ageing policy, Style Council has the responsibility to engage government-sponsored enterprises in social development business where several stakeholders can participate. By investing in dance teams, sponsors do their commercial publicity in a cost-effective way. In this process, to build a trust relationship is necessary for both sides. Dancers need to hope the background of sponsors while sponsors also hope to know the social influence of the dancing teams. Sponsors hope to employ a team with good social image and can dance in line with the advertising character.

Temporary Space for Fitness. As cities became crowded Chinese local government tried to find temporary spaces to meet the needs of fitness people. In Xishan, two kinds of temporary spaces have been used for fitness and entertainment under the help of Style Council: the market area and the primary school playgrounds.

Style Council will open 33 primary schools playgrounds to public fitness and let the market spaces be used by fitness people after lunch, when market is ended. This allows schools to be used as multi-functions places where people could go, meet and share their interests. To use these places properly, Style Council is still looking for a good way to organize these fitness activities. Management, kind of activities, organizational form and other issues are still unsettled.

Actually, this service started with a test including only one school opened for residents in the weekend. A company is managing this temporary space and charging small fee for admission.

3.3   Main Stakeholders Analysis

To know the roles of each stakeholders and the relationship among them we did some in-the-field research activities including interviews, surveys and questionnaires.

Role	Goal	Opportunity
Government	Deal with the ageing and social health problems	"Active aging policy"
Sponsor	Work for corporate social responsibility	Invest in the fitness movement
	Brand behavior	
	Advertisement	
Fitness participants	Health needs	Do fitness
	Emotional needs	Attend the fitness movement
	Sense of belonging	Same sport clothes
		Cultural and recreational activity
Coaches	Personal passion	Being paid for the coach work

The analysis of the stakeholders put the base for a scenario including a a new fitness life style built on two main factors:

1. "Active ageing policy" which encourages the elders to join the nationwide fitness programs and eliminate social discrimination against elders.
2. A new form of co-management system with such broad participation including sponsors, residents and coaches.

In Xishan, many Government departments (Worker Clubs, Culture Palace, Labor Unions. etc.) are working for the community fitness. Style Council is in charge of organizing the fitness events and coaches payment while Sports Administration, Culture Palace and Elders Universities are invited to train the coaches. Such a big and complex system did not work effectively because every administrators treat their job as temporary work. Although there are many coaches do regular work but they are mainly volunteers, their motivation totally depends on their personal interest.

Another driving factor for the coaches is self-fulfillment, sharing skills bring self-gratification to them.

4 Challenges and Opportunities

To create a new fitness lifestyle, we conclude the main challenges from the consumer's perspective as below:

Trust: There is always a barrier between the sponsors and dancers, especially for small shop owners because they are not well-known for residents. Dancers know a little about the advertising content and the background of sponsors, so they always do not want to be responsible for the advertisements. As the result, most of the sponsors we know are estate agent or state-owned enterprises like banks. A "bridge" and "agency" between dancers and sponsors to build trust relationship is needed.

Accessibility: Distance, time cost and the fitness content are all accessibility issues. The new fitness service system should allow elders to take part in freely. According to an in-the field research among 100 elderly people done in November 2014 we figured out that they are not good at using tickets, credit card or smartphone to approach the fitness place and pay for the service, a new way for them to enter the fitness space is needed (Fig. 2).

Information: Elders like to get the information in a traditional way, talking directly or mention them with physical advertisement are more effective than SMS.

Fig. 2. Field research to find best way to access fitness activities

A low-technical communication which is suitable for their living habits should be established for the elder fitness people. Traditional information platform, like the newspaper reading board, posters and Propagandist Manual should be used. For the sponsors and other residents, they need quick and detailed information, so an online platform is needed.

Space: Fitness activities fit into the space features. Although some of the activities are done according to the characteristics of public space, others are spontaneous. They happen on "found spaces", places intended for other uses (Rivlin 2007). Different from spontaneous "found spaces", some "fixed-site" made by sponsors, Community Council and shop owners absorb more professional dancers and coaches. These "fixed-site" are formed by regular fitness activities of specific group or person who know others well. As "found spaces" always course troubles like traffic jam, noisy near school or resident area, "fixed-site" are more friendly for others.

Health: "Health" has rich meanings, it is referred to as physical, mental, and social well-being. "Participation" which can improve both mental health and social well-being is in turn understood as a multifaceted array of activities by older persons in social, economic, cultural, spiritual, and civic affairs in addition to their participation in the labor force. Elders can improve their social adaptation through attending fitness. We also see that multifaceted array of fitness can build up different types of social relations which can bring people a life full of variety.

Through analyzing insight above, we find that the main problem is management, one of the solution is to invite companies nearby to manage it, but it brings cost to residents.

5 Strategy Solutions

To deal with the challenges, we set up several strategies as below.

5.1 Fitness People as Asset

According to the theory "People as asset" raised by Ezio Manzini, people and their activities can be used as asset for racial social innovation. We can see the value of the fitness activities as asset are various: it not only bring physical and mental health to fitness people through group activities, it brings social vitality and business opportunities as well. Both social and economic benefit can be achieved through wide participation of social members.

In order to fully use the asset including fitness activities, sponsors and policy, what we should do is "to recognize people's capabilities and help people use those to solve the problems they face (Sidorenko and Zaidi 2013)."

5.2 Open Information Platform for All Residents

An adjustable fitness system which can be adjusted according to the attitude of other people can reduce the negative impact of fitness activities. A social friendly life style need fully communication with local residents in order to change flexibly according to their feedback. The platform—both online and offline—is needed for fitness people to know the comments of other residents.

5.3 Coach-Driven

Coaches can be seen as "Lead Users"[2] in public fitness system. They are pioneers of experiencing new fitness activities. They fully use the public and private fitness resources, improve it then create their personal fitness lifestyles. Others learn from them and then join their groups.

Coaches are influenced by other stakeholders, especially the Style Council. Because coaches benefit from the training supported by government, they have the mission to follow the instructions of Style Council.

As we see the coaches are trained from volunteers to specialist, it is easy to understand that coaches are the people with passion and connect deeply with other residents. So the coaches can organize fitness team effectively and become a "bridge" between government department and fitness people, then a reliable cooperation can be made by coaches. Based on the effort of coaches, two kinds of reliable cooperation can be improved: one is between sponsors and dancing teams while another is an internal cooperation among dancers.

5.4 Space Meet the Affection Need

Elders need more warmth and behavioral confirmation, especially for the migrant elders who lost their former social network. So the space should not only offer equipment but also emotional service, friendship and communication program.

5.5 Fitness Lifestyle with Multi-experience Activities

Monotonous fitness program cannot absorb people for a long time. A healthy and sustainable lifestyle should involve cultural activities, social activities with broad participation. A multi-experience fitness lifestyle can bring new meaning and value to people.

6 Service

After the field research and interview, we got the final concept solutions: "FANG" which is a service system includes three separate parts. Each phases is improved from existing solutions.

---

[2] Customers who adapt, modify, or transform a proprietary offering (Berthon et al. 2007) http://en.wikipedia.org/wiki/Lead_user.

6.1   Start-up: Coach Training

Coaches are not only users of this service but also organizers. They get salary from Style Council and prize from sponsors. Their work are various: from training the fitness people, advertising for sponsors to managing the temporary space.

If someone hope to work as a coach, they should apply through Community Council, if approved, be trained at local Culture Palace[3] and Senior-Citizen University[4]. CSSI[5] and Sports Administration will send instructors to train these applicants.

After the training program, qualified applicants will get coach license ranking from 3rd to top. Local Style Council will employee these coaches to manage this service system.

6.2   Phase One: Street Fun

Style Council send coaches to tutor dancers in regular place and post the timetable and content of the fitness program on the newspaper reading board[6]. When the coaches working on the street, they will encourage core team members to express themselves or even tell their personal stories. Coaches record their words and images and then upload these information on the website. On the other hand, local residents and also comment on the website.

The sponsors will choose dancing team to cooperate with according to the data of group member, coach, place or the comment of other people on the website. After they find the right team, they submit their application with the information about their identity, amount of financial support and advertisement content on the website. Style Council will check the application under the help of local government then give coaches suggestions.

Coaches will make the decision for the cooperation according to the feedback of core team members and suggestions from Style Council.

Dancers can benefit from the uniform and equipment given by sponsors, their income depend on the performance of their advertisement activities (Fig. 3).

6.3   Phase Two: The Playground with Children's Wishes

According to the Xishan Fitness Plan in 2015, 33 primary school playgrounds will be opened to the local fitness people in the night. After analyzing the feedback of questionnaires and interview, we find that people prefer to do recreational activities like watching film or walking along the street in the night. This means some leisure and entertainment activities can bring a better multi-experience to fitness people.

---

[3] A place of cultural entertainment, people can learn dance, sports skills there.

[4] In China, mainly to help elders to learn new skills like using computer, mobile phone. There are also fitness curriculum.

[5] Chinese Administration of Social Sports Instructor are in charge of training coaches, especially part time coaches.

[6] A kind of board or wall where people can read newspaper or other timely posted information.

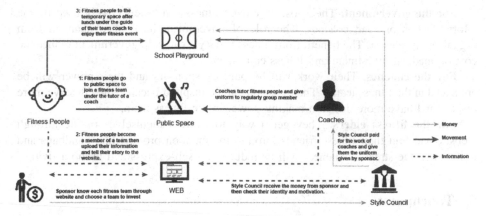

Fig. 3. The system map of service

In our concept, not only the playground, but also some classrooms will be opened to the local people, which means they can watch film and TV programs in the classroom after dinner.

Coaches will manage this temperature space and charge for the service in these schools. School will not only be an entertainment space, it can bring more love and greeting to visitors through interaction between students and visiting fitness people. For example, students will write down their wishes for visitors on blackboard in festival while fitness people can write down their feedback on the board, too (Fig. 4).

7 Value Offered

For the sponsor companies. Their advertisement can be more effective because they find the right person who can performance the culture and images of their companies/products. They can also estimate the cost and social influence through the comments posted on the website. Furtherer more, they can title the fitness match team to advertise on fitness event and then build up a new relationship with residents.

Fig. 4. School be used as temporary fitness space

For the government. Their cost on citizen fitness can be effectively used by the effort of sponsors and coaches. The role of government have been changed from organizer to investor. The benefit from fitness life style can help government reduce the cost on medical investment and fitness equipment.

For the coaches. Their work will be paid by sponsors and their power will be enhanced in the fitness teams. Their passion can be inspired because they deserve more respect and have more decision-making power in the fitness team.

For the fitness elders. They get a way to express themselves online through website and find their fitness friends through the mention product like handbags and uniform on the street. Aloneness will be reduced by self-express and group activities.

8 Touchpoint

The service system consists of 2 parts: online platform and offline fitness system. The online digital platform will be managed by Style Council while the offline fitness system is organized by coaches who are send by local enterprises and community councils.

The offline touchpoints are designed according to the regular interaction and behavior of elders, while the online system is based on the attitude of working people, especially youth.

Website. Website is the main part of online platform. It can help the sponsors find the right team which is compatible with their project culture and corporate image. The fitness group members can tell their stories and post their photos on the website and the residents can comment on the website, too. The account of the sponsorship including payment of site management, employee coaches and uniforms will be showed on the website, too. Residents can give stars to these fitness teams according to their feelings and relationship with these fitness people. So the potential sponsors can get a brief account of the social influence of fitness teams.

Uniform and handbag. Uniform and handbags are not only the advertisements of sponsor companies, but also the logo of the fitness team which can improve the sense of belonging. The dancing atmosphere can be improved by wearing the same uniforms while the dance sensibility and the expressive force will be enhanced by the uniform, too. Handbag is another kind of advertising tools to show the identity of fitness group member. The other people can ask for the information about the fitness event from the people wearing handbags.

Banners and roadblock. As many sponsors use banners and roadblock to advertise, the shape and images posted on will be redesigned which can meet the requirement of both sponsor and fitness people.

Brochure. The advertise brochures show the timetable, place the coaches which help the fitness elders to find their right fitness activities. For elders, a carry-on brochure is needed to know the information of fitness activities (Fig. 5).

Event. According to the Roles for Building China National Civilized City, each district should have at least 15 fitness group and held more than 8 fitness activates every year. In Wuxi, QunFang is the biggest fitness match. In this service, QunFang Contest will not be reported on TV but also broadcast on the website and people can

Fig. 5. Brochure made to get the feedback of stakeholders

comment on it. On the contest, fitness team will wear the uniform designed by the sponsor to perform on the event.

9 Conclusions

In this social innovation process, we try to transfer a top-down public fitness system to a multicomponent service system. As grass root innovation can reflect the social needs in a wider range, we focused on marginal people and then experienced an iterative design process with stakeholders and modify the service plan according to their attitudes.

The outcome of this proposal is a service include three phases and we hope to scale it in the future.

In the service design process, we learned that it is designers' duty to rethink and refocus the resource in our daily life and then integrate social resources to bring new value and meanings to people.

References

WHO: active ageing: a policy framework, Madrid, April 2002[EB/OL]. http://www.who.int/ageing/publications/active_ageing/en/

Fassi, D., Meroni, A., Simeone, G.: Design for social innovation as a form of design activism: an action format. In: "Social frontiers: The Next Edge of Social Innovation Research" Conference Proceedings, 14–15 Nov 2013. NESTA, London. http://www.scribd.com/doc/191848489/Design-for-social-innovation-as-a-form-of-designing-activism-An-action-format

Zhang, W.I.: Ageing problem challenges China. Nat. People's Congr. China **3**, 16–21 (2011)

Chen, C.: Grandma's world: mapping dancers in Beijing. In: Proceedings of the 42nd Annual Conference of the Environmental Design Research Association, pp. 38–49 (2011)

Rivlin, L.G.: Found spaces, freedom of choice in public space. In: Franck, K.A., Stevens, Q. (eds.) Loose Space: Possibility and Diversity in Urban Life, pp. 38–51. Routledge, London (2007)

Davies, A., Simon, J.: How to grow social innovation: a review and critique of scaling and diffusion for understanding the growth of social innovation. In: 5th International Social Innovation Research Conference, 2–4 September 2013. Oxford. http://youngfoundation.org/wp-content/uploads/2013/11/Davies-Simon_Growing-social-innovation_ISIRC-2013.pdf

Sidorenko, A., Zaidi, A.: Active ageing, in CIS Countries: semantics, challenges, and responses. Current Gerontology and Geriatrics Research, Vol. 2013, p 17 (2013), Article ID 261819. http://www.hindawi.com/journals/cggr/2013/261819/

Manzini, E.: People-as-asset, a radical social innovation and a design opportunity. http://vimeo.com/71100489

Miaosen G.: Wellbeing lifestyle and social innovation: strategic design for sustainable society. https://www.academia.edu/424067/Wellbeing_Lifestyle_and_Social_Innovation_Strategic_Design_for_Sustainable_Society

Rodin, J.: Social innovation: a matter of scale. http://voices.mckinseyonsociety.com/social-innovation-a-matter-of-scale/. (quoted in Davis 2010)

A Study of the Accessible Approach to Replace the Reservoir Silt Glaze with New Formula

Chi-Chang Lu[1(✉)] and Po-Hsien Lin[2]

[1] Crafts and Design Department, National Taiwan University of Art,
Ban Ciao City, Taipei 22058, Taiwan
t0134@ntua.edu.tw
[2] Graduate School of Creative Industry Design, National Taiwan University
of Arts, Ban Ciao City, Taipei 22058, Taiwan
t0131@ntua.edu.tw

Abstract. The author engaged in the research work of utilizing Shihmen Reservoir silt to make ceramic glazes. It was shown to be specific and feasible. But due to the different accumulation of layers or batches, it has more instability. The author had ever been three times to collect silt in different sedimentation pond, and was confirmed its chemical composition to be have obvious differences by instrumental analysis. If you used a direct replacement, you could find significant differences in appearance when silt content above 20 %. The "seger's formula" of ceramic glaze was used as the theoretical basis for the composition, and then calculated by Excel's Solver tool. It was always made the similar effect with original if you gave proper constraints and the substitution principle.

Keywords: Ceramic arts · Reservoir silt · Glaze · Seger formula · Programming solver

1 Introduction

The author engaged in the research work of utilizing Shihmen Reservoir silt to make ceramic glazes. It was shown to be specific and feasible [1]:

a. Reservoir silt glaze is classified in the category of natural silt glaze, which involves more variety of trace elements and people generally consider it as a support to the performances of the glaze color and texture. According to practical results, we find that even though the Shihmen Silt Glaze production carries a smooth surface, it still preserves a reserved, implicit sheen and possesses a fine variation effect.

b. From present observation of the experimental results, the combination of the reservoir silt with feldspar, limestone, rice husk ash, and a few other materials, can create a diversity of tone, sheen, and crystalline effects for a quality glaze. And through the manipulation of the atmosphere in the kiln, whether by oxidation firing or reduction firing, we can retrieve more variation for the glaze to perform full extent.

© Springer International Publishing Switzerland 2015
P.L.P. Rau (Ed.): CCD 2015, Part I, LNCS 9180, pp. 83–95, 2015.
DOI: 10.1007/978-3-319-20907-4_8

c. Based on experiment statistics, the maturation temperature of the glaze, which mainly contains reservoir silt, has quit a large range (from 40–50 °C or higher), therefore, uneven temperature within the kiln seldom becomes a cause for failure.
d. On the aspect of material preparation, to employ the reservoir silt to the ceramic industry can almost leave out traditional process of water tossing, the screening procedure only needs to eliminate a small portion of sand grains. According to practical executing experiences, the Shihmen Reservoir silt has more than 95 % of the content that can be taken into good account, moreover, the preparation procedures are not as complicated. If mass production is possible to achieve, the prime cost of the silt will be much more efficient to the economy benefit.
e. As for the succeeding glazes, with the formulas, which uses the similar modern raw material that relates to the calculation of the "Seger Method", we can find the conclusion where the Shihmen Reservoir Silt Glaze can reduce the needs of diverse raw materials, furthermore, making significant impact on narrowing down the time and labor cost.

But due to the different accumulation of layers or batches, it has more instability. The author had ever been three times to collect silt in different sedimentation pond, and was confirmed its chemical composition to be have obvious differences by instrumental analysis. If you used a direct replacement, you could find significant differences in appearance when silt content above 20 %.

2 Research Purpose

The ultimate goal of this research is to find an effective model that can more accurately and efficiently to solve the replacement of raw materials. Its purpose and its importance as follows:

a. provide the most efficient and economical means to achieve the task when the ceramics industry faced the instability of raw materials.
b. Contemporary ceramics have more stringent requirements for the glaze. This study hopes that through more detailed means to effectively recover the desired glaze forms.
c. the instability of reservoir silt component is the main question that it used in ceramic glazes. Problem solving can provide users with a higher degree of trust and for the use of reservoir silt have substantial positive environmentally friendly benefits.

3 Literature Review

3.1 Glaze Formula

Ceramic glazes are mixtures of oxides: silicon (SiO_2), aluminum (Al_2O_3) and other easy to melt oxides (mainly PbO, K_2O, CaO, Na_2O).

These oxides are positioned in the form of suspension in the surface of the already baked clay and during firing they melt (due to chemical changes). When dry, they create the glassy permanent coat.

The most common oxides that consist the synthesis of the ceramic glaze (baked or not) are: SiO_2, Al_2O_3, B_2O_3, Na_2O, K_2O, CaO, MgO, PbO. These are imported in the not baked glaze with the form of raw materials. These materials, available in the market, are mostly clays and frits. Mixing the aforementioned oxides we have a specific glaze. This mix requires specific quantities from each material, different for different baking temperatures. These quantities in percentages are the recipe of a specific glaze [2].

Glazes are expressed in several different forms:

a. recipe: a list of actual materials and weights, used directly to make the glaze.
b. Molecular formula: shows the relative proportion of molecules of flux, alumina and silica in the glaze. Must be converted to recipe to make the glaze.
c. chemical analysis: shows the percentage of oxides in the glaze. Also known as ultimate composition.
d. Seger formula: a special molecular formula, which makes it easier to compare glazes. It is also known as the "empirical formula" [3].

3.2   Seger Formula

A German ceramist, Hermann Seger (1839–1893), developed Seger cones for measuring temperatures in kilns. He also proposed writing the composition of glazes according to the number of different oxides in the glaze instead of listing the raw materials used in the glaze.

The oxides used in glazes are divided into three groups according to the way the oxides work in the glaze.

a. fluxes: This group of oxides functions as melter, and fluxes are also called basic oxides or bases. They are written RO or R_2O, where R represents any atom and O represents oxygen. So all the fluxes are a combination of one or two element atoms and one oxygen atom.
b. stabilizers: These work as stiffeners in the melted glaze to prevent it from running too much. They are considered neutral oxides and are writen as R_2O_3 or two atoms of some element combined with three oxygen atoms.
c. glass formers: These form the noncrystalline structure of the glaze. They are called acidic oxides and are written as RO_2 or one element atom combined with two oxygen atoms [3].

Above three groups can be represented by a formula: $RO \cdot xR_2O_3 \cdot yRO_2$. (x and y are the representatives for the mole ratio of R_2O_3 and RO_2.)

3.3   Benefits of Using Seger Formula

The main usefulness of the Seger formula is that it presents glazes in a way that is easy to compare. It is used for:

a. originating new glazes: Glazes with desired characteristics of color, mattress etc. can first be written as Seger formulas, selecting oxides that are known to produce the effects.
b. comparing glaze recipes: It is difficult to look at two recipes and see how they are different. If they are converted into Seger formulas, the differences can easily be seen.
c. modifying glazes: Glazes that change character, have problems etc. can be analyzed as Seger formulas, and directions for testing decided.
d. substituting materials: If a material is no longer available, other materials can be substituted by working out the quantities in the Seger formula [3].

Regarding the fourth function aforementioned: Other materials can be substituted by working out the quantities in the Seger formula, which has been reported by other studies [4–8].

3.4   Problems in the Practical Application of the Seger Formula

According to Yu and Hu (1999), the Seger formula has a considerable deficiency and limitation when it is used to express glaze. Specifically, only when the glaze has a neutral oxide of Al_2O_3 and an acidic oxide of SiO_2 can the Seger formula reflect the actual composition and properties of the glaze. When the glaze contains Fe_2O_3, Cr_2O_3, B_2O_3, TiO_2, and ZrO_2, the result produced using the Seger formula becomes complex and contains substantial errors [9].

Regarding the glaze characteristics and the numerical relationship involved in its expression, Lee (2006) reported that the numerical values and ratios (e.g., x, y, 1:y, and x:y) for predicting glaze quality and transparency by using the Seger formula were inconsistent among various studies [10].

These two studies show that despite the numerous advantages of the Seger formula, a substantial difference existed in the results obtained by previous studies because of various complex factors including glaze composition and firing conditions.

3.5   Optimal Algorithm in Glaze Recipe

Numerous software have been developed to solve problems related to ceramic calculation and databases, including Insight, GlazeChem, The Glaze Calculator, Matrix, Clayart, and GlazeMaster. These glaze calculation software and management systems provide convenient solutions to convert the chemical composition of glazes into glaze material recipes.

Some studies have proposed calculation solutions based on computer software [2, 11–18]. In particular, the office software Excel has been used for optimization calculations, and it is regarded as simple and easy and allows users to flexibly set constraints.

Both existing software and relevant studies have provided effective calculation models for converting the chemical composition of glazes into material recipes of glazes. However, whether the data obtained from calculations can be directly applied has not been clearly verified.

4   Research Methods

According to the research purpose, an experimental study was conducted to demonstrate the appearance difference in the pottery glazes produced using the new and original glaze formulas under the same firing condition. The degree of differences was observed based on the items, which are melting degree, liquidity, glossiness, shrinkage degree, transparency, crack degree, crystallinity, color, and texture, to evaluate the accuracy that can be achieved by the Seger formula used for material replacement. Figure 1 illustrates the experimental procedures and objectives.

a. The chemical composition of the used materials was remeasured to effectively concentrate on the research objectives. The selected clay carriers were identical, which were placed in the same kiln to control the firing conditions and exclude irrelevant factors.

b. To enable the recipes of the materials to approximate the numerical values constituting the Seger formula for the original glaze formula, the function of Solver in Excel was used for optimal computation. The aim of this study was to verify the accuracy of the firing results after material replacement; therefore, the factor of cost

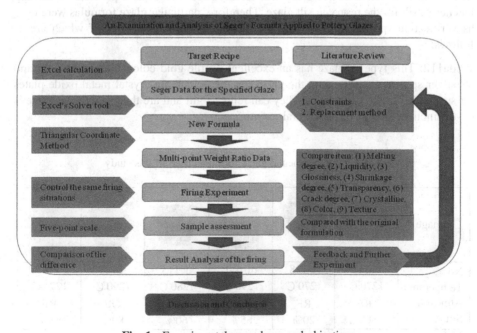

Fig. 1. Experimental procedures and objectives

(which was typically the primary consideration in previous studies) was not considered. The value differences in various oxides were summed, and the minimum value was adopted as the objective function value. Moreover, the literature was reviewed to examine the influence of x, y, 1:y, and x:y on the firing result, to set the constraints, and to enable the values in the new glaze formula to approximate that in the original glaze formula according to the theories of the Seger formula.

c. To extend the experimental points for glaze formulas, the calculated material recipes were used as the reference points for the triangular coordinate method, which was employed to perform the extended experiment based on multipoint weight ratio data, to determine the optimal glaze recipe.

d. When determining the accuracy of the firing results, the fired specimens produced using the original glaze formula were adopted as the standard samples for comparison with those produced using the new formula. The comparison was conducted based on the aforementioned items (e.g., melting degree and liquidity). To objectively determine the differences, three experts were invited to conduct the comparison by using a five-point scale. Therefore, the application of the Seger formula to the recipes of ceramic glazes can be evaluated quantitatively in terms of the result accuracy.

5 Implementation Process

5.1 Target Recipe

The primary objective of this study was to solve the replacement problem of varying batches of silt for the reservoir silt glaze. Therefore, particular glaze formulas were used as verification specimens (Table 1), the number and characteristics of which are as follows:

a. da112: This type of glaze has an excellent purple-gold color. Numerous gold and silver spots are scattered on the glaze surface, which are crystal metal oxide plates suspended in the glaze layer. They can reflect light and are thus shiny. The glaze is distinctive, similar to the natural aventurine.

Table 1. Experimental glaze formulas used in this study

Image						
No.	da112	da138	db100	dc113	rc105	rb149
Temperature	1270℃	1270℃	1290℃	1280℃	1290℃	1270℃
Atmosphere	RF	RF	OF	OF	OF	RF
Silt	50%	20%	65%	60%	80%	10%

b. da138: The color of this type of glaze is derived from iron oxide and is categorized as a temmoku glaze that features transparency. The glaze exhibits layered characteristics because of the changes in its thickness.
c. db100: This type of glaze possesses iron oxide crystals and therefore is characterized by a splashed luster. The firing result is substantially related to the content of iron oxide and the heating curve.
d. dc113: This type of glaze is black, expressing warmth and thickness. Applying underglaze iron painting can produce a decorative effect of rust color, which is a distinctive feature of the ceramics in the Song dynasty.
e. rc105: The glaze also contains crystals that produce the splashed luster effect. However, because of the melting degree and viscosity, the splashes are relatively blurred.
f. rb149: Because the content level of iron oxide in celadon should be low, the quantity of slit used in celadon is also low (only 10 %). The firing condition of the glaze is stable; the finished product is similar to the Longquan celadon in Southern Song.

5.2   Optimal Algorithm

Excel is one of the most common word processing software in MS Office. It has the function of a programming solver that can be easily used to perform optimal computations, and the constraints can be set flexibly. Therefore, this study performed optimal computations by using programming solver.

The objective function value is a key factor influencing the result of optimal computations. Lu (2007) used the objective function value to compute the lowest cost and target value of the recipe was set as the constraint [15]. Other studies on optimal computations for glazes have mostly adopted lowest cost as the objective function value. Only Wang et al. [14] provided three objective function values, which are: (a) the minimum value of the total material costs, (b) minimum value of the sum of the absolute differences between the calculated and theoretical values, and (c) maximum value of the benefit-cost ratio. In the ceramics industry, the material cost for glazes, in general, accounts for only a small proportion of the total cost. Therefore, the minimum value of the sum of the absolute differences between the calculated and theoretical values proposed by Wang et al. [14] was used as the objective function value in this study to achieve a satisfactory result.

Regarding the calculated composition value, previous studies have typically used the weight percentage of the recipe as the calculation basis. However, the interaction among the elements in glaze composition involves atoms and molecules. Therefore, the mole ratio in the Seger formula should be used to produce efficient calculation results. The minimum value of the sum of the absolute difference in mole values between the target and recipe was thus used as the objective function value in this study.

The constraints were set as follows:

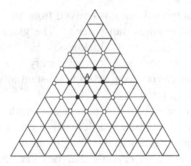

Fig. 2. Triangular coordinate method

a. Constraint 1: The glaze formulas that can be directly applied were expressed using the weight percentage of the materials. Therefore, the calculated content was set to 100.

b. Constraint 2: The weight of the used materials is included in this constraint. For example, corresponding constraints can be set for conditions where 2 % of kaolin should be used as the material for adhesion and suspension, or the amount of phosphoric acid cannot be excessively high. Because this study aimed to use reservoir silt to produce a ceramic glaze, the amount of reservoir silt was also constrained. Furthermore, this study excluded certain materials that had unstable supply or excessively high prices and set their values to 0.

c. Constraint 3: The number of material types was set. In general, using too few varieties of materials may result in the poor stability of glazes, whereas using excessively large varieties of materials may increase the time and cost of glaze compounding. Thus, the number of varieties of materials was typically less than 10.

d. Constraints 4 and 5: The absolute values of the differences in SiO_2/Al_2O_3 and $RO/(RO+R_2O)$ were set. Specifically, the absolute value of the differences in SiO_2/Al_2O_3 was set to less than 0.5, and that of the differences in $RO/(RO+R_2O)$ was set to less than 0.05. The relative ratio of SiO_2/Al_2O_3 to $RO/(RO+R_2O)$ was approximately 10:1. During the calculation, the values can be lower, such as 0.1 and 0.01, and can also be increased if a satisfactory result cannot be obtained. However, other constraints should be modified if the values are increased to 0.5 and 0.05 and no solution is obtained.

5.3   Triangular Coordinate Method

To effectively achieve the objective of original material replacement, the calculated weight ratios of the materials were used as reference points. The triangular coordinate method was adopted to perform the extended experiment based on the multipoint weight ratio data to determine the optimal glaze recipe (Figs. 1 and 2). When this method is employed, a target glaze type can be effectively realized and some unexpected findings can also be derived (Fig. 3).

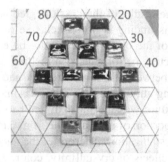

Fig. 3. Example of the triangular coordinate experiment

5.4 Replacement Method

According to the research objective, this study adopted three material replacement methods, which are: (a) replacing all materials using the Seger method, (b) replacing silt using the Seger method, and (c) replacing silt based on partial proportion. This study sought to verify whether any difference existed between the results produced by methods (1) and (2), as well as the influence of types of materials on the firing result.

6 Discussion and Conclusion

6.1 Replacement of All Materials Using Seger Method

This method was used for determining the optimal glaze recipe for replacement and for understanding the range and capability of the application of the Seger formula. Most researchers of glaze studies have agreed that the Seger formula is the most comprehensive expression among all the glaze expressions, even though it cannot be directly applied. In the Seger formula, emphasis is placed on the chemical composition of glazes; other factors such as the crystal structure of various materials are not considered. Therefore, the question as to whether the Seger formula can effectively express the final result of glazes is still open.

After firing, three experts evaluated the glaze specimens. Specifically, the following items were evaluated and scored using a five-point scale: melting degree, liquidity, glossiness, shrinkage degree, transparency, crack degree, crystallinity, color, and texture. The evaluation results are summarized as follows:

a. The firing results of the experimental glaze formula and original glaze formula were substantially different. Only a limited number of experimental glaze formulas obtained an average score higher than 4.75, indicating that the material replacement problem cannot be successfully solved using the Seger formula.
b. As the objective function value increased, the difference between the firing results and that produced using the original glaze formula also increased. Typically, the objective function value should be less than 0.2 to produce a firing result similar to the original result. This underscores the relevance of the Seger formula in glaze research.

c. Among the nine items, the results of the crack degree and transparency were most satisfactory. However, this finding is not conclusive or definite because the crack degree and transparency of the black glaze cannot be easily discerned. The specimens also showed satisfactory performance on melting degree and liquidity. Only a slight difference existed between the firing results and that of the original glaze formula regarding reducing atmosphere. In comparison, a superior performance on crystallinity, color, or texture was the most difficult to achieve. The reservoir silt glaze contains a high proportion of iron, and the iron oxide is highly sensitive to the fluxing capability and crystallization. Therefore, the success of the firing results is highly dependent on the effects of crystallinity, color, and texture.

6.2   Replacement of Silt Using the Seger Method

In this method, the replacement calculation was performed only on the Seger formula of silt. The advantage of this method is that the possible influence of the material molecular structure can be minimized because most of the materials retain the original recipes. However, an accurate replacement value with a low objective function value cannot be easily obtained using this method. The accuracy of the obtained solution was lower than that of the solution achieved by the previous method regarding the chemical composition.

After firing, the three experts evaluated the specimens. The evaluation results are summarized as follows:

a. The firing results produced using this method were superior to that produced using the first method, indicating that the molecular structure of materials is a crucial factor that should be considered in addition to the chemical composition.
b. Regarding the firing results, da138 showed optimal performance; regardless the firing atmosphere, the average scores for all the items were greater than 4.77. This superior performance may be because the original silt content in da138 was only 20 %. Except for dc113, the scores of all the other glaze specimens were greater than 4.75; only a slight modification was required to acquire the replacement recipe similar to the original recipe. The major problem of the dc113 specimen is its color. However, the replacement recipe was still obtained after slightly adjusting the content level of iron oxide.
c. Among three types of silt (i.e., silt from the Sun Moon Lake Reservoir [SMLR] and two types of silt from the Shihmen Reservoir), the replacement effect of the Shihmen Reservoir silt was superior to that of the SMLR silt. This may be primarily because the objective functional value for the replacement recipe of the SMLR silt was considerably higher than that for the replacement recipes of the two types of Shihmen Reservoir silt.
d. The evaluation results of the glaze specimens were similar to those of the specimens in the previous method. The performance on melting degree, liquidity, and glossiness significantly increased than in the first method. A superior performance on crystallinity, color, or texture was most difficult to achieve, which is actually a feature of glazes with high iron content.

6.3   Replacement of Silt Based on Partial Proportion

In our previous study, we replaced entire silt content with previous three types of silt and discovered that the glaze containing less than 20 % of silt generated an effect similar to the original effect. This method can be applied to factory manufacturing processes; that is, when new silt has been produced and old silt is still not depleted, the two materials can be combined to continue producing the same glaze color.

The three experts evaluated the glaze specimens after the firing process. The evaluation results are summarized as follows:

a. Most glaze specimens showed satisfactory firing results, indicating that replacing silt based on partial proportion is a simple and easy replacement method.
b. The firing result was substantially consistent with the properties of the glazes. For example, both the optimal computation and method of partial replacement produced the lowest effect on dc113, indicating that this type of glaze is highly sensitive to numerous factors that influence its firing result.
c. The differences in the composition among various types of silt significantly influence the firing result. The proportion of silt for replacement should be determined through experiments. The experimental result indicated that applying the partial replacement method to the same reservoir silt can produce a relatively high success rate.

6.4   Promotion and Employment Values

The discontinued production or import of raw materials often causes troubles for the industries of ceramic production and art. In particular, because the ceramic production industry typically involves a large amount of production, it may face the pressure of costs and actively search for cheap alternative materials. Thus, how to replace the original materials with new materials in a short time and achieve a similar glaze effect is a crucial topic for ceramic production.

This study demonstrated that when the glaze materials are no longer available because of unavoidable factors and should be replaced by other materials, systematic and standardized procedures can be used to generate similar recipes. Most of the recipes can be subsequently modified through experiments to become new recipes that can produce an effect similar to the original effect. While the systematic procedures can be easily implemented, the modification should be performed by experienced experts and still involves certain factors. As numerous uncertainties are involved in the material sources, a feasible and effective method indeed allows the silt glaze to be further developed (Table 2).

The application of the silt glaze is considerably more difficult than that of the commercial glaze, primarily because of the complex influence of the iron oxide. Silt glaze contains a large amount of iron oxide, which contributes additional factors that may influence firing atmosphere, crystalline, color, and texture. Compared with the silt glaze, the ceramic glaze in mass production has relatively simple requirements for glaze characteristics such as color and texture. Therefore, the proposed method can be

Table 2. Comparison of firing results between old and new recipes

No.	Firing results		No.	Firing results	
	Target	New Formula		Target	New Formula
da138 1285°C OF			da138 1250°C RF		

applied to the task of material replacement for general glazes, and the problem of unstable material sources frequently faced by the ceramics industry can be solved.

Acknowledgment. This study was partly sponsored with a grant, NSC102-2410-H-144-005, from the National Science Council, Taiwan.

References

1. Lu, C.-C., Lin, P.-H.: A study of producing ceramic glaze utilizing shihmen reservoir silt. In: Rau, P.L.P. (ed.) IDGD 2011. LNCS, vol. 6775, pp. 201–210. Springer, Heidelberg (2011)
2. Romanosoglou, C., Alexandridis, T., Tsapoga, M., Papaioannoy, E., Karadimas, N.V.: Glaze calculation software based on the Seger method with recipe mixing utilities, limit formulas and toxicity measurements. In: Recent Advances in Software Engineering, Parallel and Distributed Systems, pp. 45–49. SEPADS 2010 (2010)
3. Norsker, H., Danisch, J.: Glazes–for the Self-reliant Potter. Braunschweig, Germany (1993)
4. Cheng, T.Y.: Ceramic Glaze Study. Xu Foundation, Taipei (1975)
5. Fan, J.J.: Preparation of Glaze Ourselves. Wu-shing Books, Taipei (2002)
6. Hsueh, J.F.: Ceramic Glaze Study. Yingge Ceramics Museum, Yingge (2003)
7. Green, D.: A Handbook of Pottery Glazes. Watson-Guptill Publications, New York (1979)
8. Burleson, M.: The Ceramic Glaze Handbook: Materials, Techniques, Formulas. Baker & Taylor Books, Charlotte (2003)
9. Yu, K.T., Hu, Y.P.: Changes and additions for the theory of Seger Glaze formulas. Ceramics **2**, 12–13 (1999)
10. Lee, Z.P.: A study of the befitted numbers and rates of Seger Glaze formulas. J. Nat. Taipei Univ. Educ. **19**(2), 51–68 (2006)
11. Hsiao, C.C., Chou, F.T.: Programming for optimization calculation in glaze recipe. Porcelain Arrester **6**, 24–29 (1989)
12. She, C.T.: The development of computer-aided system for ceramic glaze formulation design. Ceram. Eng. 25–28 (1999)
13. Liu, J.J., Chang, H.C.: The software design for the study of ceramic glaze formulation. Ceramics **3**, 12–17 (2000)
14. Wang, Z.Q., Jiang, Q.Y., Wen, Q.B.: Developing the general approach for proportional optimization design in chemical industry. China Ceram. **37**(4), 37–39 (2001)

15. Lu, C.: Ceramic glaze formulation design and optimization method. China Ceram. Ind. **14** (1), 23–26 (2007)
16. Hsiang, M., Lo, H.H.: Genetic algorithms method practical application for optimizing ceramic glaze. Chin. Ceram. **2**, 59–61 (2009)
17. Yang, Y., Wang, H.F.: The optimal algorithm of semifinished product and glaze formulation of the ceramics and its realize. Funct. Mater. **8**, 1409–1412 (2009)
18. Kronberg, T., Hupa, L., Fröberg, K.: Optimizing of glaze properties. Ceram. Eng. Sci. Proc. **22**(2), 179–189 (2001)

Humanism Presented in Taiwan Cochin Ceramic Design

Huei-Mei Shih[⊠]

Graduate School of Arts and Humanities Instruction, National Taiwan
University of Arts, Daguan Rd, New Taipei City 22058, Taiwan
t0303@ntua.edu.tw

Abstract. Cochin ceramics, a low temperature and soft pottery, is one of
Taiwanese traditional arts. Originally it comes from southern part of Chinese
areas and has become a sort of architectural decoration, which has been integrated with sculpture, ceramics and painting in one. Cochin ceramics can be
seen in traditional temples and rich mansions Taiwan. In Chin dynasty (in the
18th century) with people migrating from China to Taiwan, they set foot on this
land and developed Cochin in its full scales. The research aims to offer a better
understanding of its humanism presented in traditional architectural forms. The
article covers the historical development of Cochin, its thematic analysis, its
inherent moral design, its cultural spirit, and the conclusions.

Keywords: Cochin ceramic · Thematic analysis · Folk art · Humanism

1 Introduction

Cochin ceramics, a low temperature and soft pottery, is one of Taiwanese traditional
arts. Originally it comes from southern part of Chinese areas, with people migrating
from China to Taiwan in Chin dynasty (in the 18th century). Cochin ceramics set foot
on this land and developed in its full scales. As a sort of architectural decoration, it can
be seen in traditional temples, family temples, schools and rich mansions Taiwan.
Cochin ceramics has been integrated with sculpture, ceramics, literature and painting in
one.

Traditional Taiwan architecture can be divided into three categories: town –houses,
house-hall, and quadrangles. Town-houses combine both commercial and residence
functions. Town-halls are bigger sizes. Mostly they can be found in temples, ancestral
shrines, and learning academies. Quadrangles are in the forms of residences (Lin 1990).
Not only are temples the places of people worshipping their deities but also they offer
sacrifices to gods. People would pray for their gods to protect them. The temple culture
has a significant meaning to Taiwanese people. In the temples they'll pray for their
lives to be safe. Temple culture has a great impact on ordinary people. Furthermore,
inside the temples are rich Taiwan Traditional folk arts. Also let's not forget their
architectural and decorative elements in temples which become the places of people's
spiritual and cultural shrines. Therefore, this research is based on Cochin ceramics in
temples, trying to discuss humanism presented in Taiwan Cochin ceramic design.

© Springer International Publishing Switzerland 2015
P.L.P. Rau (Ed.): CCD 2015, Part I, LNCS 9180, pp. 96–107, 2015.
DOI: 10.1007/978-3-319-20907-4_9

Under the global impact and the changing of time, people no longer have deeper recognition of their traditional culture, for their understanding of the themes of temples and the symbolic meanings of most decorations on temples become scarcer. Meanwhile a lot of precious relics are facing the crisis of being destroyed. Now a day all global nations stress on cultural identity. Only by recognition and valuing our culture can those cultural legacies be fully preserved.

The study of Cochin ceramics covers four dimensions as follows:

(1) An artistic study in terms of shapes and themes. (2) A study of craftsmen's lives and their work patterns. (3) A broader investigation of porcelain ingredients as well as cultural legacy preservations through modern scientific technology. (4) A study related to Cultural Industry in Cochin ceramics.

My study focuses on the first and second dimensions.

The method for my study, field research and documentary analysis are the main research methods. First, a review of literature and historical documents is administered. In addition, we conduct field surveys and collect data by recording the materials and interviewing with pottery craftsmen. The research covers the historical development of Cochin, its thematic analysis, its inherent moral design, its cultural spirit, and conclusions.

Research purposes are as follows:

(1) Discussing Cochin ceramic design in question. (2) Analyzing the way of expressing the theme of Cochin ceramic design. (3) Studying the symbolic meanings and fables of Cochin ceramic design. (4) Giving a clearer picture of the themes and humanism relation. (5) Upgrading the young to better understanding and recognition of their own culture.

2 About Cochin Ceramics

2.1 What Are Cochin Ceramics?

Cochin ceramics are a kind of low temperature lead glaze pottery, which brushes glaze on the surface or on the inner wall of the clay with the process of firing to certain temperatures. There are two methods. One is to fire them at the temperature of 1,200 °C. The other is to fire it at a low temperature. First it is fired into biscuit, then is brushed with lead glaze over it, and lastly is fired the second time at a low temperature (Central Academy of Fine Arts 1988). Cochin ceramics are classified into the latter. By using lead flux and colorants as mental oxides they are fired under the low temperature of 800 °C (Bian et al. 2001).

With the soft quality Cochin ceramic can't last long and easy to decay. Used as architectural decoration, it needs to be renewed every twenty or thirty years. The earliest Cochin ceramic can be traced back to Quanzhou, Fujian province. Yet this is not the final conclusion. During my field trip, in Fujian and Quanzhou Cochin ceramic still could be found in traditional ancient residences such as the West Street Old Mansion in Quanzhou's city and Tsai's Mansion group in Nanun. Both are late 19th century and early 20th century legacy. But Tsai's Mansion at Foothills in Miali, Taiwan is probably the oldest one, dating from late Jiaqing Dynasty (1796–1820)

(Shih 2008). Due to its high replacement rate of elimination it is lacking in existing evidence. Therefore the earliest era of Cochin ceramic can't be traced back.

2.2   The Origin of Low Temperature Glaze Clay

The discovery of Chinese low temperature glaze clay can be traced back to Han Dynasty (BC 202–AD 220).The glaze of that time was much simpler, only for monochrome pottery, with the color of green, yellow and brown (Zhu and Li 2000), and served as funeral utensil. When it came to Tang Dynasty (618–907 AD), with the success of producing Tang Three-color-glaze pottery, lead-glaze pottery was promoted into another higher level. The colors became more vivid. There were green, yellow, white, blue and black. The decorative techniques included engraving, printing, heaping paste, and molding (Shing 2008). The blooming of Tang Three-color-glaze pottery directly had a great impact to Song Three-color-glaze and Liao Three-color-glaze (10th–12th century), as well as on the future development of architecture color-glazed roof tile (Luo 1990). To the Ming (1368–1644) and Qing Dynasties (1644–1912) in addition to the low temperature lead-glazed pottery we noticed not only Ming Dynasty focused on plain Three-color-glaze pottery and architectural glass products such as glazed tile, glass sculpture (Shing 2008). Building along the coast of Fujian Province in Qing Dynasty tended to decorate them with low temperature lead-glaze pottery to gain the glamorous effect. In 18th century the Chinese immigrants brought low temperature pottery to Taiwan.

With the prosperity of Taiwan economy, people came across the sea to hire Chinese potters. Hence, pottery skills were also brought to Taiwan. These skillful potters passed their skills on to the locals through teaching. Therefore, the Cochin ceramic set its root in Taiwan. Now a day it has gone beyond its original habitat and become one of Taiwan's representative traditional arts.

2.3   The Name of Taiwan Cochin Ceramics

The name of Taiwan Cochin comes from Japanese teachers who lived in Taiwan in the Japanese colonial era. Originally Cochin is the name of the place which was formerly known as Fujian, Guangdong, and Guangxi areas or the region of northern Vietnam in Hanoi in between Chinese Han Dynasty to early Tang Dynasty. Those Japanese teachers were so surprised at the exquisite beauty of Cochin on Taiwan's traditional architecture. Cochin was mistaken as the incense box named *Kogou* which were used in Japanese tea art ceremony. Therefore, those Japanese teachers named it as Cochin and wrote articles and spoke highly of it. Those articles aroused the affection and attention from Japan. Therefore, the name of Cochin is used till today (Shih 2000).

However, recent archaeological researches reveal that Japanese incense boxes are not produced in Vietnam, but from Zhangzhou Pinghe Tian Pit Kiln (Fujian), its glaze are "plain three-color" (the use of yellow, green and purple glaze) (Lee 2013). Although the ceramic of Tian Pit Kilns is not necessarily related to Taiwan, but Cochin's name has been used in Taiwan for a long time. Now it has become a fixed name.

3 The Architecture and Decoration of Taiwan Traditional Temples

3.1 Folklore Religion in Taiwan

In 17th century (late Ming and early Qing Dynasty) when Chinese people immigrated to Taiwan, the initial cultivation was hard and the incomes were not abundant. By the 18th century (the mid-Qing period), due to reclamation success, Taiwan social stability and accumulation of wealth immigrants had extra money to commit the construction of temples and mansions (Li 2005). Generally they hired Chinese craftsmen to build Taiwan's temples and mansions. This was based on the ethical code they abode. Never forgot where they came from. They hired craftsmen from their birth places. Even building materials were also shipped from the mainland (Zuo 1996).

In the early reclamation, a large number of Fujian and Guangdong people who came to Taiwan led hard lives. Immigrants not only prayed for smoothly crossing the strait, but also faced the natural disasters in the natural environment and plagues. Furthermore, they had to fight with the aboriginal tribes over the land disputes. They lived in fear all day long. In the face of these difficulties and hardship, their confidence and support came from the ancestral religion. Immigrants brought their deities and beliefs with them as a spiritual reliance when they crossing the strait. Over time, religion has played an important part to the Taiwanese. That's the reason there are so many temples in Taiwan.

In Taiwan's traditional society, the function of the temples provides worshiping and praying. Also they are important places of religion spreading; it often becomes the active center. Because they locate on the corner of streets, they become the leading places of the local education, counseling and command center for villagers. Temples are the strongholds of belief, bless, protection, and teaching as well as arts, entertainment, and autonomy multiple functions in one (Kang 2004). Temples also have an important contribute to promote the prosperity and social stability to the locals.

Due to the function to fulfill the special needs of the immigrants in the early Qing period religious activities in Taiwan were active. People prayed for the survival and reproduction. They hoped to get psychological help and blessing from the gods. No sooner the economy permitted than they actively built temples. Almost pretty soon each immigrant settlement place built temples. Devotees worshiped the gods and embrace the feelings of admiration. Their devotion urged them to hire the best craftsmen, which brought the finest things to dedicate to the gods, and offer the most beautiful temples to their gods. So along wealth affluent society, the ornaments of the temples became more and more elegant. Decorative architecture and complicated building temples in Taiwan which used sculpture, painting and building reflected Taiwanese lively pursuit of lush life with psychological and aesthetic tastes.

3.2 The Decoration of Taiwan Traditional Temples

The temple is the concrete reflection of Taiwan religion. Inside each construction assembled with architectural essence of folk art which is an important public buildings

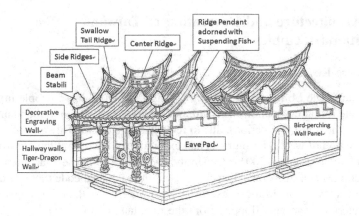

Fig. 1. Cochin ceramics are commonly found adoring. (Source: Chiayi City Koji Pottery Museum)

and art treasures. The so-called architectural decoration refers to the techniques of the traditional building craftsmen on building, stacking, painting, sculpturing, plastic, inserting, coloring (Lee 1993), and other different expression which create landscaping or symbolic meaning of flat or three-dimensional architectural elements. Taiwan's architectural researcher Noushi Kang divided the decoration of Taiwan temples into five categories (Kang 2007).

(1) Sculpture: stone carving, wood carving, brick carving. (2) Molds: Jian-nian (cut-and-paste), clay, Cochin ceramic. (3) Combinations of pile: brick, window frames, fancy brickwork. (4) Inlay: Jian-nian, marquetry wood, shell inlay, inlaid glass. (5) Painting: plane painting, relief painting, door-god painting, inscription couplet, murals. (6) Others: Terrazzo, hand-painted tiles.

Cochin ceramic as one of architectural ornaments is basically shaped in the dough-based, collect painting, literature, ceramics and other art in one, In addition to bright colors can be added to make the building look gorgeous, and Cochin subject is rich. It covers the historical stories and auspicious meaning.

Cochin fragile essence makes them easily broken, so most of them are placed in the higher places of the temples. They include center Ridge, Swallow Tail Ridge, Side Ridges, Beam Stabilizer, Gable (Ridge Pendant), Bird-perching Wall Panel, Eave Pad, Decorative Engraving Wall, Decorative Engraving Wall, Hallway walls (Tiger Gate and Dragon Gate), etc., and gold paper burning stove (furnace) roof and engraving wall (Fig. 1).

4   Themes and the Expression of Moral and Symbolic

4.1   Themes of Cochin Ceramic

Most of the traditional Cochin inherited the style of China Quanzhou. Taiwan craftsmen modeled after it, but with the personal interpretation and creativity, combined with local features or style influence, slowly forming their own characteristics. I divided the subjects of Cochin according to the results of the field trip. There are figures from the stories, auspicious animals, auspicious plants, artifacts, objects of religious symbols, calligraphy, natural phenomena, geometric patterns and landscape architecture (background). Are as follows:

4.1.1   Figures from the Stories

Most contents are drawn from traditional Chinese mythology, folklore, history, stories, literary allusions, chapter novels and drama. Characters include ghosts, loyal and virtuous, literary figures and historical figures, etc. In accordance with the plots can be divided into "civil scene" and "military scene". The civil scene refers to the scene of the combination of the literati without any martial arts scenes; or the romantic love story, elegant social story etc., such as West Chamber, Twenty-four Filial Pieties. The military scene is generally about the battles wrestling with demons or gods or plots rewriting from historical figures and many more battle scenes based, such as The Romance of The Three Kingdoms, Heroes in Sui and Tang Dynasties, Gods of Honor and Water Margin. Myth or folklore is based on well-known folk legends or mythology with the purpose of blessing and avoiding evil forces, such as representatives of auspiciousness of the Eight Immortals, the Three Official Great, Magu and other representative's immortals. Other subjects are mainly on the narrative contents including metaphor, advising people to do good deeds to promote the society to be on the track of ethical development.

4.1.2   Auspicious Animals

In addition to the general common animals, a mythological animal is imagined by the people to idealize and is widely used in a variety of decorative arts, those animals all got their names from their appearances, essences and their symbolic meaning, which presents blessing, good luck and avoiding evils in order to meet the common people's need for an ideal life. Animals are divided into two kinds, general and auspicious animals (Lin 1999). General animals include birds, animals, insects, aquatic life, etc. Auspicious animals come from the long-popular myths and legends, which gradually evolved into the concept of embracing good fortune and served to avoid evils. For example dragon, phoenix and unicorn represent auspicious animal and the crane and tortoise are regarded as a symbol of longevity. Also from homonym in Chinese, such as bats, "bat" and "blessing" are homophone, "quail" and "peaceful", "fish" and "remnants", "deer" and "prosperity" are homophone, all with auspicious meaning.

4.1.3   Auspicious Plants

Since ancient times, plant patterns with its elegant features and patterns have become commonly used objects of artistic expression. Along with the historical evolution they are given numerous symbolic meanings. With a wide variety, trees, flowers, grass and fruits are mostly common used. Such as evergreen pines represents forever youth and longevity; a section of bamboo have a gentleman ethical meaning; peony is the king of flowers, symbolizing wealth; Ganoderma, as a symbol of longevity, is believed to be able to bring immortality to people; pomegranate fruit with many seeds inside it means prosperity in the family; peaches are immortals edible fruit, symbolic of longevity. Lily is viewed a symbol of eternal love; or homonyms such as "lychee" sound like "benefit"; "sweet osmanthus flower" sound as "high position"; also available homonyms combined into auspicious meaning, such as peony and sweet osmanthus flower together are the representative of richness.

4.1.4 Artifacts

They mainly serve for daily utensils, including ritual, room appliances, home decorations and weapons; ritual such as Jazz (drinking vessel), Ding (three-legged ancient Chinese cooking vessel); common room appliances such as "Four Arts" (quadrivium, included Chin, chess, calligraphy and painting), a symbol of elegance literati, meaning all descendants will have glory future. Common home decorations vary such as vases, baskets, table, mirrors, shelves and so on; these are also commonly used to denote a symbolic meaning by combining homonyms such as "box" to "fit" homonym, "mirror" the same "territory", "vase" and "peaceful", together have "Peaceful in the whole territory" meaning, "incense" passing the torch image (generation to generation). Weapon such as halberds with flags, balls, chime form a meaning of praying for auspicious things.

4.1.5 Objects of Religion Symbol

They including religion-related objects and symbols in talisman, such as whisk, bracelets, swastika, the eight divinatory trigrams, Tai Chi, Eight treasures (Eight kinds of Buddhist magic instruments), etc. Such items are considered to have the power to avoid evils.

4.1.6 Calligraphy

Calligraphy includes the text of banners, couplets, and inscriptive poems, in addition to displaying scholarly temperament. They have the function of encouraging people to be good. Some words transforming into simple patterns or into graphs with auspicious connotations, such as patterns of swastika, "Fu" word, longevity and double happiness.

4.1.7 Natural Phenomena

They contain the moon and stars and other natural phenomena. Moon dominates the timing of life. It has god's identity. Clouds are the wagons of the deities, representing wonderland.

4.1.8 Geometric Pattern

Usually they are frames, subordinate of decorative patterns and with simple shape patterns by using a continuous, repeatable way to performance. Most commonly used are patterns of dragons, twisted trees, geometric flowers, clouds, ice cracks, waves and ripples.

4.1.9 Landscape Architectural (Background)

Mostly they are background landscape which describes the theme of time and space, and strengthens the depth of the plot and drama scene, as illustrated by the scenery with hills and waters, trees and rocks, pavilions and buildings, city walls and gates, palaces, and other pastoral scenery.

In these nine Cochin themes the first five ones are commonly used and the last three set off topic purposes. Calligraphy category appears in rich mansions.

From the above theme designed Cochin, we can clearly see that through fable and symbolic way to convey praying, avoiding evils, and educational functions. Chinese ancient dynasties all have a preference for the traditional auspicious designs; its formation can be traced back to a long time ago. According to the Chinese scholar Jitang Qiao's research, it recorded Chinese architecture ornamentation was originated, which originated in the Shangzhou and Qinhan dynasties, began in Qin and Han dynasties, and matured in Tang and Song dynasties. It was in the Ming and Qing Dynasties that it flourished (Qiao 1993). Taiwan's traditional architecture researchers Qian-Lang Li considers that Taiwan temple decoration: "was the inevitable thing from ancient architectural structures, over time, through the craftsman's imagination eventually evolved into a specific form of decoration...." (Lee 1993) Therefore, Chinese ornamentation is produced in a long tradition.

4.2   The Way of Expression the Theme

The way of the expression the theme of Cochin are as follows:

(1) Themes from mythology, folklore, historical stories, literary allusions, and Chapter Novels, etc. Parts of the story are employed to proclaim the ethical spirits of four anchors (Courtesy, Righteousness, Honesty and Honor) and eight virtues (Loyalty, Filial Obedience Humanity, Love, Trust, and Peace). They help strengthen the concept of punishing evil and promoting good. The use of these meaningful expressions in the moral stories achieves the purposes of enlightenment.

(2) Auspicious animals and plants are mostly derived the characteristics of the things itself and extended meaning for auspicious. They give auspicious ideas, or the association connection, such as lotus mean unstained characteristics, pine trees present the natural of forever green and long life, mandarin ducks on behalf of loving; turtle and the crane on behalf of longevity; pomegranate seeds on behalf of the family many descendants; gourd-vines stretches, with the meaning of descendants stretching without a break in one family. The mythological animal category is either imagined or idealized, which is deification product. These are circulated for a long time, and social customary convention with their symbolic meaning.

(3) In the homonym approach, examples are abundant: for instance, the word for "deer" is pronounced "lu", as the word "fortune"; also, the word for "pray" is read "chi", just as the word for "flag". Use different words are homonyms to achieve the symbol. The most commonly usage for architectural approach is a combinations to form auspicious semantics.

(4) The calligraphy category theme, the words themselves have special meaning. Most poets write down poems which not only shows the beauty of calligraphy but also have performs the function of teaching moral lessons and exhorting people.

Also it can use single word to show auspicious and as a simplified symbolic decorative word.

(5) Borrowing religious which has representative symbols. For the purpose of warding off evils spirits, such as the eight divinatory trigrams, Eight Immortals utensils etc.

(6) Geometric Patterns are the result of the class through the artistic processing. By decoration and using the repetition and continuous techniques to appear beauty.

Belgian poet A. Moekel (1886–1945) said, "Implied meaning is manmade and external. Symbols are natural and inherent. With the same abstract graphs implied meaning is obvious implications and the social concepts people agree." (Lee 1994) Both implied meaning and symbols are the combination of abstract feeling and perception. In other words, only through concrete variation the words and graphics can we realize their existence.

In fact, different cultural backgrounds have different interpretations of the same object, such as Taiwan's "bat" in the homonym meaning 'blessing', but in the western culture it is the incarnation of Halloween vampire on behalf of the evil. This shows that it is an experience of cultural heritage. In presenting the theme of Cochin, we must learn through cognition to learn to understand their inner spiritual meaning and symbolism.

5 Humanism Contained in Cochin Ceramics

Traditional Taiwan society is founded on agriculture. The formation of the idea of self-sufficiency in material life makes practical becomes the center of arts. Because of the need for adaptation to the natural environment the concept of the harmony between men and nature revolve (Chen 2004). Those ideas with humanism as the central ideas are demonstrated in the traditional culture in which people are urged to have a yearning for happiness. Those are embodies in the images that decorate in the temples.

Cochin in traditional temples has the decorative function using symbols to express special meaning of each thing. With the chosen motif and theme, craftsmen will add his own notation and advocate his social value in it (Lee 2003).

Taiwan Scholars Qian-Lang Li believed temple architectural decoration in Taiwan indicates the wish to seek good fortune, hope, and self-motivation. Avoiding disaster and pursuing good luck are the basic wishes of mankind. Praying is the pursuit of an ideal state. Enlightenment is to make a valuable indicator to become a model or moral. All these will have great effect on the descending generation (Li 1993). With the decorations on temples' wall provoke an educational function of being a kind and good person. Through the decorations of the temples, one can see the abstract or explicit motivations of people's yarning.

All in all I believe the rich hidden embodiment of humanism lies in Cochin ceramic. Since the Renaissance Europe has regarded humanism as the values of human natural, humanity, human values and subjectivity of human (Cheng 2003). Taiwanese former Minister of Education Wei Fan Guo stresses, "Humanism represents a humanistic spirit of selfless attitude, a social care, life purpose, and meaning of life consciousness" (Guo 1994). Therefore humanism spirit is an ideal personality shaping and affirmation.

By fieldwork I found Cochin theme contains static character scenes (civil scene), auspicious animals and plants pattern, and with lively martial fight scenes (military scene). Both the static and the dynamic scenes are of different prayers and desires. The static ones are with auspicious animals and plants. Their demand is elegance with the function of avoiding evil and pursuing good luck and encouraging descendants to gain fame and wealth. Dynamic scenes use Four Anchors and Eight Virtues as the outlines of the themes. Historical stories educate people in order to have social stability and binding effect which has strong ethics and values. Understand the value of the humanity revelation. Whether it is static or dynamic Cochin ceramic, it has the role of education in a subtle way. Through storytelling, it can lay deeper into people's minds to arouse inner spirits which are motions, hopes, ideals, morals, ideas, etc., resulting in a positive character.

6 Conclusions

Immigrants brought Taiwan's low temperature lead glaze pottery from the hometown of Fujian coastal areas. Although at present the real source can't be traced, it inherits the hometown style. Furthermore temples become the center of life and the location for spiritual worship. As the temple decoration Cochin, it inherits the historical heritage with a wide range of subjects which follow the traditional craftsmen in the selection and designing. By using their imagination, the historical stories turn into decorative patterns with a variety of symbolic themes, moral stories, symbols of natural phenomena, homonym or changing of the text, etc. It expresses the people's aspirations, the ideal life. Its images contain hidden rich cultural heritage. It conveys the adding beauty to the building, and also has aesthetic and social functions which serve as the role of appreciation and beautify the spirit.

American anthropologist Clark Wissler (1870–1947) once said that culture is a mode of life. Hence, Culture is the result of mankind's activities, a kind of accumulation instead of genetic (Jan 1998). All in all the formation of culture is from the formation of history and reflects the thoughts, feelings, and habits of mankind. People also learn a lot of tradition and experience. Craftsmen pick the themes of Cochin connecting with praying for prosperity, avoiding disaster, hoping blessing, and gaining fortune. Consequently it is believed that by going to the temples people can obtain lucks, longevity, prosperity, glory, splendor, wealth and rank from gods which are the ideal life style they wish to have.

Naturally by presenting these themes, temples craftsmen hope to make people's wishes come true. Since temples also are a place for early education, temples are the first places by presenting Cochin in a narrative story style which conveys artistic beauty, cultivating good virtue, showing awareness of Taiwanese conscience, and humanism value.

From my research it is showed that Cochin decoration is a manifestation of social culture and cultural implications with folklore thoughts. Although the building itself only serves as a beautification, the Cochin is not simply for the decorative purpose.

Any chosen theme reflects the traditional ethical norms and symbolic meaning for praying, which is a concrete manifestation of the common people's aesthetics, philosophy, social outlook, and values which lies the spirit of humanism.

References

Bian, T.S., Jio, S., Shi, Y.J.: Chinese Craft Art History, p. 17. China Light Industry Press, Beijing (2001)

Central Academy of Fine Arts: Arts and Crafts Dictionary, p. 72. Heilongjiang People's Publishing House, Beijing (1988)

Chen, T.-J.: A semiology study to interpret Chinese auspicious pattern-applied the bat auspicious pattern. Master thesis, Graduation School of Arts and Handiwork Education, National Hsinchu University of Education (2004)

Cheng, M.-C.: Probe spirit of humanism in Meine Schwester Klara. Master thesis, Graduate Institute of Children's Literature, National Taitung Teachers College (2003)

Guo, W.-F.: The Education Belief in Humanist. Wu Nan Publisher Co., Taipei (1994)

Jan, D.-L.: Explore multicultural education theory and practice. In: Multicultural Education. Taiwan Bookstore, Taipei (1998)

Kang, N.: An Illustrated Book of Taiwan Temples. Owl Publishing, Taipei (2004)

Kang, N.: An Illustrated book of Decoration of Taiwan Traditional Building. Owl Publishing, Taipei (2007)

Lee, Q.-L.: Temple Architecture. North Star, Taipei (1993)

Lee, M.M.: The Boundaries of Classical and Symbolic. Dong Da Bookstore, Taipei (1994)

Lee, C.-J.: The semiotic analysis of the wood carving in the traditional architecture —subject on ancient architecture in Changhua city. Master thesis, Graduate School of Interior Design, National Yunlin University of Science and Technology (2003)

Lee, S.-C.: Research for the origin and development, manufacture formula and technique of rouge-red glaze of Taiwan Koji pottery, p. 13. Master thesis, Graduate School of Cultural Heritage Conservation, National Yunlin University of Science and Technology (2013)

Li, C-Y.: The research of Cochin ceramic art and local culture industry development, p. 58. Master thesis, Graduate School of Fine Arts In-Service Program, National Taiwan Normal University (2005)

Lin, H.-C.: Traditional Architecture Handbook—Form and Practice, p. 21. Artist Magazine Co., Taipei (1990)

Lin, S.-C.: Decoration Arts in Penghu Local Traditional Houses. Penghu County Cultural Center, Penghu (1999)

Luo, S.J.: Etymology of low temperature glaze. Ceram. Stud. J. 5(2), 36–42 (1990). (Total No. 18, Jiangxi Province: Ceramic Research Institute of Jiangxi Province, Jiangxi Province Ceramics Science and Technology Information)

Qiao, J.: Mascot in China. Bai Guan Publisher Co., Taipei (1993)

Shih, T.-F.: Re-recognizing Taiwanese Cochin ceramic. In: To Build a Dream by Hand- The Art of Taiwan Cochin Ceramic, pp. 14–36. National Museum of History, Taiwan (2000)

Shih, H.-M.: An overview of Cochin ceramics in Taiwan with an emphasis on the influence of Hong Kun-Fu and his school –1910s to 1980s. Doctoral dissertation, University of Wollongong, Australia (2008)

Shing, S.G.: Evolution of low lead glaze, Tang three-color-glaze, glazed tile and ceramic plate painted pottery. J. Qiqihar Univ. (Philos. Soc. Sci. Ed.) 4, 172–174 (2008). Qiqihar University, Qiqihar

Zhu, B., Li, Y.: The ceramics of Qin and Han dynasties. In: The Collected Works of Chinese Ceramics 3- Qin and Han Dynasties, p. 12. Shanghai People's Fine Arts Publishing House, Shanghai (2000)
Zuo, X.-F.: A research of Taiwan Cochin ceramic (pp. 13–14). Master thesis, Graduate School of Folk Culture and Arts, National Institute of Arts (1996)

Designing Wearable Device-Based Product and Service Ecosystem

Xiaohua Sun[1(✉)], Yongqi Lou[1], Tong Li[1], and Qi Wang[2]

[1] College of Design and Innovation, Tongji University,
281 Fuxin Road, Shanghai, China
xsun@tongji.edu.cn, lou.yongqi@gmail.com,
tjlittle@126.com
[2] Eindhoven University of Technology,
Den Dolech 2, 5612 AZ Eindhoven, The Netherlands
q.wang@tue.nl

Abstract. In the design of wearable device, the focus is normally put on the device itself and functions serving individual users. However, as a product widely spread out over a large population, the consolidated data collected from the devices could be used to bring to users functions or services far beyond personal scope and increase the value of services for individual users as well. When the focus of design is switched from individual product to the overall landscape involving large amount of devices, a central data platform, and services supported by the data platform, a systematic planning of the working mechanism and services at both individual and social level become possible as the result of the scope expansion. We introduce in this paper our in-depth analysis of key issues involved in the design in this new type of ecosystem. Specifically, we use E-Wearable, a wearable device-based platform for environment protection and environmental information service to exemplify the concepts and methods we propose.

Keywords: Wearable device · Social innovation · Environmental information service · Environment protection

1 Introduction

With rapid development of sensing and mobile technologies, wearable devices have emerged in various forms and brought to people new functions and services in sports, health, and many other fields. In the design of most of the wearable devices, designers tend to focus on the product itself and functions serving individual users. Even though some of the functions do involve with the utilization of user data, its value is mostly constraint to personal use. However, rich data collected from large quantities of wearable devices could provide services at the social scope and increase the value of personal services at the same time. There are already explorations along this direction such as the MTA Relay by Frog Design [4], yet there lacks in-depth study of design from this expanded scope. When the focus of design is switched from individual products to the overall landscape including both the platform and the devices,

P.L.P. Rau (Ed.): CCD 2015, Part I, LNCS 9180, pp. 108–115, 2015.
DOI: 10.1007/978-3-319-20907-4_10

one needs to find out the running mechanism, define the system structure, and design the products and services in a systematic way.

In order to better exemplify the focus switch concept and the related design methods we propose, we implement them in E-Wearable, a wearable device-based social innovation platform for environment protection and environmental information service. We choose to experiment with the environment topic for the following two reasons: (1) Environment protection requires participation at the social scope, (2) Ubiquitous and crowd-sourced data collection is typical for environmental information gathering [2, 6–9]. In the following sections, we will explain in detail (1) How to construct a full-fledged ecosystem by defining the key components, (2) How to establish a running system through the construction of a contribution-benefit mechanism, (3) How to come up with specific product and service design by refining and combining the ecosystem components, (4) How to use modules at the platform level to both lower down the development cost of service applications and provide users with consistent experience.

2 Construction of the Ecosystem

As illustrated in the left part of Fig. 1, the platform that could consolidate large amount of user data is often out of designers' focus. Data collected by a device is normally treated as a property of the device itself and is mostly used by individual users. However, if the scope of design is expanded to what is illustrated in the right part of Fig. 1, designers will then be able to start from the central data platform, make connections with different products of a user or with products of large quantities of users.

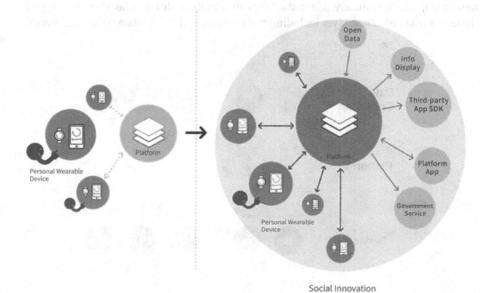

Fig. 1. The concept of focus switch

They can also link the platform with related data sources besides those collected from wearable devices. On top of this rich data set, services could be lineated out in various ways. The ecosystems thus formed are mainly of two types: association-oriented and crowdsourcing-based.

For association-oriented platform, it is important to pull in different kinds of data from as many types of products and data sources as possible and then make associations over them. Taking Apple's HealthKit [5] as an example, in the construction of the ecosystem, it is necessary to find out various types of health-related data along with their data source (e.g. EHR data) or collecting applications and devices (Jawbone, Up Move, Withings, Misfit Shine, etc.) and then make the platform connect to or be compatible with them. Services could then be derived out both directly in the form of personal applications and indirectly (through ReserachKit) as health data-based research serving hospitals, insurance companies, etc.

In crowdsourcing-based platform, the amount of devices or users involved is crucial. In the design of the ecosystem, one should think about how to incorporate large quantities of data through various types of devices and derive both public and personal services on top of the consolidated data. In designing E-Wearable, we first outline possible directions for further development of potential products, e.g. by data concerned, by wearing methods, by sensing capabilities, and by using scenarios. In order to complement data collected by wearable devices, we also include in the ecosystem devices put on vehicles, facilities installed in public environment, and open environmental data provided by the government. When deriving the services, we start by looking into services for both professional (e.g. government and IT companies) and individual users. For individual users, we further look for services provided to them by different parties: platform, third party, and government. These services could again include different modules, e.g. environmental information display, travel path recommendation, etc. Specifically, we come up with a system structure as shown in Fig. 2. There is a data collection layer including both private and public data collection devices

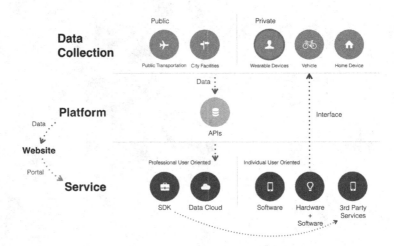

Fig. 2. System structure of E-Wearable platform

or facilitates, a platform layer for data processing and consolidation, and a service layer with services for professional and individual users.

3 Establishment of the Contribution-Benefit Mechanism

In order to keep the ecosystem running, it is essential to establish a contribution-benefit mechanism to attract more users and encourage them to make contributions. Specifically, designers should derive from users' contribution as many benefits as possible. There are mainly three types of contribution-benefit relationships to refer to while constructing this system:

1. Benefit made possible by the accumulation of certain type of data contributed or activities performed by the users
2. Benefit come into being through the association of multiple types of information contributed by the users
3. Benefit provided by another party other than the platform based on users' contribution.

In E-Wearable, there are different types of user contributions that can lead to accumulation-based benefit. Various types of environmental data collected by users at different locations across time can form together the environmental information map for users to check directly or for more services to build on top of, e.g. environmental status of people the user cares about or recommendation of traveling path with better air quality. Large quantities of user comments about the afforestation rate and other general appearance of the environment can complement with the data collected from sensing devices and enrich the environmental information map. Environment protection activities by users can also help to improve the environmental quality accumulatively. However, the resulted benefit could not be sensed immediately. The platform needs to provide an organizing and rewarding mechanism to encourage such activities. In E-Wearable, we designed an environment protection game for this purpose, in which users join different groups to accomplish environment protection or improvement tasks of certain areas in the city. Both virtual (game points or credits) and real (coupons or wearable devices) awards are given to the participants as encouragement.

For association-based benefit, one example in E-Wearable is that users can get environmental condition alerts or protection wear suggestions based on their health status and the surrounding environmental information. One example for benefits provided by other parties is that the government could take environment improvement actions, such as increasing afforestation coverage or installing environment protection facilitates, based on environmental information contributed by the users and their reports of environmental problems.

4 Design of the Products and Services

We explain is this section how we derive product and service design in E-Wearable through refinement and combination of the ecosystem components. Refinement refers to the process of specifying product and service attributes along the main categories of the key components, and combination refers to the process of deriving product and service concept through associating the refined attributes from both the data collection and the service side.

For data collection, based on the type of data concerned, the products can be refined into those for pregnant women, for people with breathing diseases, for people allergic to dust, etc. By wearing methods, they can be refined into devices in the form of glasses, necklace, wristband, ring, mask, shoes etc. By sensing capabilities, they can be refined into products sensing air quality, humidity, noise intensity, radiation intensity, vehicle exhaust pollution level, etc. And by using scenarios, they can be refined into products for people to wear or use while taking a walk, biking, or driving.

From the service side, for different types of users, there are data cloud service for the government, development SDK for third-party developers, and a variety of services for individual users which can be further refined by service provider, service module, and characteristic of the users. Services provided by the platform may include environmental information map, path recommendation, warnings towards the change of the environmental status, comments on environmental problems etc. Those provided by the government may include public environmental information display, construction of environment protection facilities, pollution treatment etc. And services provided by third-party can be refined into applications supporting specific hardware, protection wear suggestion, radiation alert, etc.

Shown in Fig. 3 are a set of products derived through the process introduced above. Considering of different data emphasis and wearing methods, we designed phone case, wristband, and ring that can collect data of the surrounding environment. Considering of the different using scenarios, we designed devices placed on bicycles and cars. Services associated with these devices are mostly provided through mobile applications. Some of the devices themselves are also able to give lighting cues or alerts regarding environmental quality. In order to complement the sensing capability and using scenario of wearable devices, we also designed sensing facilities installed in parks, on the street, and on building facades. Main services they provide are real-time environmental information displays in public.

5 Application Design at the Platform Scope

As part of the ecosystem, there would be many applications affiliated with the data platform. Besides the platform official application, there are also third party applications and applications for different devices. Not only sharing the same set of data from the platform, these applications may also have in common many service modules closely binded with the platform. For example, in E-Wearable, environmental data visualization, path recommendation based on real-time environmental information,

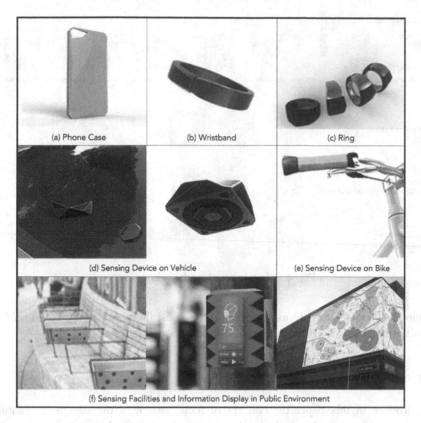

(a) Phone Case   (b) Wristband   (c) Ring

(d) Sensing Device on Vehicle   (e) Sensing Device on Bike

(f) Sensing Facilities and Information Display in Public Environment

Fig. 3. Example products and services in E-Wearable system

comments about environmental status etc. may be modules many applications would like to include.

In order to avoid reinventing the wheel in the development of different applications, in E-Wearable, we utilize a module-based design for all the affiliated services. Core modules like those introduced above will be developed by the platform. Device or third party service providers also develop their applications as modules, such as environment protection game module and modules supporting the use of various wearable devices. The platform provides visual and development guidelines for third parties to follow during the development of their own modules. As shown in Fig. 4, the basic application and applications for users with different devices may include different modules [1, 3]. For people like pregnant woman, it is also possible to include in their applications specialized modules such as radiation intensity alert.

Such an application design at the platform level helps to bring to users consistent experience while using different services. It saves them from installing multiple applications with overlapping functions in different design. When there are more and more modules in the repository, the platform can recommend to users modules they may be interested in based on their profile information, such as health status, living habits, environmental information concerned, etc. Over the process of use,

Fig. 4. Module based application design

the application can also help users dynamically adjust their application based on their browsing preference and using habit of different modules.

6 Conclusion

We introduce in this paper the concept of focus switch in the design of wearable devices and propose to design the products and services from the perspective of a data platform-centered ecosystem. Through E-Wearable, a wearable device-based social innovation platform for environment protection and environmental information service, we exemplify in detail design concepts and methods from this expanded scope. More research along this line worth to be carried out to increase the quality of design in different application fields. Also, there are security, privacy, and other issues need to be well dealt with during the process of utilizing data collected by wearable devices. Hope the concepts and methods proposed in this paper could serve as a starting point for further research on the mechanism and design principles of wearable device-based product and service ecosystem.

Acknowledgments. This work was supported in part by the Fundamental Research Funds for the Central Universities in China (0600219044) and the Grant from the International Cooperation Project of Ministry of Science and Technology (2012DFG10280).

References

1. Alepis, E., Virvou, M., Kabassi, K.: Location based user modeling in adaptive mobile learning for environmental awareness. In: ICSOFT, vol. 1, pp. 214–217 (2011)

2. Boulos, M.N.K., Resch, B., Crowley, D.N., et al.: Crowdsourcing, citizen sensing and sensor web technologies for public and environmental health surveillance and crisis management: trends, OGC standards and application examples. Int. J. Health Geogr. **10**(1), 67 (2011)
3. Ciepluch, B., Mooney, P., Jacob, R., et al.: Using openstreetmap to deliver location-based environmental information in ireland. SIGSPATIAL Spec. **1**(3), 17–22 (2009)
4. Frog Design: Mobile Ecosystems Evolving. Aricent Group, Redwood (2013)
5. Healthkit. https://developer.apple.com/healthkit/
6. Kanhere, S.S.: Participatory sensing: crowdsourcing data from mobile smartphones in urban spaces. In: Proceedings of 2011 12th IEEE International Conference on Mobile Data Management (MDM), pp. 3–6, Luleå, Sweden, 6–9 June 2011. doi:10.1109/MDM.2011.16
7. Saenz, A.: Japan's nuclear woes give rise to crowd-sourced radiation maps in Asia and US. http://singularityhub.com/2011/03/24/japans-nuclear-woes-give-rise-to-crowd-sourced-radiation-maps-in-asia-and-us/. Accessed 24 Mar 2011
8. Sense Your City. http://datacanvas.org
9. Stevens, M., D'Hondt, E.: Crowdsourcing of pollution data using smartphones. In: Workshop on Ubiquitous Crowdsourcing (2010)

From OEM to OBM - A Case Study
of Branding Taiwan

Hui-Yun Yen[1(✉)], Yu-Ju Lin[2], Yige Jin[3], and Rungtai Lin[2]

[1] Department of Advertising, Chinese Culture University, Taipei 11114, Taiwan
pccu.yhy@gmail.com
[2] Graduate School of Creative Industry Design,
National Taiwan University of Arts, Ban Ciao, Taipei 22058, Taiwan
anicole362124@hotmail.com, rtlin@mail.ntua.edu.tw
[3] Shanghai Art and Design Academy, Shanghai, China
yigeqll@sina.com

Abstract. Recently, product design in Taiwan has entered the original brand manufacturer era, which involves the evolution of Taiwan design development. Taiwan is eager to transform its economic development to "branding Taiwan." Based on previous studies and experience in Taiwan, this study proposes a conceptual framework to study Taiwan design development, which has transitioned from "use" to "user," "function" to "feeling," and "hi-tech" to "hi-touch." Hence, this study aimed to provide designers, companies, and organizations with a design strategy that is tailored to the current market. The results are presented herein to provide an interface for examining Taiwanese design development across cultures and to illustrate the relationship between local design and the global market in Taiwan's economy, industry, and design development.

Keywords: Branding Taiwan · Product design · OEM · ODM · OBM

1 Introduction

Taiwanese economic development is a fusion of design-technology (dechnology) and humanity-art (humart): from the original equipment manufacturer (OEM) to the original design manufacturer (ODM) to the original brand manufacturer (OBM). The OEM, ODM, and OBM stages reflect that Taiwanese design development is transitioning from "use" to "user," "function" to "feeling," and "hi-tech" to "hi-touch." Recently, product design in Taiwan has entered the OBM era, which involves the evolution of Taiwanese design development. Taiwan is eager to transform its economic development to "branding Taiwan."

In Taiwan, vendors have advanced their production technologies, and the market has become highly competitive. Product function and engineering design no longer give products advantages in the market. Invisible factors, including product aesthetics and symbolic attributes, have become the key factors that influence consumers' decisions to purchase of certain brand products. Product design is critical for brand image; the product should be consistent with the brand image (Levy 1959; Davis 2000;

© Springer International Publishing Switzerland 2015
P.L.P. Rau (Ed.): CCD 2015, Part I, LNCS 9180, pp. 116–127, 2015.
DOI: 10.1007/978-3-319-20907-4_11

Wang et al. 2008). This trend shows that consumers are no longer content to satisfy ordinary daily needs and feel "longing" and "desire," which are generated by admiration for a brand or product. The CEO of one of the world's top ten brand marketing companies, Gobe (2009), stated that the current era is dominated by emotions. Consequently, brands should invest primarily in creating an appropriate emotional atmosphere for consumers. Gobe (2009) also mentioned that, in the twenty-first century, consumers and companies are on both ends of a market catalyzed by emotion, where emotion serves as the bridge that connects a brand to its products.

This study therefore focused on Taiwanese and global brands to investigate how the function, design, and feeling factors (the emotional atmospheres created by the products) of products affect various brands. Furthermore, this study evaluates the effects of various brands on the function, design and feeling factors (the emotional atmospheres created by the products) of products. Hence, this study aimed to provide designers, companies, and organizations with a design strategy that is tailored to the current market.

2 Background

To consumers, brand image represents product appearance. Consumers link product information with the brand. Products symbolize brands, and the brand summarizes consumer's feelings toward products. Therefore, qualia product design can develop brand image (Keller 1993; Yen et al. 2014a, b). Product design is integral to a brand and a major driver of brand equity. Product design can drive consumer preferences and create a sustainable competitive advantage for a brand (Kumar et al. 2014). The current era values beauty, because beauty generates happiness, which encourages consumers to pursue aesthetic experiences.

People pursue beauty because beauty produces pleasure. Consumers desire to have their needs and wants satisfied by their experience of products (Lin 2013). This shows a transition into the era of user-centered product marketing, which conforms to Redstrom's (2006) proposal that "user-centered design" is a relatively recent innovation. The feeling of happiness is imposed on a tangible object, giving people a sense of surprise and sensation. Emotional qualia are the phenomenological representations of the end products of appraisal processes. To consumers, qualia distinguishes one product from another. A product's qualia is determined by its quality, including the attractiveness, beauty, and creativity rendered in the product's external features. Therefore, a successful product design meets or exceeds the emotional needs of users beyond utility and quality (Bermond 2008; McLoone et al. 2012). Yen et al. (2014a, b) proposed that qualia products can support the future development and growth of an aesthetic economy. In other words, qualia products satisfy user's needs for products to have practical function, appealing aesthetics, and the ability to emotionally connect with users.

Ashby and Johnson (2003) proposed that products have "psychology" and "physiology" and involve rational conditions for consumer use but do not lack emotional appeal. Norman (2004) published his classic article that identified how visceral design relates to appearances. Behavioral design relates to pleasure and effectiveness of use. Reflective design involves the rationalization and intellectualization of a product. In the past, "production thinking" provided product function through technology that emphasized products' "universal" and facilitated comfort. Currently, "design thinking" conveys product feelings through creativity and design that emphasizes products' uniqueness and enhances happiness. Therefore, a design transition exists from "function to feeling" and "use to user" (Lin 2014). Based on the previously mentioned research, a user-centered course of the designer perception in this section of the function, design to feeling. Modern product design should not merely aim to satisfy the functional demands of consumers; it must also consider user experience.

The pioneers of design thinking postulated that innovations should start with a focus on desirability, but should ultimately satisfy three perspectives: human desirability, technical feasibility, and economic viability (Brown 2008; IDEO 2012). "Feasibility" indicates a product's functionality; "viability" indicates what can be achieved with a product within a company's sustainable business model, and "desirability" represents what people want or will eventually want, which is a product's customer appeal. Therefore, the center of the design process is the intersection of technical feasibility, economic viability, and desirability regarding users. This intersection of OEM, ODM, and OBM can be applied for illustrating how to transform the local culture into a global market (Plattner et al. 2010; Lin 2014). Based on the previously mentioned research, the product be manufactured process of the maker perception in this section of technical feasibility, economic viability (product innovation), and desirability to users.

3 Research Method

3.1 Study Framework

The relationship between technology and humart, which were merged into a design framework to explore Taiwanese and global design development, was investigated in this study. Whether the function, design, and feeling factors (the emotional atmospheres created by the products) of products affected brands in Taiwan and globally was investigated.

The conceptual framework presented in this paper was used to study the trends in Taiwanese and global design and development from "use" to "user," "function" to "feeling," and "hi-tech" to "hi-touch." Additionally, Taiwanese design development was explored, and the OEM, ODM, and OBM stages were identified to illustrate how to transform the local culture into a global market through adaptive design development in Taiwan. Three perspectives (user, designer, and maker) were also included in the conceptual framework, which included feelings regarding functional design and representatives of the desired course of the user, representatives of the user-centered course of the designer, and representatives of the OEM to OBM course of the maker. This paper proposes a design approach for branding Taiwan by using Taiwanese designs, which can be adopted by Taiwan in the future. Hence, this study aimed to provide designers, companies, and organizations with a design strategy that is tailored to the current market. Based on literature review, products' were measured by brand

	Needs	Wants	Desires
User perception	Practical Function Quality	Aesthetics Qualia	Symbol Brand
Designer perception	Visceral Function	Behavioral Design	Reflective Feeling
Maker perception	Feasibility OEM	Viability ODM	Desirability OBM

Fig. 1. Study framework

performance in this study. The "use" to "user" was generated from product "qualia factors" that included practical function, aesthetics, and emotional connection (Lin 2014). The "function" to "feeling" was generated from "visceral level of emotional design" that included visceral, behavioral, and reflective (Norman 2004). The "hi-tech" to "hi-touch" was generated from "design thinking" that included feasibility, viability, and desirability (Brown 2008) (Fig. 1).

3.2 Research Process and Tools

Three steps were involved in this study: (1) screening domestic and international brands with manufacturing capabilities; (2) performing measurements to confirm the reliability and validity of the questionnaire before conducting the survey; and (3) conducting the formal survey.

Selection of brands and products: This phase consisted of the selection and filtering of the brands tested. Two steps were involved in this phase: (1) Because this study aimed to understand product function, design, and feeling factors (the emotional atmospheres created by the products) in the current market, 100 large companies in Taiwan and well-known international brands were referenced, and 50 brands with manufacturing capabilities were selected. (2) Expert groups were invited to perform investigations of brand familiarity, and the top 13 brands were selected, as shown in Table 1.

Measuring scales for product function, design, and feeling factors (the emotional atmospheres created by the products): In this study, the survey questions on the product function (need), design (want), and feeling (desire) factors were based on literature review. Each variable had six questions, as shown in Table 2. All the questions in Table 2 are the same as those in Table 3 but pertain to different measurement variables (Fig. 2).

Measuring scales for users, designers, and makers: In this study, the survey questions on user, designer, and maker perception factors were based on the literature

Table 1. Experimental subjects

review. Each variable had six questions, as shown in Table 3. All the questions in Table 3 are the same as those in Table 2 but pertain to different measurement variables.

Table 2. Variables of the product function, design and feeling questionnaire

Position		Measurement variables	Description of items		Theoretical sources
1	The upper left cell	Product function (need)	PFU1	The product of this brand is easy to use	Yen et al. (2014a, b)
			PFU2	This brand has durable products	
4	The middle left cell		PFU3	The product of this brand has good appearance form	Norman (2004), Hsiao and Chen (2010)
			PFU4	The product of this brand has meticulous modeling structure	
7	The lower left cell		PFU5	This brand has a sophisticated production technology	Tzokas et al. (2004), Brown (2008)
			PFU6	The product of this brand has good quality	Slater et al. (2011), Brown (2008)
2	The upper middle cell	Product design (want)	PDE1	The product of this brand has a sense of design	Yen et al. (2014a, b)
			PDE2	The product of this brand uses materials with ingenuity	
5	The center cell		PDE3	The product of this brand is easy to understand	Norman (2004), Hsiao and Chen (2010)
			PDE4	The product of this brand can produce feelings of pleasure	
8	The lower middle cell		PDE5	The product of this brand has clear idea and meet customer needs	Khurana and Rosenthal (1998), Brown (2008)
			PDE6	The product of this brand has innovated	Slater et al. (2011), Brown (2008)
3	The upper right cell	Product feeling (desire)	PFE1	The product of this brand has the story	Yen et al. (2014a, b)
			PFE2	The product of this brand has the fashion sense	
6	The middle right cell		PFE3	The product of this brand contains some implications	Norman (2004), Hsiao and Chen (2010)
			PFE4	The product of this brand has attractive and memorable	Norman (2004), Ashby and Johnson (2003)
9	The lower right cell		PFE5	The product of this brand is differentiated and uniqueness	Ranscombe et al. (2012), Brown (2008)
			PFE6	The product of this brand has brand recognition	Brown (2008)

Table 3. Variables of the users perception, designers perception and makers perception

Position		Measurement variables	Description of items		Theoretical sources
1	The upper left cell	User perception	PFU1	The product of this brand is easy to use	Yen et al. (2014a, b)
			PFU2	This brand has durable products	
2	The upper middle cell		PDE1	The product of this brand has a sense of design	
			PDE2	The product of this brand uses materials with ingenuity	
3	The upper right cell		PFE1	The product of this brand has the story	
			PFE2	The product of this brand has the fashion sense	
4	The middle left cell	Designer perception	PFU3	The product of this brand has good appearance form	Norman (2004), Hsiao and Chen (2010)
			PFU4	The product of this brand has meticulous modeling structure	
5	The center cell		PDE3	The product of this brand is easy to understand	Norman (2004), Hsiao and Chen (2010)
			PDE4	The product of this brand can produce feelings of pleasure	
6	The middle right cell		PFE3	The product of this brand contains some implications	Norman (2004), Hsiao and Chen (2010)
			PFE4	The product of this brand has attractive and memorable	Norman (2004), Ashby and Johnson (2003)
7	The lower left cell	Maker perception	PFU5	This brand has a sophisticated production technology	Tzokas et al. (2004), Brown (2008)
			PFU6	The product of this brand has good quality	Slater et al. (2011), Brown (2008)
8	The lower middle cell		PDE5	The product of this brand has clear idea and meet customer needs	Khurana and Rosenthal (1998), Brown (2008)
			PDE6	The product of this brand has innovated	Slater et al. (2011), Brown (2008)
9	The lower right cell		PFE5	The product of this brand is differentiated and uniqueness	Ranscombe et al. (2012), Brown (2008)
			PFE6	The product of this brand has brand recognition	Brown (2008)

	Needs	Wants	Desires
User perception	1 **PFU1.** The product of this brand is easy to use. **PFU2.** This brand has durable products.	2 **PDE1.** The product of this brand has a sense of design **PDE2.** The product of this brand uses materials with ingenuity	3 **PFE1.** The product of this brand has the story **PFE2.** The product of this brand has the fashion sense
Design perception	4 **PFU3.** The product of this brand has good appearance form **PFU4.** The product of this brand has meticulous modeling structure	5 **PDE3.** The product of this brand is easy to understand **PDE4.** The product of this brand can produce feelings of pleasure	6 **PFE3.** The product of this brand contains some implications **PFE4.** The product of this brand has attractive and memorable
Maker perception	7 **PFU5.** This brand has a sophisticated production technology **PFU6.** The product of this brand has good quality	8 **PDE5.** The product of this brand has clear idea and meet customer needs **PDE6.** The product of this brand has innovated	9 **PFE5.** The product of this brand is differentiated and uniqueness **PFE6.** The product of this brand has brand recognition

Fig. 2. Tables 2 and 3 comparison chart

3.3 Preliminary Verification

Seventy undergraduates with a background in advertising and marketing were invited to participate in this study, and 63 valid questionnaires were returned. A 7-point Likert scale was used in the experiment, in which 1 point indicated that the sample did not have emotional appeal or did not look or feel comfortable, 4 points indicated that the sample was moderate in its emotional appeal or looked or felt fairly comfortable, and 7 points indicated that the sample possessed strong emotional appeal or looked or felt extremely comfortable. Confirmatory factor analysis was conducted using SPSS 22.0, and the results were as follows. Questionnaire reliability: A substantial interrater reliability of .95 ($p < .001$) was achieved by each dimension and the overall scale of the product function, design, and feeling questionnaire.

Questionnaire validity: The matrix of factor loadings of each question of the product function, design, and feeling questionnaire of the longitudinal 3×3 grid was greater than 0.85, and the variance explained for each dimension of the product function, design, and feeling questionnaire was greater than 85 %. The matrix of factor loadings of each question of the product function, design, and feeling questionnaire of the transverse 3×3 grid was greater than 0.80, and the variance explained for each dimension of the product function, design, and feeling questionnaire was greater than 80 %. The questionnaire reliability and validity are shown in Tables 4 and 5.

Correlation coefficient analysis: The Pearson product-moment correlation coefficients were computed to assess the relationship between each of the networks and variables (N = 63 for all tests; Tables 6 and 7).

Grouping analysis: Confirmatory grouping analysis of the official samples was performed during this stage. The brands' product function, design, and feeling, which

Table 4. The questionnaire reliability and questionnaire validity of longitudinal of 3 × 3 grid (N = 63).

Measurement variables	Items	Cronbach's α	Factor	Variance explained
Product function (need)	PFU1	0.984	0.933	92.691 %
	PFU2		0.971	
	PFU3		0.971	
	PFU4		0.953	
	PFU5		0.966	
	PFU6		0.982	
Product design (want)	PDE1	0.980	0.966	90.810 %
	PDE2		0.913	
	PDE3		0.964	
	PDE4		0.963	
	PDE5		0.969	
	PDE6		0.942	
Product feeling (desire)	PFE1	0.970	0.892	86.990 %
	PFE2		0.944	
	PFE3		0.967	
	PFE4		0.956	
	PFE5		0.963	
	PFE6		0.870	

Table 5. The questionnaire reliability and questionnaire validity of transverse of 3 × 3 grid (N = 63).

Measurement variables	Items	Cronbach's α	Factor	Variance explained
Users perception	PFU1	0.953	0.860	82.019 %
	PFU2		0.952	
	PDE1		0.971	
	PDE2		0.919	
	PFE1		0.837	
	PFE2		0.888	
Designers perception	PFU3	0.977	0.942	90.015 %
	PFU4		0.943	
	PDE3		0.953	
	PDE4		0.966	
	PFE3		0.930	
	PFE4		0.959	
Makers perception	PFU5	0.982	0.978	92.016 %
	PFU6		0.965	
	PDE5		0.974	
	PDE6		0.956	
	PFE5		0.963	
	PFE6		0.918	

Table 6. The matrix of correlation coefficients of longitudinal of 3 × 3 grid (N = 63)

	Mean	SD	1	2	3
1. Product function (need)	5.423	0.915	0.984		
2. Product design (want)	5.311	0.882	0.958[a]	0.980	
3. Product feeling (desire)	5.178	0.894	0.892[a]	0.957[a]	0.970

[a]Level of significance is 0.01 (Two-tailed), Significantly related. Diagonal: Cronbach's alpha

Table 7. The matrix of correlation coefficients of transverse of 3 × 3 grid (N = 63)

	Mean	SD	1	2	3
1. Users perception	5.280	0.899	0.953		
2. Designers perception	5.284	0.884	0.976[a]	0.977	
3. Makers perception	5.348	0.871	0.965[a]	0.987[a]	0.982

[a]Level of significance is 0.01 (Two-tailed),Significantly related. Diagonal: Cronbach's alpha

Fig. 3. Comparison of the overall average

constituted the major focus of our study, were investigated. This stage involved 208 participants, who were all familiar with the brands included in our study. If participants gave blank answers or omitted a high number of questions, their results were discarded. Ultimately, 203 valid results were obtained. Most of the participants were between the ages of 21 and 30 and had university degrees. Grouping analysis was conducted using SPSS 22.0.

4   Results and Discussion

Comparison of the overall average: A comparison of the overall average and a median average configuration were confirmed to construct the grouping, as shown in Fig. 3.

Comparison of the average of longitudinal and transverse 3 × 3 grids: The averages of the six questions of each longitudinal and transverse 3 × 3 grid were compared with one another for each brand. The highest score of the longitudinal 3 × 3 grid achieved a position with the highest score of the transverse 3 × 3 grid achieved a position. The location of each brand was determined at the intersection of the two positions, as shown in Tables 8 and 9 and Fig. 4.

Each cell of the 3 × 3 grid was compared with one another: Each cell of the 3 × 3 grid of two questions' average was compared for each brand, and the highest score of the 3 × 3 grid achieved a position of each single one brand, as shown in Figs. 5 and 6.

Table 8. The average of each brand of transverse of 3 × 3 grid.

Brand	Function (Need)	Design (Want)	Feeling (Desire)
ASUS	4.98***	4.78***	4.51***
Tatung	5.47***	5.02***	5.09***
IKEA	5.50***	5.83***	5.57***
ACER	4.97***	4.76***	4.56***
PHILIPS	5.30***	5.03***	4.84***
HTC	5.20***	5.17***	5.04***
MUJI	5.88***	5.95***	5.87***
Giant	6.04***	5.68***	5.57***
Apple	6.09***	6.13***	6.21***
Franz	5.58***	5.51***	5.61***
Sony	5.76***	5.49***	5.39***
Alessi	5.25***	5.29***	5.31***
BenQ	4.82***	4.57***	4.44***

Table 9. The average of each brand of transverse of 3 × 3 grid.

Brand	User perception	Designer perception	Maker perception
ASUS	4.70***	4.67***	4.90***
Tatung	5.16***	5.08***	5.35***
IKEA	5.643***	5.62***	5.644***
ACER	4.702***	4.700***	4.89***
PHILIPS	5.02***	4.98***	5.18***
HTC	5.088***	5.089***	5.23***
MUJI	5.88***	5.90***	5.91***
Giant	5.73***	5.71***	5.85***
Apple	5.98***	6.13***	6.31***
Franz	5.44***	5.59***	5.67***
Sony	5.45***	5.53***	5.65***
Alessi	5.29***	5.18***	5.37***
BenQ	4.58***	4.55***	4.71***

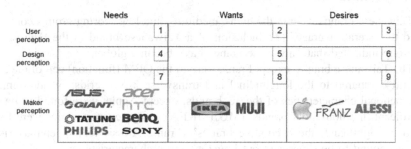

	Needs	Wants	Desires
User perception	1	2	3
Design perception	4	5	6
Maker perception	7 ASUS GIANT TATUNG PHILIPS acer hTC BenQ SONY	8 IKEA MUJI	9 Apple FRANZ ALESSI

Fig. 4. The location of each brand

ASUS

5.03	4.71	4.36
4.78	4.84	4.38
5.13	4.78	4.79

TATUNG

5.95	4.72	4.80
4.91	5.34	4.98
5.55	5.00	5.50

IKEA

5.43	5.93	5.57
5.69	5.75	5.41
5.39	5.79	5.75

acer

4.94	4.68	4.49
4.87	4.85	4.39
5.11	4.77	4.80

BenQ

4.83	4.51	4.39
4.71	4.63	4.31
4.93	4.58	4.63

PHILIPS

5.27	5.11	4.68
5.26	4.99	4.68
5.38	4.92	5.15

hTC

5.16	5.17	4.94
5.20	5.22	4.84
5.23	5.12	5.33

MUJI

5.89	6.06	5.70
5.94	5.98	5.77
5.80	5.81	6.13

GIANT

5.95	5.74	5.51
5.98	5.74	5.42
6.19	5.57	5.77

Apple

5.62	6.24	6.09
6.37	6.04	5.99
6.28	6.11	6.55

FRANZ

4.96	5.77	5.59
5.894	5.39	5.48
5.892	5.36	5.75

SONY

5.59	5.53	5.24
5.77	5.51	5.31
5.91	5.44	5.61

ALESSI

4.91	5.68	5.29
5.43	4.91	5.20
5.40	5.27	5.45

Fig. 5. Each cell of 3 × 3 grid of two questions' average compared each other of every single one brand.

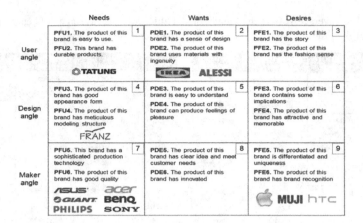

Fig. 6. The position of each single one brand

5 Conclusion

This study reached three conclusions.

(1) Taiwanese brands were in the high-, medium-, and low-scoring groups compared to the overall average. The inclusion of a Taiwanese brand in the high-scoring group indicated that Taiwanese brands have become global.
(2) The Taiwanese brands, except Franz, were in the OEM (function) cell of the 3 × 3 grid compared to the longitudinal and transverse 3 × 3 grids. In addition, the functional characteristics of the 3C brands, except Apple, were found to be significant; the household brands' (MUJI, IKEA) design characteristics were found to be significant; the decorative brands' (Franz, Alessi) feeling characteristics were found to be significant but Franz's feeling characteristics.
(3) Most Taiwanese brands were in the OEM (function) cell of the 3 × 3 grid based on a comparison of the results of each 3 × 3 grid. The Taiwanese brands had sophisticated production technology, and the products were of high quality. Among the Taiwanese brands, HTC had particular uniqueness and brand recognition among consumers.

Through the previous results and the distributions of brands in the study framework, the global position of Taiwan's brands can be compared with those of global brands. The results were presented herein to provide an interface for examining Taiwanese design development across cultures and illustrate the relationship between local design and the global market in Taiwan's economy, industry, and design development. The power of innovation inspires designers and managers to develop successful new products and services. For designers, the product is the most direct medium connecting the designer and the consumer, and the designer's creativity must be transferred through product design to consumers. For managers, successful innovative products should have clear and definite properties and target markets. An innovative product is commercially successful only when it is accepted by consumers in quantities sufficient to return a satisfactory profit to the manufacturer.

Acknowledgements. The authors gratefully acknowledge the support for this research provided by the Ministry of Science and Technology under Grant No. MOSY-103-2410-H-144-003 and MOST-103-2221-E-144-001.

References

Ashby, M., Johnson, K.: The art of materials selection. Mater. Today **6**(12), 24–35 (2003)

Bermond, B.: The emotional feeling as a combination of two qualia: a neurophilosophical-based emotion theory. Cogn. Emot. **22**(5), 897–930 (2008)

Brown, T.: Design thinking. Harvard Bus. Rev. **86**(6), 84 (2008)

Davis, S.M.: Brand Asset Management: Driving Profitable Growth Through Your Brands. Jossey-Bass, San Francisco (2000)

Gobe, M.: Emotional Branding. Allworth Press, New York (2009)

Hsiao, K.A., Chen, P.Y.: Cognition and shape features of pleasure images. J. Des. **15**(2), 1–17 (2010). (in Chinese, semantic translation)

IDEO: IDEO website. http://www.ideo.com/about/ (2012)

Keller, K.L.: Conceptualizing, measuring, and managing customer-based brand equity. J. Mark. **57**, 1–22 (1993)

Khurana, A., Rosenthal, S.R.: Towards holistic "front ends" in new product development. J. Prod. Innov. Manage **15**(1), 57–74 (1998)

Kumar, M., Townsend, J.D., Vorhies, D.W.: Enhancing consumers' affection for a brand using product design. J. Prod. Innov. Manage. (2014). doi:10.1111/jpim.12245

Levy, S.J.: Symbols for sale. Harvard Bus. Rev. **37**(4), 117–124 (1959)

Lin, R.: From curatorial design to creative brokerage. J. Des. **18**(4), 1–9 (2013). (in Chinese, semantic translation)

Lin, R.: Cultivate Oneself, Put the Family in Order, Govern the State, and Pacify the World. Rungtai Lin, Taipei (2014). (in Chinese, semantic translation)

McLoone, H., Jacobson, M., Goonetilleke, R.S., Kleiss, J., Liu, Y., Schütte, S.: Product design and emotion: frameworks, methods, and case studies. In: Proceedings of the Human Factors and Ergonomics Society Annual Meeting, vol. 56, no. 1, pp. 1940–1941. SAGE Publications (2012)

Norman, D.A.: Emotional Design: Why We Love (or Hate) Everyday Things, pp. 63–98. Basic Books, New York (2004)

Plattner, H., Meinel, C., Leifer, L.: Design Thinking: Understand–Improve–Apply. Springer, Berlin (2010)

Ranscombe, C., Hicks, B., Mullineux, G., Singh, B.: Visually decomposing vehicle images: exploring the influence of different aesthetic features on consumer perception of brand. Des. Stud. **33**(4), 319–341 (2012)

Redstrom, J.: Towards user design? On the shift from object to user as the subject of design. Des. Stud. **27**(2), 123e139 (2006)

Slater, S.F., Olson, E.M., Finnegan, C.: Business strategy, marketing organization culture, and performance. Mark. Lett. **22**(3), 227–242 (2011)

Tzokas, N., Hultink, E.J., Hart, S.: Navigating the new product development process. Ind. Mark. Manage. **33**(7), 619–626 (2004)

Wang, H.X., Chen, J., Hu, Y.C. Ye, M.: The consistency of product design and brand image. In: Computer-Aided Industrial Design and Conceptual Design, pp. 1142–1144 (2008)

Yen, H.Y., Lin, P.H., Lin, R.: A study of cultural products and the characteristics of qualia. In: The Design Research Society's 2014 conference, Umeå University, Sweden, 16–19 June 2014a

Yen, H.Y., Lin, P.H., Lin, R.: Cognition and product features of emotional branding. In: The Kansei Engineering and Emotion Research international conference, Linköping University, Sweden, 11–13 June 2014b

Research on Service-Driven Feature of Industrial Designers Under the Background of Industry Convergence

Qing Zhang[1], Chen Cheng[2(⊠)], Junnan Ye[1], and Wei Ding[1]

[1] School of Art Design and Media, East China University of Science and Technology, M.BOX 286 No. 130, Meilong Road, Xuhui, Shanghai 200237, China
zhangq@ecust.edu.cn, yejunnan971108@qq.com, dw.6789@163.com
[2] Shanghai Institute of Technology, No. 120, Caobao Road, Xuhui, Shanghai 200233, China
caca_hyuk@163.com

Abstract. Over the past thirty years of development, China has become a strong economic power and manufacturer, and entered the middle stage of the development of industrialization. However, the deficiency in the innovation capability has become a serious obstacle restricting China's development. As one of the eight industries in modern service, industrial design has been ranked as key development strategies in China. How to further reinforce industrial designers' awareness of modern design service, strengthen the understanding of the service-driven feature, and better satisfy the society's demands for industrial design of the time under the background of industry convergence; how to assist enterprises and customers realizing innovative transformation through industrial designers' design service in technological means; how to really exert the value of design in industry through industrial designers' philosophy in design service by means of coordination and innovation in a "harmonious and smooth" mode will be another issue of critical concern in the industrial design field.

In the background of industry convergence, the paper has combed evolution of design service contents and new development of industrial designers from the early 19th century to now. Based on literature review, the paper has summarized the specific work contents of the current industrial designers and then put forward the contents of three-layer service-driven characteristics of industrial designers: firstly, driving the transformation and upgrade of traditional manufacturing industries by design power; secondly, helping manufacturing industries to shape brand by design innovation; thirdly, accelerating the transferring of scientific and technological achievements and linking technology with market. In study, the paper has found that industrial designers should become joint and mutual adhesive with various experts of the enterprise. Based on the training of service awareness of innovative design, application of comprehensive perceptual test means, establishment of design concept of collaborative innovation and others, industrial designers can better serve enterprise manufacturer and consumer. In the meantime, the industrial designer's responsibility consciousness should be transformed from simple delegate object to society and from

P.L.P. Rau (Ed.): CCD 2015, Part I, LNCS 9180, pp. 128–138, 2015.
DOI: 10.1007/978-3-319-20907-4_12

simple service-oriented design to organization-oriented design, that is, from customer subject consciousness to social subject consciousness.

Keywords: Industry convergence · Industrial designer · Design service · Service-driven

1 Introduction

In the background of rapid development of economic globalization and new and hi-tech industries, industrial structure emerges the trend of diversification and complication. In order to further improve enterprise's production efficiency and competitiveness, different industries or different industries in the same industry mutually penetrate and intercross, and gradually converge and develop into new development mode or industrial organization form, which is industry convergence. Industry convergence can be divided into three types of industrial penetration, industrial intersection and industrial restructuring. In the background, a large number of new industries, new type of business, new technology and new mode ("four-news" for short) are born. It becomes an important research topic that how traditional entrepreneurs break through traditional management idea and old mode of thinking and explore the development and management innovative mode of new industries and truly realize the industrial transformation in face of the above-mentioned new things and new economic development trend.

Over the past 30-odd years of development, China has become a strong economic power and manufacturing power and entered the medium term of industrialization development. However, the deficiency in the innovative capability has also become a serious obstacle which restricts China's development. As one of the eight industries in modern service industry, innovative cultural industry has been listed on China' development strategy. On March 14th, 2014, the State Council's Some Opinions about Promoting the Integrative Development of Cultural Innovative Industry and Design Service and the Corresponding Industries issued by China's State Council, focused on the importance of cultural creation and design service and development path of "industry convergence", and also put forward a new topic that how service-driven characteristics of industrial designers effectively worked in the background of industry convergence.

Industrial design is the important technical means by which original equipment manufacturer (OEM) can turn into original design manufacturer (ODM) and then into original brand manufacturer. For modern industrial designers, industrial design is not the simple creative activity, and involves various disciplines such as machinery, materials, information, social psychology, statistics, marketing, building and resource and environment. In 2006, International Industrial Design Association pointed out in the latest industrial design that industrial design aimed at a comprehensive and creative activity, including utensil form, processing procedure, design service and system related to the entire human life, and was the key factor of humanization of innovative technology and cultural and economic exchanges.

Industrial design faces another important topic on how to further strengthen service awareness of modern design of industrial designers and the understanding of service-driven characteristics, and better satisfy the social demands of the time on industrial designers in the background of industry convergence; how to realize technically innovative transformation of the enterprise by design service of industrial designers; how to truly play the value of design value in the industry.

2 Evolution and New Development of Design Service Contents of Industrial Designer

2.1 Evolution of Design Service Contents of Industrial Designer

Industrial designers' role keeps evolving in the enterprise. With the rise of mass production in the 19th century, industrial designers began to emerge in the manufacturing industry and often served as product inventor or engineer. In 1919, Staatliches School (Staatliches Bauhaus) was founded in Weimar, Germany, and established a set of complete design education curriculum, which marked that design became an independent discipline. The core idea of Bauhaus is "the unity of arts and technology" in design, and still has profound influence now (Catherine Best 2008) [21].

From the 1920s to 1950s, with the wide recognition of the Bauhaus though in the world, the profession of industrial designer began to emerge, and industrial designers mainly designed beautiful, fashionable and durable products to satisfy consumer needs.

From the 1960s to 1970s, industrial designers became more professional. At the moment, there were many famous design organizations, such as Japan Industrial Design Association, (America) Aspen International Design Association. These associations provided industrial designers with exchange platform; in the meantime, they also promoted the form of design culture worldwide.

In the 1980s, industrial designers began to realize the important role of brand in the enterprise. Famous design companies, such as Alessi, Gucci and Ralph Lauren were founded in this period, and industrial design activities in Britain were also launched at this stage.

In the 1990s, industrial designers began to become the link between market demand and product development, and took as their main tasks how to effectively analyze the market demand information and convert it into a reasonable product. At this time, it became an important research topic that how industrial designers effectively cooperated with other technical personnel in the enterprise.

After 2000, industrial designers began to become the leader of enterprise product development, grasp product design process in all directions and coordinate the tasks of all links such as market, technology, manufacture and publicity (Table 1).

2.2 New Development of Industrial Designers in the Background of Industry Convergence

The rapid development of network technology has an impact on design service of industrial designer from design environment, design methods and tools, design objects, design thought and other aspects. In the background of industry convergence, new

Table 1. Evolution of main tasks of industrial designers

Period	Main task of industrial designers
The early 19th century	Unification of art and technology, auxiliary function of product manufacturing
The 1920s and 50s	Design becomes a kind of occupation. Designers produce beautiful, fashionable and durable products according to the demands of consumer
The 1960s and 70s	Design becomes a kind of major. Based on the original design, designers promote to form design culture in the world
The 1980s	Based on the original design, designers become the leader of brand
The 1990s	Based on the original design, designers effectively analyze market demand information and convert it into reasonable products
After 2000	Designers comprehensively grasp design process of products, and coordinate the tasks of each link such as market, technology, manufacturing and publicity

development of design service of industrial designer is mainly embodied in the following aspects:

Firstly, in the background of industry convergence, innovation is the important technical means, and will bring the enterprise huge economic benefits. And industrial designer is just the organizer and performer of the creative activity, will get higher and higher position in the enterprise in the future and become the important talent safeguard of the enterprise in the competition.

Secondly, with the continuous improvement of people's living standards, people obtain the satisfaction of the basic material needs; in the meantime, they more urgently need to obtain the satisfaction of products or personalized spiritual needs of services. It is the higher requirement for industrial designers that how they obtain the latest science and technology, the information of market changes and consumer needs, and put forward the best personalized design plan at the fastest speed in the basis of manufacturing ability of enterprise design.

Thirdly, with the arrival of the era of big data, industrial designers not only take physical product design as design object, but also include all aspects of periphery of product design, such as brand design, service design and interactive design.

3 Cooperative Work Contents of Industrial Designers in the Background of Industrial Convergence—Prona Illumination Design as an Example

In the background of industry convergence, service mode of traditional design has changed, and design will become transboundary fusion that serves "new technology, new industry, new type of business and new mode", and thus industrial design plus information plus brand and business model innovation will be the effective collaborative innovation design. In November, 2014, "Prona" intelligent illumination system designed by Torjan Horse was newly displayed at China International Industry Fair, see Fig. 1. As one of application projects of public service of intelligent city construction, it gathers photovoltaic power generation, LED illumination, micro base station, urban video probe, multimedia advertising, information release, intelligent interaction, convenience services, charging piles and other equipments, and thus realizes the fact that city streetlight is not only lighting tool, but also has communication equipment and city information platform of the information interaction system and management and supervision system of city network. Led by design, Prona intelligent illumination product is new integrated innovative achievement, and involves many industrial areas such as industrial design, energy-saving technology, electronic message, mobile communications, and digital application. Among them, industrial designer plays an important role and better explains specific collaborative work contents of industrial designer in the background of industry convergence.

Fig. 1. Product renderings of scheme C product of Prona intelligent illumination

Collaborative design of "Prona" intelligent illumination system is mainly run by innovative league as main unit. Based on innovative league as core layer, it cooperates with Torjan Horse design, Lin Stone technology, Xin Yi technology and Hua Wei and other industrial designs, energy-saving technology, electronic message, mobile communications, digital application and other enterprises, and does product strategic cooperation, that is, strategic cooperation layer. By effectively collaborating with the industries in many ways, it has got sharing application in five aspects of innovative design, applied technology, information application, marketing promotion and operation and maintenance of the project, namely, sharing application layer, and thus realized product's expanded application, superposed software, implanted hardware and other functions. Finally, under the support of innovative league, innovative base, industry funds and personnel training base ("four in one" for short), it realizes the market operation of the product. See Fig. 2.

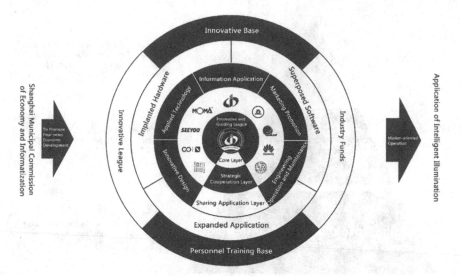

Fig. 2. System diagram of development mode of collaborative design of "Prona" intelligent illumination system

In the background of industry convergence, industrial designer's work contents keep updating with the change of extension of design service contents, and the environment that has an impact on design service also keeps changing. As dissipative theory points out, in an open system far from equilibrium, by continuously changing material, energy, information with the outside and making the change of the outside condition get a certain threshold, the original disordered state turns into the ordered state in time, space or function [5]. Industrial designer's service-driven contents also refer to effectively integrate design resources inside and outside the enterprise and make the enterprise effectively collaborate the inner and exterior of the enterprise, and finally promote the promotion of innovative ability of the enterprise and get stronger competitiveness and economic benefits.

4 Three-Layer Service-Driven Characteristics of Industrial Designers

More and more enterprises have realized that design plays an important role in enterprise competition. Based on the research on evolution of design service contents and new development and work contents of industrial designers, the author has summarized and put forward three-layer service-driven characteristics of industrial designers in the background of industry convergence (Fig. 3).

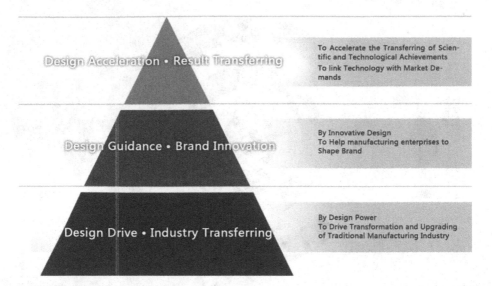

To Accelerate the Transferring of Scientific and Technological Achievements
To link Technology with Market Demands

By Innovative Design
To Help manufacturing enterprises to Shape Brand

By Design Power
To Drive Transformation and Upgrading of Traditional Manufacturing Industry

Design Acceleration • Result Transferring

Design Guidance • Brand Innovation

Design Drive • Industry Transferring

Fig. 3. Three-layer service-driven characteristics of industrial designers

4.1 Design Drives Industrial Upgrading

Innovation is the core element of industrial upgrade. By formative innovation, functional innovation, methodological innovation, cultural innovation and other innovative technological means, industrial designers do product innovation and finally realize the industrial upgrade of the manufacturing industry [11]. Famous Chinese design expert Mr. Xu Ping thinks that if design can pull and re integrate traditional manufacturing industry or service industry and form new industrial system with more innovative vitality and sensual charm, the then 'design' will turn into 'leading' type of business from the previous simple 'subordinate' type of business, and innovative, intuitive and preferred overall effect characteristics owned by design thinking will be amplified to the atmosphere of the whole new economic activity and creative development and get the promotion of humanized quality in the whole economic and cultural update and economic products in this sense [12].

Jointly promoted by Prof. Cheng Jianxin and Ding Wei etc. from School of Art Design and Media, East China University of Science and Technology and the government of Bao Ying County, Jiangsu Province, "County-based Design Plan" has become the important attempt of the Yangtze River Delta region to actively promote collaborative innovation development and realize that design drives industrial upgrading [20]. From there, we can found that industrial design is the core in innovative industries and knowledge economy. Only when industrial designers integrate advanced manufacturing technology, communication technological sources, traditional cultural resources, industrial resources and agricultural resources by innovative design, traditional manufacturing industry truly can realize industrial upgrading.

4.2 Design Leads Brand Innovation

Brand innovation means that with the change of enterprise business environment and consumer demand, brand connotation and manifestation also keep changing [13]. Brand innovation and protection can further promote enterprise market competitiveness, and brand value truly embodies enterprise soft power. When the enterprise grows to a certain stage, it undoubtedly needs the support of the brand, and industrial designer is the advocate and executor of brand innovation. Based on "family intelligent terminal" project developed jointly by our school and ZTE, the paper had found that design-led brand innovation can be embodied in the following aspects:

Image Update. In order to further promote enterprise competitiveness, the enterprise needs to determine own uniform image system, including Behavior identity (BI), mind identity (MI) and Visual identity (VI), which are the important tasks of industrial designers. And with the change of market and social environment, manifestation modes and marketing means also need to be constantly updated.

Product Innovation. While industrial designers establish the brand, they further improve the innovation on product shape, structure, color, technology, function, specifications, and so on according to the change of consumer demands; they particularly divide target market and accurately position the products, so that they can take effective product strategies.

To correctly make Good use of Brand Extension Strategy. Brand extension means that the enterprise promotes new products under the name of the original brand. Industrial designers can develop a series of products, and position brand on a series of products by the higher reputation of a brand and make many products share a brand. In this way, industrial designers not only ensure the smooth extension of the brand, but also make the original brand get a new appealing embodiment.

To expand Brand Promotion. Brand publicity and expansion have a direct impact on promotion and application of brand innovation. Industrial designers can adopt diversified means of publicity and ways of promotion and realize the comprehensive display of the brand and interaction between brand and customer. Only when brand is exchanged, it can win support among the people and has standing brand effect.

To Strengthen Trademark Management. In brand (trademark) innovation, the enterprise must establish and perfect brand management system, do good jobs of brand registration, filing, acceptance check and use, design the anti-fake label, set up brand management institution and brand protection network, appoint specialized management personnel, and faithfully implement the effective management of enterprise trademark right.

4.3 Design Accelerates the Transferring of Results

As a new product design concept and method, industrial design not only becomes the important method of market competitiveness, but also the powerful weapon of the economic development of the whole country and nation. Industrial design dynamically integrates realization of human demand and technological humanization, and becomes the bridge of the transferring of technological achievements [14]. Industrial designers scientifically and skillfully combine advanced scientific and technological achievements and market demand by creative thinking and put forward solutions and make them realistic, which is the process that design accelerates the technological achievements into products. Based on OLED product developed jointly by our school and Nanjing first Photoelectricity, the paper summarizes result conversion accelerated by design is mainly embodied in the following aspects:

Functionality Creation. Simple technological achievements only exist on paper or in the laboratory, and cannot enter into people's daily life. For example, the research and development of Nanjing OLED technology is also in the leading position in the world, but cannot be applied to specific life products. At this time, based on the analysis of consumer demand, industrial designers do social adjustment and reorganization of technological achievements, create new function and target products that meet the demands of consumers, and thus realize functionality creation of the products and accelerate result transformation.

To Create Beauty in Form. Like OLED technology, if such modern hi-tech achievements are not innovatively designed, they cannot directly face consumers at all. The creation of beauty in form means that industrial designers effectively combine simple technological achievements and aesthetic form of products by industrial design technology, and thus realize the high-tech sense consistent with the inherent quality and aesthetic form consistent with operative function of products. See Fig. 4.

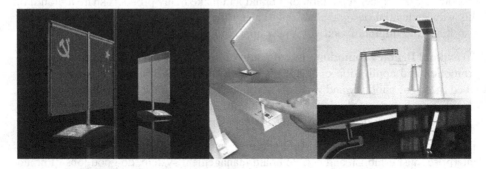

Fig. 4. Design plans of parts of OLED table lamp

To Create New Way of Life. People's way of life depends on the corresponding social material conditions. Product design is equal to people's behavior style design with the help of product, which will have a direct impact on people's daily life. The transformation of technological achievements means that industrial designers create way of life consistent with public value system and achieve the goal that new technology and new products are recognized by society by instillation and guidance.

5 Conclusion and Outlook

In the background of industry convergence, the paper has combed evolution of design service contents and new development of industrial designers from the early 19th century to now. Based on literature review, the paper has summarized the specific work contents of the current industrial designers and then put forward the contents of three-layer service-driven characteristics of industrial designers: firstly, driving the transformation and upgrade of traditional manufacturing industries by design power; secondly, helping manufacturing industries to shape brand by design innovation; thirdly, accelerating the transferring of scientific and technological achievements and linking technology with market.

In study, the paper has found that industrial designers should become joint and mutual adhesive with various experts of the enterprise. Based on the training of service awareness of innovative design, application of comprehensive perceptual test means, establishment of design concept of collaborative innovation and others, industrial designers can better serve enterprise manufacturer and consumer. In the meantime, the industrial designer's responsibility consciousness should be transformed from simple delegate object to society and from simple service-oriented design to organization-oriented design, that is, from customer subject consciousness to social subject consciousness, which is the organizational process of design behavior, and can be further deeply developed in the future academic research.

References

1. Yang, X.: Reflection on value of industrial designer of a new era. Design **10** (2014)
2. Hua, Y., Pi, Y.: Research on development strategy of industrial design in the background of low carbon economy. Strategy and Decision. The 6th International Seminar on Soft Science, 2010 (x) 007
3. Zi, L.: Enterprise strategic thinking in industry convergence. Soft Sci. **2**, 80 (2003)
4. De Mozota, B.B.: Design Management: Using Design to Build Brand Value and Corporate Innovation. Allworth Press, New York (2003)
5. Gleick, J.: Chaos Theory: A New Science. Social Scientific Document Press (1991)
6. Chen, X.: Study on Evolution of Design-driven Creative Mechanism and Design Mode. Zhejiang University, Zhejiang (2011)
7. Cheng, J.: Design value needs to be verified in the industry. Design **203**, 6 (2014). (Beijing)
8. Cheng, J., Zhang, Z.: Train innovative talents by collaborative way—exploration of training mode of industrial design undergraduate in the background of industry convergence. Design (Theor. Issue) **203**, 115–117 (2014)
9. Cheng, J.: Collaborative innovation—indicate icebreaking ways for the training of innovative design talents. In: Scientific and Artistic Convergence. The 2013 International Seminar Essays of Interdisciplinary Collaborative Innovative Design, The China Academy of Fine Arts Press, Beijing (2013)
10. Zhang, Q., Ye J.: Competition tests the ability of actual combat, and innovation casts design soul. In: The 2012 Excellent Graduation Works Set of Design and Innovation of Shanghai Universities, pp. 8–10, Shanghai (2012)

11. Keheng, Z.: Model analysis of industry upgrading Changzhou equipment manufacturing industry promoted by industrial design. Mech. Des. **6**, 123–125 (2013)
12. Xu, P.: Innovative economy: policy orientation and cultural selection. In: Industrial Design and Innovative Industry—Selected Thesis of Industrial Design Branch of China Association for Science and Technology Annual Meeting, p. 166. Mechanical Industry Press, Beijing (2007)
13. Cheng, Z.: Motivation and strategies of brand innovation. Manage. Modernization **6**, 39–40 (2014)
14. Zhu, H.: Industrial design—bridge of transformation of technology achievements. Electromech. Eng. **17**(1), 6–8 (2000)
15. Farr, M.: Design Management. Hodder and Stoughton, Warwick (1996)
16. Huang, W., et al.: Design Management: European and American Classical Cases. Design Management Association. Polytechnic University Press (2008)
17. INNO-GRIPS: Global Review of Innovation Intelligence and Policy Studies (2008)
18. Jacoby, R., Rodriguez, D.: Innovation, growth, and getting to where you want to go. Des. Manage. Rev. **18**(1), 10–20 (2007)
19. Jenkins, J.: Creating the right environment for design. Des. Manage. Rev. **19**(3), 16–22 (2008)
20. Zhang, H., Ye, J.: Plan the development of small and medium-sized enterprises from the perspective of design management—development program of crystal enterprises in Baoying county, Jiangsu province as an example. Chin. Sci. Technol. Aspect **10**, 259–260 (2014)
21. Catherine Best: Advanced tutorial of The American design management, Shanghai people's fine arts publishing house (2008)

Cross-Cultural Design Methods
and Case Studies

Comparison of User Responses to English and Arabic Emotion Elicitation Video Clips

Nawal Al-Mutairi[1]($^{\boxtimes}$), Sharifa Alghowinem[2,3], and Areej Al-Wabil[1]

[1] King Saud University, College of Computer and Information Sciences,
Riyadh, Saudi Arabia
{nawalmutairi,aalwabil}@ksu.edu.sa
[2] Australian National University, Research School of Computer Science,
Canberra, Australia
sharifa.alghowinem@anu.edu.au
[3] Ministry of Education, Kingdom of Saudi Arabia, Riyadh, Saudi Arabia

Abstract. To study the variation in emotional responses to stimuli, different methods have been developed to elicit emotions in a replicable way. Using video clips has been shown to be the most effective stimuli. However, the differences in cultural backgrounds lead to different emotional responses to the same stimuli. Therefore, we compared the emotional response to a commonly used emotion eliciting video clips from the Western culture on Saudi culture with an initial selection of emotion eliciting Arabic video clips. We analysed skin physiological signals in response to video clips from 29 Saudi participants. The results of the validated English video clips and the initial Arabic video clips are comparable, which suggest that a universal capability of the English set to elicit target emotions in Saudi sample, and that a refined selection of Arabic emotion elicitation clips would improve the capability of inducing the target emotions with higher levels of intensity.

Keywords: Emotion classification · Basic emotions · Physiological signals · Electro-dermal activity · Skin temperature

1 Introduction

Recognizing emotions had a great interest lately, not only to create an intelligent and advanced affective computing system, but also to have a better understanding of human psychology, neurobiology and sociology. For instance, an intelligent tutoring application uses emotional states to interactively adjust the lessons' content and tutorial level. For example, an intelligent tutoring application could recommend a break when a fatigue sign is detected [1]. Another example is an emotion-responsive car, which detects drivers' state, such as level of stress, fatigue or anger that might impair their driving abilities [2]. Recognizing the emotional state has potential to play a vital role in different applied domains. For example, it can provide insights for helping psychologists diagnose depression [3], detect deception [1,4], and identify different neurological illnesses such as schizophrenia [5].

© Springer International Publishing Switzerland 2015
P.L.P. Rau (Ed.): CCD 2015, Part I, LNCS 9180, pp. 141–152, 2015.
DOI: 10.1007/978-3-319-20907-4_13

To study and build any emotion intelligent system, emotional responses have to be collected in a measurable and replicable way, where a standardized method to elicit emotions is required. There are several methods to elicit a universal emotional state [6]. The most effective way is through emotion elicitation video clips, where the most popular set of clips is Gross and Levenson's set [7].

However, researchers found that emotional expressions are different between cultures, which often rely on emotion triggers [8]. The essential differences between southern and northern Americans' reactions to the same emotion eliciting stimuli were explained in [8]. They reported three sources of variability: genes, environment and acquired different beliefs, values and skills [8]. Therefore, the same emotion elicitation stimuli could produce different results based on the subject's cultural background.

Studies that explore emotional responses to stimuli on Arab cultures are rare. Given the Arab conservative culture [9], it is not possible to predict the effect of the cultural acceptance of stimuli content to the emotional response. Therefore, in this paper we compare and evaluate emotional responses to emotion elicitation clips from a commonly used Western set [7] with an initially selected Arabic set.

2 Background

For the past few decades, affective state recognition has been an active research area and has been used in many contexts [1]. For example, emotion recognition research involved psychology, speech analysis, computer vision, machine learning and many others. With all the advantages that the diversity of these research areas introduce, it also comes with controversial approaches to achieve an accurate recognition of affect. For example, defining emotion is controversial due to the complexity of emotional processes. Psychologically, emotions are mixed with several terms such as affect and feeling. Moreover, emotions are typically conjoined with sensations, moods, desires and attitudes [10]. In [11], emotion was defined as spiritual and uncontrollable feelings that affect our behavior and motivation. In literature, emotional states have been divided into different categories such as positive and negative [12], and into dimensions such as valence and arousal dimension [13], as well as into a discreet set of emotions such as Ekman's basic emotions [14]. In this paper, we use Ekman's six basic emotions (happiness, sadness, surprise, fear, anger and disgust) [14]. This was mainly for its simplicity and its universality between cultures, which would reduce variability that might affect this investigation of cultural differences [8].

Emotions can be expressed via several channels and the most common channels are facial expressions and speech prosody [15]. Other channels include physiological signals such as: heart rate, skin conductivity, brain waves, etc. Physiological signals occur spontaneously, since they reflect the activity of the nervous system. Therefore, these signals cannot be suppressed as with the facial and vocal expressions. Ekman argued that emotions have discriminative pattern generated by the Autonomic Nervous System (ANS) [16]. These patterns reflect the changes in human physiological signals when different emotions were elicited. Ax was the first to observe that ANS response is different between fear and anger

[17]. This observation led to several attempts, which have been conducted, to analyse emotional physiological response patterns. In this work, we analyse skin conductivity as a physiological response to emotion elicitation, which include skin conductance and temperature.

Electro-dermal Activity (EDA) represents electrical changes in the skin due to the activity of sweat glands that draw input from the sympathetic nervous system. Several studies noted that high EDA is linked to increased emotional arousal [18,19], which has also been used as a polygraph lie indicator [4]. Moreover, high level of arousal is an indication of high difficulty of task level [20], challenge, frustration, and excitement [19]. EDA response to stimuli contains two measures: skin conductance level (SCL), which is a tonic reaction, and skin conducted response (SCR), which reflects phasic reactions. Researchers have found that tonic parameter is most likely to reveal the general state of arousal and alertness while phasic parameter is useful for studying attentional processes [21]. Interestingly, a significant increase of SCL is more responsive to negative emotions [22] especially those associated with fear [21,23] whereas a decrease is associated with pleasure emotion states [23].

Skin temperature fluctuates due to the change in blood flow caused by vascular resistance or arterial blood pressure. A complicated model of cardiovascular was used to describe arterial blood pressure variations, which is modulated by the autonomic nervous system. Therefore, skin temperature has been used as autonomic nervous system activity indicator, and as an effective indicator of emotional state. Using skin temperature measurements, several studies found that fear is characterized by a large decrease in skin temperature, while anger and pleasure is characterized by an increase in skin temperature [16,21,23].

Despite the various studies conducted on emotion expressions, studies on cultural differences in expressing emotions are still in their infancy. As an attempt to investigate the cultural aspect, eliciting emotions using the validated clips in [7] has been used in different cultures. In [24], 45 German subjects participated in a study by rating the elicited emotions from four video clips from [7] set. They concluded that the selected video clips were able to elicit the target emotions in German culture. Moreover, 31 Japanese volunteers were invited to watch English video clips selected from [7] that elicit six different emotions [25]. The study concluded that most of the video clips have a universal capability to elicit the target emotions. However, due to the unique characteristics of the Japanese culture, some of the clips have elicited non-target emotions as well. For example, one of the video clips that elicit amusement also induced surprise, interest, and embarrassment [25].

Given the differences of Arab culture compared with the Western and Japanese cultures, it is not clear whether the [7] set of emotional elicitation clips have the capability of eliciting the target emotions in Arab subjects. Therefore, in this work, we investigate and compare emotional responses to the clips in [7] with an initial selection of Arabic emotion elicitation clips on Saudi subjects. The purpose of the Arabic set is to investigate the cultural acceptance effect on the elicited emotions in comparison with the English set. For validation, skin physiological responses are measured and analysed to identify the differences between emotional responses in both English and Arabic emotion elicitation video clips.

Table 1. List of English [7] and Arabic film clips used as stimuli

Emotion	Clip	Total Duration (mm:ss)	Elicitation Start Time	Elicitation End Time
English Clips				
Amusement	"Bill Cosby, Himself"	02:00	00:12	02:00
Sadness	"The Champ"	02:44	00:55	02:44
Anger	"My Bodyguard"	03:24	00:15	03:24
Fear	"The Shining"	01:22	00:16	01:22
Surprise	"Capricorn One"	00:44	00:42	00:44
Disgust	Amputation of a hand	01:05	00:01	01:05
Arabic Clips				
Amusement	"Bye-Bye London"	02:54	00:16	02:54
Sadness	"Bu kreem with seven woman"	00:59	00:34	00:59
Anger	"Omar"	02:13	01:35	02:13
Fear	"Mother is a Basha"	00:50	00:09	00:49
Surprise	"Tagreebah Falestineeah"	00:45	00:37	00:45
Disgust	"Arab Got Talent"	00:30	00:05	00:30

3   Method

3.1   Stimuli and Data Collection

In this study, we investigate the six emotions suggested by Ekman [14]. To elicit these emotions, one video clip for each emotion was selected from [7] emotion elicitation clips. Even though the [7] set of video clips have more than one clip for each emotion with different levels of eliciting target emotions, the selected video clips in this study were based on complying to the Arabs' ethical and cultural constraints. Thus, the video clips used here are not selected based on the highest level of eliciting target emotions. For example, the 'When Harry MetSally' clip acquired the highest level to elicit amusement among two other clips [7]. However, this clip was perceived as inappropriate in the relatively conservative Saudi culture. For this reason, the second highest level of eliciting amusement acquired by the 'Bill Cosby, Himself' clip has been selected in this study, despite that it contains some cursing and disrespecting words. The final selected clips in this paper are shown in Table 1. In order to save original emotion expressions from the speech, clips were not dubbed, yet had Arabic subtitles. In addition to the selected English clips, initial Arabic clips set have been selected from a small poll of video clips gathered by the project team members. The selected clips are shown in Table 1.

While 29 volunteers were watching the emotion elicitation clips, skin response was measured using the Affectiva Q-sensor, which is a wireless wrist-worn sensor. All 29 participants in the sample were Saudi females, age ranged from 18-45 years, and all had normal or corrected-to-normal vision. Prior to the recording,

Table 2. Number of selected segments for each emotion

	Amusement	Sadness	Anger	Fear	Surprise	Disgust
English Clips	16	23	19	19	19	22
Arabic Clips	24	16	17	19	17	22

the aims and procedures were explained to the participants, then a consent and a demographic questionnaire were obtained individually.

An interface was coded to automatically show the 12 emotion elicitation clips (both English and Arabic) in a specific order. To reduce the emotional fluctuation between two different emotions, English video clips were played followed by Arabic video clips for the same emotion in the following order: amusement, sadness, anger, fear, surprise, and disgust. In order to clear the subject's mind, a five seconds count down black screen was shown between clips. Participants were asked to watch the video clips as they do at home and feel free to move their head. By the end of the recording, participants were asked to answer a post-questionnaire and rate the elicited emotions they felt while watching each clip. The emotion rating scale range from (0 not felt -10 felt strongly), which is a modified Likert scale [26]. Since not every video clip had elicited the target emotion in all participants, only segments where the participants have felt the target emotions are included in analysis (i.e. target emotion self-rating ≥ 1). This selection criteria gave an average of 22 segments per clip as detailed in Table 2.

3.2 Feature Preparation and Extraction

As mentioned earlier, the Affectiva Q-sensor was used to record the skin responses to emotional stimuli. The sensor was not attached to the computer, however, its raw data is time-stamped. Therefore, to prepare the data for analysis, the time-stamp was used to segment the data for each subject and each clip. This pre-processing step was performed offline using a Matlab code, which matches the time-stamped data with the starting time and duration of each clip for each subject's recording. Moreover, most video clips start with setting the scene and giving a background as preparation before eliciting the target emotion. Hence, in our analysis we only used the data from the clips where the target emotions were presumed to be elicited. The start and end time of each clip where the target emotions are elicited are presented in Table 1.

The Q-sensor records several raw data features in 32 sampling rate (32 fps). These raw features could be categorized as: (1)Electro-dermal activity features, and (2) skin temperature. As mentioned in the background section, the EDA features are divided into two main categories: skin conductance level and skin conductance response. In this work, we extract several statistical features from SCL, SCR and skin temperature data. Moreover, initial feature extraction and analysis from SCR data were performed, where none of the extracted features were effective for the analysis of emotional response, which is inline with the literature [21]. Therefore, only SCL and skin temperature are included in this study. From both SCL and skin temperature data, we extracted:

- Max, Min, Mean, Range, STD, and Variance (6 × 2).
- Max, Min, Means, Range, STD and variance of the slops (6 × 2).
- Max, Min and Average values of the peaks and valleys (3 × 2 × 2).
- Average number of peaks and valleys in second (1 × 2).
- Duration (number of frames) above and below a threshold (i.e. 0.01 for SCL and 37° for skin temperature) (2 × 2).
- Max, Min, Means, Range, STD and Variance of temperature velocity and acceleration (6×2×2).

3.3 Analysis and Classification

The extracted features were analysed using a one-way between groups analysis of variance (ANOVA). ANOVA is a statistical test to study the difference between groups on a variable. In our case, the test was one-way between groups ANOVA using the six emotions as the groups for each of the extracted features, with significance level $p <= 0.01$. ANOVA test was used here for two purposes: (1) to identify the features that significantly differentiate emotions, and (2) as a feature selection method to reduce the data dimensionality of the classification problem. To insure affair comparison, features extracted from the English and Arabic clips are analysed individually, and then the common features that are significantly different in all emotion groups in both languages are selected for the classification.

For classifying emotions automatically using the selected features, we used Support Vector Machine (SVM) classifier. SVM is one of the discriminative classifiers that separate classes based on the concept of decision boundaries. Lib SVM [27] was used as an implementation of SVM in this paper. To increase the accuracy of the classification result, SVM parameters must be adjusted. Therefore, we searched for the best gamma and cost parameters using a wide range grid search with radial basis function (RBF) kernel. The classification is performed in multiclass (6 emotion classes) in a subject-independent scenario. Since the SVM is mainly used to discriminate binary classes, we used one-verses-one approach for multiclass classification. In the one-verses-one approach, several SVMs are constructed to separate each pair of classes, and then a final decision is made by the majority voting of the constructed classifiers. Moreover, to mitigate the effect of the limited amount of data, a leave-one-segment-out cross-validation is used without any overlaps between training and testing data. Dealing with features of different scales a normalization is recommended, to ensure that each individual feature has an equal effect on the classification problem. In this work, we used Min-Max normalization, which scales the values between 0 to 1 and preserve the relationships in the data.

The emotion elicitation self-ratings of the target emotions reported by the subjects were statistically analysed to compare the English and Arabic video clips in emotion elicitation. To compare the emotion elicitation self-ratings of the target emotion from the two language group video clips, two-sample two-tailed t-test was used assuming unequal variance with Significance $p = 0.05$.

4 Results

To compare the emotion elicitation levels between the English and Arabic clips, the reported self-rating of target emotions were analysed statistically using T-test. The average self-rate of target emotions of each clip is illustrated in Fig. 1.

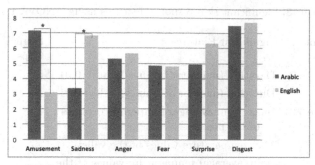

* indicates a statistically significant difference ($p < 0.05$)

Fig. 1. Average self-rate of the target emotion elicited by English and Arabic clips

Using T-test, only amusement and sadness clips were significantly different in eliciting the target emotion from Arabic and English video clips, as marked in Fig. 1. The results showed that both English and Arabic clips induced the target emotion similarly, with the exception of amusement and sadness clips. Moreover, this reveals that the English videos clips have a universal capability to induce the target emotions, with the exception of the amusement clip. For the complexity of jokes interpretation, it has been recommended to use amusement clips from participants' cultural background [28]. Furthermore, the similarity in inducing emotions from an initial set of Arabic emotion elicitation clips compared to the validated English clips, suggests that a refined selection of Arabic emotion elicitation clips might improve the levels and intensity of the induced emotions. A full framework for developing a refined selection of emotion elicitation clips for Arab participants has been suggested in [29].

In order to characterize the skin physiological changes in response to emotional stimuli, we statistically analyse the extracted features. Table 3 shows the features that are significantly different between emotions ($p \leqslant 0.01$) using ANOVA test in English and Arabic clips. Analysing EDA features, only the duration above and below the 0.01 threshold[1] were significant between emotions. This result is inline with [2], where the duration features of EDA has been found to be robust for emotion recognition. Moreover, analysing skin temperature features, several features were significantly different between emotions inline with [30]. An increase or a decrease in skin temperature associated with emotional states have been found in several studies [16,21,23]. Inline with these studies, skin temperature changes represented by velocity, acceleration and slop of the temperature values were statistically significant in this study to differentiate emotions. We have also used the normal body temperature (37°) as a threshold, where the duration of the temperature being below 37° was significantly different between emotions.

Moreover, the ANOVA test was performed on the extracted features from English and Arabic emotion elicitation clips individually (see Table 3). Most features were commonly significant between emotions in both English and Arabic

---

[1] Note that the threshold of 0.01 is widely used for the analysis of EDA signal [23].

Table 3. Significant skin response features using ANOVA test

Measurement	#	Significant Features	English Clips	Arabic Clips
EDA	2	Duration (number of frames) above 0.01	✓	✓
		Duration (number of frames) below 0.01	✓	✓
Temperature	21	(max, min, average) temperature values of the peaks	✓	✓
		Max temperature values of the valley	✓	✓
		(min, average) temperature values of the valley	✓	
		(range, STD) of temperature	✓	✓
		(variance) of temperature		✓
		(max, min, range) temperature velocity	✓	✓
		Mean temperature velocity		✓
		(max, min, range) temperature acceleration	✓	✓
		Max slop	✓	✓
		(min, mean, range) slop		✓
		Duration (number of frames) below 37°	✓	✓

STD: standard deviation

clip sets, which could suggest that both language video clip sets were able to elicit the target emotions. Arabic clips features had a few more features that were significant between emotions than the features extracted from English elicitation clips. These features include changes in temperature represented by velocity and slop statistical features (as shown in Table 3). On the other hand, only two features (minimum and mean of temperature valleys) were significant in English elicitation clips but not in Arabic elicitation clips. The differences in the significant features between English and Arabic emotion elicitation clips might be caused by the different levels of eliciting the target emotions.

In order to further compare and validate the EDA response to emotion elicitation from English and Arabic video clips, we classified the elicited six emotions using SVM. To ensure fair comparisons of English and Arabic clips classification, we used the common features that were significant between emotions using ANOVA in both English and Arabic clip sets (see Table 3). Figure 2 shows the confusion matrix of the multiclass emotion classification from Arabic and English clips individually.

Comparing the overall accuracy of classifying emotions from English and Arabic clips, English clips performed a higher classification accuracy (94 %) compared to the Arabic classification accuracy (70 %). The lower classification in the Arabic emotion elicitation clips might be caused by one of two reasons: (1) the level of eliciting the target emotion might not be consistent between subjects, or (2) more of the significant features in Arabic clips were not common with the

Arabic Clips

Emotion Class		Actual Labels					
		Amusement	Sadness	Anger	Fear	Surprise	Disgust
Predicted Labels	Amusement	96%	6%				
	Sadness	4%	29%	6%	5%	16%	48%
	Anger			82%	5%		
	Fear			12%	84%	5%	
	Surprise				5%	74%	4%
	Disgust		65%			5%	48%
						Accuracy	70%

English Clips

Emotion Class		Actual Labels					
		Amusement	Sadness	Anger	Fear	Surprise	Disgust
Predicted Labels	Amusement	100%	4%				
	Sadness		96%				
	Anger			100%			
	Fear				100%		9%
	Surprise					85%	4%
	Disgust					15%	87%
						Accuracy	94%

Fig. 2. Confusion matrix of classifying emotions from Arabic and English clips

English clips where they have not been selected. This reduction in the selected features might have an effect on the final classification result of the Arabic clips.

The confusion matrix of emotion classification from the English clips has less confusion than the Arabic ones. Looking at the confusion matrix of the Arabic clips, sadness and disgust emotions have been confused with each other in both sadness and disgust emotion elicitation clips. The low classification of sadness from Arabic clips could be justified by the low average self-rate of sadness. However, the classification of amusement in the English clip was high, even though the average self-rate was low. Furthermore, the disgust classification is also below chance levels, even though the average self-rate was high. At this point, it is difficult to find a correlation between the self-rate and the classification result, where more data is needed. Furthermore, a regression classification could be used in combination with the emotion classification, where the self-rate of the target emotion could be used to detect the level of arousal of the targeted emotion.

When classifying multiple emotions, emotions with similar features are often confused. For example, when using speech features to detect emotions, joy and surprise or anger and surprise, were often confused [31], and when using facial expressions, the most likely confused expressions were sadness with neutral or fear, and disgust with anger [32,33]. To overcome this issue, some studies group the confused emotions in one class and then use separate classifiers across groups as well as within the same group to get more accurate results as in [34,35]. However, the confusion of sadness and disgust emotions only occurred in Arabic elicitation clips, which suggests that the features used for the classification are not differentiating these emotions. That might be caused by the reduction in the selected features from the Arabic clips.

Given the English clips were successful in eliciting the target emotions, the classification results are encouraging, which suggests the robustness of using the skin response features in emotion recognition. However, since the self-rate of the target emotions in English clips reported by the participants varies, more data are required to confirm this results.

5 Conclusion

Recognizing emotional state, contribute in building an intelligent application in affective computing systems, education and psychology. Several methods have been developed to elicit emotions in a replicable way in order to study emotional response patterns, where emotion elicitation clips are the most effective method. Given cultural and language differences, the same stimuli might not have a similar emotional response between subjects from different backgrounds. In this paper, we compare emotional responses from English emotion elicitation clips from [7] with an initial selection of Arabic emotion elicitation clips on a Saudi Arabian sample.

Focusing on the universal six emotions suggested by Ekman, we measured skin physiological signals in response to emotion elicitation clips on 29 Saudi female participants. Analysing the self-rate of targeted emotions reported by the participants between the English clips and the initial Arabic clips, most self-rate were not statistically significant between the two language clips, the exceptions were in the amusement and sadness clips. This finding has two folds: (1) the English clips have a universal capability to elicit target emotions in Saudi sample, and (2) a refined selection of Arabic emotion elicitation clips will be beneficial in eliciting the targeted emotions with higher levels of intensity.

To characterize emotions, we extracted several statistical features from the skin response signal, which have been analysed statistically using ANOVA. Moreover, to compare the emotion elicitation from the English and Arabic clips, the ANOVA tests were performed on the two language clip sets individually. The significant features that differentiate emotions based on the ANOVA test are inline with the literature, and most of them were significant in both English and Arabic clips. The similarity in the significant features from English and Arabic, suggests that both language clip sets have the ability to elicit the target emotions. On the other hand, the differences in these features between the two language clip sets could indicate differences in the intensity of eliciting the target emotions.

To further compare and validate the effectiveness of skin response features in differentiating emotions, we classify the elicited six emotions using multiclass SVM. The common features in English and Arabic clips that were significant based on ANOVA test are used in the classification. Classifying emotions from English and Arabic clips were performed individually for comparison, where the English set performed higher (94 %) than the Arabic set (70 %). The lower classification result in the Arabic set compared to the English set is caused by the confusion of classifying sadness and disgust with each other, which might be caused by the reduction in the selected features. Nevertheless, the high performance in classifying emotions from the English set suggests robustness of using the skin response features in emotion recognition, given that the clips are successful in inducing the target emotions.

6   Limitation and Future Work

A known limitation of this study is the relatively small sample size, and that the participants are drawn from a narrow Saudi region. Moreover, the comparable performance of the initial selection of the Arabic emotion elicitation clips to the validated English clips suggest that refined selection of Arabic emotion elicitation clips might improve the levels and intensity of the induced emotions. Future work will aim to develop such a refined selection of emotion elicitation clips for Arab participants as suggested in [29].

Acknowledgment. The authors extend their appreciation to the Deanship of Scientific Research at King Saud University for funding the work through the research group project number RGP-VPP-157.

References

1. Fragopanagos, N., Taylor, J.G.: Emotion recognition in human-computer interaction. Neural Networks **18**(4), 389–405 (2005)
2. Singh, R.R., Conjeti, S., Banerjee, R.: A comparative evaluation of neural network classifiers for stress level analysis of automotive drivers using physiological signals. Biomed. Signal Process. Control **8**(6), 740–754 (2013)
3. Alghowinem, S.: From joyous to clinically depressed: Mood detection using multimodal analysis of a person's appearance and speech. In: 2013 Humaine Association Conference on Affective Computing and Intelligent Interaction (ACII), pp. 648–654, September 2013
4. Jiang, L., Qing, Z., Wenyuan, W.: A novel approach to analyze the result of polygraph. In: 2000 IEEE International Conference on Systems, Man, and Cybernetics, Volume 4,pp. 2884–2886. IEEE (2000)
5. Park, S., Reddy, B.R., Suresh, A., Mani, M.R., Kumar, V.V., Sung, J.S., Anbuselvi, R., Bhuvaneswaran, R., Sattarova, F., Shavkat, S.Y., et al.: Electrodermal activity, heart rate, respiration under emotional stimuli in schizophrenia. Int. J. Adv. Sci.Technol. **9**, 1–8 (2009)
6. Westermann, R., Spies, K., Stahl, G., Hesse, F.W.: Relative effectiveness and validity of mood induction procedures: a meta-analysis. Eur. J. Soc. Psychol. **26**(4), 557–580 (1996)
7. Gross, J.J., Levenson, R.W.: Emotion elicitation using films. Cogn. Emot. **9**(1), 87–108 (1995)
8. Richerson, P.J., Boyd, R.: Not by Genes Alone: How Culture Transformed Human Evolution. University of Chicago Press, Chicago (2008)
9. Al-Saggaf, Y., Williamson, K.: Online communities in saudi arabia: Evaluating the impact on culture through online semi-structured interviews. In: Forum Qualitative Sozialforschung/Forum: Qualitative Social Research, vol. 5 (2004)
10. Solomon, R.C.: The Passions: Emotions And The Meaning of Life. Hackett Publishing, Cambridge (1993)
11. Boehner, K., DePaula, R., Dourish, P., Sengers, P.: How emotion is made and measured. Int. J. Hum.-Comput. Stud. **65**(4), 275–291 (2007)
12. Cacioppo, J.T., Gardner, W.L., Berntson, G.G.: The affect system has parallel and integrative processing components: form follows function. J. Pers. Soc. Psychol. **76**(5), 839 (1999)
13. Jaimes, A., Sebe, N.: Multimodal human-computer interaction: a survey. Comput. Vis. Image Underst. **108**(1), 116–134 (2007)
14. Dalgleish, T., Power, M.J.: Handbook of cognition and emotion. Wiley Online Library (1999)
15. Brave, S., Nass, C.: Emotion in human-computer interaction. In: The Human-computer Interaction Handbook: Fundamentals, Evolving Technologies And Emerging Applications, pp. 81–96 (2002)
16. Ekman, P., Levenson, R.W., Friesen, W.V.: Autonomic nervous system activity distinguishes among emotions. Science **221**(4616), 1208–1210 (1983)
17. Ax, A.F.: The physiological differentiation between fear and anger in humans. Psychosom. Med. **15**(5), 433–442 (1953)

18. Kim, K.H., Bang, S., Kim, S.: Emotion recognition system using short-term monitoring of physiological signals. Med. Biol. Eng.Comput. **42**(3), 419–427 (2004)
19. Mandryk, R.L., Atkins, M.S.: A fuzzy physiological approach for continuously modeling emotion during interaction with play technologies. Int. J. Hum.-Comput. Stud. **65**(4), 329–347 (2007)
20. Frijda, N.H.: The Emotions. Cambridge University Press, Cambridge (1986)
21. Henriques, R., Paiva, A., Antunes, C.: On the need of new methods to mine electrodermal activity in emotion-centered studies. In: Cao, L., Zeng, Y., Symeonidis, A.L., Gorodetsky, V.I., Yu, P.S., Singh, M.P. (eds.) ADMI. LNCS, vol. 7607, pp. 203–215. Springer, Heidelberg (2013)
22. Drachen, A., Nacke, L.E., Yannakakis, G., Pedersen, A.L.: Correlation between heart rate, electrodermal activity and player experience in first-person shooter games. In: Proceedings of the 5th ACM SIGGRAPH Symposium on Video Games, pp. 49–54. ACM (2010)
23. Boucsein, W.: Electrodermal Activity. Springer, New York (2012)
24. Hagemann, D., Naumann, E., Maier, S., Becker, G., Lürken, A., Bartussek, D.: The assessment of affective reactivity using films: validity, reliability and sex differences. Personality Individ. Differ. **26**(4), 627–639 (1999)
25. Sato, W., Noguchi, M., Yoshikawa, S.: Emotion elicitation effect of films in a Japanese sample. Soc. Behav. Pers. Int. J. **35**(7), 863–874 (2007)
26. Likert, R.: A technique for the measurement of attitudes. Archiv. Psychol. **22**(140), 1–55 (1932)
27. Chang, C.C., Lin, C.J.: LIBSVM: a library for support vector machines. ACM Trans. Intell. Syst. Technol. **2**(3), 27:1–27:27 (2011). http://www.csie.ntu.edu.tw/cjlin/libsvm
28. Raskin, V.: Semantic Mechanisms of Humor, vol. 24. Springer, Netherlands (1985)
29. Alghowinem, S., Alghuwinem, S., Alshehri, M., Al-Wabil, A., Goecke, R., Wagner, M.: Design of an emotion elicitation framework for arabic speakers. In: Kurosu, M. (ed.) HCI 2014, Part II. LNCS, vol. 8511, pp. 717–728. Springer, Heidelberg (2014)
30. Haag, A., Goronzy, S., Schaich, P., Williams, J.: Emotion recognition using biosensors: first steps towards an automatic system. In: André, E., Dybkjær, L., Minker, W., Heisterkamp, P. (eds.) ADS 2004. LNCS (LNAI), vol. 3068, pp. 36–48. Springer, Heidelberg (2004)
31. Cahn, J.E.: The generation of a ect in synthesized speech. J. Am. Voice I/O Soc. **8**, 1–19 (1990)
32. Cohen, I., Sebe, N., Garg, A., Chen, L.S., Huang, T.S.: Facial expression recognition from video sequences: temporal and static modeling. Comput. Vis. Image Underst. **91**(1), 160–187 (2003)
33. Soyel, H., Demirel, H.O.: Facial expression recognition using 3D facial feature distances. In: Kamel, M.S., Campilho, A. (eds.) ICIAR 2007. LNCS, vol. 4633, pp. 831–838. Springer, Heidelberg (2007)
34. Tato, R., Santos, R., Kompe, R., Pardo, J.M.: Emotional space improves emotion recognition. In: INTERSPEECH (2002)
35. Yacoub, S.M., Simske, S.J., Lin, X., Burns, J.: Recognition of emotions in interactive voice response systems. In: INTERSPEECH (2003)

Understanding Gratifications of Watching Danmaku Videos – Videos with Overlaid Comments

Yue Chen[⊠], Qin Gao, and Pei-Luen Patrick Rau

Department of Industrial Engineering, Tsinghua University, Beijing, China
chenyue14@mails.tsinghua.edu.cn,
{gaoqin,rpl}@tsinghua.edu.cn

Abstract. Danmaku comment is a comment technology that overlays user comments directly on the video and creates a co-viewing experience. It originates from Japan and becomes increasingly popular on video sharing sites in China, particularly among the young generation. This exploratory study investigates reasons for watching Danmaku videos through two focus group studies. The results show that the users who watch Danmaku videos found it a way to entertain themselves, to be in company, to have the sense of belonging, and to seek information. Those who do not watch Danmaku videos, however, complained about the abundance of information, the imperfect information quality, and the look and feel. We summarized scenarios suitable for Danmaku commenting from three perspectives: the content, the complexity of information, and the number of viewers. Possible improvements and new applications of Danmaku commenting were discussed.

Keywords: Danmaku comment · Gratifications · Co-viewing · Video-sharing sites

1 Introduction

In 2006, nicovideo.jp, the biggest video-sharing site in Japan, introduced a feature that projects user comments directly onto the video display [1]. These comments are scrolled across the screen, synchronized to the specific playback time point at which the users send the comments. At key moments of videos, there can be so many comments that the video is almost covered with user comments, which look like a bullet curtain, or "Danmaku" in Japanese. With the movement and synchronization of comment text, users feel like co-viewing the videos with other users who watch the same videos, but at different time and different places [2]. Figure 1 shows a screenshot of videos in bilibili.com (a popular Danmaku video website in China).

Danmaku video websites became increasingly popular in Eastern Asia. On February 13, 2015, the Alexa Rank of nicovideo.jp was 92 in global and 8 in Japan [3], and the rank of bilibili.com was 377 in global and 56 in China [4]. At first, online videos with Danmaku comment in China were only popular among comics, animations, and games communities. Recently, mainstream video sharing websites in China, including tudou.com, iqiyi.com, and letv.com, begin to introduce Danmaku comment.

P.L.P. Rau (Ed.): CCD 2015, Part I, LNCS 9180, pp. 153–163, 2015.
DOI: 10.1007/978-3-319-20907-4_14

Danmaku comments

Settings such as Filters for
screening comments

Input field of comments

All comments

Fig. 1. A screen shot of a video about Chinese food in bilibili.com (source: http://www.bilibili.com/video/av543853/).

In August 2014, Danmaku comment was even displayed on two movies in the cinema in China (i.e., The Legend of Qin and Tiny Times 3) [5]. Viewers in the cinema sent the comments via mobile phones.

Whereas objectors of Danmaku comment found overlaying comment on videos can cause distractions and destroys the aesthetics of the videos, supporters of Danmaku comment are enthusiastic and find that it provides unparalleled experience. It appears that Danmaku comment fulfills unique needs for users viewing certain types of content under certain contexts. Understanding of these needs would help designers build better user experience and provide inspirations for developing innovative forms of online co-viewing systems.

This paper reports an exploratory study to understand why the Danmaku users want to watch Danmaku videos and the gratifications they receive from such videos. We also investigated why the non-users refuse Danmaku comment. Furthermore, we explored the scenarios that are suitable for Danmaku commenting.

2   Content of Danmaku Comments

Unlike traditional post-viewing comments, users make Danmaku comments during viewing. Therefore the Danmaku comments can specifically tell about the current time point. This unique feature creates some content different from traditional video comments. After viewing popular videos in bilibili.com and the Danmaku comments in these videos, we listed some examples of Danmaku comments in Table 1.

Table 1. Examples of content of Danmaku comments

Content	Examples
Self-expression (To express their feelings, or ideas by Danmaku comment.)	• A viewer simply shows that she or he is laughing by sending "2333" or "www" when the current content is funny.
	• A fan expresses enthusiasm when his or her idol appears in the video.
	• A viewer uses a short phase or sentence to ridicule something at current content humorously.
Company (To feel having the company with other viewers.)	• A viewer sends a comment "+1" to agree with the comments from other viewers.
	• A viewer sends a comment "I'm also in XX (a place)" when she or he sees a comment "I'm in XX".
	• A viewer sends a comment "7488 viewers, good morning!" when she or he is watching the video in the morning and notices that 7488 viewers are watching this video at that time.
	• A viewer sends a comment "High energy warning ahead!" when something surprising, frightening, or shocking will happen after a few seconds.
Information (To provide or ask for information.)	• A viewer sends the name of the background music at the current time point, when she or he sees a comment "What is the current background music".
Entertainment	• A viewer sends a transliteration of foreign lyrics in the video. The transliteration has interesting meaning that is usually different from the original meaning.
	• A viewer sends pieces of JavaScript code. These advanced Danmaku comments display special effects or applications (e.g., Minesweeper), and may have no relation with the video.
	• A viewer uses a short phase or sentence to ridicule something humorously.

3   Uses and Gratification Theory

We study why to view Danmaku videos based on uses and gratifications theory. This theory explains how and why people use media in a social and psychological way [6, 7]. It suggests that a user's selection of whether to use media is goal-directed and motived [8]. Therefore by understanding gratifications we can answer the question why to view Danmaku videos. This theory was originally used in the studies of traditional media such as newspapers and televisions [9, 10]. With the development of the Internet and other new media, the theory was improved and also applied in studies of new media [11].

Danmaku commenting provides a way to co-view. In a study about co-viewing with YouTube [12], researchers studied the motivations of viewing and sharing YouTube videos by uses and gratifications theory. They suggested that the motives of viewing YouTube included entertainment, information seeking, social interaction, and co-viewing.

Danmaku comment is produced by users, therefore we can see Danmaku videos as a kind of user-generated media (UGM). The content of UGM is created by users who may not be professional, with a certain amount of voluntary creative effort, and available publicly [13]. By uses and gratifications theory, previous research summarized gratifications from UGM in three ways: consuming the content (for information seeking and entertainment), participating in UGM (for social interaction needs and for community development) and producing new content (for self-expression and for self-actualization) [14].

4 Method

We used focus group method to explore general information about Danmaku comment and why people watch Danmaku videos. We chose focus group method because it can provide desirable information such as the perceptions, feelings and thinking of people about issues [15]. We conducted two focus group interviews to learn about why they like or dislike viewing Danmaku videos. We prepared questions for discussion, mainly about the gratifications of watching Danmaku videos, the criticisms about Danmaku comment, and the scenarios suitable for Danmaku commenting, but participants were also encouraged to say anything about Danmaku comment.

Participants. We recruited 11 participants in 2 focus groups. All participants had the experience of watching Danmaku videos. The information of them is shown in Table 2. We assigned both participants who usually watch Danmaku videos and participants who almost do not watch Danmaku videos in each group. Because participants have different opinions on Danmaku comment, they may express more information and provide new ideas that they may never think before.

Procedures. In each interview, after the moderator's introduction of this study, participants signed the informed consents and filled the background questionnaires. Then participants and the moderator sat around a table, got to know each other, and discussed issues about questions mentioned above. Drinks and snacks were provided to make the atmosphere relaxing and comfortable. The focus group interviews were recorded by video and audio recording, and transcribed after interviews. Then we tried to develop a framework from the records for answering the research questions and extract the related quotes in the records to support the framework. Finally we tried to explain the results and give answers to the questions.

Table 2. Participants of focus group interviews

Participant ID	Group 1	Group 2
A	F, 28, Master student, low, low; Movies, UGC, music	M, 23, PhD student, medium, low; Dramas, movies, news
B	M, 23, Master student, high, medium; UGC	M, 23, Master student, high, medium; Animations, UGC, music
C	F, 22, PhD student, high, medium; Variety shows	F, 21, PhD student, medium, low; Dramas, animations, movies
D	M, 27, Engineer, high, low; Dramas, UGC	M, 23, Master student, high, high; Animations (2-D is from Taiwan)
E	F, 21, Unemployed, high, high; Dramas, animations, UGC, music, games	M, 24, Master student, high, low; Dramas, movies, news
F	M, 23, Master student, medium, low; Animations, variety shows	

• Each interviewee's item contains their gender (F for female and M for male), age, occupation, frequency of watching online videos, frequency of watching Danmaku videos; genres that she or he usually watches (UGC means user generated contents).
  • For frequency, high means 3 times per week and above. Medium means once or twice per week. Low means the frequency lower than once per week.

5 Results

By analyzing the interviews, we explain why people like or dislike watching Danmaku videos from three perspectives: gratifications that viewers gained from watching Danmaku videos, negative factors that make some people dislike Danmaku comment, and the scenarios suitable for Danmaku comment.

5.1 Gratifications of Watching Danmaku Videos

We extracted four types of gratifications from Danmaku comment: entertainment, feeling of being in company, sense of belonging, and information seeking.

Entertainment. People watch Danmaku videos for entertainment. They see Danmaku comments as interesting re-creations. The synchronicity of the video and comments creates a special way to entertain. As 2-B said, many interesting points can only be pointed out instantly but not after viewing. Participants in both of the two groups mentioned that they watch Danmaku comment to see humorous comments, interesting transliteration of songs in foreign languages, and special effects from advanced comments such as JavaScript codes or special characters.

All experienced viewers said to see humorous comments is an important reason why they like watching Danmaku videos. Most of these comments are short phases or sentences to humorously ridicule the people or things at current time point. For example, in a video about astronomy, a big black hole is shown in the viewer's screen, the narrator is saying "the absolute extinction is coming", and the atmosphere is chilling. Just at this time, there flies over a comment "I can only see my face" (because of the reflection of the screen). This sentence is called "TuCao" in Chinese or "Tsukkomi" in Japanese. In two focus groups, the word "TuCao" appeared 45 times in total. 1-E said sometimes Danmaku comment is even more interesting than the video.

Feeling of Being in Company. People watch Danmaku videos as a way of co-viewing. 1-E said sometimes she hardly finds a friend watch an animation with her, but she can easily find many co-viewers in Danmaku comment. She also said she enjoys the exciting atmosphere when dense Danmaku comments cover the screen. The comment "High energy warning ahead!" (i.e., something surprising, frightening, or shocking will happen a few seconds later) makes her feel like interacting with the user who probably watched the same video several days ago and sent this comment. 2-B said that when something scaring appears in the screen, many comments will also appear to cover it, and the video will not scare him. 1-D said he watches Danmaku comment usually when he is watching videos alone (except the situation that he just wants to watch Danmaku comment). 2-D summarized that Danmaku comment is like a "cloud friend" who watches videos with him. Sometimes it is a learned scholar, sometimes it is a funny comedian.

Sense of Belonging. People watch Danmaku videos because they feel like belonging to a group that shares same interest of them. As 1-B said, at first Danmaku commenting was popular in animation, comics, and games community. He said many of these people enjoy staying indoor and therefore have less time meeting friends face to face, but they still need to belong and want to communicate with others, especially people who have common interests and opinions with them. Danmaku commenting provides a good way to fulfill these needs. 2-B also said that he sees Danmaku comment as a form of online forums, where people with common interests discuss with others.

Sympathy between users is important. 1-E said Danmaku comments are interesting when users have the same interest and sympathy with each other. 1-B also said he dislikes the Danmaku comments from the user who has nothing in common with him. Other participants, including non-users, also agree to the importance of sympathy in Danmaku comment.

Although people watch Danmaku videos for company and for the need to belong, most viewers do not have social interaction with other viewers. The experienced viewer 2-D said he never made friends by Danmaku videos. He may discuss with other comments, but does not care who sent these comments. 1-B even said he had viewing Danmaku videos for four years, but had no account at any Danmaku video website.

Information Seeking. People watch Danmaku videos for information. 1-C and 1-E said sometimes they enjoy the background music at a specific time point in a video and want to know the name of the music. They can always find the name in Danmaku comments. 1-B and 2-D said sometimes they can find translations in Danmaku comments when they are watching videos in foreign languages without subtitles. Also, when they cannot understand the story at a specific time point because they lack the knowledge about related allusions or background information, they can find explanations in Danmaku comments. 2-B also regards the "High energy warning ahead", mentioned by 1-E above, as useful information. 1-A, 2-C and 2-B also said they watch Danmaku comments when they want to see opinions from other people.

5.2 Negative Factors

Some people do not watch Danmaku videos for three main reasons: the abundance of information, the imperfect information quality, and the look and feel. First, 1-A, 1-D, 1-F, 2-A, and 2-E said the information of Danmaku comments is too abundant. The abundant information distracts them when watching videos. 2-E said Danmaku comment is garish and adds cognitive loads to him. Second, the content of some Danmaku comments is not satisfying. 1-B, 1-E, and 2-E said Danmaku comment contains too much individual expression of emotion. 1-B is tired of the conflicts between fans in Danmaku comment. 1-E said she has to accept all opinions including those she does not agree with, because viewers cannot reply to or argue with other commenters. 1-A, 1-B, and 2-B also complained that some comments contain spoilers about endings and reduce the suspense of stories. Third, 2-C and 2-E think the look and feel of Danmaku comment, such as font styles and colors, still needs improvement. 1-A and 2-C think Danmaku comment destroys the artistic conception of videos.

Although non-users think the information is too abundant, experienced participants seems not to care about this. 1-E said the atmosphere is exciting and the video looks funny with a thick covering of comments. 1-B also said he sometimes does not watch a video until the amount of Danmaku comments is large enough. When non-user 2-E said one or two comments on the screen is good, 2-B disagreed and said he thinks the comments should cover 1/3 area of the screen. 1-D also said many comments at the same time usually convey the same meaning, and therefore actually the information is not abundant. In addition, to reduce distraction, users can set the transparency of comments in some Danmaku video websites such as bilibili.com.

For the content, many Danmaku video websites provide different kinds of filter functions (e.g., the NG function in nicovideo.jp) to shield users from disgusting information. Users can hidden the disgusting comments by keywords, user IDs, algorithms by the website, etc.

For the look and feel issues, experienced viewers in the two interviews did not reply to non-users' statements about the imperfect look and feel of Danmaku. They may not care about it.

5.3 Scenarios

We summarized the scenarios that are suitable for Danmaku from the following three perspectives.

Content. A video may be suitable for Danmaku commenting if it is relaxing, such as a funny comedy, a variety show, or a user-generated video. 1-D said he likes to turn on the Danmaku function when he is watching humorous animations. 1-B and 1-E said they think many of their friends who like animations, like watching animations with Danmaku comment. 2-D also watches animations with Danmaku comment. 1-C said when she thinks the video is witless, she sometimes turns on Danmaku function to see interesting TuCao or Tsukkomi (i.e., short phases or sentences to ridicule the people or things humorously) from others. On the contrary, Danmaku commenting is not suitable for some serious videos. 1-E thinks that many Danmaku comments are emotional and short, and therefore not suitable for discussing something seriously. 2-B thinks that Danmaku comments make serious videos relaxing. He does not turn on Danmaku function when watching a serious video at the first time. 2-A also said he likes watching serious videos such as news and military but dislikes watching Danmaku videos.

Complexity. A video may be suitable for Danmaku commenting if the content is not complicated for viewers. 2-E said the amount and complexity of information that a video conveys can influence whether the video is suitable to play with Danmaku comment. For example, 1-B said he watches videos about games with Danmaku comment because these game videos do not require much thinking. 2-D said he thinks the stories of most animations move on slowly, and this is one of the reasons why he watches animations with Danmaku comment. 2-B and 2-C said they would like to see Danmaku comment when watching a video for the second time (or more). Because they have already known the content, they can pay more attention to Danmaku comments. 1-C said she does not want to see Danmaku comment when watching videos requiring much thinking, such as the stories of Holmes.

The Number of Viewers. A video may be suitable for Danmaku commenting if the viewer is watching the video alone. People regard Danmaku commenting as a way of co-viewing. 1-B and 2-D said when they are watching videos with friends, they usually do not need Danmaku comment (unless they specially want to watch Danmaku comment for entertainment or information).

For movies, all participants said that it is not suitable to present Danmaku comments in the cinema for three reasons. First, as 1-C and 1-E said, a viewer in the cinema cannot turn off the Danmaku comment if she or he does not want to see it, whereas the Danmaku comment in the online videos can be turned off. In the cinema, viewers cannot set the transparency or filters, which they can set in online videos. Therefore currently, Danmaku comment in the cinema forces viewers to see it, and this may annoy viewers. Second, 2-B pointed out that a comment delays and is actually not synchronized to the related time point, because viewers cannot pause the movie and then send out comments as they usually do in websites. Also, viewers hardly come up with interesting high quality comments in such a short time in the cinema. Third, as 2-C and 2-E said, Danmaku comments may destroy the artistic conception, which is important for movies.

6 Discussion and Conclusion

The most distinctive feature of Danmaku comment is that comment text are scrolled simultaneously with the video. This feature satisfies gratifications that users cannot get from the traditional post-viewing commenting videos.

Danmaku commenting provides a special way of entertainment and information retrieval. When watching traditional online videos, viewers usually comment after watching the video. They tend to make comments from an overall perspective and many details are hard to recall. However in Danmaku videos, the synchronic feature makes it possible to mark the interesting points and other information related to the current playback time.

Danmaku commenting also satisfies needs for company and belonging and provides a way for social media co-viewing. The focus groups highlighted the importance of sympathy between users. People feel more comfortable if users who sent Danmaku comments have common interests with them. Therefore we think besides transparency and filter functions, grouping users by interest can also reduce the discontent about unpleasant information. If users can join in different groups like in online forum websites and have the choice to only see the Danmaku comments from his or her groups, the amount of information may be acceptable for more people and viewers will be less likely to see unpleasant comments.

We also found that people who like watching Danmaku videos may tend to have higher polychronicity (the preference to involvement in two or more events at the same time [16]) and seek for more information. Participant 1-B and 2-B, who usually watch Danmaku videos, said that they like multitasking. 2-A and 2-E, who rarely watch Danmaku videos, clearly said they dislike multitasking. Danmaku videos require viewers to watch the video and comments at the same time. Therefore watching Danmaku videos can be considered as multitasking. Previous research shows that the overall behavior intention to multitasking with multiple smart devices can affected by motivations [17]. One of these motivations is perceived usefulness. Computer polychronicity is a key driver of perceived usefulness [18]. Therefore it is reasonable to assume that higher polychronicity may lead to more Danmaku watching, but it still needs further research.

From the function of providing information, we think Danmaku comments can also be used to automatically abstract tags of a video and used for searching. During-viewing Danmaku comments are more likely to record the details of the videos than traditional post-viewing comments. If we have effective algorithms to screen these abundant comments, Danmaku comment can be useful for video searching. Besides this potential new application, 2-D said Danmaku comments can be used to detect key time points of the video and add key frames for previewing, because at key time points, the number of comments is usually larger than that at other time points. 2-D also thinks Danmaku commenting can be used in online course videos. The Danmaku comments may provide helpful information or knowledge from other learners. It will make the viewer feel like having an intelligent desk mate.

There are some limitations. We only conducted two focus groups. Some researchers suggested that for a simple research question, the necessary number of focus group may be three or four [19]. Also, the participants were not diverse enough to represent the main Danmaku users. The participants ranged in age from 21 to 28, all with high education levels. Main Danmaku users are the 90 s generation [20], and thus future research of teenagers is necessary. In addition, except one viewer from Taiwan, we only investigated viewers in mainland China. Many Danmaku viewers are in other countries and territories in Eastern Asia, such as Japan. Therefore cross cultural research is needed.

Despite of these limitations, we provided an overview of Danmaku comment. People watch Danmaku comments for entertainment, satisfying the need for company and the need to belong, and information seeking. Non-users complained about the abundance of information, the imperfect information quality, and the look and feel. Danmaku commenting is suitable when the video is relaxing, the content is not complex for the viewer, or the viewer is watching the video alone. We also proposed some possible improvements and new applications of Danmaku commenting. Future research may explore (1) the detailed reasons for watching Danmaku videos by investigating more diverse users and considering more factors such as the individual characteristics, and (2) improvements and new applications of Danmaku commenting.

References

1. Johnson, D.: Polyphonic/Pseudo-synchronic: animated writing in the comment feed of nicovideo. Jpn. Stud. **33**, 297–313 (2013)
2. Cohen, E.L., Lancaster, A.L.: Individual differences in in-person and social media television coviewing: the role of emotional contagion, need to belong, and coviewing orientation. Cyberpsychology Behav. Soc. Netw. **17**, 512–518 (2014)
3. nicovideo.jp Site Overview. http://www.alexa.com/siteinfo/nicovideo.jp
4. Bilibili.com Site Overview. http://www.alexa.com/siteinfo/bilibili.com
5. Theaters in China Screen Movies, and Viewers' Text Messages. http://sinosphere.blogs.nytimes.com/2014/08/20/theaters-in-china-screen-movies-and-viewers-text-messages/
6. Klapper, J.T.: Mass communication research: an old road resurveyed. Public Opin. Q. **27**, 515–527 (1963)
7. Katz, E., Blumler, J.G., Gurevitch, M.: Uses and gratifications research. Public Opin. Q. **37** (4), 509–523 (1973)
8. Rosengren, K.E.: Uses and gratifications: a paradigm outlined. Uses Mass Commun. Curr. Perspect. Gratif. Res. **3**, 269–286 (1974)
9. Kippax, S., Murray, J.P.: Using the mass media need gratification and perceived utility. Commun. Res. **7**, 335–359 (1980)
10. Palmgreen, P., Rayburn, J.D.: Uses and gratifications and exposure to public television a discrepancy approach. Commun. Res. **6**, 155–179 (1979)
11. Ruggiero, T.E.: Uses and gratifications theory in the 21st century. Mass Commun. Soc. **3**, 3–37 (2000)
12. Haridakis, P., Hanson, G.: Social interaction and co-viewing with youtube: blending mass communication reception and social connection. J. Broadcast. Electron. Media. **53**, 317–335 (2009)
13. Wunsch-Vincent, S., Vickery, G.: Participative Web and User-Created Content: Web 2.0, Wikis and Social Networking. OECD, Paris (2007)
14. Shao, G.: Understanding the appeal of user-generated media: a uses and gratification perspective. Internet Res. **19**, 7–25 (2009)
15. Krueger, R.A., Casey, M.A.: Focus Groups: A Practical Guide for Applied Research. Sage Publications, Thousand Oaks (2000)
16. Hall, E.T.: The Silent Language. Anchor Press, New York (1973)

17. Zhang, Y., Mao, M., Rau, P.-L.P., Choe, P., Bela, L., Wang, F.: Exploring factors influencing multitasking interaction with multiple smart devices. Comput. Hum. Behav. **29**, 2579–2588 (2013)
18. Davis, J.M., Lee, L.S., Yi, M.Y.: Time-user preference and technology acceptance: measure development of computer polychronicity. Am. J. Bus. **24**, 23–32 (2009)
19. Rabiee, F.: Focus-group interview and data analysis. Proc. Nutr. Soc. **63**, 655–660 (2004)
20. Definitely the best securities analysis of the 90 s generation (绝对是史上最牛逼最in的90后券商分析报告). http://finance.sina.com.cn/stock/report/20140826/161020124902.shtml

User's Individual Needs Oriented Parametric Design Method of Chinese Fonts

Qijun Duan and Xiaoli Zhang[✉]

School of Design Arts & Media, Nanjing University of Science & Technology,
200, Xiaolingwei Street, Nanjing 210094, Jiangsu, China
pylduan@aliyun.com, 2418416417@qq.com

Abstract. The rapid development of technology and the changes in reading ways have promoted the research related to Chinese characters, while the new patterns of information acquisition, dissemination and communication based on modern internet technology have posed requirements for individualized design of Chinese characters. In this paper, for providing a new rational and personalized design method for Chinese characters, 3 kinds of parameters as shape parameters, structure parameters and effect parameters of Chinese characters are defined. A database of common characters, stored in the cloud and developed in a Crowdfunding way, is designed for providing design elements. Parametric Design System and the relevant application prototype is established, which is based on the rule of form and structure of Chinese characters, and the analysis of application interface characteristics. Then, the parametric design of Chinese characters can mark the information dissemination with a personal imprint in the context of modern technology and culture.

Keywords: Chinese character · Strokes · Structure · Parameter · Design

1 Preface

Mobile internet entered into our daily life at the beginning of the twenty-first century. People's reading ways have changed significantly that electronic reading now dominates. The emergence of various social networks, including but not limited to Facebook, Twitter, WeChat and QQ, influenced most people's social networking patterns. Fundamental changes have taken place in information communication. While technology revolution brings us convenience in information communication, it also, to some extent, eliminates the personality traits in communication and results in fast-food style affective interaction. Joy brought by one simple handwriting letter is now nowhere to be found. In the process that the carrier of text changes from visible to invisible, it is worthwhile for us to endeavor to retain the personal, emotional and aesthetic value of characters.

Although the transmission ways of culture around the world are still diverse today, development of the technology of communication and transportation has brought substantive changes in the scale and speed of culture transmission. Resource sharing has become one of the themes of social development. Collaboration and teamwork have become the inevitable trend of development. In such circumstances, the character,

P.L.P. Rau (Ed.): CCD 2015, Part I, LNCS 9180, pp. 164–175, 2015.
DOI: 10.1007/978-3-319-20907-4_15

as a basic carrier of cultural transmission and communication, is playing an increasingly important role. Furthermore, from the perspective of cultural inheritance and development, design and research related to characters is indispensable.

2 Design of Chinese Characters

2.1 Attributes

Characters mainly have three aspects of properties: (1) They are visible and readable. Characters concrete the voice in the form of visual symbols. (2) They serve as carrier of culture inheritance and communication. Characters can break the constraints of time and space, record knowledge and convey thought. (3) They can be redesigned. Since characters are visual symbols created by human, they can be redesigned if necessary. The design of forms should be based on the requirements in application.

2.2 The Evolution of Chinese Characters

China is one of the oldest civilized countries in the world. As an important part of Chinese civilization, Chinese characters originated in hieroglyphs and have a history of more than 3300 years. In this history, Chinese characters evolved through several different handwriting font types, including Jinwen (inscriptions on ancient bronze objects), Zhuanshu (seal character), Lishu (official script), Kaishu (regular script), Xingshu (running script) and Caoshu (cursive script) [1]. After the application of printing technology, a variety of printing fonts, including Song and boldface, are widely used in books, newspapers, magazines and all kinds of electronic media. Evolution of Chinese characters is a modeling process (Fig. 1).

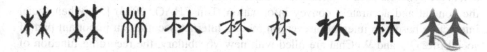

Fig. 1. The development of Chinese characters and the transformation of attributes

2.3 Design Method of Chinese Characters

Because design of Chinese characters is one of the important means to transmit Han culture, abundant design products have been achieved and applied in this field. Chinese characters have the attributes of both the graphics and text. Existing relevant research mainly focuses on the graphic attributes of Chinese characters. However, Germany Sinologist Lothar Ledderose proposed a modular system of Chinese characters in his book Ten Thousand Things: Module and Mass Production in Chinese Art, by which the Chinese characters are divided into several parts and can be reconstructed [2]. This is a thinking way of design that treats the Chinese art and social culture from the formal logic perspective.

Generally, the design work on Chinese characters can be categorized into font design and graphic design.

Font Design of Chinese Characters. With the development of technology, computers are increasingly applied in font design. Currently, there are more than a dozen common used computer font types and tens if not hundreds of fonts in each type. In font design, professional designers complete the design of a set of characters systematically on the basis of certain features of structure or shape of Chinese characters. The design cycle is long, and each character of the same font must be unified in details. Typical design procedures are as follows: (1) a new font is designed by processing and reformatting a basic font such as Song or boldface. (2) a handwritten font with individual features can be designed through handwriting, scanning and redesigning.

Graphic Design of Characters. In graphic design, designers creatively make changes in the structure, color and/or texture of a single or several Chinese characters on the basis of the characteristics of the characters to get a good visual effect. This process endows the characters with profound meaning and it is widely used in the design of logo, poster, packaging, etc.

2.4   Requirements of Chinese Characters Design in the Context of Modern Society and Technology

Psychological Mechanism of Font Users: Today, the main application way of the characters has turned to information transmission based on digital technology. Because the word to express emotion can be copied easily now, the communication way with personal imprinting becomes precious.

New Requirements in Design by Evolution of Recording Function: Chinese characters are symbols used in writing and expression. They should be able to fully reflect the content and accurately convey information (Bin ZHAO, 1993) [3]. When social interaction based on internet or even on mobile internet becomes an important part of social life, QQ and WeChat are filled with new vocabulary, the recording function of Chinese characters altered accordingly. The influence of this alternation manifests as the creation of new characters or new usage of existing characters through processes including using varied characters, changing or increasing strokes of characters, recreating characters, etc.

Protection and Inheritance of Cultural Resources: In the long history of Chinese civilization, a large amount of character design resources has been accumulated. Taking advantage of these cultural resources to complete the recreation of Chinese character culture, we can see new requirements and have new perspectives in the study and design of Chinese characters.

3 Parametric Design Method of Chinese Characters

According to the statistics of Chinese Characters National Standard (GB2312-1980), primary and secondary library contain 6763 characters [4]. Along with the changes of cultural context, Chinese characters have evolved gradually from original hieroglyphic to abstract symbols, which are constructed by points and lines cutting a rectangular space. Chinese characters of the same font are graphic symbols with similar dimension and style.

3.1 Deconstruction & Structure Analysis of Characteristics

Analysis of Characteristics. Chinese characters can be deconstructed into four levels, including character, component, stroke and detail drawing (stroke with a specific shape).

Table 1. Structure of Chinese characters and definition of parameters (秋as an example)

Structure level		Sample	Parameters	Contents
Character		秋	EPs (effect parameters)	Overall effect (including silhouette, proportions, etc.)
Compo-nents	Structural style	禾 火	StPs (structural parameters)	Structural style (left vs. right)
	Parts			Relationships between strokes, node information, etc.
Strokes		一一丨八丿丶八	ShPs (shape parameters)	Basic shape and proportion of strokes
Drawings		秋		

Types of Chinese Character Structure. According to number of components, Chinese characters can be divided into two classes as simple characters (Table 2) and

Table 2. Structural features of simple characters

Features	Samples	Features	Samples
Symmetric	田、中	Well-proportioned	三、川、王
Balanceable	天、大、人	Changed appropriately	日、目、曰

compound characters (Table 3: according to the relationships among components, they can be divided into 12 types).

Table 3. Tactic forms of compound characters

No.	Structural relationship	Samples	No.	Structural relationship	Samples
a	⊞(left vs. right)	挣、伟	g	◰(Right down surround)	建、连
b	⊟(upper vs. down)	志、苗	h	⊓(Upper 3 sides surround)	同、问
c	Ⅲ(left, middle & right)	湖、脚	i	⊔(Lower 3 sides surround)	击、凶
d	☰(upper, middle & down)	奚、罄	j	⊏(Left 3 sides surround)	区、巨
e	◰(upper right surround)	句、可	k	▣(Completely surround)	囚、团
f	◸(upper left surround)	庙、病	l	▦(Mosaic structure)	坐、爽

All the Chinese characters can be categorized into the types above.

3.2 Shape Parameters

According to the hierarchical relationships of structure, a series of ShPs (shape parameters) can be defined to describe the shape of strokes. There are 31 types of common stroke of Chinese characters (shown in Table 4).

Classification of Strokes. Strokes are the basic units of Chinese characters. The same strokes can have different shapes due to differences in length, angle and bending form (for instance, in Table 1, there are three different shapes of PIE ("ノ")). Different strokes have different number and mode of ShPs. Strokes can be categorized according to these principles as follows: (1) There are 6 kinds of single basic strokes, including dot (DIAN), horizontal stroke (HENG), vertical stroke (SHU), left-falling stroke (PIE), right-falling stroke (NA) and rising stroke (TI). (2) Compound strokes are classified according to the first stroke. (3) Compound strokes with a *bending* drawing are relatively complex, so they are categorized into a special type.

Therefore, a classification of strokes is established (Table 5). According to this classification, we can determine the code of each stroke. For instance, the code of PIE ("ノ") is *"31"*. This code can be applied in the subsequent design processes.

Spline Curves Introduced to Describe the Bending Shape of Strokes. In order to accurately describe the strokes with a bending drawing, we introduce B-spline curve (NURBS). B-spline curve is defined by some given control points and related knot vectors. Spline curves pass through ordered data points and have continuities of first and second derivatives at these points. This feature allows spline curves to well describe the curve feature of strokes of Chinese characters, and provide space for adjustments of the drawing (Fig. 2a).

Definition of Shape Parameter. ShPs are defined according to the classification of strokes:

Table 4. Strokes name of Chinese character

❶ 一	一	⓫ 一	买	⓴ 丿	豚
❷ 丨	卜	⓬ 乚	儿	㉑ 乛	九
❸ 丿	八	⓭ 乚	去	㉒ 乚	四
❹ 乀	八	⓮ 乚	以	㉓ 乚	没
❺ 丶	主	⓯ 乚	山	㉔ 乛	仍
❻ 乛	口	⓰ 乀	女	㉕ 乛	风
❼ 一	地	⓱ 乚	写	㉖ 乛	及
❽ 乛	周	⓲ 乚	戈	㉗ 乚	专
❾ 丨	小	⓳ 乛	那	㉘ 乚	鼎
❿ 7	水	⓴ 乛	课	㉙ 乚	凹
				㉚ 乛	凸

Table 5 Stroke classification & codes

	1	2	3	4	5	6	7	8	9
1 横	一	㇀	㇖	㇕	㇇	㇆	㇙	㇉	㇅
2 竖	丨	㇗	亅	㇄	㇟	㇚	㇊	㇌
3 撇	丿	㇒	㇄
4 捺	乀
5 点	丶
6 提	㇀
7 弯	乚	㇄	㇉	㇈	㇋	㇙	㇆	㇇

The ShPs of single basic strokes including dot (DIAN), horizontal stroke (HENG), vertical stroke (SHU) and rising stroke (TI) are the coordinates of both ends. Because the left-falling stroke (PIE) and right-falling stroke (NA) are curve, the relevant ShPs include a group of control points besides both ends.

All composite strokes can be constructed by basic strokes according to the strokes' classification in Table 5. Therefore, ShPs includes the coordinates of 3 kinds of points: (1) both ends and middle point of stroke, (2) turning points, (3) and data points of Spline curve (Fig. 2b). Controlling and adjusting the positions of these 3 kinds of points, we can change the shape of strokes effectively. While the code of stroke is known, the number of ShPs required is determined.

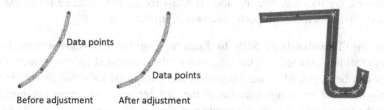

Before adjustment   After adjustment

a. Spline curve fits bending strokes   **b.** Composite strokes

Fig. 2. a. Spline curve fits bending strokes **b.** Composite strokes

3.3 Structural Parameters

According to the analysis of Chinese characters structure above, StPs (structural parameters) can be defined to describe the composition of components and the construction relationships of the strokes.

First Structural Problem: Type and Structural Form. Chinese characters can be categorized into simple characters and compound characters. The structural features of simple characters are totally decided by the relationships among strokes. There are twelve types of forms of compound characters, so the structural features of compound characters depend not only on the relationships among strokes, but also on the composition of components.

We define the first type of StPs for the following aims: (1) Distinguishing different types of character (the code of simple character is *10*, and the codes of compound character are *2a, ...,2 l*, shown in Table 3). (2) Adjusting (moving, rotating or scaling) the positions and dimensions of components if the character is a compound character (Fig. 3 shows different fonts created by modifying StPs).

秋 秋 秋 秋

Fig. 3. Different fonts created by modifying StPs

Second Structural Problem: Stroke Construction. There are only two types of relationships between strokes: intersect or non-intersect. (For instance, in the character 秋 in Table 1, HENG intersects with SHU, but DIAN does not intersect with any strokes) Therefore, the relationship between strokes can be described by whether the intersection exists. The second StPs should include: (1) The number of strokes in relevant character or component (i.e. the total number of strokes for a simple character, and the number of stroke in relevant component for compound character); (2) Whether the intersection exists and the relevant position of strokes to determine the relationships among strokes. By moving, rotating and scaling strokes, the structure relationship can be adjusted. (3) Dimension proportion between strokes.

Study on the Thresholds of StPs to Ensure Cognition of Characters. Chinese characters shall be designed and the structure shall be adjusted on the premise that the characters can be cognized. Some characters are composed by same strokes but have completely different meanings because of the differences in structure parameters. To figure out the thresholds on StPs, we conducted a cognition experiment by adjusting the StPs of 4 groups of typical characters. Sixty volunteers participated in this experiment. Experimental data is shown in Table 6.

Through the cognition experiment, we have three findings: (1) Thresholds on StPs definitely exist. If the StPs are beyond the allowed range, the cognizability of the character will be compromised. (2) Different characters require StPs with different thresholds. (3) The operating context (font size and characters around the experimental character) will have certain influence on the cognizability.

3.4   Effect Parameters

EPs are defined mainly to control the basic characteristics of Chinese characters. The traditional outline of Chinese characters is rectangle. By stretching, flattening, leaning or changing the outline into rounded rectangle or trapezoid, we can have different character designs. Furthermore, although this method is based on boldface font, we can still change the thickness and other details of strokes to achieve personalized design of characters (Fig. 4).

Table 6 Recognition experiment of Chinese character

Test sample1		土	土	土	土	土	土	土
Ratio 1		−15%	−10%	−5%	0	5%	10%	15%
tǔ 土	1	2	1	3	29	55	58	57
	2	0	1	2	20	57	60	59
shì 士	1	58	59	57	31	5	2	3
	2	60	59	58	40	3	0	1
Test sample2		日	日	日	日	日	日	日
Ratio 1		−30%	−20%	−10%	0	10%	20%	30%
rì 日	1	57	56	51	39	0	0	0
	2	51	56	52	35	5	0	1
yuē 曰	1	3	4	9	21	60	60	60
	2	9	4	8	25	55	60	59
Test sample3		申	申	申	申	申	申	申
Ratio 3		0	5%	10%	15%	20%	25%	30%
yóu 由	1	60	45	34	11	2	0	0
	2	60	51	42	15	2	0	1
shēn 申	1	0	15	26	49	58	60	60
	2	0	9	18	45	58	60	59
Test sample4		人	人	人	人	人	人	人
Degree 4		-15	-10	-5	0	+5	+10	+15
rén 人	1	57	56	59	60	17	0	2
	2	60	60	60	59	8	0	0
rù 入	1	3	4	1	0	43	60	58
	2	0	0	0	1	52	60	60

Notes: (1) Ratio 1 means the length proportion between two parallel lines.
(2) Ratio 2 = (Length-Width)/Height
(3) Ratio 3 describes the states of extension of the middle vertical line.
(4) Degree 4 is the skew degree of left/right stroke.
(5) Two different size samples are used for Recognition Test; the bigger is used in text 1.

Fig. 4. Characters designed by adjusting Eps

3.5   Technical Solutions to Parametric Design of Chinese Characters

Reference Frame for Parametric Design of Chinese Characters. A reference frame (500*500px, with addible structure lines for design) is established to provide a base, which can be used for determining the positions of strokes and adjusting the forms of strokes and characters (Fig. 5). When the design work on strokes' shape and relevant structure is finished, the comprehensive sketch of character can be achieved by adjusting the shape and proportion of this reference frame.

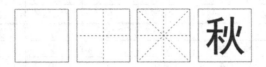

Fig. 5. Reference frame for parametric design

Database System for Parametric Design of Chinese Characters. To parameterize Chinese characters, we need to parameterize and store the relative position and proportional relationship of strokes and components, as well as the shape of strokes. As has been analyzed above, the shape of strokes can be expressed through three types of data points. However, the expression and storage of characters and components is really complex because that there are thousands of different Chinese characters. Therefore, database system should be established, which includes: (1) a database of ShPs (the code of strokes and relevant number, and positions of three types data points); (2) a database of common characters stored in the cloud with open data structure for expansion and data sharing, a database that can provide design elements with two kinds of StPs; (3) and a customized database to store personalized fonts and application.

The data accumulation of second database for design can be achieved in two ways: (1) The basic data of common Chinese characters can be input when the database is established; (2) The database can be expanded through *Crowfunding*, i.e. allowing people not limited to professional designers other than common ones design and import the data into the cloud database. Chinese characters have a history of thousands years. Chinese people know the shape of strokes and the structure of characters well. This is the cultural foundation of the *Crowdfunding* database.

Application Program for Parametric Design of Chinese Characters. Based on the boldface, the parametric design application program of Chinese font (PDAPCF) can be constructed by three different function modules: (1) new character forming;

(2) character design; (3) and information input (Fig. 6). Storing operation can be related to the basic database or customized database. Users can choose to save into two databases or not.

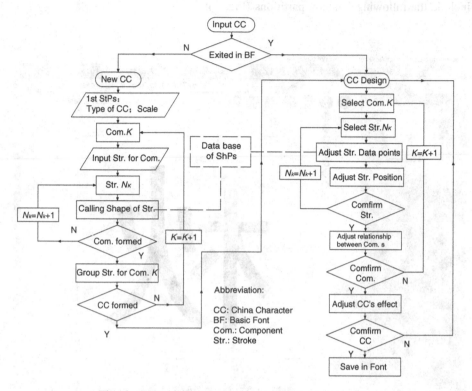

Fig. 6. Parametric design process of Chinese characters

3.6   Analysis of Interaction Characteristics of PDAPCF

This paper aims to provide common users with technical solutions to personalized Chinese characters design and related application. Therefore, the PDAPCF should have the following properties: (1) It ensures the regularity of structure and the cognizability of characters; (2) It lays emphasis on the interactive features and provides user-friendly operating experience; (3) It offers the convenience and efficiency of sharing font designs through cloud database given the users' willingness; (4) It emphasizes the interestingness of the design process and provides users with an opportunity to show personality and aesthetic orientation through the design results.

3.7 Prototype of PDAPCF

According to the foregoing analysis of technical solutions and interactive features of related application program, we can confirm that the basic application interface should include the following function partitions (Fig. 7):

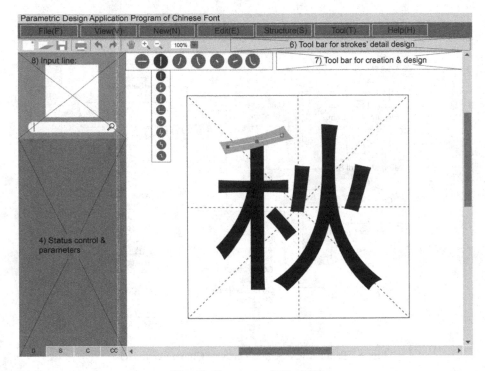

Fig. 7. Prototype of PDAPCF

1. **Command set**: dropdown menu adopted for defining and classifying all the operation command.
2. **Standard icon bar**: including common used window's operation commands; display control commands such as *Zoom* and *Pan*; and *Group* or *Explode*; etc.
3. **Design space**: providing design reference frame and addible structural lines; highlighting the data points or structural features according to the design status related to character, component and stroke.
4. **Status control icon bar**: implementing the switching operation between drawing, stroke, component and the whole character.
5. **Grouped list of strokes**: providing basic elements for new character forming (each stroke with a special code as is shown in Table 5); showing the structural features in design space (based on the database of ShPs, highlighting and applying the data points of stroke according to the relevant code).

6. **Tool bar for strokes' detail design**: providing stroke thickness adjustment function; providing characterization tool for endpoints and turning points of strokes (further statements are not here because of the space limit). Considering the basic interface should be simple and convenient to use, this bar can be designed in pop-up window.
7. **Tool bar for creation & design**: including the commands as *Stretch, Enlarge, Shorten, Lessen, Move, Rotate, Copy*, etc.
8. **Input area**: inputting and displaying the character being designed.
9. **Help & information area**: providing operating hints.

4 Conclusion

New demands for the individual design of Chinese characters have risen since information acquisition, exchange and dissemination based on modern network technology, such as online reading, social networking site, e-mail and personal web page, became popular. Parametric Design System of Chinese fonts may offer a realizable method for common people to design personalized Chinese characters. The Parametric Design of Chinese characters can mark the information dissemination with a personal imprint in the context of modern technology and culture.

Design results of PDAPCF will be stored in the custom database; the mapping relationship with commonly used font and input method is established. Then the design results can be applied in all kinds of application software, such as OFFICE, CAD and social networking software. As a result, the user's personalized features can be embodied in information communication and social interaction based on internet.

This paper ignored the application of pattern recognition technology in the design of Chinese characters (although there are abundant researches on the pattern recognition of Chinese characters). The proposed research idea and relevant result of this paper is based on printing fonts and digital communication, for the purpose of making application system simple and operable. The Crowdfunding module proposed for database expansion gives this research growth potential and good interactivity. Of course, by integrating research results of Chinese character pattern recognition, it is likely to provide common users with resources for personalized font design, thereby to inherit and develop Chinese language and cultural heritage. Therefore, we should look forward to subsequent integration of pattern recognition technology and parametric design technology of Chinese characters.

References

1. English Chinese concise dictionary of China classical. literature. http://blog.sina.com.cn/s/blog_4c86306b01013t7w.html
2. Ledderose, L.: Ten Thousand Things: Module and Mass Production in Chinese Art [M]. Joint Publishing, Shanghai (2005)
3. Bin, Z.: Palaeography outline [M], p. 5. The Commercial Press, Beijing (2009)
4. Code of chinese graphic character set for information interchange; Primary set. Beijing: Chinese Standards Press, May 1981

Dramatic Sketches: A New Interaction Design Resource for Communicating Contextual Factors

Fuad Ali EL-Qirem[1](✉) and Gilbert Cockton[2]

[1] Department of Software Engineering, Al-Zaytoonah University of Jordan,
Amman, Jordan
fqirem@yahoo.com
[2] Faculty of Arts, Design and Social Sciences, Northumbria University,
Newcastle upon Tyne NE1 8ST, UK
gilbert.cockton@northumbria.ac.uk

Abstract. User-centred design approaches focus on understanding usage contexts and evaluating usage through primary data. Collecting primary data is more feasible for contexts that project teams can directly access. Otherwise, secondary sources may be the only practical source of contextual information (and even when it is not, secondary data can still be valuable). When designing software for localization across global markets, comprehensive collection of primary data may be infeasible, but existing secondary data could be made more accessible via an appropriate design resource. In this paper, we present Dramatic Sketches as a resource for representing cultural factors. We relate a set of Dramatic Sketches to three field research studies in Jordan and show how a few Dramatic Sketches and auxiliary Micro Sketches can compactly communicate many cultural factors.

Keywords: Dramatic Sketches · User-Centered design · Contextual user and usage research · Culturally-sensitive design for arab countries

1 Representations for User-Centred Design

User-Centred Design (UCD) provides two important groups of practices to Interaction Design. Firstly, it has developed and disseminated practices for collecting and analyzing primary data relating to intended usage contexts and users. Secondly, UCD has advanced practices for empirically evaluating interactive systems. In both cases, the results of these activities need to be documented and shared within design teams. This paper focuses on the representation of potentially relevant usage contexts fora wide range of software design projects that are unknown at the time of authoring. The aim is to provide re-usable understandings of cultural factors for localization of global software products and services. The case study presented here collected data in Jordan, but much of this will generalize to the Arab Middle East, and some more generally to Islamic cultures.

Existing UCD representations are almost all aimed at specific software development projects. For example, *Personas* (Pruitt and Adlin 2006) need information

© Springer International Publishing Switzerland 2015
P.L.P. Rau (Ed.): CCD 2015, Part I, LNCS 9180, pp. 176–185, 2015.
DOI: 10.1007/978-3-319-20907-4_16

skeletons that are fine tuned for specific project needs, corresponding to, for example, a project team's specific interests in relevant behaviour patterns, user goals, skills, and attitudes, and usage environments. Each persona skeleton is then filled with information, for example from interviews. A few added fictional personal details can then bring a persona to life. Similarly, *Contextual Design Models* (Holtzblatt et al. 2005) are also not well suited to communicating general cultural factors, since they have a broad focus on concrete aspects of computer usage contexts as identified in field studies that are focused on a specific project's needs.

In contrast, one existing UCD representation, *Scenarios,* could be given the generality needed to disseminate re-usable understandings of cultural factors for localization of global software products and services. Scenarios can avoid the fixed common skeletons of project-specific personas, and also the narrowly focused predefined models of Contextual Design. They may thus be better suited than personas and contextual design models for re-usable communication of cultural contextual factors. However, scenarios have many alternative forms, and thus we must identify a form that will appeal and be readily comprehensible for software designers who need to understand users from cultures different to their own, such as the Middle East.

A suitable scenario format could provide software designers with information on computer usage and preferences in Middle East countries, the problems that users face, how these arise in relation to cultural variables, and how these problems could impact usage. A creative synthesis of existing HCI approaches to expressing usage contexts could enable rapid familiarisation with Middle Eastern or other cultures by quickly exposing software designers to unfamiliar cultural factors that could affect computer usage in a range of cultures, without the need for extensive original primary research. This paper presents Dramatic Sketches and Micro Sketches as novel scenario formats for re-usable communication of cultural contextual factors.

2 Supporting Culturally Sensitive Design for Arab Countries

The computer has become a part of life in Arab countries at work, for study and for social and entertainment purposes, but still less so than in Western countries. However, experience and expertise in computer usage is rapidly evolving across the developing world. To gain an understanding of computer usage in Jordan, we carried out three field studies, one based on repeating a US study in Jordan (EL-Qirem and Cockton 2012) in between two interview studies. The results of these studies were combined with factors from a literature survey to create a comprehensive *Diamond Model* of cultural factors in computer usage (EL-Qirem and Cockton 2011). This novel compact design resource identified 46 cultural factors, which were grouped and organised into hierarchies. Information from the field studies was used to populate this model with Jordanian instances of cultural factors, where some had been discovered. This was not possible for some factors from the literature survey.

The identified factors were too extensive to combine within one or a few persona skeletons, and the resulting personas could add further unnecessary complexity to the cultural insights from our field research. At the same time, the general forms of example Jordanian instances for the Diamond Model could lack the focused specificity associated with well-designed personas, for example, the specific goals for users of a specific new software design. We thus needed an alternative format, potentially scenario based, to communicate Jordanian instances for Diamond Model factors. Dramatic Sketches emerged as this format.

There is no expectation that software developers would be given a Diamond Model with national instances and be expected to author Dramatic Sketches themselves. An initial set of sketches would be written by researchers familiar with the field research and the resulting instances of cultural variables. However, software developers may be able to extend a set of Dramatic Sketches provided to them by reference to the instances of a Diamond Model's cultural variables.

3   Dramatic Sketches

A Dramatic Sketch has two components: a scene and a dialogue. Scenes are introduced in forms similar ones used at the start of a scene in a play (hence *dramatic*). The second component is a dialogue. Scenes are set sparingly, and dialogues are informal in tone (hence *sketches*).

The combination of a scene sketch with a dialogue between fictitious individuals can allow a relatively large number of cultural factors to be represented within a single Dramatic Sketch. This can be more engaging and compact than scenarios as typically authored for specific software design projects. This would allow a relatively low number of Dramatic Sketches to cover all instances of the cultural factors for computer usage in Jordan that were discovered or confirmed by our field research. The expectation is that software designers could quickly read through these Dramatic Sketches to improve their understanding of Jordanian users and computer usage, and thus design more effective, efficient and enjoyable software.

There is no single specific recommended method for authoring Dramatic Sketches. Instead, the authoring of Dramatic Sketches is an *approach* (Woolrych et al. 2011) that openly and flexibly combines an (incomplete) set of (incomplete) design *resources*.

For each Dramatic Sketch, an author could choose a 'cast' of factors from the Diamond Model. This would require access to and familiarity with the Diamond Model and its associated instances, which would be aided by familiarity with the originating field work. Dramatic Sketches would thus be authored by researchers who are familiar with the cultural model and instances on which they are based. This familiarity, often extending to knowledge of the original field research, allows a researcher to select instances that support scene setting and dialogue generation. These instances are then combined a lively communication of experiences of, and attitudes towards, computers. However, Dramatic Sketches are not tied to the Diamond Model. Alternative informative resources could be used as a source of cultural factors and local examples long as there are narrative aspects to these examples.

Each Dramatic Sketch has a cast of Jordanian instances that can cover a range of cultural variables in the Diamond Model. Each time we write Dramatic Sketches, we could begin with a story skeleton and then fill in the detail with instances of cultural instances that can be connected into dialogues between people. Preparation for Dramatic Sketch authoring could start by listening to recorded interviews as a basis for identifying a story skeleton and selecting a cast of instances, based on the many usage and evaluation stories that were shared during the interviews.

3.1 Example Jordanian Dramatic Sketches

Dramatic Sketches are intended to complement, and not replace the Diamond Model. Therefore each example sketch is related to (specific instances of) cultural variables in the Diamond Model, and may also comment further on the role of these variables in the dialogue. Designers with access to the Diamond Model and sets of local instances for each factor can then use the Dramatic Sketch as an index into a more formal, detailed structured model. We now present four example sketches.

Dramatic Sketch 1: Ahmad and Dr. Lila. *Ahmad is an IT expert who works at AL Zaytoonah University of Jordan, Ahmad is a specialist in IT support who help students and employees' at the university to solve computer problems, such as technical problems, software problems, hardware problems, and network problems. Ahmad is 29 years old and has worked at the university for 6 years, so he has good experience in solving the computer problems that face the users in the university. Ahmad works every week day from Sunday to Thursday, from 9:00 am to 5:00 pm. He works at the computer centre (computer service for students and employees). One day, Ahmad is sitting at his desk working on his computer, programming some database tables for the registration department of the university, while he was seating in his office his phone rang, and he answered. A member of staff working at the nursing school needs help to solve her problem.*

Ahmad: Dr. Lila, what is the problem in your computer?
Dr. Lila: this morning I try to turn on my computer but it doesn't work.
Ahmad: did you turn the power on?
Dr. Lila: yes I did, and it's still not working.
Ahmad: then give me half an hour, I have some work to do after I finish it I will come to your office to solve the problem.
After 45 min Ahmad arrives late at Dr. Lila's office.
Ahmad: sorry I am late I had a problem in some programs on my computer and it took time to solve.
Dr. Lila: no problem, could you please check what is the problem in my computer?
Ahmad: sure, that's why I am here, let me see your computer please.

Then Ahmad looks at the computer and checks that the computer is connected to the electricity and it was connected. After that, he press the power button and the computer works, but still nothing appears on the screen, then Ahmad looks at the screen but the power light on the screen is not lighting. Ahmad presses the power button on the screen, then it's turned on and works.

Ahmad: the screen was not turned on therefore you can't see anything appear on the screen. You thought that the computer was broken and does not work, and the only problem is that the computer screen was not turned on.
Dr. Lila: really, I am so sorry, I didn't know because my computer knowledge is so poor.

The first Dramatic Sketch: Ahmad and Dr. Lila, involves a cast of Jordanian instances of Diamond Model variables (e.g., attitude to time, individualism, power distance, and personal experience/knowledge). For example, we draw attention to Jordanian attitudes to time keeping in the Dramatic Sketch above. Note that the weekend is different in Islamic countries and that power distance is high in Jordan. This is the basis for authoring a Dramatic Sketch, i.e., the author reviews the Diamond Model for a coherent set of instances that could be formed into a short story. This 'cast' of instances are then assembled into a Dramatic Sketch, filling in some details fictionally if necessary. Ideally, it should be possible to form the scene setting and dialogue wholly from instances for a specific culture.

Dramatic Sketch 2: Amjad and Tariq. Computers should help to accelerate work and make it easier, but not all cultures want to be speeded up. In Jordan, employees may enjoy the rest that can accompany a computer breakdown. When their computer stops working, they don't feel any responsibility to solve the problem or even call the IT support until they've had a rest. In a second Dramatic Sketch, the 'cast' is formed from Jordanian instances for cultural variables of attitude to time, individualism vs. collectivism, power distance, and attitudes to work. These are used to set a scene and form a dialogue.

Amjad is 30 years old and has worked in IT support a mobile company, (The Global for Mobile Phone Services) for more than 10 years. Amjad works at the company all weekdays (Sunday to Thursday) from 8:00am to 5:00 pm. He works in the programming department and also in IT support, helping employees to solve technical problems with their computers. There are another 5 IT support workers in the same department.

Amjad faces lots of technical problems during his work because most work at his company depends on computers such as connecting the mobile phones to the computer to update data and for programming mobile phones for customers.

Tariq works in the data-entry department and most of his work depends on computers. One day, Tariq's computer breaks down and by default Tariq should call the IT support to fix his computer and solve the problem, but this does not happen, and Tariq stays in his office sitting in his chair and relaxing. He didn't tell anyone immediately about his computer. At the same time, Tariq is supposed to have some work at the computer to submit to his manager today. While Tariq is sitting in his office, the phone rings, Tariq's manager is calling him to ask about the paper that Tariq should submit today.

> *Manager:* when will it be finished?
> *Tariq:* I am sorry I can't finish it today, because my computer has broken down and I can't continue my work now, I will wait until the computer is fixed and then I will continue my work.
> *Manager:* OK, I will wait until your computer is fixed and then I need the papers.

After the manger finished his call with Tariq, he calls IT support to check to ask if fixing the computer will take much more time, because Tariq had lots of work to do today. Amjad answers the phone.

> *Manager:* Hi, your department received today a computer from Tariq to fix, and I need you to fix the computer as soon as possible please because he has lots of work to do today.
> *Amjad:* one minute please I will check with my colleagues.

Amjad; sorry, but we haven't received Tariq's computer and also he did not call us today to ask for any help.
Manager: Ok, thank you I will check that with Tariq.

After that, Amjad called Tariq immediately and asked him if his computer has broken down or not.

Amjad: Hello Tariq, did you have any problem in your computer or not?
Tariq: Yes, my computer has been broken from more than 4 h.
Amjad: Then why you don't call us to fix your computer today?
Tariq: In fact, I don't want to call the IT support centre to fix my computer now.
Amjad: Why?
Tariq: I came in today and I found my computer broken and I don't want to call you to fix the problem, because I had lots of work to do today, and I need to have a rest and relax. Therefore when I saw the computer was broken, I decided not to call IT support to fix it. I will call them later to fix it, and during this time I will take a break from the work.
Amjad: But I knew from your manger that you have work to submit today.
Tariq: Yes that's right, but I prefer to have a rest from the work and tell my manager that my computer broke down and we need time to fix it. And you know Amjad that any problems with a computer will take time to solve and my manger will accept that.

Dramatic Sketch 3: Anas and his Teacher. The third Dramatic Sketch communicates how the English language could be useful to learn in Jordan. The cast of instances is formed from Diamond Model variables: English fluency and the role of the educational systems; attitudes towards Western Technology; familiarity with English spelling; Government Language Policy; text direction (language and semiotics); and authority and policy of companies. This wide diverse cast of cultural variables is combined into a Dramatic Sketch that covers a range of factors that will affect the usage of computer, e.g., forcing use of English software rather than Arabic. Also, government policies are different to private sector ones, as users should use Arabic software but in the private sector, Jordanian companies use English software. Private and public sector practices differ: most private companies use English software to communicate with the world. But government sectors use Arabic software as it will be simpler for users (the Jordanian public) who don't all speak or write English.

Anas is a student at Jordan University, who studies computer science. Anas uses his computer at home for studying, playing, graphic design and for internet use. Anas and his friends are in the same school, studying most subjects in English and using English software. One day, one of Anas' teachers asks students whether they prefer English software or software translated from English to Arabic.

Anas: Truly, I use some Arabic programs translated from English to Arabic and I face lots of problem, therefore I decide to use the English versions.
Teacher: Why Anas? And what are the problems that you face?
Anas: Some Arabic programs translate the word directly without anyone thinking about what it really means. Therefore it causes some changes in the meaning and sometimes causes confusion for us.
Teacher: what else Anas?
Anas: Also, when I use English software I develop my English language by reading and learning some new words. Typing and reading will be in English, therefore I will learn more and get more experience with the English language.
Teacher: That's true but sometimes we need to use Arabic programs, especially in the government and education sectors, because most of them use Arabic software.

Anas: Yes, but on the other hand there are private companies who prefer their employees to speak and write English fluently, and also have skills in using English software.

Dramatic Sketch 4: Nasser and Jamal. Some Diamond Model factors that form the cast of variables for a fourth Dramatic Sketch are: patterns of thinking and values, access to, and experience with, Technology, and affordability of internet access.

Nasser, 30 years old, has worked at bank in Jordan for more than 8 years, Nasser is using the computer all the time, at work or out of work. Nasser uses the internet most of time for chatting and sending email for his friends or family inside or outside Jordan.

Nasser: Most of time I am busy in the official holidays with my family and relatives and I don't find enough time to visit my friends therefore, I use the internet to send an electronic card by email to my friends at work and out of work.
One day he faced a weird situation, as Nasser himself told us:
It was special event (Eaid EL-ADHA) and I thought about sending an electronic card to all my friends before one day of the Eaid, because during the Eaid day I don't have enough time to use the computer, send e-card or even visit my friends. Therefore, I sent the e-card to more than 6 friends and all my friends received it.

After that, when Nasser returned to his work, he saw his friend at work Jamal (38 years old) who was one of Nasser's friends who was sent an e-card at the Eaid. Jamal looked angrily at Nasser, saying: I don't accept your greetings of the Eaid this year.

Nasser: Why Jamal, if there is something wrong? I sent to you and all my friends an e-card.
Jamal: And do you think that is greeting, it just an electronic card that is available on the internet.
Nasser: You don't like the e-card?
Jamal: No, the problem not in the e-card. The problem is the idea itself, and the principle of this idea.
Nasser: What principle?
Jamal: The tradition on this special day is to visit each other, sit and talk or even talk through the phone, not just send an e-card. Also I don't have an expensive internet connection in my home and I don't check my email all the Eaid's days therefore I just saw the e-card yesterday.
Nasser: But I thought that the e-card was a good substitute for a visit.
Jamal: No, that's not acceptable for me in our society; we must visit each other or at least talk by phone.
Nasser: I am sorry Jamal, next time I will visit you and not just send e-card.
Jamal: I prefer that, thank you.

3.2   Micro Sketches

In four Dramatic Sketches, we have covered an extensive range of relevant cultural variables. This supports the conjecture that a relatively set of Dramatic Sketches could cover most common cultural variables and their Jordanian instances. However, it may not be efficient or effective to cover the remaining variables via complete Dramatic Sketches for a range of reasons. It may result in unhelpful inefficient repetition, forced and ineffective story lines, or unrealistic scenes.

We have therefore complemented Dramatic Sketches with an additional more compact design resource. These *Micro Sketches* comprise little scene setting (or none) and a very short dialogue (or even a monologue or a single response from an interview). Generally, it is best to have some scene setting and not expect a short quote to speak for itself. Also, while Micro Sketches need not simply correspond to quotes from field data, there is no point in adding to or revising quotations that clearly communicate Jordanian instances of cultural variables.

Both forms of sketch are a good complement to the Diamond Model because they can express specific moments of time and place that we encountered as snapshots of, and flashbacks about usage, which simultaneously provide an accessible impression of people, their work and their work place.

Micro Sketch 1. The cultural variables that influence computer usage for this Micro Sketch are attitude to work and family obligation and relationships. Where there is no dependency on using the computer for most work, users will not be frustrated when facing problems, and won't care about usage problems very much. Here, the micro-sketch is just a quote from an interview:

Most of my work doesn't depend on computer and if the computer stops working, I have other work to do until IT support fix my computer

Inefficiencies in Jordanian workplaces are often related to the social or economic situation, including the income of employees, which can leave them inadequately motivated about their work. Also we found issues that may be rarer in western countries such as Nepotism in employment, which causes overstaffing at work that increase the number of employees and delays work by passing it between different people.

Micro Sketch 2. *After I finish my work I go home to do some works such as cooking, cleaning, take care of her child, visiting family or friends*

The main cultural variables that affecting usage in this Micro Sketch are: gender roles, and family obligation and relationships. The social life of woman in Jordan affects usage of computers. Woman return home after work to prepare food and take care of children, and thus don't have enough time to use computer at home. .

Gender roles impact usage of computers, letting men use computers more than women, which could affect computer skills by increasing the experience of the men when compared to women.

Micro Sketch 3. *Sometimes older people at work don't accept people younger than them teaching them how to use computers*

In this Micro Sketch the main cultural variables that affecting the usage are patterns of thinking and values, and age differences In this final example Micro Sketch, differences in age between teachers and learners impact usage of computer in Jordan. Older people reject learning from younger people, which could cause trouble for a company to convince them to learn from experts who are younger than them.

3.3 Analysis

The four Dramatic Sketches and three Micro Sketches cover 17 of the Diamond Model's 46 factors. Some variables are unlikely to apply in all HCI settings, such as material culture variables where there strong relation between these variables and computer usage is restricted to physical (ubiquitous) computing, which remains rare in Jordan. So, although it may be possible, using a similar range of cast sizes to the examples above, to cover all 46 identified cultural variables using 11 dramatic and 8 Micro Sketches, and fewer should be required to cover the Jordanian instances identified in this research. The expectation is that such a set of Dramatic and Micro Sketches would be more understandable and memorable than a textual Diamond Model with Jordanian instances. For reference, the factors and Jordanian instances that covered through Dramatic and Micro Sketches above are:

1. Attitude to Time
2. Individualism vs. Collectivism
3. Power Distance
4. Personal Experience/Knowledge
5. Attitudes to Work
6. English Fluency
7. Role of the Educational Systems
8. Familiarity with English Spelling Across Cultures
9. Government Language Policy
10. Text Direction
11. Companies' Policies
12. Patterns Of Thinking And Values
13. Access to, and Experience with, Technology
14. Affordability of Internet Access
15. Family Obligation and Relationships
16. Gender Roles
17. Age Differences

For other factors or variables in the Diamond Model, see EL-Qirem and Cockton (2011). We created Dramatic Sketches to explore alternative formats to the comprehensive text hierarchy of the Diamond Model. We did not think that this thorough text format would be easy to internalise and reflect on. We feel that the informal narrative formats of Dramatic and Micro Sketches are more approachable and will trigger thought and reflection on the part of software designers.

Dramatic and Micro Sketches have not been tested yet with actual software designers. We have presented detailed examples above to allow HCI researchers and Interaction Design practitioners to judge for themselves as to whether Dramatic and Micro Sketches are an effective format for rapid communication and challenge.

It is important to avoid stereotypes in culturally-sensitive Interaction Design. The sketches above are not true reflections of all Jordanian computer users, nor are they exclusive to Jordanian computer users. Their role is not to represent a single true reality, but to present examples of Jordanian culture in ways that expose and challenge software designers' assumptions. They illustrate how computer usage in another culture can differ from usage in software designers' home cultures. However, subcultures may exist in software designers' home markets that are similar to Jordan. For example, female roles and responsibilities could reduce the digital literacy in many software markets. Poor motivation at work, non-meritocratic employment and promotion practices, age hierarchies and similar factors are not unique to developing countries.

Our expectation is that our Dramatic Sketches can also promote reflection from software designers who are not targeting products and services at Arab markets, and expose the risks of assuming that all users are highly motivated digital experts who will be frustrated and annoyed by usage factors (EL-Qirem and Cockton 2012).

4   Conclusions

Selected casts of Diamon Model instances can be used as a basis to author the scene setting and dialogues for Dramatic Sketches, a more accessible and appealing format for communicating cultural differences to software designers. As with travel, our hope is that culturally specific Dramatic Sketches will broaden readers'minds by challenging established Western stereotypes and values, as well as reducing the time spent on familiarisation with Jordanian or other cultures. However, systematically evaluating the effectiveness of our novel promising communication formats is a task for future research.

References

EL-Qirem, F., Cockton, G.: Computer usage and user experience in jordan: development and application of the diamond model of territorial factors. In: Jacko, J.A. (ed.) Human-Computer Interaction, Part III, HCII 2011. LNCS, vol. 6763, pp. 490–499. Springer, Heidelberg (2011)

EL-Qirem, F.A., Cockton, G. : Repeating an experiment from the USA as a cultural probe into experiences of computer usage in Jordan. In: Strano, M., Hrachovec, H., Sudweeks, F., Ess, C. (eds.) Proceedings of Cultural Attitudes towards Technology and Communication (CATAC), Murdoch University, Australia, pp. 121–134 (2012). issuu.com/catac/docs/catac12_proceedings_part_1/204

Holtzblatt, K., Wendell, J., Wood, S.: A How-to Guide to Key Techniques for User-Centered Design. Morgan Kaufmann, San Francisco (2005)

Pruitt, J., Adlin, T.: The Persona Lifecycle: Keeping People in Mind throughout Product Design. Morgan Kaufmann, San Francisco (2006)

Woolrych, A., Hornbæk, K., Frøkjær, E., Cockton, G.: Ingredients and meals rather than recipes: a proposal for research that does not treat usability evaluation methods as indivisible wholes. IJHCI 27(10), 940–970 (2011)

A Formal Method for Evaluating the Performance Level of Human-Human Collaborative Procedures

Dan Pan[1] and Matthew L. Bolton[2(✉)]

[1] Department of Industrial Engineering, Tsinghua University, Beijing 100084,
People's Republic of China
pand10@mails.tsinghua.edu.cn
[2] Department of Industrial and Systems Engineering, University at Buffalo,
State University of New York, Amherst, NY 14260, USA
mbolton@buffalo.edu

Abstract. Human-human interaction is critical to safe operations in domains like nuclear power plants (NPP) and air transportation. Usually collaborative procedures and communication protocols are developed to ensure that relevant information is correctly heard and actions are correctly executed. Such procedures should be designed to be robust to miscommunications between humans. However, these procedures can be complex and thus fail in unanticipated ways. To address this, researchers have been investigating how formal verification can be used to prove the robustness of collaborative procedures to miscommunications. However, previous efforts have taken a binary approach to assessing the success of such procedures. This can be problematic because some failures may be more desirable than others. In this paper, we show how specification properties can be created to evaluate the level of success of a collaborative procedure formally. We demonstrate the capability of these properties to evaluate a realistic procedure for a NPP application.

Keywords: Formal method · Human communication · Human error

1 Introduction

Human collaboration is essential to team performance. By collaborating, team members perform different tasks and share information to ensure mutual understanding. Although the importance of human collaboration is self-evident, its successful execution is anything but guaranteed. Failures and breakdowns in human collaboration have been associated with many accidents and incidents. For example, communication errors have been implicated in a significant percentage of accidents in the workplace in general [12], roadway accidents [10], medical deaths [14] and aviation accidents [6]. Communication error is also one of the main causes of accidents and incidents in nuclear power plants (NPPs). For example, 25 % of Japanese [8] and 10 % of German [12] NPP incidents were caused by communication failure.

From these data, we can conclude that if the human teammates could communicate and collaborate better, the safety of many systems would be improved. Standard

P.L.P. Rau (Ed.): CCD 2015, Part I, LNCS 9180, pp. 186–197, 2015.
DOI: 10.1007/978-3-319-20907-4_17

collaborative procedures and communication protocols are used to ensure effective and efficient collaboration in many safety-critical systems. Such procedures are used in air traffic control communications, operations in the MCR of nuclear power plants, practices of surgical teams, and handoff of care protocols in hospitals. However, ensuring that collaborative procedures are robust to all operational conditions is difficult. There is concurrency between the parts of procedures which different operators execute, which can induce unanticipated interactions between people. Further, humans are fallible and can miscommunicate. Thus, it can be difficult to evaluate the safety of collaborative procedures using conventional analyses like experimentation and simulation since they can miss unexpected interactions.

Formal verification, which is a form of mathematical proof, offers analysis techniques capable of considering all of the possible interactions. While formal methods have been used to evaluate machine communication protocols, these methods are ill-suited for use with human collaborative procedures for several reasons. First, humans behave differently from machines. Humans follow tasks as opposed to machine code and human communication must be contextualized as part of a task [13]. Second, humans are fallible in ways that are different from machines. Thirdly, human collaborative procedures are inherently less fragile because of the looser dynamics of human-human communication. As such, the outcome of a human communication may represent degrees of success beyond the binary (correct or incorrect). For example, if two operators are attempting to diagnose a problem, it is problematic if the operators end up with only one reaching the correct conclusion. However, this is better than if both reach the same incorrect conclusion because the incorrect conclusion has a better chance of being identified and corrected as humans continue to collaborate.

Work has evaluated procedures in both collaborative and non-collaborative contexts formally to determine if they are safe, even with generated erroneous behavior and/or miscommunications [2, 3]. However, these analyses are still limited in that they only consider the binary success of human collaboration. This is constraining because it does not give analysts the tools they need to fully evaluate the robustness of such procedures. Thus, there is a real need for an approach that will account for miscommunication while giving analysts metrics for evaluating the degrees of a procedure's success in different conditions.

In this paper, we extend an approach [12] to allow an analyst to model human collaborative procedures in the context of a task analytic modeling formalism and use model checking to evaluate the degrees of a procedure's success.

2 Background

2.1 Formal Method

Formal methods are tools and techniques for proving that a system will always perform as intended [5]. Model checking is an automated approach to formal verification. In model checking, a system model represents of a system's behavior in a mathematical formalism (usually a finite state machine). A specification represents a formal description of a desirable property about the system, usually in a temporal logic.

Finally, model checking produces a verification report either a confirmation or a counterexample. A counterexample illustrates incremental model states that resulted in the specification being violated.

There are a variety of temporal and modal logics that have been used for specification. The most common one, and the one used in the presented work, is linear temporal logic (LTL). LTL allows one to assert properties about all of the paths through a model. It does this using model variables and basic Boolean logic operators ($\land$, $\lor$, $\neg$, $\Rightarrow$, and $\Leftrightarrow$). Additionally, it has temporal operators that allow for assertions about how variables ordinally change over time. Thus, using LTL, an analyst can assert that something (Φ) should always be true G Φ; that it will always be true in the next state X Φ; that it will be true in the future F Φ; or that it will be true until something else (Ψ) is true Φ U Ψ.

2.2 Formal Methods for Human-Human Communication and Coordination

While formal methods have traditionally been used in the analysis of computer hardware and software systems [12], a growing body of work has been investigating how to use them to evaluate human factors issues [3]. However, when it comes to issues of human-human communication and coordination, there has been very little work. Paternò et al. [11] extended the Concur Task Trees formalism to allow for the modeling of human-human coordination and communication, where communications could have different modalities (synchronous or asynchronous, point-to-point, or broadcast). They used this to formally evaluate pilot and air traffic control radio communications during runway operations using different shared task representations. While useful, this method did not easily distinguish between separate and shared operator tasks, nor did it account for potential miscommunications. Both limitations were addressed by the Enhanced Operator Function Model with Communications.

2.3 Enhanced Operator Function Model with Communication (EOFMC)

EOFMC [1] extended the Enhanced Operator Function Model (EOFM) [4] to support the modeling of human-human communication and coordination as shared task structures between human operators. Specifically, EOFMC represents groups of human operators engaging in shared activities as an input/output system. Inputs represent human interface, environment, and/or mission goal concepts. Outputs are human actions. The operators' task models (local variables) describe how human actions are produced and how the internal state of the human (perceptual or cognitive) changes.

Each task in an EOFMC is a goal directed activity that decomposes into other goal directed activities and, ultimately, atomic actions. Tasks can either belong to one human operator, or they can be shared between human operators. A shared task is explicitly associated with two or more human operators, making it clear which human operators perform each part of a task.

Activities can have preconditions, repeat conditions, and completion conditions (collectively referred to as strategic knowledge). These are represented by Boolean expressions written in terms of input, output, and local variables as well as constants. They specify what must be true before an activity can execute (precondition), when it can execute again (repeat condition), and what is true when it has completed execution (completion condition).

An activity's decomposition has an operator that specifies how many sub-activities or actions (acts) can execute and what the temporal relationship is between them. In the presented work, only the following decomposition operators are important:

sync – all acts must be performed synchronously (at the exact same time);
xor – exactly one act must be performed;
and_seq – all of the acts must be performed, one at a time, in any order;
ord – all of the acts must be performed, one at a time, in the order listed; and
com – a communication action is performed (this is discussed subsequently).

Actions occur at the bottom of EOFMC task hierarchies. Actions are either an assignment to an output variable (indicating an action has been performed) or a local variable (representing a perceptual, cognitive, or communication action). Meanwhile, decomposition can specify how many sub-activities or actions can execute and what the temporal relationship is between them. Shared activities can explicitly include human-human communication using the com decomposition. In such decompositions, communicated information from one human operator can be received by other human operators (modeled as an update to a local variable). By exploiting the shared activity and communication action feature of EOFMC, human-human communication protocols can be modeled as shared task activities.

EOFMC has formal semantics that specify how an instantiated EOFMC model executes. Each activity or action has one of three execution states: Ready (waiting to execute), Executing, and Done. An activity or action transitions between states based on the state of itself, its parent activity (if it has one), the other acts in the given decomposition, the children that decompose from it, and its strategic knowledge. These semantics are the basis for the EOFMC translator that allows EOFMC models to be automatically incorporated into the input language of the Symbolic Analysis Laboratories family of model checkers.

Bass et al. [1] used EOFMC to model and evaluate communication protocols used to convey clearances between air traffic control and pilots. Bolton [2] extended the EOFMC infrastructure to enable the automatic generation of miscommunications in EOFMC models. In miscommunication generation, any given communication action can execute normatively, have the source of the communication convey the wrong information, have one or more of the communication recipients receive the wrong information, or both. In all analyses, the analyst is able to control the maximum number of miscommunications that can occur (Max). The net effect of this is that analysts can evaluate how robust a protocol is for all possible ways that Max or fewer miscommunications can occur. Bolton used this to evaluate the robustness of different protocols air traffic control could use to communicate clearances to pilots.

A limitation of all of these EOFMC studies is that they only considered specifications that would indicate whether or not the evaluated protocols always accomplished their goals, where perfect performance was required for the specification to prove true. For example, in [2], formal verifications would only return a confirmation if, at the end of a given protocol, the entered clearance matched what was intended by the air traffic controller. While useful, such analyses do not give analysts nuanced insights into the performance of the protocol or the criticality of the failure.

3   Objectives

There is a real need for an approach that will allow analysts to evaluate the degree to which a human-human collaborative procedure succeeds with and without miscommunication. This paper describes an extension of the approach found in [1, 2] that addresses this need. Specifically, we introduce novel specification criteria capable of allow analysts to diagnostically evaluate the performance of a human-human collaborative procedure, where each specification asserts that the procedure must perform at a different level of success; that is, assert an outcome that falls along an ordinal continuum of desirable outcomes. By formally verifying the specifications, the analyst will be able to determine what level of performance can be guaranteed with a given collaborative procedure and a given number of miscommunications. Because human-human collaborative procedures can vary drastically from one application to another, there is no clear way to develop generic diagnostic specifications for all procedures. Thus, we contextualize our work in terms of a specific application.

In the following sections, a NPP application is used to demonstrate how our method works. Firstly, the background of this application, a Steam Generator Tube Rupture (SGTR) scenario, is described. A procedure for diagnosing a SGTR with two operators and a human-human communication protocol are then introduced. We next use EO-FMC to model the SGTR diagnosis procedure and translate it into SAL. Different versions of the SAL file are created, each allowing for different maximum numbers of miscommunications. Then, we identify six performance levels associated with SGTR diagnosis procedure and formulate them as specifications that are formally verified with model checking. We present these results along with an interpretation of their meaning. Finally, we discuss the results and outline future areas of research.

4   Application

In pressurized water reactors (PWR), a SGTR accident is quite frequent since a variety of degradation processes from the steam generator tubing system can lead to tube cracking, wall thinning, and potential leakage or rupture [9]. The SGTR accidents involve a leak from the reactor coolant system (RCS) to the steam generator (SG) that leads to the primary coolant flowing into the secondary system. If the safety systems are unavailable, or operators take incorrect or late actions, the secondary pressure will increase rapidly. The secondary water or vapor with radioactive substances will be released into the environment. Even more seriously, the loss of reactor coolant may cause core damage. Once the core damage occurs, and if the containment is bypassed, serious radioactivity release will happen [9]. With its high occurrence frequency and capacity for causing serious radioactivity consequences, the operators' successful intervention after a SGTR accident is vital for system safety.

The example used in this study occurs in a 900MWe pressurized water reactor NPP where an alarm indicates if safety injection has lasted over 5 min. Two operators (operator 1 and operator 2) in main control need to collaborate to diagnose whether it is a SGTR accident.

4.1 SGTR Diagnosis Procedure and Communication Protocol

For safety purposes, human operators are expected to strictly follow the SGTR diagnosis procedure and associated human-human communication protocol. When an alarm sounds indicating safety injection has lasted over 5 min, operators need to collaboratively diagnose the situation using the procedure in Fig. 1.

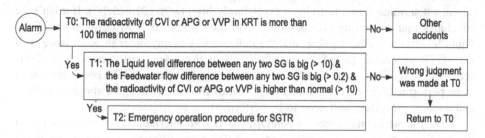

Fig. 1. SGTR diagnosis procedure

At T0, the operators must observe the CVI, APG, and VVP radioactivity and judge whether they are more than 100 times their normal values. If not, the operators should conclude that it is not a SGTR accident and proceed to other diagnostic procedures (not discussed here). If true, the operators should proceed to T1.

At T1, the operators should observe the liquid level and feedwater flow rates of all three SG and judge whether (a) the liquid level difference between any two SG is big, namely more than 10 %, (b) the feedwater flow difference between any two SG is big, namely more than 0.2 E5 kg/h, and (c) one or more of the CVI, APG, and/or VVP radioactivity parameters are higher than normal. If (a), (b) and (c) are true, the operators should conclude that an SGTR accident has occurred and that the emergency operation procedure for an SGTR accident (a T2 procedure) should be performed. If not, the operators should conclude that something other than a SGTR accident has occurred and perform other diagnostic procedures (see [7]).

During the collaborative diagnostic process, two operators have to obey a communication protocol for confirming the iterative conclusions (reached through the diagnosis of the liquid, feedwater flow, and radioactivity levels) and final conclusion (whether or not to perform at T2 procedure) that are reached. In this protocol, operator 1 (Op1) takes the lead and is responsible for confirming conclusions with operator 2 (Op2). It proceeds as follows:

1. Op1 comes to a conclusion about the system.
2. Op1 communicates his[1] conclusion to Op2.
3. Op2 checks the system to see if he agrees with Op1's conclusion.
4. Op2 states whether he agrees or disagrees with Op1.
5. If Op1 hears a confirmation ("agree"), then he proceeds to a different diagnostic activity. If not, Op1 must re-evaluate his original conclusion.

4.2   Modeling

The SGTR diagnosis procedure was implemented as an instantiated EOFMC (visualized in Figs. 2, 3 and 4). This model has two human operators: Op1 and Op2. Op1 is responsible for working through the SGTR diagnosis procedure (Fig. 2). In this, when an alarm sounds, Op1 attempts to diagnose the procedure by first dismissing previous conclusions he may have made about the system (aResetConclusions). Then, he must determine if radioactivity is exceedingly high (aOp1CheckT0). If it isn't, he concludes that something else is wrong with the system. If it is, he must check the liquid levels, the feedwater flow, and the radioactivity in any order in accordance with the SGTR procedure (aOp1CheckT1). If all of these are consistent with a SGTR accident, he should conclude (aOp1FormConclusion) that the T2 procedure needs to be performed. However, if at any point one of the checks fails, he should conclude that another procedure will need to be performed.

At any stage in this process, when Op1 reaches an intermediate or final conclusion (that radioactivity is too high, that feedwater flows are different, that liquid levels are different, that procedure T2 must be performed, etc.), he must confirm that conclusion with Op2 before he can complete the associated activity.

This confirmation process occurs via the previously discussed communication protocol, which is represented in the model as a shared task (Fig. 3). In this, when Op1 has an unchecked conclusion, he must communicate that conclusion to Op2. If Op2 agrees with the conclusion he will communicate back an "Agree", otherwise he will communicate a "Disagree". Note that at the beginning and end of the communication protocol, variables are reset to ensure proper communications between the different tasks (Figs. 2, 3 and 4) in the model.

Op2 is responsible for the procedures he uses to determine whether he agrees or disagrees with Op1's conclusions using the tasks pattern in Fig. 4. Op2 has separate tasks for confirming or contradicting each of the conclusions (final or otherwise) that Op1 has reached using the same criteria as Op1.

The complete, instantiated EOFMC task model was converted into the language of the Symbolic Analysis Laboratory (SAL) using the EOFMC java-based translator [4]. The SAL version of the model was then modified to create different versions for analyses. Specifically, in each version of the model, the maximum number of communication errors (Max) was set from 0 to 4 in increments of 1.

---

[1] Note that in the Chinese NPP used as the basis for this work, all operators are male.

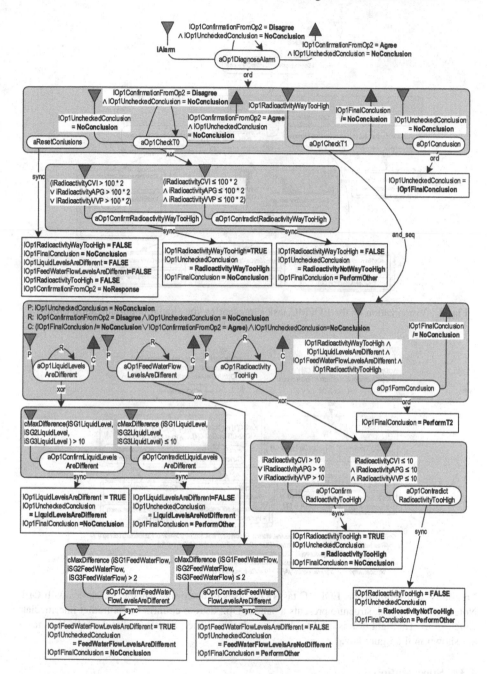

Fig. 2. Visualization of the instantiated EOFMC collaborative procedure representing the task performed by Op1.

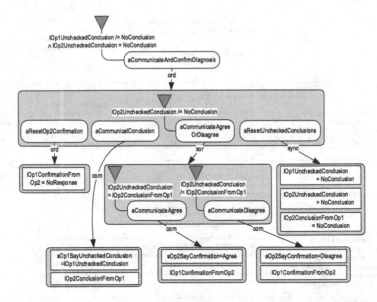

Fig. 3. Visualization of the EOFMC task representing the shared communication protocol

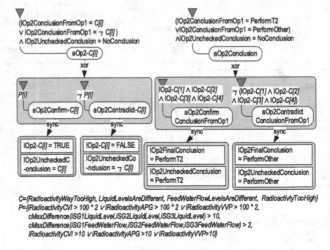

Fig. 4. Visualization of the EOFMC tasks Op2 uses to determine whether he agrees with Op1. Note that the left task structure presents a pattern Op2 uses to confirm or contradict intermediate conclusions. The right task is used for final conclusions. The parameters that describe both tasks are shown in the figure key.

4.3 Specification

To assess the degree of success of this procedure for different maximum numbers of miscommunications, we needed to derive specifications representing different outcomes indicative of different levels of performance. To accomplish this, we observed that the goal of the procedure was to ensure that the operators achieved an accurate consensus about the system and what to do in response to the alarm. Within the model, this could be indicated by the final and intermediate conclusions reached between the two operators. Thus, we identified the different ways that agreement could manifest after the performance of the procedure based on the final conclusions reached by each and, if they were correct, if the intermediary conclusions were consistent. We considered the safety implications of each of these outcomes and ordered them based on their desirability going from A (most desirable) to F (least desirable) (Table 1).

Table 1. Diagnosis outcomes

	Description
A	Op1 and Op2 reach the correct final conclusion and the same intermediary conclusions
B	Op1 and Op2 reach the correct final conclusion but differ on the intermediary conclusions
C	Op1 has the correct final conclusion and Op2 does not
D	Op2 has the correct final conclusion and Op1 does not
E	Op1 and Op2 have different wrong final conclusions
F	Op1 and Op2 have the same wrong final conclusion

In the most desirable outcome (A), both Op1 and Op2 reach the correct final conclusion and the same intermediate conclusions. In the second most desirable outcome (B), they both reach the same final conclusion, but have different intermediate conclusions. This is a slightly less desirable outcome to A because the difference in intermediary conclusions represents a disagreement in the situational understanding between the operators that could potentially lead to confusion in later processes. Any situation where wrong final conclusions are reached (C – F) is undesirable. However, it is more desirable for Op1 to reach the correct final conclusion (C) since he is in charge of leading the response. This is slightly better than outcome D, where Op1 has reached the wrong final conclusion but Op2 the right one. This is still more desirable than latter outcomes because Op2 having the right final conclusion will increase the chances that the discrepancy will be noticed and that corrective action will be taken. In situations where both Op1 and Op2 reach the wrong final conclusions (E and F), it is more desirable for Op1 and Op2 to reach different conclusions as this could allow them to potentially discover their disagreement as activities proceed. Finally, a situation where Op1 and Op2 both reach the same wrong final conclusion is clearly the worst outcome, because they are more likely to proceed based on their wrong conclusion without noticing any disagreement.

The levels were expressed specification properties (Table 2). Each was designed so that, if it verified true, its corresponding level of performance was guaranteed.

4.4   Formal Verification and Results

Formal verifications were performed using SAL's Symbolic Model Checker (SAL-SMC). For each system model with different values of Max, all six of the specifications (Table 2) were checked starting with I and working towards VI. At any

Table 2. Specifications of different performance levels

Performance Level	Specification
I	G (A)
II	G (A or B)
III	G (A or B or C)
IV	G (A or B or C or D)
V	G (A or B or C or D or E)
VI	G (A or B or C or D or E or F)

Note. A – F are diagnostic outcomes (Table 1) expressed logically using model variables.

point in this process, if a specification verified to true, verifications on that model stopped. The specification that verified to true indicated the performance level guaranteed by that model. These analyses revealed that this collaborative procedure achieves different performance levels in different conditions. For no miscommunications, the model performed at level I. For all other values of Max, the model performed at level III (guaranteeing at least an outcome of C). Given that the models consistently performed at level III as the maximum number of miscommunications increased beyond 0, it is very likely that this perform level would continue to be observed if Max was further increased. This is a positive result for the procedure because it indicates that the lead operator will always reach the correct conclusion. Since the lead operator is responsible for executing interventions based on the conclusion he reaches, this means that the procedure will likely be successful even with miscommunications.

5 Discussion and Future Work

The presented work constitutes a significant contribution in that it gives analysts the ability to better assess the robustness of human-human collaborative procedure using formal verification. Specifically, by allowing analyst to assess the level of performance guaranteed by a procedure, analysts can gain additional insights into how well it will perform. The application described in this study is illustrative of the power of our approach. Specifically, if the presented procedure were formally evaluated in the traditional way, just at level I, it would be considered a failure for all Max values greater than 0. By verifying our novel specifications, it is now clear that, although it does not provide perfect performance, the procedure does provide some guarantees that the correct conclusion will be reached. Thus, the presented work gives analysts who wish to formally evaluate human-human communication and coordination procedures formally deeper analysis capabilities.

There are a number of directions that could be explored in future work. First, besides miscommunication, other erroneous human behavior can be generated in the formal representation of the EOFMCs [3]. Future work will investigate this possibility. Second, an analyst may wish to compare the performance of different procedures. The presented approach should give analysts means of doing this based on procedure performance levels. Future work should explore how our method could be used to compare procedures. Finally, the specifications presented here are specific to the application we used. Ideally, we would be able to create specifications representing different performance levels for any procedure or domain based on a generic theory. Future work should investigate if such a generic approach is possible.

References

1. Bass, E.J., Bolton, M.L., Feigh, K., Griffith, D., Gunter, E., Mansky, W., Rushby, J.: Toward a multi-method approach to formalizing human-automation interaction and human-human communications. In: 2011 IEEE International Conference on Systems, Man, and Cybernetics, pp. 1817–1824 (2011)
2. Bolton, M.L.: Model checking human-human communication protocols using task models and miscommunication generation. J. Aerosp. Comput. Inf. Commun. doi:10.2514/1. I010276. (in press, 2015)
3. Bolton, M.L., Bass, E.J., Siminiceanu, R.I.: Using formal verification to evaluate human-automation interaction: A review. IEEE Trans. Syst. Man, Cyberne.: Syst. **43**(3), 488–503 (2013)
4. Bolton, M.L., Siminiceanu, R.I., Bass, E.J.: A systematic approach to model checking human–automation interaction using task analytic models. IEEE Trans. Syst. Man Cybern. Part A Syst. Hum. **41**(5), 961–976 (2011)
5. Clarke, E.M., Wing, J.M.: Formal methods: state of the art and future directions. ACM Comput. Surv. (CSUR) **28**(4), 626–643 (1996)
6. Connell, L.: Pilot and controller communication issues. In: Methods and Metrics of Voice Communication, pp. 19–27 (1996)
7. Dong, X.: Influence of Human-system Interface Design Method and Time Pressure on Human Error. Master thesis. Tsinghua University, Beijing, China (2010)
8. Hirotsu, Y., Suzuki, K., Kojima, M., Takano, K.: Multivariate analysis of human error incidents occurring at nuclear power plants: several occurrence patterns of observed human errors. Cogn. Technol. Work **3**(2), 82–91 (2001)
9. MacDonald, P.E., Shah, V.N., Ward, L.W., Ellison, P.G.: Steam generator tube failures. NUREG/CR-6365, INEL-95/0393. Nuclear Regulatory Commission, Washington, DC, United States (1996)
10. Murphy, P.: The role of communications in accidents and incidents during rail possessions. In: Engineering Psychology and Cognitive Ergonomics, vol. 5, pp. 447–454 (2001)
11. Paternò, F., Santoro, C., Tahmassebi, S.: Formal models for cooperative tasks: concepts and an application for en-route air traffic control. In: Markopoulos, P., Johnson, P. (eds.) Proceedings of the 5th International Conference on Design, Specification, and Verification of Interactive Systems, pp. 71–86. Springer, Vienna (1998)
12. Strater, O.: Investigation of communication errors in nuclear power plants. Communication in High Risk Environments. Linguistische Berichte, Sonderheft **12**, 155–179 (2003)
13. Traum, D., Dillenbourg, P.: Miscommunication in multi-modal collaboration. In: AAAI Workshop on Detecting, Repairing, And Preventing Human–Machine Miscommunication, pp. 37–46 (1996)
14. Wilson, R.M., Runciman, W.B., Gibberd, R.W., Harrison, B.T., Newby, L., Hamilton, J.D.: The quality in Australian health care study. Med. J. Aust. **163**(9), 458–471 (1995)

The Effect of Tactile Feedback on Mental Workload During the Interaction with a Smartphone

Peter Rasche[1(✉)], Alexander Mertens[1], Christopher Schlick[1], and Pilsung Choe[2]

[1] Chair and Institute of Industrial Engineering and Ergonomics of RWTH Aachen, Aachen 52062, Germany
p.rasche@iaw.rwth-aachen.de
[2] Department of Mechanical and Industrial Engineering, Qatar University, Doha, Qatar
pchoe@qu.edu.qa

Abstract. This empirical study examines the adequacy of tactile feedback to present status information about the progress of Internet-based services on mobile devices and possibilities to compensate age-related changes in users performance. Therefore the user experience of mobile browsing was compared using three different vibration signals and two different levels of process times. In this experiment the participants had to perform two tasks simultaneously. The participants experienced six different (combinations treatments) permutations in treatment with regard to 'vibration type' and 'process time.' The user experience was measured by the Technology Acceptance Model and the subjective mental workload by the NASA Task Load Index using a questionnaire. The experiment revealed that a short vibration signal at the end of a process is capable of increase the user experience. Therefore, 'perceived enjoyment' as well as 'perceived usefulness' improved. However, the characteristic factor 'mental workload' decreased with usage of tactile feedback.

Keywords: Design for social development · Demographic change · Aging-appropriate design

1 Introduction

The mobile use of Internet and web application and services often leads to problems regarding interference. Raskin [1] defines interference in the context of human-computer-interaction as a trade off a user has to conduct in order to perform more than one simultaneous task, which cannot be automated (such as navigating to a desired destiny). In such situation the user has to divide his attention to cope with the tasks. Usually users' performance decreases in such situations. This problem is specially critical in the context of using mobile devices in complex situations of daily life. An example of a complex situation is a pedestrian, who uses a mobile device during the crossover of a multi-lane road. An increased risk of accidents is verified as a result of the operation of a mobile device [2]. Furthermore, the individual risk increases, if the

© Springer International Publishing Switzerland 2015
P.L.P. Rau (Ed.): CCD 2015, Part I, LNCS 9180, pp. 198–208, 2015.
DOI: 10.1007/978-3-319-20907-4_18

user's age is considered due to age-related changes of the perception, cognition and motor skills [2]. Considering the demo graphic change, the problem of interference during operation of mobile devices is a critical problem. Internet-based services will have a growing importance for social participation, enhancing the quality of life and medical care for the aging society today and in the future. More than 50 % of the over 50-year-old women and men in Germany are already connected to the Internet by mobile devices and their barrier-free and secure access to Internet-based services. Even in complex situations of daily life, it is an extremely effective tool for a self-determined and fulfilled life [3, 4].

The problem described above can be addressed by providing features that enable users of mobile devices to focus the attention on the primary task (e.g. crossing a street) during non-productive portions of the secondary activity (e.g. loading new information during the use of Internet-based services). A state of the art solution for this problem is a loading-bar as known from stationary computers. Information about the progress of a process is passed on visually to the user. Using such an interface on a small screen increases the problem of interference and thereby exposes the user to unnecessary high stress and risk of accidents [5]. Therefore this empirical study examines, based on Brewster and King [6], whether a tactile feedback is appropriate to present the status information about the progress of data download on mobile devices and thereby could compensate age-related changes in user performance. Using an appropriate tactile feedback, the user should be able to focus on the primary task during phases in which no user interaction within the secondary task is necessary, although the user has continuous information about the status of the secondary task [1]. The term vibration-loading interface is defined in the context of this experiment as an interface presenting a visual progress bar, which is enhanced by a vibration signal.

2 Research Model

User experience is a common approach to determine whether software meets users' needs. One common and robust attempt to determine user experience is to evaluate the user's attitude toward usage of the examined technology, which is measured by the Technology Acceptance Model (TAM) [7]. It describes the influence of the techno-logical innovation factors of 'perceived usefulness' and 'perceived ease of use' on the user's behavioral intention to use this innovation. During the last decade, this model has been modified several times to meet the constantly evolving challenges of new technologies and users' needs. It was extended by several factors, such as 'perceived enjoyment' [8] or redesigned to meet the upcoming challenges of the smartphone industry [9, 10]. As shown by all of these researches TAM is a powerful tool, which is why it will be used as basis for the research model in this experiment [11, 12]. Based on the research assumptions the dependent variables 'perceived enjoyment', 'perceived usefulness' and 'mental workload' have influence on the usage of a vibration-loading interface. The first two variables are accepted in the context of user experience and the TAM model [13–15]. The dependent variable 'perceived enjoyment' measures the users' enjoyment of the entire situation during each treatment. Therefore, it should be possible to determine a vibration-loading interface that is accepted by users in multitasking situations. The dependent variable 'perceived usefulness' should support this by measuring whether the users think the experienced vibration-loading interface is useful during the performance of the multitasking situation. At least, the dependent variable 'mental workload' should validate the measurements of the first two variables, because an enjoyable and useful vibration-loading interface is expected to decrease users' mental workload during the experiment. This variable will be evaluated by the NASA Task Load Index will measure the subjective 'mental workload'. The NASA TLX tool, developed by NASA in 1988, divides mental workload into six different factors. These factors are 'mental demand,' 'physical demand,' 'time pressure,' 'expended effort,' 'achieved performance level' and 'experienced frustration' [16].

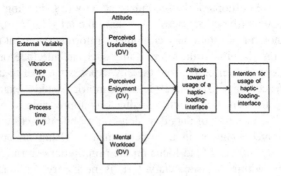

Fig. 1. Research model

To measure the influence of vibration feedback on the user experience, two independent variables were defined (see Fig. 1). The first is called 'process time' and the second is called 'vibration type' according to the research model. Roto and Oulasvirta [5] found that vibration feedback is useful for interaction pauses lasting longer than 4 s. If the process time is shorter than this, users may feel annoyed by it. To avoid this problem, the minimal process time in this experiment was set to 5 s. Beneath the 5-second process time participants experienced, a second, longer process time. The duration of the second should be longer than 10 s, as this time frame is known in the context of the 10-second-response rule among certain experts [17]. According to this rule, users shift their attention toward other things and away from the performed computer task if a process lasts longer than 10 s. It is assumed that this rule is also valid for users in a mobile environment. This is indicated by an experiment performed by Oulasvirta et al. [18]. During their experiment, smartphone users shifted their attention up to eight times away from the smartphone and back during a process depending on their mobile environment. Furthermore, it was reported by their experiment indicated that the average time a user spends glancing at the display of a smartphone also differs according to the environment [5]. On the other hand, the process time should not be too long, otherwise users could be annoyed [19]. Therefore, the second level of the independent variable 'process time' was 12.5 s. The second independent variable 'vibration type' has three levels 'continuous vibration', 'end vibration' and 'no vibration'. The first vibration type 'continuous vibration' is defined as a continuous vibration signal that will last as long as the process proceeds. 'End vibration' is defined as a short vibration signal with fixed frequency and a duration of 500 ms. The vibration signal occurs when the process is completed and the vibration-loading interface is closed. The frequency of the vibration signals was the default vibration signal provided by the smartphone Samsung GT-S5830. The last vibration type, 'no vibration' is a vibration-loading interface which provides no tactile feedback. This level is used as baseline and increases the possibilities of interpreting the results of this experiment. Based on the combination of the independent variables' levels, the mobile application simulates six different treatments with individual vibration-loading interfaces, consisting of 'vibration type' and 'process time' (see Fig. 2). Hence, participants experienced each vibration type during a long- and a short-lasting process.

		Vibration Type		
		Continuous Vibration	End Vibration	No Vibration
Process Time	Short	Treatment 1	Treatment 3	Treatment 5
	Long	Treatment 2	Treatment 4	Treatment 6

Fig. 2. External variables and configuration matrix

3 Methods

Participants. This experiment was carried out at Tsinghua University in Beijing, China in 2013. 30 participants (24 male and six female) with a European cultural background took part in the experiment. All participants were smartphone users who were highly familiar with Internet functions of their smartphones.

Experimental Design. This experiment evaluated the user experience of participants during the simultaneous performance of two tasks [20, 21]. The primary task was to watch a short movie, presented on a laptop (Apple MacBook Pro mid2012 OSX 10.8.2). Watching the information video should animate the participants and draw their attention away from the smartphone. Each short movie had the same duration of 2:30 min. The second task participants performed was a search task on a provided smartphone. The mobile application necessary for the search task was developed in MIT Appinventor on a MacBook Pro (2012, OSX 10.8.2) and was installed on a Samsung GT-S5830 under Android 2.2 Froyo for the experiment. To minimize the necessary number of participants, each participant experienced all six different treatments and thereby six different vibration-loading interfaces. The order of the movies was the same for every participant. However, the order of treatments was randomized for each participant. That means, no participant watched the same movie during the same treatment, nor did they perform different treatments in the same order. This was necessary, since the experiment provided no training with the mobile application. Furthermore, a random order should serve to eliminate the influence of learning effects on the results of this experiment. To underscore this approach, the participants were not informed which combination of the independent variables each treatment had. The smartphone was held in the right hand.

Apparatus. The environment of this experiment was challenging in terms of minimizing the effects of environmental disturbance. The participants were provided with headphones to avoid the possibility of hearing the vibration signal or other environmental sounds. The whole laboratory setting is shown in Fig. 3. The used application provided six different vibration-loading interfaces. The implemented vibration-loading interface presented a visual process-progress bar, which was improved by a vibration signal depending on the independent variable 'vibration type'. The interface stayed visible as long as the independent variable 'process time' corresponded to the treatment defined. Further, the application should require mental involvement of its users, which was achieved by asking the users to accomplish a search task. This task was based on a certain question the users were presented with in the application during the experiment. The answer of each question was presented after the user completed the right search path within the application. The search paths were designed according to a search path of an Internet search on a desktop computer. The search task simulates the use of different webpage links to achieve a certain page or information. Since this experiment focused on the user experience of vibration-loading interfaces, the user-based input was minimized to clicking certain buttons during the search task. Three screens within the application, which provided six different buttons from which to choose, were established to further increase mental effort. These screens are called search screens in the following Figure (see Fig. 3). All the presented buttons on these screens were related to the answer to the asked search question. The user selected one of these buttons depending on their opinion. To make it more realistic and to increase the mental demand, a time limit of five seconds per screen was implemented. By selecting the necessary buttons on the different screens, users created the needed search path. After pushing a button, the users experienced the treatments' vibration-loading interface and were referred to the next screen. To ensure that each screen was viewed, participants had to confirm each screen by at least one button click. To simulate a realistic scenario of mobile browsing, a certain 'trial and error' possibility within the desired application was implemented, and users could make use of the common backward button of an Android phone to navigate. If the users had used the backward button, they would experience the vibration-loading interface to make the simulation of mobile browsing as realistic as possible. In this process, a search task with a high number of mistakes might influence the user's opinion in an unintended way because of the disproportional experience of the certain interface. Therefore, users were led to an error screen after they experienced the vibration-loading interface if they chose the wrong button. The error-screen then asked users to start the entire treatment over. Further, the implementation of the error screen should prevent misuse of the backward function, since the number of possible search paths is limited within the application and thus mental involvement is substitutable by a high number of button clicks [22]. To avoid an accumulation of error screens, the search task was defined as easy as possible without neglecting mental involvement. The following figure shows a schematic illustration of the defined search paths within the application (see Fig. 3).

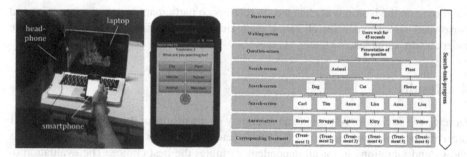

Fig. 3. Laboratory setting during the experiment (left), Search screen within the mobile application (middle) and schematic illustration of search paths implemented in the mobile application (right).

Questionnaire. The questionnaire consisted of eight pages and was divided into three main stages with 81 questions in total. The first stage asked participants three questions about their mobile Internet usage via a smartphone and demographic background data in terms of age, gender and handedness. The second stage posed questions designed to evaluate the two categories of user experience, which refer to the dependent variables of 'perceived enjoyment' and 'perceived usefulness.' Both variables were assessed by three similar questions based on the corresponding categories of the TAM model. The questions provided a 7-likert scale for the participants to rate their answers. Further questions were modified during a pre-test to make them more understandable to participants [23]. In addition to these questions, this stage also contained questions related to the NASA TLX to measure the subjective mental workload of each treatment. The third stage of the questionnaire provided space for further comments of the participants on the experiment or their experiences.

Procedure. Each experiment began with a participant choosing a random order for the six treatments of the experiment. An oral introduction to the experiment and the handling of the application was presented afterwards. This introduction, informed the participants that they had to write down the answer found for each search task in the questionnaire. The participants were also informed about the 5-second time limit of the application. After this introduction, participants began to see the movie and to use the application simultaneously. First, the application showed a waiting screen of 45 s to allow participants the chance to become involved with the presented movie. Following this, the application gave a short vibration signal (duration: 500 ms) to inform users that they could continue with the search task. The next step was to choose the random sorted treatment the application should perform. Afterward, the search question was presented, which participant had to confirm with a button click. The following three screens were the earlier-described search screens with six different buttons. If participant chose the right search path in the search screens, they were finally led to the answer screen. This screen displayed the answer to the search question. During a correctly performed search process the participants experienced the vibration-loading interface a total of five times. After completing the search task and watching the corresponding movie, participants completed the designated portion of the questionnaire. During this time, the application was rebooted to handle the next treatment, and the movie on the laptop was changed. In total, each participant watched six movies and performed six different search tasks, each time with a different combination of the independent variables.

4 Results

Descriptive Statistics. To provide an overview of the results of this experiment, Table 1 presents the descriptive statistics for the dependent variables evaluated. As the results show "end vibration" is for all dependent variables the best choice. The evaluation of the dependent variable "perceived enjoyment" reveals that "continuous vibration" is less enjoyable then "no vibration". But the participants evaluated "continuous vibration" as well as "no vibration" in both cases higher in terms of "perceived usefulness" than the baseline. The evaluation of the subjective mental workload shows that the usage of a continuous and no vibration signal leads to a high mental workload.

Table 1. Descriptive statistics of perceptions and 'mental workload'

Process time	Vibration type		Perceived enjoyment (points/7)	Perceived usefulness (points/7)	Mental workload (points/150)
short	continuous-vibration	Mean	4.98	5.10	47.93
		SD	1.677	1.359	13.901
	end-vibration	Mean	5.96	6.08	41.07
		SD	1.113	0.834	13.814
	no-vibration	Mean	5.12	2.43	51.20
		SD	1.723	1.617	21.157
long	continuous-vibration	Mean	5.06	5.08	50.87
		SD	1.452	1.453	14.012
	end-vibration	Mean	5.74	5.72	41.47
		SD	1.246	1.257	13.796
	no-vibration	Mean	5.32	2.13	49.60
		SD	1.615	1.432	18.713

N = 30 for each combination of process time and vibration-type.

t-Test and Repeated Measures ANOVAs. The internal consistency of the questionnaire used was investigated by the Cronbach's Alpha test (Cronbach, 1951).The calculated coefficients were all higher than 0.700 and ranged from 0.839 to 0.921 (0.921 for 'perceived enjoyment', 0.839 for 'perceived usefulness' and 0.858 for 'mental work-load'). Therefore, the questionnaire was statistically significant for internal reliability and convergence validity.

t-Tests as well as repeated measurement ANOVAs were performed by SPSS to prove the hypotheses. The Mauchly's Test of Sphericity was performed to verify the necessary statistical assumptions. For all three dependent variables, this test was not significant ($p > 0.05$; N = 30), so a repeated measures ANOVA could be used for each variable. The repeated measures ANOVA was performed three times, independently for each dependent variable. In the first ANOVA, the influence of the independent variables on the dependent variable 'perceived enjoyment' was examined. The result showed that only the vibration-type significantly influenced the 'perceived enjoyment' (df = 2, F = 6,0908, p = 0.002). The variable 'process time' as well as the interaction of the variables 'vibration type' and 'process time' had no significant influence on the 'perceived enjoyment' according to the ANOVA performed (df = 1, F = 0,023, p = 0.880 for 'process time' and df = 2, F = 0,455, p = 0.637 for the interaction). The second variable examined by a repeated measurement ANOVA was 'perceived usefulness.' The results showed that only 'vibration type' significantly influenced this variable (df = 2, F =73,391, p < 0.001). The results for 'process time' showed no significance at α = 0.05 (df = 1, f = 3,175, p = 0.085). For the interaction of the independent variables no significant influence was discovered (df = 2, F = 1,009, p = 0.371). The third dependent variable, which was examined with a repeated measurement ANOVA, was 'mental workload'. The results of this ANOVA showed that only 'vibration type' significantly influenced 'mental workload' (df = 2, f = 9,153, p < 0.001). The independent variable 'process time' (df = 1, F = 0,092, p = 0.764) and the interaction of these variables (df = 1, F = 1,019, p = 0.367) had no significant influence on 'mental workload' according to the results of this ANOVA.

After these ANOVAs, it was still unclear whether the significant influences of the independent variables represent a positive or a negative contribution to the user experience; therefore, different t-Tests were performed as the ANOVA revealed, 'process time' had no significant influence on 'perceived enjoyment.' The t-Tests showed no significant difference between the values of 'perceived enjoyment' for the two process times of each vibration type. Further results showed significant differences for 'perceived enjoyment' during the 'short' process time (df = 29, t = -3,442, p = 0.002) as well as the 'long' process time (df = 29, t = -2,468, p = 0.020). A comparison between the treatments with a 'continuous vibration' signal and a 'no vibration' signal showed no significant differences for both levels of 'process time' (df = 29, t = -0,398, p = 0.694 for the 'short' process time and df = 29, t = -0,760, p = 0.453 for the 'long' process time). Thus, only the 'end vibration' signal had a positive effect on 'perceived enjoyment'. In all examined cases the usage of the 'end vibration' signal led to the highest value in terms of 'perceived enjoyment' (See Fig. 4). The examination of 'perceived usefulness' by t-Tests proved the results of the performed ANOVA in nearly every case.

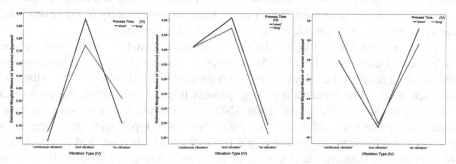

Fig. 4. Estimated Marginal Means of 'perceived enjoyment' (left), estimated marginal means of 'perceived usefulness' (middle) and estimated marginal means of 'mental workload' (right).

The t-Tests showed that the variation of the variable 'process time' had no significant influence on the measured 'perceived usefulness' of the vibration-loading interface employed. The value for 'perceived usefulness' differs by usage of the three different vibration signals, as the ANOVA had already implied. The results in Fig. 4 show that the 'end vibration' signal was evaluated to be the most useful vibration type, and that vibration has a positive overall effect on 'perceived usefulness.' What remains is the question whether the significant influences of the vibration-signals on 'mental workload' were positive or negative. The performed t-Tests showed that 'mental workload' during usage of the 'end vibration' signal differed significantly from the values measured during usage of the other vibration-types. The comparison between the 'continuous vibration' and the 'end vibration' signal showed significant differences ($df = 29$, $t = 2,807$, $p = 0.009$ for the 'short' process time and $df = 29$, $t = 3,962$, $p < 0.001$ for the 'long' process time). A further comparison between the 'end vibration' and the 'no vibration' signal also showed significant differences ($df = 29$, $t = -3,813$, $p = 0.001$ for the 'short' process time and $df = 29$, $t = -2,454$, $p = 0.020$ for the 'long' process time). In all of these cases usage of the 'end vibration' signal led to a higher mean value (see Fig. 4). Consequently, the 'end vibration' signal has a proven positive effect on 'mental workload.'

5   Conclusions

As a result of this research, it is possible to extend the findings of Brewster and King [7] to the field of smartphones. It was proven that a vibration-loading interface is capable and useful in presenting the process progress on a smartphone. The 'mental workload' of the participants was significantly decreased. Accordingly such a vibration-loading interface is able to improve user experience.

According to the NASA TLX, the level of stress, smartphone users experience decreases. A lower level of stress results in a smaller number of attention switches between the smartphone and the mobile environment [5, 18]. In this experiment it was proven that a vibration-loading interface could decrease 'mental workload' and, from this, the number of attention switches also decreases. Although the experiment was staged in laboratory surroundings, the results should endure in real-life-environments as a comparison between laboratory and field testing by Kallio and Kaikkonen [24] revealed. The small number of attention switches further results in a lower distraction levels among smartphone users, which could result in higher safety of the smartphone users in a mobile environment, as Stavrinos et al. [25] implied.

The performed ANOVA detected a slightly significant influence of the process time on 'perceived usefulness' ($p = 0.085$), whereas the mean values for the long process time were higher than the values for the short process time. This implies that vibration feedback is useful in the context of long process times. Nevertheless, the performed t-Tests did not support the results of the ANOVA as the differences between the mean values of 'perceived usefulness' for each 'vibration type' were not significant ($p = 0.891$ for 'continuous vibration', $p = 0.106$ for 'end vibration' and $p = 0.144$ for 'no vibration'). Therefore, it is correct to deny an influence of process time on all vibration types in terms of the examined process times. However, what this experiment proved in this context is that the annoyance factor of process times, which was described by Roto and Kaikkonen [19], could be superimposed by a more annoying factor. In this case the 'continuous vibration' signal. It was identified by the participants to be really annoying, especially in the case of the longer process time. This circumstance is supported by the mean values of 'perceived usefulness', which are nearly equal (5.10 for the 'short' process time and 5.08 for the 'long' process time). Furthermore, the experiment supported the assumption of Roto and Oulasvirta [18] that vibration feedback for processes lasting longer than 4 s would be appreciated by users.

The performed experiment proved further that vibration feedback during mobile browsing improves user experience on smartphones. Through the usage of a vibration-loading interface with a short vibration signal at the end of a process, it was possible to improve 'perceived enjoyment' and 'perceived usefulness' during a search task. In addition this vibration-loading interface supports users' performance in dual tasking situations as the interface decreased the 'mental workload' of participants. Conclusively, it should be emphasized that a vibration-loading interface is able to increase the safety of smartphone users in a mobile environment, which was one of the motivations for this research.

6 Outlook

Future research should evaluate if the user experience of a vibration-loading interface is truly independent from process time. In this experiment, two exemplary times were used (5 s and 12.5 s). A further experiment with a higher number of different process times and even a sequence of different process times during a search task might lead to a different conclusion than the ANOVA for 'perceived usefulness' indicated in this experiment.

In this research two simple vibration signals were investigated. Even between these two signals, a significant difference in terms of experienced enjoyment was discovered. Further research should explore this effect to optimize the vibration signal and thereby the user experience of smartphone users.

Acknowledgements. This publication is part of the research project "TECH4AGE", which is funded by the German Federal Ministry of Education and Research (BMBF, Grant No. 16SV7111) supervised by the VDI/VDE Innovation + Technik GmbH.

References

1. Raskin, J.: The Humane Interface: New Directions for Designing Interactive Systems. ACM Press, New York (2000)
2. Neider, M.B., Gaspar, J.G., McCarley, J.S., Crowell, J.A., Kaczmarski, H., Kramer, A.F.: Walking and talking: dual-task effects on street crossing behavior in older adults. Psychol. Aging **26**(2), 260–268 (2011)
3. Verclas, S., Linnhoff-Popien, C.: Mit Business-Apps ins Zeitalter mobiler Geschäftsprozesse. Xpert.press. Springer, Heidelberg (2012)
4. Fettweis, G.: Positionspapier Das Taktile Internet, Doctoral dissertation, Technische Universität Dresden

5. Roto, V., Oulasvirta, A.: Need for non-visual feedback with long response times in mobile HCI. In: Special Interest Tracks and Posters of the 14th International Conference on World Wide Web, pp. 775–781. ACM (2005)

6. Brewster, S., King, A.: An investigation into the use of tactons to present progress information. In: Costabile, M.F., Paternó, F. (eds.) INTERACT 2005. LNCS, vol. 3585, pp. 6–17. Springer, Heidelberg (2005)

7. Davis, Jr., F.D.: A technology acceptance model for empirically testing new end-user information systems: theory and results, Doctoral dissertation, Massachusetts Institute of Technology (1986)

8. Venkatesh, V.: Determinants of perceived ease of use. Integrating control, intrinsic motivation, and emotion into the technology acceptance model. Inf. Syst. Res. **11**(4), 342–365 (2000)

9. Lu, J., Yu, C.-S., Liu, C., Yao, J.E.: Technology acceptance model for wireless internet. Internet Res. **13**(3), 206–222 (2003)

10. Park, Y., Chen, J.V.: Acceptance and adoption of the innovative use of smartphone. Ind. Manag. Data Syst. **107**(9), 1349–1365 (2007)

11. Hertzum, M., Clemmensen, T., Hornbæk, K., Kumar, J., Shi, Q., Yammiyavar, P.: Personal usability constructs. how people construe usability across nationalities and stakeholder groups. Int. J. Hum.-Comput. Interact. **27**(8), 729–761 (2011)

12. Hong, S.-J., Thong, James Y.L., Moon, J.-Y., Tam, K.-Y.: Understanding the behavior of mobile data services consumers. Inf. Syst. Frontiers **10**(4), 431–445 (2008)

13. Straub, D., Keil, M., Brenner, W.: Testing the technology acceptance model across cultures. A three country study. Inf. Manag. **33**(1), 1–11 (1997)

14. Shin, D.H.: The evaluation of user experience of the virtual world in relation to extrinsic and intrinsic motivation. Intl. J. Hum.-Comput. Interact. **25**(6), 530–553 (2009)

15. Wixom, B.H., Todd, P.A.: A theoretical integration of user satisfaction and technology acceptance. Inf. Syst. Res. **16**(1), 85–102 (2005)

16. Hart, S.G., Staveland, L.E.: Development of NASA-TLX (Task Load Index). Results of empirical and theoretical research. Hum. mental workload **1**(3), 139–183 (1988)

17. Nielsen, J.: Usability Engineering. Morgan Kaufmann Publishers, San Francisco (1993)

18. Oulasvirta, A., Tamminen, S., Roto, V., Kuorelahti, J.: Interaction in 4-second bursts: the fragmented nature of attentional resources in mobile HCI. In: Proceedings of the SIGCHI Conference on Human Factors in Computing Systems, pp. 919–928. ACM (2005)

19. Roto, V., Kaikkonen, A.: Acceptable download times in the mobile internet. In: Universal Access in HCI, vol. 4 (2003)

20. Swallow, D., Blythe, M., Wright, P.: Grounding experience: relating theory and method to evaluate the user experience of smartphones. In: Proceedings of the 2005 Annual Conference on European Association of Cognitive Ergonomics, University of Athens, pp. 91–98 (2005)

21. Wasserman, T.: Software engineering issues for mobile application development. In: FoSER 2010 (2010)

22. Klastrup, L.: Death matters: understanding gameworld experiences. In: Proceedings of the 2006 ACM SIGCHI international conference on Advances in computer entertainment technology, p. 29. ACM (2009)

23. Laugwitz, B., Held, T., Schrepp, M.: Construction and evaluation of a user experience questionnaire. In: Holzinger, A. (ed.) USAB 2008. LNCS, vol. 5298, pp. 63–76. Springer, Heidelberg (2008)

24. Kallio, T., Kaikkonen, A.: Usability testing of mobile applications. A comparison between laboratory and field testing. J. Usability Stud. **1**(4–16), 23–28 (2005)

25. Stavrinos, D., Byington, K.W., Schwebel, D.C.: Effect of cell phone distraction on pediatric pedestrian injury risk. Pediatrics **123**(2), 179–185 (2009)

Brazilian Cultural Differences and Their Effects on the Web Interfaces User Experience

Tales Rebequi Costa Borges de Souza[✉], Marcelo Morandini,
and João Luiz Bernardes Jr.

School of Arts Sciences and Humanities – EACH,
University of São Paulo, São Paulo, Brazil
{tales.rebequi,m.morandini,jbernardes}@usp.br

Abstract. Having an interface that provides good user experience has become a critical factor for success in information systems. Cultural differences, however, may have a significant impact in this experience, but are seldom taken into account during interface design and evaluation, particularly in Brazil, a multi-cultural country with continental dimensions. Our goal was to investigate whether the cultural differences between the five socio-economical macro-regions of Brazil are profound enough to impact user experience in web-based interfaces and, if so, how. We performed an experiment with 110 participants, 22 per region, comparing cultural differences elicited by VSM with performance and evaluation of a fictitious Internet Banking System. Cultural differences were identified and correlated with differences in user experience, particularly in regards to the amount of information and colors shown in the interface.

Keywords: Culture · User experience · Usability

1 Introduction

Having a user interface that provides adequate usability and user experience has become a critical factor for success in information systems [1]. To achieve this, a series of best practices and empirical rules are often followed during interface design. These rules, however, seldom take in consideration cultural differences between users [2], and research across several countries and different applications shows that these cultural differences do affect user experience, and often describes how the experience is affected country [3, 4].

In the context of Brazil, on the other hand, we could find no research showing whether or how cultural differences affect user experience. Brazil is a large country, with continental dimensions and a large market of Internet users that is growing very quickly. The country is often conceptually divided in five socio-economical macro-regions, and past research shows that there are indeed significant cultural differences between these five regions [5].

The North is the region with the lowest population density and has an economy based mostly on vegetable, and mineral extraction [6], with one notable exception in Manaus which shows large industrial activity due to fiscal incentives.

P.L.P. Rau (Ed.): CCD 2015, Part I, LNCS 9180, pp. 209–220, 2015.
DOI: 10.1007/978-3-319-20907-4_19

The Northeast has approximately 30 % of the country's population and has an economy based on agribusiness, particularly sugar and cocoa. On the coast there is significant oil extraction and the beaches are also focus of tourism [6].

The Midwest is home to the nation's capital. The economy has been based on gold and diamonds mining but is currently based in livestock [6].

The Southeast occupies only 10 % of the territory but is home to 40 % of the population, being the region with the highest urban population. The region has a developed and industrialized economy, accounting for 50 % of production in the country [6].

The South is the region with the smallest area in the country (6 %). The economy is based on agriculture and industry and has received a new industrial park in recent years [6].

Systems that observes these differences have a competitive advantage [4] and could offer a better user experience, increasing the user satisfaction [7]. Translations and layout reformatting are not enough to resolve the impact of cultural differences in user experience, it is necessary to reevaluate the design completely [8, 9] and to contemplate the subjective culture of each user [2].

Our goal, then, is to investigate whether these cultural differences between the five socio-economic regions of Brazil are deep enough to affect user experience in web-based interfaces and, if so, how.

This study may indicate that Brazilian companies should prepare their information systems taking these differences into account, since this is an important challenge in a globalized society, where the companies need to keep the right balance between internationalization and localization [10]. In future works, other types of platforms and systems should also be tested, but here we focus in web-based interfaces, particularly for Internet Banking.

"Culture" can be considered one of the most complex words that exist. Initially, its was a material process derivative of agricultural cultivation. But it evolved to a term that denote features "of the soul", such as moral or intellectual characteristics. The definition of culture shows a profound historic transition, from rural to urban, from strict definitions to wider definitions, and other philosophical questions [11]. Culture can be defined as a collective programming of the mind distinguishing the members of one group or category of people from others [12] and this is possibly the definition used most frequently in HCI [10].

In 1970, Hofstede was invited to run a study to understand why some of IBM's organizational rules of IBM succeeded in some countries but failed in others. By designing a questionnaire for this purpose and analyzing its answers, Hofstede pro-posed that there are cultural dimensions that differ between countries and created a way to measure and to represent these cultural difference: the Values Survey Module (VSM) [12].

Some authors contradict Hofstede, claiming that his methodology is not correct in an anthropological context [13]. But the concept of culture has been explored in many other points of view and, is a complex concept that does have definitions prior to Hofstede's that agree with his view [14].

Usability is one of the aspects of a system that affects user experience and, just like this experience, may in turn be affected by these cultural differences. It is defined by

ISO as the set of characteristics such as appropriateness, recognizability, learnability, operability, user error protection, user interface aesthetics and accessibility [15]. Usability analysis has always served as a parameter for creating good products, but in these days of extreme competition and greater consumer awareness, it is no longer considered sufficient and it is necessary to also develop and study a user experience (UX) [16].

There are many definitions of UX [17], but one of the most accepted definitions is a person's perceptions and responses that result from using a product, system or service [18]. Therefore, UX involves usability, but also includes other user feelings, instead taking only product design in consideration [16], and one of the most basic reasons to offer a great UX is that enjoyment is fundamental to many aspects of life [19].

In this work we made use primarily of questionnaires and interviews. But before saying more about the tests, we discuss cultural differences and user experience.

2 Related Work

To evaluate whether cultural differences influence the UX, the most used method was the application and evaluation of questionnaires. As mentioned above questionnaires play a key role in UX evaluation [20] and, in the revised papers, they were used to identify the importance of UX attributes [21–26] and to detail the user experience [27–36]. In second place, Task Performance Measurements were used in some studies [4, 27, 29, 30, 32–34, 37] measuring the rate of success in tasks and the time to finish them. The questionnaire method and task method can evaluate the UX in two distinct moments, during use and afterward, and were combined in several works [27, 29, 30, 32–34]. Three studies conducted only bibliographic analysis [38–40].

Out of the 23, only three studies could not very the impact of cultural differences in UX. All other 20 studies verified and showed differences between users from distinct cultures. The papers that reported a positive result capture what were the main values in each culture, measured user experience or usability and performance on tasks, and then compared results between populations with different cultural roots preserved. On the other hand, two the articles that report a negative results showed problems on the methodology, either using children (who are often considered not to have their culture fully assimilated yet) as the population [36] or failing to measure whether there were actual cultural differences between participants [27]. The last study with negative results [30] says that, while they did not find sufficient evidence to conclude that the tested cultural dimensions affected performance, the performance levels by participants attained suggested that the usability of the interfaces was increased for all users as a result of accommodating high uncertainty avoidance, masculinity, collectivism and high power distance characteristics into the design of the interfaces.

When the interface was culturally adapted in two studies, they reported improvements in performance [4, 37], therefore showing not only a difference in user experience but a real, measurable improvement when users interacts with an interface well-suited to their culture. On both quantitative and qualitative ways, it seems clear that culture influences UX. Users of different cultures value different attributes, react differently to interfaces and have different performances in performing tasks in an identical interface.

EUA and China were the most analyzed countries in these studies. Several countries in Europe and some others in Asia were also analyzed, but Brazil was not contemplated in any study.

3 The Experiment

Five state capitals were chosen to represent their macro-regions: (1) Belém in Para representing the North; (2) Salvador in Bahia representing the Northeast; (3) Goiânia in Goiás representing the Midwest; (4) Sao Paulo in Sao Paulo representing the Southeast; and (5) Porto Alegre in Rio Grande do Sul representing the South.

Our goal was to have at least 20 users from each of these cities, for a total of 100 participants.

Instead of testing for a large number of different web pages or types of pages, we restricted our tests to the specific application of Internet Banking, which is widely used in all regions and complex enough to exhibit more details about the user experience during testing. While other applications, such as e-commerce, are just as popular, or even more so, and just as complex, one of the authors has previous experience with user interfaces for Internet Banking and we decided to take advantage of this experience.

3.1 Population

In order to reduce the influence of other cultural and socio -economics differences, we choose banking employees of Itaú Unibanco Bank aged 18 to 40. In this way, we could guarantee that the population has very similar characteristics with respect to salary range, educational level, educational area, work activities and banking knowledge. Employees of other banks could also present these characteristics, but Itaú was chosen due to the easy access of one of the authors.

Another key requirement was that participants had always lived in the same mac-ro-region they were born, to reduce the chances that the culture from another macro-region could have affected the participant. Our choice of study population brought two risks to the validity of the experiment. First, that the culture in the chosen state capitals was not representative of the entire region and, second, that our particular choice of Itaú Bank employees could constitute a subculture in itself, with more in common among its members due to this common factor than differences due to regional culture.

3.2 Procedure

One author traveled to all five macro-regions of Brazil, and asked for volunteers in bank branches during working hours. The participants were informed about the study's objectives and the entire procedure, particulary its voluntary character, and then invited to read, fill in and sign Terms of Consent.

The test starts with a warm-up chat, during which the user's basic information such as age, level of education and hometown were elicited. Then the user fills out Hof-stede's standardized Values Survey Mode (VSM) questionnaire. Users then perform five tasks in our fictitious Internet Banking System, using a notebook computer (log-ging in and out, checking their account balance, making a payment, a transfer be-tween accounts, and requesting a loan). Finally, after completing the tasks, users fill out a QUIS questionnaire, evaluating several aspects of the interaction, and are inter-viewed, making comments about their experience and preferences. The average time for this entire procedure was approximately 15 min for each user.

3.3 The System

Instead of using an existing banking system, or a mockup of an existing system, which would introduce another variable in the tests (the user's previous experience with the particular system chosen), we opted to create a fictitious and slightly simplified Internet banking system, called NOVbank. We validated its user interface with heuristic evaluation from other experts in the area that work specifically with the banking application.

Figure 1 illustrates its homepage. All figures showing the banking system show text in Portuguese, since this was the language used for the experiment.

Fig. 1. NOVbank Internet Bank - Home Page

After performing the login, the logged-in homepage was displayed. The user can be easily consult account balance, bank statement and manager information (as shown Fig. 2). On the top of the page, the user had a menu with all transaction options: bank statement, savings, payments, transfers, loans, investments, vouchers and contact.

Fig. 2. NOVbank Internet Bank - Logged Home Page

All transactions were made up of three steps: filling in data, where users fills the necessary information and chooses options; confirmation, where user confirms all information; and voucher, where the system confirms the transaction.

3.4 Questionnaires

Besides using the VSM to elicit cultural differences, we used the Questionnaire for User Interaction Satisfaction (QUIS). QUIS is a tool developed in the Human-Computer Interaction Lab (HCIL) at the University of Maryland at College Park. It evaluates users' subjective satisfaction with specific aspects of the human-computer interface [41].

This questionnaire contains 133 questions divided into 12 categories. The two first categories evaluate user knowledge in using computers and the system. In other categories users must evaluate the system with a score (1-9, lowest being negative and highest positive).

To reduce the time of each experiment and focus on issues related to our particular system, we removed some QUIS categories with questions about features not present in the system: past user experience, manuals, tutorials, teleconferencing and software installation.

4 Results

On average 22 volunteers participated the study by region, with more female participants than male, except in São Paulo (see Fig. 3).

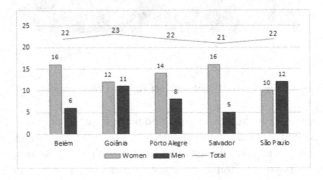

Fig. 3. Number of participants by sex

The average age of users was 30 years old. All were university graduates and 97 % from humanities courses. 95 % use Internet Banking and, for 71 %, that is the main channel to bank.

VSM results show that there were indeed many cultural differences between participants from these capitals in different Brazilian macro-regions, as seen in Table 1.

PDI results showed that São Paulo and Porto Alegre, with high scores, have a greater acceptance of hierarchy and social inequalities. Belém and Salvador, on the

Table 1. VSM results

	Belém	Goiânia	Porto Alegre	Salvador	São Paulo
PDI	15,91	22,83	32,73	15,24	36,14
IDV	1,59	10,65	1,59	6,67	23,86
MAS	9,55	12,17	4,77	21,67	17,50
UAI	-40,91	-49,13	-18,86	-33,33	-31,36
LTO	9,09	19,57	15,68	-7,62	9,32
IVR	62,27	61,30	77,73	63,81	92,27

other hand, had a low scores. It is possible see is a pattern in the regions, with the score growing towards the South, while the Midwest had an intermediate score.

IDF results showed São Paulo again with the highest score, which represents a more individualistic culture. Unlike happened with PDI, we did not find a simple geographical pattern to IDV: Salvador and Goiânia showed an intermediate score and Belém and Porto Alegre had a minimal score.

Except for Salvador, MAS results were similar to ITV. This correlation is common, with collectivist societies tending to be collaborative societies. Salvador showed a different result that represents a society with high scores of both collectivism and competition.

UAI results showed Porto Alegre with the highest score, indicates a culture with high uncertainty avoidance that thus accepts more rules, laws and bureaucracy. Salvador and São Paulo had similar scores, and Belém and Goiânia showed low uncertainty avoidance.

Porto Alegre showed a high score on LTO too. This correlation is natural because uncertainty avoidance encourages the society to make long time plans. Goiânia, however, despite having shown a low level of uncertainty avoidance, showed the highest score on long-term orientation.

All five Brazilians macro-regions showed high scores on IVR, showing that Brazilians in general assign a high value to quality of life, especially in São Paulo, which showed the higher score.

These results indicate that the Brazil's macro-regions, and particularly our experimental population within these regions, do indeed have significant cultural differences.

Figure 5 shows the average times for completion of all tasks, in minutes, for each macro-region. All participants concluded all tasks successfully, but with different time performances (see Fig. 4).

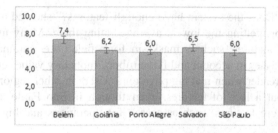

Fig. 4. Time performance on tasks

Participants in Belém took the highest mean time to conclude all tasks, with 7.4 min, while São Paulo and Porto Alegre had the lowest with 6 min. In addition to performance differences, the observer noticed that 30 % of users preferred consulting the bank statement from the home page in Goiânia and Porto Alegre, while only 20 % did so in São Paulo and 10 % in Belém and Salvador.

Other noticeable difference was that approximately 60 % of users from Belém and Salvador checked their bank balance before paying a bill during the experiment, which avoided the display of the error message "out of balance". In Goiânia and Porto Alegre this rate was approximately 50 % and in São Paulo only 20 %, possibly due to the speed in the execution of tasks.

QUIS' results were analyzed question by question, but are shown in Fig. 5 grouped in 6 categories: Reaction, Screens, Terminology, Learning, Performance and Media. While analyzing individual questions, we noticed a clear pattern. In nearly all questions, Porto Alegre and Goiânia users assigned the highest average scores, Salvador assigned somewhat lower scores, and São Paulo and Belém the lowest, with small but statistically significant differences. We assumed that this variation was either a function of the context of experiment in each city (in Belém, for instance, the experiment coincided with difficulties in the computer system used by the participants at work) or with cultural differences that were of little interest to us in this particular experiment, since they would apply across the board, not to different aspects of the user experience. What we did, then, was to have a closer look at those questions which violated this pattern (for instance, with São Paulo assigning the highest average score), and then correlated the answers to these QUIS questions with certain qualitative comments made during the interviews.

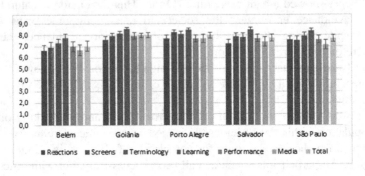

Fig. 5. QUIS' Results

The question "Does the system have enough features?" showed a violation of the pattern in Salvador, getting the lowest average rating there. Many users in Salvador wanted additional features, such as masks in form fields (i.e. automatically showing dots, commas or dashes in account and ID numbers, monetary values etc.) or the option to use a bar code reader when making payments. Users in other regions in general did not complain about a lack of features, even though in São Paulo some users gave suggestions for more features, such as search for operations and highlighting certain information.

Salvador also broke with the pattern in the question "Does the error messages clarify the problem?", getting a low score. As mentioned above, 60 % of Salvador's user checked the balance before making a payment and, because of this, did not see any error messages (this was the only error likely to occur during the test).

In the question "Is the organization of elements on the screen is useful or useless?", Porto Alegre's score was well above average. 70 % of the users in that city said during the interviews that they approved of the system's layout. In addition, users in the South praised that balance information and manager contact information showed right on the home page.

In questions related to security, the pattern was maintained but all scores were lower. Many users in all regions said they believed the system should require an additional security check, since the system required only one password and they were all used to having to enter at least two passwords (one to log in, one to confirm most operations).

Regarding design matters, Belém and Porto Alegre had completely opposite scores. Porto Alegre's users considered the design adequate, with clear colors and basic information, while Belém's users wanted more and vibrant colors, larger and rounded fonts and more information presented on the screen. This phenomenon also occurs with nearby macro-regions, Salvador had a score and opinions similar to Belém and Goiânia and São Paulo was similar to Porto Alegre. This was the aspect that, in this experiment, showed the greatest impact of the design on user experience. It is also interesting to notice that the correlation between wanting more information and more colors makes some sense (with more information shown all at once, more colors might help in telling the information apart).

5   Conclusion

Our goal was to investigate whether these cultural differences between the five Brazilian regions are deep enough to affect user experience in web-based interfaces. Our results showed that, even in a somewhat homogenous group (in our case, bank workers), the cultural differences between regions are notable. These differences not only existed, but can also be correlated with differences in user experience when using the same information system. The five Brazilians macro-regions had very different VSM results and showed differences in task performance, when evaluating the aspects of the system with QUIS and when voicing their opinions and suggestions in the inter-views. The most important difference between regions was regarding the amount of information and colors shown in the interface, with North, Northwest and Midwest favoring more of both and Southwest and South preferring less. Users in the North-east were also affected more negatively by the lack of certain optional features.

Our work suggests several interesting possibilities for further investigation. The first one is to analyze others platforms, such as mobile, to see if and what other important patterns emerge. Other types of system, such as e-commerce systems, are also of interest for further analyses, especially to compare those results with ours and see if the patterns we found extend to such systems (we believe they do, since the questions and the differences we noted are more general, not specific to Internet

Banking like the problem with security and two checks was, but this belief should be investigated). Other sources of cultural differences, such as age, genre and income, and how they affect user experience could also be investigated. Finally, even for web-based inter-faces and Internet Banking in particular, these differences could be further investigated, either analyzing aspect by aspect in more detail or measuring performance and satisfaction when using culturally adapted interfaces (for instance, one with more colors and information presented and one with less) across different regions.

Our culture is a large part of who we are and it must be represented in the products we buy, the services we consume and the experiences we enjoy. We believe that, with this work, we have collaborated with the understanding of cultural differences in Brazil and that, with this understanding, we can begin making better, more pleasant systems and interfaces to our users.

References

1. Lindgaard, G., Dudek, C.: What is this evasive beast we call user satisfaction? Interact. Comput. **15**(3), 429–452 (2003)
2. Smith, A., et al.: A process model for developing usable cross-cultural websites. Interact. Comput. **16**(1), 63–91 (2004)
3. Callahan, E.: Cultural similarities and differences in the design of university web sites. J. Comput. Mediated Commun. **11**(1), 239–273 (2005)
4. Reinecke, K., Bernstein, A.: Improving performance, perceived usability, and aesthetics with culturally adaptive user interfaces. ACM Trans. Comput. Hum. Interact. (TOCHI) **18**(2), 8 (2011)
5. Hofstede, G., et al.: Comparing regional cultures within a country: lessons from Brazil. J. Cross Cult. Psychol. **41**(3), 336–352 (2010)
6. Ministry of External Relations of Brazil – Cultural Department. http://dc.itamaraty.gov.br/publicacoes/textos/portugues/revista1.pdf/view
7. Nielsen, J.: Usability 101: Introduction to usability (2003)
8. Carey, J.M.: Creating global software: a conspectus and review. Interact. Comput. **9**(4), 449–465 (1998)
9. Boor, S., Russo, P.: How fluent is your interface. designing for international users. INTERCHI 93, 346 (1993)
10. de Castro Salgado, L.C., Leitão, C.F., De Souza, C.S.: A Journey Through Cultures: Metaphors for Guiding the Design of Cross-Cultural Interactive Systems. Springer Science & Business Media, New York (2012)
11. Eagleton, T.: The Idea of Culture. Wiley, New York (2013)
12. Hoftede, G., Hofstede, G.J., Minkov, M.: Cultures and Organizations: Software of the Mind: Intercultural Cooperation and Its Importance for Survival. McGraw-Hill, London (2010)
13. Baskerville, R.F.: Hofstede never studied culture. Acc. Organ. Soc. **28**(1), 1–14 (2003)
14. Hofstede, G.: What is culture? A reply to Baskerville. Acc. Organ. Soc. **28**(7), 811–813 (2003)
15. ISO, ISO. "IEC 25010: 2011: Systems and software engineering–systems and software quality requirements and evaluation (SQuaRE)–System and software quality models." International Organization for Standardization (2011)

16. Hartson, R., Pyla, P.S.: The UX Book: Process and Guidelines for Ensuring a Quality User Experience. Elsevier, Waltham (2012)
17. Forlizzi, J., Battarbee, K.: Understanding experience in interactive systems. In: Proceedings of the 5th Conference on Designing Interactive Systems: Processes, Practices, Methods, And Techniques. ACM (2004)
18. Law, E.L.-C., et al.: Understanding, scoping and defining user experience: a survey approach. In: Proceedings of the SIGCHI Conference on Human Factors in Computing Systems. ACM (2009)
19. Hassenzahl, M., Beu, A., Burmester, M.: Engineering joy. IEEE Softw. **18**(1), 70–76 (2001)
20. Alva, M.E.O., Hernán Sagástegui Ch, T., López, B.: Comparison of methods and existing tools for the measurement of usability in the web. In: Lovelle, J.M.C., Rodrguez, B.M.G., Gayo, J.E.L., del Ruiz, M.P.P., Aguilar, L.J.(eds.) ICWE 2003. LNCS, vol. 2722. PP.386–389. Springer, Heidelberg (2003)
21. Young, K.L., Bayly, M., Lenné, M.G.: Cross-regional in-vehicle information system design: the preferences and comprehension of Australian, US and Chinese drivers. IET Intel. Transp. Syst. **6**(1), 36–43 (2012)
22. Wallace, S., et al.: Culture and the importance of usability attributes. Inf. Technol. People **26** (1), 77–93 (2013)
23. Zaharias, P.: Cross-cultural differences in perceptions of e-learning usability: an empirical investigation. Int. J. Technol. Hum. Interact. (IJTHI) **4**(3), 1–26 (2008)
24. De Angeli, A., Kyriakoullis, L.: Globalisation vs. localisation in e-commerce: cultural-aware interaction design. In: Proceedings of the Working Conference on Advanced Visual Interfaces. ACM (2006)
25. Frandsen-Thorlacius, O., et al.: Non-universal usability? A survey of how usability is understood by Chinese and Danish users. In: Proceedings of the SIGCHI Conference on Human Factors in Computing Systems. ACM (2009)
26. Lin, C.J., Sung, D., Yang, C.-C., Jou, Y.-T., Yang, C.-W., Cheng, Lai-Yu.: Designing globally accepted human interfaces for instant messaging. In: Aykin, N. (ed.) HCII 2007. LNCS, vol. 4560, pp. 150–159. Springer, Heidelberg (2007)
27. Chang, C.-L., Yelin, S.: Cross-cultural interface design and the classroom-learning environment in Taiwan. Turk. Online J. Educ. Technol. TOJET **11**(3), 82–93 (2012)
28. Zaharias, P., Papargyris, A.: The gamer experience: investigating relationships between culture and usability in massively multiplayer online games. Comput. Entertainment (CIE) **7** (2), 26 (2009)
29. Noiwan, J., Norcio, A.F.: Cultural differences on attention and perceived usability: investigating color combinations of animated graphics. Int. J. Hum Comput Stud. **64**(2), 103–122 (2006)
30. Ford, G., Gelderblom, H.: The effects of culture on performance achieved through the use of human computer interaction. In: Proceedings of the 2003 Annual Research Conference of the South African Institute of Computer Scientists and Information Technologists on Enablement Through Technology. South African Institute for Computer Scientists and Information Technologists (2003)
31. Yan, Qifeng, Gu, Guanyi: A remote study on east-west cultural differences in mobile user experience. In: Aykin, Nuray (ed.) HCII 2007. LNCS, vol. 4560, pp. 537–545. Springer, Heidelberg (2007)
32. Marcus, A., Alexander, C.: User validation of cultural dimensions of a website design. In: Aykin, N. (ed.) HCII 2007. LNCS, vol. 4560, pp. 160–167. Springer, Heidelberg (2007)
33. van Dam, N., Evers, V., Arts, F.A.: Cultural user experience issues in e-government: designing for a multi-cultural society. In: van den Besselaar, P., Koizumi, S. (eds.) Digital Cities 2003. LNCS, vol. 3081, pp. 310–324. Springer, Heidelberg (2005)

34. Ahtinen, A., et al.: Design of mobile wellness applications: identifying cross-cultural factors. In: Proceedings of the 20th Australasian Conference on Computer-Human Interaction: Designing for Habitus and Habitat. ACM (2008)
35. Cyr, D., Head, M., Larios, H.: Colour appeal in website design within and across cultures: a multi-method evaluation. Int. J. Hum Comput Stud. **68**(1), 1–21 (2010)
36. Sim, G., Horton, M., Danino, N.: Evaluating game preference using the fun toolkit across cultures. In: Proceedings of the 26th Annual BCS Interaction Specialist Group Conference on People and Computers. British Computer Society (2012)
37. Rau, P.-L.P., Choong, Y.-Y., Salvendy, G.: A cross cultural study on knowledge representation and structure in human computer interfaces. Int. J. Ind. Ergon. **34**(2), 117–129 (2004)
38. Zahed, F., Van Pelt, W.V., Song, J.: A conceptual framework for international web design. IEEE Trans. Prof. Commun. **44**(2), 83–103 (2001)
39. Hillier, M.: The role of cultural context in multilingual website usability. Electron. Commer. Res. Appl. **2**(1), 2–14 (2003)
40. Clemmensen, T., et al.: Cultural cognition in usability evaluation. Interact. Comput. **21**(3), 212–220 (2009)
41. Questionnaire For User Interaction Satisfaction. Questionnaire For User Interaction Satisfaction. Web, 20 February 2015. http://www.lap.umd.edu/QUIS/index.html

A Pilot Study of Exploring the Relationship Between Dechnology Product and Product Personality

Wen-Zhong Su[✉], Hsi-Yen Lin, Chi-Ying Hung, and Pei-Hua Hung

Graduate School of Creative Industry Design, National Taiwan
University of Arts, Ban Ciao District, New Taipei City 22058, Taiwan
{orpheussu, p3yann, yumeeiren, paywhathome}@gmail.com

Abstract. Cultural creative products emphasize personalization to meet the needs of consumers who hope to be unique and different. The purpose of this study is to explore whether if there is a correlation between consumers' dominant or recessive personality traits and their selection of or preference for products. This study is divided into three stages, the first stage finds the relationship between personality traits and the five aspects of product personalization through literature review; the second stage is an experiment that recruits 105 college juniors in day school and night school, and asks them to complete a PDP personality test to learn the personality traits of these college consumers; the third stage provides a manual containing 41 designed Dechnology products and asks the subjects to intuitively choose products based on their own preference. The subjects are not under any pressure and do not need to evaluate the products' design, functions or aesthetics. After data collection is completed, subjects' personality traits are categorized and the product voting results are analyzed. Finally, this study concludes that there is a significant correlation between consumers' personality traits and their preference for Dechnology products. After compiling statistics on similar and different selections made by subjects with each personality trait, this study found that products selected by subjects with different personality traits also have multiple personalities. This study also found that consumers with different personality traits showed different preferences when selecting products, and analysis of products' design and functions showed that product personality was consistent with consumers' personality trait. Results of this study can serve as reference for product planners, designers and marketing personnel.

Keywords: PDP · Dechnology · Personality traits · Product personality

1 Introduction

The cultural creative industry has become a major trend of this century, and large numbers of cultural creative products have appeared in the market. However, among the vast number of creative products, what designs are accepted by consumers? Or, what preferences do target consumers have? Designers and distributors are all searching for the answer to these questions. Hence, "consumer" purchase behavior discussed under

© Springer International Publishing Switzerland 2015
P.L.P. Rau (Ed.): CCD 2015, Part I, LNCS 9180, pp. 221–231, 2015.
DOI: 10.1007/978-3-319-20907-4_20

marketing strategy has become a popular research topic. Robert Lauterborn (1990) proposed the 4C theory in contrast with the 4P of traditional marketing, emphasizing the importance of customer. Even so, "Product" in the 4P theory is still related to "Customer" in the 4C theory. Take automobile brands for example, M-Benz represents "luxury" and "comfort"; BMW represents "speed"; Audi represents "technology." All of these automobiles are represented by a "product personality," and the customers that purchase them are also different, but most are related to their dominant or recessive personality traits.

McCrae and Costa (1987) proposed the "five personality traits" to explain the values and preferences of different personality traits. Human resource departments of many enterprises adopt the PDP (Professional Dynamitic Program) personality test to examine the behavioral style of employees. PDP stands for Professional Dynamitic Program, which divides personalities into dominant (tiger), expressive (peacock), patient (koala), precise (owl), and hybrid (chameleon). People with different traits have different personalities, and the test reveals that personality.

Cultural creative products have been emphasizing personalization to meet the needs of consumers who hope to be unique and different. Product personalization is when consumers project their personality traits, both positive and negative, onto products (Sirgy 1982).

PDP personality test has been widely applied in enterprises, governments and private organizations, but it has not been applied in research on creative design. By revealing the personality traits of consumers, we can learn if consumers with different personality traits will have different preferences for product design, which will allow us to find product attributes that are viewed as the product's personality. This will enable us to further analyze if consumers' personality traits are correlated with the personality of products they buy.

2   Literature Review

Consumers' personality and behavioral pattern is referred to as their "personality traits," "personality" refers to a combination of individual characteristics that determine how a person interacts with the surrounding environment, while "trait" refers to a continuous aspect that is used to explain the "consistency" of a person's behavior under different situations (Gatewood and Field 1998). Therefore, "personality trait" is the most stable and important composition of a person's life (Costa and McCrae 1992).

At present, most Taiwanese enterprises adopt the PDP personality test to understand personality traits of their employees or potential future employees. It is a tool that reveals a person's "basic behavior," "reaction to their environment," and "predictable behavioral pattern" (www.pdp.com.tw/index.php). Allport (1937) defined personality trait as follows: "Personality is the dynamic organization within the individual of those psychophysical systems that determine his characteristics behavior and thought." The personality test provided by the PDP divides personality traits into dominance (tiger), extroversion (peacock), conformity (koala), patience (owl), and integration (chameleon) (Table 1).

Table 1. Strengths and weaknesses of personality traits organized by this study

Personality trait	Strength	Weakness	Suitable occupation
Dominance (Tiger)	1. Strong leadership	1. Inconsiderate	Supervisor, general
	2. Adventurous	2. Impatient	
	3. Decisive	3. Does not know how to please others	
	4. Fearless	4. Arrogant	
Extroversion (Peacock)	1. Optimistic, likes attention	1. Unrealistic	Public relations, sales representative
	2. Creative	2. Impulsive	
	3. Energetic	3. Poor concentration	
Conformity (Koala)	1. Listener	1. Too cautious	Administration, customer services
	2. Emotionally stable	2. Does not like change	
	3. Tolerant	3. Indecisive	
Patience (Owl)	1. Careful consideration	1. Picky	Accountant, engineer
	2. Organized	2. Complicates issues	
	3. Logical		
Integration (Chameleon)	1. Adaptive	1. Changeable	Personal assistant
	2. Strong integration ability	2. Unpredictable	

Many studies on the perception of product design have explained that products have personalities, and that there are two advantages to this. The first is that it helps consumers understand products (Mugge et al. 2009); the second is that it attracts consumers because consumers will purchase products that fit their image (Govers and Mugge 2004; Govers and Schoormans 2005). These theories establish the connection between consumers and product personality. Yang and Yu (2008) explored the personalities of Alessi products, and found that consumers did indeed associate with product personality. Aaker (1997) proposed five aspects of developing brand personality, namely sincerity, excitement, competence, sophistication and ruggedness. These five aspects correspond to the five personality traits proposed by the PDP, and their relationship is shown in Table 2:

Table 2. Personality trait corresponding to product personality

PDP personality	PDP personality trait	Product/brand characteristic	Product/brand
Koala (Conformity)	1. Stable	1. Down-to-earth	Sincerity
	2. Patient	2. Honest	
	3. Listener	3. Wholesome	
		4. Cheerful	
Peacock (Extroversion)	1. Likes attention	1. Spirited	Excitement
	2. Creative	2. Spirited	
	3. Charismatic	3. Imaginative	
	4. Interactive	4. Up-to-date	
Owl (Patience)	1. Calculating	1. Reliable	Competence
	2. Thoughtful	2. Intelligent	
	3. Logical	3. Successful	
Chameleon (Integration)	1. Adaptive	1. Upper	Sophistication
	2. Integration	2. Charming	
		3. Patience	
Tiger (Dominance)	1. Practical ability	1. Outdoorsy	Ruggedness
	2. Decisive	2. Tough	
	3. Dominant	3. Masculine	

Consumers are inclined to purchase products that fit their personality and image. Even though consumers sometimes like the design of products, they still will not purchase the product because they symbolic meaning of the product does not fit them (Creusen and Schoormans 2005). When evaluating the aesthetic value of Dechnology products, Lewalski (1988) believed that aesthetic value is divided into three levels X, Y and Z; the lowest level X represents the aesthetic design of the product's exterior; the middle level Y represents the customer's understanding of the product function; the upper level Z represents the feeling that the product gives customers, which is the product's personality. The emotional intensity that these three levels give consumers becomes stronger from X to Z (Chou 2001). Lin and Kreifeldt (2014) also proposed the three levels of a design concept model, including "appearance perception", "semantic perception" and "intrinsic perception," once again supporting the perceptive relationship between consumers and products. The relationship is shown in Table 3.

Table 3. Different levels of consumer perception of products

Lewalski (1988)	X level	Y level	Z level
	Exterior	Function	Feeling
Lin and Kreifeldt (2014)	Appearance perception	Semantic perception	Intrinsic experience

3 Methodologies

Consumers will project their personality traits onto products and personalize products (Sirgy 1982). This means that consumers create product personality, e.g. M-Benz represents "luxury," "comfort" and "dignity." Hence, the dominant or recessive personality of consumers, to a certain extent, is related to this product. Jordan (1997) proposed product personality assignment. He asked subjects to evaluate the personality of products and their preferences, and asked them to define their own personality, using this process to verify if consumers will prefer products with similar personalities as themselves. This study conducts a questionnaire survey to explore if there is a connection between consumers' personality traits and product personality. The research methodology is explained below:

This study on the correlation between personality traits and product personality is divided into three stages: Stage one as described above includes literature review and theoretical foundation. Stage two involves sample selection, personality test, and product preference questionnaire, in which 41 products of the "Dechnology 2014 New Collection" were used as the sample. Before testing subjects' preference for products, subjects first took a PDP personality test to learn their personality traits, after which the product preference questionnaire survey was conducted. Stage three categorizes the personality traits of subjects, compares results of the product preference questionnaire survey, analyzes research results, and then arrives at the conclusion and recommendations. The research framework is shown in Fig. 1.

This study uses the 41 products of the 2014 Dechnology to Humart as the product sample. Dechnology stands for "Design" and "Technology." The Department of Industrial Technology, Ministry of Economic Affairs launched the Dechnology Value-added Project in 2009, and brought together many departments to incorporate technology into the product design cycle and create applications based on "Dechnology." The project output 250 innovative products each year, and the 41 products in the sample were selected from the Dechnology 2014 New Collection (www.dechnology.com.tw).

The questionnaire survey was design based on theories of personality traits and product personality described in the literature review, and consists of two stages, the first stage is a PDP personality test, all subjects are taking the test the first time, in which questions are divided into A and B parts, each part has 10 items with a total of 20 items. The second stage provides each subject with a manual of the 41 products in the Dechnology 2014 New Collection to Humart, the manual contains the product number, name, image, and description, and each subject selects 10 products based on personal preference. Procedures of the two parts are further described below:

Stage One: Parts A and B of the PDP Personality Test. This test includes 20 items of the PDP personality test, subjects are not under any pressure when answering the questions, and their scores for parts A and B are added together. Analysis results of their personality traits are displayed in a quadrant diagram, A represents the decisive of individual behavior and B represents the reaction of individual behavior, an intersection is found to determine their personality trait.

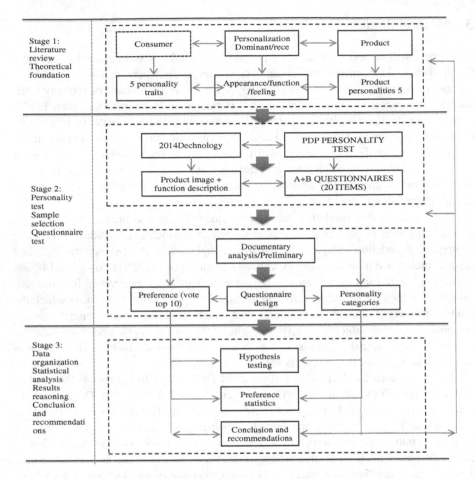

Stage 1:
Literature
review
Theoretical
foundation

Stage 2:
Personality
test
Sample
selection
Questionnaire
test

Stage 3:
Data
organization
Statistical
analysis
Results
reasoning
Conclusion
and
recommendati
ons

Fig. 1. Research framework

Stage Two: Selection of 41 Products in the 2014 Dechnology New Collection. This test provides a manual containing 41 products in the Dechnology 2014 New Collection to Humart to subjects. Subjects are under no pressure when intuitively selecting 10 products that they prefer by circling the number of the product on the questionnaire.

Subjects of this study are mainly juniors in college, including day school and night school. A total of 105 students between the ages of 19 ~ 21 took part in this study. The students were mainly from the department of business administration and the department of marketing management. Subjects are all current or future consumers who have not received any professional training in aesthetics. They choose the products intuitively based on their preference. There are not any additional requirements to evaluate product attributes or aesthetics.

4 Results and Discussion

The number of subjects that took part in the first stage PDP personality test was 105, 98 questionnaires were effective. The results are as follows: koala (51 subjects), owl (15 subjects), peacock (20 subjects), tiger (9 subjects), and chameleon (3 subjects); the distribution of subjects by gender and personality trait is shown in Fig. 2:

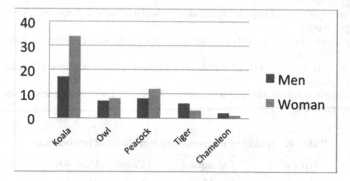

Fig. 2. Distribution of personality traits

After subjects complete the personality test in stage one, they intuitively choose 10 products they prefer from the 41 products of Dechnology 2014 New Collection to Humart. The statistical analysis is carried out in three parts, the first is to organize the number of votes for each product and personality traits into a table for hypothesis testing; the second is to find products that received the most votes; and the third is to compare the similarities and differences between popular products and personality traits. Results of the statistical analysis are described below.

The 10 products selected by subjects with each personality trait are tallied, and a line chart is used to show the distribution of product preferences of different personality traits, in which the X axis indicates product number and Y axis indicates the number of votes. The distribution of points shows the preference of each personality trait for each product. The number of votes is shown in Fig. 3: personality trait is represented by the first letter K(Koala), O(Owl), P(Peacock), T(Tiger), and C(Chameleon).

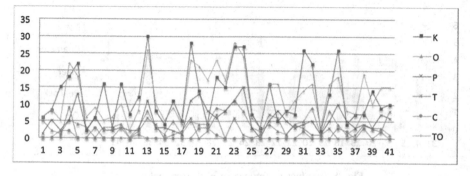

Fig. 3. Product preference of different personality traits

This study hypothesized that different personality traits are significantly correlated with preference for Dechnology products, and thus tests the hypotheses using the products selected by consumers from the questionnaire, which contains 41 products of the Dechnology 2014 New Collection to Humart. The five hypotheses are as follows (Table 4):

H1: The koala personality trait is significantly correlated with consumers' preference for Dechnology products.
H2: The owl personality trait is significantly correlated with consumers' preference for Dechnology products.
H3: The peacock personality trait is significantly correlated with consumers' preference for Dechnology products.
H4: The tiger personality trait is significantly correlated with consumers' preference for Dechnology products.
H5: The chameleon personality trait is significantly correlated with consumers' preference for Dechnology products.

Table 4. Testing of independence with different personalities

Hypothesis	Chi-Square	Criteria (d.f. = 40)
H1	59.65*	55.76
H2	59.92*	55.76
H3	59.89*	55.76
H4	59.70*	55.76
H5	59.66*	55.76

Note:* means Chi-square value higher than bracket criteria.

With 95% confidence level, The Chi-square values from H1 through H5 are all between Chi-square = 59.65 − 59.92, which are higher than bracket criteria 55.76. Such results verify that there exists a significant correlation between the five personality traits and preference for Dechnology products. In other words, consumers' product choice is influenced by their personality traits, which results in specific product preferences.

Products that received 50 % or more votes from each personality trait are shown in Fig. 4:

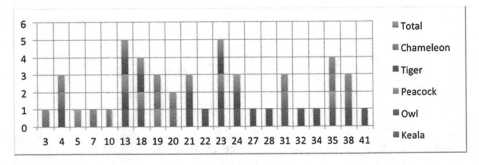

Fig. 4. Product preference of each personality trait

Table 5. Products with multiple personalities

Product	Name	Product personality
#13	Smart Gas Communicator	1. Communication technology product 2. Gas detection and fire alarm 3. Household protection 4. Automatic recording and monitoring
#18	I-hover (I-hover: Baby Bedside Hanging Bell)	1. Prevents injuries 2. Facial detection technology 3. Remote monitoring 4. Automatically determines the baby's condition
#23	Siproperly (sit properly)	1. Posture adjustment reminder 2. Automatically adjusts force 3. Pressure sensor technology 4. Alleviates pressure of the upper body

In the bar chart shown in Fig. 4, X indicates product number and Y represents the number of personality traits that preferred the product. The chart shows the distribution of product preferences of different personality traits, many of the products were preferred by multiple personality traits, e.g. product No.3 was preferred by consumers with Koala, Owl, Peacock, and Tiger personality traits. Preliminary analysis of the product showed two possibilities, one is that its design and attributes include technology, detection, safety, communication, automation, etc., and was determined to have multiple personalities. Products number 18, 23 and 24 also had similar personalities. Another possibility is that product personalities are given by consumers, and different consumers therefore interpret products differently, meaning that the same product may have different personalities (Table 5).

In the unique case of Tiger, products preferred numbers were 27, 28 and 41, which means that all these three products selected by only one personality trait. The product personalities corresponding to personality traits, as shown in Table 6, range from exterior design to intrinsic attributes. Observations from all these three products are transportation related, the intrinsic attributes are all rugged, and all have the dominant personality of consumers with Tiger personality traits.

Table 6. Product personality corresponding to personality trait

Product	Product personality	Personality trait
#27		
#28	Ruggedness 1. Outdoorsy 2. Tough 3. Masculine	Tiger 1. Practical ability 2. Decisive 3. Dominant
#41		

5   Conclusions and Suggestion Recommendations

In the two stages of tests, this study first learns the personality traits of the subjects, and then issues a manual of 41 products in the Dechnology 2014 New Collection to Humart for the subjects to choose 10 from. Subjects were asked to choose the products intuitively based on their preferences. This study assumes that there is a significant correlation with consumers' preference for Dechnology products, and that product personalities are correlated to consumers' personality traits. Conclusions of this study are as follows:

1. The hypothesis testing found that the personality traits of consumers are significantly correlated with Dechnology products. Consumers' personality traits will affect their product selection, meaning that consumers with different personality traits will have specific product preferences.
2. After analyzing the differences and similarities of product choice by consumers with different personality traits, this study found that consumers with different personality traits have specific preferences when choosing products. Preliminary analysis of the products' exterior design to intrinsic attributes showed that the products' personalities were consistent with the personality traits of consumers that chose them.
3. Observing the products selected by consumers with different personality traits, some products have multiple personalities that are preferred by consumers with different personality traits. Preliminary analysis of the product showed two possibilities, one is that its design and attributes include technology, detection, safety, communication, automation, etc., and was determined to have multiple personalities. Another possibility is that product personalities are given by consumers, and different consumers therefore interpret products differently, meaning that the same product may have different personalities.

In recent years, many creative products have emphasized personalization to satisfy the needs of consumers who hope to be unique and different. This study concluded that consumers' personality traits are correlated with product personalities, and that the product is worth further research. Further studies will conduct a matching test and use fuzzy evaluation to explore issues concerning the perception of product personality(Lin and Chang 2008).

Acknowledgements. The authors gratefully acknowledge the support for this research provided by the Ministry of Science and Technology under Grant No. MOSY-103-2410-H-144-003 and MOST-103-2221-E-144-001. The authors also wishes to thank Prof. Jhon. G. Kreifeldt and Po-Hsien Lin, especially, Prof. Rungtai Lin.

References

Aaker, J.L.: Dimensions of brand personality. J. Mark. Res. **34**, 354 (1997)

Allport, G.W.: Personality: A Psychological Interpretation. Holt, Rinehart & Winson, New York (1937)

Costa Jr., P.T., McCrae, R.R.: NEO—PIR: Professional Manual. Psychological Assessment Resources, FL (1992)

Creusen, M.E.H., Schoormans, J.P.: The different roles of product appearance in consumer choice. J. Prod. Innov. Manage. **22**(1), 63–81 (2005)

Gatewood, R.D., Field, H.S.: Human Resource Selection. The Dryden Press, Forthworth (1998)

Govers, P., Mugge, R.: 'I love my jeep, because its tough like me': the effect of product-personality congruence on product attachment. Paper presented at the Proceedings of the Fourth International Conference on Design and Emotion, Ankara, Turkey (2004)

Govers, P., Schoormans, J.P.: Product personality and its influence on consumer preference. J. Consum. Mark. **22**(4), 189–197 (2005)

Jordan, P.W.: Producst as personalities. Paper presented at the Contemporary Ergonomics, Hanson, MA (1997)

Lewalski, Z.: Product Esthetics – An Interpretation for Designers. Design & Development Engineering Press, Carson City (1988)

Lin, H.T., Chang, W.L.: Order selection and pricing methods using flexible quantity and fuzzy approach for buyer evaluation. Eur. J. Oper. Res. **187**(2), 415–428 (2008)

McCrae, R.R., Costa Jr. P.T.: Validation of the five-factor model of personality across instruments and observers. J. Pers. Soc. Psychol. **52**(1), 81–90 (1987)

Mugge, R., Govers, P., Schoormans, J.P.: The development and testing of a product personality scale. Des. Stud. **30**, 287–302 (2009)

Sirgy, M.J.: Self-concept in consumer behavior: a critical review. J. Consum. Res. **9**(3), 287–300 (1982)

Lin, R., Kreifeldt, J.G.: Do Not Touch: The Conversation Between Dechonology and Literature of Art (2014)

Zhou, Z.J.: The Shaping of Complexity Image-Based on the Characteristics of Style. Chenkong University, Tainan (2001)

Yang, M.Y., Yu, W.L.: The product traits of Alessi products. Res. Des. J. **11**(1), 1–22 (2008)

An Innovation Design for Hazardous Chemical/Gases Disaster Detection and Analysis Equipment by Using Cross-Cultural User Scenarios and Service Design

Sheng-Ming Wang[1], Cheih Ju Huang[2(✉)], Lun-Chang Chou[3], and Pei-Lin Chen[4]

[1] Department of Interaction Design, National Taipei University of Technology, Taipei, Taiwan
ryan5885@mail.ntut.edu.tw
[2] Department of Commercial Design, Chienkuo Technology University, Changhua, Taiwan
samenh@gmail.com
[3] Department of Civil Engineering, Graduate Institute of Civil and Disaster Prevention Engineering, Chienkuo Technology University, Changhua, Taiwan
lcchou@ctu.edu.tw
[4] Commercialization and Industry Service Center, Industrial Technology Research Institute, Hsinchu, Taiwan
mia-chen@itri.org.tw

Abstract. Unexpected releases of toxic, reactive, or flammable liquids and gases in processes involving highly hazardous chemicals or gas explosions have been reported for many years. The recent incident happened in Taiwan at 31st July, 2014 shows that a series of gas explosions occurred in the Cianjhen and Lingya districts of Kaohsiung in Taiwan, following reports of gas leaks earlier that night claimed 31 lives and injured other 309 people. In this study, we organized an interdisciplinary team that contains scholars from university, leaders from firefighter department, high rank officers from disaster management agencies, researchers and project managers from research institute and gases detector manufacture company and product designers to work together to propose an innovation design for hazardous chemicals/gases detection and analysis equipment. Based on the QFD analysis, operation for air detection is the most important feature. The results shown in the QFD Matrix, was further analyzed using a questionnaire that polled 6 inter-disciplinary experts in order to collect the pair-wise comparison results in AHP. The top 3 feature from the AHP are similar to the QFD weight: Air Type (20.05 %), Air Concentration (19.71 %), and Air Detection (17.44 %) The results of this research point out that the innovation product design should also include the design of service mechanism in order to meet users' requirement. For cross-cultural user scenarios perspective, design thinking method that use diagram and pictures for providing info-graphic results and the usability of user interface (UI) are two major factors should be included in the design process. The conclusions of this study suggest that the integration of product design and service design, and the co-working

P.L.P. Rau (Ed.): CCD 2015, Part I, LNCS 9180, pp. 232–240, 2015.
DOI: 10.1007/978-3-319-20907-4_21

mechanism among interdisciplinary team play very important role in the innovation design for hazardous chemicals/gases detection and analysis equipment.

Keywords: Service design · Cross-Cultural scenarios · Usability · Hazardous chemical/gases · Disaster management

1 Introduction

Unexpected releases of toxic, reactive, or flammable liquids and gases in processes involving highly hazardous chemicals or gas explosions have been reported for many years. Incidents continue to occur in various industries that use highly hazardous chemicals/gases, which may be toxic, reactive, flammable, or explosive, or may exhibit a combination of these properties. The recent incident happened in Taiwan at 31st July, 2014 shows that a series of gas explosions occurred in the Cianjhen and Lingya districts of Kaohsiung in Taiwan, following reports of gas leaks earlier that night claimed 31 lives and injured other 309 people. Eyewitness reported that smell of gas and white smoke was coming out from manholes over three hours prior to the incident. Although the firefighter rushed to the scene immediately after receiving 911 call and setup the alert zone, they could not prevent the explosion since the failure on identifying the type of leaking gas. The importance of related equipment design that can be used to detect and analyze the hazardous chemicals/gases in the disaster management cycle is aroused after this catastrophic incident.

In this study, we organized an interdisciplinary team that contains scholars from university, leaders from firefighter department, high rank officers from disaster management agencies, researchers and project managers from research institute and gases detector manufacture company and product designers to work together to propose an innovation design for hazardous chemicals/gases detection and analysis equipment. In order to integrating coworkers to work on creating the operation procedure and mechanism of the designed equipment, we hosted two workshops by using service design approach for interdisciplinary integrating. We also used cross-cultural user scenarios to ensure the design results can fulfill the international standard, such as standard for process safety management of highly hazardous chemicals (Occupational Safety and Health Administration in the United States 2011), the Clean Air Act Amendments (CAAA) (United States Environmental Protection Agency 2014).

Unlike follow the principles of traditional product design that is focused on "perfect-form" with "multiple-functions" based on well-organized design method, the innovation design for hazardous chemicals/gases detection and analysis equipment should follow the requirements proposed in the disaster management cycle as well as the operation mechanism of firefighters, and the decision making procedures of disaster management agencies.

Thus, this research begins from the exploration of hazardous chemicals/gases disaster management cycle by interviewing several research scholars in university and high rank officers of disaster management agencies to build up the scope of managing hazardous chemicals/gases disaster in Taiwan. Then, meetings with the firefighter who had experiences on responding to the hazardous chemicals/gases disaster are arranged to know the operation procedures and the scenarios of using hazardous chemicals/gases detectors. Thirdly, service design workshops with interdisciplinary team work together to propose the Quality Function Deployment (QFD) matrix and cross-cultural user scenarios of the innovation design for hazardous chemicals/gases disaster detection and analysis equipment. Thereafter, the product designer will follow the results from the workshop to design and produce the equipment prototype. Finally, World Cafe and Analytic Hierarchy Process (AHP) are implemented to review the prototype and user experiences.

2 Literature Review

The response time for the emergency response team to react is very short when facing chemical/gases leakage and spillage. In order to reduce the casualties, how to efficiently detect chemical/gases leakage and spillage is very pivotal when activating emergency response plan. According to the emergency management domain from several countries such as: the United States (Emergency Management Institute 2015), Canada (Canadian Environmental Assessment Agency (CEAA) 2013), and Japan (ASIAN DISAS-TER REDUCTION CENTER 2011), the mission statement basically includes four missions: (1) Prepare for emergency plan, (2) Respond to emergency center, (3) Recover the place, and (4) Mitigate the disaster. For more detailed measures and complicated situations, re-prepare for unpredictable disasters in the future is also important in the statement as shown in Fig. 1.

Based on this review, how to design hazardous chemicals/gases detection and analysis equipment should put emphasis not just multiple-function, to meet the user requirements would be the first target for the motivations. In this study, in-depth interviews with scholars from university, leaders from firefighter department, and high rank officers from disaster management agencies would put forward for "how and what to detect on site" when chemical/gases leakage and spillage disaster occurred. More-over, the recent gas explosions incident timeline happened in Taiwan was the basic analysis and research scenario event (Fig. 2). If hazardous chemicals/gases detection can start when or even before the fire starts, the casualties would be reduced.

Fig. 1. Emergency management mission statement

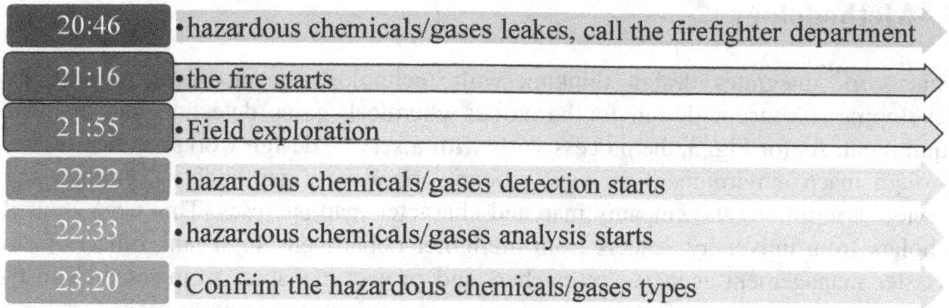

20:46	• hazardous chemicals/gases leakes, call the firefighter department
21:16	• the fire starts
21:55	• Field exploration
22:22	• hazardous chemicals/gases detection starts
22:33	• hazardous chemicals/gases analysis starts
23:20	• Confrim the hazardous chemicals/gases types

Fig. 2. Timeline for the recent gas explosions incident timeline in Taiwan (2014)

After first contacting and interviewing with the interviewees, no matter the profession language, working patterns, and even the focus were totally different. Service design is a method for transferring traditional product design and interface design to the commercial service in the society (Birgit 2006). It includes the environment for providing service, the serving process, and even the training for these service personnel (Koskinen 2008). It is a permanent feedback that requests and constantly updating process, in which the response of the users are continually being observed and monitored. Moggridge asserted that "service design is the design of intangible experiences that reach people through many different touch-points". That is, service design is a process of continual updates based on the cross-cultural responses of users who are observed and monitored.

In addition to the service design approach, the QFD Matrix and AHP are also been used simultaneously to systematically evaluated the classes and features derived from service design. QFD is a systematic approach to design, based on a close awareness of customer desires, coupled with the integration of corporate functional groups. The ultimate goal of QFD is to translate subjective quality criteria into objective ones that can be quantified and measured and which can then be used to design and manufacture the product. However, this simple point scale system used by the QFD Matrix has two weaknesses: the first one is it does not prioritize the customer requirements; the second one is the weights are of subjective value and depend on the consensus of the panel experts.

To address the above-inherited weaknesses, several researchers and practitioners have advocated using AHP to determine the weights of customer requirements (CRs). AHP is a structured technique for dealing with complex decisions (Saaty 1990; Saaty and Vargas 2012). The combined AHP-QFD approach has been used successfully to assess customer needs based on a multiple-choice decision analysis (Gupta et al. 2011) review the combination of QFD-AHP for the evaluation and selection methodology for an innovative product design concept.

The methodology combining QFD-AHP was mainly used as a multi-criteria decision method for evaluating user requirements. By considering the hazardous chemicals/gases detection and analysis of service design, this work uses this methodology to evaluate the development of hazardous chemicals/gases detection and analysis equipment.

3 Methodology

This work integrates design thinking with technology development process for developing a concept design for hazardous chemicals/gases detection and analysis equipment. As for Fig. 3, the process starts with a service design workshop that moves through macro environment analysis, product opportunity gap analysis, product and service description, and empathy map and character map analyses. This work invited scholars from university, leaders from firefighter department, high rank officers from disaster management agencies, researchers and project managers from research institute, gases detector manufacturing company and product designers to brainstorm at a 2-day workshop, with the goal of defining the features of hazardous chemicals/gases detection and analysis equipment using the service design approach. The features selected from service design results are further analyzed and used to compose the QFD matrix. The AHP is then used to prioritize and weight each criterion. A process of delivering ideas to define the features of hazardous chemicals/gases detection and analysis equipment starts by cross-cultural profession experts in a brainstorming process. The process of investigating service design is used to simplify discussions. Sticky notes were used, as "IDEO" favors this method as it helps cross-disciplinary team members describe their innovations.

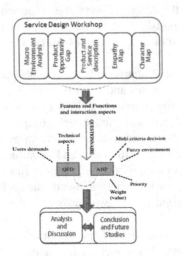

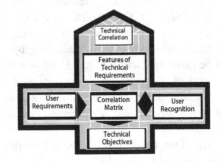

Fig. 3. Implementation processes

Fig. 4. Conceptual diagram of quality function deployment.

All features derived from the workshop are listed in a QFD matrix. Figure 4 presents the conceptual diagram of the QFD.

The QFD matrix shows the importance of each feature via correlation analysis of user requirements and features of technical requirements. It also shows user recognition by describing their experiences to competitors by giving a value to their importance. The importance range is 1–5 and their thinking is limited to strong, moderate, or poor. This method tells us how strongly the features (product characteristics) are related to user requirements and reflects the strengths of existing products. This work uses the QFD matrix to systematically list the features of the hazardous chemicals/gases detection and analysis equipment design.

The three basic AHP steps in this research are as follows.

1. Describe a complex decision-making problem as a hierarchy.
2. Use pairwise comparison techniques to estimate the relative priority of various elements on each level of the hierarchy.
3. Integrate these priorities to develop an overall evaluation of decision alternatives.

4 Result and Discussion

For the interdisciplinary team that contains scholars from university, leaders from firefighter department, high rank officers from disaster management agencies, researchers and project managers from research institute and gases detector manufacturing company and product designers to work together in this project, service design workshops were to propose an innovation design for hazardous chemicals/gases detection and analysis equipment. In Figs. 5 and 6, an interdisciplinary team that contains scholars from university, leaders from firefighter department, high rank officers from disaster management agencies, researchers and project managers from research institute and gases detector manufacture company and product designers to worked together for brainstorming workshop and created a sticky notes idea map.

Fig. 5. Brainstorming workshop   **Fig. 6.** Sticky notes idea map from cross-disciplinary team.

Following the conclusion of the brainstorming workshop, Fig. 7 shows the QFD Matrix results of hazardous chemicals/gases disaster detection and analysis equipment. Based on the QFD analysis, operation for air detection is the most important feature. SOP, user, and director are the second important features. In comparison to the technical features, air degree, data records, and auto-save are highly demanded by the respondents. The results shown in the QFD Matrix, was further analyzed using a

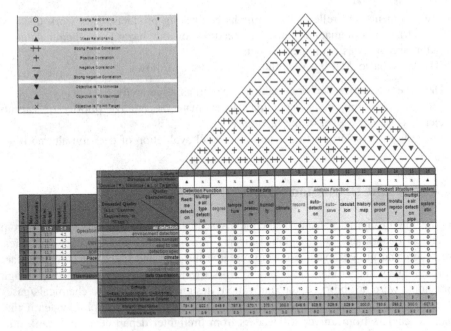

Fig. 7. QFD matrix result

questionnaire that polled 6 inter-disciplinary experts in order to collect the pair-wise comparison results. The AHP template was used to analyze the results and generate the weights and priorities of each feature.

As shown in Table 1, there is a correlation between the QFD Matrix's weight scale and the weights and ranking from AHP method. The most demanded features of hazardous chemicals/gases disaster detection and analysis equipment is *Operation*

Table 1. The QFD-AHP comparison table

Class	Features	AHP percentage	AHP priority	QFD	QFD priority
Operation 26.07 %	Air Detection	17.44 %	3	5.62	1
	Environment	8.63 %	5	5.06	2
User 3.19 %	Mobile Handset	3.19 %	9	5.06	2
	Easy to Use	7.97 %	6	5.06	2
SOP 6.91 %	Detection Spec	6.91 %	7	5.06	2
Place 3.05 %	Climate	3.05 %	10	3.93	4
Director 3.95 %	Diffusion	3.95 %	8	4.49	3
	Air Type	20.05 %	1	5.62	1
	Air Concentration	19.71 %	2	5.62	1
Transmission 9.10 %	Response Time	9.10 %	4	3.93	4

(26.07 %) and then *Transmission (9.10 %)*. There are not much difference between the *Director (22 %), User (3.19 %) and Place (3.05 %)*. The top 3 design priority for hazardous chemicals/gases disaster detection and analysis equipment are: *Air Type (20.05 %), Air Concentration (19.71 %)*, and *Air Detection (17.44 %)*.

The top 3 feature from the AHP are similar to the QFD weight. Further more than the research, the user scenario and concept design was implemented then. In Fig. 8, combining with the QFD and AHP matrix results with deep interview with firefighters, the user scenario was visualized for described the operation situation and behaviors. For detection the air type, air concentration, and efficiently detected, "plug-and-play" is the core for operating this hazardous chemicals/gases disaster detection and analysis equipment. Also, cooperated and integrated with the firefighter on site working process, all the operations were related to the original firefighter on site working process. In Fig. 9, the concept images were purposed to the features and user scenario visualization.

Fig. 8. User scenario visualization

Fig. 9. Concept images

5 Conclusion and Future Works

The results of this research point out that the innovation product design should also include the design of service mechanism in order to meet users' requirement. To solve the problems with how to design a propriety product with required service, service design provides a practical and flexible method for concept design. For cross-cultural user scenarios perspective, design thinking method that use diagram and pictures for providing info-graphic results and the usability of user interface (UI) are two major factors should be included in the design process. Furthermore, the ideas and scenario pictures generated from the co-work brainstorming in the service design workshop could not only provide the analysis on the functions and techniques details that product designer can be used for prototype implementation, but also can be used to develop applications and procedure plans that can be included in the hazardous chemicals/gases disaster management cycle. Finally, the results from the World Café and AHP, which integrates the opinions and suggestions from domain experts, provide the priority and importance of the factors and problems, such as operation efficiency, mobility, visual communication interface, requirement of heterogeneous display device for analysis results, and cross-cultural user experiences evaluation. The results also provide a mechanism for verifying the prototype of product design. The conclusions of this study suggest that the integration of product design and service design, and the co-working mechanism among interdisciplinary team play very important role in the innovation design for hazardous chemicals/gases detection and analysis equipment.

Acknowledgements. The authors gratefully acknowledge the support for this research provided by the Industrial Technology Research Institute of Taiwan, R.O.C.

References

Asian Disaster Reduction Center: Emergency Response Management in Japan. Asian disaster reduction center (2011)

Birgit, M.: Design Dictionary: Service Design. Service design review, p. 355 (2006)

Canadian Environmental Assessment Agency (CEAA). Emergency Management Basics (7 July 2013), Environment Canada. http://www.ec.gc.ca/ouragans-hurricanes/default.asp?lang=En&n=31DADDF5-1. Accessed 2 February 2015

Emergency Management Institute. Emergency Management Institute Mission (13 February 2015), Emergency Management Institute. https://www.fema.gov/resources-national-disaster-recovery-framework. Accessed 17 February 2015

Gupta, P.C., Garg, S., Maheshwari, S.: Evaluation and selection methodology for an innovative product design concepts. Int. J. Eng. Sci. Technol. (IJEST) 3(4), 3553–3561 (2011)

Koskinen, J.: Service Design. Servicedesign.tv, Finland (2008)

Moggridge, B., Atkinson, B.: Designing Interactions. MIT press, Cambridge (2007)

Occupational Safety and Health Administration in the United States. List of Highly Hazardous Chemicals, Toxics and Reactives (Mandatory) (December 27 2011), United States, The Department of Labor. https://www.osha.gov/pls/oshaweb/owadisp.show_document?p_id=9761&p_table=standards. Accessed 16 February 2015

Saaty, T.L., Vargas, L.G.: How to Make a Decision Models, Methods, Concepts & Applications of the Analytic Hierarchy Process, pp. 1–21. Springer, New York (2012)

United States Environmental Protection Agency. The Plain English Guide to the Clean Air Act (October 29 2014), United States Environmental Protection Agency. http://www.epa.gov/air/caa/peg/. Accessed February 16 2015

Based on Action-Personality Data Mining, Research of Gamification Emission Reduction Mechanism and Intelligent Personalized Action Recommendation Model

Yangbo Xu[1(✉)] and Yi Tang[2(✉)]

[1] Tongji University, Shanghai, China
yangbo@tongji.edu.cn
[2] EWAVES Design Co. Ltd., Shanghai, China
yit@ewaves.com.cn

Abstract. To the emission reduction activities, use gamification design method to implant resonance and great meaning into mainstream residents' implicit goals, so that set up the personalized challenging ways to their goals and help them transit to more sustainable lifestyle. For making up a deficiency of the correlated "action A-B" recommendation model, this paper puts forward a new causal "action-personality" data-mining model, and finally establishes an intelligent personalized behavior recommended model to help residents to achieve the emission reduction goals.

Keywords: Emission reduction · Recommendation system · Gamification design · Incentive mechanism · Data mining · Motivation · Operation action · Resulting action · Sustainable development

1 Introduction

Mr. Nicolas Hulot, the global environment ambassador appointed by French President Hollande said that, "Promoting low-carbo n economy and reducing greenhouse gas emission are not burdens to everyone pushing each other, but to make a responsible decision around the world in order to ensure the sustainability of the Earth civilization" [1].

This passage leads to the first question: Why have people still regarded promoting low-carbon economy and reducing greenhouse gas emission as burdens, but not for interest?

The second question: Currently, 30 % CO_2 emissions were caused by the residents' living behavior and their economic activities. Although residents' reduction goals are consistent, their motivation and ability are vastly different. How can we recommend personalized reduction behavior to each resident, according to his own situation, so that he will complete the reducing emission task happily?

P.L.P. Rau (Ed.): CCD 2015, Part I, LNCS 9180, pp. 241–252, 2015.
DOI: 10.1007/978-3-319-20907-4_22

2 Goal

Looking for an on-going excitation mechanism lead residents to change. Including: active mainstream residents by human's resonance value; ignite them powerful motivations to participate in sustainable reduction activities; active mainstream residents by personality value; guide the different residents, participate in different emission reduction activities in different ways.

3 Roadmap Leading to Goal

- Analysis of the relationship between "Goal - Action - Personality";
- Analysis of the relationship between "Gamification Design" and the "Goal - Action - Personality" of the emission reduction activities;
- Analysis of the relationship between "The Internet of Things", "Big Data", and the "Goal - Action - Personality" of the emission reduction activities;
- Based on data mining, propose an intelligent model to identify resident's personality through "operation action"; and combines this one with behavior recommendation model to establish a personalized behavior recommendation.

4 Mainstream Residents Lack Goals and Actions Involved in Sustainable Development Activities

Cario Vezzoli, Ezio Manzini noted that the past 50 years, mankind has always faced the possibility of self-destruction. Fortunately, it has been realized that human beings are living in an unpredictable state. The root causes of human self-destruction are their ways of life. People have always regarded possession of material as happiness, so that a lot of products and consumer goods have been emerged. We also regarded modern machinery as slaves to work for us, so that we could enjoy easier life. People have used to the standard of happiness, which are reducing the strength, hours of work, or even the ability [1].

Therefore, the goals and actions of the mainstream residents in their daily lives are lack of the spirit of sustainable development. We need to guide the residents to change their goals and behavior, build up a new standard of happiness, "participation in sustainable activities".

5 Analysis of the Relationship Between "Goal - Action - Personalities"

5.1 Freud's Personality Structure Give Us Inspiration

Freud believed that personality structure is composed of three parts: id, ego and superego. "id" is the original me, refers to the original oneself, including the basic desire, impulse and vitality to survive; "ego", is to realize the implementation of thinking, feeling, judgment or memory part; "superego," is representing the ideal part of the personality structure, is formed through internalization of moral norms, social and cultural value when the individual growing up.

Id, ego and superego, each of these three has its own goal. When the three goals are in a state of balance, individual will be in a comfortable state. Earth's ecological crisis, warns that people must change the values, from the happiness of "owning material", to "participation in sustainable development" as their new standard of happiness. This is not just the value transformation. In addition to changing the "superego", but also rebuild a new id, ego, superego balance system of the three goals. Although it's difficult to earth residents, we must change.

This paper will explore an incentive mechanism to guide mainstream residents to sustainable development-oriented transformation. Including three parts: goals, action, and personality.

5.2   Goal System

- Explicit goal: it refers specifically target determined in accordance with external influences.
- Implicit goal: it refers to an abstract goal driven by some intrinsic motivation [2].

5.3   Action System

About the behavior system, the paper cites the Jess Schell's classification. Action is the external activity driven by the explicit goal and the implicit goal. Such as: make a movement, make a noise. We can define resident's action from two angles.

- Operation Action: these actions refer to the basic actions to complete the task [2]. Although everyone uses the similar operation action when complete the same task, the details of operation action (such as rhythm, duration, frequency etc.) will be different because of the different implicit goal.
- Resulting Action: these actions are combined with a series of operation actions based on the strategic need. They are strategic actions of the residents in order to realize the goal, but not part of the task rules. Resulting action list is much longer than operation action [2]. The score, medal, ranking and other encouragements can represent the performance of resulting action.

5.4   The Relationship Between Personality, Goal and Action

Personality refers to a person's total psychological characteristic, which is relatively stable, with a certain tendency, influences his whole behavior and psychological characteristic to make difference with others. It includes: temperament, character, motivation, interest and ideal. Personality is the sustained, stable, consistent performance in different situations, can be used to describe the differences between people. Decoding one's personality will help to explain his implicit goal and preference motivation.

The goal will cause people's action, and personality makes different people choose different action to achieve goal.

A task has not only a final goal, but also a series of midway targets leading to it. People with different personalities will complete the same final task through different behavior paths to realize it. We need to describe all the sub goals one by one, and to understand how they are related.

Jesse Schell pointed out: good goal has 3 important features: specific, achievable, with a reward [2]. Of course, people with different personalities choose different actions (operation action and resulting action) to achieve the goal, and yearn different rewards.

6 Gamification Design Stimulates Resident's Instinct and a Sense of Mission

The real question is that, for the mainstream residents who used to enjoying material comforts, emission reduction means giving up some interests, so these tasks are not resident's preferred goals. In other words, people are in the Freud's ego state, more care about the interests of the pros and cons.

How to make people willing to complete the task of reducing emissions as an important implicit goal? How to make them meet the passion, overcome obstacles to achieve the goal? How to make this transition process sustainable? Introducing systematic game elements, exploring the potential of "id" and "superego", these problems will be solved.

6.1 From the Resonance and Great Mission, Promote Reduction Activities Top-to-Down

Jane McGonigal pointed out that compared with the game, the reality is negligible. Game makes us plunge into more ambitious undertakings, and bring us great significance [3].

So, what is the game? According to Jess Schell's definition: game is a fun activity to solve problem [2].

Why does game should create resonance and great meaning?

Jess Schell noted that resonance and great meaning is always based on truth. It passes a core experience clearly. When this experience resonates with one of the resident's fantasy or desire, it will quickly become an important experience for him. Think of "Titanic", why is it so moving? It has a resonant and great meaning: "love is more important than life, more powerful than death" [2].

Jane McGonigal said the meaning is that all of us desire for getting more stuff: more methods to create the miracles, more opportunities to leave our marks on this world, more curious and respectful moments in our own community or project [3].

We combine above view with Phil Rarden's view of the goal value, and then raise one question: can we keep resident's explicit goal (emission reduction goal) unchanged, but slightly shift his implicit goal (part of superego)? Let reduction goal equivalent to the sacred mission, saving the Earth.

According to Jane McGonagal's perspective, as long as we implant a great meaning into resident's implicit goal through game, and then put the challenge into a larger social context to make every reduction activities more meaningful, so that the resident will participate the real reduction activities happily in order to complete his great virtual mission. Driven by the implicit goal (superego), guide the mainstream residents develop emission reduction habits and awareness gradually.

6.2 With the More and More Difficult Challenges, the Resident Will Gain Higher and Higher Abilities and More and More Flow Experiences Constantly, and Go Straight to the Final Goal

As implanting the great meaning into resident's implicit goal (the superego part), can we also implant motivation such as "adventure" into his implicit goal (the id part) to replace the original one "pleasure", so that change his behavior?

The game activity will stimulate the flow, so that achieve this goal.

6.3 The Gamification Reduction Activities Based on Service Process, Implement of More Feedbacks to Guide the Happiness Transition

Fortunately, with the popularity of the IOT and sensors, GDC2011 proposed gamification concept. Deterding, Dixon, Khaled and Nacke define the gamification as "the use of game design elements in non-gaming background." More and more practice prove that, gamification can effectively improve the production efficiency; it also can improve the efficiency of sustainable development activities.

In this paper, the research direction is sustainable oriented gamification design. The "non game background" is defined as sustainable oriented service scene, that is: add game elements on service design, and discuss the establishment of sustainable development-oriented gamification enabling system, guiding the mainstream residents to change. Jane McGonigal pointed out, that gamification makes our life and work into team adventures through adding unnecessary but challenging obstacles to existing living/working scene and giving players more incentive feedbacks [3].

So, the enabling system combined with service design and gamification design is powerful. To the mainstream residents, service design provides tools involved in the sustainable development activities, and gamification design gives great significance and happiness for action. Combining these two is the way to guide happiness transformation.

7 Analysis of the Relationship Between the IOT, Big Data and Emission Reduction "Goal-Action-Personality"

7.1 Quantify Emission Reduction Standards and Eco-Efficiency Goals

7.1.1 Quantify Emission Reduction Standards

In our work and life, carbon emission tough points are everywhere. As long as these tough points can be detected by sensor, they could be designed by gamification. Many experts calculate amount of details of carbon emission. These data are useful for gamification design. Such as the following: *1 kWh of electricity = 0.904 kg CO$_2$, 1 ton of water = 0.194 kg CO$_2$* etc.

7.1.2 Quantify Eco-Efficiency Goals

According to EU-funded sustainable design orientation (SDO) toolkit, we design a radar chart of environmentally sustainable eco-efficiency: Optimize the system life cycle; Reduce transportation/distribution; Reduce resource consumption; Reduce exhaust emissions/emission and waste recycling; Improved renewable/biocompatibility; Non-toxic, non-hazardous [1].

We can build a radar map to check sustainable eco-efficiency for each resident.

The system will build a model to transform the resident's reduction action to eco-efficiency assessment, and encourage him to participate in emission reduction activities continually through game score, medal and ranking.

7.2 Transparent and Accurate Measurement of Action

Today's IOT technology can accurately measure the resident's operation actions and resulting actions. Through detecting the resident's actions of the gamification touch points, such as force information, location information, body position, orientation information and time sequence parameters, etc., it can be derived his response time, support time, flight time, the action of the track, supporting force, moving distance, and related kinematic and kinetic parameters moving direction, speed and stride frequency and so on. Of course, the value of the data does not come from a single data, but out of the summary. All of these data will be gathered to the cloud, analyzed via big data to feedback the results [5].

7.3 Embodied Cognition: Recognize the Personality Through Operation Actions

Phil Barden pointed, "embodied cognition," thinks that the body level shapes all aspects of cognition. Every kind of feeling, body posture or state, even the body interaction with the environment, will all affect people's cognition. That is to say, not only the brain is able to think, but also the body does so [4].

As mentioned before, the sensor system of IOT has been able to measure various behavioral variables more and more accurately, this measurement technique can be popularized in large scale, and is transparent, no interference to the user experience.

However, the sensor can't cognize the meaning of the behavioral variables independently.

Fortunately, the human brain can understand the profound and subtle meaning of actions. This does not come from arbitrary, but has an objective basis, so there is consensus about the similar behavior representing the same meaning. Phil Barden pointed out that, as we grow up, the absorbed things by our brains are like statistical tables of our experience, which are our "environmental statistics". We use "tandem reflexing and simultaneous transmission" to learn things and build our associative memory. The entire learning process is hidden [4].

Scott Kaufman, scholar in Yale University, pointed out: the ability to identify our behavior patterns and rules in the environment is our fundamental cognition [4].

Based on experience, although the task decides operation action, the different operation actions will be tend to reflect one's stable personality. So the observer can use his brain's "environmental statistic" ability to find the corresponding relation between operation action and personality. How to combine the advantages of the human brain and machine to measure the meaning of the actions in large-scale will be discussed in Sect. 8.

7.4   Related Action-Based Recommendation System

How to do "private customized" gamification design?

At present, "guess you like", a recommendation system of online shopping is a good choice. Amazon invented it. The principle is simple: suppose when an user buys book A, the system will suggest you that most people choose book B at the same time, it guesses that you would also like to buy book B.

This recommendation based on the correlated action is also valuable in gamification enabling system, as long as replace "book" with "resulting action".

8   This Paper Proposes a Gamification Recommendation System Based on Correlated "Personality-Action"

There is a fatal defect of amazon "guess you like" recommendation model: it does not know the motivation of the resident.

"Guess you like" model emphasizes the relationship between things, but not care about causality; emphasizes the user-selected objectivity, but not subjectivity. "Guess you like" model cannot really impress resident's mind.

This paper will rebuild the "guess you like" model: binding the causation with the correlation to establish a gamification recommendation system, which may really impress the resident's implicit goal.

For example, it is assumed that when a resident takes A resulting action, the gamification recommendation system will tell you to take B resulting action, because the most majority residents with similar personalities do so (Fig. 1).

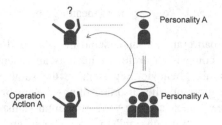

Fig. 1. Recommendation model base on correlated personality. Assuming a user takes resulting action A, the system will tell you that most people, with the similar personality, take action B after A, who buy goods A simultaneous buy goods B, it is recommended that you take resulting action B. (source: by author)

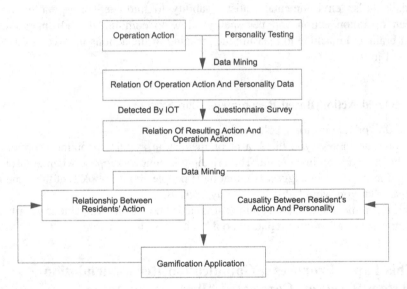

Fig. 2. The adaptive reduction action recommendation model based on the "personality – action" data mining techniques. (Source: by author)

How to make a machine to identify the human personality? Including 2 specific problems. How to build up a prototype of gamification recommendation system? How the prototype improve itself in operation. This is the solution (Figs. 2 and 3).

8.1   The First Stage: Build up the Prototype of Gamification Recommendation System

Purpose

- Build up simplified model to identify the "personality" from "operation action"(the key point);

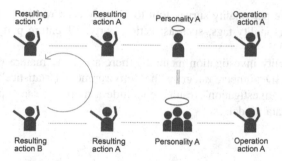

Fig. 3. The recommendation model combined with causality of "personality-action" and relationship of "resulting action A-B" (Source: by author)

- Build up model associated model the resident's existing "resulting action A" with recommended "resulting action B";
- Establish integrated model: both meet the causal relationship of "personality - operation action" and the relationship of "resulting action A-B", in order to recommend "resulting action B+"

8.2 Build up Simplified Model to Identify the "Personality" from "Operation Action" (the Key Point)

In Sect. 7.1.1, we get a result: machine sensor can finely measure people's action, but not understand the meaning of these behavioral data.

In Sect. 7.1.2, we get another result: people can recognize someone else's body language (embodied cognition) by the brain "environmental statistics", and to identify his personality. The result of "environmental statistics" is the establishment of correspondent relationship of "operation action– personality". This is a causal relationship between action and personality.

Our approach: let sensor capture different users' operation action data; build up simplified clustering relationship through data mining;insight the personality types behind these clusters; establish the initial "operation action– personality" data model; at the same time, through online surveys to investigate each resident's personality; validate and improve the "operation action – personality" data model.

- Select a number of sample residents to participate in the testing activities, assign an ID number for each one.
- Collect resident's reduction action data. Including: historical data of resident's emission reduction actions collected via IOT, real-time data of resident's operation actions collected via sensor.
- Using clustering algorithm tool to cluster the "operation action".
- For each resident cluster, tag personality label through a brain "environmental statistics" analysis.

- Through online personality survey tool to identify each resident's personality, and label them personality tags, such as: action party, adventure party, creation party etc.
- About personality investigation methods, there are many mature ways.
- By resident's ID number, integrate the "environmental statistics" results and the "questionnaire investigation" results, conclude a more precise "operation action – personality" data model.

8.3   Build up Model Associated Model the Resident's Existing "Resulting Action A" with Recommended "Resulting Action B"

Then, establish the relevance between existing "resulting action A" and recommended "resulting action B". That is whether the resident who participate in activity A will be interested in B?

- Design gamified emission reduction activities, including target, rules, feedback system, voluntary participation way, and various personalized task to the goal or sub goal.
- Each resulting action of the gamification activity is corresponding to a sub goal.
- Choose a group of sample resident to participate testing activity, tag each one an ID number.
- Organize them to participate in the gamification activities; there are different activities and goals for chosen.
- After the activity began, resident could choose any sub goal to achieve with his voluntary resulting actions. System will label each typical resulting action, prepared to recommend others.
- We are concerned that, when the resident actualize a resulting action, what is another action he interested? For example, does a resident have some interest to participate daily paper saving activity after the energy saving activity? If interested, how is the degree? Whether is it worth to recommend?
- The correlation algorithm tools of data mining can solve this problem. Through the analysis of relevance between different resulting actions, decide to recommend which one. These relations include: support, confidence, and lift.
- After a sufficient amount of data, according to these indexes to establish "resulting action A – B" data model. The data model is correlated with resident's ID number. This part of work is partially similar to Amazon's "guess you like" approach.

8.4   Establish Integrated Model: Both Meet the Causal Relationship of "Personality - Operation Action" and the Relationship of "Resulting Action A-B"

- Integrate "operation action – personality" data model and "resulting action A – B" data model through the resident's ID number to form a final recommendation, which called "resulting action B+" in this paper. For example: a resident is interested in saving electricity. After analyzing "resulting action A – B" found he liked running also; after test of "operation action – personality", found his personality, outgoing and sociable; so the system recommended him to take part in running party activities (resulting action B +).

8.5   The Second Stage: Establish Operation Database of Adaptive Gamification Recommendation System

Operational database is perfected based on the prototype of recommendation system. In the practical application, automaticly identify resident's "personality type" and "resulting action", then recommend new "resulting action+", and self-improve the failure. Through this process, improve and expand seed database to form a more accurate operation database. It is suitable for the whole process from small database to large one.

- When the resident chooses and executes a gamification task, the system will track to measure his "operation action" and "resulting action" data.
- When the system collects some resident's "operation action" data, it will automatically find the corresponding his "personality" from the "operation action - personality" data model. To infer causal This part of the work belongs to speculating the causal relationship of "operation action" and "personality".
- When the system collects a resident's existing "resulting action A" data, it will automatically find "resulting action B" which is worthy to recommend form the "resulting action A – B" data model.
- The system automatically integrate the speculation of the causality and correlation, and recommends resident the final "resulting action B+"
- In this process, if one's "operation action" data is not corresponding to the "operation action - personality" data model, the system will add this data to redo the clustering analysis, update or add new "personality" label to make the system more perfect and accurate. This is the self-study process. With the processing from small data to big data, the "operation action – personality" data model will be more and more accurate.
- At the same time, "resulting action A – B" data model is a story making machine, more and more stories will be created by the residents participating the gamification activities. This process will attract more residents to join.
- Under the continually driven by the model of "operation action – personality" and "operation action A – B", I believe that more and more residents will participate the activities and transform from existing personality structure to higher one (id, ego, superego).

9   Conclusion

The earth is facing ecological crisis, humanity's survival way must change to sustainable development- oriented. But there are two questions.

The first question: the residents will not change their inherent habits only excited by the real goals (explicit goal).

The proposed solution A in this paper is: set up a gamification enabling system of goal incentive mechanism.

Using the gamification method to implant resonance and great meaning into resident's "superego" implicit and explicit goal, guide him improve his original implicit goal top to down; through gamification challenges inspire resident's "I" implicit goals, guide him improve his original implicit goal down to top. Residents realize the emission reduction goal ("ego" explicit goal) through participation to gamification activities (resulting action). In the process, easily change habits.

The second question: the behaviors, personalities and motivations of the residents are diversification. How to automatically adapt these diverse needs and recommend different residents their preferred reduction activities accurately?

The proposed solution B in this paper is: put forward an innovational adaptive reduction action recommendation model based on "operation action – personality" data mining technique. Combine this model with author's "resulting action A – B" model, to realize accurate "resulting action B+" recommendation through gamification goal-action-personality system.

Solution B, from the personalized value of each person induces people to change habits, transit to sustainable development smoothly.

How to motivate people's goals and actions change towards sustainable development? This paper proposes a complete system from theory, mechanism and intelligent solutions. This system is universally applicable for clothing, food, housing, transportation, travel, education and other aspects. It is expected that the system have a great role in promoting the transition towards sustainable development.

References

1. Vezzoli, C., Manzini, E.: Design for Environmental Sustainability, 2008th edn. Springer, London (2008)
2. Schell, J.: The Art of Game Design: A Book of Lenses, 2nd edn. A K Peters/CRC Press, Natick (2014)
3. McGonigal, J.: Reality is Broken. Penguin Press, New York (2011)
4. Barden, P.: The Science Behind Why We Buy, 1st edn. Wiley, Chichester (2013)
5. Wu, M.Q.: The Internet of Things and Public Safety. Publishing House of Electronics Industry (in Chinese, 2012)

Design of a Clothing Shopping Guide Website for Visually Impaired People

Huiqiao Yang, Qijia Peng[✉], Qin Gao, and Pei-Luen Patrick Rau

Department of Industrial Engineering, Tsinghua University, Beijing,
People's Republic of China
pqj92@hotmail.com

Abstract. Millions of visually impaired people cannot enjoy the convenience brought by e-commerce due to the inaccessibility and complexity of existing online shopping websites. The user experience of online shopping website for visually impaired people needs to be improved. This study aims at designing a clothing shopping guide website for visually impaired people in support of choosing satisfying garment conveniently and efficiently. We designed and completed a prototype, and then a test and an interview were conducted to summarize requirements in operation and content for online clothes shopping of visually impaired users, and put forward improvements of our prototype.

Keywords: Visually impaired · Accessibility · Usability

1 Introduction

Shopping online has become an indispensable activity in people's life. Online shopping sites not only provide convenient services to the life of sighted people, but also have invaluable benefits to visually impaired users. At present, the total amount of Chinese blind is more than 6.5 million. One important benefit is that users can get details of clothing much easier than in the shops without others' help (Takagi et al. 2007). Though e-commerce services anticipate bringing great convenience for blind people, almost all e-commerce webpages have poor accessibility and usability (Fuglerud 2011). Blind people have a strong desire to interact with Web. But when they interact with Web through screen reader, the interaction process is inefficiency and high cognitive loaded (Babu et al. 2010). But blind users cannot understand complex layouts in seconds with assistive technologies (Francisco-Revilla and Crow 2009, 2010). In this study, we try to design an online shopping guide website to meet accessibility and usability needs of visually impaired people.

Accessibility: Accessibility allows users access to system functionality (Goodhue, 1988). Web accessibility guidelines define the requirements a webpage has to satisfy for purpose of providing accessible content. The most widely accepted sets of guidelines are the Web Content Accessibility Guidelines (World Wide Web Consortium 2008). However, strong domination of visually oriented business logic and rapid changes of items are other reasons for many online shopping sites inaccessible (Takagi et al. 2007).

© Springer International Publishing Switzerland 2015
P.L.P. Rau (Ed.): CCD 2015, Part I, LNCS 9180, pp. 253–261, 2015.
DOI: 10.1007/978-3-319-20907-4_23

Usability: Accessibility alone is not enough to evaluate webpages. Even if pages are accessible, usability also plays a key role since pages may be difficult to traverse (Vigo et al. 2009). Usability is the degree to which a system conforms to users' cognitive perceptions of accomplishing a task using the system (Goodwin 1987). Online shopping websites often use modular layouts. Multi-dimensional nature impedes blind users to comprehend information in the pages (Francisco-Revilla and Crow 2009).

Visually impaired users' frustrations on the web can be categorized as alt text, links, forms, plug-ins, navigation, layout, failures, and other. Among them, navigation is one of the most important factors that can frustrate blind user through screen reader (Lazar et al. 2007).

For complex webpages, such as online shopping sites, "ease of navigation" is one of the important elements for blind usability (Takagi et al. 2007). Navigation consists in moving around in a hypertext documents, deciding at each step where to go next. The main problems for a blind user navigating through screen reader are lack of page context and information overload due to excessive sequential reading (Leporini and Paternò 2008). Takagi et al. (2007) suggested several ways to support landmark-oriented navigation. The suggestions include improvement of HTML/XHTML specification, simplification of navigation interface, integration of transcoding functions and so on.

In order to ameliorate blind people's information overload and excessive sequencing when using online shopping sites, Takagi et al. (2004) proposed a method called "Blind Usability Visualization" to help designers to recognize their pages' usability effectively. Mahmud et al. (2007) developed a method to remove information overload by capturing the context of the selected link. Bigham et al. (2009) developed a method to reduce task completion time in interactive Web.

Leporini and Paternò (2004) developed a set of usability guidelines of accessible pages. Eighteen usability guidelines for blind users are grouped four main principles: structure and arrangement, content appropriateness, multimodal output and consistency. Fukuda et al. (2005) raised possible metrics basis on navigability and listenability to evaluate accessibility in usability terms.

2 Prototype Design

2.1 Requirement Summary

Interview summary. We interviewed 9 undergraduate students (5 female, 4 male) from the Special Education College of Beijing Union University in focus group methodology. All students were visually impaired and could use computer and online services skillfully with screen reading software. They all had experience on online shopping.

The complaints about existing webpages included: too many advertisements, poor typed divisions and annoying interaction design such as identifying codes. Therefore, the page should be easily for software to read, unified layout for divisions and few meaningless advertisements. The interviewees showed high expectation for the convenience of online shopping, but in existing websites, they worried that they could not get enough information to support their decision. Therefore, the information should contain all parameters in current websites, and emphasize important information such as material, model and color. The layout should support screen reading software well.

Defects of existing online shopping websites

Confusion in classification. In some selection page of existing online shopping websites, the order of options in categories has no specific ranking method. Therefore, users may find it hard to perceive the categories logically and have to memorize all options during selection, which would possibly lead to confusion and increment in mental workload.

Excessive options in some categories. According to George A. Miller, the average limit of human short-term memory capacity is around 7 items. If the number of options in one category is too large (more than 20 in some websites), visually impaired users have to remember all options and then make a choice, in which their memory workloads may greatly increase.

Lack of alternative description for pictures. The information given by a picture for a garment is far more important than any other goods. However, in most existing online shopping websites, there are no alternative descriptions for pictures, and thus visually impaired users would be probably confused when browsing a page with lots of pictures without descriptions.

Tedious long names. The names of garments are as long as 30 Chinese characters, and have no standard rule. There are repetition of meanings, confusion in arrangement and lack of logic in the order of words in a name like that. When users read such a name, they may not only find it hard to memorize, but difficult to know the features of the garment as well.

Excessive and unstandardized garment parameters. Similar to garment names, parameters in detail information pages also have excessive information and poorclassification in different brands. The lack of uniform standard of parameters ignoresspecial needs of visually impaired users, and thus makes it difficult for them to getinformation they really want from the parameters.

Lack of detailed description in words. In detailed information pages in existing websites, information showing clothes details and style is in pictures, but not words. For normal users this might be a vivid description, yet for visually impaired users this information is inaccessible. The lack of descriptive words will have serious damage on their online shopping experience.

2.2 Design of the Prototype

For the feature selectin page, the filtering column contained six classes: style, sleeve length, material, fashion, color and price. We developed a unified rule to classify options for each category to avoid confusion. In order to reduce user's memory workload, we controlled the number of items in one category less than 9. We completed functions of modification, skipping over the next category, and stopping selection for purpose of the improvement of users' operating efficiency (Fig. 1).

For the selection result page, the garment information from result included 6 parts: name, characteristic, picture, price, sales volume and a hyperlink. We develop a unified

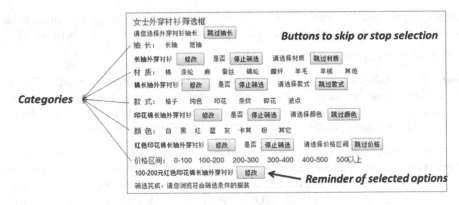

Fig. 1. Design of filtering column

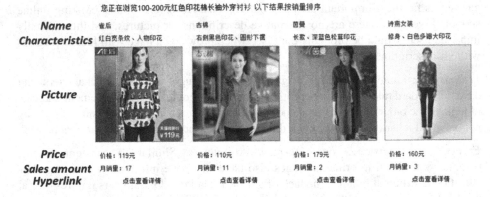

Fig. 2. Design of selection result list

and standardized naming rule for each garment. Product name consists of brand name and the remaining features not selected in the previous page. The name was put in the first line for each garment so that users can determine whether to continue browsing the rest. We also displayed additional characteristics of garments below their names (Fig. 2).

For clothes detail information page, we improved the existing garment parameters by adding information related to tactility to product parameters in this page. Also, we displayed detailed descriptions of garments in words instead of pictures (Fig. 3).

3   Test and Interview Methodology

3.1   Participants

Participants were 10 visually impaired undergraduate students (5 male and 5 female) aged from 20 to 22, who were recruited from the Special Education College of Beijing Union University. All participants had rich experience in computer and Internet and have at least 1 year experience in online shopping.

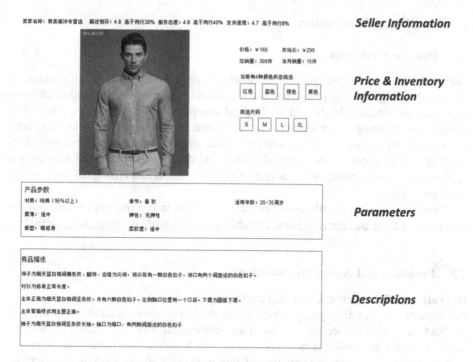

Fig. 3. Design of detailed information page

3.2 Procedure

Participants were asked to browse the 3 pages, and used the functions, and then completed tasks accordingly: in feature selection page, participants were asked to select a combination of features in the filter column, and repeat all features selected after the selection. In the page of selection result list, they were required to browse several clothes in the list and identify the differences. In the page of clothes detail information, participants were asked to browse all detail information about one specific garment and then summarize the features. In the procedure of our test, we used "think aloud" method, which allowed the participants to speak out and express what they thought during their tasks. After the completion of the task of each page, we had a short interview with participants about their opinions and comments about operation, content and process design of tasks in each page.

3.3 Recording and Counting Method

All comments are classified into 3 categories. Comments concerning on such as scanning hot keys or input feedback, would be classified as "operation"; comments on such as classification of filtering in feature selection page or whether brief or detailed description of garments information, would be classified as "content"; comments concerning such as whether they could tell the difference between garments, or how well they understood the details, would be classified as "effects".

4 Result and Discussion

4.1 Positive Feedbacks

During the interview, some positive feedbacks were given by these visually impaired users to the designs in our prototype. The classification of category in feature selection page was considered clearly and methodical compared with existing websites. The information of garment characteristics in selection result list page was believed to help them to identify garments. They could get unique and accuracy information other than the "tags" such as colors and style. Moreover, the description in detailed information page received much praise and was considered most important among all contents by these participants.

However, there were still many problems revealed in the process of task and the interview, and we put forward some possible solutions to them in the next section.

4.2 Problems and Alternative Solutions

Operation Habits. Tendency to skip back and forth within a page.
Participants said that they just wanted to skip the information unattractive to them or get back to a previous section in a rapid and convenient way. It is inconvenience for them to control the scroll bar as normal users, which means they have to use frequent skip by keyboards to get the structure of this page, as well as skipping information. Design ignoring this habit could cause confusions. For instance, in selection result page, the hyperlink is on the bottom of each table, but when the users skip to it, all information above is also skipped. The users had to skip back to browse the missing information, which led to lots of comments in this page.

The participants preferred switching focus rapidly using "tab" in the keyboard, or other hot keys defined in the webpage. For our prototype, we did not design a direct way to switch focus across the divisions in feature selection page. It seems that our original design of skipping category was still complex and hard to use. Buttons provided excessive focus in the page and much more time to switch using the "tab" key.

For feature selection page, to support frequent skipping across divisions, we can decrease the number of focus in the page by replacing buttons with combo box and multiple choice checkbox, and then allow shortcut keys to skip back and forth. In this way, each press of the "tab" key can skip exactly one category, and hot keys can be used to switch across divisions. For selection result page, we can change the position of hyperlinks to the top of each table, and thus the words of the hyperlinks must change to clothes name. In this way, it will be clearer when visually impaired users skip to the hyperlinks and easier to browse other information about the same garment. Moreover, switch by shortcut keys should also be supported in this page, so that users can skip the clothes that are not attractive to them.

Expectation for feedback. We noticed comments about feedbacks of operations were mentioned quite a lot in feature selection page. Apart from feedbacks given by screen reading software, additional information especially designed for blind users to remind their options. It is worth mentioned that the feedback can also take place when all choice are made and the users want to confirm them. For our prototype, we added confirmation after each choice, which might contradict with reading software according to some of the participants. Simplification should be made to refine the feedback information.

Content requirements: Tendency for a wider range of selection.

Participants would like more categories for selection, such as ratings or sales record, and more options for existing categories like color and style. The more detailed the selection, the more information users receive and the more precise their feeling about the garment, thus the more possible to find a satisfactory garment. In our original design, we chose fewer options to decrease mental workload, yet the participants did not care about that. Compared with the benefits of wider range of selection, the additional mental workload was not worried by the participants.

Since the increasing amount of information in categories wouldn't cause mental overload, we can use full options in categories just the same as other clothes online shopping websites. Also, we can add more categories into the filtering column, such as ratings of seller credit and sales record. Moreover, order of the categories can be changed as well according to the relative importance from the view of visually impaired users. Multiple choices are also allowed for improvement.

Demand for information content: brief in title, explicit in detail. Two kinds of information about clothes were provided: short and brief information in title (usually words or phrases) in selection result list, and long information as a paragraph in clothes detail pages. For titles, participants would like a brief title with exactly "key words", which only show the distinguishable features of clothes. For descriptions in detailed information page, participants all hoped the descriptive paragraph to be as precise as possible, containing details such as detailed pattern or ornaments of clothes.

Higher ranking for more important information. The information order is quite important to visually impaired users, for the only way to indicate importance by screen reader is the reading order, and other UI design cannot apply to these users. If the order is confusing, visually impaired users may find it hard to understand the structure and hence cannot get important information they want. In detail information page, participants suggested that more important information, including comments, descriptions and sales record, should rank higher. Therefore, the only way to display information importance clearly and rapidly in a text-based webpage for visually impaired users is ordering.

In selection result page where we display sales amount as well as credit rating of sellers or prices for each clothes, we can design a changeable order method, in which users can get different rankings as they wish. In this way different requirements of "important information" would be satisfied. In detailed information page, we give higher ranking of detailed description of garments, and add a new division of comments. The new order of display would be: price, sales amount, detailed description, parameters, comments, seller and stock information.

Comments from other customers or volunteers. For visually impaired users, the comments for a garment are vivid descriptions that provide information from a different aspect. Comments from other customer or volunteers can provide additional descriptions, usually in garment quality, credit of seller or even delivery time about a garment, thus may alleviate their worries to some extent. In the interview, many participants requested a higher ranking of the comments among all divisions, which showed the importance of comments from their point of view.

In existing online shopping websites, comments about goods are written by other customers, which usually concern service quality and price. We would display these comments as well in our pages. For visually impaired users, we discovered a special way of interaction between customers and the "volunteers". These volunteers are usually sighted relatives or friends of visually impaired people. They have already played an important part in the decision making for visually impaired people in clothes shopping. At present, visually impaired users would send the information to those volunteers by instant messaging software; then, volunteers provide feedback to customers including comments about information that is hard for them to access. Visually impaired people have enough confidence in the personalized service given by volunteers. Thus, if we add comments given by those volunteers, more information focusing on the need of users would be shown, such as the fabric comfort or color matching.

Alternative explanation for terms or original concepts. Some blind participants said they had no idea about special or original concepts that was familiar to us normal users. With the pictures the styles were visible to normal users, but for visually impaired users, the detailed meaning was not clear as its name implied. Some participants suggested we describe people suitable for this style.

To solve this problem, we can add information about "suitable people" in detailed information page. Words or phrases can be used to describe people that suit the clothes or style well. The description should include age, gender, profession and body size or height.

Acknowledgments. The authors thank Professor Zhong and the students from the Special Education College of Beijing Union University for participant recruitment in this study.

References

Babu, R., Singh, R., Ganesh, J.: Understanding blind users' Web accessibility and usability problems. AIS Trans. Hum.-Comput. Interact. 2(3), 73–94 (2010)

Bigham, J.P., Lau, T., Nichols, J.: Trailblazer: enabling blind users to blaze trails through the web. In: Proceedings of the 14th International Conference on Intelligent User Interfaces, pp. 177–186. ACM, February 2009

Francisco-Revilla, L., Crow, J.: Interpreting the layout of web pages. In: Proceedings of the 20th ACM Conference on Hypertext and Hypermedia, pp. 157–166. ACM, June, 2009

Francisco-Revilla, L., Crow, J.: Interpretation of web page layouts by blind users. In: Proceedings of the 10th Annual Joint Conference on Digital Libraries, pp. 173–176. ACM, June 2010

Fuglerud, K.S.: The Barriers to and Benefits of Use of ICT for People with Visual Impairment. In: Stephanidis, C. (ed.) Universal Access in HCI, Part I, HCII 2011. LNCS, vol. 6765, pp. 452–462. Springer, Heidelberg (2011)

Fukuda, K., Saito, S., Takagi, H., Asakawa, C.: Proposing new metrics to evaluate web usability for the blind. In: CHI 2005 Extended Abstracts on Human Factors in Computing Systems, pp. 1387–1390. ACM, April 2005

Goodhue, D.: I/S attitudes: toward theoretical and definitional clarity. ACM SIGMIS Database **19** (3–4), 6–15 (1988)

Goodwin, N.C.: Functionality and usability. Commun. ACM **30**(3), 229–233 (1987)

Lazar, J., Allen, A., Kleinman, J., Malarkey, C.: What frustrates screen reader users on the web: A study of 100 blind users. Int. J. Hum.-Comput. Interac. **22**(3), 247–269 (2007)

Leporini, B., Paternò, F.: Increasing usability when interacting through screen readers. Univ. Access Inf. Soc. **3**(1), 57–70 (2004)

Leporini, B., Paternò, F.: Applying web usability criteria for vision-impaired users: does it really improve task performance? Intl. J. Hum.-Comput. Interac. **24**(1), 17–47 (2008)

Mahmud, J.U., Borodin, Y., Ramakrishnan, I.V.: Csurf: a context-driven non-visual web-browser. In: Proceedings of the 16th International Conference on World Wide Web, pp. 31–40. ACM, May 2007

Takagi, H., Asakawa, C., Fukuda, K., Maeda, J.: Accessibility designer: visualizing usability for the blind. In: ACM SIGACCESS Accessibility and Computing, no. 77–78, pp. 177-184. ACM, October 2004

Takagi, H., Saito, S., Fukuda, K., Asakawa, C.: Analysis of navigability of Web applications for improving blind usability. ACM Trans. Comput.-Hum. Interac. (TOCHI) **14**(3), 13 (2007)

Vigo, M., Leporini, B., Paternò, F.: Enriching web information scent for blind users. In: Proceedings of the 11th International ACM SIGACCESS Conference on Computers and Accessibility, pp. 123–130. ACM, October, 2009

World Wide Web Consortium, Web content accessibility guidelines (WCAG) 2.0 (2008)

Co-design: An Investigation Through Interviewing Expert in Europe

Shu Yuan[1], Hua Dong[1]([✉]), and Zi Chen[2]

[1] Tongji University, 1602 Zonghe Building, 1239 Siping Road,
Shanghai 200092, China
donghua@tongji.edu.cn
[2] Department of Tuberculosis Prevention, Wuhan Pulmonary Hospital,
28 Baofeng Road, Wuhan 430030, China

Abstract. This paper summarized the study of the co-design expert interviews in Europe. Seven interviews were conducted, recorded, transcribed and then analyzed with the general inductive approach. Twelve categories were divided into the upper level of the principles about co-design and the lower level of the practical experiences and techniques. At last, the authors extracted the most impressive perceptions from the twelve categories based on the Chinese co-design experiences.

Keywords: Co-design · Participatory design · Expert interviews

1 Introduction

During the latter half of the 20th century, design research circle in Europe had undergone a steady transformation in its attitude with the various stakeholders involved in the design process, especially in between users and designers. From the original conception of "designing for people," it evolved to "designing with people" and eventually arrived at this novel conception of "designing by people". In the wake of all these changes, the notion of co-design (or participatory design) emerged as it was carefully studied and constantly mentioned first by the Scandinavians and then throughout the western hemisphere during the fall of last century and well into the century that we are living now. In the process of its growing influence and application, co-design saw the development and introducing of various tools and methods applicable in this design-led research. These include generative tools [1], design probes [2], context-mapping [3] and design games [4]. Generative tools was firstly raised and put into practice by Liz Sanders in the US. It was then adapted by Pieter Jan Stappers of TU Delft, where some PhD students employed the method and applied it into co-design practices, and context-mapping, a derivative of their own developed by Froukje Sleeswijk Visser when she was a PhD in TU Delft. At the same time, the Nordic researchers also explored co-design methods and tools, which help designers to gain more empathy on users (design probes by Tuuli Mattelmäki) and ease user participation during design process (design games by Eva Brandt).

In combination with co-design literatures of the Nordic countries and the Netherland, this retrospective study went through live interviews of respective co-design

P.L.P. Rau (Ed.): CCD 2015, Part I, LNCS 9180, pp. 262–273, 2015.
DOI: 10.1007/978-3-319-20907-4_24

researchers. The experts are Pieter Jan Stappers, Froukje Sleeswijk Visser and Christine de Lille from TU Delft, Julia Cassim from the UK, Pelle Ehn from Sweden, Tuuli Mattelmäki from Finland and Eva Brandt from Denmark. They were selected because they have published work relating to co-design, and they were available for interviewing for the time specified. All the interviewees' responses on co-design will be synthesized using a general inductive approach.

After introducing the co-design expert interviews in Europe, the latter part of this paper will discuss the implications from the expert interviews for the co-design practices in China.

2 The Expert Interviews

By reviewing relevant literatures, a number of experts in co-design and participatory design fields were identified. The main purpose of the expert interviews was to map a larger picture of co-design through understanding the perspectives from various specialists and to experience in person how co-design is practiced in Europe. Finally this study attempts to establish shared practices which sublimate common principles and demonstrate different techniques which have been employed by these experts up until now.

All the seven interviews were conducted face to face and each lasted from one to one and a half hours. There was a questionnaire for the interview, which included two parts. The questionnaire started from simpler questions for letting both interviewees and the interviewer quickly immerge into the current scene, i.e., the definition of co-design, or name one most impressive co-design experience. Then it went into their practical experiences, i.e., they would be asked to name the advantages and the challenges when conducting co-design sessions, the useful tools and techniques which they have employed during co-design practices. All these interviews were conducted under different circumstances because of the time limitation, varied site conditions (some interviews were conducted in offices while others were during conference breaks) and varied interviewees' preferences (some preferred to talk beyond the confinement of the questions while others responded strictly within). In consequence, this expert interview study was an open one with clear motivations.

2.1 Methods of Analyzing the Expert Interviews

All the interviews were recorded and then transcribed. A general inductive approach [5] was employed to analyze the transcriptions. Essentially a coding method, such approach enabled an effective deciphering mechanism peeking into the miscellaneous of raw materials, through which seemingly irrelevant free talks can be extracted into meaningful categories. All the categories were then sorted out into two main parts, namely, the upper level of principles about co-design from the experts' perspectives and the lower level of the practical experiences and techniques of practicing co-design. The analysis proceeded in the funnel form (Fig. 1). Comparing with other qualitative analysis approaches, *the general inductive approach provides a simple, straightforward approach for deriving findings [5]*. The coding process of the general inductive

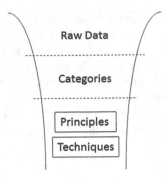

Fig. 1. The analysis funnel

Table 1. The coding process in inductive analysis (Adapted from [5])

Initial reading of text data	Identify specific text segments related to objectives	Label the segments of text to create categories	Reduce overlap and redundancy amount the categories	Classify the categories into the upper and the lower level
	$\longrightarrow$		$\longrightarrow$	
Many pages of text	Many segments of text	20 to 30 categories	12categories	6 categories in each level

approach is shown in Table 1. All the seven interviews were coded in sequence. Then the different categories from different interviewees were synthesized into two levels.

2.2 Findings of the Expert Interviews

According to the general inductive approach, twelve categories based on the transcriptions of the expert interview are summarized. Six categories are classified as the upper level of principles, namely, the definitions of co-design, the advantages and the challenges when practicing co-design, the most important factors when conducting co-design, whether the user and the designer have an equal status in co-design, being objective or not and perceptions on design probes. The other six categories are classified into the lower level of the practical experiences and techniques of practicing co-design, i.e., choosing users, engaging designers, how to use the co-design tools, being flexible, techniques for helping participants express themselves and perceptions on empathy. The synthesized categories are listed as follows.

The Upper Level: The Principles of Conducting Co-design.

Definitions of Co-design. Co-design literally means a design process that involves heavy collaborative efforts between the designers and the users to plan, adjust and

Table 2. Definitions of co-design

Interviewee	Definitions of co-design
Cassim	Co-design is that you are working with a group of people, based on equality and mutual interests. However, the creative direction and the design control have to be in the hands of the designer
De Lille	Co-design is an activity, in which the designer and the user collaborate to design a new product or service. The insights were gained through active collaboration and proactive participation among various stakeholders
Ehn	Co-design is an activity in which everything is designed with the user involved. It is like an umbrella word for all kinds of human-centred approaches, be it political or not Participatory design sprung from a different origin But the only academic conference about "Co-design" is called the Participatory Conference and the only academic journal in participatory design field is called "CoDesign". So contemporarily these are two nearly identical concepts
Mattelmäki	Four kinds of co-designs are categorized [6]. It started when the user's voice was accepted, then it went on to the development of the different kinds of tools that facilitated the user to express themselves, nowadays, not only the user, also other stakeholders were included in the co-design sessions
Sleeswijk Visser	Co-design is a design process when different stakeholders work together
Stappers	Co-design is a collaborative design process, typically when the users are involved throughout the entire design process. The users are put into the position of "experts", whose experiences the designers are interested in

facilitate the processing of a specific design endeavor [6]. Sanders and Stappers defined co-design as people designing together, an occasion when people collectively contributed their respective expertise as they participate in the design process [7]. When asked about their own definition of the co-design concept, these experts gave different responses (Table 2), which more or less reflected their own emphasis or interest of the concept. From their responses, two main trends can be observed about co-design. The first trend is that co-design and participatory design, though having different origins and at times different emphases, are becoming more and more overlapped in the contemporary view point. It is like what happened in between inclusive design and universal design, although they originated from different cradles, nowadays, they are just treated almost as if they are two different jargons about one same conception. The second trend is that co-design's purpose no longer ends at achieving better user experiences, it also has to put other stakeholders' interests into consideration.

The Advantages and Challenges When Practicing Co-design. All the experts' perspectives on this question are listed in Table 3. Organizing a co-design session is time and efforts consuming and expensive. However, just as Ehn said, things would not come out if not much time and efforts were spent. All these experts are experienced in co-design. De Lille believed that once the pre-work had been sufficiently done, the results would come naturally. However, for novices, how to handle unexpected or undesirable outcome is another challenge.

Table 3. The advantages and challenges when practicing co-design

Interviewee	The advantages	The challenges
Brandt	1. Design for the future	1. Greatly efforts consuming
		2. Lots of transferring work: Before going out: graphic work; After coming back: transform the raw field materials into design materials
De Lille	1. Co-design could accelerate the process because the designers could have users close by	
Ehn	1. It offers the chance for people to govern their own life	1. Time consuming
	2. It offers a chance to break the hegemony. It allows different voices and perspectives	2. There is no guarantee that results are good because of using co-design method
Mattelmäki	1. It brings different voices into the process, which could deepen the understanding	1. Time and resources consuming
	2. Often the involvement of non-designers helps develop	2. Users with high expectations prone to be disappointed
Sleeswijk Visser	1. If you get everything right, you get so much energy	1. Time consuming
		2. Find the right users with proper expertise.
Stappers	1. Bringing in the expertise of the user	1. Cost: time, efforts, skills, money
	2. Letting the user and the designer contact each other benefit both sides	2. The role of the designer sometimes is underestimated
	3. The end user might produce good solutions	

After synthesizing all these views, four advantages of co-design are found. First, it is more democratic as it enables the users to have their voices heard and influence the design outcomes, which later would directly impact their lives. Secondly, incorporating user ideas into the design process sometimes can be really helpful. Thirdly, with the help of the user, the designer could identify the crucial parts more accurately and quickly, thus easing the process. Fourthly, by introducing the design games, it triggers imagination that inspires designs which challenge the contemporary design norms.

The Most Important Factors When Practicing Co-design. Table 4 lists the key factors that the interviewees had contributed. They explained the essentials of co-design. It gives an outline for novices to follow.

When Brandt was preparing a design game, she always put every participant's interests into consideration and so she would have a rough idea about what he or she would like to gain from the workshop. Her focus was always on how much more engaging after the design game was introduced to facilitate a design project. Cassim

Table 4. The most important factors when practicing co-design

Interviewee	Factors
Brandt	How to engage every participant: carefully consider every participant's interests and what he or she wants to gain
Cassim	Context, budget, skill bases and the expected outcomes
De Lille	The most important qualities that co-designers need to have: Open-minded, curious, flexible
Ehn	Building trust: equality and mutually beneficial, a two way empathic relationship between the designer and the user
Mattelmäki	Treat users as humans not as research subjects; be sensitive
Sleeswijk Visser	Choosing the right users with proper expertise
Stappers	Giving some part of control to the user; Users were given certain freedom and assistance to identify the problems for themselves and even provide a solution

considered context, budget, skill bases and the expected outcomes were the four key factors for conducting co-design. Besides, clearly defining the role of the designer and the user was very important. De Lille shared her thoughts on the desirable qualities that a co-designer needed to have, i.e., a person who is open-minded, full of curiosity, being able to be flexible. Ehn highlighted the importance of building mutual trust when conducting co-design. According to his observation, empathy was often considered to be the sole responsibility on the designer's part, while trust emphasized a mutual and equal relation between the designer and the user. Mattelmäki believed that it is very important for a designer to be able to treat his or her users as human-beings, not as research subjects in a scientific experiment. Sleeswijk Visser considered choosing the right users with proper expertise was the key factor when conducting co-design. In co-design, users are put into the position of "experts" about their own life. Hence, Stappers believed that giving out certain part of control to users would be the key and the most difficult part when practicing co-design. Instead of the designer identifying the design problems for the user in the very beginning of a design process, they were given certain freedom and assistance to determine the issues for themselves and sometimes even provide a solution. When users were given some part of control, they felt their "expertise" was valued, in return they would be more inclined to collaborate with the designers to see the design process through.

Whether the User and the Designer Have an Equal Status in Co-design. De Lille and Cassim both believed that designers or researchers should take the absolute leading role in the co-design process. *"Users will never be equal partners in the design process" (from the interview of De Lille).* De Lille explained her comment, as she encountered frequently users who were just unable to image beyond the prototypes in hand. Such inability of broadened thinking can be attributed to lack of training in design fundamentals (e.g. the textile and the texture). Interaction with such users could not provide the designers with the radical insights he or she hoped to gain. In the interview with Cassim, she frequently mentioned that in order to ensure a pleasant quality of the design outcome, the designers should have a firm control over the bearing of the direction of design innovation. Cassim categorized co-design into four main types (Table 5), which reflected four kinds of designer-user relationships. And in most of these four scenarios, designers dominated the design process. Before the co-design session, the capabilities of users and the conditions in which the co-design session was going to be carried out would be carefully defined. As a result, the context of the design project would be put under control.

Table 5. The four types of co-design that Julia Cassim conducted

	Type 1	Type 2	Type 3	Type 4
People	Designers/Skilled but socially marginalized people	Designers/Addicts	Designers/People with learning disabilities	Designers/Disabled people
Roles	Creative directors and Understand the context/Makers	Creative directors and Makers/No skills	Design a template/Simple scribble	Design with the insights and expertise from disabled people/Offer lots of inputs, but do not design
Relations	An equal level of talents	Not an equal level of talents	Not an equal level of talents	An equal relation

Being Objective or Not. Both Sleeswijk Visser and Brandt maintained that it is not a necessity for researchers to be completely objective during co-design sessions. According to Sleeswijk Visser that being objective is not the purpose of a design process, trying to collaborate with users and ultimately having something created is. Sometimes absolute objectivity can be misleading, especially when the research objects are human beings, it is better to rely on one's own experiences on user research and pay more attention on deciphering the quotes of users which were deemed to be important. *"We do not say we are objective. We say we cannot be"* (from Brandt's interview). When Brandt was trying to incorporate the design game into the design process, what was on her mind wasn't how objective the design game was but rather how engaging, and that is why she also took part in the game herself.

Perceptions on Design Probes. As the pioneer of design probes, Mattelmäki explained her perceptions on it. First, she distinguished cultural probes [8] from design probes. Cultural probes were much more artistic while design probes were used as an element for evoking a dialogue, which were more empathy related. Secondly, the design probe was not only a tool, but also a process of learning, reflecting and for engaging participants. Thirdly, in the probe package, both the previous experiences of users and the potential future could be collected, just depending on how the probe package was designed.

The Lower Level: The Practical Experiences and Techniques of Conducting Co-design

Choosing Users. In regard to whom should be invited to participate in co-design sessions, Stappers believed that people of expertise to the design issue are desirable invitees. He gave an example to illustrate his definition of the expertise. In an effort to better run the operating rooms in a hospital, besides surgeons, nurses, patients and hospital administrators, the involvement of the cleaning staffs was vital as well. In terms of expertise, they have a distinctive advantage comparing to other seemingly more important partakers, they were much closer to and spending more time in the operating rooms. Sleeswijk Visser tended to regard people who have a passion on the relevant design topics as her desirable invitees. Brandt took the familiar view of Sleeswijk Visser that she preferred to invite the ones who were open, willing to participate in the topic. De Lille and Cassim also contributed their respective preferences of desirable participants. *"Thinking out of the box, who can provide you with interesting information...really think broader" (from De Lille's interview).* De Lille made a point that besides the primary users, the secondary users were also needed consideration. De Lille mentioned a project to improve the safety of stairs. A tour guide who was working in a church tower with 400 stairs was invited as an "expert" of narrow winding stairs. Cassim gave an example about participant selection when she was organizing a co-design session for designing shoes which are not only comfortable but attractive for women with rheumatoid arthritis. She invited one shoe designer, one product designer, one orthotist and one podiatrist. Three female rheumatoid arthritis patients of varied severity, different age groups and life styles were invited. Cassim had hoped to have two kinds of scenarios run simultaneously, i.e., a disability scenario and a life style scenario.

In order to cultivate a relaxed and genuine atmosphere, Stappers deliberately invited participants who were total strangers to one another as people have less if any pretence in front of strangers. A hierarchical relationship between superiors and subordinates would only hinder a genuine exchange of ideas while tacit understanding in between family members could result in an effective communication.

All in all, there are four main considerations when choosing participants; the first one is trying to find out who are the "experts" on the design topic; the second one is trying to think broader than the stereotypes; the third one is to invite the people who are open-minded and interested in the topic; finally, when considering the composition of a group of diversified participants, the people with latent understanding and can communicate freely are desirable invitees.

Engaging Designers. Sleeswijk Visser believed that only curious designers can adopt an empathic attitude towards users. She talked about two effective ways to motivate designers. The first one is trying to encourage designers to talk about their own experiences. Kouprie and Sleeswijk Visser termed it as the "connection" phase of the four phases of gaining empathy [9]. The second one is trying to avoid overloading, because designers seldom have time and patience to bear a long presentation of a bit of everything. To keep them curious, it would be better to show them ten pictures within half an hour.

How to Use the Co-design Tools. Several co-design tools were mentioned earlier in the introduction of this study. Though these tools are appealing in manifestation and look a promising solution to all the problems which could be encountered in the co-design process, all experts who commented on design tools tried to disregard the prominence of these tools if one doesn't know why, when and how to apply them. *"I think more important is in what way you will collaborate and who will you involve in… Skills and techniques are more important than tools" (from the interview of Stappers). "We should not just consider this kind of tool like probes… but it's really we should consider the competences, the processes, the whole engaging process" (from the interview of Mattelmäki). "I like tools for the specific situation"(from the interview of Sleeswijk Visser).* All these quotations reflected that these experts would not allow themselves to the confinement of these design tools, if they are irrelevant to the overall goal of the design project.

Regarding application of tools in co-design, Sleeswijk Visser asserted another view that a designer should have the awareness of incorporating multi-disciplinary tools to solve the design problem, especially in commercial design project when the deal is real. As she mentioned in a commercial project she leaded, in order to gain a fuller picture of the problem in hand, she summoned a team consisting of experts from different fields, e.g., engineers, psychologists, pharmacists. Each expert was given a slice of the problem which concerns the professions of that expert, and they were allowed to handle that slice of problem in their own professional manner, the result of such cross disciplinary collaboration was rather a success. Therefore it is always useful to approach a problem from a broader perspective.

There is another aspect when talking about co-design tools, which virtually every expert had mentioned in their respective interviews. "Flexibility".

Being Flexible. "Flexibility" meant that the tools had to be implemented according to the current situations and context. *"Being flexible and take your freedom. If this does not work, try something else and move on" (from the interview of De Lille).* De Lille gave an example, that during work hours, nurses seldom have time to join the designers for an interview session; therefore it is much more feasible to offer them something which they can complete during breaks, like place a white board with all the design issues listed as concise multiple choices for them to fill. Based on her experiences collaborating with small companies, De Lille believed that it is very important for designers to maintain a fresh perspective. Once a method or tool was met with resistance and found incompatible with the current situation, instead of insisting on the old method or tool, new ones must be tried. In Mattelmäki's view, the most important quality for a designer to possess was to be sensitive rather than being scientific and rigorous to the users. Stappers described the features of co-designing as variable, complex, unstable. He observed that once a co-design session got on the way, it proceeded according to the ever changing complexes of the situation and the instinctive and internalized experiences of the designers or the researchers. From the four types of co-design Cassim categorized, different users would be measured up and classified into different levels of capabilities, each and every design context would be carefully examined to make the whole co-design process controllable. To facing with ever-changing design context and situations, flexibility and adaptability are two very important qualities for a designer to possess. De Lille and Mattelmäki both suggested using design games to conduct co-design session, as it could be set the game rule flexibly according to the design purpose and the current conditions.

Techniques for Helping Participants Express Themselves. During co-design session, facilitating participants to express themselves was a challenge in practice. Different experts shared their experiences (Table 6).

Table 6. The techniques for helping participants express themselves

Interviewee	Techniques
Stappers	1. Using ambiguous pictures (learned from Liz Sanders)
	2. The Focus-Scope rule: when focusing on the narrow topic, talk about the broader topic to keep the conversation on
	3. Pay attention to the group dynamics: do not ignore the people who are not talkative, maybe they are good thinkers
	4. Facilitators must feel secured and encourage one of the participants to talk. Once one person broke the ice, the other participants would be more willing to join in
Cassim	1. Invite a visualizer special for users to express their ideas simultaneously
	2. Let users "make" than "draw": users are more confident when they construct something than drawing
Brandt	Adopt a turn taking rule in the design game to give everyone a chance to talk

Perceptions on Empathy. De Lille and Mattelmäki both held the view that empathy is an innate quality, which all people have a varied inheritance. Kouprie and Sleeswijk Visser divided the techniques of gaining empathy into three main classes [9]. Communication techniques [9] were the most widely used ones, for example, storytelling, visual data and original quotes. The process of gaining empathy in design practice consisted of four phases, namely, discovery, immersion, connection and detachment, in which a designer steps into the life of a user, trying to put his or her feet into the user's shoes and then detaches out of the life of that user with a deeper appreciation of the life of that individual. Sleeswijk Visser answered the question why designers had to step out of the life of the user to conclude the empathic process. *"At that moment, designers have to create something new. The mechanism of creativity is different from that of empathy, in which designers try hard to understand someone else really well. Once the designers have sufficient understanding, just leave them there and start designing. When the brainstorming mode is turned on, designers cannot understand the user deeper. I do not mean that the user is useless at this stage. They are still there. But the designers just stop trying to deepen that empathic understanding"* (from the interview of Sleeswijk Visser).

3 The Implications for China

The co-design concepts were formally introduced to China since around 2012. Subsequently two co-design workshops between professional designers and diverse users and a co-design project as a module among undergraduate students were conducted [10, 11]. From these practices, certain experiences had been accumulated while some obstacles were encountered, for example, how to properly use the co-design tools; how to effectively engage the participants, what kind of relation that the designer and the user have, etc. Through analyzing these findings from the expert's interviews, certain vague zones had been clarified according to the European pioneering experiences. The summaries of the second part can be regarded as a great attempt trying to answer the questions and the main perceptions from the synthesis are concluded as following.

- There is no need to be scientifically objective when conducting co-design.

> *"I argue for the importance of the designer's or researcher's role in making sense of an ongoing discussion, and the need to project her or his interpretations onto it and to orient it towards the design direction that she or he finds relevant." [12]*

Based on the perceptions from the interview, proper intervention is better than being absolutely objective.

- There is not a monotonous tool and rule. The researchers and the designers have to be very flexible according to the context and the conditions. Slightly change the prepared agenda according to the participants' conveniences.
- Get used to the uncertainty and ambiguity of the creative design process, especially at the early stage. Keep the purpose and the expected outcomes of the project in mind. Do not spend much time on the forms.
- Pay more attention on the participants' preferences, feelings and characters to engage everyone to be passionate in the co-design session.

4 Conclusions

This study has explored the concept of co-design through interviewing seven experts in Europe. Each expert has his/her own view on co-design, but consensus was observed, 1. Co-design and participatory design are regarded as interchangeable by the experts. 2. Different stakeholders (rather than just the end users) are brought into the co-design process. A number of key factors for practicing co-design were identified (as listed in Table 4), and each expert has his/her own viewpoints, which suggest that it is important for the individual researchers to practice co-design in his/her own way as appropriate. Practical guidance on co-design techniques was proposed, with specific tips for student researchers practicing co-design in China.

References

1. Sanders, E.B.-N.: Generative tools for co-designing. In: Scrivener, S.A.R., Ball, L.J., Woodcock, A. (eds.) Collaborative Design: Proceedings of CoDesigning, pp. 3–12. Springer, London (2000). Accessed from http://www.maketools.com/articles-papers/GenerativeToolsforCoDesig-ing_Sanders_00.pdf
2. Mattelmäki, T.: Design probes. Doctoral thesis. University of Art and Design, Helsinki, Finland (2006)
3. Sleeswijk Visser, F., Stappers, P.J., Van der Lugt, R., Sanders, E.B.-N.: Contextmapping: experiences from practice. CoDes. Int. J. CoCreation Des. Arts 1(2), 1–30 (2005)
4. Brandt, E.: Designing exploratory design games: a framework for participation in participatory design. In: Proceedings of the 9th Participatory Design Conference, pp. 57–66. ACM, New York (2006)
5. Thomas, D.R.: A general inductive approach for analyzing qualitative evaluation data. Am. J. Eval. 27(2), 237–246 (2006)
6. Mattelmäki, T., Sleeswijk Visser, F.: Lost in Co-X: Interpretations of Co-design and Co-creation
7. Sanders, E.B.-N., Stappers, P.J.: Co-creation and the new landscapes of design. CoDes. Int. J. CoCreation Des. Arts 4(1), 5–18 (2008)
8. Gaver, B., Duune, T., Pacenti, E.: Cultural probes. Interactions 6(1), 21–29 (1999)
9. Kouprie, M., Sleeswijk Visser, F.: A framework for empathy in design: stepping into and out of the user's life. J. Eng. Des. 20(5), 437–448 (2009)
10. Yuan, S., Dong, H.: Empathy building through co-design. In: Stephanidis, C., Antona, M. (eds.) UAHCI 2014, Part I. LNCS, vol. 8513, pp. 85–91. Springer, Heidelberg (2014)
11. Yuan, S., Dong, H.: Co-design in China: implications for users, designers and researchers. In: Langdon, P.M., et al. (eds.) Inclusive Designing, pp. 235–244. Springer, Heidelberg (2014)
12. Lee, J.J.: Against method: the portability of method in human-centered design. Doctoral thesis. Aalto University, School of Arts, Design and Architecture, Helsinki, Finland (2012)

Investigation into Designing of Elderly Products Intending for the User's Behavior Experiencing

Ning Zhang, Yajun Li[✉], Ming Zhou, and Zhizheng Zhang

School of Design Arts and Media, Nanjing University of Science
and Technology, Xuanwu Area, Nanjing 210094, China
lyj5088@163.com, znn1224@126.com

Abstract. Body gestures are the key point affect the elderly daily life (ADL). Seidel, D., et al. [1] An innovative designing method based on user's behavior experience is proposed in order to improve the experiencing and to mine innovative points of elderly product design. Complete interactive processes between users and products are captured through penetrating into users living scenes. A Laundry Behavior Coding (LBC) system is proposed special for the elderly in China. Ethnography methods, behavior observation, oral presentation and in-depth interviews are also deployed. 20 participants (10 young and 10 elderly) participated the study focused on drum washing machine. A special Behavior Interaction Model (BIM) is established by extracting the behavior coding gap, which is obtained by comparing the coded sets of both the old and the young. Implicit demands are discovered in order to realize innovative designing of laundry machine for the old and to enhance users' experiences.

Keywords: Elderly products · Behavior experience · Data encoding · Implicit demand · Design innovation

With 200 million people that are over 60-year-old, China has entered the acceleration period of aging in 2014. User experience is the key to verify the market and the product. However, user's sensory experience and emotional experience are always concerned while behavior analysis is ignored. Body gestures involved in ADL (a.k.a. activities of daily life) including cooking, laundering, house working and shopping, etc. are the key restrictions to the independency of elderly people's daily life [1]. However, most of the products design is aiming at young group. The significant differences of physiology including bones and muscles between the old and the young are ignored, which leads to a conditionality in using gestures of the old. The International Organization for Standardization (ISO) [2] suggests a trunk inclination of >60° and maintained for 4 + s as 'Critical' gestures. Currently 3 % of cooking and 10 % of laundry gestures accounted for critical gestures for the old [3]. Gestures including bad bending and torsion, unbalanced stretching, squatting knees and neck inclining will increase the risk of getting ill, increase the difficulty of usage while reduce the efficiency.

Understanding users' demands and abilities is a key factor in users' experiences designing [4]. The purpose of this paper is to investigate the elderly people's implicit demands from their daily life behavior data to avoid risky gestures. Meanwhile, capturing their implicit demands will become a new breakthrough in innovative designing for elderly products. Bad experiencing as well as unreasonable usages of elderly products can be resolved. In this manner, the independency of the elderly people will be advanced.

1   Introduction

The user experience concept proposed by marketing expert Betnd.H.Schmitt [5] contains five parts, the sensory, emotional, thinking, behavior and associate experience. The user experience is the key issue to validate the success of the market, and the 'behavior experience'is the most direct experience between the users and the products. All the interact information is passed from the sensory system to the behavior system. The useful product information can be obtained by the users through direct interaction with the products. Jelle Stienstra [6] described a design method based on the experience of the behavior. This method emphasizes a close loop of 'behavior – perception' which turns virtual behavior into 'tangible materiality'. In this manner, behavior activities can be used directly or indirectly into the design knowledge.

There are many research methods about working gestures in Ergonomic. Karhu decomposed the working gestures into codes of the back, arms and legs respectively through an observation method which is based on the behavior coding of OWAS (Ovako Working Posture Analysis System) [7]. Gestures can be indicated sequentially in this way. At the same time, OWAS method can be used to evaluate the coding risk level and high level risk must be improved immediately. In a similar method, REBA (Rapid - Body Assessment) [8], body postures can be divided into the trunk, neck, legs, upper arm, forearm and wrist 6 parts. The risk level of work posture can be concluded by the means of the posture angle measure .RULA (Rapid Upper Limb Assessment [9]) method is used to evaluate the work of the Upper Limb active task. It can collect and analyze the data of the wrist, arm and body gestures. The research proves the reliability of the behavior data acquisition through observation methods. However, focus of these researches lies in evaluating working gestures of adults. Gestures of the elderly people still lack of investigation.

2   Methods

2.1   Sampling

Laundry is a typical task in elderly people's daily life. The whole procedure of the laundry consists of some common gestures including neck rotation stretching, arm outstretching, trunk bending twisting and bent leg supporting, etc. Analyzing those common gestures such as bowing, kneeling and hand picking during laundry gives a guiding significance in investigating other tasks as taking a vehicle, shopping and using bathroom. Thus, the laundry task is chosen as a typical case in this study.

2.2 Data Collection Methods

Compared to the young, the elderly takes special behavioral strategies. With the purpose of investigating the implicit demands of the elderly people, a sample of 10 elderly people and 10 young people is chosen to provide the useful data. A laboratory environment rather than home environment is deployed in order to prevent experimental errors including different types of laundry machines and different factors of familiarities. Those subjects are requested to finish a preset task using the same laundry machine.

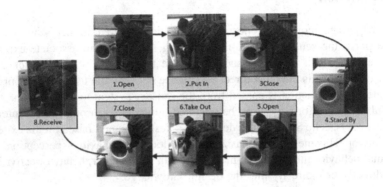

Fig. 1. Laundry procedure

(a) Preparation.

- Pretest. A video of using a laundry machine is made by the researchers in elderly people's home before the experiment, which aims at summarizing the procedures during laundry as illustrated in Fig. 1. Suggestions for environment arrangement are also shown in this video.
- Subjects choosing. The subjects in this research are classed as the young and the elderly. 10 subjects including 3 male and 7 female with the age over 70 are recruited randomly at the retired community of Nanjing University of Science and Technology. 10 subjects including 4 male and 6 female with the age between 20 and 30 are also recruited in Nanjing University of Science and Technology. All of the 20 subjects have the experience of using laundry machines.
- Testing device. A tumbling-box laundry machine for home use, a video camera and special testing caps with red marks are provided. Subjects are asked to wear the testing caps before the experiment. Red marks are also located on their shoulders, hips and knees.
- Testing missions. By reference to Fig. 1 during the pretest, the whole testing consists of opening, putting in clothes, closing, standing by, opening, taking out clothes, closing and clothes storage.
- Notes. Test can be shut down at any time if the subject feels uncomfortable or unavailable.

(b) Testing.

1. Adapting the experiment environment and learning the instruction.
2. 20 subjects with red marks performing the 8 test missions. Each one performs independently in order to prevent the behavioral learning effect.
3. Video recording is performed from the side view in order to capture the behaviors.
4. Short interviews are made after the test.

2.3   Behavior Coding Set

The position of neck, waist and knees are commonly the pain points of the elderly in China. The Laundry Behavior Coding (LBC) system is established according to the actual situation of the elderly in China and the position coding system provided by D. E. Gyi et al. [10]. Moving angles of neck, shoulder, waist and knees of the subjects are fully recorded by the camera, which leads to a whole video. The LBC System is shown in Fig. 2. Seven variables including angles of neck, trunk and knees, torsion of trunk, hand picking, leg supporting and additional aids are observed. The angle threshold values are set as 30, 60 and 90 degrees. Numbers of 1, 2, 3, and 4 are selected for coding. It should be noted that the angle of neck, which is chosen to distinguish the differences between the young and the elderly, is not a real angle as indicated in Fig. 2.

Capturing the angle of neck is realized by finding the angle between the line from the red mark to the sagittal cervical root node and the vertical line. According to the method of TO de Souza [11], the trunk angle is captured through the line from femoral greater trochanter node to shoulder center node of sagittal plane and the vertical line. The angle of knee is the angle between legs. The objects of LBC System are images. Therefore, an image of putting into/taking out clothes is captured as a combination of typical gestures including waist bending, kneeling and grabbing. The videos of 20 subjects are collected. Images are captured and processed into codes in the manner of LBC System, which is shown in Fig. 3. Coding set of the differences between the young and the elderly are obtained, which makes a preparation for further investigation.

Laundry Behavior	Action Coding			
Neck Angle (NA)	1. 0-30°	2. 31° -60°	3. 61° -90°	4. >90°
Trunk Angle (TA)	1. 0-30°	2. 31° -60°	3. 61° -90°	4. >90°
Trunk Twist (TT)	1.None	2.Left	3.Right	*
Knee Angle (KA)	1.0-30°	2.31° -60°	3.61° -90°	4. >90°
Hand Pick (HP)	1.Both	2.Left	3.Right	*
Leg Support (LS)	1.Both	2.Left	3.Right	*
Additional Aids (AA)	1. None	2.Left hands	3. Right hands	4.Other

Fig. 2. Laundry behavior coding (LBC) system

Gender / Age	Female	Male	Female	Male	Female	Female	Female	Male	Male	Female
	22	23	21	21	20	21	22	24	21	22
NA	1	2	1	4	1	4	2	2	3	2
TA	1	1	1	2	1	4	2	1	2	2
TT	1	1	1	3	1	3	1	1	1	1
KA	3	3	3	4	2	4	2	2	1	2
HP	1	2	1	1	1	3	1	3	1	1
LS	2	2	3	1	1	1	1	3	3	1
AA	1	1	1	1	1	1	1	2	1	1

Gender / Age	Male	Female	Female	Female	Female	Female	Female	Male	Male	Female
	72	74	70	76	80	80	80	72	78	72
NA	4	3	3	4	4	3	3	4	3	3
TA	3	3	3	3	3	3	3	3	3	3
TT	1	1	1	2	2	1	1	1	1	1
KA	4	4	4	4	4	4	4	4	4	4
HP	1	3	1	3	3	2	1	3	3	2
LS	1	1	1	1	1	1	1	1	1	1
AA	1	2	1	2	2	3	1	2	2	3

Fig. 3. A list of the difference codes

3 Results

3.1 Significance Level of Typical Behaviors

First of all, observation of the marked lines on subjects' bodies indicate a striking difference between the young (n = 10, mean age = 21.7 and SD = 1.1) and the elderly (n = 10, mean age = 75.4 and SD = 3.9). What's more, statistics and analysis of the codes show that obvious differences are obtained between the angles of necks (NA), the angles of trunks (TA), the angles of knees (KA), leg supporting (LS) and additional aids (AA). However, the differences between the torsion of trunks (TT) and hand picking (HP) are relatively small. With the aids of SPSS, a box plot of the codes from the young and the elderly are obtained, which is shown in Fig. 4.

- NA. ①80 % of the young subjects are classified in Code 1 and 2 with NAs less than 60°. ②All of the elderly subjects are classified in Code 3 and 4 with NAs greater than 60°.
- TA. ①50 % of the young subjects are classified in Code 1 with TAs less than 30°. 40 % of the young subjects are classified in Code 2 with TAs vary from 30° to 60°. ②All of the elderly subjects are classified in Code 3 with TAs vary from 60° to 90°.
- KA. ①All of the elderly subjects are classified in Code 4 with KAs greater than 90°. It should be noted that all of their KAs are equal or greater than 120° in actual measurements. ②50 % of the young subjects are classified in Code 1 and 2 with KAs less than 60°. 30 % of the young subjects are classified in Code 3 with KAs from 60° to 90°. 20 % of the young subjects are with KAs greater than 90°.

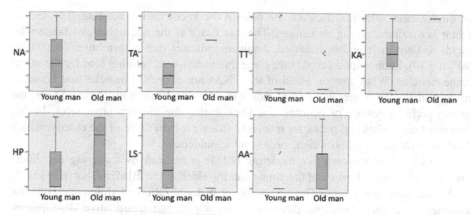

Fig. 4. Significance differences between the young and the elderly: NA: $p < 0.01$;TA:$p < 0.01$; KA:$p < 0.01$;LA:$p < 0.05$;AA:$p < 0.01$;

- LS. ①All of the elderly subjects are classified in Code 1, which means their bodies are balanced with both legs for supporting. ②50 % of the young subjects are classified in Code 2 and 3. Only left or right legs are used for supporting.
- AA. ①70 % of the elderly subjects are classified in Code 2 and 3. Additional assistances are applied using their left or right arms. ②90 % of the young subjects are classified in Code 1 with no additional assistances. Only 1 young subject are classified in Code 2 because the left arm is used for additional assistances.

3.2 Special Behavior Interactive Modeling

The testing results, which are illustrated in Fig. 5, show an obvious difference between the gestures of the young and the elderly during the laundry procedures. The main difference lies in NA, TA, KA, LS and AA. KA of elderly ($\geq 120°$, n = 10) is the key factor of the difference. In order to reach the bending scale, the elderly people have to bend much harder both in their necks and trunks, which leads to a result of unbalanced bodies. At this point, additional assistances of hands must be applied to come over the imbalance. According to the reports and interviews, KAs of the elderly are the results

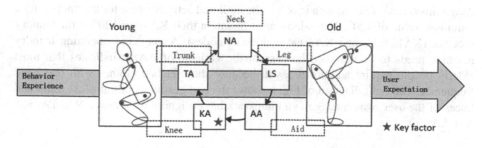

Fig. 5. BIM (behavior interactive modeling)

of three factors. The first factor is the pain in the knees during bending. The second factor is dizziness during unbending. The last factor is the additional assistance with hands to keep their bodies balanced. Analysis indicates that with a huge TA (60° to 90°, n = 10), lumber sprain could take place due to an overwhelming load for the sacral spine muscles. What's more, as all of their NAs are over 60°, muscles and bones at necks and shoulders are also under loads. On the other hand, with healthy knees, the young prefer a gesture of bending one knee during the laundry procedures. In this manner, their bodies and necks are relatively straighter than those of the elderly, which leads to a smaller load on waists, necks and shoulders.

Special behavior interactive modeling (BIM) is realized by capturing the differences between the behaviors of the young and the elderly. The BIM, as shown in Fig. 5, is divided into two stages. The first stage is materialization of difference behavior experience. In this stage, the differences are scaled into quantitative descriptions. Among the specific numbers with visualized descriptions, the key codes can be obtained. In this study, the young subjects and the elderly subjects show obvious differences in variables of NA, TA, KA,LS and AA, especially in KA, LS and AA. The second stage is the transformation from the quantified differences into special behavior demands. This paper indicates that laundry procedures for the elderly should meet the demands that KA should be equal to or greater than 120°, TA should be smaller than 60° [2], two legs for supporting and additional assistance of hands to prevent imbalance.

4 Discussion

Because of musculoskeletal degeneration and weak balance, the elderly who operating laundry machines using waist bending/kneeling postures for a long time does not conform to ergonomics. In this paper, a new design has been obtained by transforming the elderly implicit demands into visual designing knowledge using special behavior interactive modeling (BIM) system. Comparing with the young, the elderly need to interact with products more smoothly for their specific needs. An improvement for the tumbling-box laundry machine has been proposed according to LBS system and BIM mapping method.

A diagram of critical state of bending is shown in Fig. 6 (left). The green area in TA is the suggested activity range for trunk with a maximum value of 60°. The elderly must maintain their TA less than 60°in the laundry process. [2] (TA3 and TA4 are dangerous codes). The red area in KA is the inhibited activity range for the knees with a minimum value of 120°. The elderly must maintain their KA over 120° in the laundry process. (KA1, KA2 and KA3 are dangerous codes). A one-hand operating laundry machine needs to be designed because of the variable of AA. It indicates that most elderly people require additional assist, because they fetched clothes with one hand frequently. The right diagram of Fig. 6 shows the bad gesture codes at neck, trunk and knees of the user, which suggests a multi-variable designing to improve NA, TA, KA and AA.

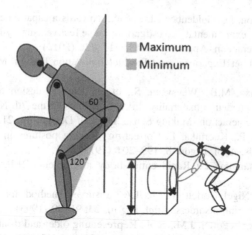

Maximum
Minimum

Fig. 6. Critical state of bending for elderly

5 Conclusion

Gestures including bad bending and torsion, unbalanced stretching, squatting knees and neck inclining will increase the risk of getting ill, increase the difficulty of usage while reduce the efficiency. Capturing the real implicit demands is the first step in understanding the elderly as their implicit demands are difficult to describe by their own. In this paper, ethnography methods, behavior observation, oral presentation and in-depth interviews have been deployed. A Laundry Behavior Coding (LBC) system have been proposed to visualize the implicit demands. This study shows a great significance in avoiding risky gestures as well as improving the independency of the elderly people. The implicit demands have been transformed into design knowledge to solve the mismatching problems occurred between elderly users' behavior experiences and product designing. Behavior cognitions and user's experiences have been advanced. Assistances have been provided for the innovative designing of the elderly products.

Acknlowledgment. The authors are grateful for the financial support provided by the research innovation project funding for graduate students of ordinary university in Jiangsu Province under Contact No. KYLX_0344.

References

1. Seidel, D., Richardson, K., Crilly, N., Matthews, F.E., Clarkson, P.J., Brayne, C.: Design for independent living: activity demands and capabilities of older people. Ageing Soc. **30**, 1239–1255 (2010)
2. ISO 11226: Ergonomics: Evaluation Of Static Working Postures. International Organization for Standardization, Geneva (2000)
3. Seidel, D., Hjalmarson, J., Freitag, S., et al.: Measurement of stressful postures during daily activities: an observational study with older people. Gait Posture **34**, 397–401 (2011)

4. Tenneti, R., Johnson, D., Goldenberg, L., et al.: Towards a capabilities database to inform inclusive design: experimental investigation of effective survey-based predictors of human-product interaction. Appl. Ergon. **43**, 713–726 (2012)
5. Luo, S., Zhu, S.: User Experience and Product Innovation Design. Machine Press, China (2010)
6. Stienstra, J., Alonso, M.B., Wensveen, S., et al.: How to design for transformation of behavior through interactive materiality. In: Proceedings of the 7th Nordic Conference on Human-Computer Interaction: Making Sense Through Design, pp. 21–30 (2012)
7. Karhu, O., Kansi, P., Kuorinka, I.: Correcting working postures in industry: a practical method for analysis. Appl. Ergon. **8**, 199–201 (1977)
8. Hignett, S., McAtamney, L.: Rapid entire body assessment (REBA). Appl. Ergon. **31**, 201–205 (2000)
9. McAtamney, L.: Nigel Corlett, E.: RULA: a survey method for the investigation of work-related upper limb disorders. Appl. Ergon. **24**, 91–99 (1993)
10. Gyi, D.E., Sims, R.E., Porter, J.M., et al.: Representing older and disabled people in virtual user trials: data collection methods. Appl. Ergon. **35**, 443–451 (2004)
11. de Souza, T.O., Coury, H.J.C.G.: Are the postures adopted according to requested lin-guistic categories similar to those classified by the recording protocols? Appl. Ergon. **36**, 207–212 (2005)

Research on Product Affective Image by the Way of Empathic Design

Meiyu Zhou, Xiaowen Yang$^{(\boxtimes)}$, Peilong Liang, and Pei Xu

School of Art Design and Media, East, China University of Science
and Technology (ECUST), M. BOX 286, NO. 130, Meilong Road,
Xuhui District, Shanghai 200237, China
zhoutc_2003@163.com,
{354434388,798491428,987375724}@qq.com

Abstract. Continuous development of science and technology and continuous innovation of products have changed users' needs. People not only pay attention to practical and functional products, but also pay more attention to satisfying emotional needs in the process of experience. In such a highly information-based era, designers actively and deeply understand users' various emotional experience instead of passively designing products only by relying on obtaining users' feedback information. Starting from design's emotional factors, this study firstly introduces empathetic design's concept and basic method, leads to the key of empathetic design method–focusing on users' experience, and then combining with theories and methods of design morphology and statistics, discusses empathetic design method applied in product design. Taking design of office chair as an example, with empathetic design's concept and method as research's foundation, this paper analyzes and carries questionnaire investigation combining with users' behavior, and demonstrates user experience's influence on formation of products' emotional imagery using contrast technique, and with the help of Chi-square test and non-parametric test. In addition, combining with product design method, based on summarizing users' demands, this paper puts forward the concept of new office chair's design.

Keywords: Empathy · User experience · Emotional imagery · Office chair

1 Introduction

With the development of social economy and improvement of life level, product design has gradually shifted from focusing on rational design of product performance to focusing on perceptual design of users' spiritual needs, so that an important design method appears–perceptual design. This method regards users' perceptual demands as the guidance and user experience's feelings as research's foundation. In the traditional process of product design, before designing products, designers often obtain users' needs through observation, investigation and interview, and then give products modeling and new quality with their own subjective imaginations. When designing products, apart from considering design factors such as function and structure, designers

© Springer International Publishing Switzerland 2015
P.L.P. Rau (Ed.): CCD 2015, Part I, LNCS 9180, pp. 283–290, 2015.
DOI: 10.1007/978-3-319-20907-4_26

should give product certain form. And the form can often reflect certain emotional factor and make products full of vitality [1]. In the process of using products, users will get emotional information through all aspects of products' quality, so as to stimulate their inner feelings.

2 Empathetic Design

Empathy refers to the process of combing perceptual image and emotion through direct combination of intuition and emotion. When people attentively appreciate the aesthetic object, they would inject their own preferences and tastes into the object, in order to make the object show emotional color and vitality. That is to say, they shift subject's emotion into the object and endow the object with subject's emotion [2]. When designing products, designers integrate emotion into products and stimulate people's association through products' various design elements [3]. Therefore, for product design, empathetic design integrates users' past emotion and experience into product design, and leads to users' association of past experience in the process of using products. Empathetic design also de-signs users' needs in more detail and redesigns user group with common experience [4]. In short, through design elements such as products' shape, color, material, texture and function, empathetic design integrates users' emotional factors into products, so that users can arouse association and resonate through products' various design elements when using products, so as to obtain spiritual pleasure and emotional satisfaction [5]. Empathetic design is mainly divided into following three steps:

The first step is to observe. After selecting user group and using environment, designers will observe users' real reactions and record them. Designers can try to imagine themselves as members of this user group, participate in using environment of user group, feel the things felt by user group, record their experiences and experience of using products, communicate and exchange with users, express their own thoughts and feelings, perceive users' inner world through emotional imagery, and can understand potential demands at the bottom of user's heart themselves which are possibly not noticed by users [6]. This empathetic design involving design personnel refers to being absorbed as the party instead of pondering emotional experience as an outsider, so that product design will trans-form from meeting users' needs into meeting their own needs. As a result, deviations caused by users' unclear expression or designers' unclear understanding in traditional mode can be avoided.

The second step is to infer. Designers will collect firsthand data obtained in the first step, and display information and various recorded data (including photos and videos) in graphic form. After induction and analysis, designers put for-ward some tentative conclusions, verify results with data obtained in the above, analyze whether hypothetical conclusion is founded or not, and find some opposite cases for reverse inference on conclusion [7]. If the selected user group is the main user group, designers can find some cases of secondary user group and user group with special needs to reversely infer.

The third step is to regard the above inference result as products' conceptual framework. The conceptual framework may be ambiguous, for the reason that in the process of observation, many users can not accurately express their feelings. In many cases, users themselves don't understand their potential demands. Only under special environment and situation, this demand will appear. It is necessary to choose secondary user group and user group with special needs for re-verse inference so as to stimulate designers' inspiration. Therefore, designers are requested to repeatedly observe and infer, stimulate their imagination, and continue to communicate with users to verify imagination. This process must be repeated until clear product conceptual framework is obtained [8].

Empathetic design method is based on user experience, but also will cause a problem that in the process of empathetic understanding, design personnel will often be immersed and lose the identity of policymakers. Therefore, the conclusion will be too subjective and ignore its objective condition, which requires finding a balance point between the two sides [9].

Empathetic design method requires constantly inference and verification in order to make research results more accurate. Therefore, this study selects 40 respondents as objects of secondary user group to be investigated.

3 Questionnaire Design and User Survey

The key of empathetic design is observing user experience, inducting and reasoning data. Taking the office chair as an example, through user experience's intuitive feelings and feelings in the process of experience, this paper analyzes users' demands for office chair's design, so that this research has designed two questionnaires. Questionnaire one is the investigation of office chair's perceptual image, has 12 questions, and mainly focuses on office chair's ten design elements: using time, material, size, backrest, color, armrest and etc.; questionnaire two has first 12 questions exactly same with questionnaire one, and adds 4 open questions about user experience. Questionnaire two requires respondents to fill in questionnaire after 15-days office chair experience. During these 15 days, respondents are requested to record their states, feelings of using office chairs and description of using environment every day.

This study has selected 40 respondents: 20 men and 20 women; 12 college students, 12 company management personnel, and 16 staff. They are divided into two groups for questionnaire survey. In the first group (direct group), 20 respondents directly fill in questionnaire without experiencing office chairs. In the second group (experience group), 20 respondents experience 15-days using office chairs. During these 15 days, every respondent firstly should record moods and weather conditions in the morning every day, should record when to start using products, their feelings and using environment, and finally summarize comprehensive situation of using products in the whole day before sleeping at night, whether their moods change, and whether they encounter problems in the process of using products. After 15-days experience, they will fill in questionnaire two.

4 Analysis of Survey Data

This paper discusses whether questionnaire data is independent, or associated. Therefore, X2 is applied to inspect whether two variables' observation values obtained from samples have special relevance. If two independent variables are independent and have no association (X2 value is not significant), it means that for one independent variable, another variable's various classification number will change in the range of sampling error. If two factors are not independent (X2 value is significant), variables are associated with each other [10]. Analysis of users' survey data is divided into two aspects:

1. Contingency table X2 (Chi-square) inspection is carried out with gender, occupation, education degree and office chair's related elements as independent variables, and with frequency as the dependent variable.
2. Independence test: mainly used for analysis of count data on two or more than two factors' multiple classification, namely studying correlation and dependency between two kinds of variables.

Assuming H0: line variable and column variable have no difference, H1: line variable and column variable have differences, when p is less than 0.1, if rejecting the null hypothesis H0, or accepting the null hypothesis.

4.1 Analysis of Users' Office Hours

According to survey data of relationship between office hours and office chair of users in two groups, by using non-parametric tests of two independent samples, men and women have no difference in office chair and office hours in direct group, experience group, and analysis of integrating two groups.

In the aspects of users' age, occupation and education degree, it can be found through non-parametric tests of various independent samples (see Table 1): There's no difference separately between direct group and experience group. However, after analyzing integration data of direct group after group and experience group, it can be found that by using non-parametric tests of multiple independent samples, Chi-Square is 7.013 and p = 0.071 (less than 0.1), which indicates that users with different occupations have different time in the office chair. The survey finds that company management personnel have time in office chair significantly higher than students, company staff and other occupations. In addition, students and company staff has time in office chair higher than other occupations, but with little difference. In the aspects of age and education degree, users have no difference in the time spent on office chair.

4.2 Analysis of Office Chair's Material

Inspection results of survey data on office chair's material can be seen in Table 2. It can be found from Table 2 that users in two groups with different genders, occupations, ages and education degrees have no obvious preference for office chair's material.

Table 1. Analysis of office hours

| Office hours | | | | | | | | |
| Direct group | | | Experience group | | | Total | | |
Variable	Chi-square	P	Variable	Chi-square	P	Variable	Chi-square	P
Occupation	5.389	0.145	Occupation	3.226	0.199	Occupation	7.013	0.071
Age	3.445	0.179	Age	3.606	0.165	Age	7.520	0.023
Education degree	3.239	0.356	Education degree	5.450	0.142	Education degree	8.016	0.046

Table 2. Analysis of office chair's material

| Office chair's material | | | | | |
| Direct group | | | Experience group | | |
Variable	Chi-square value	P	Variable	Chi-square value	P
Gender	5.254	0.154	Gender	1.385	1
Occupation	9.258	0.483	Occupation	6.32	0.366
Age	5.844	0.617	Age	6.103	0.627
Education degree	5.879	0.973	Education degree	9.835	0.455
Total					
Variable			Chi-square value		P
Group			7.549		0.045

However, through analysis from contingency table of direct group and experience group, it's found that Fisher's Exact Test value is 7.549, and P is 0.045 (less than 0.05). Therefore, users in two groups have different preference for seat's material: users in direct group prefer leather and canvas, while users in experience group prefer mesh material.

4.3   Analysis of Office Chair's Size

Inspection results of survey data on office chair's size can be seen in Table 3. Data in Table 3 shows that users with different genders and education degrees and data integration of two groups have no special tendency to office chair's size. For occupation, the direct group shows that users with different occupations have no particular preference for office chair's size. However, in the experience group, Fisher Exact Test value is 9.349 and P is 0.018 (less than 0.05), which shows that users with different occupations have different preference for office chair's size, company employees prefer office chair with wide base wide and moderate size, while college students prefer office chair with moderate size.

Table 3. Analysis of office chair's size

Office chair's size					
Direct group			Experience group		
Variable	Chi-square value	P	Variable	Chi-square value	P
Gender	1.435	1	Gender	3.851	0.171
Occupation	10.173	0.38	Occupation	9.349	0.018
Age	6.184	0.632	Age	6.54	0.098
Education degree	8.181	0.742	Education degree	5.921	0.474
Total					
Variable			Chi-square value		P
Group			3.318		0.352

4.4   Analysis of Backrest Type

Through analysis of office chair, backrest has following types: backrest's angle can be adjusted, backrest's elasticity, and backrest's height and lumbar sup-port. Results obtained after inspection of survey data are shown in Table 4: men and women in direct group and experience group have no special tendency on selecting backrest type. At the same time, people with different ages, occupations and education degrees have no difference in selecting backrest type. After inte-grating survey data in group 2, it can be found that men prefer high and flexible backrest with adjustable angle, while women prefer the backrest with lumbar support ($X2 = 9.295$, $p = 0.014$).

With direct group and experience group as line variables, and with backrest type as column variable, it's found that though analysis from contingency table, Fisher's Exact Test value is 6.13, and P is 0.072 (less than 0.1), which indicates that users in different groups have different preferences for backrest type. Users in direct investigation group prefer high backrest, while users in experience group prefer the backrest with moderate height which can adjust elasticity and angle.

Table 4. Analysis of backrest type

Backrest type					
Direct group			Experience group		
Variable	Chi-square value	P	Variable	Chi-square value	P
Gender	4.954	0.162	Gender	5.23	0.103
Occupation	12.176	0.152	Occupation	3.512	0.622
Age	5.033	0.909	Age	3.378	0.692
Education degree	8.799	0.632	Education degree	5.524	0.546
Total					
Variable			Chi-square value		P
Group			6.13		0.072

4.5   Analysis of Office Chair's Colors

We divide office chair's colors into three options: monochrome assortment, assortment of two colors and assortment of three or more colors. Results can be seen in Table 5 through analyzing survey data that men and women in direct investigation group have no difference in their preference for office chair's color style. However, in experience group, Fisher's Exact Test value is 9.055, and P is 0.018 (less than 0.1). Through analysis, it's found that men prefer dual tones with two colors' assortment, while women prefer clear and bright monochrome. The results also show that: users in direct group and users in experience group have no difference in preference for office chair's colors in aspects of occupation, age and education degree.

Table 5. Analysis of office chair's colors

Office chair's colors					
Direct group			Experience group		
Variable	Chi-square value	P	Variable	Chi-square value	P
Gender	1.974	0.75	Gender	9.055	0.018
Occupation	8.206	0.65	Occupation	4.162	0.85
Age	8.073	0.165	Age	8.339	0.184
Education degree	9.222	0.452	Education degree	9.816	0.373
Total					
Variable		Chi-square value		P	
Group		3.029		0.416	

In addition to analysis of the above 5 experience factors of office chair, this paper also discusses users' focus to purchase office chairs, and analyzes investigation data factors such as armrest type, office chair's style and adjustment frequency of chair surface's height. In the aspect of users' focus when buying office chairs, users in direct group and users in experience group mainly concern two points: good comfort and reliable function, and users in direct group also pay attention to office chair's quality. In the aspect of selecting armrest type, users in experience group are more inclined to adjustable and removable armrest with special function. In the aspect of office chair's style, users in direct group prefer classical, comfortable, fashionable and lovely style, while users in experience group prefer comfortable, simple and fashionable office chair. Users in these two groups have little difference in chair surface's adjusting frequency, but man's adjusting frequency is lower than woman's.

Through the above analysis, we determine new positioning of office chair's design concept: good comfort, reliable function, simple fashion; adjustable chair surface, adjustable and detachable armrest with additional functions; high, flexible and adjustable backrest; clear and bright color collocation, and new materials with mesh.

5 Result-Discussion

Through discussing empathetic design's theory and method, and analyzing corresponding relations between users and design elements of office chair design, it can be drawn through user investigation and data analysis that: respondents who have not experienced and respondents who have experienced for 15 days show obvious difference in office chair's emotional imagery. Respondents who have not experienced have no obvious tendency, while respondents who have experienced user experience prefer adjustable and removable handrail with additional functions, office chair's material tends to adopt mesh material, office chair's volume tends to be moderate, backrest tends to be able to adjust elastic and angle, and office chair's colors tend to be clear and bright monochrome.

References

1. Xiangwen, L.: Research on Emotional Design of Electric Vehicle. Wuhan University Of Technology, 11–13 2007
2. Chun, M.: Zhu Guangqian's acceptance and understanding about Theodor Lipps's Empathy. Theor. Stud. Lit. Art **1**, 1332–1336 (2010)
3. Norman, D.A.: Emotional Design, pp. 20–31. Electronic Industry Press, Beijing (2005)
4. Koskinen, I., et al.: Empathetic Design–User Experience in Product Design, pp. 3–12/34–41. China Architecture & Building Press, Beijing (2011)
5. Shijian, L., Shangshang, Z., Fangtian, Y., Ji, H.: Vision-behavior-emotion based product family design gene. Comput. Integr. Manuf. Syst. **12**, 2289–2295 (2009)
6. Junwei, Z.: Analysis and Study on Empathy of Product Design Based on Schema. Hunan University, pp. 22–23 (2007)
7. Jiadi, L.: Study on emotion characteristic expression and design methods of product form semantic. Art Des. **9**, 157–159 (2008)
8. Chuanxi, H., Xiao, J., Wei, X.: On user experience of aesthetic empathy. Des. User Exp. **6**, 144–147 (2012)
9. Lian, M.: Empathetic design-helping small products achieve creation. Design **2**, 46–47 (2012)
10. Jiwen, H., Quanjun, Y., Wei, C., Yabing, Z.: Research on human cognitive behavior modeling under influence of emotion. J. Syst. Simul. **3**, 515–520 (2012)

Design, Innovation, Social Development and Sustainability

A Study on the Balance and Optimization Measures in Industry-University Collaborative Innovation of Interaction Design

Jianxin Cheng, Miao Liu[⊠], and Junnan Ye

East China University of Science and Technology, Shanghai, China
cjx.master@gmail.com,
{183787975,yejunnan971108}@qq.com

Abstract. Based on the "material" homogenization tendency in the background of industrial production, this paper analyzes the current application status of interaction design in domestic product design, and discusses the reasons of five aspects. On the basis of analyzing the current situation of the interaction design, this paper combines the characteristics of the Experience Economy and the Age of Big Data, establishing the important position of market information and customer demand information in interaction design, exploring the feasibility of the corresponding method of process experience, identify experience and emotional experience in the field of interaction design, reducing the influence of human misunderstanding in this area and rising the effectiveness of interaction design. Then through analyzing the real cases, offering the theoretical foundation for the interactive technology, industrial design, new media design and other subjects and provide methodological guidance.

Keywords: Interaction design · Industry-University collaborative innovation · Optimization measures

1 Introduction

Interaction design, also known as interaction design in early stages, combines the advantages of industrial design, HCI, cognitive psychology, computer science, anthropology and sociology. It is a novel design tool in the 21st century that breaks through the classification barrier of traditional strip design. With the increase of communications between domestic and foreign universities and research institutions, Chinese designers become increasingly aware of interaction design and thus pioneer its development especially in some untraditional areas. However, many designs are deviated from the original concept because of their cognition. It has created an unbalanced situation for interaction design in China, and precluded the development of industry upgrading.

P.L.P. Rau (Ed.): CCD 2015, Part I, LNCS 9180, pp. 293–302, 2015.
DOI: 10.1007/978-3-319-20907-4_27

2 Interaction Design in China

It's been more than a decade since interaction design came into China. The recent interaction products independently designed by Chinese show that the local manufacturers have realised that availability and usability are needed to be assessed. However, the dominant players who design and implement the interaction are still engineers and product managers, which causes that human factors in interaction are limited to a superficial level, and not considered further as emotive factors. Emotive factors are usually pursued by means of emotional artistic processing rather than engineering technology. Therefore, it's doomed that interaction designer can't be replaced by engineers. On the other hand, most of the interaction designers in China can't fulfill the core part (responsibility of User Experience) of the interaction, because their professional self-cognition and the industrial position lag far behind. There are several reasons.

2.1 The Late Introduction of Interaction in the Product Development in China

Chinese interaction started appearing in the area of software design, and was sorted into the category of user interface, which is yet regarded as the external part beautifying the core function, that is to say, the least significant end of the whole design, so interaction earns little attention. The result is that the developments of user interface and core function are always independent of each other, and are not combined until the last step of the whole process. It extremely restricts the interaction and can cause high risk, as the modification of the core function in the last step may bring great costs, and the mere solution is to give up the user interface. It's obvious that this sort of speculative and gamble-like product development is hardly able to ensure a satisfying user experience.

2.2 The Block of Large State-Owned Enterprises in Interaction Development

Nowadays, in Chinese enterprises, the department of user experience basically exists as a completely new section in the original system, whose decision-making body and R&D facility mainly consist of engineers and technicians. Whereas the department of user experience is only an appendage, which plays an role as an "art designer". The reasons include:

- State-owned enterprises got inadequate knowledge about interaction design;
- Enterprises lack of motivation to change the original product development framework, because of good social and economic situation and less intense rivalry among enterprises;
- The transformation of development means requires businesses to invest a large quantity of costs and to bear high risk, which stops lots of them;
- Companies value marketing, while despise product development.

In this framework, therefore, the product manager is the actual interaction designer. As the typical organiser, product manager can effectively eases the tension among departments in a functional organisation, coordinates various marking functions, and reacts faster to the market changes. Nonetheless, without the support of across functional areas, the product development always turns out to be a lone battle, which is bad for interactive development. Moreover, compared with those of marketing, the costs of product development are much higher and riskier, its payback period is longer, and its result is less predictable. As a result, in terms of no matter risk management or cost-benefit, product manager must attach more importance to the product marking instead of development, which then results in the narrowing of production knowledge system, and invisibly weakening of the real value of user experience in the production flow.

2.3 The Ineffective Usage of User Experience Channels of the Medium and Small Private Enterprises

Plagiarizing others' ideas, ignorance of intellectual property, and the pattern of "short, adaptable and fast" has become a routine for medium and small private enterprises to develop products. Short (short duration): quickly grasping the market heats; adaptable (fair price): occupying the markets with the lowest price; fast (rapid release): shortening the product development period, and sparing time for marketing and promotion. With this pattern, proprietors incorporate interaction into daily marketing, test user demand by tentatively developing products of multi-variety and small-lot, and improve products according to the feedback gained in the distribution channel. This approach to user experience is totally random, though the only advantage is convenience – it's easy to obtain the market information because the medium and small private enterprises got more chance to keep in touch with channels, but the true value of UE has never been discovered.

2.4 The Cognitive Errors in the Process of Interaction Design

According to the microeconomic application status of China's domestic product design, the main constrains of the application and development of interactive technology has a direct relationship with the cognitive errors in the process of interaction design. There are five errors: poisoning errors of design problems, motivation errors of design basis, survey errors of user behavior, analysis errors of competition test, assess errors of user experience.

Firstly, the process of interaction design is highly dependent on the model created for the behavior of target users to understand behavioral response on performance design may be made by the users. Designers can handle the human-machine system environment better by locating the questions rightly. In today's product design projects, the products' problems are often not excavated and located by the designers, but appointed by the superior to the project design practitioners. Secondly, the core of interaction design research is transferred from the visual effects to human needs, the assessment of the design is based on the relation between design and users. As a unique group, product users are quite different with the development team of designers, engineers and salespeople, any non-user groups have biases and errors on figuring out the ultimate service goal of products. Besides, the selection of user behavior depends on the user cognitive level of human-machine work environment. The designers have to consider the manner in which this cognition be presented and the impact strength on guiding the users. Moreover, the function of specific needs should be generated in the process of product use or interaction, rather than designing driven by the positive reputation of competitors' new products. The last but not the least, there is a misunderstanding in user evaluation that formal testing methods can only be applied to mature interaction design ideas. In fact, the experimental stage product is the most valuable subjects, testing the imperfect ideas can contribute to generating new ideas. Therefore, several key issues of user experience in interaction design need to be clarified in order to break these five errors.

3   Unbalanced Development of UE in Interaction Design

With the rise of the industrial revolution and the mass production, industrial design has a long history that is closely related to interaction design. As the main carrier of interaction design, industrial design has been long debated in academic fields, especially among design research professionals. And the authenticity and reliability of user experience reports/research results are constantly questioned and challenged.

3.1   The Balance of the Aesthetic Form and Experience Nature

First of all, interactive activities occurred in the dimension of time. In evaluation of industrial products, users are not only influenced by the aesthetic appearance of the product, but also influenced by the adhesiveness developed with increased usage time. User experience and product design are intertwined and interconnected. Blurring the product design, which is giving up control of aesthetic form, will lead to both positive and negative consequences: on the one hand, users can not accurately understand the product semantics, wrong understanding may cause a negative impact; on the other hand, uncertainty of using products, may result in interesting experience in the process of using, through several times of attempt, there will be a positive impact over fulfillment.

When it comes to the focus on form design of the product itself (aesthetic) or obtaining using experience (create joyful experience), thinking method of interaction design is mainly about usability, and related to the aesthetic ideas, it is believed that awful availability may cause negative effect on the interaction of aesthetic perception. This idea leads to the following design process. The first concern is availability, and then aesthetic perception. But researchers represented by Dr. Kees Overbeeke from TU/Eindhoven also shows great interest in opposite process, which improves from the perspective of aesthetics, improve the availability. They believe that the allure from the aesthetic feeling of the appearance and interaction is part of the reason why user take interactive actions of product.

As for obtaining high quality experience, we believe it is a very efficient way to rank interactive user experience design. It is mainly based on different subjects of experience, divided into three grades from low to high, which are process experience, recognition experience, emotion experience. Among them, process experience is the lower level of the primary experience, its characteristic is the continuity, process experience itself as a kind of experience emerges from a consciousness, and it is the human being who is experiencing, triggered by external time. Recognition experience is discontinuous in time, this level of experience is recorded as the fragment (including the start, progress, results), people only are participants instead of dominants, therefore it's less controlling from people themselves. Emotion experience is the carrier to convey, summary and reflection of recognition experience. This grade of experience return control to people, because when the experience is completed, it is human who to decide how to share their experiences.

3.2 The Balance Between the Concept of Standard Design and Customized Design

In addition, since the efficiency digital integrated circuit and civilian semiconductor chip technology are becoming more mature and perfect, it can provide smoother and more convenient user experience. This should be attributed to mass production and commercial development. We should also admit that private custom with obvious personalized symbols is gradually on the rise as well as the large scales standardized design. This relies on the advancement of experiencing technology. The combine of technical quality and usability produces excellent-Performanced technological products, which directly causes the transfer from traditional products to user experience.

Interaction experience becomes a medicine to reconcile customized and industrial production. If we sum up the participation process of user experience from the perspective of production and consumption, interaction can be divided into three types. (1) Consumers purchase the components and DIY, the experience link here is at the end of consumption, consumers achieve economic and using purpose, their sense of achievement is also fulfilled, the enterprise is only responsible for producing and selling the components. (2) Consumers produce the semi products to end products in the place provided, the experience link here is in the process of consumption. In this form, consumer is buying a experience rather than a product. (3) Consumers put forward the style, function, and requirements of the design according to their own demands, the enterprise is only responsible for manufacturing the required parts and end product according to the requirements. The experience link here moves to the front of production. In this process, consumer participates in designing. It is called as consumer production, which is perhaps the direction of enterprises' future development (Figs. 1 and 2).

The experience value of Interaction design is to let the user participate in experience maximumly and resulting in sense of value. Now most of the interaction are still stay in only amusing oneself, in this case the sense of value is more of emotional value, in some ways it belongs to feeling in material aspect. However, to increase the added value of the interactive experience, the best way is to let the user to participate in the

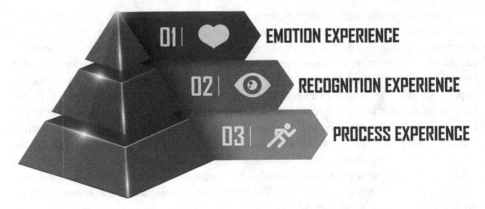

Fig. 1. Grades of interactive UE design

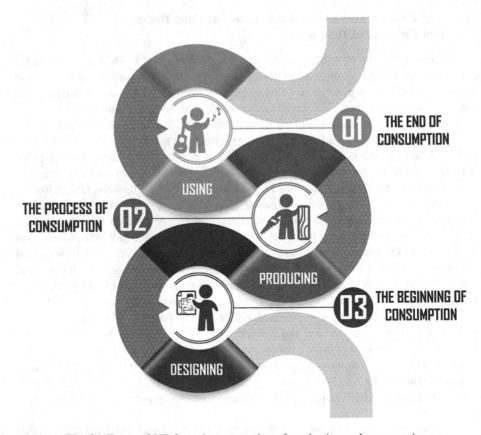

Fig. 2. Types of UE from the perspective of production and consumption

design and production processes, as in this process embodying the value which user really cares, including aesthetic value of design, science value of function, practical value of life, and self-value. Through the self realization of all these values, users will gain the needs of being respected and social value.

3.3   The Balance of Short-Term Interaction and Long-Term Interaction

In recent years, the concept of "Product" has changed completely. The traditional product more refers to physical properties, such as the length, width, height of products, surface material, the overall weight. The interactive experience of this kind of product is often short lived, even may occurring in a physical store's checkout counter, the information feedback is the user's subjective judgment. But now the products may only appear on the LCD screen and virtual network, such as a financial product of bank or network games, mobile phone games, of course, there is also a part of the products both have software and hardware. Those products' interactive experience are relatively longer, users generally requires a certain cycle to give their feed back, and the final evaluation will refers to group data, such as numbers of online game players' posts, APP download charts etc.

During the design and development period of such product with longer interactive cycle, it should be focus on design of the whole experience scenarios of users, including the predict of user's behaviour, the story board of time using, the consideration about usability and availability. Yet some enterprises will lead the consumer to act according to the expected behavior consciously from the perspective of interactive experience during the sale process. The most typical example is mobile phone industry, in which producers tends to show the colorful interactive interface, menu system, communication functions to the customers, but rarely presents its appearance or the materials. No matter how long of the feedback cycle, great experience can't only depend on the experience itself, but also need the designer to focus on creating scene structure where the experience occurred.

On the basis of agreement on the goal of user experience and interaction design, and to facilitate the best practice, the industry-university collaborative innovation need to be developed comprehensively.

4   The Optimization Countermeasures of Industry-University Collaborative Innovation(IUCI)

As a system engineering of innovation and cooperation, IUCI is the cooperation of production, learning, research, and practical application. It is the connection within technical innovation, innovative environment and the users. It deepens the understanding and practice of the education combined with production and research. With the development of information technology and the evolution of innovative forms, innovative trends characterized with user innovation and open innovation are attracting more and more attention, The role that government plays in building the open innovation platform and policy guidance is highlighted as well as the dominant position of the user in innovation process. The role of the user in the system engineering is emphasized, the education combined with production and research must be business-oriented, user-centric, and market-oriented.

4.1 Sufficient Condition to Achieve IUCI

Due to the limitations of Chinese enterprises, Industry-University Collaborative mode is most successful. With this combination approach of universities, the enterprises introduces external design institutions to assist their interactive product UE tasks. Industry-university collaboration (IUC) is often seen as a strategic alliance of two or more parties, including industrial sponsors and university research team. Different parties involved in innovative research can mutually benefit, and win what they need.

In the aspect of interest demands, the output of the strategic alliance is the technology conversion. The enterprises' most obvious benefit is to get new ideas (innovation and user experience evaluation system). They position the external institution and enrich their knowledge. So the design can play a real role in their product process. (UE department will be upgraded to the same level of engineering department and marketing department, to avoid the product manager inevitably putting more attention in marketing rather than design) Also they can pay lower the cost to obtain the potential benefits, such as graduates. In the long term, the launch of innovative products will enhance the competitiveness of the entire enterprise.

For universities in the technology conversion process can improve their social reputation as well as their influence in related research areas. From the perspective of collaborative process, the universities mainly contributes their personnel, facilities and equipment to the entire combination, while they might benefit from indirect cost savings and use license of intellectual assets.

University researchers involved in IUC activities have the opportunity to access the projects, purchase the equipment, obtain personal reputation. The participated students can also gain practical education and work experience. Overall, the faculty and students will be improved in a certain degree, and gain organizational prestige.

4.2 Necessary Condition to Achieve IUCI

Research and innovation activities will be considered as the primary task of IUCI. The research team is composed of the university faculties and some enterprise employees. They cross the border of single subject and department, and provide services for the company in the period of time with their funding. The team is very necessary while breaking through the enterprise structure bottlenecks and supplementing the existing university research activities.

Meanwhile establishing IUCI mechanisms must have the following four basic conditions:

- Be able to obtain long-term sustainable funding from enterprises or government.
- In a certain period have a fixed work place and the corresponding facilities and research equipment.

- The IUCI chairman shall be senior officer of the universities or companies.
- Research project can offer help for the higher education training program.

4.3   UE in IUCI

The traditional IUC refers to industries, universities and other research institutions cooperate with each other, exert their respective advantages, integrate research, development and production, create a strong advanced systems, and reflect the comprehensive advantages in operation. With the development of information technology, the evolution of innovation and the arrival of knowledge society, the dominant position and leading role of the user is further highlighted in the innovation process. Upgraded collaborative innovation, characterized by user innovation and open innovation, redefines the user value and the market power. The user and consumer is starting and end of the technology innovation. Thus user experience is also called the soul of IUCI.

    User directly participates in IUC, not only to reduce the blindness of technology innovation, shorten new product development cycle, but also effectively reduce the risks and costs of technology innovation. The IUCI history in China shows, in order to make IUCI achievements into actual productivity more effectively, we must strengthen the adhesion of each IUCI component by user innovation and self participation, and achieve the perfect merge of science and technology, education and economy.

4.4   iPod: A Typical Case of PaaS

Apple brought out iPod in 2008, which gave birth to the PaaS mode. After that, many companies followed but no one has surpassed Apple. It is more than a business model innovation—the UE design plays a particularly important role in Paas mode. Compared with the physical product, the PaaS product has its own peculiarities.

    The PaaS product's consumption and offering are produced at the same time—it is consumer being directly involved in the production process services, and working closely with the service provider. The fine UE has become a concrete result of production.

    Different users have different characteristics, even the same user in different states also has differences. The most effective way to provide a "considerate" product is designing based on user research and user experience.

    Physical product becomes free or directly taken the form of rent, precisely because there's no transfer of ownership in the PaaS mode, and it is the service creates real commercial profits for companies.

5   Summary

Based on the previous analysis, it is not difficult to notice that whether in the user experience design department of large enterprises in China, or the shortcut of product innovation in small and medium-sized enterprises, user experience design in China is not well be transplanted. User experience design is more like support work of verifying product availability rather than creative functions in state-owned enterprises, while in small and medium-sized enterprises, user experience is combined with marketing and sales, which weakens the focus on product design. This is closely linked to the long-term concept of emphasizing on production and technology rather than service and design. To face with the status, a professional organization or agency with flexibility and mobility that can assists different types of enterprises on completing user experience design task is highly needed in China. Universities with integral design theoretical system and sustainable investment of practitioners will be the best choice. Universities can bring human-machine dialogue and interaction without considering the system limitations of enterprises or barriers between departments. The intervention of universities can help the market to break down barriers between users and producers, make industry-university collaborative innovation a bridge between users and enterprises.

Meanwhile, in the era of product is service, the best way to optimize the user experience of enterprise is to provide users with personalized content and interactive services. Customers' loyalty for products and service comes from good experience. The key to compete for more market share is enhancing the interactive experience and optimizing the user experience design. We have reasons to believe that interaction design in China will be more and more exciting if most Chinese enterprises are truly concerned about optimizing the user experience, synchronized with, even beyond and guide the user needs.

References

1. Richard, B.: Declaration by design: rhetoric, argument, and demonstration in design practice. In: Margolin, V. (ed.) Design Discourse: History, Theory. Criticism. The University of Chicago Press, Chicago (1989)
2. Khaslavsky, J., Shedroff, N.: Understanding the seductive experience. Commun. ACM **42**(5), 45–49 (1999)
3. Forlizzi, J., Ford, S.: The building blocks of experience: an early framework for interaction designers. In: Proceedings of the DIS 2000 seminar. Communications of the ACM, New York (2000)
4. Djajadiningrat, T., Wensveen, S., Frens, J., Overbeeke, K.: Tangible products: redressing the balance between appearance and action. Tangible Interact. J. Pers. Ubiquitous Comput. **8**(5), 294–309 (2004)
5. Burrows, P.: Commentary: Apple's Blueprint for Genius. Businessweek, 21 March 2005
6. Yang, X.: "Human" is the Origination and Destination of Designs: Researches on the Concepts, Principles of Interaction Design and Significance in the Development of Chinese Contemporary Design. China Central Academy Of Fine Arts, Beijing (2011)

The Research and Practice Framework for Designing the Digital Social Innovation

Zhiyong Fu(✉) and Zirui Huang

Department of Information Art and Design, Tsinghua University,
Beijing 100084, People's Republic of China
fuzhiyong@tsinghua.edu.cn,
huangzr13@mails.tsinghua.edu.cn

Abstract. This paper focuses on the research and practice of digital social innovation (DSI). The rapid progress in the era of information provides many possibilities for social innovation. At the meanwhile, the development of science and technology has significantly boosted the breadth, depth and efficiency of social innovation. Through years' of research and practice, we improve the definition and conclude the features of DSI from a large number of case studies. Then, by combining the SET factors, we develop the general standard framework for DSI. At last, we use and confirm the righteous and effectiveness of this instruction in practice.

Keywords: Social innovation · Information technology · Framework · Grounded theory · Service design

1 Introduction

With the arrival of information age, a large amount of information is flooding our city life, and the digital form of social innovation has appeared. Digital social innovation (DSI) has become a hotspot for policy-makers, entrepreneurs, researchers, and start-ups. It presents us with a brand new vision.

Previous research like NESTA's research on DSI [1] has pioneered the field of DSI from both research questions and methods, and created many cases that laid the foundation for our research. Nowadays, for academic institutions like Parsons DESIS (Design for Social Innovation and Sustainability) Lab [2], DSI has become their new thematic group, and its work provided the theoretical basis for our study and reference. Their focus on digital technologies and platforms are considered as the organization tool for connecting community to individuals. Based on the assumptions of the previous research, we believe that digital technology is a dominant and pivotal new way to support people, customers and communities to collaborate and co-create a wide range of social needs. Consisting of a group of DESIS laboratories and partners, DSI group is currently exploring a different approach, focusing on the literal aspect of digital technology which is more technical and academic. The purpose is to investigate not only the cases and trends in social innovation, but also the corresponding design research issues and strategies in the digital, social and ubiquitous network context.

© Springer International Publishing Switzerland 2015
P.L.P. Rau (Ed.): CCD 2015, Part I, LNCS 9180, pp. 303–315, 2015.
DOI: 10.1007/978-3-319-20907-4_28

From the perspective of design, the definition and features of DSI need to be concerned. What is more important is how to apply DSI to real social practice scenarios in a standardized and process-oriented way. In order to make the project closer to reality, we worked with NGOs, charities and social enterprises to develop interdisciplinary cooperation among governments, organizations and research institutions to find new possibilities during the exploration process, Also, following the trend of globalization, we actively cooperated with Urban Studies Program at Stanford University, and formed cross-regional, cross-cultural, and interdisciplinary teams to test and practice DSI. We found that urban design is not only about physical infrastructure, but it is also about the services and amenities where infrastructure inhabits. In addition, we use four pillars of sustainability - social equity, environmental quality, cultural continuity, and economic vitality, as the framework to guide the direction of the project [3]. The four pillars have significant referential meaning to the summarized features and evaluation standard of DSI.

1.1 Society Background

According to our previous research [4], the initial prototype of the city is formed by aggregation of population and commodity exchange. A real sense of a city is to make its citizens live well with support of urban infrastructure and energy, food, water, transportation, recreation and finance system etc. The intervention of new ICT technology changes the built environment to a sensible, interactive and transferred place where support human activities in all levels, and make the city's physical space and intangible networks merge together to form a very complex ecosystem.

In the current state, the smart city is envisioned as wired and ICT-driven cities that provide better urban life [5], innovative services [6], new business opportunities [7], efficient governance and sustainable environment development [8]. More and more cities are beginning to consider civic participation, and regard the smart citizen as a new direction of smart city. Currently, governments around the world are taking actions to cooperate with their citizens in the process of designing and constructing smart cities, based on their specific situations and objectives. Social media is being widely used as a way to get citizens involved. Participatory sensing, which is empowered by the development of ICT, is also a significant approach to collecting data from citizens. Some government municipalities also launched urban sensing applications, such as the NYC 311 service [9]. New York City held its annual city hackathon 2013 with the theme of "Reinvent Green", aiming to help build digital tools and applications to support New York in leading greener lives [10].

From public benefit to social innovation, companies increasingly turn to CSR3.0 (Corporate Social Responsibility 3.0) [11]. They will focus on a more sustainable model and revolutionize our understanding on concepts such as product, consumption, wealth and inventions with new methods, ideas and technologies, for instance, in the Intel Core World Social Innovation Week [12].

1.2 Technology Background

Digital technologies and the Internet play an increasingly important role in how social innovation happens. Today's urban development is gradually turning to smart city. New technologies such as the Internet, big data, cloud computing, wearable devices, intelligent home, artificial intelligence and SNS (Social Networking Services) have been applied to social innovation [13], and extend the width and breadth of social innovation from the aspects of the process, performance and content, increasing its efficiency and reducing its complexity significantly.

The growth and development of social computing has greatly increased the complexity of the system. On the other hand, coping with complexity also brings new solutions to social innovation. Collective intelligence harvested from relationships among designers, users and organizations, and collective wisdom that acquired from things on Internet can generate greater value from the interaction between people and things. Eventually, innovative, hopeful and sustainable lifestyle can be created [14, 15].

1.3 Research Questions

We hope to offer a set of methods to contribute to DSI research in the urban context, and meanwhile to practice it and cooperate with the society from all walks of life. In the practice, we will offer insights and tools from the angle of schools.

What is the Main Participant of DSI? In recent decades, many philanthropic and charitable organizations have often turned to non-profit, especially non-governmental organizations (NGOs), to address some of the world's most intractable social problems. With the rise of those groups, the number of similar social organizations increases. However, their projects and solutions are almost homogenous, and they are also lacking in new theories or thoughts. By carefully re-tooling these organizations with the latest technology and guiding them with the best innovation practices at our disposal today, we can start fresh with a re-booted version of traditional non-governmental organizations: NGO 2.0 [16, 17].

What is the Method of DSI? With the goal of social innovation, we focus on the reflection of culture and social value on the aspects of research methods and design tools. Focusing on research questions from the community level, the more mature mode is the Bottom of the Pyramid (BOP) [18]. In the design field, collective action toolkit developed by Frog Design Company [19], HCD Toolkit developed by IDEO [20] and the DIY innovation toolkit produced by NESTA [21] are all tools for inspiring and supporting social innovation.

1.4 Methodology

Our train of thought is: first analyzing the real cases; second concluding the features of them when referring to designing process; then forming the framework of DSI suited to city sustainable background; at last testing our conclusion by practicing. During the process, we used case study and grounded theory as our method and tool.

Case Study. According to Thomas [22], "case studies are analyses of persons, events, decisions periods, projects, policies, institutions, or other systems that are studied holistically by one or more method. The case that is the subject of the inquiry will be an instance of a class of phenomena that provides an analytical frame – an object – within which the study is conducted and which the case illuminates and explicates." We studied many DSI cases in order to find a vision for the common features of DSI.

Grounded Theory. It's a systematic methodology in the social sciences involving the construction of theory through the analysis of data [23]. From our case studies, we also collected many data. After having done the statistical analysis, we conclude the statistical meaning of these data and deduce the general framework for DSI.

Contribution.
   This paper focuses on researching and practicing DSI in the urban context and makes following contributions:

- Define DSI in the urban context.
- Summarize and conclude the features and framework of DSI.
- Support the relative research.
- Support innovation teams to take part in DSI practices in the urban context.

2   Related Research

2.1   Social Innovation

There is a possible future in which services are explicitly designed to tackle social challenges such as climate change and unemployment. Social innovation is now embraced around the world as legitimate public policy in both economic and social arenas. According to the Open Book of Social Innovation [24], the three most significant problems of social innovation are intractable social problems, rising costs and paradigm.

   There is a growing interest in social innovation among policymakers, foundations, researchers and academic institutions around the world. Despite this interest, there are no a shared or common definition of social innovation. Currently, there are a large number of different definitions in circulation.

   Goldenberg defined social innovation as the development and application of new or improved activities, initiatives, services, processes, or products designed to address social and economic challenges faced by individuals and communities [25]. In 2003, Stanford had defined social innovation as "the process of inventing, securing support for, and implementing novel solutions to social needs and problems". Five years later, Stanford redefined and broadened the term. The latest approach involves "dissolving boundaries and brokering a dialogue between the public, private, and nonprofit sectors". The current Stanford definition of social innovation is "a novel solution to a social problem that is more effective, efficient, sustainable, or just than existing solutions and for which the value created accrues primarily to society as a whole rather than private individuals." It describes that, "a social innovation can be a product, production process, or technology (much like innovation in general), but it can also be a principle, an idea, a piece of legislation, a social movement, an intervention, or some combination of them" [26]. Some define social innovation as a type of innovation more broadly. Timo Hämäläinen outlines five types of innovation: technological, economic, regulative, normative and cultural [27]. According to a report of TEPSIE, it defines social innovation as "new solutions (products, services, models, markets, processes etc.), which simultaneously meet a social need (more effectively than existing solutions) and lead to new or improved capabilities, relationships and better use of assets and resources" [28].

TEPSIE found the eight common features of social innovation, which are cross-sectorial, open and collaborative, grassroots and bottom-up, pro-sumption and co-production, mutualism, creates new roles and relationships, better use of assets and resources, and develops assets and capabilities [28]. Robin Murray, Julie Caulier-Grice and Geoff Mulgan from the Young Foundation had identified six stages of social innovation from inception to impact. The six stages are [24]: prompts, inspirations and diagnoses, proposals and ideas, prototyping and pilots, sustaining, scaling and diffusion, and systemic change. In the book, they explored each of the stages in depth, and listed some of the main methods used for each one.

2.2   Case Study

Grounded theory believes that a theoretical framework can only gradually be formed through in-depth analysis of data. Therefore, we selected five typical DSI cases in the urban context, Yibo [29], Coca-Cola Hello Happiness [30], Pugedon [31], Yitu [32] and FixMyCity [33], as our primary data to analyze.

Yibo provides a novel solution to add advertisements on the Internet. It collects "404 not found" web pages that provide the advertisement service to social organizations. Now, over 200,000 websites have joined in Yibo to provide noncommercial advertisement. The advantage is that it spreads noncommercial advertisements online by fully using resources of Internet. The whole procedure can be easily recorded and traced.

Pugedon is a well-designed recycling machine. It feeds stray animals when it receives plastic bottles. At the same time, Pugedon recycles plastic materials for environment protection. On the other hand, it provides a solution to feeding stray animals. By combining these two features, Pugedon motivates people to protect environment and meanwhile care for animals.

"Hello Happiness" is a new video from Coca-Cola. In March 2014, Coke installed five special phone booths that accepted Coca-Cola bottle caps instead of coins in Dubai labor camps. In exchange for a 54-cent Coke bottle cap, migrant workers could make a three-minute international call [30]. Similar with Pugedon, Coca-Cola Hello Happiness project is totallyan offline solution. It modifies the traditional telephone booth by replacing the coins with Coke bottle caps. Apparently, Coca-Cola's innovative solution created a positive impact on the society, especially to migrant workers.

Yitu provides a multiple-field and map-based solution targeting different social problems such as environment, society and disaster. It is the first multiple-layers social map on which every person can upload and search for different social problems and requirements. Social organizations can generate corresponding social service maps based on the Yitu platform. The maps can be imbedded into the web pages to reduce the cost of development.

FixMyCity is a framework for easily building and deploying citizen reporting platforms. Based on web technologies, it enables citizens to report local issues to the responsible local authorities. Through the combination of FixMyCity platform features, bidirectional channels are created between citizens on the one side and local governments on the other. FixMyCity focuses on the extensive support to end-user mobile cross-device and the tight integration of Social Media [33].

During the research of these five DSI cases, we collected keywords in related works, such as project introductions, news and research papers, and summarized the feature descriptions as shown in table. Based on the 5W2H theory, a method in Grounded Theory for microanalysis, which is what, when, where, who, why, how, how much, we selected seven corresponding aspects - deliverable, generation, service model, object, orientation, approach, and operation to categorize the features.

We learned from other cases that the content of DSI could also be open data offered by the government or relevant departments and organizations.

3   Digital Social Innovation

3.1   Definition

DSI is the best solution to city life problems in the era of information. Science and technology have provided guarantees for many unimaginable and undoable things, making efficient and large-scale innovations possible. Today, at a time when urban lifestyle is so fast, science and technology has become more and more essential as a tool of assisting social innovation. DSI is one kind of social innovation that is based on Internet or uses digital ways. Its purposes are to improve the life quality of different groups and help raise different solutions to the same problems in digital way.

NESTA had defined DSI as "a type of social and collaborative innovation in which innovators, users and communities collaborate using digital technologies to co-create knowledge and solutions for a wide range of social needs and at a scale that was unimaginable before the rise of the Internet" [34].

In a report of NESTA [13], they proposed six areas of DSI, which are open democracy, open access, collaborative economy, awareness network, new ways of making and funding acceleration and incubation. Also they said that the technology focused on open hardware, open networks, open knowledge, and open data.

We define DSI in the urban context as a type of social innovation in which all of the society members get involved both physically and digitally through using digital technologies to co-create and co-design our neighborhood.

3.2   Features

We have concluded seven features of DSI through research and practice. They are from the seven aspects shown in Table 1. The seven features corresponding with the seven aspects come out in pairs, complement and reinforce each other. According to

Table 1. Features of the 5 typical DSI cases

Aspects	Yibo	Hello Happiness	Pugedon	Yitu	FixMyCity
Deliverable	Noncommercial advertisement platform	Pay phone	Recycling machine	Map platform	Citizen reporting platform
Generation	"404 not found" web pages Web technology	Pay with Coca-Cola bottle caps instead of coins	Put in plastic bottles Get pet food	SNS Computer-assisted data analysis Information visualization	Mobile application Web technology SNS Computer-assisted data analysis
Service Model	Online	Offline	Offline	Online	O2O
Object	Broad audience NGOs	Migrant workers	Stray animals	Grass-roots Widespread NGOs	Broad audience Responsible local authorities
Orientation	Broadcasting noncommercial advertisement	Free IDD	Environmental protect Care for stray animals	Map-based solutions for social issues	Connect citizens with authorities
Approach	Open UGC	Customized	Recycling	Open source UGC	Open source Expandable UGC
Operation	Simple operation Free	Free	Free	Simple operation Free	Cross-platform Free

Grounded Theory, the features are the substantive theory that we get from the primary data. Through practicing and validating, they gained great guidance to classify the researches on DSI.

Platform/Product. Solutions can self-generate or be improved by users on the platform and are open to many other users. A product is effective, professional, complete and validated. Usually, due to unprofessional quality or financial problems, a product comes out at the situation in which users cannot inefficiently find the solution.

Original/Reformed. Science and technology has changed our behaviors. An exited and effective social innovation will become a new DSI after digitally reformed. The development of technology has broadened our horizon and motivated social innovation. Whether social innovation is supported by a completely new technology or a combination of existing technologies, it's all original DSI.

Online/Offline. The application of Internet can be seen in almost every case of DSI. Online means state of connectivity. Offline means real activities or events. The offline part shortens the distance between innovation result and real life, while the online part provides chances for creating new business models and solutions.

Collective/Individual. Collective intelligence helps us solve complex human problems. Crowdsourcing and crowdfunding have already been new modes of generating and incubating innovation. "Collective" means the DSI is executed by the whole society, such as crowdsourcing and crowdfunding. While "Individual" means the DSI is initiated or executed by one person.

Result/Process. Results-oriented DSI emphasizes the final output – a solution or a product. While process-DSI emphasizes the middle output. It can be data or social network between the participants generated or established in the DSI process.

Open/Customized. Open indicates transparent data, self-generation, low threshold and broad audience. While customized stands for DSIs that have special requirements, targeted audiences, and experts.

Light/Heavy. Light operation means less or none cost and manpower resources, using freely, and operating simply. Heavy operation means complex development and maintenance.

3.3   Design Framework

Based on the SET factors [35], which are social, economic, and technology, we categorize the features. Then we get the formal theory, a standard DSI design framework, as the guide of our practice to evaluate the sustainability, economic benefits, and efficiency during the process of studying and practicing DSI cases. We summarize them as four evaluation indexes in our DSI design framework based on what we have learned from Tim Brown's Design Thinking [36]. The four evaluations indexes are desirability, viability and sustainability, and feasibility (Fig. 1).

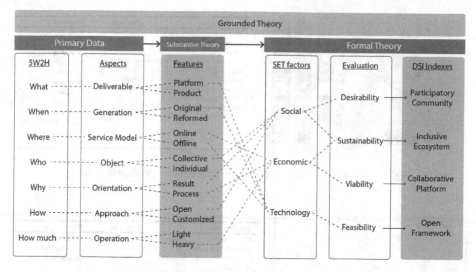

Fig. 1. Design framework of DSI

From the perspective of DSI, social desirability is about building the participatory, vibrant community to support the humanized innovation. Social and economic sustainability means it's an inclusive ecosystem that can create sustaining social values. Economic viability means aggregating the physical and digital resources to build the collaborative platform. Technology feasibility means it's an open, flexible framework based on the new technologies, such as social media, big data, and crowdsourcing. In conclusion, the four indexes of DSI are participatory community, inclusive ecosystem, collaborative platform, and open framework.

3.4   Project Practices

To explore the opportunities and services for social innovation and sustainable design patterns in the urban context, we cooperate with NGOs and public institutions to help the students to build a better concept of society problems and find the real demand, and in the same time, we apply our framework for generating solutions. There are 3 examples from the class below.

Case1: Urban Walkability and Walking Experience.

Urban walkability is a problem concentrated on sustainability of future cities from a macro perspective, and it can determine the citizens' life quality and living cost (Fig. 2).

Case2: Open Air Quality Platform for Government.

The haze and smog can directly damage human respiratory system. On one hand, limiting the airborne pollution is an important aspect; on the other hand, the communication among government, enterprises and public has a significant meaning (Fig. 3).

Description	Features	Evaluation
Through crowdsourcing, inspire citizens to participate in and spread the concept of walkability. Based on UGC, put forward scientific advices for city development, and make the measurement of walkability more meaningful.	Platform Original Online Collective Process Open Light	Participatory Community: ★★★★☆ Inclusive Ecosystem: ★★★★ Collaborative Platform: ★★★★☆ Open Framework : ★★★☆

Fig. 2. Urban walkability and walking experience – Walkability APP

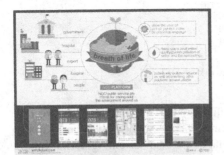

Description	Features	Evaluation
Using open data, establish an interactive relationship between the government and the public. Through crowdsourcing, the citizens can collect and upload the pollution source. Based on the map, the government and environmental organizations can upload the solutions and arrangement of environmental protect.	Platform Original Online Collective Process Open Light	Participatory Community: ★★★★★ Inclusive Ecosystem: ★★★★★ Collaborative Platform: ★★★ Open Framework: ★★★

Fig. 3. Open air quality platform for government – breath of life

Case3: Youth Hostel Service Design.

Youth hostel is a microcosm of society, which has a close relationship with youth's attitude and manner toward life. It also includes many elements: travel, making friends and accommodation (Fig. 4).

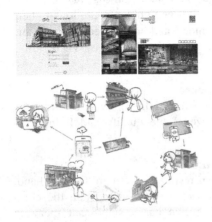

Description	Features	Evaluation
Establish a mobile app, which can socialize and share travel information. Targeting the users of the youth hostels, it provides the opportunities to find common interests and make cooperation during travelling.	Platform Original Online Collective Process Open Light	Participatory Community: ★★☆ Inclusive Ecosystem: ★★★☆ Collaborative Platform: ★★★★★ Open Framework: ★★★★☆

Fig. 4. Youth hostel service design

4 Discussions and Future Works

During our study and practice, we did a lot of research on existing related methods and tools that have already been used and practiced thousands of times. By combining and recreating them, we make our own DSI methods and tools for college students in our courses. In order to validate them in real urban context, we conducted some projects together with NGOs and other society organizations. As shown above, our projects have standardized process and completed result. Because of our expertise, our results are drawn mostly from design concern.

After this, we still have other valuable things to do:

- Firstly, build a DSI sharing platform for the organizations and companies who are planning to do DSI. The platform will contain large quantities of DSI cases and related data, which will be quite helpful for those organizations and companies especially startups. Of course there will be a committee to supervise the platform and keep it working by certain rules. If some groups profit from the platform, in return, they will share their cases and data on the platform.
- Although DSI has the social attributes, we can concern the micro aspect of the whole DSI process – the innovation groups. How to make the group more efficient and more creative is the key point. We need to discover what tools, platforms or specialties influence DSI results and how they influence.

5 Conclusions

Starting with the definition of DSI, we used case study to conclude the features of DSI, and on the basis of these features we developed the DSI's framework used on urban context. Referring to the course practices cooperated with Stanford, we practice and confirm the relevant method, and so that we believe the conclusion have the guiding significance. We will continue perfecting and verifying our conclusion and pay attention on development and promotion of creativity of innovation participant. Also, we will develop more distinctive products and services for society.

Acknowledgments. The cases are from the course of Service Design and the collaborative course – International Urbanization Seminar – with Stanford. Sincerely thanks to the hardworking teachers from Stanford – Deland Chan and Kevin Hsu. And also many thanks to our great students – Fei Yang, Yun Zhou, Lu Yao, Siyue Wang, Yang Zhou, Aihua Mu, and the team of youth hostel service design project – for their amazing ideas and works. Thanks to Xu lin's extraordinary previous work for supporting our work so well. Thanks to Tao Wan's big contribution to the public in China.

References

1. NESTA. http://www.nesta.org.uk
2. Parsons DESIS. http://www.newschool.edu/desis

3. Stanford International Urbanization Course. http://www.internationalurbanization.org
4. Fu, Z., Lin, X.: Building the co-design and making platform to support participatory research and development for smart city. In: Rau, P.L.P. (ed.) CCD 2014. LNCS, vol. 8528, pp. 609–620. Springer, Heidelberg (2014)
5. Yigitcanlar, T.: Urban management revolution : intelligent management systems for ubiquitous cities, In: The International Symposium on Land, Transport and Marine Technology (2008)
6. Naphade, M., Banavar, G., Harrison, C., Paraszczak, J., Morris, R.: Smarter cities and their innovation challenges. Computer 44, 32–39 (2011)
7. Caragliu, A., Del Bo, C., Nijkamp, P.: Smart cities in Europe. J. Urban Technol. 18, 65–82 (2011)
8. Gibson, W.: Life in the meta city. Sci. Am. 305, 88–89 (2011)
9. Salem, M., Schonowski, J., Küpper, A.: Citizen-centric smart cities: m-technology for realizing smart participatory urban sensing in e-government. Inf. Technol. Comput. Sci. 12(1), 82–92 (2013)
10. Reinvent Green Hackathon. http://www.nyc.gov/html/digital/html/opengov/reinventgreen.shtml
11. Zolli, A.: CSR commerce. Bus. Sch. 4, 038 (2007)
12. Intel Cinnovate. http://xin.cloudnpo.org/home.php
13. Growing a digital social innovation ecosystem for Europe. http://www.nesta.org.uk/publications/growing-digital-social-innovation-ecosystem-europe
14. Parameswaran, M., Whinston, A.B.: Research issues in social computing. J. Assoc. Inf. Syst. 8(6), 22 (2007)
15. Parameswaran, M., Whinston, A.B.: Social computing: an overview. Commun. Assoc. Inf. Syst. 19(1), 37 (2007)
16. NGO 2.0. http://www.ngo20.org
17. NGO 2.0: Accelerating Social Impact in a Connected World – The Hult Prize. http://www.huffingtonpost.com/hitendra-patel/ngo-20-accelerating-socia_b_1909014.html
18. El Fasiki, H.: Modes of Social Entrepreneurial Actions: MicroCredit at the Bottom-of-the-Pyramid. http://www.upublish.info/Article/Modes-of-Social-Entrepreneurial-Actions-MicroCredit-at-the-Bottom-of-the-Pyramid/727012
19. Frog Collective Action Toolkit. http://www.frogdesign.cn/work/frog-collective-action-toolkit.html
20. IDEO Human Centered Design (HCD) Toolkit. http://www.ideo.com/images/uploads/hcd_toolkit/IDEO_HCD_ToolKit.pdf
21. Development Impact & You (DIY). http://diytoolkit.org
22. Thomas, G.: A typology for the case study in social science following a review of definition, discourse, and structure. Qual. Inq. 17(6), 511–521 (2011)
23. Grounded Theory. http://en.wikipedia.org/wiki/Grounded_theory
24. Murray, R., Caulier-Grice, J., Mulgan, G.: The Open Book of Social Innovation. National Endowment for Science Technology and the Art, UK (2010)
25. Goldenberg, M.: Social innovation in Canada: how the non-profit sector serves canadians– and how it can serve them better. In: Canadian Policy Research Networks. Work Network. CPRN = RCRPP (2004)
26. Phills, J.A., Deiglmeier, K., Miller, D.T.: Rediscovering social innovation. Stanford Soc. Innov. Rev. 6(4), 34–43 (2008)
27. Hämäläinen, T.J.: Social innovations, institutional change, and economic performance: making sense of structural adjustment processes in industrial sectors, regions, and societies, vol. 281. Edward Elgar Publishing (2007)

28. Caulier-Grice J, Davies A, Patrick R, et al.: Defining social innovation [J]. A deliverable of the project:"The theoretical, empirical and policy foundations for building social innovation in Europe"(TEPSIE). In: European Commission–7th Framework Programme, Brussels: European Commission, DG Research (2012)
29. Yibo. http://yibo.iyiyun.com
30. Coca-Cola's Happiness Machines. http://www.newyorker.com/business/currency/coca-colas-happiness-machines
31. Pugedon, http://pugedon.com
32. Yitu. http://map.iyiyun.com/
33. FixMyCity. http://www.fixmycity.de/
34. Digital Social Innovation Interim Report. http://waag.org/sites/waag/files/public/media/publicaties/dsi-report-complete-lr.pdf
35. Cagan, J., Vogel, C.M.: Creating breakthrough products: Innovation from product planning to program approval. Ft Press, UK (2002)
36. Design Thinking – Tim Brown at TED. https://www.youtube.com/watch?v=UAinLaT42xY

Defining the Middle Ground: A Comprehensive Approach to the Planning, Design and Implementation of Smart City Operating Systems

Christopher Grant Kirwan[✉]

Reignwood Innovation Technology Center, Beijing 100022, China
mustafa.kirwan@gmail.com

Abstract. As cities have become more sophisticated with the introduction of advanced information technology and with the widespread use of social media, there is a need to identify a middle ground (or connective mode) which links the operating systems of the city with its citizens. In order to develop a new viable model for Smart City operating systems, an in-depth understanding of key drivers of the city will be required. This process must simultaneously integrate both top-down and bottom-up data streams to allow operating systems to grow organically and sustainably, with the following goals: (1) Permit city leaders to make more informed decisions, (2) Create an open development environment that will encourage private enterprise to infuse capital, technology and innovative business solutions, (3) Allow citizens to participate in the operation and management of their communities. The primary objective of this paper is to define the required methodology to plan, design and implement appropriate solutions to City DNA through the use of an integrated "Middle Ground" approach.

Keywords: Smart Cities · City OS · Operating Systems · System Architecture · Urban Interface · City DNA · Collective Intelligence · Citizen Participation

1 Overview

1.1 Models of City Operating Systems

City operating systems (city OS) have been predominately developed as top-down management software systems built on legacy systems that typically are accessible to specialized software engineers or proprietary operators of the system. On the opposite side of the spectrum, there have been attempts to develop open-source operating systems representing a piecemeal assembly of fragmented software elements that have not provided a comprehensive integrated platform allowing seamless connectivity and operability between city management departments. Sophisticated Smart City platforms, including Microsoft's CityNext, now make possible comprehensive development environments and business platforms for third party developers to create specialized solutions.

© Springer International Publishing Switzerland 2015
P.L.P. Rau (Ed.): CCD 2015, Part I, LNCS 9180, pp. 316–327, 2015.
DOI: 10.1007/978-3-319-20907-4_29

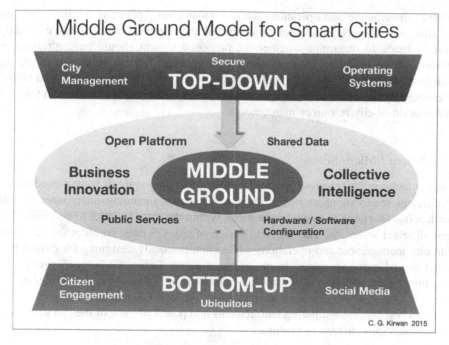

Fig. 1. Middle ground model

In many cases, the hesitation of city managers to adopt proprietary operating systems has been the perception that many large enterprises dominating the industry are locking in specific technologies that create a dependency on a singular solution rather than allowing an open-source approach. On the other hand, the open-source world has not fully been able to provide a solid, reliable platform for developers and is often overlooked by city managers for being too complicated. Therefore, the selection of smart city OS has remained a real issue for city leaders to decide on what is the best solution for managing their city and its citizens.

Figure 1 demonstrates a Middle Ground Model as described above; Top-Down refers to government, city management and the city operating systems; Middle Ground refers to a combination of business innovation and technology integration; Bottom-Up refers to the public realm, social media and citizens interface.

2 Operating System Design Factors

2.1 System Architecture

The typology of city operating systems require a holistic understanding of the unique physiology of each city in terms of the special combination of city governance structure, socio-economic environment and physical resources that assist city leaders in determining the best solution for the selection of their smart city OS. This will necessitate developing a comprehensive approach that allows the optimization of the present infrastructure and operations while simultaneously planning for future growth and change in the system based on urban growth parameters. Therefore a careful study must be made to determine whether the proposed system should be centralized or decentralized in order to facilitate the management of various city operations, for example: transportation, security, utilities monitoring, etc. This structure is also highly determined by the structure of city governance and whether the city has moved towards privatization of city resources management.

2.2   Macro / Micro Scales

A major factor in the selection and design of city operating systems is the consideration of different scales of operations from macro systems including interconnected and overlapping functions to micro applications within the city. In order to accommodate these different scales, the planning and design of city OS must consider the city from both city management and operations while simultaneously designing for citizen participation and user experience. In my previous paper, *Urban Phenomenology: Incorporating Dynamic Frames of References in the Design of Urban OS*, I elaborate on the need for adaptable, holistic systems that allow the city OS to change frames of reference to best suit these differing requirements and points of view of the end user, from city managers, to citizens to visitors.

2.3   Technical Functions: Hardware / Software

Smart City OS are a combination of hardware and software solutions and must allow the interconnectivity of various systems to create a seamless flow of information management for the operation of city systems, technologies, software applications and equipment and in many cases this also includes the management and interface with the human labor force of cities. The Smart City industry has been typically divided between hardware and software providers although some of the major players like Siemens, Honeywell and others have developed both. As mentioned in the previous paragraph, it has been a dilemma for city leaders to decide the best platform combining both hardware and software since choosing a one-solution approach limits the development of open source, competitive solutions and locks city managers into purchasing from a single company that may potentially lead to a monopoly in the market. As a consequence city leaders must look for other options.

2.4   Collective Intelligence

As cities have become increasingly more complex to manage and as technology has become ubiquitous at multiple scales, the opportunity to incorporate the individual user as part of the city operating system has become a viable dimension to create more holistic approaches that combine both top-down and bottom-up solutions. In the 1970's and 80's in the US when crime was on the rise in many cities, and in many instances the police force was not adequate to monitor and protect all neighborhoods particularly in poor districts or neighborhoods adjacent to blighted areas, the emergence of Neighborhood Watch became a viable model for self-protection. The Neighborhood Watch was made up of volunteers within the community who acted as responsible vigilantes to monitor neighborhood activities. This model became very popular across the country and was able, in many cases, to solve the issue of crime prevention and reduction. This bottom-up example illustrates how citizens can provide a valuable information network linking and augmenting city management. This citizen-centric approach has great potential today, especially with the ubiquitous nature of mobile media and the distribution of cameras and sensors throughout the city. The integration of human and computer systems, a collective intelligence, which I elaborate in the paper *Cybernetics Revisited: Towards a Collective Intelligence,* facilitates a more comprehensive solution for managing the city while allowing citizens to directly participate and influence their quality of life and at the same time providing a sense of involvement, pride and motivation in maintaining the city as a viable place to live and work.

2.5 Augmented Citizen Participation

By connecting citizens and designing solutions incorporating user experiences within city operating systems, cities can greatly benefit by the necessary human augmentation that is required to 'sense' beyond the technological limitations of current hardware and software. Of course in the future, artificial intelligence will begin to play the role of humans and human perception, however at the present stage of technology, the need for human participation within the city OS seems obvious and must be better utilized to improve both the psychological impact of citizens engagement as well as the need for real-time data collection and processing 'on the ground.' This is true for both existing city infrastructure as well as in the development of new and improved public spaces. In the paper *Ten Principles for Urban Regeneration Making Shanghai a Better City,* published by Urban Land Institute, states "The users of a place need to have a voice in its reuse. They too are experts - the most knowledgeable sources for what a site has in place and what it needs in its rejuvenation. They best know the site's history, which should inform its future. Both new forms of media and established practices can help residents' voices be heard. The intellectual capital and social infrastructure that drive contemporary cities should be integrated into urban regeneration. For example, technology can enable citizens to identify issues from potholes to cooking oil reuse."

2.6 The Role of Social Media

Social media has allowed users to create unique, personalized content while establishing broad networks for dissemination of community-based information. Much of this information has been for personal use and remains somewhat benign in terms of providing actual resourceful information to the direct management of cities. However, as big data has demonstrated, aggregating and filtering data can provide invaluable human behavioral intelligence. This information can be useful to predict individual and collective system patterns and has a wide variety of applications. On the other hand, user generated content can be overwhelming and may clutter the overall flow of information within comprehensive, efficient systems. The primary goal of the middle ground approach must be to incorporate bottom-up information through improved applications that provide useful tools for citizens to interact with local government. In addition, it will be important to apply real-time data to inform top-down decision making in the planning and operation of our communities. The purpose of establishing a middle ground is not only to serve government needs to provide better public services, but to improve the quality of life by allowing citizens to participate in the living operating system of cities. Additionally, by linking individual users with city management in a more direct way, the potential for proprietary systems to dominate information could potentially be lessened by making the communication flow more accessible, public and transparent.

2.7   Role of Business Innovation / Private Sector

Another major challenge facing cities is the issue of funding and commercialization of operating systems. The limitation of city budgets to introduce new state-of-the-art operating systems is the real constraint for cities to upgrade and adopt new technology solutions that could make these cities 'perform' better. At the same time the proliferation of mobile media and of user generated content has not necessarily provided, in its own right, a viable economic solution to assist cities in investing and financing advanced smart city OS. The role of the private sector is critical to provide market driven momentum and entrepreneurial solutions to link the top-down governance of smart city OS while connecting and harnessing the power of bottom-up citizen participatory media. Arup, a leading smart city solutions provider, estimates that the global market for smart urban systems for transport, energy, healthcare, water and waste will amount to around $400 Billion per annum by 2020.

In China, city governments have spent major investments in constructing infrastructure and have provided the required 'hardware' for the city, but have now, in many cities, run out of funding to develop the software layers of these cities. In fact, the key issue in China is the lack of software solutions both in terms of human and computer software and services. The service industry is the next wave in China, which currently is slow to develop, leaving plenty of opportunity for development.

The recent highly successful initial public offering of Alibaba on the New York Stock Exchange has ignited the imagination and spirit of Chinese entrepreneurs to seek new business ideas within the Internet of Things and the tech sector. This market momentum may be the solution to drive technology and business innovation to create the middle ground, linking the massive population's supply of data with the requirements of cities to better operate by incorporating citizens participation within the design of smart city OS.

3 Case Studies

3.1 Comprehensive Approach to Smart Cities

In order to develop a comprehensive approach to the design, planning and implementation of smart city OS, the city must be understood from the macro socio-economic point of view. Through this point of view, a multi-layered system architecture can then be developed. The following case studies were selected to represent three major aspects of the system architecture required to develop smart city OS. The first case study represents a macro system view of the city that informs the key consideration that must be factored into the design and selection of the system architecture. The second case study represents an example of an open network platform that allows a more flexible system architecture adaptable to different city requirements and configurations. The third case study presents student research projects focused on user interface and how users of the system can be engaged and participate in smart city operations.

3.2 Case Study 1: City-wide System Strategy

In order to define and program the development of adaptive, intelligence strategies for nations, Harvard professor Michael E. Porter has been a pioneer in evaluating the competiveness of individual nations based on each nation's unique combination of natural resources, industries, labor force, etc. Based on the collection and analysis of this information, a comprehensive strategy is then proposed to optimize the economic and social objectives. Porter's Diamond Model framework from *Competitive Advantage of Nations* used to evaluate the competitiveness of nations can be applied at the city level. In Porter's model, *Factor Conditions* refer to the aspects of production such as skilled labor or infrastructure, necessary for city-to-city competition. *Firm Strategy, Structure and Rivalry* refers to, when applied to city settings, how cities are organized and managed. *Demand Conditions* refer to the cities citizens demand for goods and services. *Related and Supporting Industries* refer to the presence or absence of services that are unique to each city. A strategic plan can be developed for each city that informs the way its operating systems could be developed to best serve needs of the community and preserve its competitive advantages (Fig. 2).

3.3 Case Study 2: Open Platform

It has been argued that allowing propriety legacy systems as the basis of Smart City OS is detrimental to the development of adaptable and evolutionary operating platforms by constraining the use to specific operating systems and technology solutions. In the white paper *Framework for SMART City Deployment*, the author Paul Goff argues in favor of an open system approach as the underlining architecture of the smart city OS. "A legacy approach to the deployment of information technology systems within the city will be a constraint ... Integration and convergence of physical and logical systems is the key to a successful SMART deployment."

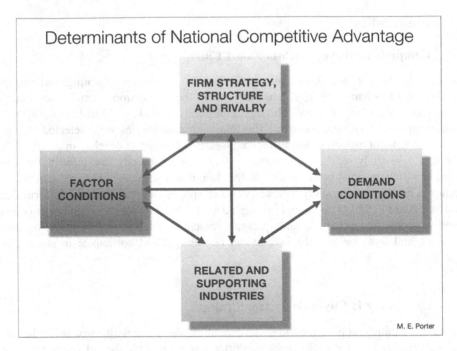

Fig. 2. Michel Porter's Diamond Model of competitive advantage

An example of a hybrid open operating system is presented in the paper *Civitas: The Smart City Middleware, from Sensors to Big Data.* The authors propose an open-middleware model that builds a flexible operating platform for multiple stakeholders to engage, share and build out the system in a more organic framework. The main feature of Civitas is a flexible cloud based IT platform that bridges city OS with third party enterprise developers and app developers with end users. The authors state "The ecosystem notion of a smart city is an abstraction that comprises the IT infrastructure deployed by governmental institutions all over the city, such as semaphores, traffic sensors, cameras, public wifi networks, etc. The Civitas platform counts on all these sources of information and actuation as its raw elements from which smart city operations can be articulated (Fig. 3)."

3.4   Case Study 3: Citizen Engagement / User Interface

Having lived and worked in China for the past six years, a period in history of Chinese development post 2008 Beijing Olympics that could be characterized as the 'Chinese Awakening,' has been an eye opening experience as a foreigner. The dichotomy arising from an accelerated opening to western influence, business and lifestyle, while maintaining China's restrained, reformist policy both to eliminate unwanted information proliferation from the west and anti-corruption measures internally within the present government, has created a back and forth situation between open and closed systems. As part of this amazing phenomenon has been the growth and proliferation of mobile

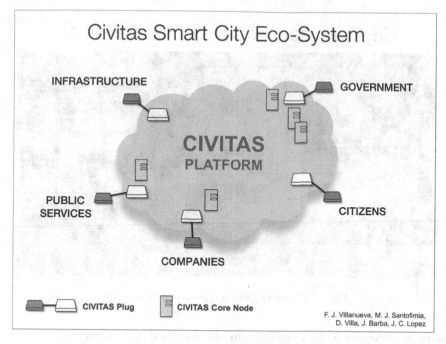

Fig. 3. Model of civitas platform

phones, social media and the new age of user interaction and participation, which would not inherently be considered a Chinese way. On the other hand this has led to numerous opportunities for Chinese citizens to influence how cities operate and to provide information that can be useful for leaders to better manage the vast developing cities that have become the symbol of China's growth and world prosperity.

As co-founder of *The Design Beijing Lab* and visiting faculty at Tsinghua University School of Art and Design, I had the opportunity, with lead faculty member Professor Fu Zhiyong, to conduct several design studios focused on research and design of citizen participation that bridge top-down and bottom-up solutions and seek to define the new concept of collective intelligence. In a studio class format, the following three projects are prototypes developed by student teams to explore the middle ground:

CityCare is a mobile app that allows citizens to post images with comments to a public BBS providing a shared platform accessible by city park managers to monitor and respond to public space maintenance. A more lyrical project, *Subscope* connects busy Beijing subways riders with city landmarks above-ground using a GPS-based function that geo-tags these specific landmarks allowing subway rider to create a collective database of personal narratives of these city landmarks. The *Smart Pedestrian Bridge* project considers how to make pedestrian bridges more effective, fun and interactive both as safe passages for pedestrians as well as to provide key traffic and other related information to automobiles and buses passing underneath. The *Smart Pedestrian Bridge* functions both as a physical bridge, as well as a digital bridge,

Fig. 4. Citycare application concept and interface

linking other Beijing bridges together into one integrated *infostructure* network. Each of these project examples seek to incorporate the design considerations discussed above including macro/micro scales, hardware/software solutions, and connect city management with citizen participation (Fig. 4).

4   The Proposed Solution / Conclusion

4.1   The Concept of City DNA

Building on Professor Michael Porter's approach, the opportunity to examine the unique combination of individual cities' advantages has led me to develop a comprehensive planning and design methodology termed City DNA to assist in defining a middle ground solution appropriate for each city. Like the concept of Brand DNA, City DNA evaluates brand identity, resources and competitive advantages among other key considerations for each city. Based on this information, the appropriate design framework is then established to develop a comprehensive system architecture. This architecture integrates a combination of government services, private enterprise solutions and end user applications that allow citizens to participate more directly in the overall smart city framework. The push-pull interaction allows the users to both access applications within the smart city framework while providing valuable user feedback data that can be used within the smart city OS to understand and improve the quality of life of the city. The data provider can be a range of entities from government agencies, corporations, and small businesses to individual users.

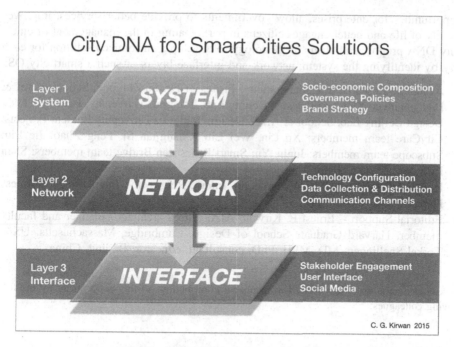

Fig. 5. City DNA for smart city solutions

4.2 Defining an Appropriate Solution for Each City

The City DNA framework has three layers System, Network and Interface that must be factored into each city DNA solution to create the unique operating system aligned with the brand and strategic positioning of the city. The importance of the brand dimension within the smart city OS design is required to provide a clear identity for each city to differentiate itself from other cities and to provide a solution tailored precisely to the unique combination of political, socio-economic and technological stage of development. Figure 5 identifies the three layers and their corresponding functions. System Layer refers to the macro level considerations that must be accounted for to select an appropriate operating system. Network Layer refers to the data collected and distributed in the cities. Interface Layer refers to the method that users interact with the system and provide data through the Interface.

4.3 Conclusion

In order to define and achieve a middle ground approach, a comprehensive understanding of the key drivers of each city is required to plan, design and implement a smart city OS appropriate for that particular community. The design must simultaneously factor in a combination of top-down and bottom-up considerations within the development of an open platform. This hybrid solution is necessary to drive the development of the smart city market that stimulates the economy of cities, creates new opportunities for enterprises, allow governments to provide better services, improves quality of life and better engages citizens in participating in the management of cities. City DNA proposes a holistic methodology to develop a customized solution for each city by identifying the system, network and interface layers of such a smart city OS.

- Academic Research & Collaboration – Professor Dr. Fu Zhiyong, School of Art & Design and co-founder of Design Beijing Lab, Tsinghua University, Beijing, China.
- Design Beijing Lab, School of Art & Design Tsinghua University Student Projects: CityCare team members: Xu Lin, Wei Liu, Changjian Si, Peng Zhao, Jie Liu; Subscope team members: Junjie Yu; Smart Pedestrian Bridge team members: Shen Li, Luobin Wang, Jingli Zhu.
- Research Assistance – Nicholas Leong, Intern, Reignwood International Business Department.
- Editorial Support – Ernest E. Kirwan, AIA, retired architect / planner and faculty member, Harvard Graduate School of Design, Cambridge, Massachusetts, USA; Torkel Snellingen, MD, MPH, PhD, consultant, educator, Beijing, China.

Acknowledgements. I am pleased to recognize contributions to this paper made by the following colleagues:

References

1. Bianchi, N., Hartman, K.: What makes a city 'smart,' anyway?(2014). http://www.modeldmedia.com/features/smart-cities-meeting-of-the-minds-102114.aspx
2. BIS Research Paper No. 136 The Smart City Market: Opportunities for the UK. Research Paper, Department for Innovation and Skills (2013)
3. CityNext Enabling Real Impact for Better Cities with a People-First Approach. Technical report, Microsoft (2013)
4. Flood, R.L., Carson, E.: Dealing with Complexity: An Introduction to the Theory and Application of Systems Science. Springer, US (1993)
5. Goff, P.: Framework for Smart City Deployment TechiCity Project Report V1.0 (2013)
6. Intelligent / Smart Cities: Open Source Community. http://icos.urenio.org/about-icos/
7. International Making Cities Livable. http://www.livablecities.org/
8. Jacobson, C.: Ten Principles for Urban Regeneration: Making Shanghai a Better City. Technical report, Urban Land Institute (2014)
9. Kirwan, C., Travis, S.: Urban media: new complexities, new possibilities – a manifesto. In: Foth, M., Forlano, L., Satchell, C., Gibbs, M. (eds.) From Social Butterfly to Engaged Citizen, pp. 235–252. The MIT Press, Massachusetts (2011)
10. Kirwan, C.: Cybernetics revisited: toward a collective intelligence. In: Lima, M. (ed.) Visual Complexity Mapping Patterns of Information, pp. 252–254. Princeton Architectural Press, New York (2011)
11. Kirwan, C.: Urban phenomenology: incorporating dynamic frames of references in the design of urban OS. In: Rau, P. (ed.) Cross-Cultural Design Cultural Differences in Everyday Life, pp. 296–302. Springer, Heidelberg (2013)
12. Lee, Y.W., Rho, S.: U-City Portal for Smart Ubiquitous Middleware (2010)

13. National Neighborhood Watch - A Division of the National Sheriffs' Association. http://www.nnw.org/
14. Open Technology Institute. http://www.newamerica.org/oti/
15. Porter, M.: The competitive advantage of nations. Harv. Bus. Rev. **68**, 73–93 (1990)
16. Porter, M.: The Competitive Advantage of the Inner City. Harvard Business Review 73 (1995)
17. Pulido, A.T.: Open Smart Cities II: Open Source Big Data. Observatorio Nacional del Software de Fuentes Abiertas (2013)
18. Villanueva, F.J., Santofimia, M.J., Villa, D., Barba, J., Lopez, J.C.: Civitas: the smart city middleware, from sensors to big data. In: 2013 Seventh International Conference on Innovative Mobile and Internet Services in Ubiquitous Computing (IMIS), pp. 445-450. IEEE Press, Taichung (2013)
19. Wilson, M.: Far From a Shooting in Florida, an Increase in Block Watchers (2012). http://www.nytimes.com/2012/06/23/nyregion/neighborhood-watches-in-new-york-far-from-trayvon-martin-case.html?_r=1

Review on Interaction Design for Social Context in Public Spaces

Xu Lin[✉], Jun Hu, and Matthias Rauterberg

Eindhoven University of Technology,
Den Dolech 2, 5612AZ Eindhoven, The Netherlands
{X.Lin, J.Hu, G.W.M.Rauterberg}@tue.nl

Abstract. This paper presents a structured literature review on interaction design for social contexts in public spaces, especially the research on designing for public interactive facilities, such as public displays, interactive installations and media façades, aiming to gain a holistic understanding on current research. A framework is also introduced to help summarize current research focuses, considering interaction process, social impacts and spatial factors as three main layers of it. Based on the framed results, the paper discusses possible design opportunities and challenges, bringing new perspectives into interaction design in public spaces.

Keywords: Public space · Social context · Interaction design

1 Introduction

Public spaces, generally considered as places where "civic, cultural and social activities occur", play an important role for public life, promoting the sense of community, enhancing the connection between people and place, and helping create a sense of belonging. It provides citizens with spaces and opportunities to exchange information and communicate on local issues, enjoying the gathered experiences with others [1].

In recent years, driven by technical and societal development in smart cities, such as the construction of sensing networks and intelligent systems, and the growth of mobile networks and the Internet of Things [2], public spaces gradually become interactive and responsive [3] both in providing basic public services and in improving urban social life. The continuously lowered cost and the increasing number of interactive facilities in public space, like public displays [4, 5], digitally augment and transform the traditional existences in urban space, such as buildings, bridges, and public statues, into public media where the social interactive experience can be sculptured with the public participation [6–8].

Meanwhile, the maturity of social networks and mobile service largely increases the means of social interaction, generally popularizes the information posting and sharing behaviour, and partially merges online activities into real spaces. Daily activities and life styles of people are changing quickly along with the technical developments, including the attitude towards online and offline social interactivity, as well as the way the space is used, which may bring new challenges to interaction design.

© Springer International Publishing Switzerland 2015
P.L.P. Rau (Ed.): CCD 2015, Part I, LNCS 9180, pp. 328–338, 2015.
DOI: 10.1007/978-3-319-20907-4_30

In this paper, we present a literature review of current research on interaction design in public spaces, especially for social contexts, through an iterated searching process and a framed analysis. Research topics mentioned frequently in research are recorded to present a general state of focuses and challenges. The findings are summarized into an initial framework, considering the interaction process, social impacts and spatial factors as three main layers of it. The derivation of this framework indicates the design possibilities in multi-place contexts that are less mentioned in reviewed papers, and brings new perspectives into interaction design in public spaces.

2 Review on Current Research

So far, there has been a large amount of research on both specific design contexts and the strategy level (e.g. research on urban interaction design [9] and smart city platform [10]) for interaction design in cities. In this paper, the search focused more on studies starting with concrete design contexts, while the potentials of interdisciplinary cooperation will also be discussed as extension.

Researchers and practitioners are taking up the challenges, exploring the potentials of interaction design for social contexts in urban space, including the research on media facades (e.g. Aarhus by Light and The Climate Wall [11]), public screens (e.g. Outdoor UBI hotspots in Oulu [12] and The Wray Photo Display [13]), mobile applications (e.g. Tiramisu [14]), and interactive art installations of which the contents and final forms may be co-created by the crowd (e.g. public art installation for Taicang [6]). Most of the research, if not all, seems to focus on concrete interaction (e.g. the form of manipulation and the material for embodiment), effects on social behaviour among citizens (e.g. the research on engagement), and spatial factors of public space.

2.1 Structured Review Searching

The review mainly went through three steps: (1) a review of related workshop paper collections; (2) a general searching and filtering with web searching tools; (3) a focused review on highly related and updated conference papers. Keywords were revised according to the results during the iterating process, except the main keywords of "public space", "interaction", "social" and "social interaction".

The review started with summarizing of position papers from CHI Workshop 2013, of which the theme was "experiencing the interactivity in public space (EIPS)" [15], gaining an initial knowledge on recent research interests and design concepts.

The second step was to conduct a general searching with keywords mentioned above via Google Scholar. The initial results were filtered again according to the titles and abstracts, as well as the re-checking of the keywords.

The last step ended with a searching for main and influential conference papers, using the same keywords and similar filtering methods, while this time the search was mainly focused on the research papers in recent five years (2010–2014).

According to the relevance of the content and citations of the paper, 77 papers were selected from the 164 searched pieces (Table 1) for the further review in detail.

Table 1. Searching results in total

CHI	PerDIS	DIS	CSCW	TEI	MobileHCI	UbiComp	Others	Total
63	16	9	7	7	7	12	43	164

*Others include: MAB, INTERACT, NordiCHI, OZCHI, Digital Creativity, MUM, AVI, and ICEGOV etc.

2.2 Summary of the Results

Tables 2 and 3 present the highly mentioned topics, which are discussed as research content and methods respectively. The numbers represent a count for papers that relatively consider the topics as main focuses or important content in their studies, while not suggesting that the rest of reviewed papers would be absolutely irrelative to

Table 2. Research topics mentioned in relatively high frequency

Themes	Sub-categories	Research topics under themes	Papers
Concrete Interaction Design	Input	Whole body interaction	12
	Mainly focusing on modality and human manipulation	Extra tools input (e.g. mobile device)	11
		Touch (multi-user contexts)	9
		Urban sensing (e.g. camera)	8
	Output	Public display	26
	Mainly focusing on presentation and interface highly combined with physical environment	Interactive installation	14
		Media facade	12
		Personal mobile device	12
		Service system	12
Social Impacts of Interaction	Human Behaviour	Communication & Share	32
		Collaboration	14
		Performativity & stage metaphor impact	6
	Cognition & Perception	Enhance user engagement	16
		Increase motivation or attention	10
		Social acceptance on interaction or social behaviour	10
Spatial Factors	Mainly focusing on spatial factors that influence on social behaviour	Spatial influences from layouts and surroundings (Mainly in co-located contexts)	17
		Societal function influence and situated factors	6

Table 3. Research types and evaluation methods mainly discussed in studies

Themes	Research topics under themes	Papers
Research	Practice (introducing experiments, field trials or case studies)	46
	Exploring design methods, frameworks or patterns	21
	Theoretical analysis and deduction	18
Evaluation	Observation	11
	Interview	7
	Questionnaire	5
	Data log in system	3

the topics. Although this record is not a precise statistics, it is helpful enough to give indications on current distribution of research attentions and trends.

Summary of research contents. As showed in record (Table 2), there are three major themes in search results: (1) concrete interaction design; (2) social impacts brought by the interaction; (3) spatial factors influencing the interaction and social behaviour. The topics are not separated from each other, but inter-connected in practice to reach specific design and research objectives. Usually, the study questions can be raised as exploring the behavioural and social impacts of specific interaction process, or discussing possibilities in interaction and space design to facilitate social experience.

Concrete interaction design is the first theme with the most-frequently mentioned topics in record, including studies like designing specific manipulation and exploring new modalities as potential interfaces. According to the basic interaction framework introduced by Abowd and Beale [16], topics are categorized by "input" and "output" process.

Research on input pays much attention to the multi-user context, and often focuses on exploring manipulations and input modalities, including gestures [15, 17] (ranging from hand gesture to whole body interaction), touch [15, 18], portable devices (e.g. smart phones), urban sensors (e.g. surveillance camera), and even sound interfaces (SI) [15]. And studies on output usually discuss about materials, platforms and technical solutions for presentation. Public display [19] is most often used in research. Media façades [11] and interactive public installations [20] are increasingly employed in large-scale design, while personal devices are popular in providing customized services. Participatory performance is also mentioned for research on human behaviour in social context [15, 21].

Social impacts of interaction look into the influence of interaction on people's behaviour and cognition. Main objectives of research include summarizing behaviour patterns and exploring how people understand, feel or get reflection on specific interaction or social relationship they are involved in.

Behavioural influences are usually studied through the observation on how specific interaction facilitates the communication between people in public spaces, including the studies on sharing, cooperating and competing behaviour, as well as the research on people's observing and reacting behaviour during the interaction (e.g. the transformation between the role of spectator and actor [22]). This research often deploys in two directions: (1) improving manipulation, modalities or tools to lower thresholds for people joining the activities; (2) improving content design or user task setting to facilitate social behaviour naturally [23].

Reviewed studies concerning the social impacts on cognition mainly discuss enticing or enhancing the user engagement [23], facilitating the feeling of connection, and exploring the range of social acceptance [15].

Spatial factors in review mainly discuss the influences brought by physical and societal features of public space on interaction process and human behaviour.

Research on physical features can be seen in the design of space layouts and surrounding environment to influence people's behaviour, including two major contexts - co-located interaction and remote interaction [24]. Combination with digitally augmented layers is also tried to enhance the spatial influence on human behaviour [15].

Societal features of different public spaces influence social behaviour of people and design of the facilities, like open space is generally used for large-scale design and short-term interaction, while indoor spaces are often used for detailed interaction or immersive experience.

Summary of research methods. Table 3 presents research types and evaluation methods used in practice, which indicates that most of the studies are based on practical design projects. There are some studies considering design methods and guidelines as major output, while fewer mainly conduct theoretical analysis or deduction, since design for interaction in public space always meets situations that cannot be foreseen or controlled in laboratory environment. The working prototypes and field trials of design play a significant role in research, especially in evaluation, which leads to a result that currently the observation (watching or video recording) combined with structured interview (with questionnaire) is considered as most feasible and practical evaluation method for user testing in wild [18].

2.3   Design Challenges in Current Reviewed Research

Being in the public spaces challenges interaction design with situations that can hardly be simulated in laboratory environment. The design can hardly be addressed specifically for certain group of regular users, and is usually defined as intuitive usage or needs to be "obtainable without prerequisites" [25]. Furthermore, there are also challenges in facilitating aesthetic communication and user experience, as well as in "utilizing the inherent qualities of public spaces to their full potential" [25].

Challenges in Design. The challenges summarized in this review paper can be discussed as dealing with the balances between several groups of trade-off relationship.

The first is to reach the balance between the single-user and multi-user context, which includes three sub-relationships: the individual operation versus the collective operation, the customized service versus the common use, and the privacy of users versus the publicity of the interaction [23].

The second important challenge is the conflict between the stable existence of the facilities and the continuous interest of people. How to keep people continuously interested in and engaged with the design is a great challenge for public space context.

The third one is to deal with the conflicts in manipulation design, including the balance between the artificial interaction and natural movements, and the combination of digital content and physical environment. The most common design question is how to design novel interaction form with appropriate affordance to entice users' intuitive manipulation.

And the last challenge is to balance the relationship between entertainment and functionality. It always requires a compromise to keep the design both entertaining and functional in use, as well as both precise and inclusive in manipulation.

Challenges in evaluation. As discussed in reviewed papers, some parameters can hardly be measured in laboratory environment, such as "effectiveness, social effects, audience behavior, and privacy implications" [5, 26]. Therefore, field studies are necessary in research to explore different design conditions, "gaining insights into relevant design parameters while still ensuring a high ecologic validity for the data" [27].

Currently, most of the evaluation is deployed as the combination of interview (questionnaire) and observation, while with technical development and changes in people's usage of public media, there is a potential to design new methods that are more efficient and suitable for evaluation in future user contexts, such as collecting feedbacks through the social media or information shared through the interaction.

3   Framed Analysis and Exploration

Base on the findings, an initial framework is introduced, showing the three layers of main reviewed factors for interaction design in public space, and aiming to gain a better understanding on the summarization of review. The framework is inspired from a progressive combination of the basic interaction framework [16], the tangible interaction framework according to Hornecker and Buur [28], and the review finding in this paper.

The basic structure of interaction from HCI perspective, introduced by Abowd and Beale [16], can be considered as a circle of four elements: user, input, system and output (Fig. 1). This structure may become more user-centered with partially considering spatial and social factors (Fig. 2), when located into physical media to enhance the connection between people and the real place, such as in tangible interaction design [28].

When designing for interaction in public space, the social and spatial factors appearing in field context become increasingly important. The studies need to not only take the original interaction structure into consideration, but also treat the social relationship and spatial influences at almost the same hierarchy. Thus, the design and research practice need to tackle a three-layer relationship, which is also indicated in review findings (Fig. 3): the interaction layer, the social layer and the spatial layer.

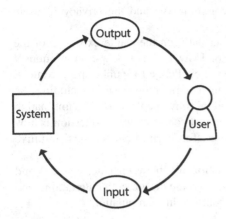

Fig. 1. Basic structure of interaction

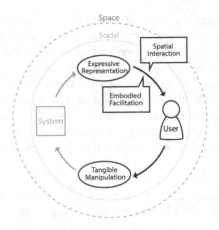

Fig. 2. Structure of tangible interaction introduced by Hornecker and Buur.

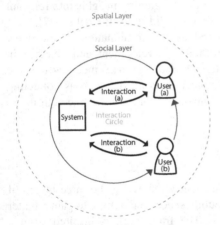

Fig. 3. Three-layer framework summarized from review findings.

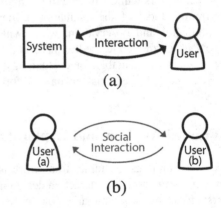

Fig. 4. Contexts that do not belong to the interaction discussed in this paper.

The interaction layer is the core of the framework. It matches the first theme in the summarization of review, and is also a basic premise of research in our review. The design without interaction, or the purely social interaction between people without interaction design intervention or mediation (Fig. 4b), may not belong to our research scope. In this circle, current research is making efforts to explore the new forms, materials and modalities of input manipulation and output presentation through the interaction process.

The social layer matches the second theme in review. It considers with the social interaction between people in the contexts (impacts on behaviour), and looks into the influences on people's thinking and feeling (impacts on cognition). When put into the public spaces, the interaction between human and interactive facilities (Fig. 4a) usually transforms into a social behaviour, due to the sociality embedded in the basic feature of public space. For instance, according to the explanation of the spectator-actor relationship, an individual usually holds an idea of being watched by the public or someone, even if he (or she) is the only person in front of the facility in public.

The spatial layer, matching third theme in review, refers to the consideration on spatial factors like the layouts of surrounding areas (no matter natural or digitally augmented) and the societal functions of different types of public spaces. As mentioned in review, these factors may have important influences on manipulation and presentation design of the interaction, as well as on people's social behaviour.

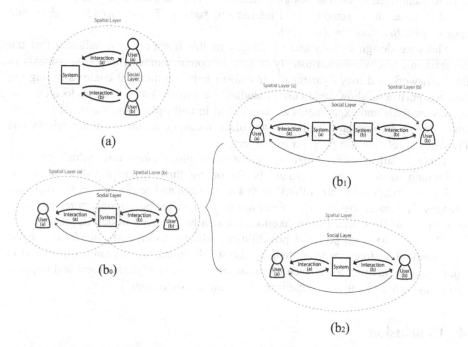

Fig. 5. Extended framework of interaction in social contexts in public space

Most of the research in review can be analyzed with this initial framework. However, differences between some contexts are not presented very clearly, for instance, the distinction between co-located situation and remote interaction context. Based on this consideration, an extension of the framework with derived contexts is employed, making it more detailed in interpretation of interaction design for social context in public space (Fig. 5).

The first context (Fig. 5a) represents one part of the basic co-located situation in public space. The users interact with the system (the public interactive facilities), and socially interact with other users during the interaction. This can be seen in many studies, especially those that focus on facilitating users' cooperation or competition behaviour through the interaction.

The second context (Fig. 5b$_2$) shows the other part of the co-located situation, in which the users interact with the system and socially interact with other users through the system without face-to-face social interaction between each other. This context can usually be seen in projects with large group of participators, such as interacting with a public screen by sending comments through mobile phones at a event [15].

The third context (Fig. 5b$_1$) describes the multi-place situation, which is rarely discussed in reviewed studies. In this context, users interact with the co-located facilities while socially interact with other users at different places through the system. It presents a situation of connecting two or more places together for interaction, which is little mentioned in current design concepts. A limited number of examples can be found in research on remote social interaction, such as *Telemurals* [24] and remote sports game *Breakout for Two* [29].

Matching design focuses and challenges to this framework, it indicates that the contexts in real environment usually present as combinations of the basic contexts in the framework and may dynamically transform between different contexts during the interaction. It also shows that current studies are usually focused on co-located contexts. Few trials and experiments are conducted in multi-place situations. At the same time, design focuses and challenges are often focusing on the problems within one layer or the relationship between two layers.

There is still a large design space for multi-place interaction, which calls for exploration to design and organize the factors in three layers together. It can be deployed through a structural thinking that is flexible and responsive to the real-time changes. The linear structure (e.g. timeline) may no longer be a dominant reference for structuring, while spatial factors like location can be involved in design process.

This discussion on potential possibilities indicates to organize the factors in the framework at a structural level, helping the whole interaction dynamically unfold in public spaces, in order to enhance the connection between digital content and physical space, as well as bring new experience into interaction design.

4   Conclusion

In this paper, we present a structured literature review for current research on interaction design for social contexts in public space. The main objective of the review is to help designers and researchers gain a holistic understanding on current research stage and explore for further possibilities, based on the summarized design focuses and challenges.

An initial three-layer framework is presented for structured analysis on review content, considering the inter-relationship between interaction process, social influences and spatial factors. The derivation of the framework helps discussing potential design opportunities in multi-place contexts, which are less mentioned in the review.

The discussion suggests organizing the factors in the three layers of the framework through a structural thinking to help the interaction unfold in multi-place situations. Although there may be new challenges coming along with the further research, the framework and its derived discussion in potentials are considered to be helpful in finding opportunities for novel interaction and user experience design. Future work on refining the framework is needed, as well as summarizing theoretical guidelines or patterns for more appropriate guidance on design practice.

References

1. Avila, M.I.M.: Factors that Influence the Social Life and Vitality of Public Open Spaces in Maracaibo-Venezuela. Case Study: Plaza de la Madre and Plaza de la República. Ph.D Thesis. Virginia Polytechnic Institute and State University (2001)
2. Townsend, A.M.: Smart Cities: Big Data, Civic Hackers, And The Quest For A New Utopia. W.W. Norton & Company, New York (2013)
3. Alves, L.J., Salem, B., Rauterberg, M.: Responsive environments: user experiences for ambient intelligence. Ambient Intell. Smart Envir. 2(4), 347–367 (2010)
4. Peltonen, P., et al.: "It's Mine, Don't Touch!": interactions at a large multi-touch display in a city centre. In: SIGCHI Conference on Human Factors in Computing Systems, pp. 1285–1294. ACM, Florence (2008)
5. Hinrichs, U., et al.: Large displays in urban life - from exhibition halls to media facades. In: CHI 2011 Extended Abstracts on Human Factors in Computing Systems, pp. 2433–2436. ACM, Vancouver (2011)
6. Hu, J., Frens, J., Funk, M., Wang, F., Zhang, Yu.: Design for social interaction in public spaces. In: Rau, P. (ed.) CCD 2014. LNCS, vol. 8528, pp. 287–298. Springer, Heidelberg (2014)
7. Hu, J., Wang, F., Funk, M., Frens, J., Zhang, Y., Boheemen, T.V., et al.: Participatory public media arts for social creativity. In: International Conference on Culture and Computing, pp. 179–180, Kyoto (2013)
8. Wang, F., Hu, J., Rauterberg, M.: New carriers, media and forms of public digital arts. In: Culture and Computing, pp. 83–93. Hangzhou, China (2012)
9. Brynskov, M., et al.: Urban Interaction Design: Towards City Making. Urban IxD Booksprint (2014)
10. Fu, Z., Lin, X.: Building the co-design and making platform to support participatory research and development for smart city. In: Rau, P. (ed.) CCD 2014. LNCS, vol. 8528, pp. 609–620. Springer, Heidelberg (2014)
11. Dalsgaard, P., Halskov, K.: Designing urban media facades: cases and challenges. In: SIGCHI Conference on Human Factors in Computing Systems, pp. 2277–2286. ACM, Atlanta (2010)
12. Ojala, T., et al.: Multipurpose interactive public displays in the wild: three years later. Computer 45(5), 42–49 (2012)
13. Taylor, N., Cheverst, K.: Supporting community awareness with interactive displays. Computer 45(5), 26–32 (2012)
14. Zimmerman, J., et al.: Field trial of Tiramisu: crowd-sourcing bus arrival times to spur co-design. In: SIGCHI Conference on Human Factors in Computing Systems, pp. 1677–1686. ACM, Vancouver (2011)
15. Väänänen-Vainio-Mattila, K., et al.: Experiencing interactivity in public spaces (eips). In: CHI 2013 Extended Abstracts on Human Factors in Computing Systems, pp. 3275–3278. ACM, Paris (2013)

16. Abowd, G.D., Beale, R.: Users, systems and interfaces: a unifying framework for interaction. In: HCI 1991: People and Computers, vol. 4, pp. 73–87 (1991)
17. Schmidt, D., et al.: Kickables: tangibles for feet. In: SIGCHI Conference on Human Factors in Computing Systems, pp. 3143–3152. ACM, Toronto (2014)
18. Jacucci, G., et al.: Worlds of information: designing for engagement at a public multi-touch display. In: SIGCHI Conference on Human Factors in Computing Systems, pp. 2267–2276. ACM, Atlanta (2010)
19. Müller, J., et al.: Requirements and design space for interactive public displays. In: International conference on Multimedia, pp. 1285–1294. ACM, Firenze, (2010)
20. Hu, J., Funk, M., Zhang, Yu., Wang, F.: Designing interactive public art installations: new material therefore new challenges. In: Pisan, Y., Sgouros, N.M., Marsh, T. (eds.) ICEC 2014. LNCS, vol. 8770, pp. 199–206. Springer, Heidelberg (2014)
21. Hansen, F.A., Kortbek, K.J., Grønbæk, K.: Mobile urban drama – setting the stage with location based technologies. In: Spierling, U., Szilas, N. (eds.) ICIDS 2008. LNCS, vol. 5334, pp. 20–31. Springer, Heidelberg (2008)
22. Goffman, E.: The Presentation of Self In Everyday Life. Anchor Press, Doubleday, New York (1959)
23. Brignull, H., Rogers, Y.: Enticing people to interact with large public displays in public spaces. In: Rauterberg, M., et al. (eds.) INTERACT 2003, pp. 17–24. IOS Press, Amsterdam (2003)
24. Karahalios, K., Donath, J.: Telemurals: linking remote spaces with social catalysts. In: SIGCHI Conference on Human Factors in Computing Systems, pp. 615–622. ACM, Vienna (2004)
25. Kortbek, K.J.: Interaction design for public spaces. In: 16th ACM international conference on Multimedia, pp. 1031–1034. ACM, Vancouver (2008)
26. Alt, F., et al.: How to evaluate public displays. In: 2012 International Symposium on Pervasive Displays, pp. 1–6. ACM, Porto (2012)
27. Hespanhol, L., Tomitsch, M.: Designing for collective participation with media installations in public spaces. In: 4th Media Architecture Biennale Conference: Participation, pp. 33–42. ACM, Aarhus (2012)
28. Hornecker, E., Buur, J.: Getting a grip on tangible interaction: a framework on physical space and social interaction. In: SIGCHI Conference on Human Factors in Computing Systems, pp. 437–446. ACM, Montréal (2006)
29. Stevens, G., et al.: Sports over a distance. Pers. Ubiquit. Comput. 11(8), 633–645 (2007)

Diagnosis on Corporate Culture and Construction

A Case Study of Limin Chemical Co., Ltd.

Lin Ma[1], Xueli Wang[2(✉)], and Xiaopeng He[1]

[1] Beihang University, Beijing, People's Republic of China
malin2014@buaa.edu.cn, 13911121009@163.com
[2] Tsinghua University, Beijing, People's Republic of China
wangxl@sem.tsinghua.edu.cn

Abstract. Along with the gradual improvement and development of China's market economy, some state-owned enterprises have gradually restructured into private ones. The culture of some enterprises has changed greatly in this structural reform process. This paper selects Limin Chemical Co., Ltd., a successfully restructured high-tech enterprise as the object of study, and extracts a method system to measure the enterprise culture through analysis of cultural differences before and after its restructuring. Based on the Denison Model of Organizational Culture, a cultural measuring model of Limin is established to diagnose current conditions of culture in Limin. According to the evaluation results, combining market trend, this paper presents the strategic object and plan of Limin's future culture construction, and discusses the establishment process of Limin's culture system in detail.

Keywords: Cultural changes · Culture diagnosis · Case study

1 Introduction

Enterprise culture is the soul of an enterprise and the driving force in its development (Kotter and Heskett 2004; William 1984). From the view of practical cases, either famous corporations like IBM, Sony, and GM, or domestic ones like Lenovo, Haier, Huawei and Beijing TRT, they all pay much attention to the construction of enterprise culture (Chen 2005). Enterprise culture is the interior quality of an enterprise that shows its personality and the highest level of business management. Only powerful enterprise culture can unite persons having different goals, beliefs and experiences together and form the centripetal force of a corporation.

Limin Chemical Co., Ltd. grows out of Xinyi County Glass Factory. It takes less than 20 years for it to be created, developed, and transformed from state-owned to private. It has now changed from a small loss-making factory to a national large-scale pesticide manufacturer that has over 1000 employees and an output value of 500 million RMB. Due to the enterprise restructuring, its organizational culture has had

P.L.P. Rau (Ed.): CCD 2015, Part I, LNCS 9180, pp. 339–348, 2015.
DOI: 10.1007/978-3-319-20907-4_31

different characteristics in different stages, which have affected the management and operation of the enterprise fundamentally.

The middle and senior managers and technical backbones bought out the property rights of the enterprise when it transformed from state-owned to private. However, this was also the most dangerous period when enterprise restructuring brought cultural innovation and broke the backward ideas that state-owned employees had for a long time, such as equalitarianism, "iron rice bowl" - a lifelong job, depending on the enterprise.

This research paper aims at helping the enterprise smoothly pull through the cultural transformation to obtain persistent competitive advantages. This paper focuses on the cultural transformation of Limin Chemical Co., Ltd., starts from theories and conducts a complete analysis of the enterprise in consideration of its current status. The paper also adopts Denison Model of Organizational Culture diagnose and rebuild the enterprise culture and to cultivate core competitiveness.

2   Cultural Changes at Different Stages

Since its bankruptcy, policy reform and reshuffling, Limin has experienced four major development stages of seeking ways out after bankruptcy, consolidation after survival, stagnation after becoming stronger and reform and innovation after hesitation. In the over 20 years of development for the enterprise, enterprise culture building has always been one of its work priorities of enterprise development and building.

When Xinyi Town Glass Factory, the predecessor of Limin, went bankrupt, the factory director led the top management team of the factory to decide to produce pesticide which was in higher demand. At the beginning of starting the new company, everything started from zero and all efforts of the enterprise had been put on seeking ways out. The joint objective for all is to "earn the basic allowance and have jobs to do". Moreover, the leaders of the enterprise displayed great charm. Therefore the employees were extremely united and dedicated. So the core of enterprise culture at this period was the organizational culture that centered ontaking painstaking efforts in starting the company and getting united for further progress. The cohesion from the strong desire for survival greatly boosted the development of the company.

In the following five years, Limin enjoyed rapid development. Compared with the start of the company, the products were initially recognized by the market. Even so, the overall technical foundation of the company was weak, the scale was small and the product competitiveness was not strong. In this period, Limin had already become aware of the importance of enhancing management. The company started to shift its focus from the external market to internal management. Drawing upon the managerial experience of foreign enterprises, it abolished the "fixed wage and no dismissal" policy, posts are determined scientifically and all posts were open for competition. The desire to be stronger and the positive attitude of the employees gradually formed the culture at this stage, mainly reflected in the dedication of employees and the sense of responsibility for taking pride in the enterprise.

Since the second half of 1996, the Chinese market had gradually become saturated and the pesticide industry had shifted toward the excessive economy. Limin was confronted with huge setbacks. Employees' sense of belonging dropped dramatically. The matching in technology, procurement, production and sales was not smooth and employees did their job in their own way. The company lingered and stagnated. To solve these problems, the enterprise adopted wage reform and boosted cost management, aiming at improving the operation efficiency. However, since the organizational culture represented by self-satisfaction was brewing in the company, employees sought for stability and lacked the motivation and initiative for creation. The reform was met with huge resistance and was not able to be implemented thoroughly.

The increasingly exposed problems in administration had affected the operation performance and the vital interests of stakeholders, thus promoting the initial agreement on internal reform within the company. Taking the opportunity of reform on the property rights of enterprise in 2004, Limin carried out bold and drastic reform and innovation and shifted from a state-owned enterprise into a private one. The middle and high-level managers and major technicians bought out all the property of the company at one swoop, fundamentally injecting vigor into the company. The managerial awareness and self-requirement of the managers underwent fundamental changes. Some fundamental management reforms were quite fruitful and effective. At that time, the company had marched through the initial stage and the middle stage for development and crossed into the mature period. The market at this stage was becoming increasingly mature and culture was likely to be the constraint of innovation development. Therefore we should lead the company to make more glorious achievements through effective culture remodeling.

3 Research Methods

3.1 Measures

This paper adopts the Denison Model of Organizational Culture (DMOC) to measure the company. After going through 20 years of research and practice, this model has been adopted by over 5,000 organizations around the world as an extremely influential measuring model for organizational culture measurement (Denison and Mishra 1995). DMOC includes 12 factors including corporate vision, strategic direction and so on (Denison 1996). This scale has displayed good reliability and validity in many organizational behavior study researches (Block 2003; Yilmaz and Ergun 2008). Considering the current situation of Limin, this research first of all invited experts for discussion and determined the completeness of dimensions and semantic clarity; secondly, a small-scale group filled out the form as a trial so that the sentences with ambiguity could be revised. Finally, the measurement scale was finalized and Likert 5 point scoring method was adopted.

3.2 Sample

The questionnaire was conducted on middle managers, grass-roots managers and some staffs selected by stratified sampling. Altogether 185 questionnaires were handed out and 185 questionnaires were collected back. The composition of the samples for the questionnaire is listed in Table 1.

Table 1. Descriptive statistics

Category	Content	Percentage	Category	Content	Percentage
Gender	Male	77.2	Degree	Below high school	17.7
	Female	22.8		High school	34.5
Age	Under 25	5.2		College and above	47.8
	26–30	51.0	Position	Middle managers	11.6
	31–35	24.6		Grass-roots managers	14.6
	36–45	19.0		Technicians	12.3
	Above 45	0.2		Other staffs	61.5

4   Results

4.1   General Analysis of the Cultural Diagnosis

According to the revised measurement scale and the Likert five-point scoring method with one point representing 20 points, the average score for each dimension is calculated to reflect the general description of current culture of the company. The result is shown in Fig. 1.

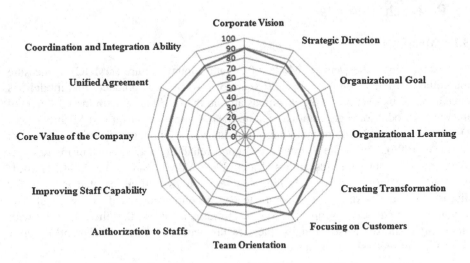

Fig. 1. General description of Limin's current Culture

Figure 1 has clearly reflected the perception of all Limin's staffs on its enterprise culture. In addition to "team orientation" and "improving staff capabilities" have got lower scores of 69.29 points and 69.45 points respectively, the score for the other dimensions is all above 70 points. The highest score is "focusing on customers" with 92.18 points. It can be seen that the company attaches great importance to customer demand.

4.2   Corporate Vision

From the survey result, it can be seen that most employees highly identify with the corporate vision with 89.36 points for this dimension. On the operation management meetings, the Board Chairman of Limin stressed for many times the corporate vision of "recruiting talents, establishing systems, creating profits, benefiting staffs, and giving back to the society". The Board Chairman also expressed for many times the strong emphasis on the interests of staffs and the corporate concept of integrating corporate benefits with customer and staff benefits. The company further prompts all staffs to work toward one goal through sharing the future vision with all staffs. This dimension is usually the weak point of a company, but due to the special growth track for Limin, the company and the staffs pull through the difficult period and grow up together and staffs have full confidence in the future of Limin.

4.3   Strategic Direction

In this dimension, the whole company has displayed a strong sense of recognition with 84.23 points. Since the company is a family enterprise, the top managers are consistent and stable. Therefore the corporate strategies can be carried out and put in place continuously. Having once pulled through the difficult period together with the company, the staffs have a strong sense of belonging. The company has also kept its promise especially in terms of performance-based reward. All departments are consistent in terms of new product R&D, talent introduction, satisfying the customer demand, and the improvement in product technology and quality and strive to realize the corporate strategic goals. Although some of the middle managers and grass-roots managers have been changed, the cultural recognition dimension of the company has not been affected due to the continuity and stability of the high-level policy implementation.

4.4   Organizational Ultimate Goal

Through the trainings organized by the enterprise, the leaders continuously convey the organizational objectives and ultimate goal of "product is the life of a company" and convert the goal into the production habits in the daily operation of staffs, including compliance with the operation standard in the production procedure and strict quality assurance. However, Limin used to be a State-owned Enterprise which went bankrupt and changed products after reform, so the egalitarianism concept has not been shifted completely. So in this dimension, the score of 74.86 points has some gap from the corporate expectation and is quite low compared with the other dimensions. In the future, the company will need to work harder on this dimension and constantly establishes the ultimate goal of "focusing on quality, improving efficiency, cultivating responsibility, studying and innovating" for staffs.

4.5 Organizational Learning

Organizational learning is the process of creating, retaining, and transferring knowledge within an organization, which will help an organization increase production efficiency, gain experience, improve the innovation capability on product, technology and management (Argote and Miron-Spektor 2011; Huber 1991). Limin has got 77.84 points for this dimension. However, in the survey, it can be found that the company attaches great importance to the technical training, but the directors rarely receive cross-position and cross-department training of multiple skills, damaging their work enthusiasm and adaptability, the optimization of corporate structure and the selection of excellent talents. In the future, the company should stress various trainings, increase exchanges in experience among colleagues, offer to share technology and resources, pull through the difficulties, and try to set up a learning organization.

4.6 Creating Transformation

In 2004, Limin was transformed into a private enterprise from a state-owned one, removed or consolidated the original functional departments, established five departments and one office while adopting a flat management style; fully implemented the position wage system linked with performance; and vigorously increased profit while cutting cost and streamlining the company. After these measures were adopted, the company had generally recognized the results of the reform. The company has got 77.57 points on average in this dimension. It is discovered from the survey that the Production Department can take preventative measures against a series of problems that affect the production tasks to guarantee the smooth production process. However, as for the clients' dissatisfaction, the company is less enthusiastic and sometimes shirks responsibilities. In the future, the company should offer to serve customers and be courageous in taking responsibilities.

4.7 Focusing on Customers

This company has a strong tendency toward meeting the demand of customers with 92.18 points for this dimension. The functional departments as well as the Production Department all focus on customer demand. This culture characteristic has been apparently shown in the concept of staffs in all departments. This company generally attaches great importance to staff training and is willing to invest a lot of time and money to let staffs constantly improve themselves and produce high-quality products efficiently and continuously. In addition, to meet the demand of customers, Limin has improved the small-scale production capability to provide high-quality, pollution and hazard-free products with a short delivery period. In addition to publicity and sales of products, the salesmen of the company also have another important function to understand the product demands of customers. The salesmen would timely communicate with the R&D Department to timely and rapidly develop products that can really meet the customer demands. To meet the needs of customers has become an indisputable rule for Limin. Due to this value, in this environment with fierce competition, businesses of Limin have continuously grown rather than shrunk.

4.8   Team Orientation

The team cooperation inside Limin leaves much to be desired because the company has only got 69.29 points for this dimension. According to the survey, under the encouragement of managers, various departments can closely cooperate with one another, but when emergencies have gone, they would come back to work independently. The organizational structure of Limin is divided according to functions. In particular, the offices under Department of Market and Department of Technology serve different customers. They just finish their own job targets and rarely cooperate with the other departments. In addition, due to the performance-based evaluation system, staffs don't like to communicate with each other in experience. So in the future, Limin should also step up efforts in strengthening the team orientation and stress the performance of a group or team and team learning. There are still such problems as impeded communication, unclear rights and obligations and shirking responsibilities in the cooperation between departments and these are the work priorities in the following cultural remolding.

4.9   Authorization to Staffs

The so-called authorization is to give corresponding rights and responsibilities to a department or a staff to boost their subjective motivation and realize the goal of the corporate objectives. The company has got 79.32 in this dimension. Limin really trusts the frontline production staffs. It is willing to authorize the staffs to formulate operation norms and standards; in addition, high-level managers and department directors are good at praising lower-level managers and staffs who take the initiative to work hard and carefully. This effectively cultivates the ability of the managers to solve problems and improve their executive forces. However, we have discovered that staffs are still not so active in improving their work on their own, which requires Limin Chemical Co., Ltd. to continue to strengthen training and study and improve staff quality in the following development to improve their responsibility and sense of ownership.

4.10   Improving Staff Capability

There are four means to improve staff capability: training, evaluation, work experience and interpersonal relationship (Zhang 2003). Limin has got a low score in this dimension with only 69.45 points. Although the company attaches great importance to the training of staffs, since there are fewer opportunities of work shift, staffs can hardly acquire work experience in the other posts. Most managers or directors have been working in one department. Only when there is a vacancy will one appropriate person be dispatched to fill the vacant post. However, new problems emerge. The new staffs have not received any training on the skills and knowledge of the new post, so it takes quite a period for them to adapt to the new post after many frictions. This has to some degree reduced the work efficiency of the company. At the same time, it has also reduced the staffs' work satisfaction. Rarely can feedbacks be provided in terms of others' behaviors, communication means and skill levels inside the company, between the superiors and the subordinates or among staffs, so staffs are not aware of their advantages and disadvantages. In addition, in the real production, many masters are reluctant to teach their skills and as a result the apprentices' ability cannot be improved. In the future, the company should try to strengthen the training of multiple skills and promote exchanges and study to cultivate the core competitiveness and innovation capability for the company.

4.11   Core Value of the Company

It takes a long time to form the core value of the company. It requires the leaders to advocate the value with the trust of staffs. Also the core value should be implemented thoroughly. After observation of this company, it can be discovered that the down-to-earth attitude, the guidance of meeting customer demand and mutual assistance among colleagues are the value advocated by the company. Under the persistent and steady advocate and insistence by the core leaders, the core value has been well implemented inside the company and become accepted corporate culture by staffs. The company has got a high score of 81.02 points for this dimension. However, how to maintain the communication between superiors and subordinates and effectively transfer the core value of the company are still the priorities for the future cultural remolding at Limin.

4.12   Unified Agreement

Since the company has sound policies for reward and punishment, strong cohesion, and the high degree of reliance and compliance by staffs to superiors, all members inside the company strictly abide by the regulations of the enterprise. The company has got 80.42 points in this dimension. The superiors have a high degree of authority. As long as superiors assign some tasks and give some requirement, the grass-roots staffs would usually follow the instructions and try to accomplish the task. However, another defect emerges. After the change of high-level leaders, will their charm sustain? In addition, the relevant regulations of the company leave much to be desired in the future.

4.13   Coordination and Integration Ability

Since the high-level leaders of the company are quite stable, the policy implementation has been smooth. The company has got a high score of 82.47 points for this dimension. Staffs trust their superiors who also keep their promises. Therefore, for the tasks assigned by the superiors, staffs would take the initiative to finish them wholeheartedly. After long-time implementation, the executive power of the company would become very strong. Compliance with the coordination and integration of the company has become the basic value of staffs.

5 Discussions

The 1990s is a transformation period for the Chinese economy from the planned economy seriously influenced by ideology to the market economy governed by the economic rules. The enterprise community is also experiencing pains and reforms. Limin began to shift to the market economy at this moment. It has embarked on a hopeful path from the initial purpose of having jobs to do and working for subsistence to becoming the leader in China's national pesticide industry. The phenomenon of Limin is a miniature for China's SME development.

This paper analyzes the corporate culture in a deep manner, considers the reality of Limin, and selects DMOC model to measure the present cultural status of Limin. The measurement result shows that in these twenty years of development, the vision for the enterprise to become stronger and the strategic goals have already enjoyed popular support from staffs; Limin has made some achievements in strategy implementation, policy execution, coordination and integration. However, team study, improving staffs' ability and cohesion building leave much to be desired urgently.

In the future, the company should strengthen the transfer of corporate strategy, prioritize staff training, specially strengthen experience exchanges among departments and colleagues, step up communications, share resources, improve staffs' quality and sense of responsibility, and try to set up a learning organization to improve the corporate culture building and the core competitiveness of the company.

Cultural measurement and evaluation are an important step in enterprise development (Schein 2006; Wang and Zhou 2002). Through Denison's DMOC scale, the paper provides a set of scientific analysis thinking methods for corporate culture; secondly, through systematically analyzing the advantages and disadvantages of Limin culture, the paper finds out the footing for cultural improvement to provide experience for the future corporate culture measurement. The defect of this paper is that it only studies the corporate cultural characteristics of one private enterprise after successful reform, so the sample is not diversified. In the future, more industries and cases are waiting to be explored to probe into the cultural characteristics of enterprises after successful reform to help more private SMEs to become successful.

Acknowledgments. This work has been supported by grants from the National Natural Foundation of China (Project Number 71421061, 71121001).

References

Argote, L., Miron-Spektor, E.: Organizational learning: from experience to knowledge. Organ. Sci. **5**, 1123–1137 (2011)

Block, L.: The leadership-culture connection: an exploratory investigation. Leadersh. Organ. Dev. J. **6**, 318–334 (2003)

Chen, Q.: "Culture" governs the world – the fortune 500 that hold high the banner of "culture governing the enterprise". Chin. Foreign Corp. Cult., **4**, 39–40 (2005) (in Chinese)

Denison, D.R.: What is the difference between organizational culture and organizational climate? A native's point of view on a decade of paradigm wars. Acad. Manag. Rev. **3**, 619–654 (1996)

Denison, D.R., Mishra, A.K.: Toward a theory of organizational culture and effectiveness. Organ. Sci. **2**, 204–223 (1995)

Huber, G.P.: Organizational learning: the contributing processes and the literatures. Organ. Sci. **1**, 88–115 (1991)

Kotter, J.P., Heskett, J.L.: Corporate Culture and Performance. China Renmin University Press, Beijing (2004) (in Chinese)

Schein, E.H.: Diagnosis and Reform of Organization Culture. China Renmin University Press, Beijing (2006) (in Chinese)

Wang, C., Zhou, J.: Corporate Cultural Studies. Economy & Management Publishing House, Beijing (2002) (in Chinese)

William, O.: Z Theory. China Social Sciences Publishing House, Beijing (1984) (in Chinese)

Yilmaz, C., Ergun, E.: Organizational culture and firm effectiveness: an examination of relative effects of culture traits and the balanced culture hypothesis in an emerging economy. J. World Bus. **3**, 290–306 (2008)

Zhang, D.: Corporate Culture Building. Tsinghua University Press, Beijing (2003) (in Chinese)

When Human-Centered Design Meets Social Innovation: The Idea of Meaning Making Revisited

Jin Ma[✉]

College of Design and Innovation, Tongji University, Fu-Xin Road 281,
Shanghai 200092, China
majin.poly@gmail.com

Abstract. Facing the challenges of sustainability, while design is seeking to play an important role in social innovation, human-centered design (HCD)—one of the most important philosophies of design—somehow appears to be fading out of the major research agenda. Based on a review of the limitations of HCD, this paper looks into the capability of the theoretical underpinning of HCD to support its potential development in social innovation from two aspects: (1) the connection between human-centeredness and the social dimension; (2) emancipating HCD from the asserted limitation of its role in innovation. The phenomenological perspective is used to support and broaden the worldview of HCD. Built upon this, the idea of meaning making is revisited to account for both questions. In addition, a preliminary framework of meaning making is proposed as a HCD tool that aims to facilitate the complex interaction in social innovation. It is argued that design as meaning making with a combined interest in exploring human experience will open up new opportunities for HCD.

Keywords: Meaning · Human-centered design · Social innovation · Phenomenological perspective · Hermeneutic spiral

1 Introduction

Ancient Greek philosopher Protagoras once said: "Man is the measure of all things." This ethos is implicitly or explicitly practiced by designers and culminates in human-centered design (HCD) practice. Facing the challenges of sustainability, however, while design is seeking to play an important role in social innovation, HCD—one of the most important philosophies of design—somehow appears to be fading out of the major research agenda.

This paper begins with a review of the limitations of HCD, particularly situated in the sustainable context where the movement of social innovation grows as an important response to sustainability challenges. Based on this review, the capability of the theoretical underpinning of HCD to support its potential development in social innovation is investigated from two aspects: (1) the connection between human-centeredness and the social dimension; (2) emancipating HCD from the asserted limitation of its role in innovation. The phenomenological perspective is used to support and broaden the worldview of HCD. Built upon this, the idea of meaning making is revisited to account

P.L.P. Rau (Ed.): CCD 2015, Part I, LNCS 9180, pp. 349–360, 2015.
DOI: 10.1007/978-3-319-20907-4_32

for both questions. At the end of the paper, a preliminary framework of meaning making is proposed as a HCD tool that aims to facilitate the complex interaction in social innovation.

2 Challenges to Human-Centered Design

According to Don Norman, HCD involves a range of methods that bear "a common framework: an iterative cycle of investigation—usually characterized by observations, an ideation phase, and rapid prototype and testing [1]," and this framework hinges on the understanding of the needs, desires, and limitations of end users of the product. HCD is a value-laden approach that has great impact on design as a means of humanizing technology by placing products in their situations of use. It points our attention to "the experience that human beings have of products—how they interact with products and how they use products as a mediating influence in their interactions with other people and their social and natural environments [2]." HCD is, however, facing increasing challenges toward its underpinning worldview, its emphasis on the notion of 'end user' that has been blurred by people's participation in design, its methods and process controlled by design professionals; and its role in design innovation.

2.1 Anthropocentric Worldview Vs. Sustainability

Although the far-sighted understanding about HCD sees products as the mediation of the interaction between people and that between people and the social and natural worlds, the emphasis on human needs and aspirations has been long overriding the care for the relationship between human beings and the world. Designers used to indulge in an anthropocentric worldview. Without seeing human beings as part of the natural, social, and economic eco-system, HCD approaches such as the "useful, usable, and desirable" principle [2] are used to stimulate endless human wants and material consumption beyond what this planet can offer.

The idea that the resources on this planet are limited was not relevant forty years ago when Victor Papanek first published his provocative book *Design for the Real World* [3] but has become a burning issue facing humanity today. Advancements in science and industry achieved in modernity have fostered Western resource-intensive consumption pattern and lifestyles that are deeply grounded on material beliefs [4]. The predominating pattern of design encourages and in turn benefits from consumerism, which speeds up the exploitative economic growth. HCD to a certain extent legitimates this circle. As a result, the current rate of production and consumption simply cannot be sustained and thus gives rise to severe environmental and social-economic ramifications. It is further expanded through globalization.

When sustainability becomes the proposition of this time, human needs that should be addressed by design have changed. The mission of HCD today is shifting beyond satisfying individual human beings' endless desires at the cost of exploitive consumption of resources. For the humanity to survive and prosper, it is necessary to move beyond the anthropocentric view of HCD. We have to ask, in which context a product is useful, usable, and desirable?

2.2 Human-Centered Design Vs. Participatory Design

HCD and participatory design [5, 6] share a fundamental emphasis on people, i.e., getting close to people and observing and analyzing their needs, but diverge at the point where the idea of "user" is delimited. For traditional HCD, users are treated as either the object or the context of design, and then absorbed into the design process as the passive information carriers for designers to dig out opportunities, collecting data, recruiting feedback to evaluate the proposed solution prototypes [7]. In vivid contract, participatory design emphasizes the need to rethink the roles of the participants, especially those who are known as users and to include users as active actors of design [8, 9]. The increasing practice of including people's participation across various stages of the design process has an impact on the conventional HCD process. The later replacement of the term "user-centered design" by "human-centered design" reflects such an impact, which renders the activity of design a democratic sense. However the conventional HCD practice remains rather conservative in terms of social inclusion.

2.3 Conventional Framework of Design Vs. Social Innovation

Design is shifting its attention from physical products design, firmly rooted in mass production rationalized for efficiency, to system design that is related to new ideas and values. For example, cities that used to be part of developed industrialized economy are suffering from long-term economic stagnation, unemployment, and the problems of aging population due to globalization and the local industrial transition. Problems of such a vast scale and complexity—sustainability, economies, politics, and overall social well-being—would not be regarded as design problems decades ago but now become burning issues, in which design is actively engaged.

While sustainability is becoming a value of necessity for the humanity to sustain, social innovation emerges as an alternative approach to address the environmental, social, and economic challenges [10]. Design for social innovation can be seen as social-purpose directed participatory design with a sustainable goal. To play an active role in social innovation, design now is seeking alternative patterns to facilitate the rich interactions inherent in the open process. However, HCD, the once prevailing design approach, is vanishing from this agenda. A significant reason rests upon the incompatibility between HCD's typical iterative investigation process controlled by professional designers and social innovation's more open and flexible process that engages various flows of active roles of designing.

The challenge to HCD's flexibility in adapting to this open and dynamic frame is great. Social innovation involves three kinds of possible processes: top-down, bottom-up, and hybrid [11]. Design culture (including the process, core competencies, knowledge, technologies, behaviors, values, dogmas) [12] burgeons from inside-out or outside-in the community, or in a combined way of the two. When design becomes "a constellation of initiatives geared toward making social innovation more probable, effective, long-lasting, and apt to spread [11]," the process is characterized by people's rotating role of designing through various phases of the process, no matter they are from inside or outside of the community. The complexity of human interaction radically grows; the boundaries between designers, users and stakeholders are blurred; the design process opens up and is no longer an iterative prototyping process neatly controlled by the designer. This shift impels the designer to work on innovation projects actively, for the frame of 'Design' is no longer given.

2.4   Incremental Improvement Vs. Radical Innovation

The literature on innovation studies divides innovation into two categories: incremental and radical. The former denotes local optimization—"improvements within a given frame of solutions"; and the latter "a change of frame." HCD is regarded as a typical approach to incremental innovation capable of enhancing the quality and value of the product in the current domain; but is claimed to have little position in radical innovation—to innovate by introducing new domains and new frames [1, 13]. Given the focus on user needs, HCD (or UCD) is believed to "be pulled by user requirements or observation [13]." A key argument for this statement is, users' interpretations are merely in line with what is happening today, how could the existing allow the designer to leap into solutions for the future? HCD tends to be seen as grounded on research in marketing, consumer behaviors, and anthropology of consumption. For example, Verganti relates market-pull (or equivalently termed as user-centered) strategy to the incremental improvement among other innovation strategies. In parallel to this view, Don Norman also illustrates HCD as a form of hill-climbing only suited for incremental innovation and having no way of informing the climber of where even higher hills might locate [1]. Hence, the repeating and testing until satisfied process is extracted as the hallmark of HCD. It further reinforces this one-sided role of HCD in innovation. In contrast with HCD's capability in incremental improvement, radical innovation is generally believed to be driven either by technology changes or by meaning changes. Apparently, in this view HCD is alienated from meaning-driven innovation.

The review of the current understanding of HCD addresses two aspects: the underlying worldview and the methods and process of HCD. The implicit anthropocentric worldview is revealed by contrasting prevailing HCD practice to the backdrop of sustainability. The iterative, well-structured design process that is predominantly controlled by the designer is challenged by the growing participation of people. Social innovation provides an even dynamic arena, which leaves little place for HCD that does not readily accommodate people's changing role of designing, the design process opened up, and complex human interactions outside of any given frame.

Given the limitations, it is pertinent to ask, is there still any possibility to develop HCD for system design as complex as social innovation? This review brings the focus of my inquiry to the potential capability of the theoretical underpinning of HCD. It can be further phrased as: (1) Is it simply impossible to grasp the big (e.g. environmental, social, and economic) context of design if individual human being is placed at the centered of design inquiry? (2) Is there any perspective that is able to open up new opportunities of HCD's role in innovation? These questions will be address through the phenomenological perspective and the idea of meaning making.

3 The Phenomenological Perspective

Phenomenology is helpful in its attitude toward the relationship between individual human being's sphere and the social sphere. According to Sokolowski, "phenomenology is the study of human experience and the ways things present themselves to us in and through such experience [14]." "Things" means everything in the world and therefore includes objects, people, environments, and activities. That is to say, even if human being's experience is personal and idiosyncratic, there is still a public realm of experience, where personal sphere is connected with the social sphere.

To understand this stance, several fundamental conceptions in phenomenology are important. First, all consciousness is consciousness "of" something. Therefore, the mind is always directed outward. In phenomenology, mind and body, subject and object of experience are united. Second, anything that is experienced is inseparable from the way it is experienced. "I" see the world through the relationship between the world and "I." Third, based on these two, our life of perception, reasoning, and knowing share a common basis, because our mind is not locked in an individual body and is not merely directing individual actions. It is possible to understand the other's experience by understanding self's experience. There is a public realm of experience, because each individual shares this fundamental relation between the world and "I" in common; and because it is the same world that we live in and interact with [15].

Therefore, there is nothing wrong with placing human at the center of understanding and designing the world, because our being in the world serves as a fundamental vehicle for us to understand the world.

The public realm of experience is where empathy comes in. Take the development of empathic design for example. Empathic design first began as the interpretive exercise of users' emotions, then moved from user-centered approach toward the co-design process centering around the concept of empathy, and is now taking an artistic and expressive turn to include empathy in design imagination [16]. This trajectory of empathic design mirrors the growth of HCD because the former is built on a long history of HCD [16]. The biggest challenge to empathic design is what HCD is facing too—how to adapt the established process and tools to design for networks and organizations that deliver services; how to expand the methods and politics to incorporate design that occurs in large systems and communities. In short, the challenge is to develop appropriate approaches to link personal-sphere based design inquiry with the processes, and methods needed by design at a social scale.

4 Meaning Making Revisited

There is a small yet increasing body of discussion on the notion of meaning in design research. Klaus Krippendorff's proposition that "design is making sense (of things) [17] " signals a meaning turn in describing the nature of design. Following this inspirational definition, design is viewed as a form of meaning making [18, 19]. Nevertheless, meaning is a word that has many meanings, whose origins can be traced back to a wide range of domains, varying from psychology to linguistics.

While Verganti addresses radical innovation driven by changes in meaning, meaning is seen as a set of emotional and symbolic values that triggers users' personal and sociocultural needs. For example, "designers give meaning to products by using a specific design *language*—that is, the set of signs, symbols, and icons (of which style is just an example) that delivers the message [13]." However, this is just one way of understanding meaning and it is symbolic (i.e., the to-be conveyed value is extracted as physical signs and symbols, and the interpretive process of meaning making is totally overlooked). To investigate whether HCD has possibilities to create significant meanings that lead to radical innovation, it would be useful to examine the notion of "meaning" and its various origins and doctrines that are influential to, or in, design.

4.1 Distinct Origins of "Meaning"

The underlying stances behind the varied understandings about meaning are described as follows.

A major strand of design studies on meaning is built upon conventional semiotics, which studies meanings *in* objects. Meaning is used "as if it were independent entity that could be attached to objects or contained in containers. [20] " Thus, it is not a coincidence that designers and design researchers, influenced by this stance, tend to turn meanings into attached properties, qualities, or attributes of things. By doing so, things do not stand in their own right, but are deprived of their original existences and extracted as *meaningful* symbols or signs. Verganti's conception of meaning is rooted in this tradition.

Cognitive Science treats human cognition as a mental process in terms of knowing, learning, and understanding. Meaning, as the product of such a process, is defined as "a thought induced in the receiver, which is originated by the contact with a design [product]. [18] " As opposed to one extreme that design is seen as artifact-centered, this view tends to ascribe the foundation of design to the faculty of the mind. In this approach, the mental process is often taken to be the entirety of a design experience.

According to Blumer's critique, meaning in its conventional psychological and sociological sense is either: (i) bypassed by merely focusing on the initiating factors (e.g. stimuli, attitudes, motives, cognition in psychology; social position, status demands, social roles, and values in sociology) and on resulting human behaviors; or (ii) is regarded as an unimportant link between the two ends and is swallowed by the initiating factors [21]. In this way, meaning is either deemed as an intrinsic part of the thing and therefore any process involved in its formation is denied; or is regarded as an expression of the elements of a person's mind (e.g. sensations, feelings, ideas, memories, motives, and attitudes), which are lodged in the psychological processes of coalescence of these elements in a person. This stance resonates with the aforementioned definitions—in conventional semiotics and cognitive science—of meaning as either attributes in objects or as mental constructions.

Meanings, in the context of symbolic interactionism, are seen as social products that arise in the process of interaction between people; instead of being established entities, meaning involves an interpretive process in its formation and it in turn shapes human action. Herbert Blumer maintains that: (i) meanings are the basis on which human beings act toward these things; (ii) the source of meanings is the process of interaction between people; and hence (iii) meanings are engaged in an interpretive process by the person who is interacting with the encountered things [21]. Symbolic interactionism provides an important perspective to contemporary interaction design.

Product semantics focuses on the communicative function of product, i.e., "what user expects the object to do [22]." In this doctrine meaning is defined as "a cognitively constructed relationship. It selectively connects features of an object and features of its (real environment or imagined) context into a coherent unity [22]." While greatly enabling designers to communicate their design intentions, the theory of product semantics, however, carries some inconsistencies in its stance toward meaning. On the one hand, it maintains that meaning is not fixed and that making sense goes around a hermeneutic circle; on the other hand, product semantics neglects personal process of meaning making, because human experience, in this approach, is viewed unable to be shared for its subjectiveness. As a result, meaning adopted in semantic theory tends to be oversimplified, as it does not account for how the object points to meaning that it "simultaneously contains and conceals [23]."

Different lines of inquiry into human experience (e.g. Dewey's analysis of the structure of an experience [24] and Polanyi and Prosh's theory on tacit knowledge [25]) indicate that meaning is related to thinking, reflecting, understanding, and knowing, and that the substrate of the meaning making process is human experience. There is an emerging body of research on experiential knowledge in the recent decade [26]. Informed by seeing experience as the basis of knowing and regarding human experience as an organic unity, meaning examined in this area carries more dynamic features of knowledge-in-action. A very important insight is: inquiry into meaning needs to restore meaning into the rich relations contained in human experience. However, one of the challenges facing this area is how to link the personal dimension to the public space so as to allow the socially relational dimensions to be revealed.

To expand the understanding of meaning by exploring the tacit and embodied dimensions of design also becomes a growing focus in phenomenological studies. For example, in order to facilitate designers to articulate more about their experiences, Jin Ma maintains that meaning provides a relational perspective, revealing both particular aspects of the world and the designer's judgments, feelings, attitudes, actions, and understandings through a hermeneutic circle [15]. Figure 1 illustrates how individual

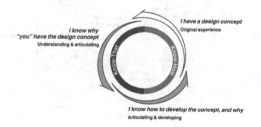

Fig. 1. The hermeneutical circle in having a design concept. (Copyright © 2013 Jin Ma)

experience can be broadened into a public dimension: meaning could be a product of co-creation arising from the interplay between constructing and reconstructing. Located in the business and social context, Marcus Jahnke develops an understanding of the contribution of design practice to innovation from the hermeneutic perspective [27]. Jahnke's study supports the idea that meaning making sits at the heart of innovation involving multi-disciplinary engagement beyond both the individual and the designerly spheres.

4.2   Positioning the Underpinning Domains of Various Conceptions of Meaning

Different studies on meaning are positioned in Fig. 2, in terms of the stances of inquiring into meaning from inside or from outside of individual experience, and approaches that focus on relations (holistic) or elements (analytic) [15]. Based on this map, relations and distinctions between the discussed research areas on meaning are further clarified. Obviously, in comparison with the other three quadrants, the upper right corner of the map remains loosely occupied. There is a limited body of studies on meaning, which is based on the structure of human experience and focuses on relations rather than elements. Especially the explorations of relations that bridge personal and social facets of meaning are scanty now.

4.3   Insights

Mapping out the landscape of studies on meaning allows us to notice the convergence of the relational nature of meaning and the personal, experience-based starting point where meaning arises. This is the area that is compatible with the ethos of HCD and may potentially bring in new dimensions to its traditional design approach.

Norman and Verganti are right in saying that meaning has not been well studied as an approach to innovation. However, their observation is flawed in that they overlooked the rich relationaility that meaning may provide when grounded on the exploration of the relational structure of human experience, and in that they did not see

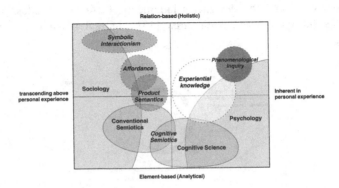

Fig. 2. The remapped landscape of research areas on meaning. (Copyright © 2014 Jin Ma)

that meaning making is an interpretative process from where new meaning may arise (e.g., it is claimed that "customers hardly help in understanding possible radical changes in product meanings as they are immersed in a sociocultural context that leads them to interpretations that are in line with what is happening today" [13]).

Meaning making involves a hermeneutic circle, or more precisely, a hermeneutic spiral [28], which intrinsically is open to something new. According to Janke's analysis on Ricoeur's critical hermeneutics, hermeneutic spiral opens up to "the 'excess of meaning' of the world, rather than locking meaning to established history and tradition;" and "'distancing' is viewed as a prerequisite for interpretation [28]." In parallel, Ma's study indicates that an experience of making sense of a design concept begins in "wonder," which presents surprisingly related things in juxtaposition to the designing person and implies the potential inclusion of the unknown. This also echoes the suggestion of Buchanan, that experience and environment are places where continuous reconstruction happens, which integrates the pluralism of past life and future possibilities in the moving present [29]. In a nutshell, grounding meaning making on human experience enables us to move beyond the claimed predicament of HCD by virtue of the fusion between the known and the unknown where new meaning emerges.

5   A Preliminary Conception on the Framework of Meaning Making

For a framework of meaning making that combines HCD with design for social innovation, two issues are considered: (1) whether the interaction between personal and social dimensions can be grasped; (2) in which way HCD can be integrated into the framework and opened up for more relational and dynamic process and social innovation. The studies on meaning with an experiential turn serves as an opener for this ongoing inquiry for its capability in accounting for both issues. They look into meaning from a holistic view and consider the human-world interactive process of meaning making process as an indispensible part of meaning study. These relationality-focused and experience-based studies provide a good starting point for seeking a way of capturing the rich meanings arising from where HCD and social innovation meets. The following is a brief description about a preliminary conception of such a framework.

While exploring the bottom line of sustainability, Stuart Walker proposes three levels of meaning: practical, social, and personal [4]. These three denote our responses respectively to environment, to other people, and to our inner self. Each level is rooted in various worldviews including modernity, postmodernity, and traditional. They together comprise a meaningful whole when sustainability issues are under considerations. This proposition nicely bridges the personal and social dimensions and links them to the world where sustainability matters occur.

Dewey in his analysis of the structure of an experience identifies three intertwining layers of an experience: practical, emotional, and intellectual, although they interdependently constitute a unity. The practical layer refers to the doing phase of an experience; the emotional refers to the undergoing phase; and the intellectual "simply names the fact that the experience has meaning [24]." Inspired by Dewey's insights,

	Practical (Environment)	Social (Community/Organization)	Personal (Self)
Knowledge	*Natural* *Societal* *Economic* *Political*	*Sociocultural* *Organizational* ...	*Tacit* *Experiential* ...
Process	*Creating business model* ...	*Building the network* *Changing the organization* ...	*Turning self into a member of the community* ...
Value(s)	*New local livelihoods* *Less deterioration of land* ...	*Better care for the aging* *Local economic revival* ...	*Self-Actualization* *Spiritual growth & Wisdom* ...

Fig. 3. Meaning Making Matrix as a HCD tool to facilitate the interaction in social innovation

I propose the process, value(s), and knowledge as three dimensions that describe the experience of design for social innovation.

The preliminary framework of meaning making is a matrix of the environmental, social, and personal aspects of meaning and the knowledge, process, and value(s) of the experience of design (see Fig. 3). By environment, here it means not only the natural world, but the surroundings/conditions, both natural and artificial, that enable the aimed changes to occur. Moreover, this Meaning Making Matrix (MMM) is intended to be used by individual persons, who are playing distinct roles in the design initiative of social innovation, as a way of articulating, reflecting, and understanding meanings arising from their own experiences in the process of social innovation. It is a tool that would facilitate the interaction between different people engaged in the process seeking a more synergistic relationship. Therefore it is fundamentally a HCD tool that allows individual participants (including designers, people from the community, or stakeholders) to voice out the meanings derived from their experiences. In particular, these meanings will by no means be limited to either personal or sociocultural sphere, and the interaction between different MMMs will introduce new meanings as well as new rounds of interpretive process.

As part of an ongoing study, the MMM requires further consolidation, modification, and evaluation through insights from concrete cases. Practical knowledge may be related to natural, societal, economic, and political environments; social knowledge may include sociological and cultural knowledge, and organizational change; personal knowledge refers to tacit knowledge or life/work experiential knowledge of that very person. Practical process (for example, if it is the designer who is using MMM) may create the business model that energizes the local resources; social process may engage people and stakeholders into a synergetic network; and personal process may include how the designer turns him/herself from the outsider into the insider of the community and brings in design culture to the community, etc. The contents of MMM vary from person to person, role to role, and case to case, especially the values. To be a usable and useful tool, relevant hermeneutic sub-categories within the matrix need to be further identified and modified.

6 Concluding Remarks

Sotamaa advocates in *The Kyoto Design Declaration*: "human-centered design thinking, when rooted in universal and sustainable principles, has the power to fundamentally improve our world. It can deliver economic, ecological, social and cultural benefits to all people, improve our quality of life and create optimism about the future and individual and shared happiness [30]." Design begins to play an active role in facilitating and enabling social innovation, in a way that is significantly different from how it contributes to consumerism culture within the traditional organizational structure and managing process. While design shifts its mission from satisfying human needs rooted in the unsustainable pattern to meeting needs of humanity for a sustainable future, conventional HCD needs to be reenergized with a consistent approach.

Seeing human beings as the measure of the artificially shaped world is still a vital perspective, however, a new set of graduations capable of capturing the previously glossed over dimensions of the world needs to be developed. Design as meaning making with a combined interest in exploring human experience will serve as an opener to address this task. The framework of meaning making proposed here is a preliminary step of an ongoing inquiry. It aims to be a tool for different roles engaged in design for social innovation to understand and to articulate their experiences, and therefore to facilitate people's interactions. This tool will open up new opportunities for HCD when situated in the contemporary sustainable challenges.

References

1. Norman, D.A., Verganti, R.: Incremental and radical innovation: design research vs technology and meaning change. Des. Issues **30**(1), 78–96 (2014)
2. Buchanan, R.: Design research and the new learning. Des. Issues **17**(4), 3–23 (2001)
3. Papanek, V.J.: Design for the Real World: Human Ecology and Social Change. Paladin press, New York (1971)
4. Walker, S.: Design and spirituality: material culture for a wisdom economy. Des. Issues **29** (3), 89–107 (2013)
5. Binder, T., Brandt, E., Gregory, J.: Editorial: design participation(-s). CoDesign **4**(1), 1–3 (2008)
6. Sanders, E.B.-N., Stappers, P.J.: Co-creation and the new landscapes of design. CoDesign **4** (1), 5–18 (2008)
7. Ho, D.K., Ma, J., Lee, Y.: Empathy @ design research: a phenomenological study on young people experiencing participatory design for social inclusion. Co-Design **7**(2), 95–106 (2011)
8. Brereton, M., Buur, J.: New challenges for design participation in the era of ubiquitous computing. CoDesign **4**(2), 101–113 (2008)
9. Lee, Y., Cassim, J.: How the inclusive design process enables social inclusion. In: Proceedings of IASDR 2009 Conference, pp.1-10 (2009)
10. Morelli, N.: Social innovation and new industrial contexts: can designers "industrialize" socially responsible solutions? Des. Issues **23**(4), 3–21 (2007)
11. Manizini, E.: Making things happen: social innovation and design. Des. Issues **30**(1), 57–66 (2014)

12. Deserti, A., Rizzo, F.: Co-designing with companies. In: Proceedings of IASDR2011 4th World Conference on Design Research, pp. 1–12, TU-Delft, Delft (2011), 1-12. (Cited in Deserti, A., Rizzo, F.: Design and the Cultures of Enterprises. Design Issues 30(1), 36–56 (2014))

13. Verganti, R.: Design, meanings, and radical innovation: a metamodel and a research agenda. J. Prod. Innov. Manage 25, 436–456 (2008)

14. Sokolowski, R.: Introduction To Phenomenology. Cambridge University Press, New York (2000)

15. Ma, J.: A phenomenological inquiry into the experience of having a design concept. Mistra Urban Futures, Gothenburg (2003)

16. Mattelmäki, T., Vaajakallio, K., Koskinen, I.: What happened to empathic design. Des. Issues 30(1), 67–77 (2014)

17. Krippendorff, K.: On the essential contexts of artifacts or on the proposition that design is making sense (of things). Des. Issues 5(2), 9–38 (1989)

18. Kazmierczak, E.T.: Design as meaning making: from making things to the design of thinking. Des. Issues 19(2), 45–59 (2003)

19. Diller, S., Shedroff, N., Rhea, D.: Making Meaning: How Successful Businesses Deliver Meaningful Customer Experiences. New Riders, Berkley (2006)

20. Krippendorff, K., Butter, R.: Semantics: meanings and contexts of artifacts. In: Schifferstein, H.N.J., Hekkert, P. (eds.) Product Experience, pp. 353–376. Elsevier Science, Amsterdam; London (2008)

21. Blumer, H.: The nature of symbolic interactionism. In: Mortensen, C.D. (ed.) Basic Readings in Communication Theory, pp. 102–120. Harper & Row, New York (1979)

22. Krippendorff, K.: On the essential contexts of artifacts or on the proposition that design is making sense (of things). In: Margolin, V., Buchanan, R. (eds.) The Idea of Design, pp. 156–184. MIT Press, Cambridge (1995)

23. Folkmann, M.N.: Evaluating aesthetics in design: a phenomenological approach. Des. Issues 26(1), 40–53 (2010)

24. Dewey, J.: Art As Experience. Perigee Books, New York (1980). (Original work published 1934)

25. Polanyi, M.: Personal Knowledge: Towards A Post-Critical Philosophy. Routledge & Kegan Paul Ltd., London (1998). (Original work published 1958)

26. Niedderer, K., Reilly, L.: New knowledge in the creative disciplines. J. Vis. Art Pract. 6(2), 81–87 (2007)

27. Jahnke, M.: Meaning in the making: Introducing a hermeneutic perspective on the contribution of design practice to innovation. University of Gothenburg, Gothenburg (2013)

28. Janke, M.: Revisiting design as hermeneutic practice: an investigation of Paul Ricoeur's critical hermeneutics. Des. Issues 28(2), 30–40 (2012)

29. Buchanan, R.: Children of the moving present: the ecology of culture and the search for causes in design. Des. Issues 17(1), 67–84 (2001)

30. Sotamaa, Y.: The kyoto design declaration: building a sustainable future. Des. Issues 25(4), 51–53 (2009)

Design Process as Communication Agency for Value Co-Creation in Open Social Innovation Project:

A Case Study of QuYang Community in Shanghai

Dongjin Song[1]([⊠]), Susu Nousala[2,3], and Yongqi Lou[1]

[1] Tongji University, 281 FuXin Road, 200092 Shanghai, China
susan.sdj@gmail.com
[2] Aalto University, 135C Hameentie, 00560 Helsinki, Finland
[3] Wuhan University of Technology, 1040 Heping Road, Wuhan, China

Abstract. Within the context of social innovation, this paper, builds on the established principle of 'positive deviance'. The purpose of this approach was to identify design processes and tools that improved the communication within the QuYang Community, one case among many creative communities. In this practical context, the design process was conducted as the communication agency for decoding and recoding socio-space components as well as stimulating, externalizing, integrating and co-creating value in the creative elderly community. Open social innovation paradigm can be considered as one way to mitigate some of the risk associated with social innovation. Emerging "creative community [1] " cases were seen as the grounded dynamic laboratories for clarifying the emerging open social innovation paradigm.

Keywords: Open social innovation paradigm · Positive deviance approach · Design tools · Creative community

1 Introduction

Social innovation refers to innovative activities and services that are motivated by the goal of meeting a social need [2], which is considered as an approach to systemic change of the existing economic and social model. Social innovation has been gaining importance both in academic and practice arena in last ten years. However, most social innovative approaches are driven by enthusiasts and fail to achieve a wider impact [3]. To date, minimal research has been undertaken to explore the reasons for social innovation failure and how to minimize the risk of social innovation process.

From 2010, several scholars illustrated that the increasing "openness" paradigm of social innovation organizations could mitigate some of the risk associated with innovation [4, 5, 9–11]. Openness of social innovation paradigm also mentioned by Italian research literature, focuses on hybrid social innovation process (combining bottom-up

P.L.P. Rau (Ed.): CCD 2015, Part I, LNCS 9180, pp. 361–371, 2015.
DOI: 10.1007/978-3-319-20907-4_33

approach and top-down approach) and collaborative interaction among stakeholders [6, 14].

In this paper, the authors build on the established principle of 'positive deviance' proposing an approach of open social innovation paradigm in the real world context. Sternin (1990) used "positive deviance" to describe the approach which looked for solutions among individuals and families in the community who are already doing well, enabled others in this community to leverage these solutions across their local communities [7].

By analyzing one particular case (QuYang Community) and conducting a collaborative workshop with the community, the authors explored (1) How could we apply *positive deviance* approach to open social innovation paradigm. (2) How could design researchers take design process as the communication agency for decoding and recoding socio-space components as well as stimulating, externalizing, integrating and co-creating value in this creative elderly community?

1.1 QuYang Community: Challenges and Opportunities

In China, social and political reality is associated with a top-down decision making model, which is often believed to restrict citizen from participating in social reforms. At the same time, the awareness of community value and social connectedness, lost in recent years needs to be reconstructed.

In QuYang Community, a group of ordinary people positively tried to organize themselves to solve problems and enhanced their awareness of wellbeing in this local elderly community for four years. But related activities were mainly initiated and organized by the elderly people with frequently moving (e.g. moved out to live with children or passed away). Our challenges were not only using design process as communication agency to understand and duplicate such "positive deviance" but also enabling the new residents to recognize and appreciate the value of QuYang Community.

Meanwhile, QuYang Community is one example of "creative community" which triggered by the real context, initiated by individuals or communities instead of experts to make good use of the local resources and promotes new ways of social exchange. The "positive deviance" approach and design tools that used in QuYang Community could also widely benefit the other creative communities.

2   Open Social Innovation Paradigm and Positive Deviance Approach

2.1   Open Social Innovation Paradigm

Social innovation, as one form of innovation (commonly seen with high failure rate behavior) has had limited growth regarding model development within the academic field after the Rome Club report in 1972 [8]. Chalmers (2011) draws from several empirical studies on social innovation and wider conceptual literature to identify common barriers of social innovation: market protectionism, risk aversion, problem complexity, access to networks and access to finance.

With the rediscovery of social innovation trends, social innovation moved from margins to the mainstream (The Young Foundation, 2009). From 2010, several scholars illustrated that the increasing "openness" paradigm could mitigate some of the risk associated with social innovation organizations [4, 5]. Chalmers (2011) first argued that social innovation field would benefit by embracing the open paradigm both within the internal organizational structure of socially innovative firms and, in the knowledge searching activities in which such organizations were engaged. The terms "open social innovation" [9] or "open societal innovation" [10, 11] refer to the adaptation use of open innovation approach from business, adapted and utilized by public and society organizations to meet social needs. This open paradigm intended to apply inbound (inside-out), outbound (outside-in) or combined (coupled) open innovation strategies to include and engage all stakeholders equally, not only politics and public administration but also civil society organizations and the citizens, when social innovators account social change as the ultimate goal of their strategy. Five exemplary approaches have been identified for open social innovation paradigm: the lead user method, the open innovation tool kit, ideas and innovation platforms, special event formats, and competitions [10].

Manzini (2014) emphasized that the "openness" and "resilience" of social innovation process could help build collaborative, participatory and transparent relationships among stakeholders. Social innovation process usually is considered as two dominate approach: top-down process & bottom-up process. Manzini defined that top-down and bottom-up social innovation process by each oriented stakeholders: Top-down model largely considered that original drivers are experts, decision makers or political activists; Bottom-up model mainly oriented by people and communities directly involved.

With the limitation and challenges of detached top-down and bottom-up process, Bright and Godwin (2010) and Manzini (2014) argued that social innovation often depends on more complex interactions between very diverse initiatives, should be as hybrid process which integrated top-down and bottom-up process, a hybrid process observed in social innovation projects. The greatest barrier to achieve social impact of social innovation initiation comes not only from people and communities but also from "experts" who seek to help them and from the authorities that preside over them.

Social innovation process were requiring openness, this meant more stakeholders involvement with more complex interaction in real social innovation process.

Openness of social innovation organization in practice and research calls for extended research over the next decade. Patterns of innovation differ fundamentally by sector; firm and strategy and thus we would expect that the paradigm and outcome of open social innovation approach would show resilience in the real world context.

2.2 Creative Communities: Grounded Dynamic Laboratories for Clarifying the Emerging Open Social Innovation Paradigm

There are a series emerging social innovation project for every day life around world, e.g. Co-housing, Car sharing, CSA (community support agriculture) and so on. Each project obviously with its own particular characteristics as well as sharing many distinguishing features in common:

- *Initiated by individuals or communities who usually are called "ordinary people" instead of experts;*
- *Triggered by the real context of needs, resources, principles and capabilities;*
- *Radical and dynamic innovations of local systems, making good use of the local resources and promoting new ways of social exchange;*

Manzini (2007) defined these communities as "creative community [1] ".

These creative communities grounded dynamic innovation of local systems which were triggered by needs, resources, principles and capabilities in real context. Creative community projects offered a broad range of concrete cases with issues, practices, knowledge and theories. Creative communities were also seen as the ideal laboratories for inspiring, exploring and defining emerging open social innovation paradigm.

2.3 Positive Deviance Approach

Positive deviance (PD) as a term was first introduced by Pascale and Sternin (2004), development of the notion comes from important research on nutrition in poor communities in Vietnam (1990). Comparing the other problem solving approach, PD is one among a broad set of participatory methods which focus on the successful exceptions, not the failing norm [7]. Individuals or group of community have discovered solution themselves, even through they share the same constraints and barriers as others. These practitioners can be called "positive deviants [12] " or "heroes [1] " in their communities.

Comparing positive deviance approach and "creative community" initiations, some of the key factors regarding community collaboration remained closely similar:

- *In real world context*
- *Initiated by ordinary people instead of expert*
- *Performing better even shared the same resource and barrier as the others*
- *Local solutions*

Positive deviance approach has been widely applied to a variety of complex social problems and achieved impressive results in these quite diverse fields: saving Antarctica, reducing gang violence, improving smoking cessation, reducing corruption, improving the end-of-life experience and quality of death, reducing the high dropout rates of minorities, the curtailment of sex trafficking of girls (www.positivedeviance.org).

PD process could be simplified as define, determine, discover, and design four basic steps, which comprise an iterative road map for the process [7].

Uncovering some of the PD approaches for creative communities, had significant elements that could be assimilated into open social innovation paradigm within the real social context.

2.4   The Role of Design

Design is recognized widely as a creative and effective catalyst of social innovation [13, 14]. In this case, the 'object' of design itself tended to turn into a 'process', and considered as knowledge exploration, generation and integration process more than a problem-solving activity.

Communities, both the physical local community and the community of the specific stakeholders, can be seen as a book written in social-space language. Once the social space code is deciphered, the community can be read. Design process could be seen as the communication agency for decoding and recoding socio-space components to understand and reflect the real world context. In such open social innovation context, new roles of design regarding the process and tools needs to be explored.

3   Marimekko-Tongji Collaborative Workshop

3.1   Contexts and Background

Marimekko-Tongji Workshop was a two weeks' workshop on the theme of "Small Changes, Big Difference", was an attempt to employ positive deviance approach and design methods to provide a platform for empowering community to tackle challenges. This workshop stimulated and externalized tacit knowledge of such a creative community, generating and integrated knowledge as a positive deviance approach towards an open social innovation paradigm.

QuYang Community, a local elderly community, located in an 18-storey old-style residential building with elevators in Shanghai, China. In this community, a group retired elderly residents organize themselves to solve problems and enhance their awareness of wellbeing. They turned the space (in front of elevators) into a community hub and named it "Warm House" in 2009.

A team of more than 40 volunteers was established to provide services, such as IT service, sewing aid and movie playing. Living in the cold concrete buildings, people can stay connected with each other and bring awareness to their daily life through such activities. This group of volunteers can be seen as positive deviance of QuYang Community and the QuYang Community as a positive deviance for other communities.

3.2   Positive Deviance Approach and Design Tools

Before the design researchers began community engagement the first author worked as coordinator involved in community leadership built a resource team of volunteers with the community in preliminary step. The general process, tools and expecting outcome to the lead group of volunteers, needed to listen to feedback and expectation of the community. The steps were modified from the *Basic Field Guide to the Positive Deviance Approach* [15]:

- *Get information on the organizational setting:* this self-government volunteer organization is named Warm House. One member of the lead group also takes responsible of neighborhood committee. It is convenient to access to the PD group and extend an invitation to potential stakeholders in QuYang community.

- *Verify the presence of volunteer team in the workshop*: there are four volunteer and their families will cooperate with and open to the design researchers. These families acted as starting point, and scaled up to the whole community afterwards.
- *Achieve the common vision of the community with the lead group:* encourage the communication of the community to enhance the wellness of daily living via the medium of Marimekko fabric. This process also established mutual trust between community and researchers.

After given the general background and trained the basic methods of finding out demands, integrating and prototyping, each four groups reframed their own research plan with the support of the initiation volunteer family. Each group shared the iterative basic PD process but choose the proper design tools in each phase according the specific context of the volunteer family (See Fig. 1).

	Group One	Group Two	Group Three	Group Four
PD Challenges	Encourage communication among people from inside and outside of community	Encourage communication among people from different culture background	Encourage communication among PDs	Encourage communication among people of different generations
Define	Interviews	Interviews	Interviews	Storytelling
Determine	Interviews	Interviews	Focus group	Interviews
Discover	Design probe kits	Matching game	Prototyping	Prototyping
Design	Co-design workshop	Co-design	Prototyping	Prototyping
Outcome	Guide book Workshop prototypes	Mailbox Lantern	Curtain Container	Photo frame

Fig. 1. The design tools and main outcomes of each four group

3.3   Enabling the Community and Designers Through Co-Design Approach

There are several basic principles when initiating the PD process in a community: the community must own the entire process as the main actor, to take it a step further, discover existing uncommon, successful behaviors and strategies, reflect on these existing solutions and adapt them to their circumstances. The initiation and participation of community members are critical to PD process.

4 Preliminary Results

4.1 Design Tools

Fig. 2. The storytelling design tools

Design Tool: Storytelling. Directed storytelling is a tool for design researcher to explore PDs' behaviors without having to do long-term ethnographic research, yet still developing empathy with the people they are designing for and with. Unused life-experience stories of the PDs can be the treasure for the next generations of this community (See Fig. 2).

Fig. 3. The design probe kits and data analysis

Design Tool: Design Probe Kits. Design Probes were given to the community members with the aim to get insight into the daily life of PDs' activities as well as relationship and touch points with inside and outside of community. The probe kits included a single-use camera, a personal dairy and guidance how to use the material. After three days, the probe kits were collected for the further exploration. A discussion with selected community members were organized in order to understand the meaning behind the pictures and diaries. (See Fig. 3)

Design Tool: Matching Game. Matching game was based on the attempt to use color and emotion perception to connect people from different culture background. Facing so many different unfamiliar materials and colors, design researchers and community

Fig. 4. The matching game

residents chould build a corresponding relation between color and emotion perception first. In this way, participants can achieve general agreement on cultural awareness (See Fig. 4).

Fig. 5. Participatory decoration processes

Design Tool: Participatory Decorations. Design researchers aimed to create scenario where constructive and meaningful communication could happen. In order to enhance the communication among PDs and others in this community, making best use of the odds and ends of cloth, design researchers inspirited by the PDs' hand written good wishes on the wall, made small cards covered with Marimekko's fabric one side and left the other side blank (See Fig. 5).

The participants can realize and express their emotions and positive attitude to the others by choosing card, writing wishes, quotations or greetings on these cards back, putting them on the others' mailbox.

Fig. 6. The co-design workshop

Design Tool: Co-Design Workshop. A co-design workshop was organized together with the community – provided with fabric, paint, colors, cardboard and various other materials, the PD volunteers of community were guided to create useful everyday items. The aim of the workshop was to both find out items frequently used in daily life as well as get inspiration for communication inside and outside of the community.

During the process of co-design, roles with different capabilities occurred and reconstructed themselves, as old relationships between organizations and neighborhood based on family unit had broken down. New relations emerged, exploring and reconstructing the community value. Base. This improved the people's awareness of their own capabilities that could be applied to the community. By way of design, ordinary people were able to participate in the process and come up with solutions in response to their demands (See Fig. 6).

5 Discussions

Creative communities that are mainly bottom-up interventions can be seen as the successful PDs among communities as well as ideal laboratory for exploring open social innovation paradigm. By using PD approach to creative communities, the change process goes from outside in to inside out, contributing to extending the boundary of social innovation organizations. PD is best suited for "problems embedded in social and behavioral patterns that resist technical fixes" [12] offering an alternative way to address certain types of social problems, which disturbing the top-down standard models.

Although the workshop didn't clarify the value of community, it connect people or groups who hadn't connected before, recognize and become aware of the shared environment and value of community. The co-design workshop process also added value by in social networks by creating healthier people who were no longer isolated.

In QuYang Community, the organized collaborative workshop encouraged the communication among people and involved more residents to raise their awareness as well as co-creating values. This aim achieved an experience for the community supported by the utility of PD approach in new settings. In each four basic phase, storytelling, design probe, matching game, participatory decorations and co-design workshop these design tools were generated, integrated and applied for different concrete context. The PD process and these design tools could be considered as a way of decoding and recoding the social-space components when design researchers and PDs actively participated in community.

Design tools, especially the co-design workshop were largely optimized for the PD process. The essential precondition of PD application was that the community defined the questions, invested time and energy to discover the answers by themselves. When design researchers organized co-design workshop and found that people needed inspiration to start the activities, but not too much guidance. Understanding context and translating individual successful solution to collective achieves is quite a hard adaptive challenge. With the active participatory of the residents and design researchers, prototyping emerged and developed out of the workshop, as an ongoing activity. As we can see, the co-design workshop created a platform transformed the social system and behavioral change by the emerging roles of stakeholders with diverse range of capabilities. There was also a role change of the design professionals from facilitators that were more concerned with processes than the objects.

Dissemination of PD depends on social systems, empowering the community to solve their own problems. However, the PD approach is a long-term process. Isolated PDs still need social process to disseminate their innovation and incorporate it into the community structure, including following up and evaluation of the ongoing process.

6   Conclusion

The process of PD approach is much more important than the PD results. PD approach is highly related to the concrete context that both the resources and barriers are unique, thus PD results of one community cannot be used as model to the others. In Chinese old saying "Give a man a fish and you feed him for a day. Teach a man to fish and you feed him for a lifetime"(Lao Tzu). Positive deviance approach process which defining, determining, discovering and design these basic iterative steps, involved and empowered the community to stimulate, externalize, integrate and co-create community value by encouraging the communication among people, especially between the PDs and the others.

Acknowledgments. Special thanks to QuYang Community and the students from Tongji University, Aalto University and Political di Milano.

References

1. Meroni, A. Creative communities. Milano: Polidesign (2007). http://scholar.google.com/scholar?hl=en&btnG=Search&q=intitle:Creative+communities+|#1
2. Mulgan, G.: The process of social innovation. Innovations: Technol. Gov. Globalization **1** (2), 145–162 (2006)
3. Caulier-grice, J., Mulgan, G., Vale, D.: Discovery, Argument & Action How Civil Society Responds to Changing Needs. Young Foundation, London (2005)
4. Leiponen, A., Helfat, C.E.: Innovation objectives, knowledge sources, and the benefits of breadth. Strateg. Manag. J. **31**, 224–236 (2010)
5. Chalmers, D.: Why social innovators should embrace the "open" paradigm. In: EMES Social Innovation Conference (2011). http://strathprints.strath.ac.uk/33561/
6. Bright, D.S., Godwin, L.N.: Encouraging social innovation in global organizations: integrating planned and emergent approaches. J. Asia-Pacific Bus. **11**, 179–196 (2010)
7. Pascale, R., Sternin, J., Sternin, M.: The Power of Positive Deviance: How Unlikely Innovators Solve the World's Toughest Problems, p. 256. Harvard Business Press, Cambridge (2013). https://books.google.com/books?id=TWw7yXNfibEC&pgis=1
8. Zhong, F.: Collaborative Service Based on Trust Building -Service design for the innovative food network in China (2008)
9. Chesbrough, H., Di Minin, A.: Open Social Innovation. In: Chesbrough, H., Vanhaverbeke, W., West, J. (eds.) New Frontiers in Open Innovation, pp. 169–188. Oxford University Press, Oxford (2014)
10. Von Lucke, J., et al.: Open Societal Innovation: The Alemannic Definition. Available SSRN 2195435 1–5 (2012)
11. Raffl, M.C., Katharina, G.: eSOCIETY across borders: regional identity and open societal innovation. In: 12th International Conference e-Society (2014)
12. Pascale, R., Sternin, J., Sternin, M.: The power of positive deviance: how unlikely innovators solve the world's toughest problems. Inform. Prim. Care **12**, 139–145 (2010)
13. Murray, R., Caulier-Grice, J., Mulgan, G.: The Open Book of Social Innovation (2010). http://desis-dop.org/documents/10157/12818/Murray,+Caulier-Grice,+Mulgan+(2010),+The+Book+of+Social+Innovation.pdf
14. Manzini, E.: Design for sustainability. How to design sustainable solutions. Sustainable Everyday Project 1–11 (2006). http://www.dis.polimi.it/manzini-papers/06.01.06-Design-for-sustainability.doc
15. Tufts University: Basic Field Guide to the Positive Deviance Approach (2010). http://www.positivedeviance.org/pdf/FieldGuide/FINALguide10072010.pdf

Design for Sustainable Behaviour

Xu Sun[1(✉)], Qingfeng Wang[2], Nan Wang[1], Charlie Sugianto So[1],
and Yan Wang[3]

[1] Product Design and Manufacture Group, Faculty of Engineering,
University of Nottingham Ningbo, Ningbo, China
{xu.sun,nan.wang,charlie.sugianto}@nottingham.edu.cn
[2] Nottingham Business School Ningbo, Ningbo, China
qingfeng.wang@nottingham.edu.cn
[3] University of Brighton, Brighton, England
y.wang5@brighton.ac.uk

Abstract. This paper explores the associated factors that lead to sustainable behaviour at home, and how design could be used to influence user behaviour in the area of pro-environmental households within China.

Keywords: Energy behaviour · Sustainable design

1 Introduction

Traditional sustainable design has a strong focus on mechanical engineering (e.g. design for disassembly, recyclability), however, sustainable technology does not automatically lead to sustainable user behaviour. Previous research that has addressed the human behaviour of energy usage and how design can contribute to the sustainability of product use is very limited [10, 19]. The behaviour component is frequently underestimated in analyses of pro-environmental households, partly because of its complexity [20, 21], and partly because it is influenced by culture, attitudes and aesthetic norms and social and economic variables [12].

Product designers shape the development of products which directly impact upon society and the environment, and the application of sustainable product design can significantly reduce lifecycle impacts [9]. Several design strategies have been identified, including Eco-feedback, which provides signs as reminders to inform users of energy consumption - (e.g. [13, 16]), behaviour steering, which encourages users to behave in sustainable ways prescribed by the designer (e.g. [7]) and persuasive technology, which applies persuasive methods to change how people think or act [5]. Little work has been done to link these strategies and techniques and to apply them in practical areas, and there is a lack of design guidelines and empirical design practices for designers briefed with influencing user behaviour [10, 19].

This study contributes by filling in the gap of lack of empirical user-centred practices to promote sustainable domestic energy consumption. It focuses on the pro-environmental domestic water use for Chinese users. This is because water scarcity is predicted to have a severe impact on the quality of life of both current and future generations, while the demand for water will outstrip supply by 25 % in 2030 in China,

© Springer International Publishing Switzerland 2015
P.L.P. Rau (Ed.): CCD 2015, Part I, LNCS 9180, pp. 372–380, 2015.
DOI: 10.1007/978-3-319-20907-4_34

if no remedial actions are taken [3]. This study explores the associated factors that lead to sustainable domestic water use behaviour, and how design could be used to influence user behaviour in the area of pro-environmental households within China.

2   Background

Sustainable design takes into account environmental, economic and social impacts enacted throughout the product lifecycle. Generally, economic and environmental concerns are well defined and understood, whereas the social sphere of sustainable design has been less well explored [9].

2.1   Design Strategy to Promote Sustainable Behaviour K

Impacts upon society and the environment during the period of use of a product are often determined by consumer behaviour, thus designers are in a position to reduce use impacts by purposefully shaping behaviour towards more sustainable practices [1, 10, 19].

Early research has identified three design interventions: (1) Eco-feedback [13]; (2) Behaviour Steering [7]; and (3) Persuasive Technology [5] as potential strategies which could be integrated into product design to influence user behaviour [9].

Eco-feedback provides information and reminders to the user concerning his or her own impacts, and aims to guide the user toward pro-environmental behaviour. In the field of psychology, it has been acknowledged that outcome feedback, and the knowledge of results, can have a positive effect on performance. Goals and feedback are intertwined, and to optimise feedback effectiveness, goal-setting can provide a standard by which the user can judge if the feedback represents good or poor performance. The energy conservation is dependent on having a goal to save energy as the primary goal of the user, while the success of goal-setting is dependent on whether the user is anticipating large monetary savings, as the amounts of possible energy and, thus monetary savings, are very small [13].

Behaviour Steering encourages users to behave in ways prescribed by the designer through constraints integrated in the product, and it has been found that this approach helps to sustain behavioural changes. For instance, Jelsma and Knot [7] applied the idea of 'scripting' to sustainable product design. Scripting was defined as the design of a product-layout guiding the behaviour of the user, in a more or less forceful way, to comply with values and intentions inscribed into the product by the designer. If it would be the designer's intention to inscribe increased likelihood of sustainable usage into the product, this would mean designing products in such a way that unsustainable behaviour is made difficult or impossible, while sustainable behaviour is made easier, or even automatic [7].

Persuasive Technology employs persuasive methods to ensure changes in how people think or act. Fogg [5] explored the role of computing products as persuasive social actors that work on five primary types of social cues: physical, psychological, language, social dynamics, and social roles. Fogg also highlighted the impact of physical attractiveness, where a computing technology that is visually attractive to target users is also likely to be more persuasive. In addition, people are also more readily persuaded by computing technology products that are similar familiar to themselves in some way. Also, computing technology that assumes roles of authority will have enhanced powers of persuasion [5].

Wood and Newborough [21] argued that the most effective energy intervention is that which captures the attention of the audience, gains involvement and is credible and useful in the users' situation. It is not simply the informational content given that is important, but the way in which the information motivates the consumer into action [21].

2.2 Sustainable Energy Behaviour Research in China

China is a typical binary economy and a socially diverse country; there is a significant difference between urban and rural regions in many respects. Therefore, it is critical to analyse the impact on energy use for the lifestyles of both urban and rural residents. It is widely recognised that China is currently a transition economy. There is a great difference between the levels of energy consumption by rural and urban populations. Rapid urbanisation, however, will bring more and more rural residents into urban areas, as a result of which there will be changes in their energy consuming behaviour and increases in the requirement for water energy resources, such as water. Subsequently, the differences in the lifestyles of rural and urban residents will gradually reduce. Meanwhile, the increased income of rural residents will lead to a greater demand for commodities and will increase their living expenditure on fast-moving-consumer goods, thus leading to greater requirements for energy. Given all the above, however, Murata, et al., 2008 argue that a '28 % reduction [of 14] in China could be achieved by the year 2020 by means of improving citizens' energy efficiency in household appliance use'. Since households can make significant contributions to energy conservation, to effectively encourage household energy-saving behaviour, first it is necessary to identify the key behavioural antecedents [17].

Energy use is influenced by technology efficiency and by personal lifestyles. Wei, et al. [18] argue that residents' lifestyles can have an important and significant impact on energy use. Wei also suggested that one of the most efficient measures for energy conservation is a change of lifestyle, which may include the transition from luxurious consumption to frugal consumption.

Based on the research conducted in Beijing by [17], the results indicate that there is significant potential to reduce unnecessary energy use from the household perspective. This, however, is not supported by the ineffective energy-saving behaviour being encouraged in Beijing. Furthermore, it is noted that economic benefits, comfort and convenience, and information are important determinants to predicting household energy-saving behaviour. Also, the study illustrates how social norms attach great importance to the reduction of unnecessary daily electricity use, while the implementation of design strategies should depend largely on these determinants. Environmental awareness, however, has been shown to have no significant influence on residents' energy-saving actions. It should also be noted that similar results were also obtained in Hangzhou, supporting the above findings in Beijing [2].

Moreover, Feng, et al. [4] concluded in their study that total indirect energy consumption differs by region in China, and household income also affects energy consumption, with higher levels for high-income compared to low-income households. The higher the income, the more diverse is the energy consumption. However, it is worth noting that, in contrast to findings in some Western countries, income is not a good indicator of environmental attitudes in China, as it mostly influences energy consumption through product purchase. Also, those with low incomes from both rural and urban samples in China showed environmental concern similar to members of higher-income groups [23].

While Chinese residents are able to conserve energy, many residents feel that when energy conservation is contradictory to the comfort and convenience of life, they will neglect or abandon conservation behaviour [22]. The importance of improving occupants' behaviour for reducing household energy consumption is often overlooked as many people are extremely addicted to advanced technologies on energy savings [15].

2.3   Cultural Impact in Energy Behavior

Culture has a profound influence on human behaviour [12]. In a cross cultural study, China was found to have lower energy consumption levels than developed countries. The study surveyed the energy consumption in Chinese households in 2012 and found that it represents approximately 44 % of that in the United States in 2009, and 38 % of that in the EU-27 in 2008 [24]. To further reduce energy consumption, it has been suggested that China could apply more advanced technologies, such as automatic control technology and heat recovery technology, which are in common use in the United States [8].

More existing research projects have found that people's age has a positive correlation with residential energy consumption, in countries such as Canada, Australia, Brazil, Denmark, India and the Netherlands. However, research analysis in China has revealed a negative correlation between occupant age and heating/cooling energy consumption [2].

3   User Studies

A series of empirical user studies has been planned to take place in different regions within China to investigate people's behaviour in household energy consumption. This paper reports a user study which was conducted in Southwest China.

3.1   Generating Concepts

Design concepts were generated based on the literature review to serve as seeds in user studies. As previous study indicates, Chinese urban household water usage can be classified into 5 categories including laundry (39 %), showering/bathing (27 %), kitchen usage (19 %), house cleaning (13 %), drinking (2 %). Clearly, the water for drinking is a fixed demand of human beings, so, the remaining four categories are the main starting points of our concepts. Furthermore, laundry and showering/bathing accounts for 66 % of the total domestic water consumption in Chinese urban areas, which makes these two aspects much more important than the remaining two. Six design concepts were derived, as illustrated in Table 1.

3.2 Participants

A total of four families took part in the study (four males and three females). The four selected families represented four typical types of family in China: (1) a couple with a child; (2) a young couple; (3) a couple with senior parents; (4) a single person (See Table 2).

3.3 Procedure

Four user workshops were conducted with a series of co-design activities at four participants' homes. In the workshop, the participants were asked to describe the ways in which their energy use relates to their behaviour, and their requirements and preferences for reducing energy usage at home. All participants were also given the six design concepts described above and were asked to decide on the contexts in which they might be most useful and how they might best be changed to be useful at home.

3.4 Analysis and Results

An emergent themes analysis was applied to gain an understanding of the collected data.

The single participant did not care about the amount of detergent used for washing, whereas the household that consists of a family living with their parents used low foam detergent and a small stream of running water to wash and rinse. Furthermore, they cleaned their tableware by using hot water and without detergent, and used paper kitchen towels to remove any oil from the tableware beforehand. This may demonstrate that elderly occupants are more familiar with, and more aware of the need for energy conservation.

Most households were aware of the water problem but were not aware of how much water they used for daily activities. The household with a family and their child paid for water every six months and only notified when the water quota is almost over. Furthermore, the household consisting of the young couple located in a water abundant area were more likely to ignore water conservation even if they were aware of water scarcity. These results are consistent with the research findings by [2] in which environmental awareness may not result in a significant influence on residents' energy-saving actions.

All of the household members interviewed thought that different utility pricing at different hours of the day would not make much difference to levels of water

Table 1. Sustainable design concepts

Concepts	Descriptions
	Concept 1: *Water saving washing machine* With a built-in laundry detergent tank, the washing machine can add just the right amount of detergent during the washing process. This method can minimise the water used for washing and rinsing and limits the amount of detergent residue. In addition, the washing machine can show the overall water consumption in a direct way to increase the water saving awareness of the user.
	Concept 2: *An electrical calendar providing information on daily water consumption* Normally, people are informed of the water consumption of their household when they pay their bill, either monthly or quarterly. Such frequency of information is insufficient to build awareness of sustainable water use. This concept divides a monthly check into a daily check to increase awareness of the water consumption.
	Concept 3: *Warning of shower time* By providing an unstable water pressure for a shower, this concept warns people who take a long time to wash. In such way, the concept can encourage direct water savings, although it may annoy people.
	Concept 4: *Collecting cold water before the shower water has heated up* This concept is based on the problem whereby shower water heats up slowly. The cold water which comes before the water heats up is often wasted. This concept promotes the collection of the cold water for other uses.
	Concept 5: *Transparent cistern for a flush toilet* Flush toilets waste a lot water because they use a whole tank or perhaps a half tank of water for each flush. This concept adapts the flush button so that it requires a continuous press, which allows users to stop the water at any moment. The transparent cistern can increase the awareness of saving water under the same method as Concept 1.
	Concept 6: *Induction area to stop the area* This concept solves the problem whereby people keep the shower water running when they are applying soap. By setting an induction area under the shower head, the shower head can stop the water when people leave this area to apply soap. This concept promotes the idea of saving water directly.

Table 2. Participants' demographic profile

Demographic profile	Number
Gender	
Male	4
Female	3
Age	
20 years and less	1
21 to 29 years	3
40 to 49 years	2
50 years and above	1
Profession	
Manager	1
Teacher	1
Student	1
Contractor	1
Government officer	1
Engineer	1
Retiree	1

conservation. This is very likely due to the fact that water is relatively cheap in China, and thus does not directly affect people's behaviour in relation to their energy consumption.

All of the household members interviewed also thought culture (i.e. social relationships) plays a role in changing user energy behaviour, as participants reflected on a community sharing concept in which data is shared amongst all members of their community; they would not want to be the household that uses/wastes the most water in the community. This indicates a change in user behaviour by providing competition in their local community.

One particular comment was made in terms of privacy concerns, whereby the user was unwilling to, and would be uncomfortable about revealing the amount of their water usage to the public.

Of the six concepts presented to the interviewees, they gave high ratings to the concepts that are related to water conservation during showering (Concepts 3 and 6).

4   Conclusion

The results have identified four areas which should be further explored in the design of sustainable energy behaviour, including people's age, the area in which they live, their perceptions of water usage and any relevant cultural factors.

Age. The study indicates a positive relationship between the participants' age and household energy conservation. Generally, households with older members tend to consume less water for both personal hygiene and cleaning purposes, as older occupants are more experienced and are more concerned about the environment than younger people.

Living area. In this study, the participants' families all live in Sichuan province, which is in the southwest of China. This is a water rich area of China, especially Luzhou city which is located at the intersection of the Yangtze River and the Tuojiang River. Such geographic characteristics seem to encourage residents to neglect water conservation in their daily activities, with the exception of the older occupants.

Awareness of water consumption (e.g. water pricing policy). Members of the participating households were aware of approximately how much water they consumed each month, and they were aware of the pricing policy for water usage in their neighbourhood. They were of the opinion that different pricing for different hours of the day would not affect their water usage behaviour, probably due to the fact that water is relatively cheap in China. The professions of the participants may also have an impact on their perception of water pricing relative to their level of income or spending.

Finally *culture* can play a role in changing user behaviour. Individuals understand their everyday practices with regards to social norms. The research identified a need for the inclusion of social context and cultural considerations in the field of energy consumption research and design.

Acknowledgements. The authors acknowledge the financial support from a NSFC grant reference 71401085, and the support from the International Doctoral Innovation Centre (IDIC) at the University of Nottingham, China.

References

1. Bhamra, T., Lilley, D., Tang, T.: Sustainable Use: Changing consumer behaviour through product design. Turin (2008)
2. Chen, J., Wang, X., Steemers, K.: A statistical analysis of a residential energy consumption survey study in Hangzhou, China. Energy Build. **66**, 193–202 (2013)
3. Economist Intelligence Unit: Report: Water for all? A study of water utilities' preparedness to meet supply challenges to 2030 (2012)
4. Feng, Z.-H., Zou, L.-L., Wei, Y.-M.: The impact of household consumption on energy use and CO_2 emissions in China. Energy **36**(1), 656–670 (2011)
5. Fogg, B.: Persuasive Technology: Using COmputers to Change What We Think and Do. Morgan Kaufmann, San Fransisco (2003)
6. Hori, S., Kondo, K., Nogata, D., Ben, H.: The determinants of household energy-saving behaviour: survey and comparison in five major Asian cities. Energy Policy **52**, 354–362 (2013)
7. Jelsma, J., Knot, M.: Designing environmentally efficient services; a 'script' approach. J. Sustain. Prod. Des. **2**(3–4), 119–130 (2002)
8. Jiu, L., Zhao, J., Liu, X., Wang, Z.: Energy consumption comparison analysis of high energy efficiency office buildings in typical climate zones of China and U.S. based on correction model. Energy **65**, 221–232 (2014)
9. Lilley, D.: Design for sustainable behaviour: strategies and perceptions. Des. Stud. **30**(6), 704–720 (2009)

10. Lockton, D., Harrison, D., Stanton, N.: Making the user more efficient: design for sustainable behaviour. Int. J. Sustain. Eng. 1(1), 3–8 (2008)
11. Lockton, D., Harrison, D., Stanton, N.A.: The Design with intent method: a design tool for influencing user behaviour. Appl. Ergonomics 41(2), 382–392 (2010)
12. Lutzenhiser, L.: A cultural model of household energy consumption. Energy 17(1), 47–60 (1992)
13. McCalley, L., Midden, C.J.: Energy conservation through product-integrated feedback: the roles of goal-setting and social orientation. J. Econ. Psychol. 23(5), 589–603 (2002)
14. Murata, A., Kondou, Y., Hailin, M., Weisheng, Z.: Electricity demand in the Chinese urban household-sector. Appl. Energy 85(12), 1113–1125 (2008)
15. Ouyang, J., Hokao, K.: Energy-saving potential by improving occupants' behaviour in urban residential sector in Hangzhou city, China. Energy Build. 41(7), 711–720 (2009)
16. Völink, T., Meertens, R.M.: Technological innovations and the promotion of energy conservation: the case of goal-setting and feedback. In: Verbeek, P.P., Slob, A. (eds.) User Behavior and Technology Development; Shaping Sustainable Relations Between Consumers and Technologies, pp. 139–148. Springer, Dordrecht (2006)
17. Wang, Z., Zhang, B., Yin, J., Zhang, Y.: Determinants and policy implications for household electricity-saving behaviour: evidence from Beijing, China. Energy Policy 39(6), 3550–3557 (2011)
18. Wei, Y.-M., Liu, L.-C., Fan, Y., Wu, G.: The impact of lifestle on energy use and CO2 emission: an empirical analysis of China's residents. Energy Policy 35(1), 247–257 (2007)
19. Wever, R., Kuijk, J.V., Boks, C.: User-centred design for sustainable behaviour. Int. J. Sustain. Eng. 1(1), 9–20 (2008)
20. Wilhite, H., Masuda, T., Yamaga, H.: A cross-cultural analysis of household energy use behaviour in Japan and Norway. Energy Policy 24(9), 795–803 (1996)
21. Wood, G., Newborough, M.: Energy-use information transfer for intelligent homes: enabling energy conservation with central and local displays. Energy Build. 39(4), 497–503 (2007)
22. Yan, S., Lifang, F.: Influence of psychological, family and contextual factors on residential energy use behaviour: an empirical study of China. Energy Procedia 5, 910–915 (2011)
23. Yu, X.: Is environment 'a city thing' in China? Rural-urban differences in environmental attitudes. J. Environ. Psychol. 38, 39–48 (2014)
24. Zheng, X., et al.: Characteristics of residential energy consumption in China: findings from a household survey. Energy Policy 75, 126–135 (2014)

Preliminary Study: Influence of Cultural Differences on the Innovation Process Between Chinese and Germans

Liuxing Tsao[1], Philip Alexander Behr-Heyder[1,2], and Liang Ma[1(✉)]

[1] Department of Industrial Engineering, Tsinghua University, Beijing, People
Republic of China
clx14@mails.tsinghua.edu.cn, liangma@mail.tsinghua.edu.cn
[2] RWTH Aachen, Templergraben 55, 52056 Aachen, German
philip.behr-heyder@rwth-aachen.de

Abstract. The success of companies in the industrial sector is highly
dependent on innovation. China is the biggest industry nation in the
world and Germany is well-known for its engineering and innovations.
The differences and conflicts between Chinese and German culture
appear in the innovation process. We designed a questionnaire based
on Hofstedes cultural model and the stage-gate innovation process to
study these differences and elaborate guidelines to encourage innovation
in Sino-German companies. We surveyed 92 participants from China
and Germany. Furthermore, four semi-structured interviews were conducted with top executives for qualitative data collection. The results
suggested that Chinese might be mainly influenced by the concept of
power-distance and face, whereas Germans might be influenced by uncertainty avoidance during the innovation process. We developed guidelines
to understand the national cultural influence on the innovation process
and to manage Chinese and German engineers in this process.

Keywords: Cross-cultural studies · International management ·
Chinese and German engineers · Innovation · Innovation process

1 Introduction

The success of companies in the industrial sector is highly influenced by the innovation power [3]. Innovation can create a balance between efficient operations and
future opportunities [4]. In the middle of the 20th century most people thought
that innovativeness is highly correlated with Research and Development(R&D)
spending. Nowadays scholars focus more on soft factors like cultural influences
as main drivers for successful innovations. Furthermore, mismatched cultural
conditions cause frictions within companies [6].

An innovation is something original, new, and important in whatever field
that breaks into a market or society [7]. Recent research shows the role of organizational culture for enabling organizations to translate innovation activities

© Springer International Publishing Switzerland 2015
P.L.P. Rau (Ed.): CCD 2015, Part I, LNCS 9180, pp. 381–391, 2015.
DOI: 10.1007/978-3-319-20907-4_35

into real performance improvements. One of the most important models is the
stage-gate innovation process. It contains six phases as shown in Fig. 1. These
six phases consist of cross-functional and parallel activities which are undertaken
by a team of employees from different departments [11]. A complete innovation
process starts from the idea generation stage, and a successful process should
pass each check gate then comes to the final market launch stage.

Fig. 1. The stage-gate model of innovation process [11, 12]

China is one of the biggest industry nations in the world and Germany is
well-known for its engineering and innovations. Due to globalization needs many
German companies build plants in China, but the two countries have very different cultural backgrounds. Yang states that Chinese management style is based
on three different pillars: Confucianism, Socialism and Capitalism, whereas German management was highly influenced by the American capitalism [13].

Culture is the patterns of thinking, emotions, and behavior in a society that
reflects traditional ideas and values [10]. Cultures are contested, ever changing
and emergent, they are invented and reinvented in social life [2]. Hofstede created
a cultural model and identified four dimensions that he named individualism
(IDV), masculinity (MAS), power distance (PDI), and uncertainty avoidance
(UAI) [9]. Yang added long-term orientation versus short-term orientation to
life (LTO) as the fifth dimension [14].

Due to different scholars' background there is not one single research approach to conduct cross-cultural research [10]. Four major groups conducting cross-cultural research are anthropologists, psychologists, statisticians, and
qualitative-minded researchers by different methods, such as interviews, experiments, statistical tools etc. To gain a broad insight into the cultural influence
on the innovation process, we author chose a combination of quantitative data
collection by surveys as well as qualitative datas via interviews. Weused Eisen-
hardts case study approach to prove framework for the research [5]. Based on
preliminary result, we made inference of the culture effects on innovation process
and developed guidelines to understand the cultural influence on the innovation
process and to manage Chinese and German engineers in this process.

2   Method

2.1   Quantitative Data Collection

There are three levels of factors influencing the innovation process of companies:
micro, meso and macro level. The micro level involves forces addressing the

companys own culture. The meso level is the transactional level consisting of market forces like suppliers or strategic alliances. The micro and meso level influences are kept to a minimum by a broad scope of participants from different companies since this study aims to analyze the macro level influenced by national cultural characters.

For measuring the influence factors on the innovation process, the authors used Archarya scaling questions. The importance of each factor was rated on a 4 step scale. The "1" meant very unimportant and "4" meant very important [1]. The final questionnaire consisted of five stages directly related to the stage-gate innovation processes including 17 questions addressing Hofstedes five cultural dimensions (see Table 1). The English questionnaire was translated into the mother tongues of the participants (Chinese and German) to avoid any misinterpretation due to a foreign language.

2.2 Qualitative Data Collection

We conducted semi-structured interviews to collect qualitative dataenhancing controversial discussion with the experts. This method enabled the authors to investigate the root causes of cross cultural issues in the innovation process. Based on Gubrium guidelines, the interviews started with a self-introduction and an expectation exchange [8]. Afterwards the improvement possibilities and problems during each of the six stages in the innovation process were discussed. These interviews ended with open questions to further investigate and to ensure a deep understanding of the ideas. The participant for the interviews were chosen based on their relevant experience of managing Chinese and German engineers in the industrial sector. Four senior executives with different education and working background took part.

3   Results

3.1   Questionnaire Results

Participants. The web-based questionnaire was filled out by 28 Chinese (36 % female, 64 % male) and 64 German (23 % female, 77 % male) managers. With most subjects in the age of 21–29. Chinese and Germany participants had similar education background (about 50 % rewarded a Bachelors Degree or equivalent).

Factors in Each Innovation Stage. Due to the limitation of the sample size and the unbalanced amount of feedbacks from Chinese and Germany participants, the author gave intuitive inferences and suggestions rather than conducting statistical comparisons. The preliminary questionnaire result revealed similar findings as previous research showed. Chinese tend to have a high score in power distance, low in individualism, and compared to Germans a long-term orientation during the innovation process.

L. Tsao et al.

Table 1. Questionnaire items regarding the five cross culture dimensions

Stage	Question	Detailed Items	Dimensions
Idea generation	Important factors and triggers	Regular formal meetings	PDI
		Internal/External sources/events	IDV
	Responsible person	None	PDI, LTO
	Key driving person	None	PDI, LTO
	Motivation tools	None	MAS
Analysis of ideas	Employees to proceed or discontinue a proposal	None	PDI
	Important factors and triggers	Personal experience, use of structured methods, knowledge of competitor/customer	UAI
		Predictability of the market	LTO
		Idea generation direction	UAI
Development	Leadership style	Led by top-management, middle manager or by engineers	PDI
		Autonomous teams	MAS
Test stage	Ways to handle problems	None	IDV
	Importance of standardized methods and tools	None	UAI
	Management style for on time test	None	UAI
Market launch	Reasons for success	Proximity to authorities	IDV
		Proximity to customers	LTO
		Innovation process management	MAS, PDI
		R&D funding	UAI
		Teams and engineers	IDV

* IDV - Individualism(MAS)
* MAS - Masculinity
* PDI - Power Distance
* UAI - Uncertainty Avoidance
* LTO - Long-term Orientation to Life

Figure 2 showed how the participants assessed the four factors regarding the generation of new ideas. For the factor formal meetings, Germans assessed it in the middle of the range important to very important while Chinese ranked this factor between important and unimportant, revealing a difference towards the idea of PDI. Thus the form of meetings should be carefully designed in a cross-cultural company in the idea generating stage.

For the responsible person of idea generation, we concluded from Fig. 3 that Chinese tended to assess managers more important for the process to generate new ideas. Germans assessed the involvement of engineers as more important in comparison to the Chinese participants. 83 % of the Chinese participants

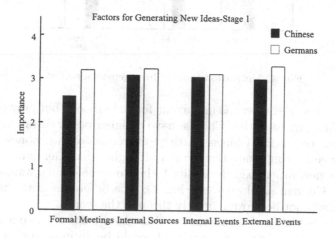

Fig. 2. Factors of generating of new ideas-Idea generation stage

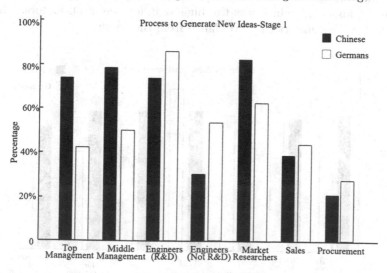

Fig. 3. The responsible person-Idea generation stage

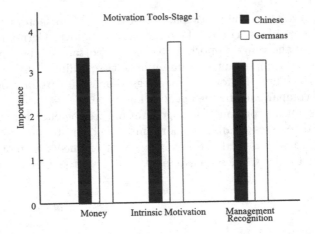

Fig. 4. Motivation tools C Idea generation stage

evaluated market researchers as important for the process, but only 63 % of the Germans. This suggested that Chinese have a higher power distance.

Regarding motivation, Chinese participants tended to rate money as motivation tool for generating innovative ideas a bit higher than German participants. The intrinsic motivation, e.g. the ability to improve something, was very important for the German employees (see Fig. 4). The difference in the masculinity dimension could not be proven directly through the scores.

Demonstrated in Fig. 5, Germans rated the knowledge of customer needs 0.5 higher than the Chinese participants. This could be an indicator for long-term orientation. Chinese evaluated the origin of the idea much higher than German participants, about 0.9 which was the biggest difference of all factors. Chinese seemed to have low uncertainty avoidance from the result.

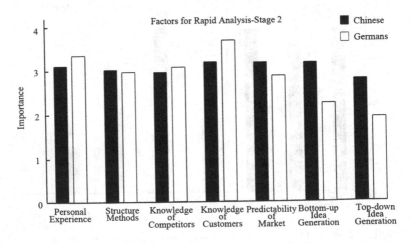

Fig. 5. Factors for rapid analysis-Rapid analysis stage

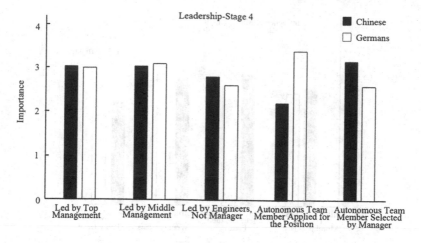

Fig. 6. Leadership style-Development stage

For the development stage, an opposite result was found regarding autonomous teams between Chinese and Germans. If members in the team were staffed by managers Chinese assess them as more important. If employees were staffed afterwards to an autonomous team, Germans evaluated it 1.2 higher than the Chinese participants. Concluding this, power distance is a big difference between these two cultures (Fig. 6).

When facing an occurred problem, Chinese tended to solve it in a team while Germans preferred to solve it individuality (Fig. 7). It revealed the difference in IDV.

A LTO difference appeared in the test stage. The Chinese participants thought that long-term planning, on a monthly or less than a monthly basis

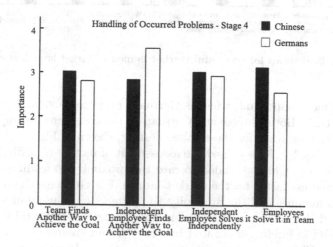

Fig. 7. Ways to handle occurred problems-Development stage

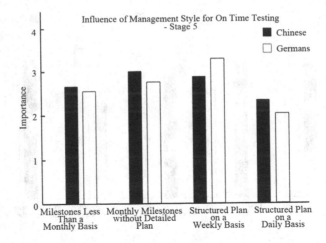

Fig. 8. Management styles for an on time testing C Test stage

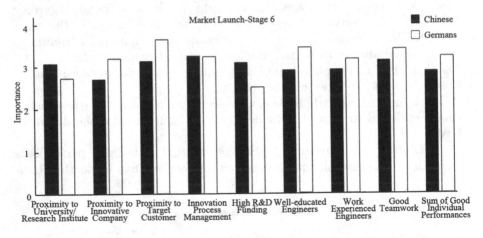

Fig. 9. Reasons for successful market launch - Market launch stage

was slightly more important, whereas Germans preferred a structured planning on a weekly basis. Both Chinese and German do not consider planning on a daily basis as really important for the on time testing, shown in Fig. 8.

The following Fig. 9 visualized the assessment of factors regarding a successful market launch. Chinese tended to rate the proximity to leading universities higher as a success factor for the market launch. For Germans the proximity to innovative companies and the proximity to customers was more important, the result blurred the difference of Germans and Chinese in IDV and LTO dimensions. High R&D funding was rated by the German engineers with a score of 2.46; whereas Chinese rated it with 3.09, indicating a lower uncertainty avoidance need. The education, work experience, good teamwork, and a sum of good individual performances was more important for the German participants showing a individualism character.

3.2   Interview Results

Overall more than seven hours of interviews were conducted with the four experts. One interview was conducted face-to-face, the other interviews were conducted via telephonical system. All interviewees agreed that the interviews were recorded for recapitulation. The quantitative insights were used to elaborate the guidelines.

Based on the interviews main improvement points for the collaboration between Chinese and German engineers are communication strategies, handling of guanxi(Chinese term of relationship), handling of a collectivist/individualistic culture, and understanding of pragmatism versus sticking to plans.

4   Conclusion

Discovered the underlying influence of culture during the innovation process in cross-cultural companies, we focused on two very important countries for innovations in the industrial sector: China and Germany. Their national cultures and their historical influences are very different. This leads to frictions and preventable problems during the innovation process in Chinese-German working environments. The authors analyzed the differences with a questionnaire for qualitative data and interviews for qualitative data gathering. Based on this data, guidelines for managers were elaborated. The result confirmed most of the factors revealed by former researchers. The derived guidelines are described in the following:

- Formal meeting structures are more important for Germans, but German managers should consider conducting 1-on1 meetings to discuss negotiable points in advance with Chinese engineers who could be afraid to lose face in bigger meetings.
- Chinese having a long-term oriented culture tend to think longer about innovative ideas before offering them. Due to this fact, foreign managers should be aware that their employees spend a lot of effort to elaborate the idea and should never directly reject them.
- Chinese engineers overall accept monthly milestones. Being aware of the possibility to pragmatically skip parts of the structured proceeding to enhance a faster innovation process and therefore more time for testing the prototype.
- Hierarchy is very important in China, thus German employees should be aware to stick to the hierarchical order.
- Chinese managers should be aware that most Germans think of engineers as most important persons and main driver for the innovation process. This can lead to conflicts with Chinese for whom hierarchy is more important than the department background.

- In Germany on-the-job trainings and further education is very popular on all hierarchical levels, but in China most companies do not spend much effort in the further education of their employees. German joint-ventures in China should try to be an exception and start with trainings, e.g. soft skills, or intercultural communication abilities. Furthermore, this probably decreases the employee fluctuation.
- According to the interviewees a lot Chinese engineers are afraid of making mistakes when they speak English. Therefore Western managers should try to create a comfortable setting while discussion in a foreign language.
- Managers could use official awards which will please both the German employees who are more driven by the intrinsic motivation to improve something and the Chinese employees whose face would be strengthen due to such an award.
- According to the interviewees the best possibility to enhance the intercultural collaboration between Chinese and German is sending the employees to the other country to get used to the specific national business habits.

Though most of the findings consist on the former studies that Chinese were less individualized and stressed more on relationship, having long-term thought rather than short-term, results on the uncertainty avoidance dimension needed to be check further since some mismatch findings occurred. It might be caused by the culture transportation and more competitive environments in the rapid innovation process.

This research dealt with national cultural influence on the innovation process. Although this process is very important for companies in the industrial sector, there are a lot more processes in companies which influence its success. Further research could analyze e.g. the national culture influence on strategic decisions or the marketing.

All in all only two different cultures C Chinese and German - were analyzed. In total 92 questionnaires were collected due to the spread method of the surveys, and the amount of the samples were unbalanced with 28 Chinese against 64 Germans. Considering this issue, the author did not conduct strict statistical comparisons to test the significance of difference on each item, but gave preliminary findings on the tendency of performance between Chinese and Germans. These tendency was used to elaborate guidelines for managers in Sino-Germany Companies to encourage innovations. In future research, more samples should be collected and statistically compared to convince the result.

Acknowledgement. This study was supported by the National Natural Science Foundation of China (NSFC, Grant Number 71101079 and Grant Number 71471095). This study was also supported by Tsinghua University Initiative Scientific Research Program under Grant Number: 20131089234.

References

1. Altermatt, B.: Questionnaire & survey design. Accessed 23 May 2011 (2006)
2. Avison, D., Malaurent, J.: Impact of cultural differences: A case study of erp introduction in china. Int. J. Inf. Manage. **27**(5), 368–374 (2007)
3. Becheikh, N., Landry, R., Amara, N.: Lessons from innovation empirical studies in the manufacturing sector: a systematic review of the literature from 1993–2003. Technovation **26**(5), 644–664 (2006)
4. Börjesson, S., Elmquist, M., Hooge, S.: The challenges of innovation capability building: Learning from longitudinal studies of innovation efforts at renault and volvo cars. J. Eng. Technol. Manage. **31**, 120–140 (2014)
5. Eisenhardt, K.M.: Building theories from case study research. Acad. Manage. Rev. **14**(4), 532–550 (1989)
6. Fitzsimmons, S.R., Stamper, C.L.: How societal culture influences friction in the employee-organization relationship. Hum. Resour. Manage. Rev. **24**(1), 80–94 (2014)
7. Frankelius, P.: Questioning two myths in innovation literature. J. High Technol. Manage. Res. **20**(1), 40–51 (2009)
8. Gubrium, J.F., Holstein, J.A.: Handbook of Interview Research: Context and Method. Sage, Thousand Oaks (2002)
9. Hofstede, G.: Organizations and Cultures: Software of the Mind. McGrawHill, New York (1991)
10. Tayeb, M.: Conducting research across cultures: overcoming drawbacks and obstacles. Int. J. Cross Cult. Manage. **1**(1), 91–108 (2001)
11. Wentz, R.C.: Die Innovationsmaschine: Wie die weltbesten Unternehmen Innovationen managen. Springer, Heidelberg (2008)
12. Wentz, R.C.: The Innovation Machine: How the World's Best Companies Manage Innovation. Createspace, Charleston (2012)
13. Yang, B.: Confucianism, socialism, and capitalism: A comparison of cultural ideologies and implied managerial philosophies and practices in the pr china. Hum. Resour. Manage. Rev. **22**(3), 165–178 (2012)
14. Yang, K.S.: Chinese values and the search for culture-free dimensions of culture. Int. J. Psychol. **18**, 143–164 (1987)

From Invisible to Visible: The Evolution of Space Formation of the Nineteenth Century Christian Missionary Work in Taiwan

Yin-Chun Tseng[1(✉)], Kun-Chen Chang[2], Fu-Kuo Mii[3],
and Chiu-Wei Chien[4]

[1] Doctoral Program in Design, College of Design,
National Taipei University of Technology, Taipei City 10608, Taiwan
ycl208@gmail.com
[2] National Taipei University of Technology, Taipei City 10608, Taiwan
kunchen@ntut.edu.tw
[3] Tamkang University, Tamsui District, New Taipei City 25137, Taiwan
072654@mail.tku.edu.tw
[4] National Taiwan University of Arts, Ban Ciao City, Taipei 22058, Taiwan
chiewei@gmail.com

Abstract. The nineteenth century, Priest Mackay carried out the missionary work in Taiwan with the permission from The Presbyterian Church in Canada. The purpose of this study was to investigate how Mackay in a foreign land pioneer the missionary gathering space. MacKay gathered believers at temples, under trees or in hotels at the early stage. As the believers became more, some families started to provide gathering space and donated. In small towns the churches were usually built in private homes or with small size while they were built tall and with Western-style in densely populated towns. Mackay established small schools where it was densely populated in order to cultivate future missionaries. Also in many churches drug stores were installed, by which it facilitated the distribution of western medication in northern Taiwan. The evolution of missionary spatial form reflected the attitude of Taiwanese people toward the foreign religion. And from the change in space it also reflected that the relationship between Taiwanese and Christianity were gradually being recognized.

Keywords: Priest Mackay · The Presbyterian Church · Church · Missionary

1 Introduction

George Leslie Mackay is an important figure in the Presbyterian Church's missionary activities in northern Taiwan. As written in the 1892 publication, From Far Formosa, George Leslie Mackay, who was both a frontier and a leader, had established a total of 60 churches. The five churches established by Mackay after his arrival in Tamsui, northern Taiwan, in 1872 included the churches in Gō-kó-khin (五股坑), Sin-káng (新港社), Chiu-nih (洲裡), and Sai-thâm-tóe Church (獅潭底). Before his first return to Canada to report his work, Mackay had established 21 churches in northern Taiwan.

© Springer International Publishing Switzerland 2015
P.L.P. Rau (Ed.): CCD 2015, Part I, LNCS 9180, pp. 392–402, 2015.
DOI: 10.1007/978-3-319-20907-4_36

After returning to northern Taiwan in 1882, Mackay further established over 40 churches in the Kabalan Plain, most of which were churches for Taiwan's Pingpu Aborigines and Han Chinese. Before his second return to Canada to report his work in August 1893, Mackay had established eight churches in the Taipei Basin and nine churches on the west coast of northern Taiwan, making this time period the heyday of Mackay's missionary work. However, as a result of damages caused by the Sino-French War and Taiwanese people's fear and anti-foreigner sentiments, at least seven mission stations in Tōa-liong-tōng (大龍峒), Bang-kahe (艋舺), Sek-khán (錫口), Sin-tiàm (新店), Chiu-nih (洲裡), Pat-li-hun (八里坌), and Gō-kó-khin (五股坑) were damaged or destroyed. Through the reconstruction of churches, the influence of Mackay's missionary work was strengthened.

When Mackay returned to northern Taiwan from Canada in November 1895, the regime in Taiwan had shifted from the Ching Dynasty to the Japanese Colonial Period, and the environment had undergone a drastic change, and Mackay made every effort to keep churches running in order to conciliate worshipers and keep mission stations running.

From his arrival in northern Taiwan for his missionary work in 1872 to dying of throat cancer in 1901, Mackay spent nearly 25 years in Taiwan, not counting his furlough to Canada for four and a half years. During his stay in Taiwan, Mackay successfully promulgated a foreign religion in northern Taiwan and established 60 mission stations. This study focuses on discussions of how 60 to 70 mission stations and preaching points, where Mackay's missionary activities were conducted, were built from intangible to tangible. Furthermore, this study examines the source of the spaces for Mackay's missionary activities, the reasons why these spaces were adapted, and the style changes of these spaces.

2 Literature Review

The literature review mainly addresses issues in relation to changes in architecture and space arrangements in the course of Mackay's missionary work.

2.1 Discussions on a Single Architecture

Publications, such as *The Blueprint for the Investigation and Repair of Tamkang Mackay Cemetery, The Blueprint for the Investigation and Repair of Oxford College (1999)* by Li Chien-Lang, *The Blueprint for the Research and Repair of a Taipei County Monument - Tamsúi Presbyterian Church (2005)* by Chou Ke-hwa and Chou Tsung-hsien, and *Architectural Treasures Designed by Mackay (2006)* by Li Chien-ling are largely historical research on a chosen architecture constructed by Mackay. Most of these publications, which cover the chosen architecture's contributions in the course of Mackay's missionary work, are merely analysis and research on a single architecture.

2.2   Discussions on the System and Architectural Styles of Presbyterian Churches in Northern Taiwan

The publication *Local Characteristics of Mackay Architecture Series in Tamsui (1994)* by Kao Tsann-rong covers a series of Mackay architectures in two different time periods. Mackay architectures in the earlier period were built by Mackay, while construction of Mackay architectures in the later period was led by Rev. William Gauld and Kenneth W. Dowie. This publication is centered on changes in the function and style of architectures, and Mackay architectures as a fusion of Chinese and Western architectures. *Christian Architectures in Tamsui in the 1880s-1930s (1999)* by Li Chien-lang consists of two parts: Mackay's architectural ideas in the first part and Rev. William Gauld architectures in the second part. Using isometric drawing to produce a pictorial representation of the Mackay Architecture series in Tamsui (including Mackay Mission Hospital, Oxford College, and Tamsúi Presbyterian Church), and offering a brief explanation of individual architecture's distinctive features, this publication is more of an analysis on construction materials and architectural features than a discussion on historical elements.

The Development of Protestants in Hsinchu in the Ching Dynasty (2002) by Chiang Tien-Chien, which was published in the 5th issue of *the Journal of Social Studies Education*, expounds on the development of churches in the Tek-chhàm (竹塹) area and the ethnic group distributions at that time. For example, the church in Sin-káng (新港) was mainly attended by the Pingpu aborigine people, while the church in Sai-thâm-tóe (獅潭底) was mainly attended by the Shēngfān (生番) aboriginal savage people. The church in Yueh-mei (月眉) was the head of all Hakka churches, and other Hakka churches in Lung-t'an (龍潭), Hsien-ts'ai-weng (鹹菜甕), and Hsin-p'u (新埔) were subsequently established.

In conclusion, existing relevant studies have no systematic analysis and discussions on all spaces where Mackay carried out his missionary activities in Taiwan.

3   Methodology

By scrutinizing historical texts that document Mackey's missionary activities in Taiwan, this study compares, analyzes, and summarizes the establishment and construction of spaces for Mackay' missionary activities. These spaces include mission stations, missionary residences, mission hospitals, and missionary training schools. In addition, regarding how spaces hidden amongst private residences were converted to western-style churches, this study offers a brief explanation on the sources of these spaces and the key to their transformation. A brief description of obtainable relevant literature: *From Far Formosa, The History of Presbyterian Churches in Northern Taiwan, and Elder John Lai's Archives* are as follows:

From Far Formosa was dictated by Mackay, and its translated version was published by Aletheia University. *From Far Formosa* documents Mackay's journey from San Francisco on November 1, 1871 to Yokohama in Japan, Guangdong in China, Hong Kong, and finally arriving in Taiwan for his missionary work. The last documented date in *From Far Formosa* is February 10, 1901. With the exception of a missing diary from 1883, *From Far Formosa* offers a complete record of Mackay's nearly three-decades of medical and missionary activities in Taiwan, and provides a window into the course of Mackay's missionary work in Taiwan, as well as important events regarding the establishment of the churches.

From Far Formosa (the Chinese translation version: A Chronicle of Events in Formosa: Memoirs of George Leslie Mackay in Taiwan) was dictated by Mackay, edited by J. A. MacDonald, and published in London, the United Kingdom, in 1896. *From Far Formosa* was not written by Mackay himself; instead, it was written by those who considered Mackay's experiences in Taiwan worth recording and being told to future generations when Mackay returned to Canada for his second furlough and described his experiences and work in Taiwan to people in Canada. As Mackay would rather dedicate himself to the arduous missionary work than have the patience to record it, all relevant information was collected and organized by compilers, and both the initial and final manuscript of *From Far Formosa* were revised according to Mackay's instructions. *From Far Formosa* is a book centering on Mackay's various experiences and memories in Taiwan.

Elder John Lai's Archives, an archive of the history of churches in Taiwan, primarily consists of three sections, and includes seven volumes of church history, Professor Lai Yung-hsiang's relevant studies, and other scholars' historical texts and documents regarding the history of churches in Taiwan. Through the collected data and literature about the development of churches in Taiwan in the era of Spanish Formosa and Dutch Formosa, as well as research papers on the development of the Presbyterian Church of England and the Presbyterian Church of Canada in Taiwan, Elder John Lai's Archives provide valuable insights into the historical setting of Taiwan at that time, and other important missionary events.

4 Results

Missionary Mackay arrived in Takao (打狗) in southern Taiwan on December 29, 1871 to meet Rev. Hugh Ritchie from the Presbyterian Church of England, and wished to learn and understand the way missionary work was carried out in Taiwan. On March 9, 1872, Mackay, Rev. Hugh Ritchie, and Dr. Matthew Dickson travelled to Tam-súi and embarked on their over-a-month surveillance excursion in the parish. During the nearly-90-day surveillance excursion, Mackay spent 26 days at the residence of Rev. Hugh Ritchie and the remaining days at different churches, village houses' storage areas, or spaces where domesticated animals were raised. As a result, shortly after his arrival in Taiwan, Mackay had already experienced life in a variety of environments.

4.1 Early Spaces for Mackay's Missionary Work (Early 1872 to Late 1874)

At his second arrival in Tam-súi on April 8, 1872, Mackay leased a barn as his first dwelling place through the introduction of English businessman John Dodd. His residence in Tam-súi became the first space for his missionary activities (Kuo 1971).

Mackay subsequently used "the 10 Commandments" flyer as a medium for his missionary work. He posted the flyer on the door of his residence, distributed copies of this flyer all across Tam-súi, and successfully recruited his first disciple and follower - Giam Chheng Hoa. In the beginning of June 1872, Mackay officially started his medical practice and built a bamboo cottage next to his residence to house patients that required medical treatments. This bamboo cottage was the first space extended from Mackay's house. After receiving treatments, patients usually participated in Mackay's worship services. Mackay used to say his small hut was like a dwelling place, a church, a hospital, and a school at the same time, although there were not many students yet (Mackay 2012).

In early days, spaces used as a mission station came from two resources. The first source was barns and spaces at home, as offered by Mackay's followers, to perform missionary activities. Some believers also offered land for the construction of mission stations, such as the mission stations in Gō-kó-khin (五股坑), Chiu-nih (洲裡), Pat-li-hun (八裡坌), Sin-káng (新港社), and Sin-tiàm (新店). Mackay also handed out flyers of "the 10 Commandments" to his followers in order the followers could post the flyers on their house doors to declare their belief in Christianity.

Another source was self-built thatched huts. Mission stations of this type included the mission stations in San-teng-po (三重埔) and Sai-thâm-tóe (獅潭底). The mission station in Sai-thâm-tóe (獅潭底), which was located in the inner mountainous area of Miaoli County, and a habitat of the Shēngfān aboriginal savage people, only lasted for three months because a missionary was mistakenly slain by the Shēngfān aboriginal savage people. In addition, in towns and cities without any mission stations, Mackay usually performed his missionary activities and handed out flyers of "the 10 Commandments" on streets, outside temples, or under the shade of large tree.

Early locations for Mackay's missionary works were mostly hidden amongst private residences, and these mission stations looked nothing like western-style mission stations. Built with simple and crude construction materials (soil blocks and thatches), these mission stations could easily be destroyed by pagans. However, such "intangible" mission stations provided Mackay with space for living and teaching. As mentioned in a record at the end of 1874, Mackay suffered from physical discomfort due to having a fever 11 times, as well as skin ulcers and abscesses twice, the cause of which were allegedly Mackey's visits to unhygienic places. However, during his illness, Mackay stayed at neighboring mission stations, where the living conditions were better. Therefore, mission stations also became an important space for living.

4.2   Spaces Built for Mackay's Early Missionary Work (Early 1875 – Late 1879)

In 1875, Rev. J.B. Fraser came to Taiwan as a doctor/pastor to assist Mackay with missionary work. Rev. J.B. Fraser also brought subsidiary funds from the Canadian Presbyterian Church for construction. Planning of the construction of two mission houses commenced in 1875, and the construction was completed in 1876 or 1877. The two mission houses were both comfortable and modern buildings, the construction of which was under the charge of Rev. J.B. Fraser, as Mackay was itinerating for his missionary work. According to historical records, Mackay converted one room of his residence into a classroom, while Rev. J.B. Fraser converted one room in his residence into a dispensary.

Mission stations built in the period between 1875 and 1870 were located primarily in the Taipei Basin, and secondarily on the west coast of northern Taiwan. Prosperous cities were sought-after locations for renting a place to set up a mission station. Mackay himself took up the matter of leasing most of time, while some followers came forward to deal with leasing matters from time to time; however, not many followers offered their own residence. At that time, the residents of two large cities, Bang-kahe (艋舺) and Tek-chhàm (竹塹) (Mackay 2007) in northern Taiwan, were swamped with anti-foreigner sentiment. The second day after Mackay hung a "Christianity" board outside his rental premise, the board was attacked and smashed. Local gangsters also threatened residents and banned them from leasing or selling their properties. Mission stations in Tōa-liong-tōng (大龍峒) (Zuo 1997), Keelung, and San-kak-éng (三角湧) (Lai 1995) were finally established after local residents' ferocious protests and the intercession of local influential people. Before returning to Canada in 1879, Mackay had set up a total of 20 churches, most of which were in the Taipei Basin. Each mission station contained a space for religious services, a space for teaching, a free private school (elementary school), a space for living, and a dispensary.

Mackay had been treating patients in both cities and rural villages, and sometimes he treated patients at patients' houses and other times on the streets. The earliest hospitals, which were established in Keelung and Tam-súi in 1879, (Mackay 2012) had only one bedroom. The hospital in Tam-súi, the location of the medical headquarters, was funded by a donation of Madame Mackay in Detroit to memorialize her late husband Captain Mackay. The hospital was equipped with hospital wards and necessary medical facilities (Mackay 2007). In addition to recruiting doctors from foreign firms to assist the hospital, Mackay organized students' internship at the hospital. In addition to providing medical treatment, the hospital was also where students received training.

4.3   Spaces for Missionary Work After Mackay Returned to Canada to Report His Work (Early 1881 – Late 1884)

Mackay left Tam-súi for Canada on December 27, 1879 to report his work, and returned from Canada to Tam-súi on December 19, 1881. After returning to Taiwan, Mackay established the Oxford College, a girls' school, Bang-kahe (艋舺) Mission Station, and Sin-tiàm (新店) Mission Station through fundraising. As the mission stations in San-chiao-p'u (三角埔) had fewer Christian followers, the mission station in San-chiao-p'u was moved to Tsúi-tng-kha (水返腳).

While carrying out his missionary work, Mackay spared no effort to educate and cultivate future missionaries. Mackay considered evangelizing to local men by local evangelists and local females by local female catechists a quick way to promulgate Christianity as there was neither language barriers nor issues with adaptation to a new environment. Finally, the Oxford College and a girls' school were built in 1882 and 1883, respectively, and male and female missionaries from the two schools were dispatched to all preaching points to preach Christianity. Both the Oxford College and the girls' school were boarding schools, which emphasized students' competency to carry out missionary work and discipline in life.

Along with a gradual increase in the number of followers in Tsúi-tng-kha (水返腳), some people offered space at their own shops as Mackay's mission stations. Furniture, including the tables and chairs at the mission station in San-chiao-p'u (三角埔), was moved to Tsúi-tng-kha (水返腳) (Lai 2002). The brick-roof mission station in Bang-kahe (艋舺) was built in 1884 on land purchased by Mackay (Mackay 2007). Spaces in the mission station included a space for religious services, a living space, a dispensary, a space for teaching, a space for operating a free private school, and dormitories for students in the free private school. Another mission station in Sin-tiàm (新店) had a total of five spaces, a pastor's bedroom, a pastor's lounge, a small lounge, a guest room, and a small room (mainly for storing medical equipment). There were five beds in four rooms, 1,000 copies of the Bible, and 100 big and small Holy Scriptures,(Chinese Academy 1962) showing the significant role of the mission station in Sin-tiàm during the course of Mackay's missionary work. However, both new mission stations were torn down in the outbreak of the Sino-French War.

As recorded in Mackay's diary in 1883, people closed their ears to Mackay's sermons, so Mackay took students to Kavalan (the modern-day Yilan County) to carry out his missionary work. Both adults and children in several villages averted and even blasphemed against him. When Mackay finally arrived in the Fan-she-t'ou (番社頭) coastal area and ran into a person who previously listened to his sermon, this person escorted Mackay and Mackay's companions to his village. A makeshift church was constructed that night and all villagers came out to listen to Mackay's sermon. Several weeks later, neighboring communities heard of Mackay and became willing to invite Mackay's missionary services to their villages, and through the chanting of hymns, aborigines in the Kavalan Plain gradually accepted Christianity. Most of the 15 mission stations set up by Mackay in 1883-1884 were self-built.

4.4   Spaces for Missionary Work After the Sino-French War (Early 1885 to 1894)

After the Sino-French War, Mackay was forced to take sanctuary in Hong Kong in October 1884 and return to Tam-súi on April 19, 1885. Most churches in northern Taiwan had been torn down. After negotiation, the Ching government made a compensatory payment in the amount of 10,000 Mexican dollars. Mackay subsequently used the compensatory payment to build six sturdy and steady mission stations. Signs and logos denoting "burned yet not ruined" were placed next to the words and logos of "Christianity". The architectural styles of the six churches can be classified into two types. The churches in Sin-tiàm (新店), Bang-kahe (艋舺), Toā-tiū-tiâ (大稻埕), and Sek-khán (錫口) were western-style mission stations with a steeple and a tall tower rising above the roof of the building. In addition to decorations, such architectural style especially dismissed Chinese feng shui as mere superstition. Another style of western-style mission stations were in Pat-li-hun (八里坌) and Chiu-nih (洲裡). Each of the six mission stations consisted of three buildings, each of which had different

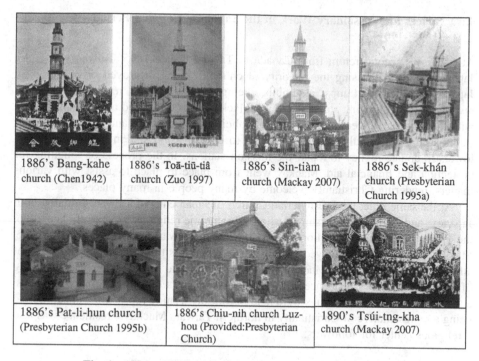

1886's Bang-kahe church (Chen1942)	1886's Toā-tiū-tiâ church (Zuo 1997)	1886's Sin-tiàm church (Mackay 2007)	1886's Sek-khán church (Presbyterian Church 1995a)
1886's Pat-li-hun church (Presbyterian Church 1995b)	1886's Chiu-nih church Luz-hou (Provided:Presbyterian Church)	1890's Tsúi-tng-kha church (Mackay 2007)	

Fig. 1. 1886 ~ 1890's churches along the bank of Tamsui river

functions: religious services, free private school, and space for living. Mackay attempted to use the modularization of architecture to declare that Christianity had taken root and grown robustly in northern Taiwan (See Fig. 1).

In 1890, the mission station in Tsúi-tng-kha (水返腳) was the voluntary donation of followers in Taiwan, and land and construction costs were covered by donations from local mission stations. Both the architectural design and construction of this mission station was supervised by Giam Chheng Hoa (嚴清華) (Mackay 2007). The property rights of the mission station belonged to churches in Taiwan, showing the self-sufficiency of churches in Taiwan at this time and missionaries' autonomy.

In 1892, the Ching government became alert to westerners' growing activities in Taiwan, and decreed that there should be a full investigation of the use of all archi-tectures built by western missionaries in Taiwan. Among the 24 mission stations in the Tam-súi River drainage basin, there were 15 western-style architectures and nine Chinese-style architectures. Only medicine was handed out in Kavalan at that time. Among the total of 23 churches, there were 18 western-style churches (three brick houses and 15 thatched huts) and five Chinese-style churches (four thatched huts and one with unidentified construction materials). In the documented four mission stations on the west coast of northern Taiwan, one had a free private school, two had a dispensary, and all were Chinese-style mission stations established on a rental premise. Among the total of 53 mission stations in northern Taiwan, there were 35 western-style architectures and 18 Chinese-style architectures. This period was considered the peak of MacKay's endeavor in setting up churches.

4.5   Spaces for Missionary Work in the Japanese Colonial Period (1895 -1901)

At Mackay's second return from Canada to Taiwan in late 1895, Taiwan was under Japanese rule. Witnessing the majority of churches being destroyed or occupied by Japanese soldiers and most assemblies being held at private residences, Mackay resorted to the following strategies. First, Mackay strived to build a good relationship with the Japanese government in order to solicit government aid and keep the mission stations intact. Secondly, Mackay traveled to each mission station to encourage followers to donate money to repair the mission stations. In the process of soliciting for protection and financial aid, Mackay went from place to place to assist with various matters, rendering Christianity welcome by many people in many places.

At the same time, the Presbyterian Church of Japan entered Taiwan. Initially, both Japanese and Taiwanese worshipers attended the same religious services. In late 1896, the first Japanese mission station was established in Taiwan with Mackay's assistance. Mackay's residence also played an important role at this time. Influential Japanese of all ranks frequently visited Mackay's museum in order to have a better understanding of Taiwan. Mackay's residence became the headquarters of his missionary activities, and all internal church meetings were held in Mackay's study room, thus, in addition to being a representative of Christianity in northern Taiwan, Mackay's residence was also a religious center for followers.

5   Summary

5.1   The Importance of Living Conditions

After Mackay returned to northern Taiwan to continue his missionary work, he gave a clear description of his temporary lodgings while visiting different preaching points, most of which were next to domesticated animals. He often recorded "spending his night in a dark, dirty, and ramshackle space". In his diary, which recorded his early missionary work in 1872-1875, he wrote that he had suffered from fever 14 times, on average five times a year. According to the record, Mackay also had smallpox, furuncles, and abscesses once a year on average (George Leslie Mackay 2012). Given the hostile living environment at the time, each preaching point became the best sanctuary for Mackay to rest and recuperate from illness, as he never stopped evangelizing and teaching activities even during his illness.

5.2   The Extension of the Teaching Space

"The Peripatetic College, a.k.a. the Itinerant College, is the first school established by Mackay in northern Taiwan. Due to Mackay's constant missionary itineration, the work of training students was performed at any time, meaning a classroom could be anywhere, such as under a banyan tree, next to a bamboo forest, seashore, mountain, valley, riversides, plain, a residential house, temporary lodging, etc. Upon the establishment of a mission station, the teaching space extended into the mission station. In addition, Mackay set up free private schools (elementary school) at several mission stations to teach male and female students over the age of 12 (Chang 1987; Lai 1992). Setting up free private schools not only provided a channel for scouting the right candidates to become future missionaries, but also eased teenagers' aversion to Christianity.

5.3   Setting up a Dispensary in Each Mission Station

In the early phase of Mackay's missionary work, he not only promulgated Christian doctrine, but became close to Taiwanese people by providing "medical treatments". In the first year, bamboo cottages were built for hospitalized patients, and there were recorded medical treatments provided at the mission stations. In 1879, Mackay subsequently established hospitals in Keelung and Tam-súi (淡水). However, the assistance provided by these establishments to followers was limited, as all medical treatments called for professional doctors. According to the records of relevant literature, the six mission stations in Sin-tiàm (新店), Bang-kahe (艋舺), San-kak-éng (三角湧), Ho-shang-chou (和尚洲), Tsúi-tng-kha (水返腳), and Sek-khán (錫口) all had a dispensary in 1885. Despite having no dispensary, the mission station in Tōa-liong-tōng (大龍峒) had a box full of western medicine books, (Chinese Academy 1962) as Mackay wished to help patients in need when medical treatments were unable to be performed. The establishment of dispensaries symbolized continuous medical aid.

5.4   The Evolution of Mission Stations

Mackay's missionary activities were initially carried out in his own residences, as well as outdoor areas, under a big tree, or next to a temple. After Mackay started to attracted followers in small towns, mission stations were built hidden among private residences or makeshift and self-built. Upon starting his missionary activities in large cities, Mackay started to establish mission stations on rental premises. After obtaining funds during his trip to Canada, Mackay built two mission stations. Following the tearing down of mission stations by mobsters in the Sino-French War, and its subsequent reconstruction, re-built mission stations started to have geo-specific distinctive styles. For example, mission stations in the Taipei Basin were built like western-style churches, mission stations in the Kavalan Plain were mostly self-built thatched western-style mission stations, and mission stations on the west coast of northern Taiwan were mostly built on rental premises. After mission stations across Taiwan were destroyed in the Japanese Colonial Period in 1895, Mackay began to request that each mission station repair their own building, which ushered in a period of self-sufficient mission stations. In Mackay's 25 years in Taiwan, he had encountered various difficulties at different stages. Political power, which was key in the destruction of mission stations, accidently became a crucial element for the reconstruction of wrecked mission stations. By setting up both tangible and intangible mission stations in cities and villages across northern Taiwan, and turning mission stations from ramshackle thatched huts to rock-solid brick buildings, Mackay had successfully planted Christian culture in northern Taiwan.

References

Chinese Academy: The File of the Negotiation of China, France and Vietnam (1962)

Mackay, G.L.: The Assembly of Presbyterian Church of Northern Taiwan. Diaries of George Leslie Mackay 1871–1901. Tipi (Translation) (2012)

Mackay, G.L.: edited by J. A. Macdonald, translated by Wan-Seng Lin, published by Avanguard. From Far Formosa¬-The Island, its People and Mission (2007)

Chen, H.-W.: The History of Presbyterian Church of Northern. The Presbyterian Church of Taiwan, Taiwan (Translation) (1942)

Kuo, H.-L.: Foreign Protestant Missionary: The Autography of George Leslie MacKay, P71. Tainan Seminary (1971)

Chang, J.: The Note of Presbyterian John Chang: The Story of A-Tsang-a, Toā-Chiu Church, April 1987

Lai, J.: 189 The Daughter-in-law: Tsang-a, History of Church, 2nd edition (1992)

Lai, J.: 280 The Establishment of Keelung Church and Gao – Zhen, History of Church, 3rd edition (1995)

Lai, J.: 576 The Establishment of Tsúi-tng-kha Church, History of Church, 6rd edition (2002)

Presbyterian Church in Taiwan: The 120th Anniversary of the Establishment of Sek-khán Church, Special Edition, pp. 1875–1995 (1995a)

Presbyterian Church in Taiwan: The 120th Anniversary of the Establishment of Pat–li–hun Church, Special Edition, pp. 1874–1995 (1995b)

Zuo, W.-H.: The 120th Anniversary of the Establishment of Toā-tiū-tiâ Church, Special Edition, 1875-1995, The Development and History of 120 years' Establishment of Toā-tiū-tiâ Church, pp. 44–45 (1997)

Exploring Socioeconomic and Sociocultural Implications of ICT Use: An Ethnographic Study of Indigenous People in Malaysia

Norazlinawati Walid[1](✉), Emma Nuraihan Mior Ibrahim[1], Chee Siang Ang[2], and Norlaila Md. Noor[2]

[1] Faculty of Computer and Mathematical Sciences, Universiti Teknologi MARA, Shah Alam, Malaysia
norazlinawati_lynn@yahoo.com.my,
emma@tmsk.uitm.edu.my
[2] School of Engineering and Digital Arts, Kent University, Canterbury, UK
csa8@kent.ac.uk, norlaila@tmsk.uitm.edu.my

Abstract. In some countries, it is revealed that the ICT usage by indigenous people is possible to be accomplished and utilized to deliver benefits. For the purpose of development and advancement of Orang Asli (one of the indigenous groups in Malaysia) and in support of the national aspirations in Vision 2020, ICT exposure to Orang Asli requires holistic implementation. Therefore, the predominant issue to be discovered comprehensively is about Orang Asli and it is imperative to understand their needs and requirements in terms of ICT acceptance, appropriation, barriers, as well as infrastructure and infostructure issues. In conclusion, we found four main aspects to be considered in research involving Orang Asli's use of ICT and benefit ICT: (i) the influential people, (ii) infrastructure barriers (iii) social development issues, and (iv) motivational factors.

Keywords: Indigenous · Orang asli · Malaysia · Socioeconomic · Sociocultural · ICT use · Focus group · Thematic analysis · Card sorting · Expert reviewer

1 Introduction

Malaysia is a multicultural and multilingual country. Based on the historical findings, the indigenous groups that originally occupied Malaysia consisted of Malays, the Orang Asli that only settled in Peninsula Malaysia [1], and the native ethnic groups in Sabah and Sarawak [2, 28]. Among the four groups, Orang Asli community was and still is a minority and their existence is less known to the public. Their socioeconomic development is not as fast as other communities in Malaysia, especially in context of technological development, particularly ICT adoption. Orang Asli's acceptance of ICT is quite slow and not comprehensive. Drawing from the work looking into the improvement of indigenous groups in other countries, it is believed that these communities can be improved with the aid of ICT projects such as website containing information on arts and culture of indigenous people, learning using multimedia in indigenous languages, e-businesses that preserve traditional crafts while strengthening local economies and so on. Besides, there are also successful projects in Malaysia

© Springer International Publishing Switzerland 2015
P.L.P. Rau (Ed.): CCD 2015, Part I, LNCS 9180, pp. 403–413, 2015.
DOI: 10.1007/978-3-319-20907-4_37

known as e-Bario and e-Bedian which were developed specifically for indigenous community in Sarawak [3]. However, the ICT project for Orang Asli as far as Department of Orang Asli Development (JAKOA) is concerned, are restricted to providing laptops for Orang Asli's children who were offered to pursue their studies at universities and another initiative is a computer training centre located in Kluang, Johor while in reality Orang Asli communities are spread across the entire Peninsular Malaysia. ICT development for them is not sufficiently implemented partly due to their lack of ICT adoption [2]. Based on the justification for socioeconomic development of Orang Asli communities, they would certainly benefit from ICT use. This is in line with Malaysia's aspiration in the Vision 2020 of the overall development for all citizens, closing the socioeconomic gap [4]. One out of nine main goals of Vision 2020 is to create a scientific and progressive society that is innovative and advanced in technology use and development. Hence, our motivation is to explore the breadth and depth of the socioeconomic and sociocultural implications of ICT use among the Orang Asli. Our aim is to understand the needs and requirements for technology acceptance and appropriation as well as the barrier of ICT adoption in the target community. This will give us an insight into their learning ability, economic capability, cognitive style, daily practice and behaviour towards ICT.

2   Research Background

2.1   Orang Asli in Malaysia

Based on the recorded history, Orang Asli originated from neighbouring Champa, Indo China, Burma and Sumatra [5] and was the earliest group of people that came to Malaya (now known as Malaysia). They settled in some parts of Peninsular Malaysia long before the Malay community. The terminology of Orang Asli as an ethnic category only existed after 1960 [2]. Previously there were many terms used by anthropologists and administrators to categorize this group such as 'Orang Darat', 'Orang Laut', 'Bersisi', 'Mantra' and 'Orang Mawas' [2] (Fig. 1).

Orang Asli in Malaysia is not a homogeneous ethnic minority. They represent a heterogeneous community because they have unique differences, particularly in terms of sociocultural for each ethnic group. The rationale behind this difference is related to the Orang Asli background itself that officially consisted of 18 tribes in Peninsular Malaysia

Fig. 1. Environment of Orang Asli

and they are categorized into three main groups based on their mother tongues and customs: they are Negrito, Senoi and Proto-Malay. Negrito, is an ethnic group which contains Kensiu, Kintak, Jahai, Lanoh, Mendriq and Bateq. For Senoi group, it comprises of the Semai tribe, Temiar, Jahut, Che Wong, Mahmeri and Memoq Beri while Proto-Malay group consists of Temuan, Semelai, Jakun, Kanaq, Kuala and Seletar [22].

In the past, a majority of them lived in the forest and practiced the traditional way of life that was deeply influenced by the natural environment and maintained the old practices of their ancestors. However, the development of Orang Asli has experienced significant changes as the results of Malaysian government transformation and approach through the establishment of JAKOA in 1954. Various drastic development programs were carried out specifically for Orang Asli after the end of crisis in late 1980 s. Among the development programs, focuses were given to providing housing aid, basic infrastructures, social facilities, educational programs, and health programs. It also aimed to increase residents' income and alleviate poverty through farming and agricultural projects [2].

2.2   Orang Asli's Socioeconomic and Sociocultural Development

The formation of a sovereign Malaysia on 16 September 1963 opened new paths for Orang Asli's socioeconomic development because JAKOA's role has been expanded to develop their socioeconomic status and living conditions. Orang Asli has shown significant improvements socioeconomically compared to 20 years ago [6] and this included family economy [7, 22], education [8, 23], healthcare [9], and technology [10]. They are no longer considered a "traditional" community that opposes self-development and advancement. Generally, Orang Asli was exposed to two types of developments which are, the one designed specifically for them and the general national development that has a direct impact on them. However, at that time, the general public often assumed that Orang Asli did not want to participate in economic progress; hence they failed to contribute to the nation's development [11]. Therefore, efforts to provide development to Orang Asli community faced tough challenges. Among the key areas that need to be handled are problems of poverty, lack of education, lack of political power and attitude change.

However, JAKOA commitment in delivering development to Orang Asli has in-creased after several decades of work especially in the context of social development, education and health [9]. It also implemented with more systematic, planned approaches which are more in line with Orang Asli's culture. Despite the erosive impact of the Orang Asli culture due to some development initiatives implemented [6], these development efforts largely received positive responses from Orang Asli community. In fact, it is a matter of how the development was brought to them.

Apart from socioeconomic development, sociocultural aspects of Orang Asli are also an important part that needs to be investigated in order to know them well. 18 Orang Asli tribes each possess their own sociocultural identities. Among the ceremonies that are mostly emphasized are weddings, births, deaths, and appointment of a chief or more commonly known as Batin. Other than the diversity of their ritual practices, Orang Asli is also known to have a lot of ancestral beliefs and taboos.

Among the most significant ones are taboos in nutritional aspects, the current relationship of humans or between humans and animals, as well as medical [5, 12] beliefs.
Although every ethnic group has differences in practice of their traditional ceremonies
and taboos, it is fair to say that they share some fundamental cultural practices.

The Orang Asli community puts an emphasis in appointment of the chairman or
better known as Batin appointed among men. For each ethnic group, Batin has the
authority over all issues in the village including marital affairs and death, as head of
customs and administrative of the village's socioeconomic activities [5]. Batin's
appointment can be accomplished through heredity or by the individual's ability and
personality through villagers election, selected by management team member or the
will of previous Batin. In every Orang Asli group, Batin is highly respected. Villagers
will obey his instructions because he has the highest authority. At present, a Batin's
role has also been widely received as a liaison person with government agencies and
neighbouring villages.

Another important ceremony, known as 'Sewang' consists of music, dancing and
singing especially in the wedding celebration and sometimes is a ritual to medicinal
procedures [5]. This is because from the medical perspective, these rituals predate the
views and opinions of shaman. Normally Orang Asli will get cures from shaman
be-fore getting hospital treatments.

2.3   ICT Adoption of Orang Asli in Malaysia

In general, local researchers agree that Orang Asli does not reject ICT development [4, 10]
because the community thinks that ICT is a platform to help them advance and succeed in
the modern world. However, according to W. Amir Zal [11] the acceptance of any new
things or ideas is often related to their cognitive styles, attitudes, behaviours and norms.

It is well-known that ICT adoption among Orang Asli is very slow compared to other
communities in Malaysia [2]. Among the main contributors to this problem are the
educational and economic constrains [10]. Appropriate and effective strategies to
pro-mote Orang Asli use of ICT are still not fully grasped by the government nor NGOs.
This is evident because there are no other successful ICT projects for Orang Asli apart
from e-Bario and e-Badian which targeted Sarawak's indigenous. This indicates that
Orang Asli has somehow lagged behind in ICT use even though there are a few individuals among them who are skilled and follow the development of ICT on their own.

3   A Global View on Indigenous Groups' Attitude Towards ICT

Globally, advancements in ICT are rapid, and in some cases, even a fully developed
and semi-developed society fails to catch up with the latest technological changes.
Given this, it is not hard to imagine the difficulty faced by the indigenous groups
worldwide in regards to ICT adoption. Therefore, their ability to pursue modernization
and development of ICT has become an important topic addressed by researchers
worldwide.

Exposure to ICT usage is not only focused on the technical aspect but it is a holistic change, involving technological implications in line with their culture, language, lifestyle, as well as level of education and economic ability to accommodate the needs. Thus, studying the level of ICT acceptance of the indigenous group is inherently complex. It is therefore not surprisingly the level of ITC acceptance varies widely across the world. However, some researchers stated that the most important aspect for indigenous groups to accept ICT is their awareness [13]. They need to be exposed to the importance, benefits and values of ICT. But, for the researchers of this study, all aspects need to move in tandem so that the acceptance of ICT is not limited only to the physical capabilities which are from the aspects of cost, skills and facility but mentally and phycology as well.

Effort to provide ICT exposure to the indigenous people is very active around the world. As specified by Native American observers, the evolution of cultural change is always happening based on current technology. Unlike the past in which iron knives and horses left an impact, today, the Internet is able to provide opportunities for Native American to support themselves and their tribes [14]. Therefore, the role of ICT is reflected as being very significant and powerful.

Some administrative personnel have to work hard to provide exposure and awareness on Internet use for the indigenous group such as in Northern Territory of Australia. It is a very remote and economically backward region. However their indigenous students are supplied with wireless-enabled laptop Internet called the 'XO' for free. These devices were supplied by a charitable organization on an initiative named One Child One Laptop (OLCP) and the XO is specifically designed to survive the harsh conditions there [15].

Efforts must not only be focused on infrastructure: further work should involve the effort to expose them to "infostructure" such as system and software to receive and disseminate information relating to indigenous information. For instance, Ashninka, the indigenous communities of Peru, were introduced to Telematic Network for Indigenous Populations in 2000 as an innovative project of indigenous e-commerce that aims to provide the indigenous people with an online purchasing portal that allows visitors to buy their products, including music, handicrafts and food [16]. In addition, the eThekwini Municipal Library's Libraries and Heritage Department has developed a localized Wiki containing local knowledge and histories of indigenous community in Duban, South Africa [21].

The indigenous community in Brazil also had the opportunity to enjoy Internet connectivity when Brazilian scientists established collaboration efforts to co-write articles with scientists from 114 countries from 1995 to 1997. Therefore, the Brazilians indigenous people were able to work together in order to solve environmental, social, and political problems of common concern [14].

Although there are many positive responses from the indigenous individuals which proved that they are willing to embrace ICT and economic progress through the use of ICT, creating the awareness is not an easy process. The acceptance of ICT by the indigenous people is still not comprehensively achieved worldwide because there are areas with low percentage of ICT use such as those in Australia. Findings showed that the ICT adoption by indigenous communities in very remote areas is very low par-ticularly in using the Internet [17, 18]. The same situation also happens to the Orang

Asli in Malaysia: their acceptance of ICT usage is still low. This is supported by a report published in The Indigenous World 2014; indigenous groups over the world are lagging in a few areas such as education, work, entrepreneurship, regional development, as well as science and technology [19].

4 Methodology

In this study, we employed a qualitative approach to carry out an empirical study aiming to identify the influence of socioeconomic and sociocultural of Orang Asli towards acceptance and use of ICT. Focus groups and observations were conducted with 75 Orang Asli considered as informer from 5 villages in Peninsular Malaysia. Thematic analysis was conducted to analyse the rich qualitative data. To support the result obtained from thematic analysis, a card sorting exercise and open-ended interviews were carried out with six experts from three different fields.

4.1 Focus Group

We decided to conduct focus groups in order to collect in-depth information about this complex topic in a relatively short space of time, since the aim of the focus groups was not to achieve consensus [24] but more on the simulation of new ideas and high level of discussion. Five Orang Asli's villages were chosen for this study. Each village provided the researchers with 15 informers, resulting in a total of 75 informers, aged between 15 and 80 years old from diverse backgrounds (Tables 1 and 2).

Although some researchers favour participant selection characterized by homogeneity [20, 25, 26] such as occupation, age, gender, education level, or health problem; due to the need of considering the perspective from multiple perspectives, the homogeneity issue is not emphasized and only three aspects are taken into consideration:

- original Orang Asli – there are outsiders living in the Orang Asli's village due to inter-marriage, so they were not selected;
- past the age level of at least 15 years old – at this age he/she should able to read if he/she attends the government school as recommended;
- possess knowledge of technology –those who were selected have some minimal knowledge about television, radio, telephone and computer to ensure that they can discuss issues related to technology.

Focus groups were conducted to cover four aspects namely healthcare, education, subsistence, and ICT adoption with the aim to discover current socioeconomic

Table 1. Selected orang asli village for focus group

Category	Village
Urban	Kampung Orang Asli Bukit Lanjan, Selangor
Sub-Urban	Kampung Orang Asli Ulu Jelintoh, Perak
	Kampung Orang Asli Bukit Payung, Malacca
	Kampung Orang Asli Donglai Baru, Selangor
Rural	Kampung Orang Asli Bukit Choh, Perak

Table 2. List of expert reviewers

Name	Expert Area	Additional Information
Associate Professor Dr. Juli a/l Edo	Anthropology	Lecturer in Anthropology and Sociology of Orang Asli at University of Malaya, Malaysia and an Orang Asli descent
Dr. Wan Ahmad Amir Zal bin Wan Ismail	Anthropology	Lecturer from School of Social and Economic Development, Malaysia Terengganu University
Dr. NurulFadzilah binti Deraman	Medical Practitioner	7 years' service at Hospital Orang Asli Gombak and act as Head of Medical Section
Dr. Nabil Muhammad bin Al Kuddos	Medical Practitioner	3 years' service at Hospital Orang Asli Gombak and an active doctor in the 1Malaysia Mobile Clinic program specifically for Orang Asli.
Mr. Mohd Jiwa bin Zulkifli	Development and growth on Orang Asli community	Has served for 40 years with JAKOA: began in 1974 and he is very knowledgeable about the development of Orang Asli, as he becomes a spokesman for the museum Orang Asli Gombak and the main reference for local and international researchers.
Mrs. Jasmin	Development and growth on Orang Asli community	Has 13 years of service in JAKOA and also an Orang Asli descent from Semai tribe and her husband is from the Jakun tribe

development of Orang Asli in Malaysia. Once the data and information was gathered, thematic analysis was carried out by combining and cataloging similar patterns into high level themes and low level themes. Themes are defined as units derived from conversation topics, vocabulary, recurring activities, meanings, feelings, or folk sayings and proverbs [27]. The structure is able to provide a comprehensive view of the information and it made it easier to see a theme emerging.

At the same time, the observation was meant to find out individuals who are more likely to use technology, how far they use the technology, and are there any issues while they were handling the technology. Informer's activities of using technology will be observed for 10 h, from 8.00 am until 6.00 pm without them realizing it. The technology usage that was observed was activities involving television, radio, computer or laptop, mobile phone and any related electrical appliances.

4.2   Expert Reviewer

After the thematic analysis was finalized, the card sorting method [29] was conducted to ensure that the themes used and interpreted were in line with experts view. Six experts were involved from three different fields. In this process, other than getting views on themes that were used, they were also interviewed to gain insights related to four topics listed below:

- their opinion on cognitive style of Orang Asli
- their opinion on socioeconomic development of Orang Asli
- their opinion on sociocultural condition of Orang Asli
- their opinion on ICT usage among Orang Asli

5 Findings

The main objective of this study is to determine the socioeconomic and sociocultural situation of the Orang Asli and how these may affect their acceptance and use of ICT. From the focus groups, observation studies, and expert reviews; a summary was presented in Tables 3 and 4.

Table 3. Thematic analysis and expert interview findings

High Level Theme	Low Level Theme	Expert Interview Finding
Ability for informer who does not use ICT	Lack of Technology Knowledge and Skills	1. They do not reject the use of ICT 2. Young people are more likely to accept ICT than older ones 3. Issues in ICT adoption are literacy, costs, and lack of facilities especially network coverage and electricity 4. Tend to use ICT for entertainment
	Lack of Facilities	
	Illiterate	
	Techno-phobia	
	Aged	
	Low Necessities	
Preference in social media application	Awareness towards Technology	
	Influence by social media	
	New cultural acceptance	
Traditional cognitive style persisted	Cost Avoidance	1. Prioritize the Batin's opinion 2. They do not reject modernity 3. They still hold strongly to their customs and ancestral beliefs 4. External factors can affect their attitude 5. They like to be humble because it is an expression of being respectful to others 6. They are sensitive but do not become angry if disheartened but will not cooperate. 7. They emphasized good relations
	Fear for uncertainty	
	Easily demotivated	
	Feel Sufficient	
	Dislike force	
Motivation in receiving assistance and progress	Needs for Technical Support	
	Curiosity	
	Self-learning	
	Aspiration	

Based on the finding, it was found that there are four main aspects to be considered in efforts to attract Orang Asli to use and benefit from ICT. These are (i) influential people, (ii) infrastructure barriers, (iii) social development issues, and (iv) motivational factors.

Influential People. In their daily lives, the most 'influential individual' is the Batin and he is able to influence the villagers to be more open minded and to explore ICT. In addition, school students are influenced by school teachers as they receive formal education on ICT. Most of them have been able to use ICT effectively, probably due to

Table 4. Observation finding

Observation Aspect	Village Category	Age Group	Observation Finding
The use of technology by age group and level of technology usage	General	General	Almost all were capable of using television and radio at least by switching on and off the appliances.
	General	Elderly	A small number of mobile phones used and none used computer or laptop. Mobile phone was mainly used only to make calls for certain numbers that they remember or memorize and received calls only.
	General	Adult	Almost all use mobile phones and none use computer or laptop. Some used smart phone as well as tablet depending on income
	General	Youth	A large number of youth that have jobs were able to use mobile phones. Some used basic mobile phone and the others used smart phone depending on their job and income.
	Sub-Urban and Rural	Youth	No youth used laptop

the formal education, as well as the students' own initiative and enthusiasm due encouragement and guidance from friends of other ethnic groups. Positive response from school students can be utilized to influence others to use ICT.

Infrastructure Barriers. The second aspect is 'infrastructure barriers' since these may affect their physical ability to use ICT. There are three identified barriers which are (i) cost to be borne, (ii) lack of training materials or training centres, and (iii) lack of facilities especially network coverage and electricity. Barrier related to cost can be mostly related to their standard of living that is still relatively low. Regarding ICT training facilities, they need support from external parties such as the government, NGOs or commercial organizations to provide them.

Social Development Issues. The third aspect is 'social development issues' which relate to cognitive styles and lifestyles. We had identified two issues related social development: (i) illiteracy, and (ii) preservation of tradition and culture. Illiteracy is an issue related to their education level because awareness on education is still not strong among Orang Asli. Apart from that, Orang Asli especially adults; are very concerned about the impact of technologies on their belief and culture.

Motivational factors. 'Motivational factors' are an important aspect in regards to providing ICT facilities and services to Orang Asli. Among the factors that should be considered are (i) elements of entertainment and enjoyment, (ii) the evidence of benefits ICT can provide, (iii) positive attitudes especially to build good social relationship, and (iv) respects to their ancestral beliefs and customs. ICT projects for Orang Asli should not simply focus on addressing the basic needs such as food, education and healthcare, but should encompass wider social aspects, including entertainment, social networking, and cultural heritage.

6 Future Work

The next step of the research study will focus on the development of an application for raising the healthcare awareness among Orang Asli. From the results, it is clear to us that the application design will need to be more than just to provide basic healthcare information. Therefore, the future work is to conceptualize the requirements needed for appropriate technological design and development for this selected indigenous people group by taking into consideration the four main aspects derived from this study. Further, a prototyping of healthcare application will be developed and a series of user studies will be conducted.

References

1. Mikkelsen, C. (ed.): International Work Group of Indigenous Affairs, "Malaysia," in The Indigenous World 2013, vol. 2012, pp. 258–264. Copenhagen (2013)
2. Department of Development Orang Asli, Pelan Strategik Jabatan Kemajuan Orang Asli 2011–2015, 1st ed. Kuala Lumpur, Malaysia: Department of Development Orang Asli, Malaysia, p. 138 (2011)
3. Zen, H., Ab, K., Songan, P., Yeo, A.W., Gnaniah, J.: Bridging the Digital Divide: The E-Bario and E-Bedian Telecommunication Framework. Work with Computer System, pp. 277–281 (2004)
4. Ahlan, A.R., Arshad, Y.: The ICT social inclusion among orang asli community in gombak area. In: International Conference on Research Innovation Information System, IEEE (2011)
5. Malaysia Curriculum Development Center and UNICEF, Budaya, Pantang Larang dan Amalan Kesihatan Orang Asli Semenanjung Malaysia, First. Kuala Lumpur, Malaysia: Ministry of Education, p. 121 (1998)
6. Jamiran, M.N.S., Wee, S.T.: Kelestariaan transformasi pembangunan sosioekonomi orang aali. In: Persidangan Kebangsaan Geografi Alam Sekitar Kalike **4**, pp. 5–6 (2013)
7. Choy, E.A., Ariffin, Z.C.M., Pereira, J.J.: Sosioekonomi Masyarakat Orang Asli : Kajian Kes di Hutan Simpan Bukit Lagong, Selangor, Malaysia Pengenalan. Jurnal Melayu **5**, 295–314 (2010)
8. International Work Group of Indigenous Affairs, The Indegenous World 2013. Copenhagen, p. 531 (2013)
9. Wee, S.T., Mohamed, M., Jamiran, M.N.S., Zainal Abidin, Z.Z., Mohd Sam, S.A.: Pembangunan Sosioekonomi Komuniti Orang Asli di Malaysia. In: Persidangan Kebangsaan Geografi Alam Sekita Kali ke 4, pp. 755–761 (2013)
10. Amir Zal, W.A.: Penerimagunaan Teknologi Maklumat dan Komunikasi oleh Belia Orang Asli Selangor: Indikator Integrasi Melalui Tafsiran Nilai. Jurnal Teknologi Maklumat Multimedia **11**(2011), 49–54 (2011)
11. Amir Zal, W.A.: Nilai belia orang asli selangor terhadap teknologi maklumat dan komunikasi (ICT). J. Hum. Capital Dev. **2**(2), 49–70 (2009)
12. Rahimi, F., Rahimah, S., Marlia, M.S.: Adakah pantang larang pemakanan di kalangan orang asli mempengaruhi tahap kesihatan ibu dan anak-pengalaman daerah kuala lipis. J. Malays. Public Health Med. **3**(1), 73–77 (2003)
13. Ngcobo, K.M., Obono, S.D.E.: Modeling ICT adoption factors for the preservation of indigenous knowledge. Int. J. Comput. Inf. Syst. Control Eng. **7**(1), 58–63 (2013)

14. Lieberman, A.E.: Taking Ownership : Strengthening Indigenous Cultures and Languages Through the Use of ICTs. Academic for Educational Development (2005)
15. Taylor, A.: Information communication technologies and new indigenous mobilities? Insights from remote northern territory communities. J. Rural Community Dev. 7(1), 59–73 (2012)
16. Salazar, J.F.: Indigenous peoples and the cultural construction of information and communication technology (ICT) in latin america. In: Indigenous Peoples and the Cultural Construction of Information and Communication Technology (ICT), IGI Global, pp. 1966–1975 (2008)
17. Michael, K., Dunn, L.: The use of information and communication technology for the preservation of Aboriginal culture : the Badimaya people of Western Australia. In: Dyson, L. (ed.) Information Technology and Indigenous People, Idea Group Publishing (2006)
18. ARC Centre of Excellence for Creative Industries, T. C. for A. T. Innovation, and T. C. L. Council, Home Internet for Remote Indigenous Communities (2011)
19. International Work Group of Indigenous Affairs, The Indigenous World 2014, p. 597. Copenhagen (2014)
20. Donnell, A.B.O., Lutfey, K.E., Marceau, L.D., Mckinlay, J.B.: Health research of cross-national survey research : a study of physician decision making. Qual. Health Res. 17(7), 971–981 (2007)
21. McNulty, N.: The ulwazi programme: a case study in community-focused indigenous knowledge management. Knowl. Manage. Dev. Integr. Ser. Inf. Syst. 35, 215–232 (2014)
22. Department of Orang Asli Development (JAKOA). http://www.jakoa.gov.my/, Depart-ment of Orang Asli Development website, Retrieved on 4 March 2014
23. Nicholas, People first Orang Alsi after 50 years of merdeka. Off The Edge (2007). http://www.coac.org.my/beta
24. White, G.E., Thomson, A.N.: Anonymized focus groups as a research tool for health professionals. Qual. Health Res. 5(2), 256–261 (1995)
25. Asbury, J.: Overview of focus group research. Qual. Health Res. 5, 414–420 (1995)
26. Mary, M., Meg, S.: Using Focus Group for Evaluation. The University of Arizona, Tucson Arizona website. http://ag.arizona.edu/sfcs/cyfernet/cyfar/focus.htm. Re-trieved on 13 June 2014
27. Braun, V., Clarke, V.: Using thematic analysis in psychology. Qual. Res. Psychol. 3, 77–101 (2006)
28. International Work Group of Indigenous Affairs (IWGI). International Work Group of Indigenous Af-fairs Website, Retrieved on 13 February 2014. http://www.iwgia.org/regions/asia/malaysia
29. Nawaz, A.: A comparison of card-sorting analysis methods. In: The 10th Asia Pacific Conference on Computer Human Interaction. (APCHI2012) (2012)

Stakeholder Engagement: Applying Dechnology in a Technology-Oriented Organization

Chih-Shiang (Mike) Wu[1,2(✉)], William Huang[1], Pei-Lin Chen[1], and Tung-Jung Sung[2]

[1] Industrial Technology Research Institute, Hsinchu, Taiwan
{itri531050,williamhuang,mia-chen}@itri.org.tw
[2] National Taiwan University of Technology and Science, Taipei, Taiwan
sungtj@mail.ntust.edu.tw

Abstract. Technology revolution and the subsequent innovation can bring about a multitude of benefits for the society. However, innovation derived from a single technology push is no longer sufficient to meet the needs of the current market. While past studies have suggested that an ideal environment for innovation involves the engagement of multiple stakeholders, in practice, this ideal has remained a major challenge for many technology-oriented organizations. In 2010, the Industrial Technology Research Institute (ITRI) launched a project called Dechnology, where service design and design thinking were incorporated into the R&D process. The project developed the Dechnology innovation model, and successfully engaged stakeholders in the innovative process, which helped the collaboration between ITRI and corporations. This study looked at three cases from the Dechnology project and investigated the mechanisms applied in the Dechnology innovation model. This study further illustrated that the Dechnology project utilized three main mechanisms, which were (1) to apply the end-user voice properly, (2) to build a multidisciplinary facilitation team, and (3) to establish visualized co-creation environments.

Keywords: Stakeholder engagement · Service design · Innovation · Co-creation

1 Introduction

Innovation through technology push has been suggested by past studies (Brown et al. 2002; Lo 2005) to have a multitude of benefits for the development of the economy and society. In fact, many countries have established national level technology research organizations, such as the National Research Council in Canada and the Netherlands Organization for Applied Scientific Research, aimed at enhancing the competitiveness of their respective economies. Nevertheless, with the perpetually changing market of today, a number of studies (Rothwell 1994; Stefano et al. 2007; Verganti 2009) have suggested that technology push alone is no longer sufficient for achieving the innovation demanded by the market. Several studies (Chesbrough 2003; Lee et al. 2012) emphasized the

P.L.P. Rau (Ed.): CCD 2015, Part I, LNCS 9180, pp. 414–425, 2015.
DOI: 10.1007/978-3-319-20907-4_38

importance of breaking an organization's boundaries, being flexible in utilizing resources from inside and outside of an organization, and engaging different stakeholders for value co-creation.

However, Anthony et al. (2014) argued that, if an organization lacks the appropriate mechanisms for stakeholder engagement and value co-creation, it may impede the innovation process. Furthermore, Yang et al. (2014) highlighted that it might not be an easy feat for a non-technology oriented expertise to cast influence on the R&D process in a technology-oriented organization. In light of this situation, the main purpose of this study was to answer the following question: how to facilitate value co-creation among the internal and external stakeholders in a technology-oriented organization so as to enhance the efficiency of the innovation process?

In 2010, with support from the Taiwan government, the Industrial Technology Research Institute (ITRI), launched a project called Dechnology (an acronym from the words 'design' and 'technology'). The project utilized the methods of "service design" and "design thinking" (Hong and Haung 2013; Yang et al. 2014) and developed the innovation model (hereinafter referred to as the Dechnology innovation model) for ITRI, and helped ITRI to engage internal and external stakeholders in the innovation process. As a way of answering the aforementioned question, this study looked at the three cases from the Dechnology project to extract the mechanisms applied in the Dechnology innovation model that improved the innovation efficiency at ITRI.

The first part of this study was a literature review on the theoretical foundations of stakeholder engagement in technology push innovation and the Dechnology innovation model. Secondly, the case study research method was conducted on three cases of the Dechnology project to extract the mechanisms applied in the Dechnology innovation model. Lastly, this study compiled the mechanisms into a framework diagram as a reference for similar technology-oriented organizations looking to develop the related innovation models in the future.

2 Literature Review

The present study reviewed studies in the literature about the influence of stakeholder engagement in technology push innovation. Then, this paper illustrated the rationale and theories behind the Dechnology innovation model.

2.1 Stakeholder Engagement in Technology Push Innovation

Brown et al. (2002) and Lo (2005) pointed out that technological innovation might bring about new commercial opportunities and exert revolutionary impact on mankind's economic and social development. However, various studies (Rothwell 1994; Stefano et al., 2007; Verganti 2009) have suggested that in order to enhance the efficiency of the innovation process, organizations should consider multiple sources for innovation (such as market pull, design driven innovation) to facilitate the direction of technological innovation effectively in this rapidly changing market. Furthermore, Chesbrough (2003) indicated that for an organization to achieve both time to market and differentiated innovation, there should be effective stakeholder engagement and value co-creation mechanisms aimed at maximizing the benefits of the organization's core innovation capacity.

However, Gould (2012) noted that a lack of a proper system structure during the innovation process might lead to a loosely bound stakeholder relationship network, and may not only hamper the effectiveness of multidisciplinary resources but also lower the quality of innovation, or even heighten the risks of innovation. Moreover, research suggested that stakeholder management is a crucial factor for the success of an organization's operations (Evan and Freeman 1988; Sautter and Leisen 1999). On achieving effective stakeholder management, several studies (Ayuso et al. 2011; Gould 2012; Smith et al. 2011) advocated that an organization should not focus solely on pleasing the stakeholders; instead, it should adopt practical engagement to promote stakeholder networks and consensus.

Nevertheless, Yang et al. (2014) mentioned that it might not be an easy task to influence R&D in a technology-oriented organization with a non-technology oriented approach. Although there are plenty of studies that illustrated the need for stakeholder engagement, this study found that few studies suggested how to facilitate stakeholder engagement in a technology-oriented organization. Thus, this study illustrated the Dechnology innovation model and cases in the following section.

2.2 The Dechnology Innovation Model

ITRI was founded in 1973 with mission of creating economic value, and promoting social well-being through technology. Being the largest R&D organization technology in Taiwan, ITRI contributed to the advancement of the society and economy by sharing the fruits of its research with industries via IP transfers spin-offs, etc. Past studies (Arnold et al. 1998; Lo 2005) have pointed out that ITRI played a key role in the development of Taiwan's industry. However, with the onset of the experience economy (Pine II and Gillmore, 2003), the industries became eager to break away from the mindset of an original equipment manufacturer (Yang et al. 2014). Meanwhile, the 'technology push' that ITRI had always relied upon for innovation became less and less effective at meeting market needs.

In 2010, ITRI was supported by Taiwan's Ministry of Economic Affairs to implement the Dechnology project aimed at adding value to technology through design (Hong and Huang 2013). To meet market needs and facilitate stakeholder engagement, the project combined the methods of design thinking (Brown 2002) and service design (Mager and Sung 2011) and developed the Dechnology innovation model (Fig. 1), which were: (1) human centered for experience Design (HCED); (2) human centered for technology commercialized design (HCTCD); and (3) human centered for industrial technology development (HCITD). Together, they enabled ITRI to accelerate industry transformation in Taiwan.

Over the course of five years, a Dechnology team was formed with members from the fields of design, technology, and business. Through their efforts, over 30 traditional corporations have found innovation directions and established deep connections with

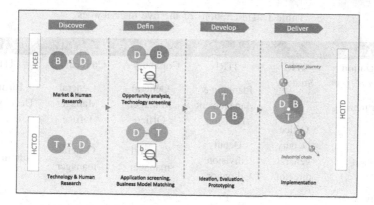

Fig. 1. The Dechnology innovation model

ITRI. Moreover, recently, the Dechnology team stepped up to introduce the external stakeholders to give impact on the R&D directions in ITRI. Thus, in order to understand how the Dechnology innovation model facilitated stakeholder engagement, this study investigated three cases of the Dechnology project in the next section.

3 Methodology

3.1 Research Process

This study, firstly, applied participant observation and in-depth interviews to find out about the progress of the three cases from the Dechnology project. Secondly, during the research process, this study collected the feedbacks from the interviewees (see Table 1), in order to extract the mechanisms that were applied in the Dechnology projects. Finally, based on these findings, this study established a framework to illustrate the mechanisms applied in the process of the Dechnology innovation model.

3.2 Three Cases in the Dechnology Project

The three cases from the Dechnology project were: (1) Case A: applying HCED in 2011 to adopt the FluxMerge thin motor technology into a home-use stairlift; (2) Case B: applying HCTCD in 2014, in exploring new value-added services for a gene chip technology; and (3) Case C: applying HCITD in 2014, in aiding the skincare industry to develop radical innovations and spur its transformation.

3.2.1 Case A: HCED

Responding to the upcoming aging society, Company A began importing stairlifts since 2001. However, Company A found that the size of stairlifts overseas were too large for installation in an average home in Taiwan where space is limited, so it is hard to enter the market. Given the situation, Company A started to develop its own stairlifts to accommodate the needs of senior citizens in Taiwan.

Table 1. Descriptions of the five interviewees

Interviewee	A1	A2	A3	A4	A5
Organization	ITRI	ITRI	Company A	Company B	ITRI
Department	Strategy and R&D Plan Office	Planning & Management Division	General Manager Office	General Manager Office	Business Development Division
Position	Deputy general director	Deputy division director	General manager	General manager	Administrator
Seniority (year)	28	10	23	2	5
Relationship with the Dechnology project	Resource allocation for the projects in ITRI	The project leader of the Dechnology project	The leader of Case A in Company A	The participant of the workshop in Case B	The project manager of Case C

Later, Company A collaborated with ITRI to build the FluxMerge thin motor technology (a technology won the R&D100 Award in 2013) into a compact size of stairlifts for Taiwan. However, during the cooperation between company A and ITRI, the development reached a halt due to their different value cognition. When the R&D team from ITRI hoped to emphasize the 'thinness' feature so as to promote the technology, the team from Company A reckoned that it would create problems in cost as it would require modifying other existing technologies. Nevertheless, when the Dechnology team intervened, the cooperation moved forward effectively (See Fig. 2).

Firstly, with HCED, the Dechnology team surveyed the preferences and needs of the target users, and the technology limitation. Next, the Dechnology team proposed a set of strategies and visualized the concepts accordingly which included: lowering the mechanical impression of the product, reducing the size of the product, and improving the overall user experience. Since the proposals were aimed at user experiences that could enhance the competitiveness of the product, Company A agreed to modify other existing technologies according to the proposal. Also, the ITRI team agreed to focus on user needs and deliever good expereince instead of insisting on emphasizing the feature of 'thinness',. The product was later launched and became the number one selling product in Taiwan with a 23 % market in 2014.

3.2.2 Case B: HCTCD

Company B was a corporation devoted to the research of gene chip technology. In order to expand the scope of its business, in recent years, Company B entered the field of prenatal diagnosis to enable pregnant women to detect earlier on if a fetus has the condition of hereditary disease. Although the company's technology had been in the market for more than one year, it still faced obstacles in capturing the market. Therefore, Company B worked with the Dechnology team in hopes of finding new opportunities and value for the company's core technology. (See Fig. 3).

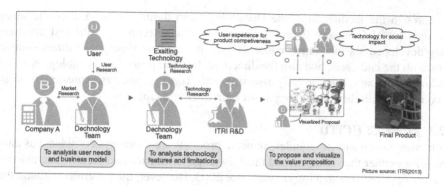

Fig. 2. The development of the stairlifts of Company A

Fig. 3. A prenatal gene chip innovative application workshop

With HCTCD, the Dechnology team began by gaining an in-depth understanding of the core technology of Company B and the related service models. The team also conducted user interviews to understand the behavior of pregnant women and their views and experiences regarding gene chip analysis. In addition, the Dechnology team interviewed different stakeholders (such as the medical doctors) to find out about their views on gene chip analysis. Having carried out the interviews and technical assessment, the Dechnology team found that although gene chip technology was valuable for older pregnant women or women with a family hereditary disease, it was limited by the current service model. The technology relied upon medical doctors as its mediator, whose recommendations often determined user decisions and may have affected the value of gene chip technology. Moreover, lacking an appropriate design for the service of the prenatal diagnosis, Company B caused the users to feel unease and anxiety during the waiting period for the examination results.

The Dechnology team then sorted the user needs and sought out other related cases in domains other than prenatal diagnosis market. Then, the aforementioned customer needs, procedural issues, and similar cases were compiled into a physical innovation toolkit, which included: a customer journey map, customer insights, and inspired cards. Finally, the Dechnology team hosted a co-creation workshop with participation from the company chairman, the general manager, the departmental managers, and the target customers of Company B.

Through the facilitation of the Dechnoloy team during the workshop, the senior management of Company B broke through their past technology-oriented mindsets. They developed six innovation concepts, which may help them make direct connections with the end-users, and also the directions for their gene chip technology research roadmap. Company B is currently assessing these concepts and has expressed its desire to cooperate with the Dechnology team on realizing them.

3.2.3   Case C: HCITD

With changing consumer attitudes, skincare products are nowadays considered as daily necessities rather than luxuries, and the Taiwan government listed the skincare industry as a key development area for Taiwan since 2003. However, the government found that the industry has been bottlenecked by its lack of certain key resource.

In 2014, the ITRI conducted a project to find the gaps in the skincare industries so as to develop the corresponding market opportunities and future R&D directions. The project originally followed ITRI's traditional innovation approach: gathering the profiles of benchmark companies to define the gaps, and then exploring the opportunities with technology professionals. However, halfway through the project, it was found that almost all of the findings were related to either 'cost reductions' or 'me too solutions''. These implied that there was little room for radial innovation. In turn, the team in charge of the project sought cooperation with the Dechnology team. (See Fig. 4).

Firstly, the Dechnology team investigated the users' behaviors during the skin care process, and found that the users were significantly influenced by 'brand marketing'. Also, the users were relatively unmoved by the skincare benefits solely brought about by technology innovation. Therefore, technology-oriented efforts such as developing new ingredients may not be sufficient to improve the industry. However, on the other hand, the Dechnology team found that there were potential needs in terms of auxiliary behavior, such as consultation, recording, and testing. Thus, the application of R&D for developing the related products may create new opportunities for the industry.

Secondly, based on the findings about user needs, the Dechnology team looked for the innovative cases from different fields to serve as sources for inspiration. A co-creation workshop was organized with participants including ITRI staff members and heavy users of skincare products (such as models) to explore innovation opportunities. By applying these materials, the workshop gave rise to 6 major innovation directions,

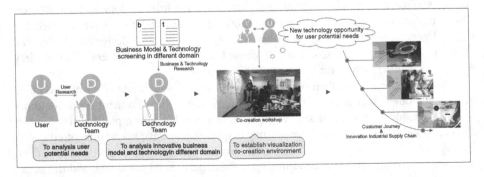

Fig. 4. Co-creation workshop and outputs

Table 2. Mechanisms and values of Dechnology innovation model

Mechanism	Value	Project
To apply the end-user voice properly	• Bridging the gap for value co-creation • Providing value proposition and vision for innovation	A, B, C
To build a multidisciplinary facilitation team	• Integrating considerations from different stakeholders • Setting strategies and goals for multidisciplinary and collaborative innovation projects	A, B, C
To establish visualized co-creation environments	• Facilitating communication among the stakeholders • Facilitating co-creation among the stakeholders	A, B, C

26 innovative concepts and related technology roadmap. Currently, the proposal from Case C has been approved by the senior management of ITRI and might become an important way of convergence for defining the future R&D direction for ITRI.

4   Discussion

The core value of a technology-oriented organization lies in technological innovation. However, technology push alone may be no longer adequate at meeting the demands of industrial transformation. Combining mothods of design thinking and service design into the technology push process, the Dechnology project gradually introduced a different innovation model for ITRI (Yang et al. 2014). This study investigated three cases of the project and found that the Dechnology innovation model utilized three major mechanisms (see Table 2) to facilitate stakeholder engagement in a technology-oriented organization, including: (1) to apply the end-user voice properly; (2) to build a multidisciplinary facilitation team; and (3) to establish visualized co-creation. Finally, this study compiled a framework of the three major mechanisms of the Dechnology innovation model into a diagram.

4.1   To Apply the End-User Voice Properly

Norman (2010) suggested that multidisciplinary cooperation among stakeholders might benefit the innovation process; however, the difference in value cognition between researchers and practitioners may lead to unsuccessful outcomes for multidisciplinary collaboration. Other studies (Stickdorn and Schneider 2011; Osterwalder et al. 2014) have pointed out that a "user-centered" approach may serve as a common language among the stakeholders, which can facilitate collaboration and co-creation and in turn to build up consensus. For example, in Case A, since the Dechnology team introduced the voice of end-users, the two parties were able to put focus on the same value proposition so as to achieve consensus.

Furthermore, Richardson (2010) has pointed out that as the challenges faced by corporations escalate in complexity, it is important to address the right issues at the initial stages of innovation processes. Therefore, rather than applying traditional marketing methods, corporations may need to immerse themselves into the users' live to discover the minute, yet unfulfilled needs. In both Case B and C, by introducing the users' behavior into the projects, the teams were able to find the hidden problems. Interviewee A5 mentioned, "*the past practices only explored the industrial gaps and technological opportunities, which were prone to the limitations of the operation mindsets, and hampered innovative thinking. However, with the user research conducted this time, it did allow us to rethink the innovation direction.*"

These findings suggested that with the Dechnology innovation model of properly using of the voice of end users, the organization could shorten the distance from research to commercialization. Moreover, the applications of end-user voice uncovered the hidden problems that led technology-oriented organization to re-evaluate the gaps from different aspects so as to explore the potential innovation directions.

4.2 To Build a Multidisciplinary Facilitation Team

Many studies (Driver et al. 2011; Perks et al. 2005) have pointed out that the roles of the designers have changed in modern innovation projects; the designers may need to possess skills including: holistic consideration, diverse information acquisition, facilitation, integration, and interpretation. With the growing complexity of needs in the market, when corporations attempt to integrate an innovative technology into a specific product, they may need to consider information from a variety of aspects. However, SMEs may often be constrained by limited resources and lack the capability of integration. Thus, even if they have found an innovative technology from ITRI, they may not be able to incorporate it into their products or services. Interviewee A1 has mentioned that "*in the present-day market, ITRI should no longer offer only technology support, rather, it should provide total solutions to effectively facilitate industrial transformation*".

In Case A, the Dechnology team considered more than just the technology aspect of the case. Rather, the team applied the expertise from multiple fields to integrate diverse information into a few concepts. This enabled the team to resolve the differences between ITRI and Company A. As interviewee A2 pointed out, "*in Case A, since the Dechnology team understood the technology and the ingenuity of the design effectively, it enabled the technical team and Company A to see the opportunity and ensured the successful implementation of the case.*"

In Case B, as the multidisciplinary Dechnology team possessed expertise in technology, business, and design, the team was able to see the limitations of the technology, the viability of the business, and the needs of the user. This enabled the team to facilitate Company B in developing concepts that were both logical and creative. Interviewee A4 pointed out that "*the facilitation efforts by the Dechnology team enabled the different departments to express their concerns and view the issues clearly, which in turn changed our way of applying our core technology.*"

On the other hand, in Case C, with Dechnology team involved, the project was able to match the user needs to technology categories and industrial supply chain in an effective way. In fact, the Dechnology team itself consisted of professionals from the fields of technology, design, and business. It was the main reason why the team was able to understand the considerations and limitations of different disciplines, and then offer the appropriate interpretations to facilitate effective communication among the stakeholders for them to reach positive co-creation results.

4.3 To Establish Visualized Co-creation Environments

Stickdorn and Schneider (2011) has suggested that co-creation is an open development model, which, if arranged properly, may promote desirable ideas that may serve as sources of inspiration later on for the core team. Moreover, Clatworthy (2011) have pointed out that by employing physical visual stimuli in workshops (such as Lego building blocks, memo stickers, and inspiring cards), it could enhance the stakeholders' imagination and communication, so as to lead to more effective co-creation.

For example, in Case A, B, and C, the Dechnology team visualized the customers' needs, the concepts, the related cases and technologies. It enabled the multidisciplinary team to effectively focus on topics one at a time and carry out in-depth discussions. Interviewee A3 pointed out that *"in the past, we've never had an opportunity to engage in such in-depth discussions. Yet, this time, with the aid of visualization, we were all able to view the issues holistically and understand each other's thoughts."*

The findings of this study suggested that through establishing visualized co-creation environments in the Dechnology project, it promoted stakeholder communication during the innovation processes and facilitated value co-creation among stakeholders, which in turn improved the effectiveness of innovation.

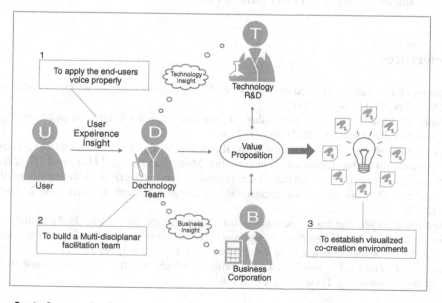

Fig. 5. A framework diagram of stakeholder engagement mechanisms in the Dechnology innovation model.

4.4   Stakeholder Engagement: The Dechnology Innovation Model

To sum up the aforementioned three mechanisms, this study compiled a framework diagram (Fig. 5) that illustrated how the Dechnology innovation model facilitated stakeholder engagement and co-creation in the innovation projects that led to improvements in the efficiency of innovation processes.

5   Conclusion

In recent years, rapid changes in the market implied that innovation derived from a single technology push is no longer sufficient. At the same time, technology-oriented organizations faced the major challenge of facilitating stakeholder engagement to promote innovation. In 2010, ITRI launched the Dechnology project that developed the Dechnology innovation model aimed at engaging multiple stakeholders in an innovation project. Therefore, in order to extract the methods, this study investigated three related cases and found three major mechanisms applied in the Dechnology innovation model, which were: (1) to apply the end-user voice properly; (2) to build a multidisciplinary facilitation team; and (3) to establish visualized co-creation environments.

The Dechnology innovation model so far has promoted the success of several innovations. However, some areas warrant further investigation. Firstly, the methodology for connecting from needs to the development of technology should be further investigated. Secondly, the way (such as web-based innovation platform) to attract stakeholders from wider areas to engage for the innovation co-creation should be established; and lastly, due to the fact that the cases in this study were mostly from Taiwan, the results of this study may require further verification and support from similar studies carried out in other countries in the future.

References

Anthony, S.D., Duncan, D.S., Siren, P.M.A.: Build an innovation engine in 90 days. Harvard Bus. Rev. **92**(12), 60–68 (2014)

Arnold, E., Rush, H., Bessant, J., Hobday, M.: Strategic planning in research and technology institutes. R&D Manage. **28**(2), 89–100 (1998)

Ayuso, S., Rodríguez, M.A., García-Castro, R., Ariño, M.A.: Does stakeholder engagement promote sustainable innovation orientation? Ind. Manage. Data Syst. **111**, 1399–1417 (2011)

Brown, K., Schmied, H., Tarondeau, J.C.: Success factors in R&D: A meta-analysis of the empirical literature and derived implications for design management. Acad. Rev. **2**, 72–87 (2002)

Chesbrough, H.W.: The era of open innovation. Sloan Manage. Rev. **44**(3), 35–41 (2003)

Clatworthy, S.: Service innovation through touch points: development of an innovation toolkit for the first stages of new service development. I. J. Des. **5**(2), 15–28 (2011)

Driver, A.J., Peralta, C., Moultrie, J.: Exploring how industrial designers can contribute to scientific research. I. J. Des. **5**(1), 17–28 (2011)

Evan, W.M., Freeman, R.E.: A stakeholder theory of the modern corporation: kantian capitalism. In: Beauchamp, T.L., Bowie, N.E. (eds.) About Ethical Theory and Business, 3rd edn. PrenticePHall, Englewood Cliffs (1988)

Gould, R.W.: Open innovation and stakeholder engagement. J. Technol. Manage. Innov. 7(3), 1–11 (2012)

Hung, W.K., Huang, W.: Creating value for technology by design: a case study of dechnology project. J. Des. 18(1), 41–64 (2013)

Lee, S.M., Olson, D.L., Trimi, S.: Co-innovation: convergenomics, collaboration, and co-creation for organizational values. Manage. Decis. 50(5), 817–831 (2012)

Lo, T.H.: Technology Innovation Management of Industrial Technology Research Institute in Taiwan. Unpublished doctoral dissertation, National Chiao Tung University, Hsinchu, Taiwan, R.O.C. (2005)

Mager, B., Sung, T.J.: Special issue editorial: designing for services. Int. J. Des. 5(2), 1–3 (2011)

Norman, D.A.: The research-Practice Gap: The need for translational developers. Interactions 17 (4), 9–12 (2010)

Osterwalder, A., Pigneur, Y., Bernarda, G., Smith, A., Papadakos, T.: Value Proposition Design: How to Create Products and Services Customers Want. John Wiley & Son, Hoboken (2014)

Perks, H., Cooper, R., Jones, C.: Characterizing the role of design in new product development: an empirically derived taxonomy. J. Product Innov. Manage. 22, 111–127 (2005)

Richardson, A.: Innovation X: Why a Company's Toughest Problems Are Its Greatest Advantag. Jossey-Bass, San Francisco (2010)

Rothwell, R.: Towards the fifth-generation innovation process. Int. Mark. Rev. 11(1), 7–31 (1994)

Sautter, E.T., Leisen, B.: Managing stakeholders: a tourism planning model. Ann. Tourism Res. 26(2), 312–328 (1999)

Smith, N.C., Ansett, S., Erez, L.: How Gap Inc., Engaged With its Stakeholders. MIT Sloan Manage. Rev. 52(4), 69–76 (2011)

Stefano, D., Gambardella, A., Verona, G.: Technology push and demand pull perspectives in innovation studies: current findings and future research directions. Res. Policy 14(8), 1283–1295 (2007)

Stickdorn, M., Schneider, J.: This is Service Design Thinking. Wiley, Hoboken (2011)

Verganti, R.: Design-driven innovation: changing the rules of competition by radically innovating what things mean. Harvard Business Press, Boston (2009)

Yang, C.F., Wu, C.S., Gong, Y., Sung, T.J.: Transformative service design: from technology to dechnology. In: The Proceedings of the 5th International Conference on Applied Human Factors and Ergonomics AHFE 2014, Kraków, Poland, 19–23 July, 2657–2668 (2014)

Author Index

Alghowinem, Sharifa I-141
Al-Mutairi, Nawal I-141
Al-Wabil, Areej I-141
Ang, Chee Siang I-403
Ariffin, Shamsul Arrieya II-3

Behr-Heyder, Philip Alexander I-381
Bernardes, João Luiz I-209
Bolton, Matthew L. I-186

Casalegno, Federico II-174
Chang, Kun-Chen I-392
Chang, Tsen-Yao I-3
Charunratanavisan, Muanphet II-121
Chen, Hao II-15
Chen, Jun-Liang II-263
Chen, Pei-Lin I-232, I-414
Chen, Tianjian II-46
Chen, Yue I-153
Chen, Zhe II-374
Chen, Zi I-262
Cheng, Chen I-128
Cheng, Chieh II-121
Cheng, Jianxin I-293
Chien, Chiu-Wei I-15, I-392
Chilana, Kulpreet II-174
Choe, Pilsung I-198, II-150, II-338
Chou, Lun-Chang I-232
Chuang, Miao-Hsien II-187, II-348
Cockton, Gilbert I-176

Dai, Linong I-49
de Souza, Tales Rebequi Costa
      Borges I-209
Ding, Wei I-128
Dong, Hua I-262
Duan, Qijun I-164
Dyson, Laurel Evelyn II-3

EL-Qirem, Fuad Ali I-176

Fan, Xinheng II-80
Fassi, Davide I-71
Fu, Paul L. II-80
Fu, Zhiyong I-303

Gao, Qin I-153, I-253
Gong, Miaosen II-57, II-384
Gulrez, Tauseef II-338
Guo, Yongyan II-328

Haferkamp, Lukas II-121
Hasheminejad, Mahdi II-150
He, Xiaopeng I-339
Hsieh, Hsiu Ching Laura II-113
Hsu, Chi-Hsien I-36
Hsu, Chiui I-24, II-307
Hu, Jun I-328
Huang, Cheih Ju I-232
Huang, Kuo-Li I-3
Huang, Na Ling II-348
Huang, Sheng II-394
Huang, William I-414
Huang, Xiaojun I-49
Huang, Zirui I-303
Hung, Chi-Ying I-221, II-68, II-197, II-209
Hung, Pei-Hua I-221, II-68, II-197, II-209,
      II-263
Hwang, Chiao Yu II-113

Ji, Xiang II-121
Jin, Yige I-116, II-307
Joardar, Satarupa II-101

Kirwan, Christopher Grant I-316
Kitkhachonkunlaphat, Kanrawi II-22
Kowalewski, Sylvia II-34
Kreifeldt, John II-263

Lachner, Florian I-58
Leckebusch, Judith II-34
Lei, Tian II-46
Li, Larry Hong-lin II-222
Li, Tong I-108
Li, Xueliang II-57, II-384
Li, Yajun I-274
Li, Zhizhong II-361
Liang, Peilong I-283
Liang, Yin I-71
Liao, Xiaojing II-230

Lidynia, Chantal   II-34
Lin, Chih-Long   I-15
Lin, Hsi-Yen   I-221, II-68, II-197, II-209,
   II-285
Lin, Nai-Hsuan   II-252
Lin, Po-Hsien   I-24, I-83, II-241, II-274,
   II-307
Lin, Rungtai   I-15, I-116, II-263, II-285,
   II-348
Lin, Ting-Yu Tony   II-15, II-318
Lin, Xu   I-328
Lin, Yu-Ju   I-116, II-307
Lindemann, Udo   I-58
Liu, Lei   II-140
Liu, Miao   I-293
Liu, Na   II-129
Liu, Xu   II-46
Liu, Zhe   II-338
Liuqu, Yanyang   II-80
Lou, Yongqi   I-108, I-361
Lu, Chi-Chang   I-83

Ma, Jin   I-349
Ma, Jui-Ping   II-187, II-348
Ma, Liang   I-381
Ma, Lin   I-339, II-140
Maniglier, Marie   II-318
Md. Noor, Norlaila   I-403
Mertens, Alexander   I-198
Mii, Fu-Kuo   I-392
Mior Ibrahim, Emma Nuraihan   I-403
Morandini, Marcelo   I-209
Motamedi, Sanaz   II-150
Mu, Qiaochu   II-15
Mueller, Florian 'Floyd'   I-58

Neuhaus, Andreas   II-121
Nousala, Susu   I-361

Pan, Dan   I-186
Peng, Qijia   I-253
Ponnada, Aditya   II-161

Rasche, Peter   I-198
Rau, Pei-Luen Patrick   I-153, I-253, II-15,
   II-121, II-318, II-338, II-361, II-407
Rauterberg, Matthias   I-328
Riaz, Nazish   II-90
Rigas, Dimitrios   II-90

Schlick, Christopher   I-198
Serot, Benoit   II-318
Seshagiri, Sarita   II-161
She, Manrong   II-361
Shih, Huei-Mei   I-96
Song, Dongjin   I-361
Su, Wen-Zhong   I-221, II-68, II-197, II-209
Sugianto So, Charlie   I-372
Sun, Meng   II-174
Sun, Na   II-121, II-318
Sun, Xiaohua   I-108
Sun, Xu   I-372
Sung, Tung-Jung   I-414

Tang, Yi   I-241
Tao, Linkai   II-328
Tsai, Wang-Chin   I-36
Tsao, Liuxing   I-381
Tseng, Jao-Hsun   II-241, II-274
Tseng, Yin-Chun   I-392
Tzou, Shwu-Huoy   II-252

Verlhac, Maxime   II-318
von Saucken, Constantin   I-58
Vorvoreanu, Mihaela   II-22

Walid, Norazlinawati   I-403
Wang, Deyu   II-129
Wang, Huiwen   II-374
Wang, Jieyu   II-101
Wang, Ming-shean   II-285
Wang, Nan   I-372
Wang, Qi   I-108
Wang, Qingfeng   I-372
Wang, Sheng-Ming   I-232
Wang, Xueli   I-339
Wang, Yan   I-372
Wang, Yuhui   II-46
Wei, Shuaili   II-46
Wu, Chih-Shiang (Mike)   I-414
Wu, Lei   II-46

Xia, Bang   II-374
Xiao, Dongjuan   II-57, II-384
Xiao, Sichun   II-394
Xiong, Luyao   II-46
Xu, Pei   I-283
Xu, Yangbo   I-241

Yang, Huiqiao   I-253
Yang, Xiaowen   I-283
Ye, Junnan   I-128, I-293
Yeh, Mo-Li   II-241, II-285
Yen, Hui-Yun   I-116, II-307
Yu, Bin   II-328
Yu, Ruifeng   II-129
Yuan, Shu   I-262

Zaman, Cagri Hakan   II-174
Zhang, Chang   II-394
Zhang, Lie   II-294

Zhang, Linghao   II-394
Zhang, Ning   I-274
Zhang, Qing   I-128
Zhang, Wen   II-294
Zhang, Xiaoli   I-164
Zhang, Yingzhi   II-338
Zhang, Yubo   II-407
Zhang, Yunhong   II-129
Zhang, Zhizheng   I-274
Zhou, Meiyu   I-283
Zhou, Ming   I-274
Ziefle, Martina   II-34

Printed in the United States
By Bookmasters